# Milestones in Motivation

Century Psychology Series

Kenneth MacCorquodale
Gardner Lindzey
Kenneth E. Clark

*Editors*

# Milestones in Motivation

*Contributions to the Psychology
of Drive and Purpose*

*Edited by*

WALLACE A. RUSSELL
*University of Minnesota*

APPLETON-CENTURY-CROFTS
EDUCATIONAL DIVISION
New York  MEREDITH CORPORATION

*To Marjorie and Pamela*

# Preface

*This book,* more than most, requires a word of explanation if it is to be of maximum use to the prospective reader. It is obviously a collection of readings about motivation. Many of them have been called historically significant. My aim, however, has been to produce something more than just another set of readings or a source book in the history of motivational psychology. It has been to present in a particular way the only approach to the psychology of motivation which, in twenty years of teaching, I have found adequate to the task of giving coherence to the field as a whole.

The approach is a longitudinal one. It identifies several different lines of development that are simultaneously influencing the present state of affairs and determining the direction of future work in motivational psychology. Each line has its own internal consistencies and its relevance for the whole. Together, they structure the field. Any temporally cross-sectional view over all of them would mask this structure and yield only an apparently chaotic picture. The longitudinal approach taken here, however, emphasizes these organizing factors. The several lines of development and their relationships to one another are dealt with explicitly in the introduction, in the discussions which precede each major section and in the briefer paragraphs prefacing each article. *In toto,* the book may be seen as an introduction to the major themes and issues of motivational psychology presented through the medium of an ordered, interconnected set of primary source materials.

The approach is implemented by means of the selections themselves and some things now need to be said about them. Everyone agrees that direct contact with primary sources is desirable, but how this can be achieved effectively and meaningfully is a difficult problem. Too often time factors or library facilities do not allow recourse to the original texts. Also, it has been my experience that brief and highly edited excerpts from such texts, as are found in most collections of readings, usually fail to serve as a substitute. Context is lacking, vocabularies seem esoteric, the author's personality and attitudes are not projected. The answer, it seems to me, is to provide the reader with a large enough segment of the work of any contributor so that he can truly speak for himself. Consequently, the readings included here consist, for the most part, of complete articles or chapters or sections with sufficient scope to acquaint the reader with the full flavor and intent of the original. The effort has been, in fact, to reproduce the original source as closely as possible. Styles of referencing and footnoting have been carried over from each individual article, and editorial changes and deletions have been kept to a minimum.

The decision to give each contributor the scope necessary to communicate his full message has had its costs. The book threatened to become too large. Although the intent to be inclusive was strong, it became necessary to omit many important writings, which were worthy of inclusion. It became impossible to add a section of recent though possibly ephemeral articles at the present frontiers of motivational research. But the advantages were also great. William James has been given room to show his real genius. Both of Clark Hull's masterly writings on the topic of purpose have been made available to present-day students. Indeed, each major strand of motivation theory has its outstanding representative, and each voice included can speak with high fidelity at full volume. There is no more valid way to become acquainted with a field of knowledge.

To the late Richard M. Elliott, long the psychology editor for Appleton-Century-Crofts, belongs the initial suggestion for a book of this sort and to him goes my first and most grateful acknowledgement. Many others also deserve recognition for assistance at various stages in the preparation of the material. The authors represented, and their publishers, have been most cooperative and their permissions are individually acknowledged in footnotes at the beginning of each article. The University of Minnesota has generously supported the project, in part through the granting of leave time and in part through a McMillan Travel Grant. The Center for Research in Human Learning and the Psychology Department of the University of Minnesota have provided indispensable time and secretarial help over a period of time which extended far longer than could have been anticipated. Miss Rose Boucher, Mrs. Mary H. DuBay, and many others have assisted mightily at a task which could not have been for them the labor of love that it was for me.

Wallace A. Russell

# Contents

# Introduction

*The psychology of motivation* concerns itself with problems of the activation and direction of behavior. This book presents an organized collection of writings which have served as milestones in the development of thought about these problems. Of all of the central issues in psychology, perhaps none has proven as recalcitrant to human understanding as those dealing with motivation. That man seeks goals and acts purposefully, at least some of the time, seems descriptively undeniable. That organisms vary from time to time in their responsiveness, in their level of excitement or arousal, seems equally obvious. Yet, in spite of the best thoughts of some of the best minds in psychology, the emergence of satisfactory explanations of such motivational phenomena has been slow relative to those in other areas of psychology, such as learning, sensation, and perception. This fact may account for the observation that the history of motivational psychology has never been written. The absence of a consensus in the field has inhibited efforts at a summing up. Nevertheless, great contributions have been made in motivational psychology and clear paths of development are discernible. They deserve to be better known. The purpose of this volume is to present those major contributions to motivational psychology which have brought the field to its present level and to do so in a context that will reveal the thematic continuities which can guide the directions of future progress.

The selection of starting points in the history of ideas is an arbitrary business. Views about the motivation of men and animals can be discovered no matter how far back one goes in the available records. Perhaps it is not profitable to search for starting points at all. Rather, it might be better to think of pivotal points in a continuous stream of ideas and to use these to get our bearings.

In motivational psychology one of the major pivotal points occurred with the appearance of the theory of evolution in the nineteenth century. Prior to the publication of Darwin's "Origin of Species by Means of Natural Selection," in 1859, it had been customary to hold that there was a qualitative difference in the motivational propensities of men and other species. "Blind instinct" was felt to be satisfactory for the explanation of animal behavior, but reason and will seemed necessary considerations when it came to man. Evolutionary thinking broke this dichotomy in a

*1*

dramatic way. When man was considered as part of the animal order it became quite acceptable to imagine, not only that animals might possess reason and will, but that man himself might be motivated by instinct. This latter hypothesis turned motivational psychology into the paths it has followed until recently and provides us with a comfortable pivotal point with which to begin our coverage.

The first section of readings consists of highlights in the variegated and convoluted history of instinct since Darwin made it respectable to apply the concept to human motivation. Essentially, it is a story of increased reliance upon the concept until the popularity of instinct reached a peak in the work of McDougall around the time of World War I. Then came a drastic decline in the acceptability of instinct during the heyday of the operationally minded and environmentally oriented behaviorists of the twenties and thirties. It was only after World War II that the observations of ethologists like Tinbergen and others, working outside of the field of psychology, and the still more recent renewal of psychological interest in genetic factors in behavior brought about the reinstatement of instinct as a topic of concern to motivational psychologists, largely in connection with the analysis of species specific behavior.

The eclipse of instinct during the years between the two World Wars allowed the evolution of a most significant alternative view of motivation, a view which took the name of drive theory. As it became the dominant formulation, it tended more and more to emphasize the problem of activation as the unique concern of motivation. In the thinking of Hull and his followers, drive became a completely nondirective energizer of behavior, a factor which increased the responsiveness of an organism but did not in itself determine the directional patterns of behavior. Ultimately, physiological findings which suggested a neural basis for such nonspecific activation led to a union of this line of thought with what has come to be known as arousal theory. This continuing theme is represented in the readings which make up the second major section of the text.

The problem of the goal-directedness of behavior is nothing less than the ancient issue of purpose, with all its philosophical entanglements. Within theoretical psychology this issue has seldom been granted the central position that it seems to warrant and the history of efforts to explain purposeful behavior has to a startling degree been repressed by recent generations of psychologists. Section three seeks to lift that repression by presenting the line of outstanding work on this topic as it extends from James, through Holt and Perry, to Hull and Tolman. In this section, too, will be found some significant contributions to the dynamics of purpose which culminate here with Lewin, but which identify a domain of activity that is currently of increasing relevance.

The frequently noted cleavage between experimental-systematic psychology and clinical-descriptive psychology is nowhere more regrettable than in the area of motivation. There is no question that a representative of the latter area, Sigmund Freud, is the greatest name in motivation if not in psychology as a whole. His ideas have been germinal in motivational thinking at the level of personality functioning. His work, and that of personalist and humanistic men like Allport, Murray, and Rogers continue to broaden the scope of motivational psychology and to provide the descriptive targets at which truly explanatory schemes must aim. It is likely that the future of motivation is being sketched out at this level. Section four contains articles which have already made their mark by pushing motivation to cope with its most difficult manifestations. It would be folly for experimentally inclined system makers to ignore the contributions of these intuitive trail-blazers.

The necessity of a firm empirical underpinning for motivational psychology must also be recognized. Clear statements of the functional consequences of motivation, experimental studies of basic processes, and efforts at quantification of relevant variables must never be overlooked in tracing the development of our complex subject. Several of the most influential writings on these aspects of motivation make up section five. When work at this level can be meaningfully related to the complex phenomena dealt with in the preceding section, the day may have come when an integrated history of motivation will at last be written.

The search for a generalized basis for motivation has never ceased and still goes on. The final section is made up of milestone contributions to this long range, general objective. It may well prove that no single basis for the problems of activation and direction in behavior will ever be found. These characteristics may be multiply determined by factors which have no common features. This possibility in no way detracts from the desirability of reaching an understanding of each facet of these vital outcomes. Nor does it vitiate the progress which has been made toward more unified treatments of motivation. The concept of homeostasis, the relevance of tissue needs, the role of hedonic processes, and other factors, all contribute to the understanding of certain broad aspects of motivation. And who can say that they may not, in some way, be approximations to a future formulation that will accomplish the unifying function which now seems such a remote possibility?

# I
# Instinct

Charles Darwin concluded that ". . . man and the higher mammals, especially the Primates, have some few instincts in common." In the wake of that conclusion has followed a series of remarkable efforts to trace man's motivational tendencies back to innate, constitutional propensities which are in some way "built in" to the biological structure of each individual. Darwin did not originate the idea of human instinct, and even in his own time other men, such as Herbert Spencer, advanced the same general notion. In Darwin, however, the concept was embedded in the most influential intellectual development of the period, namely, the theory of evolution, and one consequence of the acceptance of the latter was a prolonged effort to systematize the nature of instinct. William James, the leading American psychologist, proposed that man had many instincts and that their number and flexibility contributed to the complexity of human behavior relative to that of other animals. Later, William McDougall carried the interpretation of motivation in terms of instinct to its ultimate. "The human mind," he said, "has certain innate or inherited tendencies which are the essential springs or motive powers of all thought and action, whether individual or collective. . . ."

Even while riding the tide of evolutionary thinking, the doctrine of instinct has met strong opposition. Partly, no doubt, this opposition sprang out of the pervasive philosophical tradition of empiricism which had tended to view man as a "tabula rasa," or blank slate, upon which all human characteristics were inscribed by the all-determining hand of experience. The inclination to choose sides on the classical heredity-environment issue has always been strong, and many additional factors worked toward an emphasis on environmental determination on the part of the democratic, objective, behavioristic psychologists of America in the early years of this century. Beyond matters of philosophical preference were real logical and empirical problems with the concept of instinct. It proved fantastically difficult for some to see that by labeling a motive as instinctive no necessary progress had been made in explaining the tendencies referred to. There was great confusion over the definition of an instinct. Did it refer to some general telic urge, to specific goal-oriented families of behavior, to unlearned reflexes, or to all of these? Given at least minimal clarity of definition, what empirical procedures could establish that one was dealing with an instinct? These and other questions loomed so large that between the two World Wars there were many, among them Zing Yang Kuo, who urged that the concept be abandoned entirely. Of course, it was not. Karl Lashley,

Leonard Carmichael, and others continued to deal with the issues of unlearned behavior. Nevertheless, the pendulum had swung to an anti-instinct extreme and it seemed that the very word would disappear as a psychological term.

After World War II the careful descriptions of animal behavior occurring in natural settings, provided by ethologists like Tinbergen and Lorenz, rekindled interest in the complex behavioral adaptations manifested uniformly by all members of a given species. Chastened by previous disillusionment, psychologists once more entertained the concept of instinct, but this time with the attitude that here was a challenge rather than a substitute for explanation.

In the selections which follow, influential statements by Darwin, McDougall, Kuo, and Tinbergen represent each of the major phases of the continuing theme of instinct.

# 1 · Charles R. Darwin

## Comparison of the Mental Powers
## of Man and the Lower Animals

Twelve years after Darwin had published the *Origin of Species by Means of Natural Selection,* he felt obliged to spell out in detail how man fitted into his general theory. This he did in *The Descent of Man, and Selection in Relation to Sex.* Darwin based his argument that man has descended from lower forms on a comparison of man's bodily structure with that of other animal species and on a comparison of the mental powers of man and lower animals. This latter comparison is made in the selection reproduced here. In it Darwin speaks freely of instincts in man and of reasoning in animals. By suggesting the possibility of instincts in man, he gave impetus to a new kind of thinking and research in the area of motivational psychology.

*We have seen* in the last chapter that man bears in his bodily structure clear traces of his descent from some lower form; but it may be urged that, as man differs so greatly in his mental power from all other animals, there must be some error in this conclusion. No doubt the difference in this respect is enormous, even if we compare the mind of one of the lowest savages, who has no words to express any number higher than four, and who uses no abstract terms for the commonest objects or affections,[1] with that of the most highly organised ape. The difference would, no doubt, still remain immense, even if one of the higher apes had been improved or civilised as much as a dog has been in comparison with its parent-form, the wolf or jackal. The Fuegians rank amongst the lowest barbarians; but I was continually struck with surprise how closely the three natives on board H.M.S. "Beagle," who had lived some years in

[1] See the evidence on these points, as given by Lubbock, 'Prehistoric Times,' p. 354, &c.

England and could talk a little English, resembled us in disposition and in most of our mental faculties. If no organic being excepting man had possessed any mental power, or if his powers had been of a wholly different nature from those of the lower animals, then we should never have been able to convince ourselves that our high faculties had been gradually developed. But it can be clearly shewn that there is no fundamental difference of this kind. We must also admit that there is a much wider interval in mental power between one of the lowest fishes, as a lamprey or lancelet, and one of the higher apes, than between an ape and man; yet this immense interval is filled up by numberless gradations.

Nor is the difference slight in moral disposition between a barbarian, such as the man described by the old navigator Byron, who dashed his child on the rocks for dropping a basket of sea-urchins, and a Howard or Clarkson; and in intellect, between a savage who does not use any abstract terms, and a Newton or Shakespeare. Differences of this kind between the highest men of the highest races and the lowest savages, are connected by the finest gradations. Therefore it is possible that they might pass and be developed into each other.

My object in this chapter is solely to shew that there is no fundamental difference between man and the higher mammals in their mental faculties. Each division of the subject might have been extended into a separate essay, but must here be treated briefly. As no classification of the mental powers has been universally accepted, I shall arrange my remarks in the order most convenient for my purpose; and will select those facts which have most struck me, with the hope that they may produce some effect on the reader.

With respect to animals very low in the scale, I shall have to give some additional facts under Sexual Selection, shewing that their mental powers are higher than might have been expected. The variability of the faculties in the individuals of the same species is an important point for us, and some few illustrations will here be given. But it would be superfluous to enter into many details on this head, for I have found on frequent enquiry, that it is the unanimous opinion of all those who have long attended to animals of many kinds, including birds, that the individuals differ greatly in every mental characteristic. In what manner the mental powers were first developed in the lowest organisms, is as hopeless an enquiry as how life first originated. These are problems for the distant future, if they are ever to be solved by man.

As man possesses the same senses with the lower animals, his fundamental intuitions must be the same. Man has also some few instincts in common, as that of self-preservation, sexual love, the love of the mother for her new-born offspring, the power possessed by the latter of sucking, and so forth. But man, perhaps, has somewhat fewer instincts than those possessed by the animals which come next to him in the series. The orang in the Eastern islands, and the chimpanzee in Africa, build platforms on which they sleep; and, as both species follow the same habit, it might be argued that this was due to instinct, but we cannot feel sure that it is not the result of both animals having similar wants and possessing similar powers of reasoning. These apes, as we may assume, avoid the many poisonous fruits of the tropics, and man has no such knowledge; but as our domestic animals, when taken to foreign lands and when first turned out in the spring, often eat poisonous herbs, which they afterwards avoid, we cannot feel sure that the apes do not learn from their own experience or from that of their parents what fruits to select. It is however certain, as we shall presently see, that apes have an instinctive dread of serpents, and probably of other dangerous animals.

The fewness and the comparative simplicity of the instincts in the higher animals are remarkable in contrast with those of the lower animals. Cuvier maintained that instinct and intelligence stand in an inverse ratio to each other; and some have thought that the intellectual faculties of the higher animals have been gradually developed from their instincts. But Pouchet, in an interesting essay,[2] has shewn that no such inverse ratio really exists. Those insects which possess the most wonderful instincts are certainly the most intelligent. In the vertebrate series, the least intelligent members, namely fishes and amphibians, do not possess complex instincts; and amongst mammals the animal most remarkable for its instincts, namely the beaver, is highly intelligent, as will be admitted by every one who has read Mr. Morgan's excellent account of this animal.[3]

Although the first dawnings of intelligence, according to Mr. Herbert Spencer,[4] have been developed through the multiplication and co-ordination of reflex actions, and although many of the simpler instincts graduate into actions of this kind and can hardly be distinguished from them, as in the case of young animals sucking, yet the more complex instincts seem to have originated independently of intelligence. I am, however, far from wishing to deny that instinctive actions may lose their fixed and untaught character, and be replaced by others performed by the aid of the free will. On the other hand, some intelligent actions—as when birds on oceanic islands first learn to avoid man—after being performed during many generations, become converted into instincts and are inherited. They may then be said to be degraded in character, for they are no longer performed through reason or from experience. But the greater number of the more complex instincts appear to have been gained in a wholly different manner, through the natural selection of variations of simpler instinctive actions. Such variations appear to arise from the same unknown causes acting on the cerebral organisation, which induce slight variations

[2] 'L'Instinct chez les Insectes.' 'Revue des Deux Mondes,' Feb. 1870, p. 690.
[3] 'The American Beaver and his Works,' 1868.
[4] 'The Principles of Psychology,' 2nd edit. 1870, pp. 418–443.

or individual differences in other parts of the body; and these variations, owing to our ignorance, are often said to arise spontaneously. We can, I think, come to no other conclusion with respect to the origin of the more complex instincts, when we reflect on the marvellous instincts of sterile worker-ants and bees, which leave no offspring to inherit the effects of experience and of modified habits.

Although a high degree of intelligence is certainly compatible with the existence of complex instincts, as we see in the insects just named and in the beaver, it is not improbable that they may to a certain extent interfere with each other's development. Little is known about the functions of the brain, but we can perceive that as the intellectual powers become highly developed, the various parts of the brain must be connected by the most intricate channels of intercommunication; and as a consequence each separate part would perhaps tend to become less well fitted to answer in a definite and uniform, that is instinctive, manner to particular sensations or associations.

I have thought this digression worth giving, because we may easily underrate the mental powers of the higher animals, and especially of man, when we compare their actions founded on the memory of past events, on foresight, reason, and imagination, with exactly similar actions instinctively performed by the lower animals; in this latter case the capacity of performing such actions having been gained, step by step, through the variability of the mental organs and natural selection, without any conscious intelligence on the part of the animal during each successive generation. No doubt, as Mr. Wallace has argued,[5] much of the intelligent work done by man is due to imitation and not to reason; but there is this great difference between his actions and many of those performed by· the lower animals, namely, that man cannot, on his first trial, make, for instance, a stone hatchet or a canoe, through his power of imitation. He has to learn his work by practice; a beaver, on the other hand, can make its dam or canal, and a bird its nest, as well, or nearly as well, the first time it tries, as when old and experienced.

To return to our immediate subject: the lower animals, like man, manifestly feel pleasure and pain, happiness and misery. Happiness is never better exhibited than by young animals, such as puppies, kittens, lambs, &c, when playing together, like our own children. Even insects play together, as has been described by that excellent observer, P. Huber,[6] who saw ants chasing and pretending to bite each other, like so many puppies.

The fact that the lower animals are excited by the same emotions as ourselves is so well established, that it will not be necessary to weary the reader by many details. Terror acts in the same manner on them as on

5 'Contributions to the Theory of Natural Selection,' 1870, p. 212.
6 'Recherches sur les Mœurs des Fourmis,' 1810, p. 173.

us, causing the muscles to tremble, the heart to palpitate, the sphincters to be relaxed, and the hair to stand on end. Suspicion, the offspring of fear, is eminently characteristic of most wild animals. Courage and timidity are extremely variable qualities in the individuals of the same species, as is plainly seen in our dogs. Some dogs and horses are ill-tempered and easily turn sulky; others are good-tempered; and these qualities are certainly inherited. Every one knows how liable animals are to furious rage, and how plainly they show it. Many anecdotes, probably true, have been published on the long-delayed and artful revenge of various animals. The accurate Rengger and Brehm [7] state that the American and African monkeys which they kept tame, certainly revenged themselves. The love of a dog for his master is notorious; in the agony of death he has been known to caress his master, and every one has heard of the dog suffering under vivisection, who licked the hand of the operator; this man, unless he had a heart of stone, must have felt remorse to the last hour of his life. As Whewell [8] has remarked, "who that reads the touching instances of maternal affection, related so often of the women of all nations, and of the females of all animals, can doubt that the principle of action is the same in the two cases?"

We see maternal affection exhibited in the most trifling details; thus Rengger observed an American monkey (a Cebus) carefully driving away the flies which plagued her infant; and Duvaucel saw a Hylobates washing the faces of her young ones in a stream. So intense is the grief of female monkeys for the loss of their young, that it invariably caused the death of certain kinds kept under confinement by Brehm in N. Africa. Orphan-monkeys were always adopted and carefully guarded by the other monkeys, both males and females. One female baboon had so capacious a heart that she not only adopted young monkeys of other species, but stole young dogs and cats, which she continually carried about. Her kindness, however, did not go so far as to share her food with her adopted offspring, at which Brehm was surprised, as his monkeys always divided everything quite fairly with their own young ones. An adopted kitten scratched the above-mentioned affectionate baboon, who certainly had a fine intellect, for she was much astonished at being scratched, and immediately examined the kitten's feet, and without more ado bit off the claws. In the Zoological Gardens, I heard from the keeper that an old baboon (*C. chacma*) had adopted a Rhesus monkey; but when a young drill and mandrill were placed in the cage, she seemed to perceive that these monkeys, though distinct species, were her nearer relatives, for she at once rejected the Rhesus and adopted both of them. The young Rhesus,

---

[7] All the following statements, given on the authority of these two naturalists, are taken from Rengger's 'Naturges. der Säugethiere von Paraguay,' 1830, s. 41–57, and from Brehm's 'Thierleben,' B. i. s. 10–87.

[8] 'Bridgewater Treatise,' p. 263.

as I saw, was greatly discontented at being thus rejected, and it would, like a naughty child, annoy and attack the young drill and mandrill whenever it could do so with safety; this conduct exciting great indignation in the old baboon. Monkeys will also, according to Brehm, defend their master when attacked by any one, as well as dogs to whom they are attached, from the attacks of other dogs. But we here trench on the subject of sympathy, to which I shall recur. Some of Brehm's monkeys took much delight in teasing, in various ingenious ways, a certain old dog whom they disliked, as well as other animals.

Most of the more complex emotions are common to the higher animals and ourselves. Every one has seen how jealous a dog is of his master's affection, if lavished on any other creature; and I have observed the same fact with monkeys. This shews that animals not only love, but have the desire to be loved. Animals manifestly feel emulation. They love approbation or praise; and a dog carrying a basket for his master exhibits in a high degree self-complacency or pride. There can, I think, be no doubt that a dog feels shame, as distinct from fear, and something very like modesty when begging too often for food. A great dog scorns the snarling of a little dog, and this may be called magnanimity. Several observers have stated that monkeys certainly dislike being laughed at; and they sometimes invent imaginary offences. In the Zoological Gardens I saw a baboon who always got into a furious rage when his keeper took out a letter or book and read it aloud to him; and his rage was so violent that, as I witnessed on one occasion, he bit his own leg till the blood flowed.

We will now turn to the more intellectual emotions and faculties, which are very important, as forming the basis for the development of the higher mental powers. Animals manifestly enjoy excitement and suffer from ennui, as may be seen with dogs, and, according to Rengger, with monkeys. All animals feel Wonder, and many exhibit Curiosity. They sometimes suffer from this latter quality, as when the hunter plays antics and thus attracts them; I have witnessed this with deer, and so it is with the wary chamois, and with some kinds of wild-ducks. Brehm gives a curious account of the instinctive dread which his monkeys exhibited towards snakes; but their curiosity was so great that they could not desist from occasionally satiating their horror in a most human fashion, by lifting up the lid of the box in which the snakes were kept. I was so much surprised at his account, that I took a stuffed and coiled-up snake into the monkey-house at the Zoological Gardens, and the excitement thus caused was one of the most curious spectacles which I ever beheld. Three species of Cercopithecus were the most alarmed; they dashed about their cages and uttered sharp signal-cries of danger, which were understood by the other monkeys. A few young monkeys and one old Anubis baboon alone took no notice of the snake. I then placed the stuffed specimen on the ground in one of the larger compartments. After a time all the monkeys collected round it in a large circle, and staring intently, presented a most ludicrous appearance. They became extremely nervous; so that when a wooden ball, with which they were familiar as a plaything, was accidently moved in the straw, under which it was partly hidden, they all instantly started away. These monkeys behaved very differently when a dead fish, a mouse, and some other new objects were placed in their cages; for though at first frightened, they soon approached, handled and examined them. I then placed a live snake in a paper bag, with the mouth loosely closed, in one of the larger compartments. One of the monkeys immediately approached, cautiously opened the bag a little, peeped in, and instantly dashed away. Then I witnessed what Brehm has described, for monkey after monkey, with head raised high and turned on one side, could not resist taking momentary peeps into the upright bag, at the dreadful object lying quiet at the bottom. It would almost appear as if monkeys had some notion of zoological affinities, for those kept by Brehm exhibited a strange, though mistaken, instinctive dread of innocent lizards and frogs. An orang, also, has been known to be much alarmed at the first sight of a turtle.[9]

The principle of *Imitation* is strong in man, and especially in man in a barbarous state. Desor [10] has remarked that no animal voluntarily imitates an action performed by man, until in the ascending scale we come to monkeys, which are well-known to be ridiculous mockers. Animals, however, sometimes imitate each others' actions: thus two species of wolves, which had been reared by dogs, learned to bark, as does sometimes the jackal,[11] but whether this can be called voluntary imitation is another question. From one account which I have read, there is reason to believe that puppies nursed by cats sometimes learn to lick their feet and thus to clean their faces: it is at least certain, as I hear from a perfectly trustworthy friend, that some dogs behave in this manner. Birds imitate the songs of their parents, and sometimes those of other birds; and parrots are notorious imitators of any sound which they often hear.

Hardly any faculty is more important for the intellectual progress of man than the power of *Attention*. Animals clearly manifest this power, as when a cat watches by a hole and prepares to spring on its prey. Wild animals sometimes become so absorbed when thus engaged, that they may be easily approached. Mr. Bartlett has given me a curious proof how variable this faculty is in monkeys. A man who trains monkeys to act used to purchase common kinds from the Zoological Society at the price of five pounds for each; but he offered to give double the price, if he might keep three or four of them for a few days, in order to select one. When asked how he could possibly so soon learn whether a particular monkey would turn out a good actor, he answered that it all depended on their power

---

[9] W. C. L. Martin, 'Nat. Hist. of Mammalia,' 1841, p. 405.
[10] Quoted by Vogt, 'Mémoire sur les Microcéphales,' 1867, p. 168.
[11] 'The Variation of Animals and Plants under Domestication,' vol. i. p. 27.

of attention. If when he was talking and explaining anything to a monkey, its attention was easily distracted, as by a fly on the wall or other trifling object, the case was hopeless. If he tried by punishment to make an inattentive monkey act, it turned sulky. On the other hand, a monkey which carefully attended to him could always be trained.

It is almost superfluous to state that animals have excellent *Memories* for persons and places. A baboon at the Cape of Good Hope, as I have been informed by Sir Andrew Smith, recognised him with joy after an absence of nine months. I had a dog who was savage and averse to all strangers, and I purposely tried his memory after an absence of five years and two days. I went near the stable where he lived, and shouted to him in my old manner; he showed no joy, but instantly followed me out walking and obeyed me, exactly as if I had parted with him only half-an-hour before. A train of old associations, dormant during five years, had thus been instantaneously awakened in his mind. Even ants, as P. Huber [12] has clearly shewn, recognised their fellow-ants belonging to the same community after a separation of four months. Animals can certainly by some means judge of the intervals of time between recurrent events.

The *Imagination* is one of the highest prerogatives of man. By this faculty he unites, independently of the will, former images and ideas, and thus creates brilliant and novel results. A poet, as Jean Paul Richter remarks,[13] "who must reflect whether he shall make a character say yes or no—to the devil with him; he is only a stupid corpse." Dreaming gives us the best notion of this power; as Jean Paul again says, "The dream is an involuntary art of poetry." The value of the products of our imagination depends of course on the number, accuracy, and clearness of our impressions; on our judgment and taste in selecting or rejecting the involuntary combinations, and to a certain extent on our power of voluntarily combining them. As dogs, cats, horses, and probably all the higher animals, even birds, as is stated on good authority,[14] have vivid dreams, and this is shewn by their movements and voice, we must admit that they possess some power of imagination.

Of all the faculties of the human mind, it will, I presume, be admitted that *Reason* stands at the summit. Few persons any longer dispute that animals possess some power of reasoning. Animals may constantly be seen to pause, deliberate, and resolve. It is a significant fact, that the more the habits of any particular animal are studied by a naturalist, the more he attributes to reason and the less to unlearnt instincts.[15] In future chapters we shall see that some animals extremely low in the scale apparently

12 'Les Mœurs des Fourmis,' 1810, p. 150.

13 Quoted in Dr. Maudsley's 'Physiology and Pathology of Mind,' 1868, pp. 19, 220.

14 Dr. Jerdon, 'Birds of India,' vol. i. 1862, p. xxi.

15 Mr. L. H. Morgan's work on 'The American Beaver,' 1868, offers a good illustration of this remark. I cannot, however, avoid thinking that he goes too far in underrating the power of Instinct.

display a certain amount of reason. No doubt it is often difficult to distinguish between the power of reason and that of instinct. Thus Dr. Hayes, in his work on 'The Open Polar Sea,' repeatedly remarks that his dogs, instead of continuing to draw the sledges in a compact body, diverged and separated when they came to thin ice, so that their weight might be more evenly distributed. This was often the first warning and notice which the travellers received that the ice was becoming thin and dangerous. Now, did the dogs act thus from the experience of each individual, or from the example of the older and wiser dogs, or from an inherited habit, that is from an instinct? This instinct might possibly have arisen since the time, long ago, when dogs were first employed by the natives in drawing their sledges; or the Arctic wolves, the parent-stock of the Esquimaux dog, may have acquired this instinct, impelling them not to attack their prey in a close pack when on thin ice. Questions of this kind are most difficult to answer.

So many facts have been recorded in various works shewing that animals possess some degree of reason, that I will here give only two or three instances, authenticated by Rengger, and relating to American monkeys, which stand low in their order. He states that when he first gave eggs to his monkeys, they smashed them and thus lost much of their contents; afterwards they gently hit one end against some hard body, and picked off the bits of shell with their fingers. After cutting themselves only once with any sharp tool, they would not touch it again, or would handle it with the greatest care. Lumps of sugar were often given them wrapped up in paper; and Rengger sometimes put a live wasp in the paper, so that in hastily unfolding it they got stung; after this had once happened, they always first held the packet to their ears to detect any movement within. Any one who is not convinced by such facts as these, and by what he may observe with his own dogs, that animals can reason, would not be convinced by anything that I could add. Nevertheless I will give one case with respect to dogs, as it rests on two distinct observers, and can hardly depend on the modification of any instinct.

Mr. Colquhoun [16] winged two wild-ducks, which fell on the opposite side of a stream; his retriever tried to bring over both at once, but could not succeed; she then, though never before known to ruffle a feather, deliberately killed one, brought over the other, and returned for the dead bird. Col. Hutchinson relates that two partridges were shot at once, one being killed, the other wounded; the latter ran away, and was caught by the retriever, who on her return came across the dead bird; "she stopped, evidently greatly puzzled, and after one or two trials, finding she could not take it up without permitting the escape of the winged bird, she considered a moment, then deliberately murdered it by giving it a severe

[16] 'The Moor and the Loch,' p. 45. Col. Hutchinson on 'Dog Breaking,' 1850, p. 46.

crunch, and afterwards brought away both together. This was the only known instance of her ever having wilfully injured any game." Here we have reason, though not quite perfect, for the retriever might have brought the wounded bird first and then returned for the dead one, as in the case of the two wild-ducks.

The muleteers in S. America say, "I will not give you the mule whose step is easiest, but *la mas racional*,—the one that reasons best;" and Humboldt [17] adds, "this popular expression, dictated by long experience, combats the system of animated machines, better perhaps than all the arguments of speculative philosophy."

It has, I think, now been shewn that man and the higher animals, especially the Primates, have some few instincts in common. All have the same senses, intuitions and sensations—similar passions, affections, and emotions, even the more complex ones; they feel wonder and curiosity; they possess the same faculties of imitation, attention, memory, imagination, and reason, though in very different degrees.

[17] 'Personal Narrative,' Eng. translat., vol. iii. p. 106.

# 2 • William McDougall

## The Nature of Instincts and Their Place in the Constitution of the Human Mind

McDougall came to the United States from England at the time of the rise to dominance of the behaviorist point of view. Nevertheless, his nonbehavioristic "hormic" psychology, which stressed instinct and purpose, was greatly influential, though ultimately his excesses in the direction of teleology and animism triggered a virulent reaction against his position. In this selection McDougall demonstrates the fundamental role he assigned to instincts and describes their cognitive, affective, and conative aspects.

*The human mind* has certain innate or inherited tendencies which are the essential springs or motive powers of all thought and action, whether individual or collective, and are the bases from which the character and will of individuals and of nations are gradually developed under the guidance of the intellectual faculties. These primary innate tendencies have different relative strengths in the native constitutions of the individuals of different races, and they are favoured or checked in very different degrees by the very different social circumstances of men in different stages of culture; but they are probably common to the men of every race and of every age. If this view, that human nature has everywhere and at all times this common native foundation, can be established, it will afford a much-needed basis for speculation on the history of the development of human societies and human institutions. For so long as it is possible to assume, as has often been done, that these innate tendencies of the human mind have varied greatly from age to age and from race to race, all such speculation is founded on quicksand and we cannot hope to reach views of a reasonable degree of certainty.

The evidence that the native basis of the human mind, constituted by the sum of these innate tendencies, has this stable unchanging character is afforded by comparative psychology. For we find, not only that these tendencies, in stronger or weaker degree, are present in men of all races now living on the earth, but that we may find all of them, or at least the germs of them, in most of the higher animals. Hence there can be little doubt that they played the same essential part in the minds of the primitive human stock, or stocks, and in the pre-human ancestors that bridged the great gap in the evolutionary series between man and the animal world.

These all-important and relatively unchanging tendencies, which form the basis of human character and will, are of two main classes—

(1) The specific tendencies or instincts;

(2) The general or non-specific tendencies arising out of the constitution of mind and the nature of mental process in general, when mind and mental process attain a certain degree of complexity in the course of evolution.

In the present and seven following chapters I propose to define the more important of these specific and general tendencies, and to sketch very briefly the way in which they become systematised in the course of character-formation; and in the second section of this volume some attempt will be made to illustrate the special importance of each one for the social life of man.

Contemporary writers of all classes make frequent use of the words "instinct" and "instinctive," but, with very few exceptions, they use them so loosely that they have almost spoilt them for scientific purposes. On the one hand, the adjective "instinctive" is commonly applied to every human action that is performed without deliberate reflexion; on the other hand, the actions of animals are popularly attributed to instinct, and in this connexion instinct is vaguely conceived as a mysterious faculty, utterly different in nature from any human faculty, which Providence has given to the brutes because the higher faculty of reason has been denied them. Hundreds of passages might be quoted from contemporary authors, even some of considerable philosophical culture, to illustrate how these two words are used with a minimum of meaning, generally with the effect of disguising from the writer the obscurity and incoherence of his thought. The following examples will serve to illustrate at once this abuse and the hopeless laxity with which even cultured authors habitually make use of psychological terms. One philosophical writer on social topics tells us that the power of the State "is dependent on the instinct of subordination, which is the outcome of the desire of the people, more or less distinctly conceived, for certain social ends": another asserts that ancestor-worship has survived amongst the Western peoples as a "mere tradition and instinct": a medical writer has recently asserted that if a drunkard is fed on fruit he will "become instinctively a teetotaler": a political writer tells us that "the Russian people is rapidly acquiring a political instinct": from a recent treatise on morals by a distinguished philosopher two passages, fair samples of a large number, may be taken; one describes the "notion that blood demands blood" as an "inveterate instinct of primitive humanity"; the other affirms that "punishment originates in the instinct of vengeance": another of our most distinguished philosophers asserts that "popular instinct maintains" that "there is a theory and a justification of social coercion latent in the term 'self-government.'" As our last illustration we may take the following passage from an avowedly psychological article in a recent number of the *Spectator:* "The instinct of contradiction, like the instinct of acquiescence, is inborn. . . . These instincts are very deep rooted and absolutely incorrigible, either from within or from without. Both springing as they do from a radical defect, from a want of original independence, they affect the whole mind and character." These are favourable examples of current usage, and they justify the statement that these words "instinct" and "instinctive" are commonly used as a cloak for ignorance when a writer attempts to explain any individual or collective action that he fails, or has not tried, to understand. Yet there can be no understanding of the development of individual character or of individual and collective conduct unless the nature of instinct and its scope and function in the human mind are clearly and firmly grasped.

It would be difficult to find any adequate mention of instincts in treatises on human psychology written before the middle of last century. But the work of Darwin and of Herbert Spencer has lifted to some extent the veil of mystery from the instincts of animals, and has made the problem of the relation of instinct to human intelligence and conduct one of the most widely discussed in recent years.

Among professed psychologists there is now fair agreement as to the usage of the terms "instinct" and "instinctive." By the great majority they are used only to denote certain innate specific tendencies of the mind that are common to all members of any one species, racial characters that have been slowly evolved in the process of adaptation of species to their environment and that can be neither eradicated from the mental constitution of which they are innate elements nor acquired by individuals in the course of their lifetime. A few writers, of whom Professor Wundt is the most prominent, apply the terms to the very strongly fixed, acquired habits of action that are more commonly and properly described as secondarily automatic actions, as well as to the innate specific tendencies. The former usage seems in every way preferable and is adopted in these pages.

But, even among those psychologists who use the terms in this stricter sense, there are still great differences of opinion as to the place of instinct in the human mind. All agree that man has been evolved from pre-human ancestors whose lives were dominated by instincts; but some hold that, as man's intelligence and reasoning powers developed, his instincts atrophied, until now in civilized man instincts persist only as troublesome vestiges of his pre-human state, vestiges that are comparable to the vermiform appendix and which, like the latter, might with advantage be removed by the surgeon's knife, if that were at all possible. Others assign them a more prominent place in the constitution of the human mind; for they see that intelligence, as it increased with the evolution of the higher animals and of man, did not supplant and so lead to the atrophy of the instincts, but rather controlled and modified their operation; and some, like G. H. Schneider [1] and William James,[2] maintain that man has at least as many instincts as any of the animals, and assign them a leading part in the determination of human conduct and mental process. This last view is now rapidly gaining ground; and this volume, I hope, may contribute in some slight degree to promote the recognition of the full scope and function of the human instincts; for this recognition will, I feel sure, appear to those who come after us as the most important advance made by psychology in our time.

Instinctive actions are displayed in their purest form by animals not very high in the scale of intelligence. In the higher vertebrate animals few instinctive modes of behaviour remain purely instinctive—*i.e.*, unmodified by intelligence and by habits acquired under the guidance of intelligence or by imitation. And even the human infant, whose intelligence remains but little developed for so many months after birth, performs few purely instinctive actions; because in the human being the instincts, although innate, are, with few exceptions, undeveloped in the first months of life, and only ripen or become capable of functioning, at various periods throughout the years from infancy to puberty.

Insect life affords perhaps the most striking examples of purely instinctive action. There are many instances of insects that invariably lay their eggs in the only places where the grubs, when hatched, will find the food they need and can eat, or where the larvæ will be able to attach themselves as parasites to some host in a way that is necessary to their survival. In such cases it is clear that the behaviour of the parent is determined by the impressions made on its senses by the appropriate objects or places: *e.g.*, the smell of decaying flesh leads the carrion-fly to deposit its eggs upon it; the sight or odour of some particular flower leads another to lay its eggs among the ovules of the flower, which serve as food to the grubs. Others go through more elaborate trains of action, as when the mason-wasp lays its eggs in a mud-nest, fills up the space with caterpillars, which it paralyses by means of well-directed stings, and seals it up; so that the caterpillars remain as a supply of fresh animal food for the young which the parent will never see and of whose needs it can have no knowledge or idea.

Among the lower vertebrate animals also instinctive actions, hardly

[1] "Der thierische Wille." Leipzig, 1880.
[2] "Principles of Psychology," London, 1891.

at all modified by intelligent control, are common. The young chick runs
to his mother in response to a call of peculiar quality and nestles beneath
her; the young squirrel brought up in lonely captivity, when nuts are
given him for the first time, opens and eats some and buries others with
all the movements characteristic of his species; the kitten in the presence
of a dog or a mouse assumes the characteristic feline attitudes and behaves
as all his fellows of countless generations have behaved. Even so intelligent an animal as the domesticated dog behaves on some occasions in a
purely instinctive fashion; when, for example, a terrier comes across the
trail of a rabbit, his hunting instinct is immediately aroused by the scent;
he becomes blind and deaf to all other impressions as he follows the trail,
and then, when he sights his quarry, breaks out into the yapping which is
peculiar to occasions of this kind. His wild ancestors hunted in packs,
and, under those conditions, the characteristic bark emitted on sighting
the quarry served to bring his fellows to his aid; but when the domesticated terrier hunts alone, his excited yapping can but facilitate the
escape of his quarry; yet the old social instinct operates too powerfully
to be controlled by his moderate intelligence.

These few instances of purely instinctive behaviour illustrate clearly
its nature. In the typical case some sense-impression, or combination of
sense-impressions, excites some perfectly definite behaviour, some movement or train of movements which is the same in all individuals of the
species and on all similar occasions; and in general the behaviour so
occasioned is of a kind either to promote the welfare of the individual
animal or of the community to which he belongs, or to secure the per-
petuation of the species.[3]

In treating of the instincts of animals, writers have usually described
them as innate tendencies to certain kinds of action, and Herbert
Spencer's widely accepted definition of instinctive action as compound
reflex action takes account only of the behaviour or movements to which
instincts give rise. But instincts are more than innate tendencies or dispositions to certain kinds of movement. There is every reason to believe
that even the most purely instinctive action is the outcome of a distinctly
mental process, one which is incapable of being described in purely mechanical terms, because it is a psycho-physical process, involving psychical
as well as physical changes, and one which, like every other mental process,
has, and can only be fully described in terms of, the three aspects of all
mental process—the cognitive, the affective, and the conative aspects; that
is to say, every instance of instinctive behaviour involves a knowing of

---

[3] In many cases an instinct is excitable only during the prevalence of some
special organic condition (*e.g.,* the nest-building and mating instincts of birds, the
sitting instinct of the broody hen); and some writers have given such organic conditions an undue prominence, while neglecting the essential part played by sense-
impressions.

something or object, a feeling in regard to it, and a striving towards or away from that object.

We cannot, of course, directly observe the threefold psychical aspect of the psycho-physical process that issues in instinctive behaviour; but we are amply justified in assuming that it invariably accompanies the process in the nervous system of which the instinctive movements are the immediate result, a process which, being initiated on stimulation of some sense organ by the physical impressions received from the object, travels up the sensory nerves, traverses the brain, and descends as an orderly or co-ordinated stream of nervous impulses along efferent nerves to the appropriate groups of muscles and other executive organs. We are justified in assuming the cognitive aspect of the psychical process, because the nervous excitation seems to traverse those parts of the brain whose excitement involves the production of sensations or changes in the sensory content of consciousness; we are justified in assuming the affective aspect of the psychical process, because the creature exhibits unmistakable symptoms of feeling and emotional excitement; and, especially, we are justified in assuming the conative aspect of the psychical process, because all instinctive behaviour exhibits that unique mark of mental process, a persistent striving towards the natural end of the process. That is to say, the process, unlike any merely mechanical process, is not to be arrested by any sufficient mechanical obstacle, but is rather intensified by any such obstacle and only comes to an end either when its appropriate goal is achieved, or when some stronger incompatible tendency is excited, or when the creature is exhausted by its persistent efforts.

Now, the psycho-physical process that issues in an instinctive action is initiated by a sense-impression which, usually, is but one of many sense-impressions received at the same time; and the fact that this one impression plays an altogether dominant part in determining the animal's behaviour shows that its effects are peculiarly favoured, that the nervous system is peculiarly fitted to receive and to respond to just that kind of impression. The impression must be supposed to excite, not merely detailed changes in the animal's field of sensation, but a sensation or complex of sensations that has significance or meaning for the animal; hence we must regard the instinctive process in its cognitive aspect as distinctly of the nature of perception, however rudimentary. In the animals most nearly allied to ourselves we can, in many instances of instinctive behaviour, clearly recognise the symptoms of some particular kind of emotion such as fear, anger, or tender feeling; and the same symptoms always accompany any one kind of instinctive behaviour, as when the cat assumes the defensive attitude, the dog resents the intrusion of a strange dog, or the hen tenderly gathers her brood beneath her wings. We seem justified in believing that each kind of instinctive behaviour is always attended by some such emotional excitement, however faint, which in each case is specific or peculiar to that kind of behaviour. Analogy with our own experience justifies us, also, in assuming that the persistent striving towards its end, which characterises mental process and distinguishes instinctive behaviour most clearly from mere reflex action, implies some such mode of experience as we call conative, the kind of experience which in its more developed forms is properly called desire or aversion, but which, in the blind form in which we sometimes have it and which is its usual form among the animals, is a mere impulse, or craving, or uneasy sense of want. Further, we seem justified in believing that the continued obstruction of instinctive striving is always accompanied by painful feeling, its successful progress toward its end by pleasurable feeling, and the achievement of its end by a pleasurable sense of satisfaction.

An instinctive action, then, must not be regarded as simple or compound reflex action if by reflex action we mean, as is usually meant, a movement caused by a sense-stimulus and resulting from a sequence of merely physical processes in some nervous arc. Nevertheless, just as a reflex action implies the presence in the nervous system of the reflex nervous arc, so the instinctive action also implies some enduring nervous basis whose organisation is inherited, an innate or inherited psychophysical disposition, which, anatomically regarded, probably has the form of a compound system of sensori-motor cars.

We may, then, define an instinct as an inherited or innate psychophysical disposition which determines its possessor to perceive, and to pay attention to, objects of a certain class, to experience an emotional excitement of a particular quality upon perceiving such an object, and to act in regard to it in a particular manner, or, at least, to experience an impulse to such action.

It must further be noted that some instincts remain inexcitable except during the prevalence of some temporary bodily state, such as hunger. In these cases we must suppose that the bodily process or state determines the stimulation of sense-organs within the body, and that nervous currents ascending from these to the psycho-physical disposition maintain it in an excitable condition.[4]

---

[4] Most definitions of instincts and instinctive actions take account only of their conative aspect, of the motor tendencies by which the instincts of animals are most clearly manifested to us; and it is a common mistake to ignore the cognitive and the affective aspects of the instinctive mental process. Some authors make the worse mistake of assuming that instinctive actions are performed unconsciously. Herbert Spencer's definition of instinctive action as compound reflex action was mentioned above. Addison wrote of instinct that it is "an immediate impression from the first Mover and the Divine Energy acting in the creatures." Fifty years ago the entomologists, Kirby and Spence, wrote: "We may call the instincts of animals those faculties implanted in them by the Creator, by which, independent of instruction, observation, or experience, they are all alike impelled to the performance of certain actions tending to the wellbeing of the individual and the preservation of the species." More recently Dr. and Mrs. Peckham, who have observed the behaviour of wasps so carefully, have written: "Under the term 'instinct' we place all complex acts which are performed

The behaviour of some of the lower animals seems to be almost completely determined throughout their lives by instincts modified but very little by experience; they perceive, feel, and act in a perfectly definite and invariable manner whenever a given instinct is excited—*i.e.*, whenever the presence of the appropriate object coincides with the appropriate organic state of the creature. The highest degree of complexity of mental process attained by such creatures is a struggle between two opposed instinctive tendencies simultaneously excited. Such behaviour is relatively easy to understand in the light of the conception of instincts as innate psycho-physical dispositions.

While it is doubtful whether the behaviour of any animal is wholly determined by instincts quite unmodified by experience, it is clear that all the higher animals learn in various and often considerable degrees to adapt their instinctive actions to peculiar circumstances; and in the long course of the development of each human mind, immensely greater complications of the instinctive processes are brought about, complications so great that they have obscured until recent years the essential likeness of the instinctive processes in men and animals. These complications of instinctive processes are of four principal kinds, which we may distinguish as follows:—

(1) The instinctive reactions become capable of being initiated, not

---

previous to experience, and in a similar manner by all members of the same sex and race." One modern authority, Professor Karl Groos, goes so far as to say that "the idea of consciousness must be rigidly excluded from any definition of instinct which is to be of practical utility." In view of this persistent tendency to ignore the inner or psychical side of instinctive processes, it seems to me important to insist upon it, and especially to recognise in our definition its cognitive and affective aspects as well as its conative aspect. I would reverse Professor Groos's dictum and would say that any definition of instinctive action that does not insist upon its psychical aspect is useless for practical purposes, and worse than useless because misleading. For, if we neglect the psychical aspect of instinctive processes, it is impossible to understand the part played by instincts in the development of the human mind and in the determination of the conduct of individuals and societies; and it is the fundamental and all-pervading character of their influence upon the social life of mankind which alone gives the consideration of instincts its great practical importance.

The definition of instinct proposed above does not insist, as do many definitions, that the instinctive action is one performed without previous experience of the object; for it is only when an instinct is exercised for the first time by any creature that the action is prior to experience, and instinctive actions may continue to be instinctive even after much experience of their objects. The nest-building or the migratory flight of birds does not cease to be instinctive when these actions are repeated year after year, even though the later performances show improvement through experience, as the instinctive actions of the higher animals commonly do. Nor does our definition insist, as some do, that the instinctive action is performed without awareness of the end towards which it tends, for this too is not essential; it may be, and in the case of the lower animals, no doubt, often is, so performed, as also by the very young child; but in the case of the higher animals some prevision of the immediate end, however vague, probably accompanies an instinctive action that has often been repeated; *e.g.*, in the case of the dog that has followed the trail of game many times, we may properly regard the action as instinctive, although we can hardly doubt that, after many kills, the creature has some anticipation of the end of his activity.

only by the perception of objects of the kind which directly excite the innate disposition, the natural or native excitants of the instinct, but also by ideas of such objects, and by perceptions and by ideas of objects of other kinds:

(2) the bodily movements in which the instinct finds expression may be modified and complicated to an indefinitely great degree:

(3) owing to the complexity of the ideas which can bring the human instincts into play, it frequently happens that several instincts are simultaneously excited; when the several processes blend with various degrees of intimacy:

(4) the instinctive tendencies become more or less systematically organised about certain objects or ideas.

The full consideration of the first two modes of complication of instinctive behaviour would lead us too far into the psychology of the intellectual processes, to which most of the textbooks of psychology are mainly devoted. It must suffice merely to indicate in the present chapter a few points of prime importance in this connection. The third and fourth complications will be dealt with at greater length in the following chapters, for they stand in much need of elucidation.

In order to understand these complications of instinctive behaviour we must submit the conception of an instinct to a more minute analysis. It was said above that every instinctive process has the three aspects of all mental process, the cognitive, the affective, and the conative. Now, the innate psycho-physical disposition, which is an instinct, may be regarded as consisting of three corresponding parts, an afferent, a central, and a motor or efferent part, whose activities are the cognitive, the affective, and the conative features respectively of the total instinctive process. The afferent or receptive part of the total disposition is some organised group of nervous elements or neurones that is specially adapted to receive and to elaborate the impulses initiated in the sense-organ by the native object of the instinct; its constitution and activities determine the sensory content of the psycho-physical process. From the afferent part the excitement spreads over to the central part of the disposition; the constitution of this part determines in the main the distribution of the nervous impulses, especially of the impulses that descend to modify the working of the visceral organs, the heart, lungs, blood-vessels, glands, and so forth, in the manner required for the most effective execution of the instinctive action; the nervous activities of this central part are the correlates of the affective or emotional aspect or feature of the total psychical process.[5] The excitement of the efferent or motor part reaches it by way of the cen-

---

[5] It is probable that these central affective parts of the instinctive dispositions have their seat in the basal ganglia of the brain. The evidence in favour of this view has been greatly strengthened by the recent work of Pagano ("Archives Italiennes de Biologie," 1906).

tral part; its constitution determines the distribution of impulses to the muscles of the skeletal system by which the instinctive action is effected, and its nervous activities are the correlates of the conative element of the psychical process, of the felt impulse to action.

Now, the afferent or receptive part and the efferent or motor part are capable of being greatly modified, independently of one another and of the central part, in the course of the life history of the individual; while the central part persists throughout life as the essential unchanging nucleus of the disposition. Hence in man, whose intelligence and adaptability are so great, the afferent and efferent parts of each instinctive disposition are liable to many modifications, while the central part alone remains unmodified: that is to say, the cognitive processes through which any instinctive process may be initiated exhibit a great complication and variety; and the actual bodily movements by which the instinctive process achieves its end may be complicated to an indefinitely great extent; while the emotional excitement, with the accompanying nervous activities of the central part of the disposition, is the only part of the total instinctive process that retains its specific character and remains common to all individuals and all situations in which the instinct is excited. It is for this reason that authors have commonly treated of the instinctive actions of animals on the one hand, and of the emotions of men on the other hand, as distinct types of mental process, failing to see that each kind of emotional excitement is always an indication of, and the most constant feature of, some instinctive process.

Let us now consider very briefly the principal ways in which the instinctive disposition may be modified on its afferent or receptive side; and let us take, for the sake of clearness of exposition, the case of a particular instinct, namely the instinct of fear or flight, which is one of the strongest and most widely distributed instincts throughout the animal kingdom. In man and in most animals this instinct is capable of being excited by any sudden loud noise, independently of all experience of danger or harm associated with such noises. We must suppose, then, that the afferent inlet, or one of the afferent inlets, of this innate disposition consists in a system of auditory neurones connected by sensory nerves with the ear. This afferent inlet to this innate disposition is but little specialised, since it may be excited by any loud noise. One change it may undergo through experience is specialisation; on repeated experience of noises of certain kinds that are never accompanied or followed by hurtful effects, most creatures will learn to neglect them [6]; their instinct of flight is no longer excited by them; they learn, that is to say, to discriminate between these and other noises; this implies that the perceptual disposition, the afferent inlet of the instinct, has become further specialised.

[6] As in the case of wild creatures that we may see from the windows of a railway train browsing undisturbed by the familiar noise.

More important is the other principal mode in which the instinct may be modified on its afferent or cognitive side. Consider the case of the birds on an uninhabited island, which show no fear of men on their first appearance on the island. The absence of fear at the sight of man implies, not that the birds have no instinct of fear, but that the instinct has no afferent inlet specialised for the reception of the retinal impression made by the human form. But the men employ themselves in shooting, and very soon the sight of a man excites the instinct of fear in the birds, and they take to flight at his approach. How are we to interpret this change of instinctive behaviour brought about by experience? Shall we say that the birds observe on one occasion, or on several or many occasions, that on the approach of a man one of their number falls to the ground, uttering cries of pain; that they infer that the man has wounded it, and that he may wound and hurt them, and that he is therefore to be avoided in the future? No psychologist would now accept this anthropomorphic interpretation of the facts. If the behaviour we are considering were that of savage men, or even of a community of philosophers and logicians, such an account would err in ascribing the change of behaviour to a purely intellectual process. Shall we, then, say that the sudden loud sound of the gun excites the instinct of fear, and that, because the perception of this sound is constantly accompanied by the visual perception of the human form, the idea of the latter becomes associated with the idea of the sound, so that thereafter the sight of a man reproduces the idea of the sound of the gun, and hence leads to the excitement of the instinct by way of its innately organised afferent inlet, the system of auditory neurones? This would be much nearer the truth than the former account; some such interpretation of facts of this order has been offered by many psychologists and very generally accepted.[7] Its acceptance involves the attribution of free ideas, of the power of representation of objects independently of sense-presentation, to whatever animals display this kind of modification of instinctive behaviour by experience—that is to say, to all the animals save the lowest; and there are good reasons for believing that only man and the higher animals have this power. We are therefore driven to look for a still simpler interpretation of the facts, and such a one is not far to seek. We may suppose that, since the visual presentation of the human form repeatedly accompanies the excitement of the instinct of fear by the sound of the gun, it acquires the power of exciting directly the reactions characteristic of this instinct, rather than indirectly by way of the reproduction of the idea of the sound; *i.e.*, we may suppose that, after repetition of the experience, the sight of a man directly excites the instinctive process in its affective and conative aspects only; or we may say, in physiological terms, that the visual disposition concerned in the

---

[7] It is, *e.g.*, the interpretation proposed by G. H. Schneider in his work "Der thierische Wille"; it mars this otherwise excellent book.

elaboration of the retinal impression of the human form becomes directly connected or associated with the central and efferent parts of the instinctive disposition, which thus acquires, through the repetition of this experience, a new afferent inlet through which it may henceforth be excited independently of its innate afferent inlet.

There is, I think, good reason to believe that this third interpretation is much nearer the truth than the other two considered above. In the first place, the assumption of such relative independence of the afferent part of an instinctive disposition as is implied by this interpretation is justified by the fact that many instincts may be excited by very different objects affecting different senses, prior to all experience of such objects. The instinct of fear is the most notable in this respect, for in many animals it may be excited by certain special impressions of sight, of smell, and of hearing, as well as by all loud noises (perhaps also by any painful sense-impression), all of which impressions evoke the emotional expressions and the bodily movements characteristic of the instinct. Hence, we may infer that such an instinct has several innately organised afferent inlets, through each of which its central and efferent parts may be excited without its other afferent inlets being involved in the excitement.

But the best evidence in favour of the third interpretation is that which we may obtain by introspective observation of our own emotional states. Through injuries received we may learn to fear, or to be angered by, the presence of a person or animal or thing towards which we were at first indifferent; and we may then experience the emotional excitement and the impulse to the appropriate movements of flight or aggression, without recalling the nature and occasion of the injuries we have formerly suffered; *i.e.*, although the idea of the former injury may be reproduced by the perception, or by the idea, of the person, animal, or thing from which it was received, yet the reproduction of this idea is not an essential step in the process of reexcitement of the instinctive reaction in its affective and conative aspects; for the visual impression made by the person or thing leads directly to the excitement of the central and efferent parts of the innate disposition. In this way our emotional and conative tendencies become directly associated by experience with many objects to which we are natively indifferent; and not only do we not necessarily recall the experience through which the association was set up, but in many such cases we cannot do so by any effort of recollection.[8]

Such acquisition of new perceptual inlets by instinctive dispositions, in accordance with the principle of association in virtue of temporal con-

[8] In this way some particular odour, some melody or sound, some phrase or trick of speech or manner, some peculiar combination of colour or effect of light upon the landscape, may become capable of directly exciting some affective disposition, and we find ourselves suddenly swept by a wave of strong emotion for which we can assign no adequate cause.

tiguity, seems to occur abundantly among all the higher animals and to be the principal mode in which they profit by experience and learn to adapt their behaviour to a greater variety of the objects of their environment than is provided for by their purely innate dispositions. In man it occurs still more abundantly, and in his case the further complication ensues that each sense-presentation that thus becomes capable of arousing some emotional and conative disposition may be represented, or reproduced in idea; and, since the representation, having in the main the same neural basis as the sense-presentation, induces equally well the same emotional and conative excitement, and since it may be brought to mind by any one of the intellectual processes, ranging from simple associative reproduction to the most subtle processes of judgment and inference, the ways in which any one instinctive disposition of a developed human mind may be excited are indefinitely various.

There is a second principal mode in which objects other than the native objects of an instinct may lead to the excitement of its central and efferent parts. This is similar to the mode of reproduction of ideas known as the reproduction by similars; a thing, or sense-impression, more or less like the specific excitant of an instinct, but really of a different class, excites the instinct in virtue of those features in which it resembles the specific object. As a very simple instance of this, we may take the case of a horse shying at an old coat left lying by the roadside. The shying is, no doubt, due to the excitement of an instinct whose function is to secure a quick retreat from any crouching beast of prey, and the coat sufficiently resembles such a crouching form to excite the instinct. This example illustrates the operation of this principle in the crudest fashion. In the human mind it works in a much more subtle and wide-reaching fashion. Very delicate resemblances of form and relation between two objects may suffice to render one of them capable of exciting the emotion and the impulse which are the appropriate instinctive response to the presentation of the other object; and, in order that this shall occur, it is not necessary that the individual shall become explicitly aware of the resemblance between the two objects, nor even that the idea of the second object shall be brought to his consciousness; though this, no doubt, occurs in many cases. The wide scope of this principle in the human mind is due, not merely to the subtler operation of resemblances, but also to the fact that through the working of the principle of temporal contiguity, discussed on the foregoing page, the number of objects capable of directly exciting any instinct becomes very considerable, and each such object then serves as a basis for the operation of the principle of resemblance; that is to say, each object that in virtue of temporal contiguity acquires the power of exciting the central and efferent parts of an instinct renders possible the production of the same effect by a number of objects more or less resembling it. The conjoint operation of the two principles may be illustrated by a simple example: a child is terrified upon one occasion by the violent behaviour of a man of a peculiar cast of countenance or of some special fashion of dress; thereafter not only does the perception or idea of this man excite fear, but any man resembling him in face or costume may do so without the idea of the original occasion of fear, or of the terrifying individual, recurring to consciousness.

As regards the modification of the bodily movements by means of which an instinctive mental process achieves,[9] or strives to achieve, its end, man excels the animals even to a greater degree than as regards the modification of the cognitive part of the process. For the animals acquire and use hardly any movement-complexes that are not natively given in their instinctive dispositions and in the reflex co-ordinations of their spinal cords. This is true of even so intelligent an animal as the domestic dog. Many of the higher animals may by long training be taught to acquire a few movement-complexes—a dog to walk on its hind legs, or a cat to sit up; but the wonder with which we gaze at a circus-horse standing on a tub, or at a dog dancing on hind legs, shows how strictly limited to the natively given combinations of movements all the animals normally are.

In the human being, on the other hand, a few only of the simpler instincts that ripen soon after birth are displayed in movements determined purely by the innate dispositions; such are the instincts of sucking, of wailing, of crawling, of winking and shrinking before a coming blow. Most of the human instincts ripen at relatively late periods in the course of individual development, when considerable power of intelligent control and imitation of movement has been acquired; hence the motor tendencies of these instincts are seldom manifested in their purely native forms, but are from the first modified, controlled, and suppressed in various degrees. This is the case more especially with the large movements of trunk and limbs; while the subsidiary movements, those which Darwin called serviceable associated movements, such as those due to contractions of the facial muscles, are less habitually controlled, save by men of certain races and countries among whom control of facial movement is prescribed by custom. An illustration may indicate the main principle involved: One may have learnt to suppress more or less completely the bodily movements in which the excitement of the instinct of pugnacity naturally finds vent; or by a study of pugilism one may have learnt to render those movements more finely adapted to secure the end of the instinct; or one may have learnt to replace them by the habitual use of weapons, so that the hand flies to the sword-hilt or to the hip-pocket, instead of being raised to strike, whenever this instinct is excited. But one exercises but little, if any,

[9] It would, of course, be more correct to say that the creature strives to achieve its end under the driving power of the instinctive impulse awakened within it, but, if this is recognised, it is permissible to avoid the repeated use of this cumbrous phraseology.

control over the violent beating of the heart, the flushing of the face, the deepened respiration, and the general redistribution of blood-supply and nervous tension which constitute the visceral expression of the excitement of this instinct and which are determined by the constitution of its central affective part. Hence in the human adult, while this instinct may be excited by objects and situations that are not provided for in the innate disposition, and may express itself in bodily movements which also are not natively determined, or may fail to find expression in any such movements owing to strong volitional control, its unmodified central part will produce visceral changes, with the accompanying emotional state of consciousness, in accordance with its unmodified native constitution; and these visceral changes will usually be accompanied by the innately determined facial expression in however slight a degree; hence result the characteristic expressions or symptoms of the emotion of anger which, as regards their main features, are common to all men of all times and all races.

All the principal instincts of man are liable to similar modifications of their afferent and motor parts, while their central parts remain unchanged and determine the emotional tone of consciousness and the visceral changes characteristic of the excitement of the instinct.

It must be added that the conative aspect of the psychical process always retains the unique quality of an impulse to activity, even though the instinctive activity has been modified by habitual control; and this felt impulse, when it becomes conscious of its end, assumes the character of an explicit desire or aversion.

Are, then, these instinctive impulses the only motive powers of the human mind to thought and action? What of pleasure and pain, which by so many of the older psychologists were held to be the only motives of human activity, the only objects or sources of desire and aversion?

In answer to the former question, it must be said that in the developed human mind there are springs of action of another class, namely, acquired habits of thought and action. An acquired mode of activity becomes by repetition habitual, and the more frequently it is repeated the more powerful becomes the habit as a source of impulse or motive power. Few habits can equal in this respect the principal instincts; and habits are in a sense derived from, and secondary to, instincts; for, in the absence of instincts, no thought and no action could ever be achieved or repeated, and so no habits of thought or action could be formed. Habits are formed only in the service of the instincts.

The answer to the second question is that pleasure and pain are not in themselves springs of action, but at the most of undirected movements; they serve rather to modify instinctive processes, pleasure tending to sustain and prolong any mode of action, pain to cut it short; under their prompting and guidance are effected those modifications and adaptations of the instinctive bodily movements which we have briefly considered above.[10]

We may say, then, that directly or indirectly the instincts are the prime movers of all human activity; by the conative or impulsive force of some instinct (or of some habit derived from an instinct), every train of thought, however cold and passionless it may seem, is borne along towards its end, and every bodily activity is initiated and sustained. The instinctive impulses determine the ends of all activities and supply the driving power by which all mental activities are sustained; and all the complex intellectual apparatus of the most highly developed mind is but a means towards these ends, is but the instrument by which these impulses seek their satisfaction, while pleasure and pain do but serve to guide them in their choice of the means.

Take away these instinctive dispositions with their powerful impulses, and the organism would become incapable of activity of any kind; it would lie inert and motionless like a wonderful clockwork whose mainspring had been removed or a steam-engine whose fires had been drawn. These impulses are the mental forces that maintain and shape all the life of individuals and societies, and in them we are confronted with the central mystery of life and mind and will.

[10] None of the doctrines of the associationist psychology was more profoundly misleading and led to greater absurdities than the attempt to exhibit pleasure and pain as the source of all activities. What could be more absurd than Professor Bain's doctrine that the joy of a mother in her child, her tender care and self-sacrificing efforts in its behalf, are due to the pleasure she derives from bodily contact with it in the maternal embrace? Or what could be more strained and opposed to hundreds of familiar facts than Herbert Spencer's doctrine that the emotion of fear provoked by any object consists in faint revivals, in some strange cluster, of ideas of all the pains suffered in the past upon contact with, or in the presence of, that object? (*cf.* Bain's "Emotions and the Will," chap. vi.; and H. Spencer's "Principles of Psychology," vol. i. part iv. chap. viii. 3rd Ed.)

# 3 • Zing Yang Kuo

## *Giving Up Instincts in Psychology*

Kuo's radical denial of all instincts represents the sharp reaction against the promiscuous use of the concept. Kuo was not alone in his position. L. L. Bernard published an attack on the misuse of instinct in the same year and later dealt with the topic in a book, *Instinct, a Study in Social Psychology.* In order to show the chaos in the use of instinct as an explanatory word, Bernard reported a survey of nearly 500 texts in which he found reference to a total of 5759 different classes, or types, of instincts. Small wonder that many agreed that the usefulness of the term was at an end!

*In the present paper* an attempt is made to repudiate the current views of instinct and to suggest a new interpretation of the native equipment of man on a purely objective and behavioristic basis.

## INSTINCT IN MODERN PSYCHOLOGY

Although the theory of instincts is as old as the history of psychology, it is only recently that they have been applied so universally in nearly all of the fields of psychology. They were formerly conceived of as a specific faculty possessed only by brutes. People of ancient and medieval times believed that animals lived by instinct while human beings lived by reason. Even up to the middle of the nineteenth century there was little discussion of instincts in human psychology. Darwin and Spencer were, among others, responsible for first calling our attention to the rôle played by instincts in human behavior. But the traditional belief persisted and many writers still held that human instincts were irrational and undesirable forms of behavior and hence must be supplanted by reason. It was J. H. Schneider and William James who assigned to instincts a leading rôle in the determination of human motives. James asserted that man had

This article is reproduced in full from the *Journal of Philosophy,* 1921, *17,* 645–664. Reprinted by permission of the *Journal of Philosophy.*

more instincts than animals and that there was no material antagonism between instinct and reason.

Partly due to the influence of James, the rôle of human instincts turns to the other direction. Not only are instincts no longer looked upon with suspicion, but they are regarded as the mainspring of human behavior. Instinct has become a current fad in psychology. Behavior of man, origin of social institutions, religious motives, and the like—all these different human activities are to be explained in terms of instinct. Recent social unrest and the labor movement are again attributed to the failure on the part of society to satisfy the instinctive impulses. Writers on the psychology of war almost identify the war motive with the herd instinct, the instinct of pugnacity, and other allied instincts. For the Freudian psychologists the sex instinct becomes the most fundamental thing in human nature.

Thousands of passages might be quoted from modern literature of psychology to show how much stress has been laid upon the significance of instinct in human behavior. But the following quotations will suffice to illustrate: "The human mind has certain innate or inherited tendencies which are the essential springs or motive powers of all thought and action, whether individual or collective, and are the bases from which the character and will of individuals and of nations are gradually developed under the guidance of the intellectual faculties." [1] "The behavior of man in the family, in business, in the state, in religion, and every other affair of life is rooted in his unlearned original equipment of instincts and capacities. All schemes of improving human life must take account of man's original nature, most of all when their aim is to counteract it." [2]

There have been some protests among psychologists against the looseness of the usage of the term "instinct." A reader of modern literature on the subject of instincts will be struck by the fact that no two psychologists will agree upon the definition of and what constitutes human instincts. In spite of all these divergencies, however, there are certain generalities that characterize the current views on instincts.

In the first place, instinct is usually defined in either one of two ways: as an innate tendency to action, or as an inherited combination of reflexes. We take Parmelee's as an illustration of the latter: "An instinct is an inherited combination of reflexes which have been integrated by the central nervous system so as to cause an external activity of the organism which usually characterizes a whole species and is usually adaptive." [3] This view seems most acceptable to the students of animal psychology and behaviorists. The former view is adopted by introspectionalists and students of social psychology who find it more satisfactory to define instincts in psychological than in biological terms. McDougall illustrates this view-point

---

[1] McDougall, *Soc. Psychol.*, p. 29.
[2] Thorndike, *Educ. Psychol.*, Vol. I., p. 4.
[3] Parmelee, *The Science of Human Behavior*, p. 226.

in his definition: "We may, then, define an instinct as an inherited or innate psycho-physical disposition which determines its possessor to perceive, and to pay attention to objects of a certain class, to experience an emotional excitement of a particular quality upon perceiving such an object, and to act in regard to it in a particular manner, or at least, to experience an impulse to such action." [4]

In the second place, instinct is usually viewed as adaptive or teleological; that is, every instinctive performance always tends to accomplish some biological end or to adapt the organism to its environment: thus the biological purpose of anger is "the defense of the organism by removing the offending object"; that of fear is "the defense of the organism by removing it from the offending environment" and so on.[5] This view is conceded by most of the biologists and psychologists as well.

Thirdly, instinct is assumed either as fixed and stereotyped, or, as capable of modification. The latter point of view is the prevailing one in our modern literature. Psychologists have dealt with the problem of the modification of instincts in various ways: (1) Simply as an increase in perfection of the performance of instinct through practise; (2) that it takes place through changes in the original mode of response or in sensory perception; and (3) that it occurs by becoming integrated into the more complex types of responses.[6] Hunter emphasizes the point that instincts may be modified, before their first appearance, by experience of the organism or through social influence.[7] A great many psychologists maintain that instincts appear at certain periods of life and that they may be lost through disuse.

Fourth, instincts are sometimes conceived by psychologists as a specific response to a specific stimulus, or merely as a general tendency to respond to a variety of stimuli. Thorndike and many of his followers are in agreement with the former view; while McDougall, Drever, and many others, subscribe to the latter.

Three general methods are used by modern psychologists for the study of instincts. (1) The genetic method is used for the observation of the reactions of the infant. If certain reactions function from the birth on with a considerable amount of effectiveness, we assert that they are specific instincts. Nursing is perhaps the only instinct which is supposed to appear at birth. (2) In the experimental method, the experimenter observes the organism under certain controlled conditions in which there is no chance for the organism to acquire certain forms of reactions. If, in spite of such prevention of learning, the organism still can perform such

[4] *Soc. Psychol.*, p. 29.

[5] W. H. Hunter, "The Modification of Instinct," *etc.*, in *Psychol. Rev.*, 1920, Vol. 27, p. 265.

[6] See J. R. Kantor's "Functional Interpretation of Human Instincts," *Psychol. Rev.*, 1920, Vol. 27, No. 1, p. 52.

[7] *Psychol. Rev.*, 1930, Vol. 27, pp. 255–261.

reactions, we conclude that they are specific instincts. Spalding's experiment on the flight of birds and Scott's on the social influence on the singing of birds are examples of the second method of studying instincts. (3) In the observational method, we simply observe the characteristic activities of a race. If certain activities characterize the whole species, they are regarded as instinctive. Thus, the mouse-hunting reaction is supposed to be an instinct that belongs to the cat because it is a characteristic reaction of the whole species.

## NON-EXISTENCE OF SPECIFIC INSTINCTS [8]

1. We have stated that there is no general agreement among the students of instincts as to the number and kinds of instincts. Writers on the subject arbitrarily list them in accordance with their own purposes. If the writer is interested in social psychology, his list of instincts will be based on those reactions that are socially significant. If his interest is in economics or in religion his list will inevitably be a quite different one. As the purposes are varied so the classifications of instincts are unlimited and uncertain.

2. The so-called instincts are in the last analysis acquired trends rather than inherited tendencies. By an acquired trend is simply meant a habitual tendency to act in a certain way under certain conditions. In this connection it must be kept clearly in mind that a trend or tendency to action is different from an actual act; the former is simply a potential behavior which becomes an actual act when the organism is properly stimulated. A behavior tendency can only be developed as a result of the previous experience of the organism—that is, as a result of previous performance of an actual act in the presence of adequate stimuli. To assume any inborn tendency is to assume *a priori* relation between the organism and stimulating objects; for every behavior is an interaction between the organism and its surrounding objects. Such as assumption is no less objectionable than the theory of innate ideas. As a matter of fact both the theory of instinct and that of innate ideas are based on the same conception; namely the conception of *a priori* relation of the organism to external objects. If it is true that one can not have an idea of a tree before one has actually seen or learned about a tree, it must be equally true that one can not have any food trend before one has ever eaten food.

[8] The central position of this paper is quite different from that of Professor Knight Dunlap. (*Cf.* "Are there any Instincts?" in *J. abnorm. Psychol.*, 1919, Vol. 14, 307–311.) A careful examination of Professor Dunlap's article will show that he has by no means denied the existence of instinct. What he seems to have objected to is the teleological groupings of instincts which are to him unpsychological. In the present paper we attempt to deny not only the classification of instincts, but their very existence.

To illustrate how our trends of action are developed let us consider the following hypothetical cases: A new-born babe, when stimulated by a certain object, displays a number of random acts. If some of these acts incidentally result in satisfaction, it is likely to be repeated on similar occasions. If, on the other hand, it results in pain, it is likely to be avoided. Through a number of trials and errors the ill-adaptive acts are eliminated, perhaps inhibited by the emphasis on the favorable reaction, and the adaptive ones are selected. If these selected acts are called forth frequently enough, by similar stimuli or "conditioning" stimuli, they tend to become habitual trends of reaction. If a child is first presented a number of wooden blocks he reacts to them in various ways: he pushes some of them away, pulls some near to him, puts some of then into his mouth, kicks them with his legs, slashes them with his arms, *etc.* In such cases, there is nothing that can be called purposive; all of them are random in character. But, if he incidentally puts some of them together and derives more pleasure from this than from other act (the reason why it gives more pleasure is probably due to certain reflex bodily effects, or it may be due to the fact that, as M. Meyer has suggested, the sensory impression in the pile of blocks is more intensive than a single block; or, it may be due to the approval and encouragement of the attendant or nurse for this particular reaction, the putting together of blocks) he is more likely to react in this way when the blocks are again presented to him on the next occasion. Now, if such a reaction is called out often enough, there is built in the child a habit of putting blocks together, and when this reaction is transferred to other objects (conditioned response) we may reasonably conclude that a rudimentary trend of construction is formed.

The habit of acquisition is generated and developed in exactly the same way. Through imitation or encouragement by persons surrounding him, the babe may form a habit of gathering his playthings together. And when this reaction is later transformed to other objects, there is bred in him a trend-of-collecting reaction.

Again, the so-called moral instinct is a result of the combined influences of various social forces. From birth on the child is subject to social impressions. These impressions and the reactions of the child tend to modify the cortical structure and leave their permanent registration in the cerebral neurons. On proper occasions these cerebral neurons are aroused and the similar reactions are likely to be reproduced by the child. But owing to his inability to recollect the sources of these influences, he may reproduce them as if they came directly from his original nature. Our conscience is a product of various social sanctions. The authorities are first imposed upon the child from without, but gradually they are transformed into the internal authority, which gives rise to conscience. The transformation takes place so slowly and so gradually that the organism is not aware of the process. A child is repeatedly told not to do a certain thing, and that if he does do it he will be punished by some authority. He refrains from doing it at first merely because he fears the punishment, but finally it becomes habitual through frequent exercise, and he feels his duty not to do such a thing even though there be no threat of punishment for the breaking of the habit at all. In case the habit should be changed, it will involve a deep feeling of uneasiness which is commonly regarded as the awakening of conscience. Many psychologists who observe his behavior fail to trace the sources from which this habitual trend of action is developed and attribute it to an instinct.

Other trends of action are developed in the same manner. If we watch the stages of the development of human behavior closely enough, we shall not have any difficulty to trace the sources of social influences. To call an acquired trend of action an instinct is simply to confess our ignorance of the history of its development.[9] Many psychologists have denied the moral and religious trends as specific instincts. But is there any difference between these and trends such as parental care, sex, acquisition, fighting, self-display, curiosity, *etc.?* Why can we not on the same basis deny them? Whatever has been denied as an instinct is simply referred back to some other instinct. We are told that there are no religious and moral instincts as such; they are simply a combination of other instincts. But these other instincts few psychologists have ever attempted to analyze further.

3. Psychologists frequently speak of instinct in terms of purpose or teleology. Certain reactions accomplish certain ends. If these end reactions are performed without previous education, they are called instincts. Thus, if a bird has never seen other birds build a nest or has never been taught to build it, the first nest that it builds is considered as the result of an instinct. But an end reaction may involve a great number of mechanisms or subordinated acts most of which may be acquired, and yet all of these acquired mechanisms or subordinated acts may be overlooked because of interest in the end reaction, the "instinct." Walking is usually asserted to be the result of instinctive action. But how many acquired mechanisms are involved in the walking process? The movements of the trunk, of the head, of the legs and feet, hands and arms, in fact almost every part of the body, must be coordinated before walking can take place. Are we justified, then, in calling walking an instinct while the mechanisms involved in the process are acquired? How many mechanisms or other activities are involved in fighting, in sex, in parental care, *etc.?* How many of these mechanisms are not acquired? We are told that certain instincts can not function until certain mechanisms necessary for these reactions are ready. Sex instinct, they say, is not capable of functioning until the mechanisms necessary for the sexual performance have been

[9] Pillsbury seems to have frankly confessed that we call those responses instincts because they can not be explained by experience. See his *Essentials of Psychology,* 1920, p. 268.

acquired. But since these instincts have no ready-made mechanisms of their own, do we have any right to call them inherited responses? Moreover, the same acquired activities or mechanisms may be combined in different ways to produce different end reactions. The constituent acts of the fighting instinct may be identical with those involved in flights; the mouse-hunting activities of a cat may be identical with those involved in play; and do we not sometimes spend the same energy and employ the same mechanisms to construct something as to destroy something? What may sometimes seem to be unlearned activity is a new combination; its constituent acts may be as old as the life history of the organism.

That an instinct has a definite inherited neural pattern few students will deny. But such a conception can not be applied to many of the supposed instincts. General observation tends to show that the so-called instinctive reactions are very variable. Swindle has reported that even nest-building in birds, which is always supposed to be perfect and definite, involves a great deal of variability of response.[10] When we can not find any definite responses in instincts, we wonder as to the definiteness of inherited neural patterns. The teleological conception of instinct seems to reduce it to a "trend" or tendency of action, and gives up its neural correlate altogether.[11] But we have shown that the trend is acquired rather than inherited.

4. The methods used in investigating instincts are unreliable. The genetic method seems more advantageous than the others, but it has so far yielded few positive results. What it has found in the young babe is a number of random and unorganized acts. Nothing that we can call a specific instinct has been found to have ever appeared at birth, or even shortly after birth. If the student of instincts limits his list to these random and unorganized acts, we shall have no particular objection to his using the term "instinct"; but we do object to the calling of any reaction an instinct if it does not appear at birth or shortly after birth; for, as we shall see, all the activities of the organism in later life are various organized reactions of elementary movements.

The general observation method is altogether inadequate; according to this, when we find a certain reaction which is characteristic of the species, it is an instinct. But a careful analysis will show that the members of the species have similar reactions, not because they have inherited the same instincts, but, rather, because they have inherited the same action system and live in a similar environment. Given an action system in a given situation the two organisms will react in identically the same way, if their past experiences and the physiological states of the moment are identically the same; change the environment and a different reaction results.

---

[10] *Amer. J. Psychol.*, 1919, Vol. 30, pp. 173–186.
[11] *Cf.* E. C. Tolman's "Instinct and Purpose" in *Psychol. Rev.*, 1920, Vol. 27, pp. 217–233, especially page 222.

Furthermore, social influences also play a very important rôle in assimilating behavior, both in human beings and in animals. They begin to work on the organism from birth on. The results of Scott's experiments on the social influence on the songs of birds have clearly shown that the mere observation of the common types of behavior possessed by the members of the same species can not give us any warrant for the conclusion of the existence of instincts.

Those experiments on animal instincts that have yielded negative results will, of course, discredit instincts; but even those that have yielded positive results may still be subject to criticism. As we have shown, the end reaction may be performed by the organism without previous education, but its constituent acts or the mechanisms employed to produce the result are as old as the life history of the organism. There may be a new combination or a reintegration of old activities under the demand of new environment which tends to produce new result; but there is no new mechanism involved. If the experimenter can prove that birds can build nests without being taught or seeing the same activities of other birds, he must be reminded of the fact that the mechanisms and the subordinated or constituent activities which are combined to produce a complete reaction of nest building are practically the same as those that they have employed in eating, mating, fighting, flight, etc.

We may even question the validity of Spalding's experiment on the flight of birds. He confined newly hatched birds in small boxes so that they were prevented from stretching their wings and were not allowed to see the flight of other birds These birds were not released until they reached the normal age at which other birds of the same species began to fly. Spalding found that these birds could fly well upon being released. He thus concluded that flight was an instinct. Such a conclusion is erroneous. That the birds could fly without previous education was rather due to the maturity of action system (wings, and other flying mechanisms). Given a mature action system and given an environmental demand a definite reaction can be fairly predicted. It is no more natural than that birds with well developed flying mechanisms will fly when conditions demand such reaction. In other words, the so-called unlearned acts are not manifestation of innate responses but rather the direct effect of new situations and of the action system which possesses the possibility of such acts. The behavior of an organism must always be described in terms of its relation to the surrounding objects and its action system rather than in terms of inherited responses. The organism possesses no "preformed" reactions any more than germ cells possess a "preformed" embryo. The preconception of instinct has often betrayed the psychologist into overlooking the new environmental factors which are chiefly responsible for the supposedly unlearned acts. Instead of observing and describing the situations which call forth new acts he attempts the discovery of instincts.

This leads us to the rejection of the theory of periodical appearance of instincts. The so-called "delayed instincts" such as the sex and parental instincts, *etc.*, if they could be actually demonstrated at all, must be regarded as a result of changes in action system (for instance, changes in the structure of the sex organs at puberty which are accompanied by new intra-organic stimuli) and changes in social situations, rather than as a result of the manifestations of some mysterious forces. Any change in life situation and action system as effected by maturity of development will inevitably result in a new mode of behavior. And yet how many psychologists have not been at error in attributing it to the sudden appearance of instincts?

5. There have been at least two motives which have led the psychologist to insist on the existence of instincts and their significance in behavior. The first is the notion that every instinct has an adaptive function. Biased by the Darwinian theory of natural selection, students of psychology are apt to interpret every spontaneous reaction of the organism in terms of biological value. They argue that instincts play a very important part in the preservation of the organism and the species. These instincts, because of their adaptive value, are preserved in the race through natural selection and are handed down from generation to generation. This view is both theoretically and practically ungrounded.

In the first place, these supposed instincts might be adaptive in certain generations; but there is no guarantee that they will be adaptive in all generations and under every circumstance. Our environment is constantly changing, and new environment requires new adaptation. If instincts persist from generation to generation, they, instead of being adaptive instruments for racial or individual preservation, will become mal-adaptive in a new environment. This is especially true of those human races whose civilization has been progressing. There, the social situation changes so rapidly that no member of a new generation will have to re-capitulate the old way of reaction in which their ancestors have reacted to the former environment. Should we have inherited the same instincts as our ancestors of a few thousand years ago, how awkward we would be in adapting ourselves to modern society.

In the second place, and this is more important, actual fact does not show that every spontaneous response of the young infant is adaptive. On the contrary, our observation of the behavior of the young infant seems to indicate that except those reactions that are connected with vegetative functions, most of the responses that it makes are non-adaptive, or even ill-adaptive. An infant not infrequently reacts positively to those stimuli that are harmful and negatively to those that will do no harm or are even beneficial. It will be very ridiculous to say that the young infant attempts to grasp the fire or a harmful snake, when presented to him, because such a reaction is useful to the organism. The fact that children do survive in spite of many ill-adaptive reactions that they possess, is due to the artificial elimination by society of those harmful stimuli to which they will respond positively. Children are born in a society where the stimuli are so controlled that they have little chance to exercise ill-adaptive reactions.[12] The period of infancy is a period of helplessness. This is a period that requires social protection. To say that the so-called innate responses of the young human organism have biological value is to overlook the fact that from the moment that the child is born it is taken care of by society.

6. The second motive in the discussion of instincts I wish to combat is the motive on the part of the students of instincts to conceive an instinct as an impulse which furnishes the drive or motive power that leads the organism to action. We quote McDougall again: "The human mind has certain innate or inherited tendencies which are the essential springs or motive powers of all thought and action, whether individual or collective, and are the bases from which the character and will of individuals and of nations are gradually developed under the guidance of the intellectual faculties." [13] "Take away these instinctive dispositions with their powerful impulses, and the organism would become incapable of activity of any kind; it would be inert and motionless like a wonderful clockwork whose main spring had been removed, or a steam engine whose fires had been drawn. These impulses are the mental forces that maintain and shape all the life of individuals and societies, and in them we are confronted with the central mystery of life and mind and will." [14] Here we are obliged to take sharp issue with McDougall and all of his followers who maintain that all the motives of human activities are derived from instincts. A general observation of child behavior will show that the activities of the new born babe are aroused by external stimuli rather than by internal "drives." Professor Woodworth has well said: "But this assumption of great inertia or inertness of the organism, though it might perhaps have a semblance of truth as applied to adults, is rather grotesque when applied to children—it is to children above all that it must be applied, since it is only young children who are limited to native tendencies, older individuals having developed derived impulses, as indicated in one of the quotations above. If anything is characteristic of children, it is that they are easily aroused to activity. Watching a well-fed and well-rested babe, as it lies kicking and throwing its arms about, cooing, looking here and there, and pricking up its ears (figuratively) at every sound, one wonders what is the nature of the powerful impulse that initiates and sustains all this activity The fact is that the infant is responsive to a great variety of stimuli and that he is driven very largely by the stimuli that reach him

12 *Cf.* Watson's *Behavior*, pp. 257–258.
13 *Soc. Psychol.*, p. 19.
14 *Op. cit.*, p. 44.

from outside; though, when he is hungry, we see him driven by an inner 'powerful impulse' through a series of preparatory reactions towards the consummation of feeding. In the play of older children, also, it is difficult to find a strong incentive necessary; almost anything can be made play and then become attractive on its own account. It is true, as a general proposition, that as the individual grows up, his actions are more and more controlled by inner drives rather than by the immediately present stimuli; but even adults are less inert than McDougall seems to assume. Their activity is more easily aroused, and requires less interior motive or drive than he supposes." [15]

But in adult life the case is somewhat different. As Woodworth has pointed out, the actions of the human adult "are more and more controlled by inner drives." But these inner drives are by no means mystical forces suddenly bursting forth from the organism; on the contrary, they have their history and development: they are products of the constant interaction between the organism and its environment. There is every reason to believe that the motive forces of human behavior are largely shaped by society. Living in a given community one acquires certain motives of action. It is not that the social instincts tend to create society, but that the constant association tends to breed the social trends in the organism. The man is fond of living in a family not because he was born that way, but, rather, because he has lived in that way. No organism can be sociable unless it has social contact with other organisms. Isolate the child from human society as soon as it is born, would it still possess the motive forces that are common to human beings? McDougall and his followers, when they speak of these "powerful impulses" as the foundation of human behavior, forget that they are really dealing with the acquired trends rather than with instinct as they have defined it. McDougall cites from Galton the case which he regards as the display of gregarious instinct in the South African ox. He says, "The ox displays no affection for his fellows, hardly seems to notice their existence, so long as he is among the herd; if he becomes separated from the herd, he displays an extreme distress that will not let him rest until he succeeds in rejoining it, when he hastens to bury himself in the midst of it, seeking the closest possible contact with the bodies of his fellows." [16] McDougall here seems to be dealing with an acquired trend of the ox rather than its innate tendency of gregariousness, for it may be doubted if this ox would still react in the same way even if it had not lived in the herd before. In my own observation of pigeons, I have found that some pigeons, raised in isolation, like to stay aloof from their fellows even when social contact is possible.

One more illustration will make our point clearer. We quote it from

[15] *Dynam. Psychol.*, pp. 64–65.
[16] *Soc. Psychol.*, p. 84.

C. O. Whitman on *Behavior of Pigeons.* "If a bird of one species is hatched and reared by a wholly different species, it is very apt, when fully grown up, to prefer to mate with, the species under which it has been reared. For example, a male passenger-pigeon that was reared with ring-doves and had remained with that species, was ever ready, when fully grown, to mate with any ring-dove, but could never be induced to mate with one of his own species. I kept him away from ring-doves a whole season in order to see what could be accomplished in the way of getting him mated finally with his own species, but he would never make any advances to the females; whenever a ring-dove was seen or heard in the yard he was at once attentive." [17]

H. Carr and Hunter interpret this phenomenon as the modification of the mating instinct by habit before its first appearance. Such an interpretation is very far-fetched. It presupposes that the pigeon must necessarily possess an instinct to mate with the female of its own species. In our own opinion it is just as natural for it to mate with a female of another species as to mate with one of its own. In such a case no instinct of any sort has been modified. The difference lies only in the fact that this male pigeon was hatched and reared in a different environment, so that it developed a different type of sexual reaction. Whitman has also found that a male pigeon might be paired with another male, and a female with another female. Some male pigeons even refused to be paired with females, while insisting on securing sexual relation with some inanimate object or the hands of the experimenter.[18] All such cases must also be looked upon as normal. There is no sexual perversion on the part of the pigeon. For there is no sex instinct in the sense that it necessarily involves coition between two opposite sexes. The fact that mating always takes place between two opposite sexes of the same species is because the members of the same species always live in the same community where the hetero-sexual habit is normally developed. If, on the other hand, the organism is born and reared with other species, it may develop a habit of mating with the member of that species as we found in Whitman's pigeon; or, even, if it is reared in isolation, it may, in all probability, develop a homosexual or autoerotic habit. But from the standpoint of a natural scientist this involves no sexual abnormality whatever. We must remember that sexual perversion is merely a socio-moral problem. It has nothing to do with the physiological process. The point I am here driving at is this: that all our sexual appetites are the result of social stimulations. The organism possesses no ready-made reaction to the other sex, any more than it possesses innate ideas.

[17] Whitman, C. O. *The Behavior of Pigeons.* Carnegie Inst. Washington Publ., No. 257, 1919, p. 28.
[18] The same phenomena have been repeatedly reported by many observers; the writer also had the same observation.

## A SUGGESTED REINTERPRETATION OF MAN'S NATIVE EQUIPMENT

We are now in a position to suggest a new interpretation of man's original responses which will be totally different from most of the current conceptions of instinct. On account of the lack of adequate experimental data at present, our statement will be bound to be more or less dogmatic. But in spite of this, we shall state our position in objective terms so far as possible.

1. The human infant is endowed with a great number of units of reaction. By units of reaction I mean the elementary acts out of which various coordinated activities of later life are organized. The reaction units are what we find in the child's spontaneous activities and random acts. The new born baby is characterized by being easily aroused to action; it is exceedingly active. It performs a great number of movements, such as those of the eyes, ears, arms, legs, hands, fingers, toes, face, head and trunk, in fact, every part of the body. "Stimulate him in any way and these movements become more frequent and increase in amplitude. Under the influence of intraorganic stimulation as seen in the hyperactivity of the smooth muscle contractions in hunger and thirst, and especially in the hypersecretion of the ductless glands in rage, fear and other emotional activities, these movements become much more numerous. In pain, likewise, the number of movements is increased." [19] Such spontaneous and random acts are all that we can credit to the native endowment of man.[20] These are non-specific instincts, for they are reflexes in character and involve few, if any, complex neural patterns, as opposed to most of the conventional ideas of instincts which suppose highly complex patterns.

2. With the exception of those activities that are connected with the vegetative functions the activities of the new born babe are nonadaptive in character; and while there are certain coordinate reactions such as eye coordination, the sucking reaction, *etc.*, which appear at birth or shortly after birth,[21] we agree with Watson that in the young organism the random or unorganized and non-adaptive acts outnumber the coordinate and adaptive ones. The general observation of the behavior of the new born babe seems to support this view. Most of the babe's acts are aimless or non-teleological. It responds to almost any stimulus that can reach it; any-

---

[19] Watson: *Psychology,* p. 270.

[20] The assumption that emotions are inherited responses is very questionable. The writer expects to discuss this problem at length in the near future.

[21] It may be doubted, even, that such coordinated acts are at all genuine innate responses. Habits begin to be formed at birth, or even in the embryo. There is good reason to believe that these coordinated responses are the earliest habits of the organism.

thing that touches its hands it grasps and puts into its mouth. When it is lying on its back it kicks with its legs and slashes with its arms. All these movements have no biological significance; likewise a great many other reactions. The child must have gone through a number of failures before it can begin to stand, to crawl, or to walk. The psychologist has failed to observe how difficult it is for a child to cooordinate its movements in order that it may be able to stand, crawl or walk, when he insists that neural patterns for these reactions are inherited.

3. These reaction units are the elements out of which all the coordinated acts of the organism are integrated. Perhaps a simple type of the integration of reaction units can be illustrated by the hand-eye coordination. Watson found that the beginning of reaching for the candle, which was presented before a babe, was between the 120th and 130th days. A somewhat more complex integration in the child is found in walking which involves the coordination of the movements of the legs, feet, head, trunk, visual organs and some other parts of the body. The next more complex organizations may be found in reading and writing. The former involves the coordination of the movement of the eyes, vocal cords, lips and tongue and other related parts. The latter involves the coordination of fingers, hands, arms and eyes, and the head and the trunk which maintain the general position of the body. In playing piano, the coodination is still more complex than any one mentioned above. Here we have the movements of the legs, feet, hands, arms, general bodily position and the auditory and visual organs, and in case singing is accompanied we have to add the movements of vocal apparatus, lips, and tongue—in fact, the implicit vocal movements are involved even when the player is singing silently.

Not only the elementary acts can be integrated into a single act, but the organized acts are also capable of various combinations. A single case will be sufficient to illustrate the point. A normal child of six or seven years old has a considerable degree of coordination in walking and in the movements of various other parts of the organism. But if he is to be taught the dancing lesson, a new coordination is needed. The steps of his feet must be coordinated with his hearing, the movement of the body must follow his steps and so on. Such an act is not a direct integration from the original units of reaction but a recoordination, the elements of which are more or less coordinated in themselves.

4. There are several characteristics in the integration of the reaction units into coordinated acts which must be emphasized here.

First. The process of the integration always involves selection and elimination. We have stated that most of the acts of the new born infant are non-adaptive. What we mean to say is that in the early childhood there are few appropriate movements. The appropriate acts of the child can only be secured through a number of trials and errors. Natural selection is always operating in the random acts of the babe. But there is another factor of selection which is more significant from the standpoint of education. It is a selection controlled by society. A child is very likely to make indiscriminate reactions. We have noted that the child not infrequently responds positively to harmful stimuli and that in order to protect the child from being injured by such reactions, society removes the stimuli that will call forth ill-adaptive reactions. The educational process in one sense is to control the environment in such a way as to eliminate the possibility of wrong reactions of the child.

In this connection, there is another important function of education. We saw that the process of acquiring adaptive reaction by trial and error or through natural selection is very slow and laborious. In primitive society where life was very simple, where the demands of society upon the individual for right actions were far less complicated than they are now, we might leave him to adjust himself without the assistance of education. But since the modern social structure is so complex and the social demands are so great a child, if he is left alone, may fail to fulfill the social requirements. Furthermore, if the learning process is not shortened, the time and energy of the individual will not be sufficient for him to acquire all the necessary social adjustments. Herein lies the fundamental justification for education. The fundamental motive of education is to assist the individual to adapt himself to society in a most economical and effective way. Through instruction, useless and ill-adaptive movements in learning may be avoided and the appropriate acts be quickly performed. The chief function of education, in other words, is time-economy and labor-saving; the main problem in educational psychology is the problem of efficiency of learning.

Second. If the stimuli that have aroused certain responses in the organism appear so often that the bond between the stimuli and responses becomes fixed, we have specialized responses or what is ordinarily called habitualized acts. Our habitual acts are stereotyped acts that have been integrated from the elementary acts. In general, the oftener the same stimuli appear the more specialized the reaction to these stimuli becomes and the more rigid and fixed is the habit.

Third. On the other hand, on account of the demands of novel environment, our habitualized activities may be reorganized so that the organism will be enabled to adjust itself to the new situation. It is only a truism to say that there are different possibilities of reorganization of early acquired habits in different individuals. There are individuals whose habits are so fixed and stereotyped that they are almost incapable of reorganization of any sort. Individuals of this kind often fail to adapt themselves to novel environment. On the other hand, there are individuals whose habits are so plastic that they are easily reintegrated under the demands of new situation. On the whole, the plasticity of habits depends on the richness of experience of the organism. The more experience or the more variety of stimuli it has, the less fixed and rigid are its organized reactions.

This leads us to an emphasis on the importance of liberal education. Liberal education means from the standpoint of psychology that kind of education which provides great varieties of experience for the individual in such a way as to enable him to adapt himself readily to novel situations. The training of adaptability is more important than that of specialization in education. I do not mean to minimize the importance of specialization, but in modern education there is great danger in over-emphasizing this phase of training. Vocational education is often secured at the expense of general education. We must not forget that the more specialized the individual is, the less adaptive to novel environment will he become.

Fourth. (And this is simply to restate the chief element of our contention in this paper.) The type of integration of the elementary acts into complex reaction systems largely depends on the nature of the environment. Our daily acts are organized as a result of environmental demands; our trends of actions are products of the constant interplay between the organism and environment. If a man is born and raised in a highly civilized community, he may acquire a powerful trend of parental care which he extends to humanity as a whole and even to animals. On the other hand, if he is brought up in a savage tribe where the custom of cannibalism prevails, he may acquire a habit of taking pleasure in killing. At times the same native equipment may be developed into compassion, while at others it may be developed into cruelty. The tender-hearted Buddha differs from a bloodsucker not so much in his native constitution as in his acquired characteristics. This principle also holds true of animals. The passenger pigeon when hatched and reared with the ring-doves will refuse to mate with the female of its own species. The goslings, when reared away from water will refuse to go to water. Chickens, when hatched and reared in the absence of a hen, may follow any moving object and refuse to follow any hen. We need not assume that the instincts wane or are modified in order to explain such phenomena. The theories of waning and modification of instincts have no scientific ground whatever. Psychologists have often been misled by the assumption that certain reactions which are common to the species must belong to the category of instinct while deviation from any such common reactions must be regarded as the waning or modification of instinct. If it is realized that the organism possesses no specific instincts whatever and that different types of behavior simply result from different environmental demands, these two theories will at once become superfluous.

The fact that the nature of environment determines the organization of reaction systems accounts for both social solidarity and individual differences in occupations and in types of behavior.[22] In every society there are certain kinds of social stimulation that are common to all members of the group, a fact which makes similar reactions among the members possible. On the other hand social influences are so complicated and so varied that no two individuals will happen to live in an identical situation. Different experiences and different training tend to produce individuality.

There are more possibilities for the organizations of the original units of reaction into a complex system, then society can supply stimuli. Man possesses more latent potentialities than he has actually realized. On the other hand, society furnishes more opportunities for individual development than the organism can make use of. One individual can not at the same time be a politician, a scientist, an educator, a poet, carpenter, a miner and fruit raiser. When the development of the individual reaches its limit, it becomes very hard for him to acquire any new organization of reaction systems. Everyone realizes how difficult it is for an individual to change his vocation or to acquire a new skill after the age of thirty or so, in spite of the fact that he possesses all these possibilities.

Fifth. That the original units of reaction are the elements out of which our organized activities are directly developed is more true of children than of adults. In adults the habit formation consists more in the reintegration of the old habits than in the direct integration of the original elementary acts. The development of human behavior is from simple to complex, from unorganized to organized. Human reaction systems are always organized in hierarchies; each new habit utilizes some of the previously formed habits; we build our more complex organizations of reaction system upon the simpler ones. In other words, the units of the acquisition of new habits in later life are not the original units of reaction but the earlier acquired habits. We never learn how to walk in order to learn how to dance, we never learn how to coordinate the movements of eyes and hand in order to learn how to use a typewriter, for all such simpler coordinations have been acquired in early childhood; the only thing we have to do in learning these things, to repeat, is to organize these simpler ones into a more complex system. Watson says that it takes the child a longer time to learn to drive a nail well than it takes an adult engineer to build an airplane. This is literally true, for in the child the systems of reaction are so simple that little can be utilized in new learning, while in the adult highly complex systems of organization have been achieved that can be made use of in a new acquisition.

---

[22] Individual differences that are due to heredity are simply the differences in the degree of latent possibilities in the integration of the elementary acts into various complex reaction systems. The theory of native capacities as advocated by Woodworth, Thorndike and others is as untenable as that of instincts.

The development of human behavior is essentially the increase of complexity in the organization of reaction systems. This fact has been overlooked by most geneticists. Genetic psychology in the past has been largely devoted to the study of the periodical appearance of instincts. The geneticists have failed to analyze the complex forms of behavior into their simple elements. To be sure, they investigate the different stages of development. But they have seldom scrutinized how each stage is related to its previous and subsequent stages. They have occasionally noticed the spontaneous and random movements in the new-born babe, but have never realized that all the complex activities in the adult can be analyzed into such simple acts; they tell us rightly or wrongly that at certain ages the child displays certain types of behavior, but how they come about they have failed to investigate altogether. Such failure is, of course, partly due to lack of adequate experimentation but more largely to the preconceptions of instinct, especially that of the periodicity of instincts. Indeed, genetic psychology in the past has practically failed and the need to start it all over again on a purely objective and experimental basis is now imperative. To do so we must first discard all presumptions of instinct altogether and study the development of behavior in terms of increase in complexity of the organization of reaction systems as they are integrated in various ways either directly or indirectly from the original units of reaction. And, further, greater attention should be paid to the study of environmental factors which affect the organization of the reaction system; we should look to the specific stimuli or situation rather than the instincts for the explanation of the development of behavior. It is no small handicap to the genuine understanding of the development of behavior to assume instincts existing as specific faculties in the organism.

5. There are a number of elementary acts that are not integrated with other reaction systems and remain relatively independent acts throughout the life of the organism. They may respond to stimuli independently of other organized reactions which concern the organism as a whole. Such acts belong in the categories of reflexes, such as knee-jerk, winking, sneezing, yawning, etc.

By way of conclusion, we may state that such a theory we have so far advanced is not an altogether new one. The importance of the spontaneous and random activities of the young organism has been duly emphasized by Professor Watson.[24] But we can not agree with him that, besides the activities of this sort, there is another group of innate reactions or instincts. In fact, the results of his investigation on the behavior of the new-born babe do not indicate any appearance of specific instincts, except a vast number of random movements. Having failed in discovering specific instincts in the young babe, he is forced to accept the theory of

---

[24] See *Behavior*, Chaps. 4 and 6, and *Psychology*, Chaps. 7 and 8.

temporal order of appearance of instincts which has not any scientific proof and has been rejected altogether in this paper. Further, he has done violence to his own definition of instinct when he accepts many of the conventionally listed instincts. For, as we have seen, the responses of these instincts involve a great deal of variability and it is very hard to find in them any definite inherited neural patterns which is his essential conception of instinct. We are, therefore, obliged to repudiate all his theories of instinct. For we have found that the random or unorganized acts in the young babe are sufficient to account for all complex and organized forms of behavior in adults, and that it is not only superfluous but harmful to our genuine understanding of human behavior to assume the existence of any specific instinct.

·

# 4 • Niko Tinbergen

## *An Attempt at a Synthesis*

Tinbergen was a leader among the European ethologists who forced a reconsideration of instinct upon American psychology. His *Study of Instincts,* and particularly the chapter presented here, had a most significant impact, even though Tinbergen himself now considers the material outdated. In spite of the many revisions in thinking about instinct as it relates to species specific behavior which have been made in recent years, the observations and works of the ethologists have continued to keep the issues of unlearned behavior in the forefront of continuing themes in motivational psychology. As a germinal treatment of its topic, the following article has earned a permanent place in the history of the field.

*We have now* arrived at a point where it is necessary to review our results in order to evaluate and appreciate their significance in relation to our main problem, that is, the problem of the causation of instinctive behaviour.

The foregoing chapters have led to the following conclusions.

Instinctive behavior is dependent on external and internal casual factors. The external factors, or sensory stimuli, are of a much simpler nature than our knowledge of the potential capacities of the sense organs would make us expect. Yet they are not so simple as the word 'stimulus' would suggest, for the 'sign stimuli' have *gestalt* character, that is to say, they release configurational receptive processes. The various sign stimuli required for the release of an instinctive activity co-operate according to the rule of heterogeneous summation. These facts led us to the postulation of Innate Releasing Mechanisms, one of which is possessed by each separate reaction. Apart from releasing stimuli, directing stimuli play a part, enabling or forcing the animal to orient itself in relation to the environment. The internal causal factors controlling, qualitatively and quantitatively, the motivation of the animal may be of three kinds: hormones, internal sensory stimuli, and, perhaps, intrinsic or automatic nervous impulses generated by the central nervous system itself. Instinctive 'reactions' are of varying degrees of complexity; even the simplest type, the 'fixed pattern', depends on a system of muscle contractions which is of a configurational character.

These results are incomplete in more than one respect. First, the evidence is still very fragmentary, and the generalizations are still of a very tentative nature. Second, the work done thus far has been mainly analytical, and no attempt has yet been made to combine the separate conclusions into a picture of the causal structure underlying instinctive behaviour as a whole. We have, however, gained one thing: we are realizing more and more clearly that the physiological mechanisms underlying instinctive behaviour are much more complicated than we were able to see at the start. Previous attempts at synthesis, such as Pavlov's reflex theory and Loeb's tropism theory, now appear to be grotesque simplifications.

While thus realizing both the relative paucity of analytical data and the complexity of the casual structure, we will nevertheless venture to sketch, in rough outline, a synthetic picture of the organization of the partial problems within the main problem as a whole.

## DIFFERENCES IN DEGREE OF COMPLEXITY OF 'REACTIONS'

So far I have been using the terms 'reaction', 'motor response', 'behaviour pattern', 'movement' for muscle contractions of very different degrees of complexity. This fact is of paramount importance, and I will emphasize it by presenting some more instances.

As we have seen, the swimming of an eel is a relatively simple movement. In every somite there is alternating contraction of the longitudinal muscles of the right and the left half of the trunk. In addition, the pendulum movements of successive somites are slightly out of step, each somite contracting a short time after its predecessor. The result is the propagation of the well-known sinusoid contraction waves along the body axis (Gray, 1936).

The swimming movements of a fish like *Labrus* or *Sargus*, as described by von Holst (1935*b*, 1937), are more complex. The pectoral fins, moving back and forth in alternation, are also in step with the dorsal, caudal, and anal fins, each of which makes pendulum movements as well.

The movement of a male stickleback ventilating its eggs is of a similar type. The pectorals make pendulum movements alternately. This motion is directed forward, resulting in a water current from the fish to the nest.

In order to counteract the backward push this exerts upon the fish, forward swimming movements of the tail are made in absolute synchronization with the rhythm of the pectorals.

Although locomotion might be considered merely an element of a 'reaction' in the sense in which I have been using this term, the stickleback's ventilating movement is a complete reaction, responding in part to a chemical stimulus emanating from the nest.

The reaction of a gallinaceous chick to a flying bird of prey is, again, somewhat more complicated. It may consist of merely crouching, but often it consists of running to shelter provided by the mother or by vegetation, crouching, and continuously watching the pedator's movements.

Finally, a male stickleback in reproductive condition responds to visual and temperature stimuli of a rather simple type by behaviour of a very complicated pattern: it settles on a territory, fights other males, starts to build a nest, court females, and so on.

## HIERARCHICAL ORGANIZATION

A closer study of these differences in complexity leads us to the conclusion that the mechanisms underlying these reactions are arranged in a hierarchical system, in which we must distinguish between various levels of integration.

The reproductive behaviour of the male stickleback may be taken as an example.

In spring, the gradual increase in length of day brings the males into a condition of increased reproductive motivation, which drives them to migrate into shallow fresh water. Here, as we have seen, a rise in temperature, together with a visual stimulus situation received from a suitable territory, releases the reproductive pattern as a whole. The male settles on the territory, its erythrophores expand, it reacts to strangers by fighting, and starts to build a nest. Now, whereas both nest-building and fighting depend on activation of the reproductive drive as a whole, no observer can predict which one of the two patterns will be shown at any given moment. Fighting, for instance, has to be released by a specific stimulus, viz. 'red male intruding into the territory'. Building is not released by this stimulus situation but depends on other stimuli. Thus these two activities, though both depend on activation of the reproductive drive as a whole, are also dependent on additional (external) factors. The influence of these latter factors is, however, restricted; they act upon either fighting or building, not on the reproductive drive as a whole.

Now the stimulus situation 'red male intruding', while releasing the fighting drive, does not determine which one of the five types of fighting will be shown. This is determined by additional, still more specific stimuli.

For instance, when the stranger bites, the owner of the territory will bite in return; when the stranger threatens, the owner will threaten back; when the stranger flees, the owner will chase it; and so on.

Thus the effect of a stimulus situation on the animal may be of different kinds. The visual stimulus 'suitable territory' activates both fighting and nest-building; the visual situation 'red male in territory' is specific in releasing fighting, but it merely causes a general readiness to fight and does not determine the type of fighting. Which one of the five motor responses belonging to the fighting pattern will be shown depends on sign stimuli that are still more restricted in effect. The tactile stimulus 'male biting' releases one type of fighting, the visual stimulus 'male threatening' another type. The stimulus situations are not of an essentially different order in all these cases, but the results are. They belong to different levels of integration and, moreover, they are organized in a hierarchical system, like the staff organization of an army or of other human organizations. Fig. 4.1 illustrates the principle. The facts (1) that

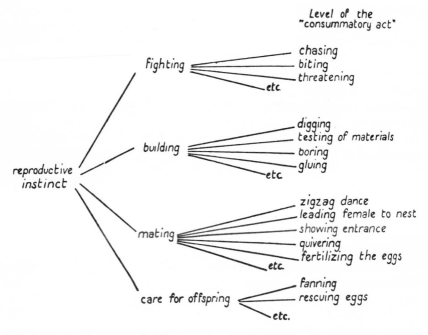

Figure 4.1.   The principle of hierarchical organization illustrated by the reproductive instinct of the male three-spined stickleback. After Tinbergen, 1942.

at each of the levels an external stimulus can have a specific releasing influence and (2) that each reaction has its own motor pattern, mean that there is a hierarchical system of IRMs and of motor centres. So far as we can judge at present, each IRM is able to collect sensory impulses according to the rule of heterogeneous summation, and each motor centre controls a configurational pattern of muscle contractions.

The principle of hierarchical organization has been tested in but three cases: the digger wasp *Ammophila campestris* (Baerends, 1941), the three-spined stickleback (Tinbergen, 1942), and the turkey (Räber, 1948), and although the principle is undoubtedly sound, nearly nothing is known in detail about the way it works out in the various drives and in different species of animals. Before a more detailed discussion can be attempted, a closer consideration of motor responses is necessary.

## APPETITIVE BEHAVIOUR AND CONSUMMATORY ACT

The activation of a centre of the lowest level usually, perhaps always, results in a relatively simple motor response: biting, chasing, threatening, &c, in the case of fighting in the stickleback; actual eating, actual escape, actual coition, &c., in other instincts. This type of response has been the object of our analysis in most of the cases treated in the preceding chapters. This is no accident; it is the natural outcome of the tendency to analyse which leads to a conscious or (more often) unconscious selection of relatively simple and stereotyped phenomena.

These relatively simple responses are, usually, the end of a bout of prolonged activity, and their performance seems to 'satisfy' the animal, that is to say, to bring about a sudden drop of motivation. This means that such an end-response consumes the specific impulses responsible for its activation. Fighting, eating, mating, 'playing the broken wing', &c., are, as a rule, 'self-exhausting'. Craig (1918), in a most remarkable paper that has not received the attention it deserves, was the first to single out these elements of behaviour; he called them 'consummatory actions'. Lorenz (1937*b*), realizing that they constitute the most characteristic components of instinctive behaviour, that is to say those components that can be most easily recognized by the form of the movement, called them *Instinkthandlungen,* thereby greatly narrowing the concept of instinctive act. This use of the term gives rise to continuous misunderstandings and hence should be dropped

The centres of this lower type of movement rarely respond to the external stimulus situation alone. As a rule, they get their internal impulses from a superordinated centre. The activation of these higher centres may result either in a mere increase in readiness of the animal to react with one of a number of consummatory actions, or, more often, in a type of movement often called 'random movement', 'exploratory behaviour', 'seeking behaviour', or the like. Contrary to the consummatory action it is not characterized by a stereotyped motor pattern, but rather by (1) its variability and plasticity and (2) its purposiveness. The animal in which a major drive, like the hunting drive, the nest-building drive, the mating drive, is activated starts searching or exploratory excursions which last until a situation is found which provides the animal with the stimuli adequate for releasing the consummatory act.

As mentioned above, Craig recognized these two types of behaviour, viz. the variable striving behaviour and the rigid consummatory action; and, moreover, he saw their mutual relationships as components of instinctive behaviour as a whole. He called the introductory striving or searching phase 'appetitive behaviour' to stress the fact that the animal is striving to attain some end.

Appetitive behaviour may be a very simple introduction to a consummatory action, as in the case of a frog catching a prey; the preparatory taxis (turning towards the prey) is true purposive behaviour, and is continued or repeated until the prey is within range and in the median plane.

More complicated is the appetitive phase of feeding in a *Planaria* mounting a stream against a scent-loaded current.

Heinroth (1910) describes a still higher form of appetitive behaviour in mated ducks exploring the country for a nesting-hole.

In extreme cases the appetitive behaviour may be prolonged and highly adaptable, as in the migratory behaviour of animals.

It will be clear, therefore, that this distinction between appetitive behaviour and consummatory act separates the behaviour as a whole into two components of entirely different character. The consummatory act is relatively simple; at its most complex, it is a chain of reactions, each of which may be a simultaneous combination of a taxis and a fixed pattern. But appetitive behaviour is a true purposive activity, offering all the problems of plasticity, adaptiveness, and of complex integration that baffle the scientist in his study of behaviour as a whole. Appetitive behaviour is a conglomerate of many elements of very different order, of reflexes, of simple patterns like locomotion, or conditioned reactions, of 'insight' behaviour, and so on. As a result it is a true challenge to objective science, and therefore the discrimination between appetitive behaviour and consummatory act is but a first step of our analysis.

A consideration of the relationships between appetitive behaviour and consummatory act is important for our understanding of the nature of striving in animals. It is often stressed that animals are striving towards the attainment of a certain end or goal. Lorenz has pointed out not only that purposiveness, the striving towards an end, is typical only of appetitive behaviour and not of consummatory actions, but also that the end of purposive behaviour is not the attainment of an object or a situation itself, but the performance of the consummatory action, which is attained as a consequence of the animal's arrival at an external situation which provides the special sign stimuli releasing the consummatory act. Even psychologists who have watched hundreds of rats running a maze rarely realize that, strictly speaking, it is not the litter or the food the animal is striving towards, but the performance itself of the maternal activities or eating.

Holzapfel (1940) has shown that there is one apparent exception to this rule: appetitive behaviour may also lead to rest or sleep. As I hope to show further below, this exception is only apparent, because rest and sleep are true consummatory actions, dependent on activation of a centre exactly as with other consummatory actions.

Whereas the consummatory act seems to be dependent on the centres of the lowest level of instinctive behaviour, appetitive behaviour may be activated by centres of all the levels above that of the consummatory act. As has been pointed out by Baerends (1941), appetitive behaviour by no means always leads directly to the performance of a consummatory act. For instance, the hunting of a peregrine falcon usually begins with relatively random roaming around its hunting territory, visiting and exploring many different places miles apart. This first phase of appetitive behaviour may lead to different ways of catching prey, each dependent on special stimulation by a potential prey. It is continued until such a special stimulus situation is found: a flock of teal executing flight manoeuvres, a sick gull swimming apart from the flock, or even a running mouse. Each of these situations may cause the falcon to abandon its 'random' searching. But what follows then is not yet a consummatory action, but appetitive behaviour of a new, more specialized and more restricted kind. The flock of teal releases a series of sham attacks serving to isolate one or a few individuals from the main body of the flock. Only after this is achieved is the final swoop released, followed by capturing, killing, plucking, and eating, which is a relatively simple and stereotyped chain of consummatory acts. The sick gull may provoke the release of sham attacks tending to force it to fly up; if this fails the falcon may deftly pick it up from the water surface. A small mammal may release simple straightforward approach and subsequent capturing, &c. Thus we see that the generalized appetitive behaviour was continued until a special stimulus situation interrupted the random searching and released one of the several possible and more specific types of appetitive behaviour. This in its turn was continued until the changing stimulus situation released the swoop, a still more specific type of appetitive behaviour, and this finally led to the chain of consummatory acts.

Baerends (1941) came to the same conclusion in his analysis of the behaviour of the digger wasp *Ammophila campestris* and probably the principle will be found to be generally applicable. It seems, therefore, that the centres of each level of the hierarchical system control a type of appetitive behaviour. This is more generalized in the higher levels and more restricted or more specialized in the lower levels. The transition from higher to lower, more specialized types of appetitive behaviour is brought about by special stimuli which alone are able to direct the impulses to one of the lower centres, or rather to allow them free passage to this lower centre. This stepwise descent of the activation from relatively higher to relatively lower centres eventually results in the stimulation of a centre or a series of centres of the level of the consummatory act, and here the impulse is finally used up.

This hypothesis of the mechanism of instinctive behaviour, though supported by relatively few and very fragmentary facts and still tentative therefore, seems to cover the reality better than any theory thus far advanced. Its concreteness gives it a high heuristic value, and it is to be hoped that continued research in the near future will follow these lines and fill in, change, and adapt the sketchy frame.

## NEUROPHYSIOLOGICAL FACTS

### The Relatively Higher Levels

The hypothesis presented above, of a hierarchical system of nerve centres each of which has integrative functions of the 'collecting and redispatching' type, has been developed on a foundation of facts of an indirect nature. If it is essentially right, it should be possible to trace these centres by applying neurophysiological methods. As I have said before, it must be considered as one of the greatest advantages of objective behaviour study that by using essentially the same method as other fields of physiology it gives rise to concrete problems that can be tackled by both the ethologist and the physiologist.

Now in recent times several facts have been brought to light which indicate that there is such a system of centres, at least in vertebrates.

I have already mentioned the fact that the work of Weiss, von Holst, Gray, Lissmann, and others proves that the spinal cords of fishes and amphibians must contain mechanisms controlling relatively simple types of co-ordinated movements, such as the locomotory contraction waves of the trunk muscles in fish or the locomotory rhythm of alternating contraction of leg muscles in axolotls. And although doubts have been raised concerning the absolute independence of these centres from external stimulation—doubts which have been discussed in Chapter III— the integrative, co-ordinative nature of the movements controlled by the motor centres is beyond doubt.

Other evidence of the same sort is given by the work of Adrian and Buytendijk (1931) on the respiratory centre in the medulla of fish.

However, all these facts concern the very lowest type of centre we have postulated, that of the consummatory action or, more probable still, that of its least complex component, the fixed pattern.

Now it seems to me to be of the highest importance that recently Hess (1943, 1944; Hess and Brügger, 1943, 1944; Brügger, 1943) has succeeded, by application of strictly local artificial stimuli, to elicit behaviour of a much higher level of integration. Hess succeeded in bringing minute electrodes into the diencephalon of intact cats. In this way he could apply weak stimuli to localized parts of the brain. By systematically probing the hypothalamic region he found areas where the application of a stimulus elicited the complete behaviour patterns of either fighting, eating, or sleep. His descriptions make it clear that all the elements of the pattern were not only present but were displayed in perfect co-ordination. Moreover, the response was initiated by genuine appetitive behaviour; the cat looked around and searched for a corner to go to sleep, it searched for food, &c. By combining this experiment with anatomical study the position of the centres of these patterns could be determined (Fig. 4-2).

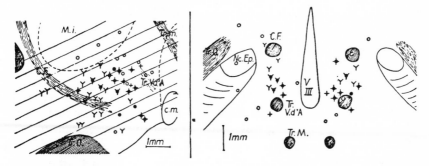

• Food seeking (1)
+ "General motor urge" (2)
Y Fighting in defence (3)
+ (1) and (2) combined
Y (1) and (3) combined
° No effect

Figure 4.2.   Sagittal (left) and horizontal (right) section through hypothalamic 'centres' of a cat. Symbols indicate results of local stimulation. After Brügger, 1943.

These results are of considerable interest in two respects.

First, Hess appears to have found the anatomical basis of the centres controlling instinctive patterns as a whole. A mere electric shock, surely a very simple type of stimulation, releases a complex pattern, an integrated whole of movements of the highest instinctive level. This lends support to our conclusion that somewhere between receptors and effectors there must be a mechanism that takes qualitatively different, configurational impulse-patterns coming from the receptors, combines them in a purely quantitative way, and takes care of redispatching them in reintegrative form so that a configurational movement results. Hess seems to have hit a station somewhere in this mechanism.

Second, the location of these centres is of interest in connexion with the findings about the functions of the spinal cord discussed above. While the spinal cord and the medulla seem to control only certain components of the instinctive patterns, the hypothalamus contains the highest centres concerned with instinctive behaviour. Our analysis of the hierarchical layout of behaviour patterns justifies the prediction that further research along the lines initiated by von Holst, Weiss, Gray, and Hess will lead to the discovery of a whole system of centres belonging to levels below the hypothalamic level as found by Hess, centres which are subordinate to the hypothalamic centres but which in their turn control centres lower still.

I should like to emphasize that this future work could only be done by workers who are fully acquainted with the instinctive behaviour as a whole and with its analysis, and at the same time are in command of neurophysiological methods and techniques. Our science is suffering from a serious lack of students with these qualifications, and it is an urgent task of ethologists and neurophysiologists to join efforts in the training of 'etho-physiologists'.

It is specially interesting that the hierarchical organization has not only been found in vertebrates but in insects as well. According to Baerends's results a wasp with a decentralized system of ventral ganglia and its relatively small 'brain' presents essentially the same picture as vertebrates.

*Instinct and instincts.*   The recognition of the hierarchical organization raises some problems of terminology. There is an enormous confusion around the use of the terms 'instinctive activity' or 'instinctive act'. Some authors maintain that instinctive behaviour is highly variable and adaptive in relation to a goal—in other words that it is purposive or directive—and that, because the goal remains constant while the movements, and hence the mechanisms employed, change, it is futile to attack instinctive behaviour with physiological methods. We have seen that this only applies to the appetitive part of behaviour, and moreover, that even in this purposive element of behaviour the number of possible movements and hence the number of available mechanisms is restricted. Other authors stress the rigidity, the stereotypy of instinctive behaviour.

Now it seems that the degree of variability depends entirely on the level considered. The centres of the higher levels do control purposive behaviour which is adaptive with regard to the mechanisms it employs to attain the end. The lower levels, however, give rise to increasingly simple and more stereotyped movements, until at the level of the consummatory act we have to do with an entirely rigid component, the fixed pattern, and a more or less variable component, the taxis, the variability of which, however, is entirely dependent on changes in the outer world. This seems to settle the controversy; the consummatory act is rigid, the higher patterns are purposive and adaptive. The dispute about whether 'instinctive behaviour' is rigid or adaptive has been founded on the implicit and entirely wrong assumption that there is only one type of instinctive activity.

The fact that the controversy is settled does not, of course, mean that the problem of purposiveness is solved. But the fact that even purposive behaviour appears to be dependent on quantitative activation of a centre and that it comes to an end whenever one of the lower centres has used the impulses shows that purposiveness as such is not a problem which cannot be studied by physiological methods. The fundamental problem is not to be found in the physiological mechanisms now responsible for purposive behaviour but in the history, the genesis of the species.

Returning now to our nomenclatural difficulty, the question naturally arises, What is to be called an instinctive act? Is it the pattern as a whole, or is it one of the partial patterns, or even, as Lorenz has proposed, the consummatory act? I would prefer to apply the name to all levels. For instance, reproductive behaviour in the male stickleback is, as a whole, an instinctive activity. But its component parts, nest-building and fighting, may also be called instinctive activities. A solution could be found by distinguishing instinctive acts of, for example, the first level, the second level, and so on. But here we meet with the additional difficulty that most probably the various major instinctive patterns of a species do not have the same number of levels. If we begin to count from the highest level, we would come to the absurd situation that various consummatory acts, though perhaps of the same degree of complexity, do not belong to the same level. If we begin at the level of the consummatory act, the major instincts would get different rank. This state of affairs renders it impossible to devise a universal nomenclature of instinctive behaviour as long as our knowledge is still in this fragmentary state.

It is of great importance for our understanding of instinctive behaviour as a whole to realize that the various instincts are not independent of each other. We have rejected the reflex hypothesis of behaviour and we have seen that each instinctive mechanism is constantly primed, that is to say, prepared to come into action. Such a system can only work because blocking mechanisms prevent the animal from performing continuous chaotic movements.

Now chaos is further prevented by another principle, viz. that of inhibition between centres of the same level. As a rule, an animal can scarcely do 'two things at a time'. Although there is a certain amount of synchronous activity of two instincts, this is only possible at low motivation, and, as a rule, the strong activation of instinctive behaviour of one kind prevents the functioning of another pattern. Thus an animal in which the sexual drive is strong is much less than normally susceptible to stimuli that normally release flight or eating. On the other hand, when flight is released, the thresholds of the reproductive and feeding activities are raised. The same relationship of mutual inhibition seems to exist between centres of lower levels. Intensive nest-building, for instance, renders the male stickleback much less susceptible than usual to stimuli normally releasing fighting, and vice versa.

Although the physiological basis of this inhibitory relationship will not be discussed here, it should be pointed out that its very existence has been the implicit origin of the distinction between various 'instincts' which has been made by numerous authors. So far, many authors who accepted a distinction between different instincts have defined them in terms of the goal or purpose they serve. A consideration of the neurophysiological relationships underlying instinct leads to a definition of 'an instinct' in which the responsible nervous centres and their mutual inhibition are also taken into account. It makes us realize that the purposiveness of any instinct is safeguarded by the fact that all the activities forming part of a purposive behavior pattern aimed at the attainment of a certain goal depend on a common neurophysiological mechanism. Thus it is only natural that any definition of 'an instinct' should include not only an indication of the objective aim or purpose it is serving, but also an indication of the neurophysiological mechanisms. Because of the highly tentative character of my picture of these neurophysiological relationships it may seem a little early to attempt a definition of 'an instinct'; yet in my opinion, such an attempt could be of value for future research. I will tentatively define an instinct as a hierarchically organized nervous mechanism which is susceptible to certain priming, releasing and directing impulses of internal as well as of external origin, and which responds to these impulses by coordinated movements that contribute to the maintenance of the individual and the species.

For the same reason, it seems too early to attempt an enumeration of the various instincts to be found in animals and man. First, while we know that, in the cat, eating, fighting, and sleep must each be called a major instinct because each is dependent on the activation of a hypothalamic centre, there are patterns which almost certainly are equally dependent on a relatively high centre ( e.g., escape, sexual behaviour, &c.) but of which nothing of the kind has yet been proved. Further, different species have different instincts. For instance, while many species have a parental instinct, others never take care of their offspring and hence probably do not have the corresponding neurophysiological mechanisms. However, such things are difficult to decide at present, because, for instance, it has been found that males of species in which the care of the young is exclusively an affair of the female can be brought to display the full maternal behaviour pattern by injecting them with prolactin. Though this example concerns individuals of the same species, we could not reject *a priori* the possibility that, for instance, a species might lack a certain instinct because, having lost it relatively recently, it retained the nervous mechanism but not the required motivational mechanism.

So long as we know nothing about such things, it would be as well to refrain from generalizations.

However, it is possible to point out some inconsistencies in the present views on instincts to be found in the literature. Contrary to current views, there is, in my opinion, no 'social instinct' in our sense. There are no special activities to be called 'social' that are not part of some instinct. There is no such thing as the activation of a system of centres controlling social activities. An animal is called social when it strives to be in the neighbourhood of fellow members of its species when performing some, or all, of its instinctive activities. In other words, when these instincts are active, the fellow member of the species is part of the adequate stimulus situation which the animal tries to find through its appetitive behaviour. In some species all instincts, even the reproductive instinct and the instinct of sleep, have social aspects. In many other species the social aspect, while present in feeding or in all non-reproductive instincts, is absent from the reproductive instinct. This is especially obvious in many fishes and birds. In many amphibians the situation is just the reverse. Further, in many species there are differences of degree, or even of quality, between the social elements of different instincts. For instance, in herring gulls there is a tendency to nest in colonies. But in mating and nest-building there is only a weak social tendency, limited to the fact that individuals select their nesting site in the neighbourhood of an existing colony; attacking a predator, one of the other sub-instincts of the reproductive instinct, is a much more social affair.

There is no instinct for the selection of the environment, no *Funktionskreis des Milieus* as von Uexküll (1921) claims. Here again reactions to habitat are parts of the reproductive instinct or of other instincts.

There is, however, an instinct of sleep. Sleep is a readily recognizable, though simple behaviour pattern and has a corresponding appetitive behaviour pattern; further, it is dependent on the activation of a centre. Moreover, sleep can appear as a displacement activity (see below), a property found in true instinctive patterns only.

There is, further, an instinct of comfort, or rather of care of the surface of the body.

There is not one instinct of combat. There are several sub-instincts of fighting. The most common type of fighting is sexual fighting, which is part of the reproductive pattern. Sexual fighting has to be distinguished from defence against a predator, for it has a different IRM and, often, a different motor pattern.

*Displacement activities.* Another set of interrelations, though in itself perhaps not of primary importance in the organization of behaviour, has to be considered now: those revealed by the occurrence of 'displacement activity'. This phenomenon will be discussed in some detail, because it is not generally known and yet seems to be of great importance for our understanding of the neurophysiological background of instinct.

It has struck many observers that animals may, under certain circumstances, perform movements which do not belong to the motor pattern of the instinct that is activated at the moment of observation. For instance, fighting domestic cocks may suddenly pick at the ground, as if they were feeding. Fighting European starlings may vigorously preen their feathers. Courting birds of paradise wipe their bills now and then. Herring gulls, while engaged in deadly combat, may all at once pluck nesting material, &c. (Fig. 4.3). In all the observed instances the animal gives the impression of being very strongly motivated ('nervous'). Rand (1943) has called such movements 'irrelevant' movements. Makkink (1936) gave an implied interpretation by using the term 'sparking-over movements', suggesting that impulses are 'sparking over' on another 'track.' Kirkman (1937) used the term 'substitute activities' which I adopted in 1939 (Tinbergen, 1939). Later the term 'displacement activity' was proposed (Tinbergen and Van Iersel, 1947; Armstrong, 1948), and this term will be used here.

The phenomenon has been clearly recognized and analysed independently by Kortlandt (1940a) and by Tinbergen (1939, 1940). An examination of the conditions under which displacement activities usually occur led to the conclusion that, in all known cases, there is a surplus of motivation, the discharge of which through the normal paths is in some way prevented. The most usual situations are: (1) conflict of two strongly activated antagonistic drives; (2) strong motivation of a drive, usually the sexual drive, together with lack of external stimuli required for the release of the consummatory acts belonging to that drive.

1. A conflict between two antagonistic drives is found with animals fighting at the boundary line between their territories. Numerous instances, apart from those already mentioned, have been observed. Male sticklebacks, when meeting at the boundary between their territories, adopt the attitude seen in the picture serving as a frontispiece for this book. At first sight the movements seem very similar to feeding movements, and so they were at first described (Tinbergen, 1940). It has since been discovered, however, that with very strong motivation, when the movement

---

Figure 4.3.   Various displacement activities.

1. Nesting movements in herring gull as an outlet of the fighting instinct. Moderate intensity. After Tinbergen, 1940.
2. Nesting movements in herring gulls as outlets of the fighting instinct. High intensity.
3. Sleeping attitude in European oyster-catcher as an outlet of the fighting instinct.
4. Sleeping attitude in European avocet as an outlet of the fighting instinct. After Makkink, 1936.
5. Sand-digging in male three-spined stickleback as an outlet of the fighting instinct. After Tinbergen, 1947b.
6. Preening in sheldrake as an outlet of the sexual instinct. After Makkink, 1931.

Figure 4.3. (Legend Continued)

7. Preening in the garganey as an outlet of the sexual instinct. After Lorenz, 1941.

8. Preening in the mandarin as an outlet of the sexual instinct. After Lorenz, 1941.

9. Preening in the mallard as an outlet of the sexual instinct. After Lorenz, 1941.

10. Preening in the European avocet as an outlet of the sexual instinct. After Makkink, 1936.

11. Food-catching movement in the European blue heron as an outlet of the sexual instinct. After Verwey, 1930.

12, 13, and 14. Sexual movements in the European cormorant as outlets of the fighting instinct. After Kortlandt, 1934b.

15. Food-begging movements in herring gull as outlets of the sexual instinct. After Tinbergen, 1940.

16. Food-pecking movements in domestic cocks as an outlet of the fighting instinct.

becomes more complete, it develops into complete digging, and cannot be distinguished from the movements of digging a pit for the nest. This movement does not belong to the fighting drive but to the nesting pattern.

It is a striking fact that displacement activities often occur in a situation in which the fighting drive and the drive to escape are both activated. Within its own territory, a male invariably attacks every other male. Outside its territory, the same male does not fight, but flees before a stranger. In between the two situations, that is, at the territory's boundary, opposing males perform displacement activities. The natural conclusion, viz. that displacement activities, in this situation, are an outlet of the conflicting drives of attack and escape (which of course cannot discharge themselves simultaneously, because their motor patterns are antagonistic), has been tested experimentally (Tinbergen, 1940). A red dummy was offered to a male stickleback in its territory and was duly attacked. Instead of withdrawing the dummy, it was made to 'resist' the attack by hitting the attacking male with it. When this 'counter-attack' is carried out vigorously enough, the territory-holding male can be defeated in its own territory. It withdraws and hides in the vegetation. If the dummy is now held motionless in the territory, it will continuously stimulate the male's fighting drive. The tendency to flee, however, diminishes with time. Gradually the fighting drive regains its superiority over the tendency to flee, and after a few minutes the male will attack the dummy again. Just before this happens, however, the male performs displacement digging. This shows, therefore, that displacement digging occurs when the two drives involved are in exact equilibrium. There is little doubt that the various displacement activities occurring during territorial fights must be explained in the same way.

2. In many species the male, even when strongly sexually motivated, is unable to perform coition as long as the female does not provide the sign stimuli necessary for the release of the male's consummatory act. A male stickleback, for instance, cannot ejaculate sperm before the female has deposited her eggs in the nest. The appearance of a female strongly arouses his sexual impulses. When the female does not respond to his zigzag dance by following him to the nest—a common phenomenon in incompletely motivated females—the male invariably shows nest-ventilating movements, often of high intensity and of long duration (Fig. 4.4). The amount of displacement fanning can even be used as a very reliable measure of the strength of his sexual motivation (Van Iersel and Tinbergen, 1947). This doubtless is the reason why so many displacement activities are parts of courtship patterns. Male ducks, for instance, regularly preen their plumage during courtship; birds of paradise, as mentioned above, and also European jays, wipe their bills. Herring gulls and many other birds (see Lack, 1940) feed their mates during courtship; it is not at all improbable that this courtship feeding is displacement feed-

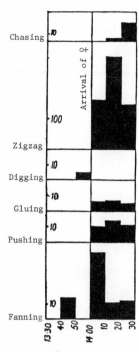

Figure 4.4. Frequency graph of reproductive activities in male three-spined stickleback before and after visual stimulation by a female. Abscissa: time in hours and minutes. After Tinbergen and Van Iersel, 1947.

ing. Numerous other examples have been mentioned in the literature (Kortlandt, 1940; Tinbergen, 1940; Lorenz, 1941).

A comparative review of displacement activities reveals that they are always innate patterns, known to us from the study of other instincts. Recognition is often difficult because the displacement activity is usually incomplete. This turns upon the intensity of the motivation, for with very strong motivation the displacement act may be complete. An example is given by Tinbergen and Van Iersel: if male sticklebacks are forced to nest very closely together, they will show nearly continuous displacement digging and the result is that their territories are littered with pits, or even become one huge pit (Figs. 4.5, 4.6). Another cause of difficulty in recognizing displacement activities is the 'ritualization' which a certain group of them secondarily undergo, a phenomenon which will be discussed later. The remarkable stereotypy of displacement reactions, the fact that they resemble innate motor patterns of other instincts, and the fact that they are typical for the species and do not differ from one member to another, suggests that the motivation of an instinct when prevented from discharging through its own motor pattern finds an outlet by discharge through the centre of another instinct. The facts known thus far are well in accordance with the 'centre-theory' of instinct presented above and elaborated below (p. 75). The incompleteness of displacement activities shows that the sideways discharge meets with considerable resistance.

It is a very remarkable fact that our present knowledge of displace-

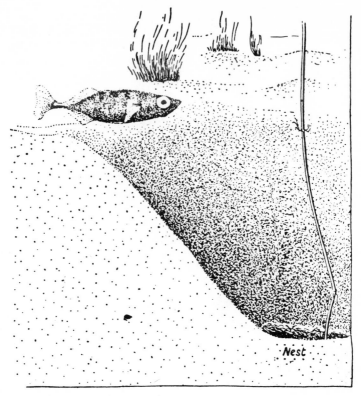

Figure 4.5.   Male three-spined stickleback with nest in deep pit made by displacement digging. After Tinbergen and Van Iersel, 1947.

ment activities confirms our conclusion that care of the body surface, and also sleep, are true instincts depending upon special nervous motivational (excitatory) centres, for they both appear as displacement reactions. It may be recalled that sleep, like instinctive consummatory acts, has a special kind of appetitive behaviour directed towards attaining a fitting situation (p. 65); further that sleep, like true instinctive activities, depends on the activation of a centre in the hypothalamus (p. 65). In these respects, therefore, sleep behaves as an instinctive activity, and there is no doubt, in my opinion, that sleep should be called an instinct. On the other hand, there are, so far as we know, no instances of displacement activities that could be interpreted as 'social activities' or as 'activities in relation to the environment', and this confirms our conclusion that there is no such thing as 'a social instinct' or a *Funktionskreis des Mediums*.

As will be clear later, displacement activities are by no means rare in man. Many instances of 'nervousness' concern displacement activities. The situation in man, however, is more complicated than in animals.

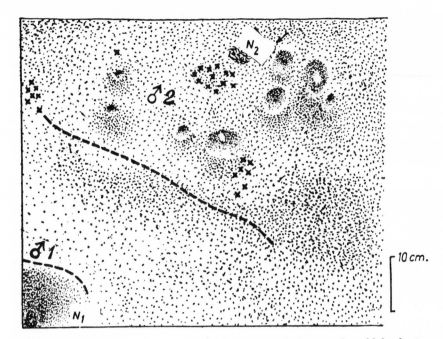

Figure 4.6.   Territories of two neighbouring male three-spined sticklebacks in crowded tank, with pits due to displacement digging. Broken lines: boundaries where owners are threatening; the ground between them is no-man's-land. Crosses indicate *Elodea* and *Batrachium* vegetation. $N_1$, nest belonging to male 1 (the male of Figure 4.5); $N_2$, nest belonging to male 2. After Tinbergen and Van Iersel, 1947.

The fact that a displacement activity is an expression, not of its 'own' drive (of autochthonous motivation, as Kortlandt (1940) called it) but of a 'strange' drive (of allochthonous motivation), makes it possible for it to act as a signal to fellow members of the same species, provided it can be distinguished from the 'genuine' activity, activated by its 'own' drive. As a matter of fact, many displacement activities are different from their 'models' and do act as signals. Thus displacement digging in stickle-backs is actually understood by other sticklebacks as a threat (as an expression of the fighting drive); it is different from its 'model', true digging, in that the spines are erected. The fact that displacement reactions may in this way embark upon an evolutionary development of their own by acquiring a social function will be discussed further below.

### The Lower Levels

The principle of hierarchical organization has been studied from a different point of view in the lower levels of integration. As we have seen, the consummatory act is the lowest or simplest element that appears in most cases of overt behaviour. It is, however, obvious that in most consummatory acts we have to do with co-ordinated movements of a great number of muscles. Now many facts show that there is hierarchical organization within each consummatory act too.

The ventilation or fanning movement of the stickleback may serve as an example. It consists of alternating forward and backward movements of the pectoral fins and, synchronous with their rhythm, sinusoid swimming movements of trunk and tail. The unity of this movement as a whole breaks down under certain conditions, e.g., when the fish is diseased. The pectorals may still move in alternation, but the trunk moves in an independent rhythm.

The movements of each separate fin are, as a rule, a co-ordinated system of swinging movements of a number of separate fin rays. Each ray swings to the left and the right in a regular alternating rhythm, and between successive rays there is a definite phase difference. Von Holst (1934) found in the goldfish that under certain conditions of anaesthesia the co-ordination within each fin may be disturbed; the rays begin to flutter in disorder. However, he reports that even then the movements of each separate ray remain perfectly regular, each ray swinging in perfect left-right alternation; it is merely the co-ordination between the rays that is disturbed. In these cases, therefore, it appears that the consummatory act is a co-ordinated activity of a number of fins, each of which may, under certain conditions, become independent. The movements of the fin as a whole are composed of still lower units which may also act independently of each other. One step farther down brings us on the level of the separate muscle contractions, for each fin ray is moved by a set of two muscles to the right and two to the left, the left and right pair contracting in alternation, and each pair acting as one muscle.

The argument for a hierarchical organization in behaviour as a whole, from the level of a major instinct down to the consummatory act, is different from that for the lowest levels. As we saw above, the existence of mutually inhibiting relations between different reactions (between the centres of the same level)—which enables the animal to confine its activities to one thing at a time—makes it possible to distinguish between more or less independent units within each level. Within the consummatory act, on the other hand, there is co-operation instead of inhibition, and the independence of component parts becomes apparent in quite another way, viz. when they occasionally follow their own rhythms under conditions that break down the power of the co-ordinating agents. While it is beyond my power to give an exhaustive review of the work done on integrative mechanisms at these lower levels, I want to mention the important work done by von Holst. This author made a thorough analysis of the co-ordinating principles at work in the swimming movements of fishes. As we have seen, the separate fins usually move in strict alternation or synchronization. Von Holst proved, with the aid of a wealth of material, that this co-ordination was due to two principles. First, the rhythm of one centre, for instance that of the pectoral fins, may be superimposed upon the rhythm of another centre such as that of the caudal fin. This superposition effect may vary over a wide range of intensities, from nearly zero to practically absolute dominance.

The second type does not concern the intensity of the separate contractions but their frequency or rhythm. In many cases pectorals and caudal fins have different rhythms. Usually one of them is dominant and, in some unknown way, can force the other to fall into step (Fig. 4.7).

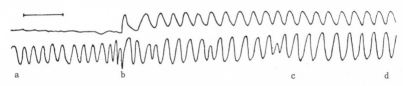

Figure 4.7.   The 'magnet effect'. Registration of the movements of the pectoral fin (dominant, above) and the dorsal fin (dependent, below) of *Labrus*, *a—b*, the dominant rhythm is at rest; the dependent rhythm appears in pure form. *b—c*, the dependent rhythm follows the dominant rhythm's tempo incompletely. *c—d*, the dependent rhythm is completely 'caught'; increase in amplitude is caused by superposition. After von Holst, 1936.

This influence too may be of varying intensity, and von Holst shows many cases ranging from weak to strong dominance. In cases of slight dominance the co-ordination is not absolute but relative, and von Holst shows that absolute co-ordination is but an extreme case of relative co-ordination.

The nature of this influence is unknown.

A few remarks may be inserted here on the configurational character of many processes involved in behaviour. Configurational processes may be found both on the receptor and on the motor side of behaviour. At the receptor side, the evidence suggests that in the eye the retina itself has synthesizing powers. Moreover, simple motor responses display configurational qualities. Although the configurational character of perceptual processes has often been stressed in a descriptive way, no attempt has been made, so far as I know, to analyse 'configurational' stimuli and the inter-relationships responsible for them. This is because correlation of ethological and neurophysiological findings is, at present, more promising at the effector side than at the receptor side of behaviour. The reason for this is that neurophysiology is much more developed in the domain of motor response than in that of receptor processes. 'The laboratory usage for obtaining reflexes is often direct stimulation of bared afferent nerves, a plan which eschews selective excitation of specific receptors and precise knowledge of the receptive field, and thus renounces serviceable guides to the functional purposes of the reflex' (Creed, Denny Brown, Eccles, Liddell, and Sherrington, 1932, p. 104).

In the domain of the motor response, von Holst (1941) has shown that the phenomenon called the magnet effect, which in itself seems to be open to quantitative description, may unite two rhythms into a movement of a higher order which displays all the characteristics of a configurational process, in which relations (between the tempi of dominant and dependent rhythm) are more constant than quantities (the absolute tempi). This is, so far as I know, the first attempt to attack the problem of *Gestalt* along physiological lines.

### P. Weiss's Concept of Nervous Hierarchy

The concept of a hierarchial organization of the nervous system is, of course, not new. And it is especially interesting to see how ethological study has led to the recognition of the hierarchical structure of innate behaviour quite independently of the conclusions drawn by neurophysiologists.

Now the ethologist has been considering higher levels of integration than the neurophysiologist. As a result, a combined picture of neurophysiological and ethological facts shows more levels than those recognized by neurophysiologists.

Weiss (1941a) enumerates the following levels from the lowest upward.

1. The level of the individual motor unit.
2. All the motor units belonging to one muscle.
3. Co-ordinated functions of muscular complexes relating to a single joint.
4. Co-ordinated movements of a limb as a whole.
5. Co-ordinated movements of a number of locomotor organs resulting in locomotion.
6. 'The highest level common to all animals', the movements of 'the animal as a whole'. (Weiss, 1941a, p. 23).

The levels 3, 4, and 5 are those studied by von Holst in his work on co-ordination in fishes. As will be clear, level 6 in Weiss's scheme really consists of a number of levels, in fact all the levels from the 'fixed pattern' up. It is interesting that Weiss's classification stops just here, because it is just at this level that one type of co-ordination changes into another type. But it will be clear that the hierarchical principle is the basis of the organization of these higher levels too.

Here again is an illustration of the fundamental identity of the neuro-physiological and the ethological approach. The only difference between them is a difference in level of integration.


## CONCLUSION


To conclude this section on the physiology of instinctive behaviour, it would be of advantage to present the results obtained in the form of a graphic picture of the nervous mechanisms involved. I should like to emphasize the tentative nature of such an attempt. While such a graphic representation may help to organize our thoughts, it has grave dangers in that it tends to make us forget its provisional and hypothetical nature.

We have seen that the causal factors controlling innate behaviour are of two kinds, viz. internal and external. In most cases both kinds exert an influence and they supplement each other. Usually the internal factors do not themselves evoke the overt response; they merely determine the threshold of the response to the sensory stimuli. Therefore, the internal factors like hormones, internal stimuli, and intrinsic impulses determine what the psychologist calls the motivation; and I will call them motivational factors. As we have seen, it is highly probable that in many cases external stimuli may also raise the motivation, and some of them therefore also belong among the motivational factors.

Another category of external stimuli, viz. those activating releasing mechanisms, must be distinguished from the motivational factors; I shall call them releasing factors.

Beach (1942), in a discussion of the factors effective in arousing the male sexual behaviour in rats, postulated a central excitatory mechanism (CEM) which is receptive to sensory stimuli and hormone influences and which dispatches impulses to the neural circuits of the behaviour pattern.

When we compare his presentation (Fig. 4.8) with the results discussed above, it is clear that, although Beach gives due attention to the cooperation of internal and external factors, his picture does not take into account (1) the hierarchical organization and (2) the different functions of motivational and releasing factors.

Concerning the first point, it seems that the single CEM postulated by Beach is rather a system of CEMs of different levels. Each 'centre' in our system is a CEM in Beach's sense, as each of these centres has its own afferent and efferent connexions.

Of no less importance is the difference between motivational and releasing factors. For, as we have seen, the motivational factors influence the CEM itself while the releasing factors activate a reflex-like mecha-

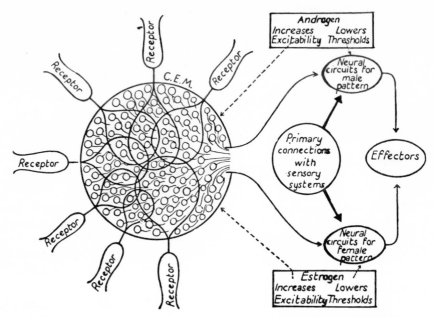

Figure 4.8.    The 'central excitatory mechanism.' After Beach, 1942.

nism, the IRM, removing a block that prevented the outflow of impulses along the efferent paths.

The system C(entral) E(xcitatory) M(echanism)–I(nnate) R(eleasing) M(echanism) is tentatively presented in Figs. 4.9 and 4.10. Let us first consider Fig. 4.9, which represents one centre of an intermediate level.

The centre is 'loaded' by motivational impulses of various kinds. First it receives impulses from the superordinated centre of the next higher level. Impulses from this higher level flow to other centres as well, in fact to all the centres controlled by the higher centre. Second, centre 1 may receive impulses from an 'automatic', self-generating centre belonging especially to it. Third, a hormone might contribute to the motivation, either by acting directly on centre 1, or through the automatic centre. As discussed previously, it is probable that hormones act exclusively on the higher centres. Fourth, internal sensory stimuli may help to load centre 1. Fifth, external sensory stimuli might also act directly upon the centre and contribute to its motivation.

This system together represents a CEM in Beach's sense, belonging to one level of the hierarchical system.

Outgoing impulses are blocked as long as the IRM is not stimulated. When the adequate sign stimuli impinge upon the reflex-like IRM, the block is removed. The impulses can now flow along a number of paths. All but one lead to subordinate centres of the next lower level. However,

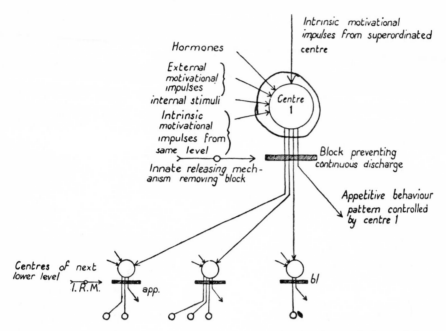

Figure 4.9. Tentative representation of an instinctive 'centre' of an intermediate level. Explanation in text.

all these centres are prevented from action by their own blocks, and most of the impulses therefore flow to the nervous structures controlling appetitive behaviour. This appetitive behaviour, as we have seen (p. 59), is carried on until one of the IRMs of the lower level removes a block, as a result of which free passage is given through the corresponding centre of this next lower level. This 'drains away' the impulses from the appetitive behaviour mechanism and conducts them to the appetitive behaviour mechanism of the lower centre.

Fig. 4.10 suggests how centres of this type might be organized within one major instinct. The reproductive instinct of the male three-spined stickleback has been taken as a concrete example. The hormonal influence, presumably exerted by testosterone, is acting upon the highest centre. This centre is most probably also influenced by a rise in temperature. These two influences together cause the fish to migrate from the sea (or from deep fresh water) into more shallow fresh water. The highest centre, which might be called the migration centre, seems to have no block. A certain degree of motivation results in migratory behaviour, without release by any special set of sign stimuli, which is true appetitive behaviour. This appetitive behaviour is carried on—the fish migrates—

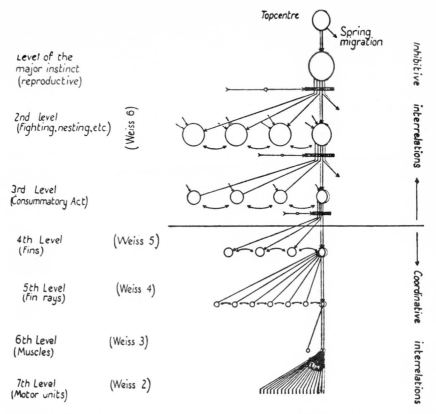

Figure 4.10.   The hierarchical system of 'centres' underlying a major instinct, viz. the reproductive instinct of the male three-spined stickleback. Explanation in text.

until the sign stimuli, provided by a suitable territory (shallow, warm water and suitable vegetation) act upon the IRM blocking the reproductive centre *sensu stricto,* which might be called 'territorial centre'. The impulses then flow through this centre. Here, again, the paths to the subordinated centres (fighting, nest-building, &c.) are blocked as long as the sign stimuli adequate to these lower levels are not forthcoming. The only open path is that to the appetitive behaviour, which consists of swimming around, waiting for either another male to be fought or a female to be courted, or nest material to be used in building.

    If, for instance, fighting is released by the trespassing of a male into the territory, the male swims towards the opponent (appetitive behaviour). The opponent must give new, more specific sign stimuli, which will remove a block belonging to one of the consummatory acts (biting, chasing, threatening, &c.) in order to direct the impulse flow to the centre of one of these consummatory acts.

The various centres located at the various levels are, therefore, not organized in exactly the same way. The very highest centre has no block. If there were blocks at these very highest centres, the animal would have no means of 'getting rid' of impulses at all, which, as far as we know, would lead to neurosis. The next centre responds, in comparison to the lower centres, to a relatively higher number of motivational factors.

The next centres of the male stickleback's reproductive behaviour pattern, represented, for example, by fighting and nest-building, are loaded primarily by the impulses coming from the higher centre. Whether there are special motivational factors for each of these centres besides those coming from the higher centre is not certain, but I think there are, because the fighting drive displays the phenomenon of afterdischarge, and, moreover, seems to be motivated (not merely released) by external stimuli. In general it seems, that the lower we go, the more pronounced the influence of external releasing stimuli becomes.

Arrows between the centres of one level indicate interrelationships suggested by the existence of mutual inhibition and of displacement activities. It should be emphasized that it is quite possible that these interconnexions do not in reality run directly from one centre to the other, but go by way of the superordinated centre, and that the 'inhibition' of one centre by the other may in reality be competition, the 'inhibiting' centre by decrease of resistance 'draining away' the impulse flow at the expense of the 'inhibited' centre.

Thus the motivation is carried on through a number of steps, which may be different in different instincts, down to the level of the consummatory action. Here the picture is changed. When the block of the consummatory centre is removed, a number of centres come into action simultaneously, between which horizontal co-ordinative forces are effective. With fish, these centres below the consummatory level are arranged in two or three planes, the lowest of which is the centre of the right or left fin-ray muscle, which is a relatively simple type of nervous centre. The relation between sub-consummatory centres of the same level are represented by horizontal lines.

It should again be emphasized that these diagrams represent no more than a working hypothesis of a type that helps to put our thoughts in order.

# II
# Drive and Arousal

Instinct theory has always manifested a primary concern for unlearned sources of direction in behavior. It was this concern which led early views to stress the purposiveness of assumed instincts, their orientation towards particular goals or end-states. Many views, like those of McDougall, were explicitly stated in teleological terms which were anathema to psychologists determined to make their subject matter an orthodox science. It seemed that a description of behavior that relied upon the "pull" of goals which were often not physically present and had reference to some future state of affairs was in flagrant contradiction to the enterprise of providing a causal account of behavior in which causes were respectably placed prior to their effects. It was the effort to replace the instinctive pull from the goal with some kind of push from behind that brought about the rise of drive theory, the subject of the articles in this section.

Drive theory evolved gradually after R. S. Woodworth first used the term. Using the analogy of a machine, which consists of a power source and a mechanism that is activated by that source, Woodworth saw drive as a force which "powers" the behavioral "mechanisms" to make us do what we do. This rather crude notion proved amenable to successively more sophisticated elaboration. The machine analogy gradually faded as the search for the sources of drive shifted to the study of those physiological states, such as hunger and thirst, which seemed likely to provide a firm basis for psychological activation. The article by E. B. Holt contrasts this emphasis with classical instinct approaches. In the work of Clark Hull the concept of drive became formalized, not so much in physiological terms, as a construct in a hypothetico-deductive behavior system. Thus conceived, it was deemed necessary to state as precisely as possible the unique functional properties which distinguished drive, symbolized by the letter $D$, from other constructs in the system. The unique function attributed to $D$ was that of a general energizer of behavior. Drive was seen as a construct which had a multiplicative relationship to habits, that is, it tended to enhance the response strength of any and all tendencies associated with the situation in which the individual found himself. Since $D$ was in large part considered to increase as a function of such antecedent events as food deprivation, it could still be recognized as the "push from behind" which early drive theorists had sought. In the process of refinement, however, drive had lost any capacity to give direction to behavior. It was seen only as an activator, a kind of general excitation which increased the responsiveness of an organism but did not directly influence the orientation of its behavior. Drive came to be formulated as a determiner of the intensity but not the quality of behavior. Serious efforts were made to equate motivation with drive, a semantic ploy which did not succeed. The separation of motivation from the problems of direction in behavior apparently flew too much in the face of conventional usage, and furthermore, it proved empirically difficult to confirm that even simple deprivational operations resulted in states which nonselectively enhanced all behavior. Nevertheless, drive theory inspired a vast amount of fruitful investigation, resulted in great gains in knowledge about motivational variables, drew attention to significant distinctions which needed to be made, and emphasized, albeit to the exclusion of directional factors, that motivation did involve variation in activation. When advances in neurophysiology led to the discovery of brain centers which exercised control over the general arousability of living organisms, a development which is related in D. O. Hebb's article in this section, it was an easy step from the previous drive theories to the more recent psychophysiological formulations of what has come to be called "arousal theory." If motivation deals with problems of the activation and direction of behavior, it is through drive theory that the understanding of activation as part of the area has most conspicuously developed.

# 5 • Robert S. Woodworth

## On a Distinction Between "Drive" and "Mechanism"

In formulating the concept of drive, as distinct from mechanism, Woodworth foreshadowed much that was to come in motivational thinking over the next 30 years. His view that mechanisms may, if strong, become drives was original. His emphasis on the role of the consummatory reaction—behavior such as eating or drinking—turned psychological thought toward the motivational implications of such conditions as hunger and thirst as primary motivations, or drives, and suggested the importance of what Hull was later to call "anticipatory goal reactions." For Woodworth, drive could be general, "a condition of readiness for a yet undetermined stimulus," and it could also act selectively to facilitate certain mechanisms and inhibit others. That is, in Woodworth one can see a clear first statement of the energizing and directing functions of motivation.

A *beginner in psychology*, approaching the subject from the side of common interests and unworried as yet by controversies within the ranks of psychologists, would be inclined to suppose that the aim of the science was fairly clear, and to express it as an attempt to understand the 'workings of the mind'. He wishes to be informed how we learn and think, and what leads people to feel and act as they do. He is interested, namely, in cause and effect, or what may be called dynamics.

This is not only the commonsense point of view, but also the point of view that is most in evidence in the history of psychology. Locke, one of the prime movers in psychological study, expressed himself as designing to give "some account of the ways whereby our understandings come to attain those notions of things we have" [1]; Berkeley, in his *Essay towards a New Theory of Vision*, begins by saying, "My design is to show the

---

[1] *Essay Concerning Human Understanding*, Book I, Chap. I, Sect. 2.

tter, and many similar
uestions are asked with
y science has come to
substitute the question
question 'Why?' always
: finality is reached in
'How?' is always good
ldom if ever complete.
of drive is reducible to
justification for making
s of action of human
l attention to them.
m may become clearer
rive here is the power
n is made to go, and is
relative, since the ma-
the direction that shall
of the mechanism as
results. But the mech-
g in disposable energy.
led gun, stored energy
ate this stored energy,
of mechanism is rather
contain stored energy,
the stimulus that nor-
g along a motor nerve.
ning out along a motor
in the nerve cells con-
mselves excited to dis-
from a sensory nerve.
elf driven by a stimulus
reflex mechanism, con-
nerve and muscle, can
xternal stimulus.
and consisted of direct
reat significance in the
ve would simply be the
hole organism. On the
thing internal, and the
ay up from the drive

ts of 'reinforcement' or
ural terms, the coming
ult in some cases that

nagnitude and situa-
t in his *Inquiry Con-*
in some degree, the
ind is actuated in its
and forces, by which
ted." Even in recent
efined as the descrip-
psychologists, as re-
his problem of cause

—since we no longer
gain a clear view of
its minute elements
ities occur, and what
orderly fashion. Now
it system of processes
ent system, because
usness goes on below
dered as a series of
ecause it leaves out
ilus and the reaction,
provide a coherent
ng between stimulus
have to look to brain
ntil brain physiology
after it has done so,
nalysis which we can
thods of psychology.
t of view, and to be
side of vital activity,
vs offered us by the
ior, but endeavoring
sults of brain physiol-
processes of mental

ology is gained, two
med the problem of
problem, how we do
ces us to do it. Take
lem of mechanism is
unt of curve, and co-
nd. The problem of
aged in this exercise
other, why he rouses

himself more against one than against another
questions. It will be noticed that the mechanism
'How?' and the drive questions with 'Why?' N
regard the question 'Why?' with suspicion, and t
'How?' since it has found that the answer to the
calls for a further 'Why?' and that no stability
this direction, whereas the answer to the questic
as far as it is accurate, though, to be sure, it is
It may be true in our case, also, that the questio
a question of mechanism, but there is *prima faci*
the distinction. Certainly the motives and spri
life are of so much importance as to justify spec

This distinction between drive and mechan
if we consider it in the case of a machine. The
applied to make the mechanism go; the mechani
relatively passive. Its passivity is, to be sure, onl
terial and structure of the mechanism determine
be taken by the power applied. We might spe
reacting to the power applied and so producing t
anism without the power is inactive, dead, lacki

In some forms of mechanism, such as a lo
is present, and the action of the drive is to lib
which then does the rest of the work. This sort
similar to that of a living creature. The muscle
which is liberated by a stimulus reaching them
mally reaches them being the 'nerve impulse' com
The nerve drives the muscle. The nerve impulse c
nerve originates in the discharge of stored energ
trolling this nerve; and these central cells are th
charge by nerve impulses reaching them, perhap
The sensory nerve drives the motor center, being i
reaching the sense organ from without. The whol
sisting of sense organ, sensory nerve, center, moto
be thought of as a unit; and its drive is then the

If all behavior were of this simple reflex type
responses to present stimuli, there would be no
distinction between drive and mechanism. The dr
external stimulus and the mechanism simply the
other hand, what we mean by a 'motive' is som
question thus arises whether we can work our
as external stimulus to the drive as inner motive.

The first step is to notice the physiological fa
'facilitation' and of 'inhibition'. These mean, in n
together of different nerve impulses, with the re

manner wherein we perceive by sight the distance, magnitude and situation of objects"; and Hume hoped, as he expressed it in his *Inquiry Concerning Human Understanding,* to discover, at least in some degree, the secret springs and principles by which the human mind is actuated in its operations, just as Newton had "determined the laws and forces, by which the revolutions of the planets are governed and directed." Even in recent years, while psychology has usually been formally defined as the descriptive science of consciousness, the actual interests of psychologists, as revealed by the problems taken up, have centered on this problem of cause and effect.

What is meant by a study of cause and effect—since we no longer hope to discover ultimate causes—is an attempt to gain a clear view of the action or process in the system studied, both in its minute elements and in its broad tendencies, noting whatever uniformities occur, and what laws enable us to conceive the whole process in an orderly fashion. Now neither consciousness nor behavior provides a coherent system of processes for causal treatment. Consciousness is not a coherent system, because much of the process that is partly revealed in consciousness goes on below the threshold of consciousness; and behavior, considered as a series of motor reactions to external stimuli, is incoherent because it leaves out of account the process intervening between the stimulus and the reaction. Nor do consciousness and behavior taken together provide a coherent system, since much of the internal process intervening between stimulus and reaction is unconscious. We shall undoubtedly have to look to brain physiology for a minute analysis of the process; but until brain physiology is able to give us such an analysis, and probably even after it has done so, we shall derive some satisfaction from the coarser analysis which we can derive from the introspective and behavioristic methods of psychology. But the essential thing is to keep the dynamic point of view, and to be working always toward a clearer view of the mental side of vital activity, refusing to be contented with the fragmentary views offered us by the exclusive students of either consciousness or behavior, but endeavoring to utilize the results of both these parties, and the results of brain physiology as well, for an understanding of the complete processes of mental activity and development.

Once the point of view of a dynamic psychology is gained, two general problems come into sight, which may be named the problem of 'mechanism' and the problem of 'drive'. One is the problem, how we do a thing, and the other is the problem of what induces us to do it. Take the case of the pitcher in a baseball game. The problem of mechanism is the problem how he aims, gauges distance and amount of curve, and coordinates his movements to produce the desired end. The problem of drive includes such questions as to why he is engaged in this exercise at all, why he pitches better on one day than on another, why he rouses himself more against one than against another batter, and many similar questions. It will be noticed that the mechanism questions are asked with 'How?' and the drive questions with 'Why?' Now science has come to regard the question 'Why?' with suspicion, and to substitute the question 'How?' since it has found that the answer to the question 'Why?' always calls for a further 'Why?' and that no stability or finality is reached in this direction, whereas the answer to the question 'How?' is always good as far as it is accurate, though, to be sure, it is seldom if ever complete. It may be true in our case, also, that the question of drive is reducible to a question of mechanism, but there is *prima facie* justification for making the distinction. Certainly the motives and springs of action of human life are of so much importance as to justify special attention to them.

This distinction between drive and mechanism may become clearer if we consider it in the case of a machine. The drive here is the power applied to make the mechanism go; the mechanism is made to go, and is relatively passive. Its passivity is, to be sure, only relative, since the material and structure of the mechanism determine the direction that shall be taken by the power applied. We might speak of the mechanism as reacting to the power applied and so producing the results. But the mechanism without the power is inactive, dead, lacking in disposable energy.

In some forms of mechanism, such as a loaded gun, stored energy is present, and the action of the drive is to liberate this stored energy, which then does the rest of the work. This sort of mechanism is rather similar to that of a living creature. The muscles contain stored energy, which is liberated by a stimulus reaching them, the stimulus that normally reaches them being the 'nerve impulse' coming along a motor nerve. The nerve drives the muscle. The nerve impulse coming out along a motor nerve originates in the discharge of stored energy in the nerve cells controlling this nerve; and these central cells are themselves excited to discharge by nerve impulses reaching them, perhaps from a sensory nerve. The sensory nerve drives the motor center, being itself driven by a stimulus reaching the sense organ from without. The whole reflex mechanism, consisting of sense organ, sensory nerve, center, motor nerve and muscle, can be thought of as a unit; and its drive is then the external stimulus.

If all behavior were of this simple reflex type, and consisted of direct responses to present stimuli, there would be no great significance in the distinction between drive and mechanism. The drive would simply be the external stimulus and the mechanism simply the whole organism. On the other hand, what we mean by a 'motive' is something internal, and the question thus arises whether we can work our way up from the drive as external stimulus to the drive as inner motive.

The first step is to notice the physiological facts of 'reinforcement' or 'facilitation' and of 'inhibition'. These mean, in neural terms, the coming together of different nerve impulses, with the result in some cases that one strengthens the other, and in some cases that one weakens or suppresses the other. Take the familiar 'knee-jerk' or 'patellar reflex' as an example. This involuntary movement of the lower leg, produced by some of the thigh muscles, can only be elicited by a blow on the tendon passing in front of the knee (or some equivalent, strictly local stimulus). But the force of the knee-jerk can be greatly altered by influences coming from other parts of the body. A sudden noise occurring an instant before the blow at the knee will decidedly reinforce the knee-jerk, while soft music may weaken it. Clenching the fist or gritting the teeth reinforces the knee-jerk. The drive operating the knee-jerk in such cases is not entirely the local stimulus, but other centers in the brain and spinal cord, being themselves aroused from outside, furnish drive for the center that is directly responsible for the movement. If one nerve center can thus furnish drive for another, there is some sense in speaking of drives.

Still, the conception of 'drive' would have little significance if the activity aroused in any center lasted only as long as the external stimulus acting upon it through a sensory nerve; for, taken as a whole, the organism would still be passive and simply responsive to the complex of external stimuli acting on it at any moment. It is therefore a very important fact, for our purpose, that a nerve center, aroused to activity, does not in all cases relapse into quiescence, after a momentary discharge. Its state of activity may outlast the stimulus that aroused it, and this residual activity in one center may act as drive to another center. Or, a center may be 'sub-excited' by an external stimulus that is not capable of arousing it to full discharge; and, while thus sub-excited, it may influence other centers, either by way of reinforcement or by way of inhibition. Thus, though the drive for nerve activity may be ultimately external, at any one moment there are internal sources of influence furnishing drive to other parts of the system.

This relationship between two mechanisms, such that one, being partially excited, becomes the drive of another, is specially significant in the case of what have been called 'preparatory and consummatory reactions' (Sherrington). A consummatory reaction is one of direct value to the animal—one directly bringing satisfaction—such as eating or escaping from danger. The objective mark of a consummatory reaction is that it terminates a series of acts, and is followed by rest or perhaps by a shift to some new series. Introspectively, we know such reactions by the satisfaction and sense of finality that they bring. The preparatory reactions are only mediately of benefit to the organism, their value lying in the fact that they lead to, and make possible, a consummatory reaction. Objectively, the mark of a preparatory reaction is that it occurs as a preliminary stage in a series of acts leading up to a consummatory reaction. Consciously, a preparatory reaction is marked by a state of tension.

Preparatory reactions are of two kinds. We have, first, such reactions as looking and listening, which are readily evoked when the animal is in a passive or resting condition, and which consist in a coming to attention and instituting a condition of readiness for a yet undetermined stimulus that may arouse further response. The other kind consists of reactions which are not evoked except when the mechanism for a consummatory reaction has been aroused and is in activity. A typical series of events is the following: a sound or light strikes the sense organ and arouses the appropriate attentive reaction; this permits a stimulus of significance to the animal to take effect—for example, the sight of prey, which arouses a trend towards the consummatory reaction of devouring it. But this consummatory reaction cannot at once take place; what does take place is the preparatory reaction of stalking or pursuing the prey. The series of preparatory reactions may be very complicated, and it is evidently driven by the trend towards the consummatory reaction. That there is a persistent inner tendency towards the consummatory reaction is seen when, for instance, a hunting dog loses the trail; if he were simply carried along from one detail of the hunting process to another by a succession of stimuli calling out simple reflexes, he would cease hunting as soon as the trail ceased or follow it back again; whereas what he does is to explore about, seeking the trail, as we say. This seeking, not being evoked by any external stimulus (but rather by the absence of an external stimulus), must be driven by some internal force; and the circumstances make it clear that the inner drive is directed towards the capture of the prey.

The dog's behavior is to be interpreted as follows: the mechanism for a consummatory reaction, having been set into activity by a suitable stimulus, acts as a drive operating other mechanisms which give the preparatory reactions. Each preparatory reaction may be a response in part to some external stimulus, but it is facilitated by the drive towards the consummatory reaction. Not only are some reactions thus facilitated, but others which in other circumstances would be evoked by external stimuli are inhibited. The dog on the trail does not stop to pass the time of day with another dog met on the way; he is too busy. When an animal or man is too busy or too much in a hurry to respond to stimuli that usually get responses from him, he is being driven by some internal tendency.

'Drive' as we have thus been led to conceive of it in the simpler sort of case, is not essentially distinct from 'mechanism'. The drive is a mechanism already aroused and thus in a position to furnish stimulation to other mechanisms. Any mechanism might be a drive. But it is the mechanisms directed towards consummatory reactions—whether of the simpler sort seen in animals or of the more complex sort exemplified by human desires and motives—that are most likely to act as drives. Some mechanisms act at once and relapse into quiet, while others can only bring their action to completion by first arousing other mechanisms. But there is no absolute distinction, and it will be well to bear in mind the possibility that any mechanism may be under certain circumstances the source of stimulation that arouses other mechanisms to activity.

# 6 • Edwin B. Holt

## Instinctive and Appetitive Drives

The shift of emphasis from instinct to a stress upon physiological states as internal initiators of activity is shown in this chapter by Holt. His tendency to regard such states as stimuli within the organism is representative of one strand of interpretation within drive theory. It is seen later in the work of Neal Miller, who regarded drives as originating in any intense stimulation, and William Estes, who proposed an interpretation of drive in strict stimulus-response terms. Other critics of the necessity of positing an energizing function in drive have also sought to interpret motivational phenomena as elicited responses to stimulus conditions. Holt, however, continued the movement toward formulations of drive as a nondirectional "push" by noting the random restlessness which may result from states of deprivation.

*An organism equipped* with adient and avoidant responses, with chain reflexes, movements of progression, equilibration, and the other varieties of adience that we have so far studied, is ready to do much. The neural paths of lowered resistance which mediate these responses are 'engrams': but, as we have seen, they have all been learned and not inherited. They are all reflexes. And with this elementary equipment the animal begins to evince what must be called 'conduct.' It is the various acquired habits of this rather elementary sort, which have commonly been called 'instincts'; and this word is a good one if we remember that it is merely a name for these activities, and that it does not explain their mechanism or their causal origins. These origins we have briefly surveyed in the foregoing pages; so that we are in a position now to speak of instincts and to mean thereby, not faculties, but the activity of reflex mechanisms whose function we can define and whose structure we fairly well understand. In doing this, we shall not be repeating the error of the instinct-faculty psychology, for whatever we try to explain will be explained not by the *name* of the phenomenon but by the physiological mechanism which produces it (*cf.* Craig, 1918).

The instinct psychology, besides treating instincts as explanatory causal categories and as inherited, commits the third blunder of attempting to list them in so and so many 'fundamental' groups. And this is as factitious as would be an attempt to list the 'fundamental' shapes of constellations in the sky. There are no outstanding groups and, as Prof. Dewey (1922) has said, no grounds for restricting "original activities to a definite number of sharply demarcated classes of instincts." . . . "For any activity is original when it first occurs. As conditions are continually changing, new and *primitive* activities are continually occurring. The traditional psychology of instincts obscures recognition of this fact. It sets up a hard-and-fast preordained class under which specific acts are subsumed, so that their own quality and originality are lost from view." It is not to be wondered at that the 'fundamental instincts' as listed by the various writers on the subject differ so preposterously. Moreover, there is no thoroughgoing uniformity of instinctive behaviour from individual to individual, and so far as there is any uniformity it is merely because the individuals of a species develop under tolerably similar conditions, but the uniformities are absurdly exaggerated by most of the writers.

As a result of his studies in the psychology of the Hymenoptera Dr. L. Verlaine has invaded the central citadel, as it were, of the 'instinct' psychology; for it has been customary to assert that the insects are so far the perfect examples of distinct, phylogenetically invariant and inherited instincts that they exhibit no other activities. They have been supposed to be incapable, at any period of their lives, of learning; while at the same time the marvellous 'perfection' of their preformed mechanisms ('blind instincts') has been held up for admiration. Speaking of wasps and bees, Verlaine (1925) says, "The psychology of these insects differs from human psychology only in the simplicity of its manifestations, although these are far from being as elementary as has been often supposed." . . . "The psychology of the Hymenoptera and human psychology are ruled by the same laws and determined by natural factors. There are not two psychologies, that of animals and that of men, but one general psychophysiology with its manifold and varied aspects." Having insisted that, "There are no innate characters" ("The class of 'innate characters' and that expression itself should be abolished. There exist only acquired characters"). Verlaine goes on to say: "The numerous criteria of instinct that have been so far proposed, have all at various times been found gravely defective." . . . "Instinct and intelligence are labels placed by us on groups of phenomena which are separated only in our mind but not in that of the organisms producing the phenomena; and while these phenomena may differ considerably if considered in their final form, they do not so differ when one studies their causation and their mechanism."

It is worth noting, further, that the lists of 'fundamental instincts' tend to be absurdly prettified. So that for the future convenience of instinct-faculty psychologists I will suggest a few obvious additions, all being of course 'strictly innate and inherited':—the instincts of wanton destructiveness (surely an authentic 'instinct' if any is), ostentation, greed, hatred, mendacity, treachery, larceny, cruelty, self-mutilation (apparently an exclusive attribute of *homo sapiens*), lechery and the whole array of sexual perversions. Let these not be neglected when we discuss 'our God-given inheritance.'

Among the instinctive activities many of the older writers, as for instance Erasmus Darwin (1794), drew a distinction which of late has been too often ignored by psychologists. This distinction was preserved by Alexander Bain (1864) when he divided the simpler forms of habit into 'instincts' and 'appetites.' Some stimulators, namely, are contained within the organism's own body, and these, being inescapable, force the organism to activities which Bain, following precedent, called 'appetites.' Bain's list is: the appetites for food (including water and oxygen), exercise, sleep and repose, and (developing later) the sexual appetite ("Sleep, Exercise, Repose, Thirst, Hunger, Sex"). It seems to me that there is some question about an appetite for exercise; though Erasmus Darwin (1794) also mentions a 'propensity' to action due to "accumulation of the spirit of animation." Circular reflexes, as we have learned, when once stimulated will perpetuate themselves until inhibited by some other reflex, and this gives the appearance of an autonomous 'craving for exercise' on the part of the organism. I suspect this to be the phenomenon which Bain had in mind. An activity like this which must first be stimulated from outside, but which will then continue its own stimulation, is clearly intermediate between an instinct and an appetite; and strictly is neither the one nor the other. To the list must be added defæcation and micturition, and in woman an appetite to give suck to her offspring. This last was included by Darwin.

While biologists and physiologists, in general, recognize the importance of distinguishing appetites from instincts, internally stimulated activities from externally stimulated activities, there are relatively fewer contemporary psychologists who, like Dr. James Drever, realize the significance of this distinction. In a discussion on the classification of the instincts, at the Seventh International Congress of Psychology (Oxford, 1923) Dr. Ernest Jones (1924) said: "The main hint Dr. Drever himself gives of a classification is after all into two groups only, the appetitive and reactive ones. The distinction is evidently a valid one, though how useful it may prove is another matter. As a criterion to be applied to the whole gamut of instincts it could be justified only if the difference between the two classes is both fundamental and important. Clinical observations make it doubtful whether the difference is fundamental. Thus many mani-

festations, for instance most sexual ones, are both appetitive and reactive."
Dr. Jones seems to forget that the *reactive* apparatus is of course necessarily the same for both instincts and appetites, namely, the bony skeleton
with the muscles that actuate it. How else could, say, the hunger appetite
'manifest' itself? The distinction, however, is assuredly both fundamental
and important: fundamental, as the distinction between extero- and interoceptor sense-organs; important, because a self-contained (interoceptive)
irritation can be allayed only by very specific modes of response, and not
along the ordinary lines of 'avoidance.' It is precisely, I take it, because
the appetite stimulators always travel with the organism and so continue
to irritate it, that repression of the sex appetite, for instance, is so dangerous. That Dr. Jones should minimize such a distinction is rather amazing,
but instructive. The whole Freudian psychology, with its Herbartian slant,
has in fact persistently (and I incline to say completely) ignored the
physiology which some modern psychologists have so profitably consulted.
It is no wonder, then, that Freudians are a little hazy as to just what
should or should not be repressed; that, for instance, after discovering that
sex repression is the source of most functional nervous disorders, they
can proceed to *recommend* sex repression under the sanctified name of
'sublimation.' An interesting and logically necessary corollary of this
sublimation doctrine is that satisfactorily married men and women must
be 'culturally' the least effective!

The great point about the appetites is that since their stimuli are
contained within the organism, these cannot be evaded by any ordinary
avoidance response (locomotion, etc.), but will keep the organism restless
until it acquires, by trial-and-error, very different and often intricate
modes of response which will allay the internal stimulation. The appetites,
when active, are imperative. And any reflex habits which are acquired
as motor outlet for the appetitive stimuli, which may justly be called
'annoyers' in the physiological sense (that is, stimuli which produce a
general restlessness), are bound to be touched off spontaneously and at
more or less regular physiological periods: whereas reflexes that are released by external stimuli often go for years without being activated. Thus
an ability to speak a foreign language (for this also is reflex) may lie
fallow for many years, and gives no trouble; not so an appetite.

While the distinction between instinct and appetite is solely one as
to the source of stimulation, all appetitive stimuli being resident within
the organism, and while this has its implications, yet in both cases alike
that which is stimulated and driven to action is the general motor, and
indeed the sensori-motor, apparatus of the organism. It is not necessary
here, nor is the writer competent, to treat of the internal appetitive
processes in any great detail; specially since here the vegetative or autonomic nervous system is more or less involved. Very broadly speaking,
however, three problems are here presented: first, as to the actual appeti-

tive stimuli; second, as to the receptor organs which these stimuli excite; and third, as to the response patterns which develop as outlets for the afferent appetitive impulses.

The appetitive stimuli appear to be of two sorts, mechanical pressures and chemical substances. The former occur in the case of 'hollow viscera' (*cf.* E. J. Kempf, 1918; G. H. Wang, 1923), that is, of secretory and excretory glands which possess regular ducts for the discharge of their contents. The accumulating contents exert a pressure (distention) on the walls of these glands, which initiates the physiological 'craving' for discharge. The appetites for defæcation, micturition, lactation, and the sexual appetite appear to depend on such a mechanism. On the other hand the appetites for sleep (repose), oxygen, water, and other foods appear to originate from chemical stimuli contained, probably, in the blood. In the case of sleep the stimuli are probably chemical products of fatigue, and particularly perhaps those which the blood has received from fatigued muscle tissue (lactic acid?); in the case of oxygen-need the deficiency of oxygen in the blood leaves an excessive hydrogen-ion concentration, which is the appetitive stimulus;[1] with water depletion the serum of the blood carries more crystalloidal substances (salts) than normally, and these are the stimuli of thirst (*cf.* L. R. Müller, 1924).[2] These last two cases are conveniently termed 'deficit stimuli.' The appetite for other foods is doubtless due to similar deficit stimuli (Müller, 1924); and here it may be questioned whether there is not a considerable variety of specific stimuli, as R. Turró (1911) believes, corresponding to a deficiency in the blood of various essential food elements: whether, too, these deficit stimuli may not be identical with some of the 'hormones.'

As physiological annoyers or appetitive drives, the deficit stimuli should be capable of stimulating, *i.e.* of initiating nerve impulses in, some portion of the sensori-motor system. Yet I am not convinced that any of the chemical constituents of the blood (deficit stimuli, hormones) have been conclusively shown actually to excite nerve impulses at any points in this system—although it is a widely accepted view that they do so. Perhaps the best established case of hormone action is that of adrenaline which, as has been shown by W. B. Cannon and others, in a series of papers, intensifies (sensitizes?) a variety of physiological processes all of which in turn facilitate the (otherwise excited) muscular activity of the

[1] Just possibly, however, it is the depleted air itself which acts as a chemical stimulus. In one place Sherrington (1922, p. 346) speaks of "the delicate mechanism linking the condition of the air at the bottom of the lungs with that particular part of the nervous system which manages the ventilation of the lungs." In this case the 'craving' for oxygen would not be in the strictest sense of the term an appetite. Or again, both modes of stimulation may be operative.

[2] Here too there may be another, more properly external, stimulus—namely, a parched condition of the mucous lining of the mouth and throat (*cf.* Cannon, 1918).

organism, and depress digestive and other 'vegetative' processes. It seems uncertain whether adrenaline or any other hormone directly excites the central nervous system, though it may well be that this and several other hormones indirectly qualify behaviour in various ways. Some of the physiological effects even of adrenaline are under dispute. And at the present time the functions of the endocrine (ductless) glands are in general too obscure to be brought very definitely into our picture (*vide* Swale Vincent, 1922).

As for the receptor organs, secondly, which the appetitive stimuli excite, they are in the case of hollow viscera thought to be sensory cells lying in the walls of the viscus, which are mechanically compressed (or stretched?) when the walls of the viscus are distended by accumulated contents. It may be questioned, incidentally, whether this pressure as exerted on the sphincter muscles of such viscera, does not primarily assist in keeping these sphincters contracted (stretch or myotatic reflex); if so, the evacuation of such viscera would have to be effected by nervous impulses from some other source, such as the pressure receptors in the walls of the same viscus, coming to inhibit the myotatic contraction of the sphincters. Such a reservoir would be 'self-tripping,' while the contraction of the sphincters might still receive extraneous re-enforcement or inhibition from remoter parts of the nervous system. This is partly conjectural; but it seems to be certainly ascertained that when the hollow viscera in question are distended, pressure receptors pertaining to them are stimulated, and so send afferent impulses to the central nervous system, which, if the viscus remains distended, produce a general restlessness of the organism.

The chemoceptors which are excited by 'deficit stimuli,' presumably in the blood, are generally believed to be various 'centres' or motor ganglia in the mid-brain or medulla, each of which 'controls and regulates' such muscular activity as will repair the deficit by which each particular 'centre' is specifically stimulated (Bayliss, 1915; L. R. Müller, 1924). Thus in a depleted atmosphere an organism will have too little oxygen in its blood and an excessive hydrogen-ion concentration, which latter, according to current notions, will stimulate chemically its central 'respiratory centre' and so produce both faster and deeper breathing. Or again, the temperature of the body is supposed to be regulated by a 'thermal centre' which is directly and selectively stimulated by the temperature (!) of the blood.

This altogether prevalent conception of medullary and mid-brain 'centres' which, as their normal function, are selectively stimulated by various chemical constituents of the blood, and then 'regulate' the various appetitive activities, is supported by experimental evidence, of a sort; and it is doubtless true that there are in the central nervous system fairly definite regions ('centres') which if artificially stimulated will exalt or depress this or that vegetative function. Yet I am obliged to believe that this theory of 'regulatory centres' is mere word magic. The notion of "breathing regulated by a breathing-centre," or feeding regulated by a hunger-centre, may seem wonderfully adequate provided that one does not see that it is wonderfully and absolutely verbal. It presents the same methodological disabilities as do the notions of talking regulated by a 'speech-centre,' thinking regulated by a ratiocinative centre, and philoprogenitiveness (F. J. Gall) by a bump of philoprogenitiveness. An animal nervous system is a network of conduction paths, where impulses that come in go continuously through and out; and any imputation of 'centres' lying between afferent and efferent paths is, if you consider it squarely, a survival of ghost-soul psychology—which is to say, of theology. To retain the 'centres,' as does the theory under consideration, and cut out the afferent paths by making the 'centres' also chemoceptors, permits the optimist to hope that the centres will 'regulate' everything most intelligently, and that the motor strands therefrom will have been connected (by heredity or Divine Providence, or both) with precisely the right effector organs—the optimist, that is, who is also a mere verbalist.

In the general animal economy the cells of the central nervous system are specialized as conduction tissue, while sensitivity (the initiation of nerve currents), and selective sensitivity to specific sorts of stimuli, are the function of sense-organs. The histology of ganglia of the central nervous system does not suggest their functioning as specific sense-organs; and I am unacquainted with any reputable evidence that these ganglia differ from one another, chemically or otherwise, as they undoubtedly must differ if they are to have that selective, and very specific, irritability which the theory imputes to them. In short, it seems to me that the safe and sober view here is that the deficit stimuli (chemical) probably exist, that they may (or may not) exist in the blood, that they stimulate specifically different receptor organs, and that at present nobody has the faintest idea what or where these receptor organs are.

Our third point for consideration is the response patterns which develop as outlets for the afferent appetite impulses. The appetites pertain primarily to the internal animal economy, and the first path of motor discharge (path of *lowest* resistance) for any appetitive stimulus is usually on autonomic channels and to effector tissues that are in close relation to the organ from which the appetitive afferent impulses come; giving rise to internal processes of a relatively local character. The case of oxygen hunger will illustrate this. By a moderate deficiency of oxygen in the air some chemoceptors (perhaps in the lungs: *cf.* Sherrington, 1922) are stimulated and these afferent impulses find their readiest (most deeply canalized) motor outlet into the muscles that inflate and deflate the lungs, causing heightened breathing. But if the oxygen deficiency becomes more extreme, the chemoceptors in question are more strongly stimulated, and their afferent impulses now *spread* to the general body musculature, and the animal becomes restless. It remains so until its movements bring it into a region of fresher air (or else, until it dies of asphyxiation and exhaustion). If we undertook to study these more or less local appetitive mechanisms we should be led to consider the entire internal (vegetative) economy of organisms; and of course this is not our present quest. It is my belief that all of these internal reflex processes are *learned* from random beginnings, in ways strictly analogous to those which we have studied; but they are learned during the fœtal growth, when function and organ are developing hand in hand. For, as Prof. Child has said, "development is a process of functional construction." The embryonic behaviour pattern survives in later life partly as the vital organs, and partly as the (now stereotyped and automatic) functions of these organs. (It would be intelligent, I think, to *look* for the appetitive chemoceptors in these vital organs.) But this great industry, largely automatic as it is, is not isolated from the rest of the animal economy. Its afferent impulses normally spread (and when intense spread very widely) into the great skeletal musculature.

The afferent appetitive impulses which spread more widely in the nervous system, and so reach the general body muscles, are of course those which produce the open and obvious behaviouristic manifestations of appetite. And here it is plain, particularly in the cases of the hunger and sexual appetites, that the habits learned under appetitive stimulus are learned by trial-and-error. As Turró has said, all the early impulses of newly-born vertebrates are 'blind' impulses.

The first outward manifestation of any appetite, in young organisms, is general random restlessness. In a totally inexperienced young individual of any of the higher animals the restlessness of hunger would have no other termination than death. But maternal care, guaranteed in the case of mammals by the mother's mammary appetite, carries the young offspring safely on to a point where it has acquired such ('instinctive') activities as locomotion, smelling, looking, listening, seizing, eating and the like. These activities are now the ones which, at the time of weaning, are excited by internal deficit stimuli, and the young animal prowls about restlessly but randomly, smelling, looking, listening, with a very fair chance that one of these adiences will lead it to food. Lastly, the swallowing of food allays, though not immediately, the deficit stimuli, and the hunger cycle is completed. But the appetite is inexorable, and if food is not secured the restlessness becomes more and more extreme, with brief remissions, until finally the animal becomes too weak for further exertions, goes into a state of coma, and dies. The appetites for oxygen and water, depending likewise (in all probability) on deficit stimuli, function in a similar way.[3]

The remaining four appetites (for copulation, lactation; defæcation and micturition) all depend, it is fairly safe to say, on afferent impulses of pressure arising from the distention of hollow viscera, which is due to accumulation of the respective secretion or excretion. They appear to be alike further in that in each case a tonic closure of the viscus by a sphincter muscle (myotatic reflex?) has first to be acquired: and the pressure or distention is superimposed on that. Then, as in the other cases, these afferent impulses reach the central nervous system by paths which have at first no established motor outlets, and so, although the impulses are not at first of high intensity (as they are in the case of 'noxious' stimuli), they are persistent enough to produce a general motor restlessness, which will cease only when (according to the trial-error-and-success pattern) the random activities have brought about a release (inhibition) of the sphincter muscles of the hollow viscus. In all these cases the relief-giving activity is vastly more elaborate and specific than mere locomotion, and the period of trial-and-error learning is correspondingly protracted. This learning, too, is subject to grave idiosyncrasy and mishap.

The sexual appetite is so hedged about by taboos, superstitions, and lies, that any true statement about it will meet with a thousand frenzied denials. So if I say that the sexual appetite, like all other appetites, is imperative and like the others does not brook indefinite delay, there will be loud cries of dissent, to the general purport that "pure thoughts, hard exercise, cold water and prayer" will divert the sexual appetite for a lifetime. To those in whom the sexual appetite arouses 'impure thoughts' I make no doubt that cold water and prayer will prove beneficial. For indeed I suppose that the most, and perhaps the only, impure thought connected with sex is the thought to perpetuate the stereotyped lies about it. But if there is anybody who honestly imagines that this appetite ever has been or ever will be beguiled by any such precautions, he should find his attention instantly claimed by the attractive themes of sexual perversion and the neurotic disorders, and *why they happen*. He will also find it interesting and profitable to study the phenomena of 'cultural' mendacity, and the 'as if' hypocrisies. And yet even the Freudians, who ought to know better, follow the accepted superstitions with their theory of

---

[3] Several investigators (Cannon and Washburn, 1912; Cannon, 1915, pp. 251–264; Carlson, 1916, pp. 9–13, 62–71; Richter, 1922; Müller, 1924, p. 526) see in the so-called 'hunger contractions' of the empty stomach the probable cause of conscious 'hunger pangs,' and of the appetitive hunger restlessness. It may be so, but the cause producing the hunger contractions is not, so far as I can learn, satisfactorily made out. And as Carlson (1916, p. 63) has remarked, whatever causes the hunger contractions could just as well cause the hunger sensation (and restlessness) directly. Cannon (1918) and Müller (1924, pp. 530–537) assign an analogous rôle to 'thirst contractions' of the œsophagus, which appear when its mucous lining becomes parched.

sexual 'sublimation'—a colossal blunder—and the unctuous rubbish about 'cultural' (*kulturelle*) aims. Of course, if by artificial, 'educational' means this or any other appetitive restlessness *is* drafted off into motor channels other than those that appease the appetite, the individual is successfully wrecked.

In short, all of the appetite drives are persistent afferent impulses coming from organs situated within the body, and producing (in addition to visceral and other internal processes) at the outset, that is previously to trial-and-error learning, merely random movements of general restlessness. These impulses commence at a mild intensity, but if the appetite remains unappeased they gain in strength (often with rhythmical remissions of longer or shorter duration) until, unless the animal chances to do something that allays the appetite, he perishes. This chancing is a process of trial-and-error learning, exactly similar to that by which avoidance reactions to overstrong external stimuli are established; except that in the latter case some form of locomotion is very often that which terminates the annoying afferent stimulation, while the appetitive annoyers are appeased usually only by a more highly differentiated course of action. As in all trial-and-error learning, the 'end' is set in advance, that is, the restlessness of an appetite will not cease until the internal excitation is abolished. Notwithstanding that all conduct which is driven by an appetite, and particularly so in the cases of hunger and sex, has strongly the appearance of *seeking* an end (in fact later it transformatively becomes this), it is important to remember that in its primary mechanism such conduct is always *avoidance*. Perhaps all learning by trial-and-error is at bottom learning to avoid.

In his chapter on *Instinct* Prof. Holmes remarks: "Several modern writers have over-emphasized the element of responsiveness in instinct, as if an animal were like an instrument played upon by outer forces and had its actions fatally determined by the action of those forces on its own inner mechanism. Other writers have treated instinct as determined by a sort of internal impulsion. . . . It is without question that internal states form the promptings of many instinctive acts. . . . It is of course difficult in many cases to ascertain whether activity results, perhaps indirectly, from outer stimulations or from internal changes" And very often, of course, the sensory pattern is made up of impulses from both these sources. The fact that appetitive stimuli, when present, are persistent and of increasing intensity until the appetite is 'gratified,' after which they are for a while probably completely absent, fully justifies Bain's use of a separate term, 'appetite,' for internally initiated activities.

# 7 · Clark L. Hull

## *Primary Motivation and Reaction Potential*

Hull made a giant step toward the formalization of motivation theory. He continued Woodworth's distinction between drive and mechanism and clarified the directional-energizing issue by introducing the concept symbolized by the letter "D" to refer to the energizing function and that of "$S_D$," the drive stimulus, to stand for the capacity for deprivational states to act as cues for particular direction-providing responses. As can be seen below, even in Hull, drive (*D*) was not entirely without some capacity to influence the selection of responses, since a relevant drive was attributed a greater energizing effect upon responses learned in its presence than upon responses for which it was an irrelevant drive. Later neo-Hullians, such as Judson Brown, have tended to abandon even this distinction and to treat *D* as a fully nonselective energizer for any and all responses elicited from an organism. The difficulties of confirming such a general claim for drive have led many to be critical of such simple statements of the energizing function. Some have acted as though the theoretical usefulness of the concept rested solely upon such a general claim. Hull's distinction between *D* and $S_D$ encouraged more precise statements of the functions of each and proved enormously productive of further experimentation.

*It may be recalled* that when the problem of primary reinforcement was under consideration, the matter of organic need played a critical part in that the reduction of the need constituted the essential element in the process whereby the reaction was conditioned to new stimuli. We must now note that the state of an organism's needs also plays an important rôle in the causal determination of which of the many habits possessed by an organism shall function at a given moment. It is a matter of common observation that, as a rule, when an organism is in need of food only those acts appropriate to the securing of food will be evoked, whereas when it is in need of water, only those acts appropriate to the securing of water will be evoked, when a sexual hormone is dominant only those acts appropriate to reproductive activity will be evoked, and so on. Moreover, the extent or intensity of the need determines in large measure the vigor and persistence of the activity in question.

By common usage the initiation of learned, or habitual, patterns of movement or behavior is called *motivation*. The evocation of action in relation to secondary reinforcing stimuli or *incentives* will be called *secondary motivation;* a brief discussion of incentives was given above in connection with the general subject of amount of reinforcement. The evocation of action in relation to primary needs will be called *primary motivation;* this is the subject of the present chapter.

## THE EMPIRICAL ROLES OF HABIT STRENGTH AND DRIVE IN THE DETERMINATION OF ACTION

Casual observations such as those cited above often give us valuable clues concerning behavior problems, but for precise solutions, controlled quantitative experiments usually are necessary. In the present context we are fortunate in having an excellent empirical study which shows the functional dependence of the persistence of food-seeking behavior jointly on (1) the number of reinforcements of the habit in question, and (2) the number of hours of food privation. Perin (*12*) and Williams (*20*) trained albino rats on a simple bar-pressing habit of the Skinner type, giving separate groups different numbers of reinforcements varying from 5 to 90 under a standard 23 hours' hunger. Later the groups were subdivided and subjected to experimental extinction with the amount of food privation varying from 3 to 22 hours.

The gross outcome of this experiment is shown in Figure 7.1, where the height of each column represents the relative mean number of unreinforced reactions performed by each group before experimental extinction yielded a five-minute pause between successive bar pressures. The positions of the twelve columns on the base shows clearly the number of reinforcements and the number of hours' food privation which produced each. It is evident from an examination of this figure that *both* the number of reinforcements and the number of hours of food privation are potent factors in determining resistance to experimental extinction. Moreover, it is clear that for any given amount of food privation, e.g., 3 or 22 hours, the different numbers of reinforcements yield a close approximation to a typical positive growth function. On the other hand, it is equally clear that for a given number of reinforcements, e.g., 16, the number of hours

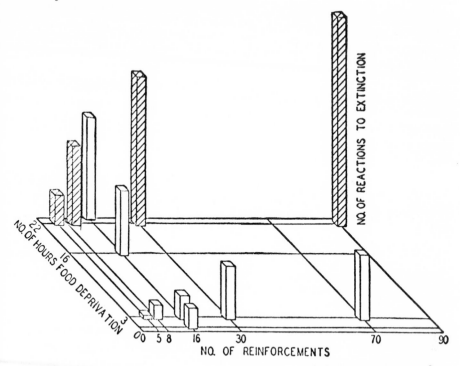

Figure 7.1.   Column diagram of the Perin-Williams data showing quantitatively how the resistance to experimental extinction in albino rats varies jointly with the number of reinforcements and the number of hours of food privation at the time the extinction occurred. The cross-hatched columns represent the groups of animals reported by Williams (*20*); the non-hatched columns represent the groups reported by Perin. (Figure reproduced from Perin, *12*, p. 106. By permission of the American Psychological Association.)

of food privation has an almost linear functional relationship to the resistance to experimental extinction.

For a more precise analysis of these functional relationships it is necessary to fit two-dimensional curves to the data. The results of this procedure are presented in Figures 7.2 and 7.3. Figure 7.2 shows that resistance to extinction at the 16-reinforcement level is a slightly positively accelerated function of the number of hours' food privation for the first 22 hours. Figure 7.3 shows that a positive growth function fits both "learning" curves fairly well. An examination of the equations which generated these curves reveals that the asymptotes differ radically, clearly being increasing functions of the number of hours of food privation, but that the rates at which the curves approach their respective asymptotes are practically identical (*F* equals approximately 1/25 in both cases). Finally it may be noted that both curves, when extrapolated backward to where the

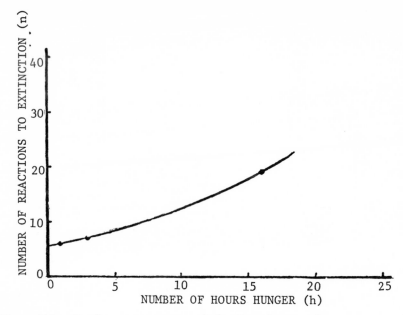

Figure 7.2. Graphic representation of the data showing the systematic relationship between the resistance to experimental extinction (circles) and the
number of hours' food privation where the number of reinforcements is constant at 16. The smooth curve drawn through the sequence of circles represents
the slightly positively accelerated function fitted to them. This function is believed to hold only up to the number of hours of hunger employed in the
original habit formation process: in the present case, 23. (Figure adapted from
Perin, *12*, p. 104, by permission of the American Psychological Association.)

number of reinforcements would equal zero, yield a *negative* number of
extinctive reactions amounting to approximately four. This presumably is
a phenomenon of the reaction threshold which will be discussed in some
detail later; it is believed to mean that a habit strength sufficient to resist
four extinction reactions is necessary before reaction will be evoked by
the stimuli involved.

For a final examination of the outcome of the experiment as a whole,
the curves shown in Figures 7.2 and 7.3 were synthesized in such a way
as to yield a surface fitted to the tops of all the columns of Figure 7.1.
This surface is shown in Figure 7.4. An examination of this figure reveals
the important additional fact that when the surface is extrapolated to
where the number of hours' food privation is zero, the resistance to experimental extinction presumably will still show a positive growth function
with *n*-values of considerable magnitude. As a matter of fact, the asymp-

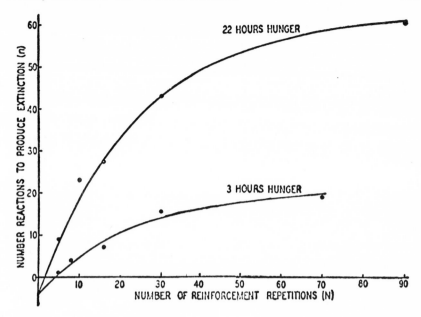

Figure 7.3. Graphic representation of the two "learning" curves of Figure 7.1, shown in the same plane to facilitate comparison. The solid circles represent the empirical values corresponding to the heights of the relevant columns of Figure 7.1; the one hollow circle represents a slightly interpolated value. The smooth curves drawn among each set of circles represent the simple growth functions fitted to each set of empirical data. (Figure adapted from Perin, *12*, p. 101, by permission of the American Psychological Association.)

tote of the growth function where $h = 0$ (satiation) is 28 per cent of that where $h = 22$ hours.

These last results are in fairly good agreement with comparable values from several other experimental studies. Measurements of one of Skinner's published graphs, reproduced as Figure 7.5, indicate that his animals displayed approximately 17 per cent as much food-seeking activity at satiation as at 25 hours' food privation. Finch (*3*) has shown that at satiation a conditioned salivary reaction in nine dogs yielded a mean of 24 per cent as much secretion as was yielded at 24 hours' food privation. Similarly, Zener (*22*) reports that the mean salivary secretion from four dogs average at satiation 24 per cent as much as at from 21 to 24 hours' food privation. The considerable amounts of responsiveness to the impact of conditioned stimuli when the organism is in a state of food satiation may accordingly be considered as well established.

The continued sexual activity of male rats for some months after

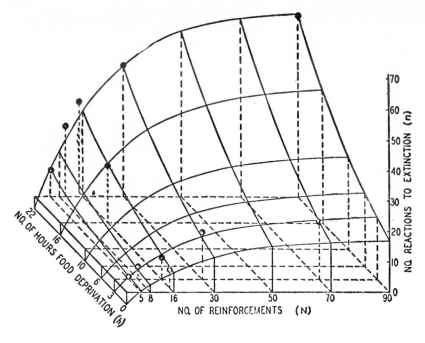

Figure 7.4.   Three-dimensional graph representing the fitted "surface" corresponding quantitatively to the action of the number of reinforcements and the number of hours of food privation following satiation, in the joint determination of the number of unreinforced acts of the type originally conditioned which are required to produce a given degree of experimental extinction. (Figure adapted from Perin, *12*, p. 108, by permission of the American Psychological Association.)

castration points in the same direction. Stone (*15*) reports that male rats which have copulated either shortly before or shortly after castration, when an adequate supply of hormone would be present, continue to show sexual behavior sometimes as long as seven or eight months after removal of the testes. According to Moore *et al.* (*10*), Stone (*15*), and Beach (*1*), this operation removes within 20 days not only the source of testosterone but, through the resulting atrophy of accessory glands, also the source of other specifically supporting secretions. A few weeks after castration, therefore, when the normal supply of sex hormones in the animal's body has been exhausted, the sex drive is presumably in about the same state as is the food drive after complete food satiation. The continued sexual activity of these animals thus presents a striking analogy to the continued operation of the food-release bar by Perin's rats after food satiation. While not absolutely convincing, this evidence from the field of sexual

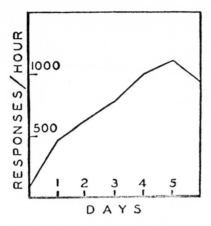

Figure 7.5. Graph showing the relationship of the action potentiality as a function of the length of food privation following satiation. First note the fact that there is an appreciable amount of action potentiality at the beginning of this graph, where the amount of food privation is zero. Next, observe that the curve is relatively high at one day of food privation, which was the degree of drive under which the original training occurred. Finally, note that the rise in action potentiality is fairly continuous up to about five days, after which it falls rather sharply. This fall is evidently due to exhaustion, as the animals died soon after. The function plotted as the smooth curve of Figure 7.2 corresponds only to the first section of the present graph and clearly does not represent the functional relationship beyond a point where the number of hours of food privation is greater than 23. (Figure reproduced from Skinner, *13*, p. 396, by permission of Appleton-Century-Crofts.)

behavior suggests that the performance of learned reactions to moderate degrees in the absence of the specific drive involved in their original acquisition may be sufficiently general to apply to all primary motivational situations.

Closely related to this same aspect of Perin's investigation is a study reported by Elliott (*2*). Albino rats were trained in a maze under a thirst drive with water as the reinforcing agent until the true path was nearly learned, when the drive was suddenly shifted to hunger and the reinforcing agent to food. The outcome of this procedure is shown in Figure 7.6. There it may be seen that on the first trial under the changed condition of drive there was an appreciable disturbance of the behavior in the form of an increase in locomotor time; there was also an increase, of about the same proportion, in blind-alley entrances. On the later trials, however, the learning process appeared to proceed much as if no change had been made in the experimental conditions.

As a final item in this series there may be mentioned an empirical

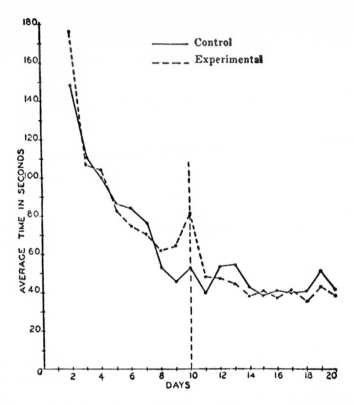

Figure 7.6.    Graphs showing the disruptive influence on a maze habit set up in albino rats on the basis of a water reinforcement, of having the drive (on the tenth day) suddenly shifted from thirst to hunger. (Reproduced from Elliott, 2, p. 187, by permission of the University of California Press.)

observation of Pavlov concerning the effect on an extinguished conditioned reaction of increasing the drive. On the analogy of Perin's experiment, it might be expected that this would again render the reaction evocable by the stimulus; and this in fact took place. In this connection Pavlov remarks (*11*, p. 127):

To illustrate this last condition we may take instances of differential inhibitions established on the basis of an alimentary reflex. If, for example, the dog has been kept entirely without food for a much longer period than usual before the experiment is conducted, the increase in excitability of the whole alimentary nervous mechanism renders the previously established differential inhibition wholly inadequate.

## EMPIRICAL DIFFERENTIAL REACTIONS TO IDENTICAL EXTERNAL ENVIRONMENTAL SITUATIONS ON THE BASIS OF DISTINCT DRIVES

A second important type of motivational problem was broached in an experiment reported by Hull (6). Albino rats were trained in the rectangular maze shown in Figure 7.7. On some days a given animal would be run in the maze when satiated with water, but with 23 hours' food privation, whereas on other days the same rat would be run when satiated with food but with 23 hours of water privation. The two types of days alternated according to a predetermined irregularity. On the food-privation days the reinforcement chamber always contained food and the left entrance, say, to the chamber was blocked so that access could be had only by traversing the right-hand side of the rectangle. On the water-privation days the reinforcement chamber always contained water, and

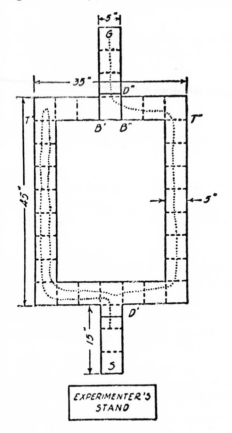

Figure 7.7. Diagram of the maze employed in Hull's differential drive experiment. $S$ = starting chamber; $G$ = food chamber; $D'$, $D''$ = doors manipulated by cords from the experimenter's stand; $B'$, $B''$ = barriers across passageway, one of which was always closed. The course pursued by a typical rat on a "false" run is shown by the sinuous dotted line. Note that the animal went down the "wrong" side of the maze far enough to see the closed door at $B'$ and then turned around. (Reproduced from Hull, 6, by permission of the American Psychological Association.)

the right-hand entrance to the reinforcement chamber would be blocked so that access to the water could be had only by traversing the left-hand side of the rectangle. The outcome of this experiment is shown in Figure 7.8. There it may be seen that while learning was very slow, the animals of the experimental group gradually attained a considerable power of making the reaction which corresponded to the drive dominant at the time.

The capacity of rats to learn this type of discrimination was later demonstrated more strikingly by Leeper (8), in a substantially similar investigation. Leeper's experiment differed, however, in the detail that two distinct reinforcement chambers were employed and no passageways were blocked at any time, so that if on a "food" day the rat went to the water side he always found water, and if on a "water" day he went to the food side, he always found food. Under these conditions the animals learned to perform the motivational discrimination with great facility; Leeper's animals needed only about one-twelfth the number of trials required by the original Hull technique, though again the process of acquisition was gradual.[2]

## DOES THE PRINCIPLE OF PRIMARY STIMULUS-INTENSITY GENERALIZATION APPLY TO THE DRIVE STIMULUS ($S_D$)?

A factor with considerable possible significance for the understanding of motivation is the relationship between the degree of similarity of the need at the time of reinforcement and that at the time of extinction, on the one hand, and the associated resistance to experimental extinction on the other. No specific experiments have been found bearing exactly on this point, but several incidental and individually inconclusive bits of evidence may be mentioned as indicating the general probabilities of the situation.

The first of these was reported by Heathers and Arakelian (4). Albino rats were trained to secure food pellets by pressing a bar in a Skinner-Ellson apparatus. Next, half of the animals were partially extinguished under a weak hunger, and the remainder were extinguished to an equal extent under a strong hunger. Two days later the animals were subjected to a second extinction, half of each group under the same degree of hunger

---

[2] This striking difference is attributed in part to the operation of spatial orientation and in part to the fact that when rats are deprived of either food or water they do not consume a normal amount of the other substance; this prevents genuine satiation of the supposedly satiated drive. For example, thirsty rats supposedly satiated with food will, after receiving even a few drops of water, very generally eat if food is available (6, p. 270); and rats, like humans, frequently drink while eating dry food if water is available. Thus after the first trial Leeper's animals were presumably operating under both drives, and one drive or the other was reinforced no matter which path was traversed.

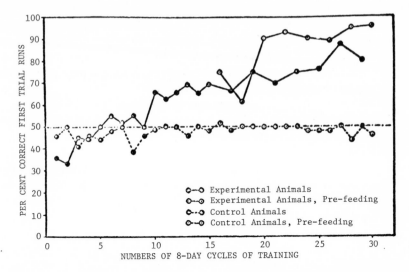

Figure 7.8. Composite graphs showing the per cent of correct choices at the first trial of each experimental day in the discrimination by rats between hunger and thirst motivation. (Figure reproduced from Hull, 6, p. 263, by permission of the American Psychological Association.)

as in the first extinction, and the remaining half under a drive equal to the first-extinction hunger of the other group. Combining the state of food privation of the first and second extinctions, there were thus four hunger-extinction groups:

1, strong-strong; 2, strong-weak; 3, weak-strong; 4, weak-weak.

The authors report that a statistical pooling of the results from these four groups of animals revealed a tendency of the rats extinguished twice on the same drive to resist extinction less than did those animals which were extinguished the second time on a drive different from that employed on the first occasion. In two independent studies this difference amounted to approximately 4 and 6 per cent respectively; the latter results are reported to have a probability of 8 in 10 that the difference was not due to chance. This experimental outcome is evidently related to the primary generalization of stimulus intensity and suggests that *perseverative extinction effects are to some extent specific to the primary drive or need intensity under which the extinction occurs.*

By analogy, the stimulus-intensity generalization gradient apparently found in the case of extinction effects just considered strongly suggests the operation of the same principle in the case of reinforcement effects. Now, such a gradient has been demonstrated experimentally by Hovland; it naturally has its greatest value at the point of reinforcement. Con-

sequently it is to be expected that in a curve of motivation intensity such
as that of Skinner (shown in Figure 7.5) a special elevation or inflection
would appear at the drive intensity at which the original reinforcement
occurred. Whether a mere coincidence arising from sampling errors or
not, exactly such an inflection may be seen in Skinner's empirical graph
at one day of food privation, which was in fact the drive employed by
Skinner in the training of the animals in question. The present set of
assumptions implies that if Skinner's curve as shown in Figure 7.5 were
to be plotted in detail by hours rather than days, it would present a positive acceleration from zero to one day of food privation. Now, Perin's
study did plot this region in some detail, and Figure 7.2 shows that a
positively accelerated function was found. These facts still further increase the probability that the principle of stimulus-intensity generalization applies to the drive stimulus ($S_D$).

## THE INFLUENCE OF CERTAIN DRUGS ON EXPERIMENTAL
## EXTINCTION AND ITS PERSEVERATIONAL EFFECTS

Certain drugs are known to influence markedly the phenomena of
experimental extinction. Switzer (18) investigated the effect of caffeine
citrate on the conditional galvanic skin reaction in human subjects, using
a control dose of milk sugar. He found that caffeine increased resistance
to experimental extinction; incidentally he also found that caffeine increased the amplitude of the unconditioned galvanic skin reaction and
decreased the reaction latency.

Pavlov (11, p. 127) reported a somewhat related experiment performed by Nikiforovsky. An alimentary salivary conditioned reflex had
been set up to a tactile stimulus on a dog's forepaw. This reaction tendency
generalized to other parts of the animal's skin, including a point on the
back which subsequently was completely extinguished. At the latter stage
of training the stimulus on the paw yielded five drops of saliva during
the first minute of stimulation, whereas stimulation of the extinguished
spot on the back yielded a zero reaction. Thereupon, the animal was
given a subcutaneous injection of 10 c.c. of 1 per cent solution of caffeine.
A few minutes later the stimulus when applied to the forepaw evoked
four drops during the first minute, and when applied to the previously
extinguished spot on the back, yielded three drops (11, p. 128), thus
indicating a major dissipation of the extinction effects.

Miller and Miles (9) have contributed to this field. They demonstrated in albino rats traversing a 25-foot straight, enclosed runway that
an injection of caffeine sodio-benzoate reduced the locomotor retardation
due to experimental extinction by about two-thirds. In the same study it

was shown that the retardation in locomotor time due to satiation was reduced by the caffeine solution approximately one-half (9).

Benzedrine is another substance which when thrown into the blood stream has the power of greatly retarding the onset of experimental extinction. This was demonstrated by Skinner and Heron (14) to hold for the Skinner bar-pressing habit.

## SEX HORMONES AND REPRODUCTIVE ACTIVITY

As a final set of empirical observations concerning motivation we must consider briefly the relation of sex hormones to reproductive behavior. Within recent years an immense amount of excellent experimental work has been performed in this field, though only brief notice of it can be taken in this place. An account of two typical bits of this work was given above. In a recent comprehensive summary by Beach (1) the following propositions appear to have fairly secure empirical foundation:

1. Animals of practically all species which through castration have become sexually unresponsive to ordinary incentive stimulation, become responsive promptly on the injection of the appropriate hormone—usually testosterone proprionate for males and estrogen for females.

2. Presumptively normal male rats differ greatly in their sexual responsiveness, all the way from those which will attempt copulation with inanimate objects to those which will not react even to an extremely receptive and alluring female. The injection of testosterone usually raises the reactivity of all but a few of the most sluggish animals. Alternatively, the presentation of an especially attractive incentive tends to have the same objective effect, though to a lesser degree (17).

3. Destruction of the cerebral cortex decreases sexual reactivity roughly in proportion to the extent of such destruction, very much as occurs in the case of food habits. If destruction has not been too great, injection of the hormone will largely restore sexual responsiveness to appropriate incentives. The presentation of an exceptionally attractive incentive will, however, have much the same effect upon the objective behavior of such organisms.

4. Virgin male organisms which are unresponsive to an ordinary receptive female, after a few copulations under the influence of an injection of the hormone will remain responsive long after the hormone has presumably disappeared from the animal's body. This is believed to be caused by the learning resulting from the incidental reinforcement which occurred when the animal was under the influence of the hormone (1).

5. Many intact individuals of both sexes in most species occasionally manifest a portion of the behavior pattern characteristic of the opposite sex. Injection of the sex hormone of the opposite sex in castrated individuals of either sex tends strongly to the evocation of the sexual behavior pattern char-

acteristic of normal organisms of the opposite sex on appropriate stimulation; this, however, is not usually as complete as the gross anatomical equipment of the organisms would seem to permit. Curiously enough, large doses of testosterone given to male rats make possible the elicitation of all elements of the typical female sexual behavior (*1*).

## PRIMARY MOTIVATIONAL CONCEPTS

With the major critical phenomena of primary motivation [3] now before us, we may proceed to the attempt to formulate a theory which will conform to these facts.

At the outset it will be necessary to introduce two notions not previously discussed. These new concepts are analogous to that of habit strength ($_sH_R$) which, it will be recalled, is a logical construct conceived in the quantitative framework of a centigrade system.

The first of the two concepts is *strength of primary drive;* this is represented by the symbol $D$. The strength-of-drive scale is conceived to extend from a zero amount of primary motivation (complete satiation) to the maximum possible to a standard organism of a given species. In accordance with the centigrade principle this range of primary drive is divided into 100 equal parts or units. For convenience and ease of recall, this unit will be called the *mote,* a contraction of the word *motivation* with an added *e* to preserve normal pronunciation.

Because of the practical exigencies of exposition the second of the new concepts has already been utilized occasionally in the last few pages, where it has been referred to as the "reaction tendency," a term in fairly general use though lacking in precision of meaning. For this informal expression we now substitute the more precise equivalent, *reaction-evocation potentiality;* or, more briefly, *reaction potential.* This will be represented by the symbol $_sE_R$. Like habit ($_sH_R$) and drive ($D$), reaction-evocation potential is also designed to be measured on a 100-point scale extending from a zero reaction tendency up to the physiological limit possible to a standard organism. The unit of reaction potentiality will be called the *wat,* a contraction of the name *Watson.*

It should be evident from the preceding paragraphs that $D$ and $_sE_R$ are symbolic constructs in exactly the same sense as $_sH_R$, and that they share both the advantages and disadvantages of this status. The drive concept, for example, is proposed as a common denominator of all primary motivations, whether due to food privation, water privation, thermal deviations from the optimum, tissue injury, the action of sex hormones,

---

[3] The empirical phenomena of secondary motivation, including such matters as incentive, fractional anticipatory goal- and subgoal-reactions, cannot be treated in the present volume because space is not available.

or other causes. This means, of course, that drive will be a different function of the objective conditions associated with each primary motivation. For example, in the case of hunger the strength of the primary drive will probably be mainly a function of the number of hours of food privation, say; in the case of sex it will probably be mainly a function of the concentration of a particular sex hormone in the animal's blood; and so on. Stated formally,

$$D = f(h)$$
$$D = f(c)$$
$$D = \text{etc.},$$

where $h$ represents the number of hours of food privation of the organism since satiation, and $c$ represents the concentration of a particular hormone in the blood of the organism.

Turning now to the concept of reaction-evocation potentiality, we find, thanks to Perin's investigation sketched above (p. 100 ff.), that we are able at once to define $_sE_R$ as the product of a function of habit strength $(_sH_R)$ multiplied by a function of the relevant drive $(D)$. This multiplicative relationship is one of the greatest importance, because it is upon $_sE_R$ that the amount of action in its various forms presumably depends. It is clear, for example, that it is quite impossible to predict the vigor or persistence of a given type of action from a knowledge of either habit strength or drive strength alone; this can be predicted only from a knowledge of the product of the particular functions of $_sH_R$ and $D$ respectively; in fact, this product constitutes the value which we are representing by the symbol $_sE_R$.

## SUMMARY AND PRELIMINARY PHYSIOLOGICAL INTERPRETATION OF EMPIRICAL FINDINGS

Having the more important concepts of the systematic approach of primary motivation before us, we proceed to the formulation of some empirical findings as related to motivation.

Most, if not all, primary needs appear to generate and throw into the blood stream more or less characteristic chemical substances, or else to withdraw a characteristic substance. These substances (or their absence) have a selective physiological effect on more or less restricted and characteristic portions of the body (e.g., the so-called "hunger" contractions of the digestive tract) which serves to activate resident receptors. This receptor activation constitutes the drive stimulus, $S_D$. In the case of tissue injury this sequence seems to be reversed; here the energy producing the injury is the drive stimulus, and its action causes the release into the blood of adrenal secretion which appears to be the physiological motivating substance.

It seems likely, on the basis of various analogies, that, other things equal, the intensity of the drive stimulus would be some form of negatively accelerated increasing function of the concentration of the drive substance in the blood. However, for the sake of expository simplicity we shall assume in the present preliminary analysis that it is an increasing linear function.

The afferent discharges arising from the drive stimulus ($S_D$) become conditioned to reactions just the same as any other elements in stimulus compounds, except that they may be somewhat more potent in acquiring habit loadings than most stimulus elements or aggregates. Thus the drive stimulus may play a rôle in a conditioned stimulus compound substantially the same as that of any other stimulus element or aggregate. As a stimulus, $S_D$ naturally manifests both qualitative and intensity primary stimulus generalization in common with other stimulus elements or aggregates in conditioned stimulus compounds.

It appears probable that when blood which contains certain chemical substances thrown into it as the result of states of need, or which lacks certain substances as the result of other states of need, bathes the neural structures which constitute the anatomical bases of habit ($_sH_R$), the conductivity of these structures is augmented through lowered resistance either in the central neural tissue or at the effector end of the connection, or both. The latter type of action is equivalent, of course, to a lowering of the reaction threshold and would presumably facilitate reaction to neural impulses reaching the effector from any source whatever. As Beach (1) suggests, it is likely that the selective action of drives on particular effector organs in non-learned forms of behavior acts mainly in this manner. It must be noted at once, however, that sensitizing a habit structure does not mean that this alone is sufficient to evoke the reaction, any more than that caffeine or benzedrine alone will evoke reaction. Sensitization merely gives the relevant neural tissue, upon the occurence of an adequate set of receptor discharges, an augmented facility in routing these impulses to the reactions previously conditioned to them or connected by native (inherited) growth processes. This implies to a certain extent the undifferentiated nature of drive in general, contained in Freud's concept of the "libido." However, it definitely does not presuppose the special dominance of any one drive, such as sex, over the other drives.

While all drives seem to be alike in their powers of sensitizing *acquired* receptor-effector connections, their capacity to call forth within the body of the organism characteristic and presumably distinctive drive stimuli gives each a considerable measure of distinctiveness and specificity in the determination of action which, in case of necessity, may be sharpened by the process of patterning to almost any extent that the reaction situation requires for adequate and consistent reinforcement. In this respect, the action of drive substances differs sharply from that of a pseudo-drive substance such as caffeine, which appears to produce nothing corresponding to a drive stimulus.

Little is known concerning the exact quantitative functional relationship of drive intensity to the conditions or circumstances which produce it, such as the number of hours of hunger or the concentration of endocrine secretions in the blood. Judging from the work of Warden and his associates (*19*), the relationship of the hunger drive up to two or three days of food privation would be a negatively accelerated increasing function of time, though a study by Skinner (Figure 7.5) suggests that it may be nearly linear up to about five days. For the sake of simplicity in the present explorational analysis we shall assume the latter as a first approximation.

Physiological conditions of need, through their sensitizing action on the neural mediating structures lying between the receptors and the effectors ($_sH_R$), appear to combine with the latter to evoke reactions according to a multiplicative principle, i.e., reaction-evocation potentiality is the product of a function of habit strength multiplied by a function of the strength of drive:

$$_sE_R = f(_sH_R) \times f(D).$$

In the next section it shall be our task to consider in some detail what these functions may be; if successful we shall then possess the main portion of a molar theory of primary motivation.

## THE QUANTITATIVE DERIVATION OF $_sE_R$ FROM $_sH_R$ AND $D$

Since we have taken Perin's experiment as our main guide in the analysis of the primary motivational problem in general, it will be convenient to take the need for food as the basis for the detailed illustration of the working of the molar theory of motivation; this we now proceed to develop.

Turning first to the habit component of $_sE_R$, we calculate the values of $_sH_R$ as a positive growth function; we use in this calculation the fractional incremental value ($F$) found by Perin to hold for the learning processes represented in Figure 7.3, which was approximately 1/25 for each successive reinforcement. On this assumption the values at various numbers of reinforcements, e.g., 0, 1, 3, 9, 18, 36, and 72, have been computed. These are shown in column 2 of Table 7.1.

The habit-strength values of column 2, Table 7.1, consist of the physiological summation of the habit-strength loadings of the stimulus components, represented by the original drive stimulus $S_D'$ and the non-drive components, which we shall represent by $S_I$. Assuming as a matter of convenience that $S_D'$ and $S_I$ have equal loadings, the value of each (see fifth terminal note) is easily calculated for the several numbers of reinforcements. These values are shown in column 3 of Table 7.1.

Turning next to the matter of drive, it will be assumed that the original learning took place under a 24-hour food privation. Assuming further that drive is a linear function of the number of hours' hunger and that (Figure 7.5) the maximum of 100 motes would be reached at five days or 120 hours, Perin's periods of food privation may be converted into units of drive strength by multiplying the number of hours' food privation by the fraction 100/120. In this way we secure the following drive or $D$-values.

| Number of hours' food privation ($h$): | 0 | 3 | 8 | 16 | 24 |
|---|---|---|---|---|---|
| Strength of drive in motes ($D$): | 0 | 2.5 | 6.667 | 13.333 | 20 |
| Deviation ($d$) of possible $D$'s from the drive ($D'$) of original learning: | 20 | 17.5 | 13.333 | 6.667 | 0 |

Now, $S_D$ is assumed to be approximately a linear function of $D$. It follows from this and the principle of primary stimulus generalization that action evoked under any other intensity of drive (and drive stimulus) than that involved in the original habit formation must be subject to primary intensity-stimulus generalization. Assuming the relatively flat gradient yielded by an $F$-value of 1/50, it is easy to calculate the value of $_S H_R \atop _D$ at each degree of the five $D$-values taken above. These $_S H_R \atop _D$ values are shown in columns 4, 5, 6, 7, and 8 respectively of Table 7.1. A glance at the bottom entries of each of the columns shows that the values of $_S H_R \atop _D$ fall progressively from 46.34 at $D = 20$ (i.e., $d = 0.00$) to 30.94 at $D = 0$ (i.e., $d = 20$).

We must now combine these habit values by the process of physiological summation characteristic of conditioned stimulus compounds (neglecting the effects of afferent interaction) with the habit loading of the non-drive stimulus component of the compound which is represented by the values appearing in column 3. The physiological summation of the values in column 3 with the values of columns 4 to 8 gives us the habit-strength values shown in columns 9, 10, 11, 12, and 13 of Table 7.1. It will be noticed that this final recombination of the $_S H_R$ values where $D = 20$ yields exactly the same values as those of column 2. This is because when reaction evocation occurs at the original drive ($D'$), i.e., where $D = D'$, no distortion of the $S_D$ component of the habit results, the synthesis being exactly the reverse of the analysis which took place between columns 2 and 3.

TABLE 7.1. Table showing the preliminary steps in the derivation of a series of theoretical reaction-potential values from a varied set of antecedent reinforcements under a drive of 20 units' strength, the resulting habits being evaluated for reaction potentiality at drive-strengths of 0.00, 2.50, 6.667, 13.333, and 20.0 units.

| N | Habit Strength as Formed $(s_1+s_DH_R)$ Two Components | One Component $(sH_R)$ | Effective Habit Strength of Drive-Stimulus Component $(s_D\bar{H}_R)$ Derived from Intensity Generalization Gradient | | | | | Physiological Summation of Both Habit Strengths of Components $(s_1+s_D\bar{H}_R)$ | | | | | Reaction-Evocation Potential $(sE_R)$ as Mediated by Various Strengths of Drive | | | | |
|---|---|---|---|---|---|---|---|---|---|---|---|---|---|---|---|---|---|
| | | | $d'=$ 20.00 | $d'=$ 17.5 | $d'=$ 13.33 | $d'=$ 6.67 | $d'=$ 0.00 | $D=$ 0.00 | $D=$ 2.50 | $D=$ 6.67 | $D=$ 13.33 | $D=$ 20.00 | $D=$ 0.00 | $D=$ 2.50 | $D=$ 6.67 | $D=$ 13.33 | $D=$ 20.00 |
| 1 | 2 | 3 | 4 | 5 | 6 | 7 | 8 | 9 | 10 | 11 | 12 | 13 | 14 | 15 | 16 | 17 | 18 |
| 0 | 0.00 | 0.00 | 0.00 | 0.00 | 0.00 | 0.00 | 0.00 | 0.00 | 0.00 | 0.00 | 0.00 | 0.00 | 0.00 | 0.00 | 0.00 | 0.00 | 0.00 |
| 1 | 3.05 | 1.54 | 1.03 | 1.08 | 1.18 | 1.35 | 1.54 | 2.55 | 2.60 | 2.70 | 2.87 | 3.06 | .23 | .30 | .41 | .61 | .83 |
| 3 | 8.77 | 4.49 | 3.00 | 3.15 | 3.43 | 3.92 | 4.49 | 7.36 | 7.50 | 7.77 | 8.23 | 8.78 | .67 | .85 | 1.18 | 1.75 | 2.39 |
| 9 | 23.35 | 12.46 | 8.31 | 8.75 | 9.54 | 10.89 | 12.46 | 19.73 | 20.12 | 20.81 | 21.99 | 23.37 | 1.79 | 2.29 | 3.15 | 4.66 | 6.37 |
| 18 | 39.43 | 22.18 | 14.81 | 15.58 | 16.95 | 19.38 | 22.18 | 33.71 | 34.30 | 35.37 | 37.26 | 39.44 | 3.06 | 3.90 | 5.36 | 7.90 | 10.76 |
| 36 | 58.13 | 35.29 | 23.56 | 24.78 | 26.96 | 30.84 | 35.29 | 50.54 | 51.33 | 52.74 | 55.25 | 58.13 | 4.59 | 5.83 | 7.99 | 11.72 | 15.85 |
| 72 | 71.21 | 46.34 | 30.94 | 32.54 | 35.40 | 40.50 | 46.34 | 62.94 | 63.80 | 65.34 | 68.07 | 71.21 | 5.72 | 7.25 | 9.90 | 14.44 | 19.42 |

117

With the theoretical values of $f(_sH_R)$ available in columns 9 to 13 inclusive of Table 7.1, we may now turn our attention to the problem of $f(D)$. It is assumed that $D$ itself acts upon $_sH_R$ as a direct proportion. However, there is the complication that other or alien drives active at the time (represented in the aggregate by the symbol $\dot{D}$) have the capacity to sensitize habits not set up in conjunction with them. Let it be supposed that this generalized effect of alien drives adds 10 points to the actual drive throughout the present situation. Thus the effective drive ($\overline{D}$) operative on a given habit would necessarily involve the summation of $\dot{D}$ and $D$; in the case of the 24-hour food privation a simple summation would in the present situation amount to $10 + 20$, or 30, and at 120 hours it would be $10 + 100$, or 110. In order to maintain our centigrade system the simple summation must be divided by the maximum possible under these assumptions, or 110. Accordingly we arrive at the formula,

$$\overline{D} = 100 \, \frac{\dot{D} + D}{\dot{D} + 100},$$

where $\overline{D}$ represents the *effective drive* actually operative in producing the reaction potential.

Now, assuming that reaction evocation potentiality is essentially a multiplicative function of habit strength and drive, i.e., that,

$$_sE_R = f(_s\overline{H}_R) \times f(\overline{D}),$$

since $f(_sH_R)$ is $_s\overline{H}_R$, and $f(D)$ is $\overline{D}$, we have by substitution,

$$_sE_R = _s\overline{H}_R \times \overline{D}.$$

However, since both $_s\overline{H}_R$ and $\overline{D}$ are on a centigrade scale, their simple product would yield values on a ten-thousand point scale; therefore, to keep $_sE_R$ also to a centigrade scale we write the equation,

$$_sE_R = \frac{_s\overline{H}_R \times \overline{D}}{100}.$$

Substituting the equivalent of $\overline{D}$ and simplifying, we have as our final equation,

$$_sE_R = _s\overline{H}_R \, \frac{\dot{D} + D}{\dot{D} + 100}.$$

The second portion of this formula, with the various $D$ values substituted, is,

| $\dfrac{10 + 0,}{110}$ | $\dfrac{10 + 2.5,}{110}$ | $\dfrac{10 + 6.667,}{110}$ | $\dfrac{10 + 13.333,}{110}$ | $\dfrac{10 + 20}{110}$ |
|---|---|---|---|---|
| $= .0909$ | $.1136$ | $.1515$ | $.2121$ | $.2727.$ |

The values of $_sE_R$ are accordingly obtained simply by multiplying the several entries of column 9 by .0909, those of column 10 by .1136, and so on. These products are presented in detail in columns 14, 15, 16, 17 and 18 of Table 7.1, which are the values we have been seeking; they are shown diagrammatically by the curved surface of Figure 7.9. A comparison of the theoretical values of Figure 7.9 with the surface fitted to the empirical values represented by the circles in Figure 7.4 indicates that the theoretical derivations approximate the facts very closely indeed.

Computations analogous to the preceding have shown that the present set of postulates and constants also hold when $D > D'$ at least up to three days of food privation. The theoretical curve for all values of $D$ between 0 and 72 hours yields a positively accelerated reaction potential up to 24 hours ($D'$ in the present analysis), where there is a slight inflection; as $D$ increases above $D'$ there is at first a brief period of positive acceleration, which is followed by a protracted period that is nearly linear, the whole showing a fair approximation to Figure 7.5.

Generalizing from Table 7.1 and Figure 7.9, the following corollaries may be formulated as a kind of condensed summary of the implications of the present set of assumptions as shown by the preceding computations:

I. *When habit strength is zero, reaction-evocation potential is zero.*

II. *When primary drive strength* ($D$) *is zero, reaction-evocation potential* ($_sE_R$) *has an appreciable but relatively low positive value which is a positive growth function of the number of reinforcements.* Corollaries I and II both agree in detail with Perin's empirical findings.

As the drive ($D$) increases from zero to $D'$:

III. *The reaction-evocation potential increases with a slight positive acceleration.*

IV. *The reaction-evocation potential maintains its positive growth relationship to the number of reinforcements.* Both of these corollaries agree in detail with Perin's empirical findings.

As the drive ($D$) increases above $D'$:

V. *There is a definite inflection in the* $_sE_R$ *function at D, the slope for values of D just greater than D' being less than for those just below.*

VI. *The reaction-evocation potential above D' increases at first with a slight positive acceleration, which soon gives place to a practically linear relationship.* Both of these corollaries agree in detail with Skinner's empirical findings (Figure 7.7).

## MISCELLANEOUS COROLLARIES FLOWING FROM THE PRESENT PRIMARY MOTIVATION HYPOTHESIS

The first problem in this series is that presented by Elliott's experiment described above, the outcome of which is clearly shown in Figure 7.6.

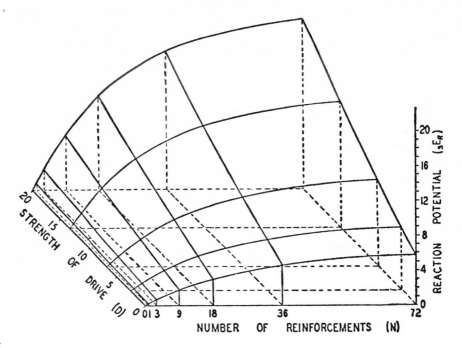

Figure 7.9. Graphic representation of the theoretical joint determination of reaction potential by various numbers of reinforcements under a drive $(D')$ of 20 units' strength when functioning under drives $(D)$ of various strengths less than that of the original habit formation. Note the detailed agreement with the comparable empirical results shown in Figure 7.4.

Here we have the case of a reaction tendency set up on the basis of one drive, showing a partial but by no means complete disruption when this drive (thirst) is abruptly replaced by another drive, that of hunger. At this point we recall the assumption stated earlier (p. 115) that all drives alike are able to sensitize all habits. Applying this to the behavior of Elliott's animals during the first critical test trial on the maze after the change in drive, it is to be expected that while hunger was then the dominant drive, certain residual amounts of various other drives (including thirst) were also active. These in the aggregate $(\dot{D})$, the hunger drive included, are presumed to operate in a multiplicative manner upon the habit strength effective at the moment in determining reaction potentiality. It is assumed that this would be enough to evoke, on the average, about 20 percent as much activity as is evoked by the thirst drive.

This means that the residual drive $(\dot{D})$ must amount to considerably more than 20 per cent of the regular thirst drive, say. For example in the detailed analysis of the preceding section, where 24 hours' hunger stood at 20 units of drive, this residual drive was placed at 10 units, which is

50 per cent as much as 20. Nevertheless, the reaction potential at 24 hours' hunger came out of 19.42 units, whereas that at satiation or zero drive stood at 4.58 units, the latter being only about 23 per cent of the former. The explanation of the paradoxical difference of 50 versus 23 per cent is significant; it arises largely from the fact that when the hitherto dominant drive ceases to be active, not only are there lost the 20 units of drive strength previously contributed by this need, but *there is also lost to the conditioned stimulus compound the sizable component made up by $S_D$, the withdrawal of which materially reduces the available habit strength associated with the situation in question, and so reduces the resulting reaction potential.*

On the basis of the above analysis we may formulate the following additions to the corollaries listed in the preceding section:

VII. *Under the conditions of the satiation of the dominant drive involved in the original habit-acquisition, there are sufficient residuals of other drives which in the aggregate yield on the average an excitatory potential amounting to around 20 per cent of that mobilized by a 24-hour hunger on a habit originally set up on the basis of this drive.*

VIII. *In case an organism is presented with all the stimuli characteristic of a habit, if the original drive is replaced by a strong second drive whose $S_D$ activates no conflicting habit tendency, the reaction potential to the execution of the habitual act will be stronger than would be the case if the irrelevant second drive were not active.* This means that if a control group with both hunger and thirst thoroughly satiated were to be added to the Elliott experiment described above, the mean retardation in the running time and the mean number of errors would increase appreciably above what resulted from a mere replacement of one drive by another (6).

A second problem concerns the relation of the experimental extinction of a reaction tendency to the drive intensity operative at the time of extinction. Now, the passage from Pavlov quoted above (p. 107) strongly suggests that *experimental extinction effects are in some sense directly opposed to reaction potential rather than merely to habit strength.* Since with a constant habit strength an increase in the drive augments the reaction potential, and since extinction effects are an increasing function of the number of unreinforced evocations, it follows that:

IX. *The number of reinforcements being constant, the stronger the relevant drive, the greater will be the number of unreinforced evocations which will be required to reduce the reaction potential to a given level.*

X. *The number of reinforcements being constant, the stronger an allied but irrelevant drive active at the time of extinction, the greater will be the number of unreinforced evocations required to reduce the reaction potential to a given level, though this number will be materially less than would be required under the same intensity of the relevant drive.*

Thus if a habit set up on the basis of a thirst drive were extinguished under a sizable hunger drive but with water satiation, the theory demands that the reaction potential would extinguish with fewer unreinforced evocations than would be the case under the same intensity of the thirst drive in conjunction with a zero hunger drive; moreover, such a habit would require more unreinforced reaction evocations to produce a given degree of extinction under a strong hunger drive than under a weak one. By the same type of reasoning it is to be expected that if a reaction tendency were set up in male rats under hunger or thirst, and if subsequently a random sample of the organisms were castrated, experimental extinction under a normal hunger drive would occur more quickly than it would in the non-castrated organisms.

At this point we turn to a more detailed consideration of Pavlov's observation just referred to, that when he had performed an experimental extinction under a given drive and then increased the drive, the conditioned stimulus would again evoke the reaction. This may be deduced rather simply: If a certain number of unreinforced evocations of a reaction have produced sufficient extinction effects to neutralize a given amount of excitatory potential, an increase in the drive will increase the excitatory potential which the existent extinction effects will no longer suffice to neutralize completely. The balance of the reaction potential will accordingly be available to evoke reaction and, upon adequate stimulation, will do so. We thus come to our eleventh corollary:

XI. *If a reaction tendency is extinguished by massed reaction evocations under a given strength of drive, and if at once thereafter the drive is appreciably increased, the original stimulation will again evoke the reaction.*

Our final question concerns an exceedingly inportant problem in adaptive dynamics. It has already been pointed out that as a rule action sequences required to satisfy a food need are different from those required to satisfy a water need, and both would ordinarily be quite different from the acts which would be required to satisfy a sex drive. This problem is posed very sharply when, as in the Hull-Leeper experiments, an organism is presented with an identical objective situation and required to make a differential reaction purely on the basis of the need dominant at the moment. These experiments confirm everyday observations that animals can adapt successfully to such situations. The question before us is how this behavior is to be explained.

At first sight it might be supposed that in this situation the animals would merely associate $S_h$ with turning to the right, say, and $S_t$ with turning to the left, and that adaptation would thereby be complete. A little further reflection will show, however, that this simple explanation is hardly adequate, because if there were really an independent and functionally potent receptor-effector connection between the hunger-drive stimulus and turning to the right the animal would, when hungry, be impelled to turn to the right continuously when in its cage or wherever it happened to be, as well as at the choice point in the maze. The animals, of course, display no such behavior, any more than we ourselves do.

The present set of postulates mediates the explanation chiefly on the basis of a secondary process known as *patterning*. Unfortunately it will not be possible to give an exposition of this exceedingly important subject until a later chapter. However, pending the detailed presentation in that place we shall here merely indicate dogmatically the nature of patterning and briefly sketch the application of this secondary principle to the problem in adaptive dynamics now before us.

By the term "patterning" we mean the process whereby organisms acquire the capacity of reacting (or not reacting) to particular *combinations* of stimuli as distinguished from the several component stimulus elements or aggregates making up the compound. At bottom this process turns out to be a case of learning to discriminate afferent interaction effects. Specifically, the principle of afferent interaction implies that in the Hull-Leeper studies afferent impulses ($s$) arising from the environmental stimuli ($S_I$) are somewhat different when stimulation occurs in combination with the hunger-drive stimulus ($S_h$) from those which result from the same stimulation in combination with the thirst-drive stimulus ($S_t$). Similarly, the afferent impulses arising from $S_h$ and $S_t$ are somewhat different when initiated in conjunction with $S_I$ from those initiated by $S_h$ and $S_t$ in the cage or other situations. If the afferent impulses arising from the environmental stimuli uncomplicated by any particular drive be represented by $s$, then these impulses when modified by the interaction with the hunger-drive stimulus may be represented by $s_h$, and when modified by interaction with the thirst-drive stimulus, by $s_t$. Since there are but two alternatives, it is to be expected that at the outset of training, reaction would be about 50 per cent correct. However, as the differential reinforcement yielded by the techniques employed in these investigations continues, the gradient of generalization between $s_h$ and $s_t$ would progressively steepen; i.e., discrimination learning would gradually take place, exactly as it does in fact. Thus we arrive at our twelfth corollary:

XII. *Organisms will learn to react differentially to a given objective situation according to the drive active at the time, and to react differentially to a given drive according to the objective situation at the time.*

## SUMMARY

The needs of organisms operate both in the formation of habits and in their subsequent functioning, i.e., in primary motivation. Because of the sensitizing or energizing action of needs in this latter rôle, they are called *drives*.

A great mass of significant empirical evidence concerning primary motivation has become available within recent years. A survey of this material, particularly as related to hunger, thirst, injury (including the action of very intense stimuli of all kinds), sex, and the action of certain substances such as caffeine, has led to the tentative conclusion that all primary drives produce their effects by the action of various chemicals in the blood. Substances like caffeine, through bathing the neural mechanisms involved, seem to operate by heightening the reaction potential mediated by all positive habit tendencies. Drive substances, such as the various endocrine secretions, are conceived either to be released into the blood by certain kinds of strong stimulation or as themselves initiating stimulation of resident receptors through their evocation of action by selected portions of the body, e.g., the intestinal tract and the genitalia. In both cases the energy effecting this receptor activation is called the drive stimulus ($S_D$).

The action of these endocrine substances, while apparently lowering the reaction threshold of certain restricted effectors (*1*, p. 184 ff.), seems also to have a generalized but possibly weaker tendency to facilitate action of *all* effectors, giving rise to a degree of undifferentiated motivation analogous to the Freudian libido. Thus a sex hormone would tend to motivate action based on any habit, however remote the action from that involved in actual copulation. This, together with the assumption that one or more other motivations are active to some degree, explains the continued but limited amount of habitual action of organisms when the motivation on the basis of which the habit was originally set up has presumably become zero. It also suggests a possible mechanism underlying the Freudian concept of sublimation. However, where differential behavior is required to bring about reduction in two or more drives, the differences in the drive stimuli characteristic of the motivations in question, through the principle of afferent interaction and the resulting stimulus patterning, suffice to mediate the necessary discrimination.

The hypothesis of the endocrine or chemical motivational mechanism and the associated principle of the drive stimulus, when coupled with various other postulates of the present system such as primary reinforcement, primary stimulus generalization, and the opposition of experimental extinction to excitatory potential, seem to be able to mediate the deduction, and so the explanation, of nearly all the major known phenomena of primary motivation.[4] In addition to the phenomena already summarized there may be mentioned the further deductions flowing from

---

[4] One class of phenomena seems to involve the action of fractional antedating goal reactions and of spatial orientation. Space is not here available for the elaboration of these mechanisms and their action in motivational situations.

the system: that resistance to extinction maintains a consistent growth function of the number of reinforcements for any constant drive; that the asymptotes of these growth functions are themselves functions of the strength of drive; that for constant habit strengths, reaction potential has a positive acceleration for increasing drives between zero and the drive employed in the original reinforcement; that if habit strength is zero, reaction tendency is zero; that an increase in drive will over-ride the total extinction of a reaction potential arising from a weaker drive; that in a given objective habit situation the abrupt shift from one drive to another will, in the absence of discriminatory training, disrupt the behavior to some extent, though not completely; that transfers of training (habits) from one motivation to another will be prompt and extensive; that organisms in the same external situations will learn to react differentially in such a way as to reduce different needs; that the conditioned evocation of endocrine secretions facilitates the evocation of muscular activity on the subsequent presentation of appropriate conditioned stimuli, which is believed to be the rôle of "emotion" in the motivation of behavior.

On the basis of the various background considerations elaborated in the preceding pages, we formulate our sixth and seventh primary molar laws of behavior:

*Postulate 6.* Associated with every drive $(D)$ is a characteristic drive stimulus $(S_D)$ whose intensity is an increasing monotonic function of the drive in question.

*Postulate 7.* Any effective habit strength $(_S\overline{H}_R)$ is sensitized into reaction potentiality $(_SE_R)$ by all primary drives active within an organism at a given time, the magnitude of this potentiality being a product obtained by multiplying an increasing function of $_SH_R$ by an increasing function of $D$.

From Postulates 5, 6, and 7 there may be derived the following corollary:

*Major corollary II.* The amount of reaction potentiality $(_SE_R)$ in any given primary motivational situation is the product of (1) the effective habit strength $(S_1 + S_D\overline{H}_R)$ under the existing conditions of primary drive multiplied by (2) the quotient obtained from dividing the sum of the dominant value of the primary drive $(D)$ plus the aggregate strength of all the non-dominant primary drives $(\dot{D})$ active at the time, by the sum of the same non-dominant drives plus the physiological drive maximum $(M_D)$.

## NOTES

### Mathematical Statement of Postulate 6

$$S_D = bf(D),$$

where

$$b > 0.$$

### Mathematical Statement of Postulate 7

$$_sE_R = f(_s\overline{H}_R) \times f(D) \tag{33}$$

## Mathematical Statement of Major Corollary II

$$_sE_R = {}_{\substack{S \ +S \\ 1 \ D}}\overline{H}_R \frac{\dot{D}+D}{\dot{D}+M_D}, \tag{34}$$

where

$D =$ the strength of the dominant primary drive at a moment under consideration

$\dot{D} =$ the aggregate strength of all the non-dominant primary drives and quasi-drives at the moment under consideration

$M_D =$ the physiological drive maximum (100 motes)

$S_1 =$ the non-drive component of the stimulus complex at the moment under consideration

$S_D =$ the stimulus specifically dependent upon the primary drive at the moment under consideration

$_{\substack{S \ +S \\ 1 \ D}}\overline{H}_R =$ the physiological summation of $_{\substack{S \\ 1}}\overline{H}_R$ and $_{\substack{S \\ D}}\overline{H}_R$

$_{\substack{S \\ 1}}\overline{H}_R =$ the effective habit loading of the non-drive component of the stimulus complex

$_{\substack{S \\ D}}\overline{H}_R =$ the effective habit loading of $_{\substack{S \\ D}}H_R$

## The Equations of Perin's Graphs

The curve drawn through the upper set of data points of Figure 7.3 was plotted from the fitted equation:

$$n = 66(1 - 10^{-.0180\,N}) - 4,$$

when $n$ represents the number of unreinforced reaction evocations to produce experimental extinction and $N$ represents the number of reinforcements in the setting up of the habit. The curve drawn through the lower set of data points of Figure 7.3 was plotted from the fitted equation:

$$n = 25(1 - 10^{-.0185\,N}) - 4,$$

where $n$ and $N$ have the same significance as in the preceding equation. Note the practical identity of the exponents, .0180 and .0185.

The curve drawn through the data points of Figure 7.2 was plotted from the equation:

$$n = 9.4(10^{.0241\,h}) - 4,$$

where $n$ means the same as above and $h$ represents the number of hours of food privation.

The surface passing among the data points of Figure 7.4 was generated by the fitted equation:

$$n = 21.45\,(10^{.0222\,h})(1 - 10^{-.0180\,N}) - 4 \tag{35}$$

in which $n$, $h$, and $N$ mean the same as before. A comparison of this equation with the preceding equations shows that it is essentially the positive growth function of the first two equations in which the asymptote has been taken by a function of the drive ($h$) derived from the third equation. Thus $n$, regarded as action potentiality, may be seen to be a multiplicative function of $h$, or motivation, and $N$, or habit strength.

## The Equations Employed in the Derivation of Table 7.1 and Figure 7.9

The positive growth function from which the values in column 2 of Table 7.1 were derived is:

$$_{S_1 + S_D} H_R = 75(1 - 10^{-.018\,N}).$$

The equation by which the values of column 3 were derived from those in column 2 is:

$$_S H_R = 100 - \sqrt{10,000 - 100_{S_1 + S_D} H_R}.$$

This equation is a special form of that representing the physiological summation of two habit tendencies given below.

The equation from which the values of the drive ($D$) were calculated from the number of hours' food privation ($h$) is:

$$D = \frac{100}{120} h.$$

The values of the drive deviations ($d'$) were calculated from the equation:

$$d' = D' - D,$$

where $D'$ represents the strength of drive employed in the formation of the habit and $D$ represents the strength of drive under which stimulation calculated to lead to reaction evocation occurs.

The equation by means of which the values of column 4, 5, 6, 7, and 8 of Table 7.1 were calculated from those of column 3 is:

$$_{S_D} \overline{H}_R = {}_{S_D} H_R (10^{-.00881\,d'}).$$

This, it may be noted, is equation 29 (Hull, p. 199 ff.), the equation of primary stimulus generalization in which $_{S_D} H_R$ represents the effective-habit-strength loading of the drive stimulus.

The equation by means of which the values of columns 9, 10, 11, 12, and 13 of Table 7.1 were calculated from those of columns 4, 5, 6, 7, and 8 is:

$$_{S_1 + S_D} \overline{H}_R = {}_{S_1} \overline{H}_R + {}_{S_D} \overline{H}_R - \frac{{}_{S_1} H_R \times {}_{S_D} H_R}{100}.$$

The values of the effective drive ($\overline{D}$) were found by the equation:

$$\overline{D} = 100 \frac{\dot{D} + D}{\dot{D} + M_D},$$

in which $D$ is supposed to be the sum of the generalized effects of all the irrelevant drives active at the time, and $M_D$ represents the maximum drive possible in a centigrade system, i.e., 100. The value of $D$ found by trial to fit the Perin data fairly well is 10. Therefore the equation becomes:

$$\overline{D} = 100 \, \frac{10 + D}{110} \, .$$

For example, in case $\overline{D}$ is maximal this equation becomes:

$$\overline{D} = 100 \, \frac{110}{110}$$

$$= 100.$$

The basic equation by means of which the values of columns 14, 15, 16, 17, and 18 of Table 7.1 were calculated from the values of columns 9, 10, 11, 12, and 13 of Table 7.1 is:

$$_sE_R = s_1 + s_D \overline{H}_R \times \frac{\overline{D}}{100} \, .$$

Substituting the equivalent of $\overline{D}$ and simplifying, this becomes:

$$_sE_R = s_1 + s_D \overline{H}_R \times \frac{10 + D}{110} \, .$$

## REFERENCES

1. Beach, F. A.   Arousal, maintenance, and manifestation of sexual excitement in male animals. *Psychosom. Med.*, 1942, *4*, 173–198.
2. Elliott, M. H.   The effect of change of drive on maze performance. *Calif. Pub. in Psychol.*, 1929, *4*, 185–188.
3. Finch, G.   Hunger as a determinant of conditional and unconditional salivary response magnitude. *Amer. J. Physiol.*, 1938, *123*, 379–382.
4. Heathers, G. L., and Arakelian, P.   The relation between strength of drive and rate of extinction of a bar-pressing reaction in the rat. *J. gen. Psychol.*, 1941, *24*, 243–258.
5. Hovland, C. I.   The generalization of conditioned responses: II. The sensory generalization of conditioned responses with varying intensities of tone. *J. genet. Psychol.*, 1937, *51*, 279–291.
6. Hull, C. L.   Differential habituation to internal stimuli in the albino rat. *J. comp. Psychol.*, 1933, *16*, 255–273.
7. Hull, C. L.   The rat's speed-of-locomotion gradient in the approach to food. *J. comp. Psychol.*, 1934, *17*, 393–422.
8. Leeper, R.   The role of motivation in learning: A study of the phenomenon of differential motivational control of the utilization of habits. *J. genet. Psychol.*, 1935, *46*, 3–40.
9. Miller, N. E., & Miles, W. R.   Effect of caffeine on the running speed of hungry, satiated, and frustrated rats. *J. comp. Psychol.*, 1935, *20*, 397–412.
10. Moore, C. R., Price, D., & Gallagher, T. F.   Rat prostate cystology and

testes-hormone indicator and the prevention of castration changes by testes extract injection. *Amer. J. Anat.*, 1930, *45*, 71–108.

11. Pavlov, I. P.   *Conditioned reflexes* (trans. by G. V. Anrep). London: Oxford Univer. Press, 1927.
12. Perin, C. T.   Behavior potentiality as a joint function of the amount of training and the degree of hunger at the time of extinction. *J. exper. Psychol.*, 1942, *30*, 93–113.
13. Skinner, B. F.   *The behavior of organisms.* New York: D. Appleton-Century Co., Inc., 1938.
14. Skinner, B. F., & Hernon, W. T.   Effect of caffeine and benzedrine upon conditioning and extinction. *Psychol. Record*, 1937, *1*, 340–346.
15. Stone, C. P.   The retention of copulatory ability in male rats after castration. *J. comp. Psychol.*, 1927, *7*, 369–387.
16. Stone, C. P.   The retention of copulatory activity in male rabbits following castration. *J. genet. Psychol.*, 1932, *40*, 296–305.
17. Stone, C. P.   Activation of impotent male rats by injections of testosterone proprionate. *J. comp. Psychol.*, 1938, *25*, 445–450.
18. Switzer, S. A.   The effect of caffeine on experimental extinction of conditioned reactions. *J. gen. Psychol.*, 1935, *12*, 78–94.
19. Warden, C. J., Jenkins, T. N., & Warner, L. H.   *Introduction to comparative psychology.* New York: Ronald, 1934.
20. Williams, S. B.   Resistance to extinction as a function of the number of reinforcements. *J. exper. Psychol.*, 1938, *23*, 506–521.
21. Young, P. T.   *Motivation of behavior.* New York: John Wiley and Sons, 1936.
22. Zener, K. E., & McCurdy, H. G.   Analysis of motivational factors in conditioned behavior: I. The differential effect of changes in hunger upon conditioned, unconditioned, and spontaneous salivary secretion. *J. Psychol.*, 1939, *8*, 321–350.

# 8 • Donald O. Hebb

## Drives and the C. N. S.
## (Conceptual Nervous System)

The notion of drive as a general energizer of behavior was for some years studied primarily at the behavioral level. Only gradually did it become apparent that a fruitful interplay between developments in neurophysiology and behavioral drive theory was possible. To be sure, efforts had been made to interpret emotions as drives and the physiology of emotions has a long history. Nevertheless, the potential equation of arousal, emotional or otherwise, as studied physiologically, with the conceptual "functions" assigned to drive was not generally recognized. D. O. Hebb in this article made a forceful presentatoin of this possibility. Since its appearance, the question of the general energizing function has become predominantly a concern for physiological psychologists.

*The problem of motivation* of course lies close to the heart of the general problem of understanding behavior, yet it sometimes seems the least realistically treated topic in the literature. In great part, the difficulty concerns that c.n.s., or "conceptual nervous system," which Skinner disavowed and from whose influence he and others have tried to escape. But the conceptual nervous system of 1930 was evidently like the gin that was being drunk about the same time; it was homemade and none too good, as Skinner pointed out, but it was also habit-forming; and the effort to escape has not really been successful. Prohibition is long past. If we *must* drink we can now get better liquor; likewise, the conceptual nervous system of 1930 is out of date and—if we must neurologize—let us use the best brand of neurology we can find.

Though I personally favor both alcohol and neurologizing, in mod-

Presidential address, Division 3, at American Psychological Association, New York, September, 1954.
This article is reproduced in full from the *Psychological Review*, 1955, 62, 243–254. Reprinted by permission of the American Psychological Association and the author.

eration, the point here does not assume that either is a good thing. The point is that psychology is intoxicating itself with a worse brand than it need use. Many psychologists do not think in terms of neural anatomy; but merely adhering to certain classical frameworks shows the limiting effect of earlier neurologizing. Bergmann (2) has recently said again that it is logically possible to escape the influence. This does not change the fact that, in practice, it has not been done.

Further, as I read Bergmann, I am not sure that he really thinks, deep down, that we should swear off neurologizing entirely, or at least that we should all do so. He has made a strong case for the functional similarity of intervening variable and hypothetical construct, implying that we are dealing more with differences of degree than of kind. The conclusion *I* draw is that both can properly appear in the same theory, using intervening variables to whatever extent is most profitable (as physics for example does), and conversely not being afraid to use some theoretical conception merely because it might become anatomically identifiable.

For many conceptions, at least, MacCorquodale and Meehl's (26) distinction is relative, not absolute; and it must also be observed that physiological psychology makes free use of "dispositional concepts" as well as "existential" ones. Logically, this leaves room for some of us to make more use of explicitly physiological constructs than others, and still lets us stay in communication with one another. It also shows how one's views concerning motivation, for example, might be more influenced than one thinks by earlier physiological notions, since it means that an explicitly physiological conception might be restated in words that have—apparently—no physiological reference.

What I propose, therefore, is to look at motivation as it relates to the c.n.s.—or conceptual nervous system—of three different periods: as it was before 1930, as it was say 10 years ago, and as it is today. . . . I hope to persuade you that some of our current troubles with motivation are due to the c.n.s. of an earlier day, and ask that you look with an open mind at the implications of the current one. Today's physiology suggests new psychological ideas, and I would like to persuade you that they make psychological sense, no matter how they originated. They might even provide common ground—not necessarily agreement, but communication, something nearer to agreement—for people whose views at present may seem completely opposed. While writing this paper I found myself having to make a change in my own theoretical position, as you will see, and though you may not adopt the same position you may be willing to take another look at the evidence, and consider its theoretical import anew.

Before going on it is just as well to be explicit about the use of the terms motivation and drive. "Motivation" refers here in a rather general sense to the energizing of behavior, and especially to the sources of energy in a particular set of responses that keep them temporarily dominant over others and account for continuity and direction in behavior. "Drive" is regarded as a more specific conception about the way in which this occurs: a hypothesis of motivation, which makes the energy a function of a special process distinct from those S-R or cognitive functions that are energized. In some contexts, therefore, "motivation" and "drive" are interchangeable.

## MOTIVATION IN THE CLASSICAL (PRE-1930) C.N.S.

The main line of descent of psychological theory, as I have recently tried to show (20), is through associationism and the stimulus-response formulations. Characteristically, stimulus-response theory has treated the animal as more or less inactive unless subjected to special conditions of arousal. These conditions are first, hunger, pain, and sexual excitement; and secondly, stimulation that has become associated with one of these more primitive motivations.

Such views did not originate entirely in the early ideas of nervous function, but certainly were strengthened by them. Early studies of the nerve fiber seemed to show that the cell is inert until something happens to it from outside; therefore, the same would be true of the collection of cells making up the nervous system. From this came the explicit theory of drives. The organism is thought of as like a machine, such as the automobile, in which the steering mechanism—that is, stimulus-response connections—is separate from the power source, or drive. There is, however, this difference: the organism may be endowed with three or more different power plants. Once you start listing separate ones, it is hard to avoid five: hunger, thirst, pain, maternal, and sex drives. By some theorists, these may each be given a low-level steering function also, and indirectly the steering function of drives is much increased by the law of effect. According to the law, habits—steering functions—are acquired only in conjunction with the operation of drives.

Now it is evident that an animal is often active and often learns when there is little or no drive activity of the kinds listed. This fact has been dealt with in two ways. One is to postulate additional drives—activity, exploratory, manipulatory, and so forth. The other is to postulate acquired or learned drives, which obtain their energy, so to speak, from association with primary drives.

It is important to see the difficulties to be met by this kind of formulation, though it should be said at once that I do not have any decisive refutation of it, and other approaches have their difficulties, too.

First, we may overlook the rather large number of forms of behavior in which motivation cannot be reduced to biological drive plus learning.

Such behavior is most evident in higher species; and may be forgotten by those who work only with the rat or with restricted segments of the behavior of dog or cat. (I do not suggest that we put human motivation on a different plane from that of animals (7); what I am saying is that certain peculiarities of motivation increase with phylogenesis, and though most evident in man can be clearly seen with other higher animals.) What is the drive that produces panic in the chimpanzee at the sight of a model of a human head; or fear in some animals, and vicious aggression in others, at the sight of the anesthetized body of a fellow chimpanzee? What about fear of snakes, or the young chimpanzee's terror at the sight of strangers? One can accept the idea that this is "anxiety," but the anxiety, if so, is not based on a prior association of the stimulus object with pain. With the young chimpanzee reared in the nursery of the Yerkes Laboratories, after separation from the mother at birth, one can be certain that the infant has never seen a snake before, and certainly no one has told him about snakes; and one can be sure that a particular infant has never had the opportunity to associate a strange face with pain. Stimulus generalization does not explain fear of strangers, for other stimuli in the same class, namely, the regular attendants, are eagerly welcomed by the infant.

Again, what drive shall we postulate to account for the manifold forms of anger in the chimpanzee that do not derive from frustration objectively defined (22)? How account for the petting behavior of young adolescent chimpanzees, which Nissen (36) has shown is independent of primary sex activity? How deal with the behavior of the female who, bearing her first infant, is terrified at the sight of the baby as it drops from the birth canal, runs away, never sees it again after it has been taken to the nursery for rearing; and who yet, on the birth of a *second* infant, promptly picks it up and violently resists any effort to take it from her?

There is a great deal of behavior, in the higher animal especially, that is at the very best difficult to reduce to hunger, pain, sex, and maternal drives, plus learning. Even for the lower animal it has been clear for some time that we must add an exploratory drive (if we are to think in these terms at all), and presumably the motivational phenomena recently studied by Harlow and his colleagues (16, 17, 10) could also be comprised under such a drive by giving it a little broader specification. The curiosity drive of Berlyne (4) and Thompson and Solomon (46), for example, might be considered to cover both investigatory and manipulatory activities on the one hand, and exploratory, on the other. It would also comprehend the "problem-seeking" behavior recently studied by Mahut and Havelka at McGill (unpublished studies). They have shown that the rat which is offered a short, direct path to food, and a longer, variable and indirect pathway involving a search for food, will very frequently prefer the more difficult, but more "interesting" route.

But even with the addition of a curiosity-investigatory-manipulatory drive, and even apart from the primates, there is still behavior that presents difficulties. There are the reinforcing effects of incomplete copulation (*43*) and of saccharin intake (*42, 11*), which do not reduce to secondary reward. We must not multiply drives beyond reason, and at this point one asks whether there is no alternative to the theory in this form. We come, then, to the conceptual nervous system of 1930 to 1950.

## MOTIVATION IN THE C.N.S. OF 1930–1950

About 1930 it began to be evident that the nerve cell is not physiologically inert, does not have to be excited from outside in order to discharge (*19*, p. 8). The nervous system is alive, and living things by their nature are active. With the demonstration of spontaneous activity in c.n.s. it seemed to me that the conception of a drive system or systems are supererogation.

For reasons I shall come to later, this now appears to me to have been an oversimplification; but in 1945 the only problem of motivation, I thought, was to account for the *direction* taken by behavior. From this point of view, hunger or pain might be peculiarly effective in guiding or channeling activity but not needed for its arousal. It was not surprising, from this point of view, to see human beings liking intellectual work, nor to find evidence that an animal might learn something without pressure of pain or hunger.

The energy of response is not in the stimulus. It comes from the food, water, and oxygen ingested by the animal; and the violence of an epileptic convulsion, when brain cells for whatever reason decide to fire in synchrony, bears witness to what the nervous system can do when it likes. This is like a whole powder magazine exploding at once. Ordinary behavior can be thought of as produced by an organized series of much smaller explosions, and so a "self-motivating" c.n.s. might still be a very powerfully motivated one. To me, then, it was astonishing that a critic could refer to mine as a "motivationless" psychology. What I had said in short was that any organized process in the brain is a motivated process, inevitably, inescapably; that the human brain is built to be active, and that as long as it is supplied with adequate nutrition will continue to be active. Brain activity is what determines behavior, and so the only behavioral problem becomes that of accounting for *in*activity.

It was in this conceptual frame that the behavioral picture seemed to negate the notion of drive, as a separate energizer of behavior. A pedagogical experiment reported earlier (*18*) had been very impressive in its indication that the human liking for work is not a rare phenomenon, but general. All of the 600-odd pupils in a city school, ranging from 6 to 15 years of age, were suddenly informed that they need do no work whatever unless they wanted to, that the punishment for being noisy and interrupting others' work was to be sent to the playground to play, and that the reward for being good was to be allowed to do more work. In these circumstances, *all* of the pupils discovered within a day or two that, within limits, they preferred work to no work (and incidentally learned more arithmetic and so forth than in previous years).

The phenomenon of work for its own sake is familiar enough to all of us, when the timing is controlled by the worker himself, when "work" is not defined as referring alone to activity imposed from without. Intellectual work may take the form of trying to understand what Robert Browning was trying to say (if anything), to discover what it is in Dali's paintings that can interest others, or to predict the outcome of a paperback mystery. We systematically underestimate the human need of intellectual activity, in one form or another, when we overlook the intellectual component in art and in games. Similarly with riddles, puzzles, and the puzzle-like games of strategy such as bridge, chess, and *go;* the frequency with which man has devised such problems for his own solution is a most significant fact concerning human motivation.

It is, however, not necessarily a fact that supports my earlier view, outlined above. It is hard to get these broader aspects of human behavior under laboratory study, and when we do we may expect to have our ideas about them significantly modified. For my views on the problem, this is what has happened with the experiment of Bexton, Heron, and Scott (5). Their work is a long step toward dealing with the realities of motivation in the well-fed, physically comfortable, adult human being, and its results raise a serious difficulty for my own theory. Their subjects were paid handsomely to do nothing, see nothing, hear or touch very little, for 24 hours a day. Primary needs were met, on the whole, very well. The subjects suffered no pain, and were fed on request. It is true that they could not copulate, but at the risk of impugning the virility of Canadian college students I point out that most of them would not have been copulating anyway and were quite used to such long stretches of three or four days without primary sexual satisfaction. The secondary reward, on the other hand, was high: $20 a day plus room and board is more than $7000 a year, far more than a student could earn by other means. The subjects then should be highly motivated to continue the experiment, cheerful and happy to be allowed to contribute to scientific knowledge so painlessly and profitably.

In fact, the subject was well motivated for perhaps four to eight hours, and then became increasingly unhappy. He developed a need for stimulation of almost any kind. In the first preliminary exploration, for example, he was allowed to listen to recorded material on request. Some subjects were given a talk for 6-year-old children on the dangers of alcohol. This might be requested, by a grown-up male college student, 15 to 20 times in a 30-hour period. Others were offered, and asked for repeatedly, a recording of an old stockmarket report. The subjects looked forward to being tested, but paradoxically tended to find the tests fatiguing when they did arrive. It is hardly necessary to say that the whole situation was rather hard to take, and one subject, in spite of not being in a special state of primary drive arousal in the experiment but in real need of money outside it, gave up the secondary reward of $20 a day to take up a job at hard labor paying $7 or $8 a day.

This experiment is not cited primarily as a difficulty for drive theory, although three months ago that is how I saw it. It *will* make difficulty for such theory if exploratory drive is not recognized; but we have already seen the necessity, on other grounds, of including a sort of exploratory-curiosity-manipulatory drive, which essentially comes down to a tendency to seek varied stimulation. This would on the whole handle very well the motivational phenomena observed by Heron's group.

Instead, I cite their experiment as making essential trouble for my own treatment of motivation (*19*) as based on the conceptual nervous system of 1930 to 1945. If the thought process is internally organized and motivated, why should it break down in conditions of perceptual isolation, unless emotional disturbance intervenes? But it did break down when no serious emotional change was observed, with problem-solving and intelligence-test performance significantly impaired. Why should the subjects themselves report (*a*) after four or five hours in isolation that they could not follow a connected train of thought, and (*b*) that their motivation for study or the like was seriously disturbed for 24 hours or more after coming out of isolation? The subjects were reasonably well adjusted, happy, and able to think coherently for the first four or five hours of the experiment; why, according to my theory, should this not continue, and why should the organization of behavior not be promptly restored with restoration of a normal environment?

You will forgive me perhaps if I do not dilate further on my own theoretical difficulties, paralleling those of others, but turn now to the conceptual nervous system of 1954 to ask what psychological values we may extract from it for the theory of motivation. I shall not attempt any clear answer for the difficulties we have considered—the data do not seem yet to justify clear answers—but certain conceptions can be formulated in sufficiently definite form to be a background for new research, and the physiological data contain suggestsons that may allow me to retain what was of value in my earlier proposals while bringing them closer to ideas such as Harlow's (*16*) on one hand and to reinforcement theory on the other.

## MOTIVATION AND C.N.S. IN 1954

For psychological purposes there are two major changes in recent ideas of nervous function. One concerns the single cell, the other an "arousal" system in the brain stem. The first I shall pass over briefly; it is very significant, but does not bear quite as directly upon our present problem. Its essence is that there are two kinds of activity in the nerve cell: the spike potential, or actual firing, and the dendritic potential, which has very different properties. There is now clear evidence (12) that the dendrite has a "slow-burning" activity which is not all-or-none, tends not to be transmitted, and lasts 15 to 30 milliseconds instead of the spike's one millisecond. It facilitates spike activity (23), but often occurs independently and may make up the greater part of the EEG record. It is still true that the brain is always active, but the activity is not always the transmitted kind that conduces to behavior. Finally, there is decisive evidence of primary inhibition in nerve function (25, 14) and of a true fatigue that may last for a matter of minutes instead of milliseconds (6, 9). These facts will have a great effect on the hypotheses of physiological psychology, and sooner or later on psychology in general.

Our more direct concern is with a development to which attention has already been drawn by Lindsley (24): the nonspecific or diffuse projection system of the brain stem, which was shown by Moruzzi and Magoun (34) to be an *arousal* system whose activity in effect makes organized cortical activity possible. Lindsley showed the relevance to the problem of emotion and motivation; what I shall attempt is to extend his treatment, giving more weight to cortical components in arousal. The point of view has also an evident relationship to Duffy's (13).

The arousal system can be thought of as representing a second major pathway by which all sensory excitations reach the cortex, as shown in the upper part of Figure 8.1; but there is also feedback from the cortex and I shall urge that the *psychological* evidence further emphasizes the importance of this "downstream" effect.

In the classical conception of sensory function, input to the cortex was via the great projection systems only: from sensory nerve to sensory tract, thence to the corresponding sensory nucleus of the thalamus, and thence directly to one of the sensory projection areas of the cortex. These are still the direct sensory routes, the quick efficient transmitters of information. The second pathway is slow and inefficient; the excitation, as it were, trickles through a tangled thicket of fibers and synapses, there is a mixing up of messages, and the scrambled messages are delivered indiscriminately to wide cortical areas. In short, they are messages no longer. They serve, instead, to tone up the cortex, with a background sup-

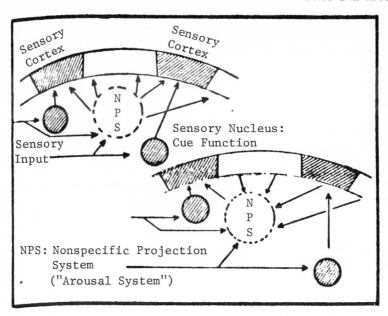

Figure 8.1

porting action that is completely necessary if the messages proper are to have their effect. Without the arousal system, the sensory impulses by the direct route reach the sensory cortex, but go no farther; the rest of the cortex is unaffected, and thus learned stimulus-response relations are lost. The waking center, which has long been known, is one part of this larger system; any extensive damage to it leaves a permanently inert, comatose animal.

Remember that in all this I am talking conceptual nervous system: making a working simplification, and abstracting for psychological purposes; and all these statements may need qualification, especially since research in this area is moving rapidly. There is reason to think, for example, that the arousal system may not be homogeneous, but may consist of a number of subsystems with distinctive functions (38). Olds and Milner's (37) study, reporting "reward" by direct intracranial stimulation, is not easy to fit into the notion of a single, homogeneous system. Sharpless' (40) results also raise doubt on this point, and it may reasonably be anticipated that arousal will eventually be found to vary qualitatively as well as quantitatively. But in general terms, psychologically, we can now distinguish two quite different effects of a sensory event. One is the *cue function,* guiding behavior; the other, less obvious but no less important, is the *arousal* or *vigilance function.* Without a foundation of arousal, the cue function cannot exist.

And now I propose to you that, whatever you wish to call it, arousal in this sense is synonymous with a general drive state, and the conception of drive therefore assumes anatomical and physiological identity. Let me remind you of what we discussed earlier: the drive is an energizer, but not a guide; an engine but not a steering gear. These are precisely the specifications of activity in the arousal system. Also, learning is dependent on drive, according to drive theory, and this too is applicable in general terms—no arousal, no learning; and efficient learning is possible only in the waking, alert, responsive animal, in which the level of arousal is high.

Thus I find myself obliged to reverse my earlier views and accept the drive conception, not merely on physiological grounds but also on the grounds of some of our current psychological studies. The conception is somewhat modified, but the modifications may not be entirely unacceptable to others.

Consider the relation of the effectiveness of cue function, actual or potential, to the level of arousal (Fig. 8.2). Physiologically, we may assume that cortical synaptic function is facilitated by the diffuse bombardment of the arousal system. When this bombardment is at a low level an increase will tend to strengthen or maintain the concurrent cortical activity; when arousal or drive is at a low level, that is, a response that produces increased stimulation and greater arousal will tend to be repeated. This is represented by the rising curve at the left. But when arousal is at a high level, as at the right, the greater bombardment may interfere with the delicate adjustments involved in cue function, perhaps by facilitating irrelevant responses (a high $D$ arouses conflicting $_sH_R$'s?).

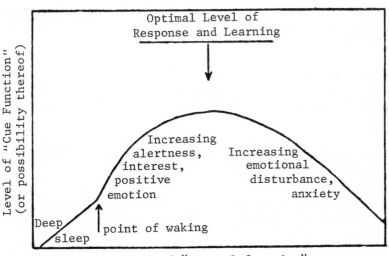

Figure 8.2

Thus there will be an optimal level of arousal for effective behavior, as Schlosberg (39) has suggested. Set aside such physiologizing completely, and we have a significant behavioral conception left, namely, that the same stimulation in mild degree may attract (by prolonging the pattern of response that leads to this stimulation) and in strong degree repel (by disrupting the pattern and facilitating conflicting or alternative responses).

The significance of this relation is in a phenomenon of the greatest importance for understanding motivation in higher animals. This is the *positive attraction of risk taking,* or mild fear, *and of problem solving,* or mild frustration, which was referred to earlier. Whiting and Mowrer (49) and Berlyne (4) have noted a relation between fear and curiosity—that is, a tendency to seek stimulation from fear-provoking objects, though at a safe distance. Woodworth (50) and Valentine (48) reported this in children, and Woodworth and Marquis (51) have recently emphasized again its importance in adults. There is no doubt that it exists. There is no doubt, either, that problem-solving situations have some attraction for the rat, more for Harlow's (16) monkeys, and far more for man. When you stop to think of it, it is nothing short of extraordinary what trouble people will go to in order to get into more trouble at the bridge table, or on the golf course; and the fascination of the murder story, or thriller, and the newspaper accounts of real-life adventure or tragedy, is no less extraordinary. This taste for excitement *must* not be forgotten when we are dealing with human motivation. It appears that, up to a certain point, threat and puzzle have positive motivating value, beyond that point negative value.

I know this leaves problems. It is not *any* mild threat, *any* form of problem, that is rewarding; we still have to work out the rules for this formulation. Also, I do not mean that there are not secondary rewards of social prestige for risk taking and problem solving—or even primary reward when such behavior is part of lovemaking. But the animal data show that it is not always a matter of extrinsic reward; risk and puzzle can be attractive in themselves, especially for higher animals such as man. If we can accept this, it will no longer be necessary to work out tortuous and improbable ways to explain why human beings work for money, why school children should learn without pain, why a human being in isolation should dislike doing nothing.

One other point before leaving Fig. 8.2: the low level of the curve to the right. You may be skeptical about such an extreme loss of adaptation, or disturbance of cue function and S-R relations, with high levels of arousal. Emotion is persistently regarded as energizing and organizing (which it certainly is at the lower end of the scale, up to the optimal level). But the "paralysis of terror" and related states do occur. As Brown and Jacobs (8, p. 753) have noted, "the presence of fear may act as an energizer . . . and yet lead in certain instances to an increase in immobility." Twice in the past eight months, while this address was being prepared, the Montreal newspapers reported the behavior of a human being who, suddenly finding himself in extreme danger but with time to escape, simply made no move whatever. One of the two was killed; the other was not, but only because a truck driver chose to wreck his truck and another car instead. Again, it is reported by Marshall (27), in a book that every student of human motivation should read carefully, that in the emotional pressure of battle no more than 15 to 25 percent of men under attack even fire their rifles, let alone use them efficiently.

Tyhurst's (47) very significant study of behavior in emergency and disaster situations further documents the point. The adult who is told that his apartment house is on fire, or who is threatened by a flash flood, may or may not respond intelligently. In various situations, 12 to 25 per cent did so; an equal number show "states of confusion, paralyzing anxiety, inability to move out of bed, 'hysterical' crying or screaming, and so on." Three-quarters or more show a clear impairment of intelligent behavior, often with aimless and irrelevant movements, rather than (as one might expect) panic reactions. There seems no doubt: the curve at the right must come down to a low level.

Now back to our main problem: If we tentatively identify a general state of drive with degree of arousal, where does this leave hunger, pain, and sex drives? These may still be anatomically separable, as Stellar (45) has argued, but we might consider instead the possibility that there is just one general drive state that can be aroused in different ways. Stellar's argument does not seem fully convincing. There are certainly regions in the hypothalamus that control eating, for example; but is this a *motivating* mechanism? The very essence of such a conception is that the mechanism in question should energize *other* mechanisms, and Miller, Bailey, and Stevenson (31) have shown that the opposite is true.

But this issue should not be pressed too far, with our present knowledge. I have tried to avoid dogmatism in this presentation in the hope that we might try, for once, to see what we have in common in our views on motivation. One virtue of identifying arousal with drive is that it relates differing views (as well as bringing into the focus of attention data that may otherwise be neglected). The important thing is a clear distinction between cue function and arousal function, and the fact that at low levels an increase of drive intensity may be rewarding, whereas at high levels it is a decrease that rewards. Given this point of view and our assumptions about arousal mechanisms, we see that what Harlow has emphasized is the exteroceptively aroused, but still low-level, drive, with cue function of course directly provided for. In the concept of anxiety, Spence and Brown emphasize the higher-level drive state, especially where there is no guiding cue function that would enable the animal to escape threat. The feedback from cortical functioning makes intelligible

Mower's (35) equating anxiety aroused by threat of pain, and anxiety aroused in some way by cognitive processes related to ideas of the self. Solomon and Wynne's (44) results with sympathectomy are also relevant, since we must not neglect the arousal effects of interoceptor activity; and so is clinical anxiety due to metabolic and nutritional disorders, as well as that due to some conflict of cognitive processes.

Obviously these are not explanations that are being discussed, but possible lines of future research; and there is one problem in particular that I would urge should not be forgotten. This is the cortical feedback to the arousal system, in physiological terms: or in psychological terms, the *immediate drive value of cognitive processes,* without intermediary. This is psychologically demonstrable, and *has* been demonstrated repeatedly.

Anyone who is going to talk about acquired drives, or secondary motivation, should first read an old paper by Valentine (48). He showed that with a young child you can easily condition fear of a caterpillar or a furry animal, but cannot condition fear of opera glasses, or a bottle; in other words, the fear of some objects, that seems to be learned, was there, latent, all the time. Miller (29) has noted this possibility but he does not seem to have regarded it very seriously, though he cited a confirmatory experiment by Bregman; for in the same passage he suggests that my own results with chimpanzee fears of certain objects, including strange people, may be dealt with by generalization. But this simply will not do, as Riesen and I noted (21). If you try to work this out, for the infant who is terrified on *first* contact with a stranger, an infant who has never shown such terror before, and who has always responded with eager affection to the only human beings he has made contact with up to this moment, you will find that this is a purely verbal solution.

Furthermore, as Valentine observed, you cannot postulate that the cause of such fear is simply the strange event, the thing that has never occurred before. For the chimpanzee reared in darkness, the first sight of a human being is of course a strange event, by definition; but fear of strangers does not occur until later, until the chimpanzee has had an opportunity to learn to recognize a few persons. The fear is not "innate" but depends on some sort of cognitive or cortical conflict of learned responses. This is clearest when the baby chimpanzee, who knows and welcomes attendant A and attendant B, is terrified when he sees A wearing B's coat. The role of learning is inescapable in such a case.

The cognitive and learning element may be forgotten in other motivations, too. Even in the food drive, some sort of learning is fundamentally important: Ghent (15) has shown this, Sheffield and Campbell (41) seem in agreement, and so does the work of Miller and his associates (3, 32, 30) on the greater reinforcement value of food by mouth, compared to food by stomach tube. Beach (1) has shown the cortical-and-learning element in sex behavior. Melzack (28) has demonstrated recently that even pain responses involve learning. In Harlow's (*16*) results, of course, and Montgomery's (*33*), the cognitive element is obvious.

These cortical or cognitive components in motivation are clearest when we compare the behavior of higher and lower species. Application of a *genuine* comparative method is essential, in the field of motivation as well as of intellectual functions (*22*). Most disagreements between us have related to so-called "higher" motivations. But the evidence I have discussed today need not be handled in such a way as to maintain the illusion of a complete separation between our various approaches to the problem. It *is* an illusion, I am convinced; we still have many points of disagreement as to relative emphasis, and as to which of several alternative lines to explore first, but this does not imply fundamental and final opposition. As theorists, we have been steadily coming together in respect of ideational (or representative, or mediating, or cognitive) processes; I believe that the same thing can happen, and is happening, in the field of motivation.

## REFERENCES

1. Beach, F. A.   The neural basis at innate behavior. III. Comparison of learning ability and instinctive behavior in the rat. *J. comp. Psychol.*, 1939, *28*, 225–262.
2. Bergmann, G.   Theoretical psychology. *Annu. Rev. Psychol.*, 1953, *4*, 435–458.
3. Berkun, M. M., Kessen, Marion L., & Miller, N. E.   Hunger-reducing effects of food by stomach fistula versus food by mouth measured by a consummatory response. *J. comp. physiol. Psychol.*, 1952, *45*, 550–554.
4. Berlyne, D. E.   Novelty and curiosity as determinants of exploratory behavior. *Brit. J. Psychol.*, 1950, *41*, 68–80.
5. Bexton, W. H., Heron, W., & Scott, T. H.   Effects of decreased variation in the sensory environment. *Canad. J. Psychol.*, 1954, *8*, 70–76.
6. Brink, F.   Excitation and conduction in the neuron. In S. S. Stevens (Ed.), *Handbook of experimental psychology.* New York: Wiley, 1951. Pp. 50–93.
7. Brown, J. S.   Problems presented by the concept of acquired drives. In *Current theory and research in motivation: a symposium.* Lincoln: Univer. of Nebraska Press, 1953. Pp. 1–21.
8. Brown, J. S., & Jacobs, A.   The role of fear in the motivation and acquisition of responses. *J. exp. Psychol.*, 1949, *39*, 747–759.
9. Burns, B. D.   The mechanism of afterbursts in cerebral cortex. *J. Physiol.*, 1955, *127*, 168–188.
10. Butler, R. A.   Discrimination learning by rhesus monkeys to visual-exploration motivation. *J. comp. physiol. Psychol.*, 1953, *46*, 95–98.
11. Carper, J. W., & Polliard, F. A.   Comparsion of the intake of glucose and saccharin solutions under conditions of caloric need. *Amer. J. Psychol.*, 1953, *66*, 479–482.

12. Clare, M. H., & Bishop, G. H.   Properties of dendrites; apical dendrites of the cat cortex. *EEG clin. Neurophysiol.*, 1955, *7*, 85–98.
13. Duffy, Elizabeth.   An explanation of "emotional" phenomena without the use of the concept "emotion." *J. gen. Psychol.*, 1941, *25*, 283–293.
14. Eccles, J. C.   *The neurophysiological basis of mind.* London: Oxford Univer. Press, 1953.
15. Ghent, Lila.   The relation of experience to the development of hunger. *Canad. J. Psychol.*, 1951, *5*, 77–81.
16. Harlow, H. F.   Mice, monkeys, men, and motives. *Psychol. Rev.*, 1953, *60*, 23–32.
17. Harlow, H. F., Harlow, Margaret K., & Meyer, D. R.   Learning motivated by a manipulation drive. *J. exp. Psychol.*, 1950, *40*, 228–234.
18. Hebb, D. O.   Elementary school methods. *Teach. Mag.* (Montreal), 1930, *12*, 23–26.
19. Hebb, D. O.   *Organization of behavior.* New York: Wiley, 1949.
20. Hebb, D. O.   On human thought. *Canad. J. Psychol.*, 1953, *7*, 99–110.
21. Hebb, D. O., & Riesen, A. H.   The genesis of irrational fears. *Bull. Canad. Psychol. Ass.*, 1943, *3*, 49–50.
22. Hebb, D. O., & Thompson, W. R.   The social significance of animal studies. In G. Lindzey (Ed.), *Handbook of social psychology.* Cambridge, Mass.: Addison-Wesley, 1954. Pp. 532–561.
23. Li, Choh-Luh, & Jasper, H.   Microelectrode studies of the cerebral cortex in the cat. *J. Physiol.*, 1953, *121*, 117–140.
24. Lindsley, D. B.   Emotion. In S. S. Stevens (Ed.), *Handbook of experimental psychology.* New York: Wiley, 1951. Pp. 473–516.
25. Lloyd, D. P. C.   A direct central inhibitory action of dromically conducted impulses. *J. Neurophysiol.*, 1941, *4*, 184–190.
26. MacCorquodale, K., & Meehl, P. E.   A distinction between hypothetical constructs and intervening variables. *Psychol. Rev.*, 1948, *55*, 95–107.
27. Marshall, S. L. A.   *Men against fire.* New York: Morrow, 1947.
28. Melzack, R.   The effects of early experience on the emotional responses to pain. Unpublished doctor's dissertation, McGill Univer., 1954.
29. Miller, N. E.   Learnable drives and rewards. In S. S. Stevens (Ed.), *Handbook of experimental psychology.* New York: Wiley, 1951. Pp. 435–472.
30. Miller, N. E.   Some studies of drive and drive reduction. Paper read at Amer. Psychol. Ass., Cleveland, September, 1953.
31. Miller, N. E., Bailey, C. J., & Stevenson, J. A. F.   Decreased "hunger" but increased food intake from hypothalamic lesions. *Science*, 1950, *112*, 256–259.
32. Miller, N. E., & Kessen, Marion L.   Reward effects of food via stomach fistula compared with those via mouth. *J. comp. physiol. Psychol.*, 1952, *45*, 555–564.
33. Montgomery, K. C.   The effect of activity deprivation upon exploratory behavior. *J. comp. physiol. Psychol.*, 1953, *46*, 438–441.
34. Moruzzi, G., & Magoun, H. W.   Brain stem reticular formation and activation of the EEG. *EEG clin. Neurophysiol.*, 1949, *1*, 455–473.
35. Mowrer, O. H.   Motivation. *Annu. Rev. Psychol.*, 1952, *3*, 419–438.

36. Nissen, H. W. Instinct as seen by a psychologist. *Psychol. Rev.*, 1953, *60*, 291–294.
37. Olds, J., & Milner, P. Positive reinforcement produced by electrical stimulation of septal area and other regions of rat brain. *J. comp. physiol. Psychol.*, 1954, *47*, 419–427.
38. Olszewski, J. The cytoarchitecture of the human reticular formation. In E. D. Adrian, F. Bremer, and H. H. Jasper (Eds.), *Brain mechanisms and consciousness.* Oxford: Blackwell, 1954.
39. Schlosberg, H. Three dimensions of emotion. *Psychol. Rev.*, 1954, *61*, 81–88.
40. Sharpless, S. K. Role of the reticular formation in habituation. Unpublished doctor's dissertation, McGill Univer., 1954.
41. Sheffield, F. D., & Campbell, B. A. The role of experience in the "spontaneous" activity of hungry rats. *J. comp. physiol. Psychol.*, 1954, *47*, 97–100.
42. Sheffield, F. D., & Roby, T. B. Reward value of a non-nutritive sweet taste. *J. comp. physiol. Psychol.*, 1950, *43*, 471–481.
43. Sheffield, F. D., Wulff, J. J., and Backer, R. Reward value of copulation without sex drive reduction. *J. comp. physiol. Psychol.*, 1951, *44*, 3–8.
44. Solomon, R. L., & Wynne, L. C. Avoidance conditioning in normal dogs and in dogs deprived of normal autonomic functioning. *Amer. Psychologist,* 1950, *5*, 264. (Abstract)
45. Stellar, E. The physiology of motivation. *Psychol. Rev.*, 1954, *61*, 5–22.
46. Thompson, W. R., & Solomon, L. M. Spontaneous pattern discrimination in the rat. *J. comp. physiol. Psychol.*, 1954, *47*, 104–107.
47. Tyhurst, J. S. Individual reactions to community disaster: the natural history of psychiatric phenomena. *Amer. J. Psychiat.*, 1951, *107*, 764–769.
48. Valentine, C. W. The innate bases of fear. *J. genet. Psychol.*, 1930, *37*, 394–419.
49. Whiting, J. W. M., & Mowrer, O. H. Habit progression and regression—a laboratory study of some factors relevant to human socialization. *J. comp. Psychol.*, 1943, *36*, 229–253.
50. Woodworth, R. S. *Psychology.* New York: Holt, 1921.
51. Woodworth, R. S., & Marquis, D. G. *Psychology.* (5th Ed.) New York: Holt, 1947.

# III
# Purpose, or Goal-Directedness, in Behavior

No one doubts that some, if not all, behavior can be most efficiently described by reference to the end toward which it is directed. Purposeful behavior is seen as characteristic of man and is often imputed to other species as well. Psychologists have most typically divided into two camps on the subject of purpose. On the one hand, there are those, like many instinct theorists, who assume purpose to be so intrinsic to all behavior that it must be accepted as a given, a postulate which in itself demands no explanation. On the other hand, there are those, like the drive theorists, who doubt that purpose can be dealt with in scientific terms at all. They tend to deny that behavior may be purposeful and to see apparent examples of purposiveness as mere artifacts of blind adaptive mechanisms. A generation of psychologists, imbued with the spirit of drive theory, seemed to repress the very problem of direction in behavior, not only in their claim that activation was the sole function of motivation but in their refusal to deal with the issue seriously under any other heading. Many were not aware that purpose had ever been a problem for psychologists.

There is no longer any necessity to avoid the topic of purpose on the grounds that it is an unscientific issue. Nor is there any need to accept purpose as a first and inexplicable principle. From the field of engineering, in the application of servo-mechanisms or feedback devices, has come plain evidence that mechano-electrical systems far simpler than living organisms can be constructed in such a manner as to seek defined end-states and in other ways show purposeful behavior. The new field of cybernetics has grown up to explore the analogies between such systems and the neural systems in human and other species. It is simply not correct to maintain in the face of these developments that purpose necessarily implies some nonscientific metaphysics or that it is in principle not explainable. Some recent treatments of purpose have been built upon the possible similarities between men and computers, and to some this has seemed a wholly new endeavor for psychologists. The articles of this section, however, show that there exists a continuity of thought from the early years of the development of psychology even for this topic. Though it was for a long time little heeded, it is a rich tradition deserving more attention than it has had. Here it will be sampled in two parts. The first group of articles has to do with the analysis of purpose and deals with the question, How is it that behavior may come to be describable with respect to an anticipated end? William James provides a convenient starting point with his classic chapter on the will. Although he was unable to divorce himself entirely from the concept of a "free" will, his discussion of ideo-motor acts provided a framework for a deterministic scheme which has undergone successive modification for over three-quarters of a century. E. B. Holt respected both Freud and Pavlov and tried to make even clearer than James had done the manner in which purposeful behavior could emerge from simpler patterns. His effort to reconcile Pavlovian reflexes with the Freudian wish stands as an intellectual achievement of the first order. Perry, and then Tolman, continue to confront the problem of defining and accounting for purpose, each presenting positions that look more modern today than they would have a few years ago. The final papers of the first group represent the classic efforts of one drive theorist who did not repress the problem to construct an account of purpose construed as a habit mechanism. Hull in these articles formulated such significant concepts as the pure stimulus act, the drive stimulus, and the fractional anticipatory goal response. He recognized his continuity with James and foreshadowed problems which are still before us.

The second group of articles in this section relates to the dynamics of purpose. Granted the possibility of purposive behavior, how do goal orientations influence the functioning of the individual? Brentano and Wundt may be taken as eponyms for the two psychological camps respecting purpose which were referred to above. Wundt saw the organism as relatively passive. Brentano viewed it as intrinsically active. For the latter, intentionality was a defining characteristic of psychic events. Brentano established the school of "act" psychology and is a key ancestor to much of the phenomenological psychology of today. Titchener provides us here with one of the clearest English language reviews of his position and contrasts it with that of Wundt. Watt was a member of the Wuerzburg School who showed how act-like determining tendencies could influence the course of thought, and Lewin built a psychology on the concept of motivation as a directed force. From him and his followers came the early formulations of conflict, level of aspiration, and the dynamics of motivation as an influence upon recall, persistence, substitution, and resumption of tasks which a person may undertake. The more recent work of McClelland and, particularly, Atkinson may be seen as continuations of these themes.

# 9 • William James

## *Will*

The Darwinian implication of instincts in man led by a devious route to
the concept of drive and the study of the mechanisms of general arousal.
Fruitful as this avenue was, it seemed, for some time at least, to have had the
effect of diverting interest away from the classic problems of goal-directed behavior, or purpose. A completely nondirected energizer of behavior, such as
generalized drive, may help greatly in understanding variations in the intensity
of behavior, but the problems of the direction, or the qualitative character of
behavior, can rarely be solved by reference to Hull's "D." Some psychologists
have contended that the problem of direction in behavior is "nonmotivational"
by virtue of their definition of motivation as the energizing function. They have
suggested that any apparent goal orientation in behavior is merely a matter of
understanding the habit mechanisms involved. Even if this should be the case,
however, it is still a psychological problem to explain how habit mechanisms
do in fact have this effect, and when this problem is confronted, we find once
again that there is a problem of purpose.

The directional aspects of motivation were formerly dealt with under the
heading of "will," and one of the most lucid writers on this topic was William
James. A large portion of his chapter on the will is reproduced here. In it can
be seen not only his engaging writing style, which attracted many young
scholars to the new field of psychology, but also his ability to analyze the difficult problem of will and purpose with an insight very untypical of his, or any
other, day. James' treatment of ideo-motor action implies a mechanistic way for
ideas of goals to result in purposive action. Worth noting, though, is his inability to push such a deterministic account to its logical end. In James' final
analysis, there is still room for some play of free, undetermined will. Nevertheless, he provided a ground from which more thoroughgoing analyses of
purpose were later to spring.

*Desire, wish, will,* are states of mind which everyone knows, and which
no definition can make plainer. We desire to feel, to have, to do, all sorts

of things which at the moment are not felt, had, or done. If with the desire there goes a sense that attainment is not possible, we simply *wish;* but if we believe that the end is in our power, we *will* that the desired feeling, having, or doing shall be real; and real it presently becomes, either immediately upon the willing or after certain preliminaries have been fulfilled.

The only ends which follow *immediately* upon our willing seem to be movements of our own bodies. Whatever *feelings* and *havings* we may will to get, come in as results of preliminary movements which we make for the purpose. This fact is too familiar to need illustration; so that we may start with the proposition that the only *direct* outward effects of our will are bodily movements. The mechanism of production of these voluntary movements is what befalls us to study now. The subject involves a good many separate points which it is difficult to arrange in any continuous logical order. I will treat of them successively in the mere order of convenience; trusting that at the end the reader will gain a clear and connected view.

The movements we have studied hitherto have been automatic and reflex, and (on the first occasion of their performance, at any rate) unforeseen by the agent. The movements to the study of which we now address ourselves, being desired and intended beforehand, are of course done with full prevision of what they are to be. It follows from this that *voluntary movements must be secondary, not primary functions of our organism.* This is the first point to understand in the psychology of Volition. Reflex, instinctive, and emotional movements are all primary performances. The nerve-centres are so organized that certain stimuli pull the trigger of certain explosive parts; and a creature going through one of these explosions for the first time undergoes an entirely novel experience. The other day I was standing at a railroad station with a little child, when an express-train went thundering by. The child, who was near the edge of the platform, started, winked, had his breathing convulsed, turned pale, burst out crying, and ran frantically towards me and hid his face. I have no doubt that this youngster was almost as much astonished by his own behavior as he was by the train, and more than I was, who stood by. Of course if such a reaction has many times occurred we learn what to expect of ourselves, and can then foresee our conduct, even though it remains as involuntary and uncontrollable as it was before. But if, in voluntary action properly so-called, the act must be foreseen, it follows that no creature not endowed with divinatory power can perform an act voluntarily for the first time. Well, we are no more endowed with prophetic vision of what movements lie in our power, than we are endowed with prophetic vision of what sensations we are capable of receiving. As we must wait for the sensations to be given us, so we must wait for the movements to be performed involuntarily,[1] before we can frame ideas of what either of these things are. We learn all our possibilities by the way of experience. When a particular movement, having once occurred in a random, reflex, or involuntary way, has left an image of itself in the memory, then the movement can be desired again, proposed as an end, and deliberately willed. But it is impossible to see how it could be willed before.

*A supply of ideas of the various movements that are possible left in the memory by experiences of their involuntary performance is thus the first prerequisite of the voluntary life.*

Now the same movement involuntarily performed may leave many different kinds of ideas of itself in the memory. If performed by another person, we of course *see* it, or we *feel* it if the moving part strikes another part of our own body. Similarly we have an auditory image of its effects if it produces sounds, as for example when it is one of the movements made in vocalization, or in playing on a musical instrument. All these *remote* effects of the movement, as we may call them, are also produced by movements which we ourselves perform; and they leave innumerable ideas in our mind by which we distinguish each movement from the rest. It *looks* distinct; it *feels* distinct to some distant part of the body which it strikes; or it *sounds* distinct. These remote effects would then, rigorously speaking, suffice to furnish the mind with the supply of ideas required.

But in addition to these impressions upon remote organs of sense, we have, whenever we perform a movement ourselves, another set of impressions, those, namely, which come up from the parts that are actually moved. These *kinæsthetic* impressions, as Dr. Bastian has called them, are so many *resident* effects of the motion. Not only are our muscles supplied with afferent as well as with efferent nerves, but the tendons, the ligaments, the articular surfaces, and the skin about the joints are all sensitive, and, being stretched and squeezed in ways characteristic of each particular movement, give us as many distinctive feelings as there are movements possible to perform.

.    .    .    .    .    .    .    .    .    .    .

If the ideas by which we discriminate between one movement and another, at the instant of deciding in our mind which one we shall perform, are always of sensorial origin, then the question arises, "Of which sensorial order need they be?" It will be remembered that we distinguished two orders of kinæsthetic impression, the *remote* ones, made by the movement on the eye or ear or distant skin, etc., and the *resident* ones, made on the moving parts themselves, muscles, joints, etc. Now do resident images, exclusively, form what I have called the mental cue, or will remote ones equally suffice?

*There can be no doubt whatever that the mental cue may be either*

---

[1] I am abstracting at present for simplicity's sake, and so as to keep to the elements of the matter, from the learning of acts by seeing others do them.

*an image of the resident or of the remote kind.* Although, at the outset of our learning a movement, it would seem that the resident feelings must come strongly before consciousness (cf. pp. 151–2), later this need not be the case. The rule, in fact, would seem to be that they tend to lapse more and more from consciousness, and that the more practised we become in a movement, the more 'remote' do the ideas become which form its mental cue. What we are *interested* in is what sticks in our consciousness; everything else we get rid of as quickly as we can. Our resident feelings of movement have no substantive interest for us at all, as a rule. What interest us are the ends which the movement is to attain. Such an end is generally an outer impression on the eye or ear, or sometimes on the skin, nose, or palate. Now let the idea of the end associate itself definitely with the right motor innervation, and the thought of the innervation's *resident* effects will become as great an encumbrance as we formerly concluded that the feeling of the innervation itself would be. The mind does not need it; the end alone is enough.

The idea of the end, then, tends more and more to make itself all-sufficient. Or, at any rate, if the kinæsthetic ideas are called up at all, they are so swamped in the vivid kinæsthetic feelings by which they are immediately overtaken that we have no time to be aware of their separate existence. As I write, I have no anticipation, as a thing distinct from any sensation, of either the look or the digital feel of the letters which flow from my pen. The words chime on my mental *ear,* as it were, before I write them, but not on my mental eye or hand. This comes from the rapidity with which often-repeated movements follow on their mental cue. An end consented to as soon as conceived innervates directly the centre of the first movement of the chain which leads to its accomplishment, and then the whole chain rattles off *quasi*-reflexly, as was described previously.

The reader will certainly recognize this to be true in all fluent and unhesitating voluntary acts. The only special fiat there is at the outset of the performance. A man says to himself, "I must change my shirt," and involuntarily he has taken off his coat, and his fingers are at work in their accustomed manner on his waistcoat-buttons, etc.; or we say, "I must go downstairs," and ere we know it we have risen, walked, and turned the handle of the door;—all through the idea of an end coupled with a series of guiding sensations which successively arise. It would seem indeed that we fail of accuracy and certainty in our attainment of the end whenever we are preoccupied with much ideal consciousness of the means. We walk a beam the better the less we think of the position of our feet upon it. We pitch or catch, we shoot or chop the better the less tactile and muscular (the less resident), and the more exclusively optical, (the more remote) our consciousness is. Keep your *eye* on the place aimed at, and your hand will fetch it; think of your hand, and you will very likely miss your aim. Dr. Southard found that he could touch a spot with a pencil-point more accurately with a visual than with a tactile mental cue. In the former case he looked at a small object and closed his eyes before trying to touch it. In the latter case he *placed* it with closed eyes, and then after removing his hand tried to touch it again. The average error with touch (when the results were most favorable) was 17.13 mm. With sight it was only 12.37 mm.[2]—All these are plain results of introspection and observation. By what neural machinery they are made possible we need not, at this present stage, inquire.

Earlier we saw how enormously individuals differ in respect to their mental imagery. In the type of imagination called *tactile* by the French authors, it is probable that the kinæsthetic ideas are more prominent than in my account. We must not expect too great a uniformity in individual accounts, nor wrangle overmuch as to which one 'truly' represents the process.[3]

[2] Bowditch and Southard in *Journal of Physiology*, vol. III. No. 3. It was found in these experiments that the maximum of accuracy was reached when two seconds of time elapsed between locating the object by eye or hand and starting to touch it. When the mark was located with one hand, and the other hand had to touch it, the error was considerably greater than when the same hand both located and touched it.

[3] The same caution must be shown in discussing pathological cases. There are remarkable discrepancies in the effects of peripheral anæsthesia upon the voluntary power. Such cases as I quoted in the text are by no means the only type. In those cases the patients could move their limbs accurately when the eyes were open, and inaccurately when they were shut. In other cases, however, the anæsthetic patients *cannot move their limbs at all* when the eyes are shut. (For reports of two such cases see Bastian in 'Brain,' Binet in *Rev. Philos.*, xxv. 478.) M. Binet explains these (hysterical) cases as requiring the 'dynamogenic' stimulus of light. They *might*, however, be cases of such congenitally defective optical imagination that the 'mental cue' was normally 'tactile;' and that when this tactile cue failed through functional inertness of the kinæsthetic centres, the only optical cue strong enough to determine the discharge had to be an actual *sensation* of the eye.—There is still a third class of cases in which the limbs have lost all sensibility, even for movements passively imprinted, but in which voluntary movements can be accurately executed even when the eyes are closed. MM. Binet and Féré have reported some of these interesting cases, which are found amongst the hysterical hemianæsthetics. They can, for example, write accurately at will, although their eyes are closed and they have no feeling of the writing taking place, and many of them do not know when it begins or stops. Asked to write repeatedly the letter *a*, and then say how many times they have written it, some are able to assign the number and some are not. Some of them admit that they are guided by visual imagination of what is being done. Cf. *Archives de Physiologie*, Oct. 1887, pp. 363–5. Now it would seem at first sight that feelings of outgoing innervation must exist in these cases and be kept account of. There are no other guiding impressions, either immediate or remote, of which the patient is conscious; and unless feelings of innervation be there, the writing would seem miraculous. But if such feelings are present in these cases, and suffice to direct accurately the succession of movements, why do they not suffice in those other anæsthetic cases in which movement becomes disorderly when the eyes are closed. *Innervation* is there, or there would be no movement; why is the *feeling* of the innervation gone? The truth seems to be, as M. Binet supposes (*Rev. Philos*, xxiii. p. 479), that these cases are not arguments for the feeling of innervation. They are pathological curiosities; and the patients are not really anæsthetic, but are victims of that curious dissociation or splitting-off of one part of their consciousness from the rest which we are just begin to understand, thanks to Messrs. Janet, Binet, and Gurney, and in which the split-off part (in this case the kinæsthetic sensations) may nevertheless remain to produce its usual effects.

I trust that I have now made clear what that 'idea of a movement' is which must precede it in order that it be voluntary. It is not the thought of the innervation which the movement requires. It is the anticipation of the movement's sensible effects, resident or remote, and sometimes very remote indeed. Such anticipations, to say the least, determine *what* our movements shall be. I have spoken all along as if they also might determine *that* they shall be. This, no doubt, has disconcerted many readers, for it certainly seems as if a special fiat, or consent to the movement were required in addition to the mere conception of it, in many cases of volition; and this fiat I have altogether left out of my account. This leads us to the next point in the psychology of the Will. It can be the more easily treated now that we have got rid of so much tedious preliminary matter.

### IDEO-MOTOR ACTION

The question is this: *Is the bare idea of a movement's sensible effects its sufficient mental cue, or must there be an additional mental antecedent, in the shape of a fiat, decision, consent, volitional mandate, or other synonymous phenomenon of consciousness, before the movement can follow?*

I answer: Sometimes the bare idea is sufficient, but sometimes an additional conscious element, in the shape of a fiat, mandate, or express consent, has to intervene and precede the movement. The cases without a fiat constitute the more fundamental, because the more simple, variety. The others involve a special complication, which must be fully discussed at the proper time. For the present let us turn to *ideo-motor action*, as it has been termed, or the sequence of movement upon the mere thought of it, as the type of the process of volition.

Wherever movement follows *unhesitatingly and immediately* the notion of it in the mind, we have ideo-motor action. We are then aware of nothing between the conception and the execution. All sorts of neuromuscular processes come between, of course, but we know absolutely nothing of them. We think the act, and it is done; and that is all that introspection tells us of the matter. Dr. Carpenter, who first used, I believe, the name of ideo-motor action, placed it, if I mistake not, among the curiosities of our mental life. The truth is that it is no curiosity, but simply the normal process stripped of disguise. Whilst talking I become conscious of a pin on the floor, or of some dust on my sleeve. Without interrupting the conversation I brush away the dust or pick up the pin. I make no express resolve, but the mere perception of the object and the fleeting notion of the act seem of themselves to bring the latter about. Similarly, I sit at table after dinner and find myself from time to time taking nuts or raisins out of the dish and eating them. My dinner properly is over, and in the heat of the conversation I am hardly aware of what I do, but the perception of the fruit and the fleeting notion that I may eat it seem fatally to bring the act about. There is certainly no express fiat here; any more than there is in all those habitual goings and comings and rearrangements of ourselves which fill every hour of the day, and which incoming sensations instigate so immediately that it is often difficult to decide whether not to call them reflex rather than voluntary acts. We have seen earlier that the intermediary terms of an habitual series of acts leading to an end are apt to be of this *quasi*-automatic sort. As Lotze says:

> We see in writing or piano-playing a great number of very complicated movements following quickly one upon the other, the instigative representations of which remained scarcely a second in consciousness, certainly not long enough to awaken any other volition than the general one of resigning one's self without reserve to the passing over of representation into action. All the acts of our daily life happen in this wise: Our standing up, walking, talking, all this never demands a distinct impulse of the will, but is adequately brought about by the pure flux of thought.[4]

In all this the determining condition of the unhesitating and resistless sequence of the act seems to be *the absence of any conflicting notion in the mind.* Either there is nothing else at all in the mind, or what is there does not conflict. The hypnotic subject realizes the former condition. Ask him what he is thinking about, and ten to one he will reply 'nothing.' The consequence is that he both believes everything he is told, and performs every act that is suggested. The suggestion may be a vocal command, or it may be the performance before him of the movement required. Hypnotic subjects in certain conditions repeat whatever they hear you say, and imitate whatever they see you do. Dr. Féré says that certain waking persons of neurotic type, if one repeatedly close and open one's hand before their eyes, soon begin to have corresponding feelings in their own fingers, and presently begin irresistibly to execute the movements which they see. Under these conditions of 'preparation,' Dr. Féré found that his subjects could squeeze the hand-dynamometer much more strongly than when abruptly invited to do so. A few *passive* repetitions of a movement will enable many enfeebled patients to execute it actively with greater strength. These observations beautifully show how the mere

---

[4] *Medicinische Psychologie*, p. 293. In his admirably acute chapter on the Will this author has most explicitly maintained the position that what we call muscular exertion is an afferent and not an efferent feeling; "We must affirm universally that in the muscular feeling we are not sensible of the *force* on its way to produce an effect, but only of the *sufference* already produced in our movable organs, the muscles, after the force has, in a manner unobservable by us, exerted upon them its causality" (p. 311). How often the battles of psychology have to be fought over again, each time with heavier armies and bigger trains, though not always with such able generals!

quickening of kinæsthetic ideas is equivalent to a certain amount of tension towards discharge in the centres.[5]

We know what it is to get out of bed on a freezing morning in a room without a fire, and how the very vital principle within us protests against the ordeal. Probably most persons have lain on certain mornings for an hour at a time unable to brace themselves to the resolve. We think how late we shall be, how the duties of the day will suffer; we say, "I *must* get up, this is ignominious," etc.; but still the warm couch feels too delicious, the cold outside too cruel, and resolution faints away and postpones itself again and again just as it seemed on the verge of bursting the resistance and passing over into the decisive act. Now how do we *ever* get up under such circumstances? If I may generalize from my own experience, we more often than not get up without any struggle or decision at all. We suddenly find that we *have* got up. A fortunate lapse of consciousness occurs; we forget both the warmth and the cold; we fall into some revery connected with the day's life, in the course of which the idea flashes across us, "Hollo! I must lie here no longer"—an idea which at that lucky instant awakens no contradictory or paralyzing suggestions, and consequently produces immediately its appropriate motor effects. It was our acute consciousness of both the warmth and the cold during the period of struggle, which paralyzed our activity then and kept our idea of rising in the condition of *wish* and not of *will*. The moment these inhibitory ideas ceased, the original idea exerted its effects.

This case seems to me to contain in miniature form the data for an entire psychology of volition. It was in fact through meditating on the phenomenon in my own person that I first became convinced of the truth of the doctrine which these pages present, and which I need here illustrate by no farther examples.[6] The reason why that doctrine is not a self-evident truth is that we have so many ideas which *do not* result in action. But it will be seen that in every such case, without exception, that is because other ideas simultaneously present rob them of their impulsive power. But even here, and when a movement is inhibited from *completely* taking place by contrary ideas, it will *incipiently* take place. To quote Lotze once more:

The spectator accompanies the throwing of a billiard-ball, or the thrust of the swordsman, with slight movements of his arm; the untaught narrator tells his story with many gesticulations; the reader while absorbed in the perusal of a battle-scene feels a slight tension run through his muscular system, keeping time as it were with the actions he is reading of. These results become the more marked the more we are absorbed in thinking of the movements which

[5] Ch. Féré: *Sensation et Mouvement* (1887), chapter III.

[6] Professor A. Bain (*Senses and Intellect,* pp. 336–48) and Dr. W. B. Carpenter (*Mental Physiology,* chap. VI) give examples in abundance.

suggest them; they grow fainter exactly in proportion as a complex consciousness, under the dominion of a crowd of other representations, withstands the
passing over of mental contemplation into outward action.

The 'willing-game,' the exhibitions of so-called 'mind-reading,' or
more properly muscle-reading, which have lately grown so fashionable,
are based on this incipient obedience of muscular contraction to idea,
even when the deliberate intention is that no contraction shall occur.[7]

We may then lay it down for certain that *every representation of a
movement awakens in some degree the actual movement which is its
object; and awakens it in a maximum degree whenever it is not kept from
so doing by an antagonistic representation present simultaneously to the
mind.*

The express fiat, or act of mental consent to the movement, comes
in when the neutralization of the antagonistic and inhibitory idea is required. But that there is no express fiat needed when the conditions are
simple, the reader ought now to be convinced. Lest, however, he should
still share the common prejudice that voluntary action without 'exertion
of will-power' is Hamlet with the prince's part left out, I will make a few
farther remarks. The first point to start from in understanding voluntary
action, and the possible occurrence of it with no fiat or express resolve,
is the fact that consciousness is *in its very nature impulsive.*[8] We do not
have a sensation or a thought and then have to *add* something dynamic
to it to get a movement. Every pulse of feeling which we have is the
correlate of some neural activity that is already on its way to instigate a
movement. Our sensations and thoughts are but cross-sections, as it were,
of currents whose essential consequence is motion, and which no sooner
run in at one nerve than they run out again at another. The popular
notion that mere consciousness as such is not essentially a forerunner of
activity, that the latter must result from some superadded 'will-force,' is
a very natural inference from those special cases in which we think of an
act for an indefinite length of time without the action taking place. These

---

[7] For a full account, by an expert, of the 'willing-game,' see Mr. Stuart Cumber-
land's article: "A Thought-reader's Experiences in the Nineteenth century," xx. 867.
M. Gley has given a good example of ideo-motor action in the Bulletins de la Société
de Psychologie Physiologique for 1889. Tell a person to think intently of a certain
name, and saying that you will then force her to write it, let her hold a pencil, and
do you yourself hold her hand. She will then probably trace the name involuntarily,
believing that you are forcing her to do it.

[8] I abstract here from the fact that a certain *intensity* of the consciousness is required for its impulsiveness to be effective in a complete degree. There is an inertia
in the motor processes as in all other natural things. In certain individuals, and at
certain times (disease, fatigue), the inertia is unusually great, and we may then have
ideas of action which produce no visible act, but discharge themselves into merely
nascent dispositions to activity or into emotional expression. The inertia of the motor
parts here plays the same rôle as is elsewhere played by antagonistic ideas. We shall
consider this restrictive inertia later on, it obviously introduces no essential alteration
into the law which the text lays down.

cases, however, are not the norm; they are cases of inhibition by antagonistic thoughts. When the blocking is released we feel as if an inward spring were let loose, and this is the additional impulse of *fiat* upon which the act effectively succeeds. We shall study anon the blocking and its release. Our higher thought is full of it. But where there is no blocking, there is naturally no hiatus between the thought-process and the motor discharge. *Movement is the natural immediate effect of feeling, irrespective of what the quality of the feeling may be. It is so in reflex action, it is so in emotional expression, it is so in the voluntary life.* Ideo-motor action is thus no paradox, to be softened or explained away. It obeys the type of all conscious action, and from it one must start to explain action in which a special fiat is involved.

It may be remarked in passing, that the inhibition of a movement no more involves an express effort or command than its execution does. Either of them *may* require it. But in all simple and ordinary cases, just as the bare presence of one idea prompts a movement, so the bare presence of another idea will prevent its taking place. Try to feel as if you were crooking your finger, whilst keeping it straight. In a minute it will fairly tingle with the imaginary change of position; yet it will not sensibly move, because *its not really moving* is also a part of what you have in mind. Drop *this* idea, think of the movement purely and simply, with all breaks off; and, presto! it takes place with no effort at all.

A waking man's behavior is thus at all times the resultant of two opposing neural forces. With unimaginable fineness some currents among the cells and fibres of his brain are playing on his motor nerves, whilst other currents, as unimaginably fine, are playing on the first currents, damming or helping them, altering their direction or their speed. The upshot of it all is, that whilst the currents must always end by being drained off through *some* motor nerves, they are drained off sometimes through one set and sometimes through another; and sometimes they keep each other in equilibrium so long that a superficial observer may think they are not drained off at all. Such an observer must remember, however, that from the physiological point of view a gesture, an expression of the brow, or an expulsion of the breath are movements as much as an act of locomotion is. A king's breath slays as well as an assassin's blow; and the outpouring of those currents which the magic imponderable streaming of our ideas accompanies need not always be of an explosive or otherwise physically conspicuous kind.

.    .    .    .    .    .    .    .    .    .    .

## PLEASURE AND PAIN AS SPRINGS OF ACTION

Objects and thoughts of objects start our action, but the pleasures and pains which action brings modify its course and regulate it; and later the thoughts of the pleasures and the pains acquire themselves impulsive and inhibitive power. Not that the thought of a pleasure need be itself a pleasure, usually it is the reverse—*nessun maggior dolore*—as Dante says—and not that the thought of pain need be a pain, for, as Homer says, "griefs are often afterwards an entertainment." But as present pleasures are tremendous reinforcers, and present pains tremendous inhibitors of whatever action leads to them, so the thoughts of pleasures and pains take rank amongst the thoughts which have most impulsive and inhibitive power. The precise relation which these thoughts hold to other thoughts is thus a matter demanding some attention.

If a movement feels agreeable, we repeat and repeat it as long as the pleasure lasts. If it hurts us, our muscular contractions at the instant stop. So complete is the inhibition in this latter case that it is almost impossible for a man to cut or mutilate himself slowly and deliberately— his hand invincibly refusing to bring on the pain. And there are many pleasures which, when once we have begun to taste them, make it all but obligatory to keep up the activity to which they are due. So widespread and searching is this influence of pleasures and pains upon our movements that a premature philosophy has decided that these are our only spurs to action, and that wherever they seem to be absent, it is only because they are so far on among the 'remoter' images that prompt the action that they are overlooked.

This is a great mistake, however. Important as is the influence of pleasures and pains upon our movements, they are far from being our only stimuli. With the manifestations of instinct and emotional expression, for example, they have absolutely nothing to do. Who smiles for the pleasure of the smiling, or frowns for the pleasure of the frown? Who blushes to escape the discomfort of not blushing? Or who in anger, grief, or fear is actuated to the movements which he makes by the pleasures which they yield? In all these cases the movements are discharged fatally by the *vis a tergo* which the stimulus exerts upon a nervous system framed to respond in just that way. The objects of our rage, love, or terror, the occasions of our tears and smiles, whether they be present to our senses, or whether they be merely represented in idea, have this peculiar sort of impulsive power. The *impulsive quality* of mental states is an attribute behind which we cannot go. Some states of mind have more of it than others, some have it in this direction, and some in that. Feelings of pleasure and pain have it, and perceptions and imaginations of fact have it, but neither have it exclusively or peculiarly. It is of the essence of all consciousness (or of the neural process which underlies it) to instigate movement of some sort. That with one creature and object it should be of one sort, with others of another sort, is a problem for evolutionary history to explain. However the actual impulsions may have arisen, they must now be described as they exist; and those persons obey a curiously narrow teleological superstition who think themselves bound to interpret them in every instance as effects of the secret solicitancy of pleasure and repugnancy of pain.[9]

It might be that to *reflection* such a narrow teleology would justify itself, that pleasures and pains might seem the only *comprehensible and reasonable* motives for action, the only motives on which we *ought* to act. That is an *ethical* proposition, in favor of which a good deal may be said. But it is not a *psychological* proposition; and nothing follows from it as to the motives upon which as a matter of fact we *do* act. These motives are supplied by innumerable objects, which innervate our voluntary muscles

[9] The silliness of the old-fashioned pleasure-philosophy *saute aux yeux*. Take, for example, Prof. Bain's explanation of sociability and parental love by the pleasures of touch: "Touch is the fundamental and generic sense. . . . Even after the remaining senses are differentiated, the primary sense continues to be a leading susceptibility of the mind. The soft warm touch, if not a first-class influence, is at least an approach to that. The combined power of soft contact and warmth amounts to a considerable pitch of massive pleasure; while there may be subtle influences not reducible to these two heads, such as we term, from not knowing anything about them, magnetic or electric. The sort of thrill from taking a baby in arms is something beyond mere warm touch; and it may rise to the ecstatic height, in which case, however, there may be concurrent sensations and ideas. . . . In mere tender emotion not sexual, there is nothing but the sense of touch to gratify, unless we assume the occult magnetic influences. . . . In a word, our love pleasures begin and end in sensual contact. Touch is both the alpha and omega of affection. As the terminal and satisfying sensation, the *ne plus ultra*, it must be a pleasure of the highest degree. . . . Why should a more lively feeling grow up towards a fellow-being than towards a perennial fountain? [This 'should' is simply delicious from the more modern evolutionary point of view.] It must be that there is a source of pleasure in the companionship of other sentient creatures, over and above the help afforded by them in obtaining the necessaries of life. To account for this, I can suggest nothing but the primary and independent pleasure of the animal embrace." [Mind, this is said not of the sexual interest, but of 'Sociability at Large.'] "For this pleasure every creature is disposed to pay something, even when it is only fraternal. A certain amount of material benefit imparted is a condition of the full heartiness of a responding embrace, the complete fruition of this primitive joy. In the absence of those conditions the pleasure of giving . . . can scarcely be accounted for; we know full well that, without these helps, it would be a very meagre sentiment in beings like ourselves. . . . It seems to me that there must be at the [parental instinct's] foundation that intense pleasure in the embrace of the young which we find to characterize the parental feeling throughout. Such a plesaure once created would associate itself with the prevailing features and aspects of the young, and give to all of these their very great interest. For the sake of the plesaure, the parent discovers the necessity of nourishing the subject of it, and comes to regard the ministering function as a part or condition of the delight" (*Emotions and Will*, pp. 126, 127, 132, 133, 140). Prof. Bain does not explain why a satin cushion kept at about 98° F. would not on the whole give us the pleasure in question more cheaply than our friends and babies do. It is true that the cushion might lack the 'occult magnetic influences.' Most of us would say that neither a baby's nor a friend's skin would possess them, were not a tenderness already there. The youth who feels ecstasy shoot through him when by accident the silken palm or even the 'vesture's hem' of his idol touches him, would hardly feel it were he not hard hit by Cupid in advance. The love creates the ecstasy, not the ecstasy the love. And for the rest of us can it possibly be that all our social virtue springs from an appetite for the sensual pleasure of having our hand shaken, or being slapped on the back?

by a process as automatic as that by which they light a fever in our breasts. If the thought of pleasure can impel to action, surely other thoughts may. Experience only can decide which thoughts do. The chapters on Instinct and Emotion have shown us that their name is legion; and with this verdict we ought to remain contented, and not seek an illusory simplification at the cost of half the facts.

If in these our *first* acts pleasures and pains bear no part, as little do they bear in our last acts, or those artificially acquired performances which have become habitual. All the daily routine of life, our dressing and undressing, the coming and going from our work or carrying through of its various operations, is utterly without mental reference to pleasure and pain, except under rarely realized conditions. It is ideo-motor action. As I do not breathe for the pleasure of the breathing, but simply find that I *am* breathing, so I do not write for the pleasure of the writing, but simply because I have once begun, and being in a state of intellectual excitement which keeps venting itself in that way, find that I *am* writing still. Who will pretend that when he idly fingers his knife-handle at the table, it is for the sake of any pleasure which it gives him, or pain which he thereby avoids. We do all these things because at the moment we cannot help it; our nervous systems are so shaped that they overflow in just that way; and for many of our idle or purely 'nervous' and fidgety performances we can assign absolutely no *reason* at all.

Or what shall be said of a shy and unsociable man who receives point-blank an invitation to a small party? The thing is to him an abomination; but your presence exerts a compulsion on him, he can think of no excuse, and so says yes, cursing himself the while for what he does. He is unusually *sui compos* who does not every week of his life fall into some such blundering act as this. Such instances of *voluntas invita* show not only that our acts cannot all be conceived as effects of represented pleasure, but that they cannot even be classed as cases of represented *good*. The class 'goods' contains many more generally influential motives to action than the class 'pleasants.' Pleasures often attract us only because we deem them goods. Mr. Spencer, e.g., urges us to court pleasures for their influence upon health, which comes to us as a good.. But almost as little as under the form of pleasures do our acts invariably appear to us under the form of *goods*. All diseased impulses and pathological fixed ideas are instances to the contrary. It is the very badness of the act that gives it then its vertiginous fascination. Remove the prohibition, and the attraction stops. In my university days a student threw himself from an upper entry window of one of the college buildings and was nearly killed. Another student, a friend of my own, had to pass the window daily in coming and going from his room, and experienced a dreadful temptation to imitate the deed. Being a Catholic, he told his director, who said, 'All right! if you must, you must,' and added, 'Go ahead and do it,' thereby instantly quenching his desire. This director knew how to minister to a mind diseased. But we need not go to minds diseased for examples of the occasional tempting-power of simple badness and unpleasantness as such. Every one who has a wound or hurt anywhere, a sore tooth, e.g., will ever and anon press it just to bring out the pain. If we are near a new sort of stink, we must sniff it again just to verify once more how bad it is. This very day I have been repeating over and over to myself a verbal jingle whose mawkish silliness was the secret of its haunting power. I loathed yet could not banish it.

Believers in the pleasure-and-pain theory must thus, if they are candid, make large exceptions in the application of their creed. Action from 'fixed ideas' is accordingly a terrible stumbling-block to the candid Professor Bain. Ideas have in his psychology no impulsive but only a 'guiding' function, whilst

> The proper stimulus of the will, namely, some variety of pleasure and pain, is needed to give the impetus. . . . The intellectual link is not sufficient for causing the deed to rise at the beck of the idea (except in case of an 'idée fixe'); [but] should any *pleasure* spring up or be continued, by performing an action that we clearly conceive, the causation is then complete; both the directing and the moving powers are present.[10]

Pleasures and pains are for Professor Bain the '*genuine* impulses of the will.'[11]

> Without an antecedent of pleasurable or painful feeling—actual or ideal, primary or derivative—the will cannot be stimulated. Through all the disguises that wrap up what we call motives, something of one or other of these two grand conditions can be detected.[12]

Accordingly, where Professor Bain finds an exception to this rule, he refuses to call the phenomenon a 'genuinely voluntary impulse.' The exceptions, he admits, 'are those furnished by never-dying spontaneity, habits, and fixed ideas.'[13] Fixed ideas 'traverse the proper course of volition.'[14]

> *Disinterested impulses* are wholly distinct from the attainment of pleasure and the avoidance of pain. . . . The theory of disinterested action, in the only form that I can conceive it, supposes that the action of the will and the attainment of happiness do not square throughout.[15]

---

[10] *Emotion and Will*, p. 352. But even Bain's own description belies his formula, for the idea appears as the 'moving' and the pleasure as the 'directing' force.
[11] P. 398.
[12] P. 354.
[13] P. 355.
[14] P. 390.
[15] Pp. 295–6.

*Sympathy* "has this in common with the Fixed Idea, that it clashes with the regular outgoings of the will in favor of our pleasures." [16]

Prof. Bain thus admits all the essential facts. Pleasure and pain are motives of only part of our activity. But he prefers to give to that part of the activity exclusively which these feelings prompt the name of *'regular outgoings'* and *'genuine* impulses' of the will,[17] and to treat all the rest as mere paradoxes and anomalies, of which nothing rational can be said. This amounts to taking one species of a genus, calling it alone by the generic name, and ordering the other co-ordinate species to find what names they may. At bottom this is only verbal play. How much more conducive to clearness and insight it is to take the *genus* 'springs of action' and treat it as a whole; and then to distinguish within it the species 'pleasure and pain' from whatever other species may be found!

There is, it is true, a complication in the relation of pleasure to action, which partly excuses those who make it the exclusive spur. This complication deserves some notice at our hands.

An impulse which discharges itself immediately is generally quite *neutral* as regards pleasure or pain—the breathing impulse, for example. If such an impulse is arrested, however, by an extrinsic force, a great feeling of *uneasiness* is produced—for instance, the dyspnœa of asthma. And in proportion as the arresting force is then overcome, *relief* accrues—as when we draw breath again after the asthma subsides. The relief is a pleasure and the uneasiness a pain; and thus it happens that round all our impulses, merely as such, there twine, as it were, secondary possibilities of pleasant and painful feeling, involved in the manner in which the act is allowed to occur. These *pleasures and pains of achievement, discharge, or fruition* exist, no matter what the original spring of action be. We are glad when we have successfully got ourselves out of a danger, though the thought of the gladness was surely not what suggested to us to escape. To have compassed the steps towards a proposed sensual indulgence also makes us glad, and this gladness is a pleasure additional to the pleasure originally proposed. On the other hand, we are chagrined and displeased when any activity, however instigated, is hindered whilst in process of actual discharge. We are 'uneasy' till the discharge starts up again. And this is just as true when the action is neutral, or has nothing but pain in view as its result, as when it was undertaken for pleasure's express sake. The moth is probably as annoyed if hindered from getting into the lamp-flame as the *roué* is if interrupted in his debauch; and we are chagrined if prevented from doing some quite unimportant act which would have given us no noticeable pleasure if done, merely because the prevention itself is disagreeable.

[16] P. 121.
[17] Cf. also Bain's note to Jas. Mill's *Analysis,* vol. II. p. 305.

Let us now call the pleasure *for the sake* of which the act may be done the *pursued pleasure*. It follows that, even when no pleasure is pursued by an act, the act itself may be the *pleasantest line* of conduct when once the impulse has begun, on account of the incidental pleasure which then attends its successful achievement and the pain which would come of interruption. A *pleasant act* and an act *pursuing a pleasure* are in themselves, however, two perfectly distinct conceptions, though they coalesce in one concrete phenomenon whenever a pleasure is deliberately pursued. I cannot help thinking that it is the *confusion of pursued pleasure with mere pleasure of achievement* which makes the pleasure-theory of action so plausible to the ordinary mind. We feel an impulse, no matter whence derived; we proceed to act; if hindered, we feel displeasure; and if successful, relief. Action *in the line of the present impulse* is always for the time being the pleasant course; and the ordinary hedonist expresses this fact by saying that we act for the *sake* of the pleasantness involved. But who does not see that for this sort of pleasure to be possible, *the impulse must be there already as an independent fact?* The pleasure of successful performance is the *result* of the impulse, not its *cause*. You cannot have your pleasure of achievement unless you have managed to get your impulse under headway beforehand by some previous means.

It is true that on special occasions (so complex is the human mind) *the pleasure of achievement may itself become a pursued pleasure;* and these cases form another point on which the pleasure-theory is apt to rally. Take a foot-ball game or a fox-hunt. Who in cold blood wants the fox for its own sake, or cares whether the ball be at this goal or that? We know, however, by experience, that if we can once rouse a certain impulsive excitement in ourselves, whether to overtake the fox, or to get the ball to one particular goal, the successful venting of it over the counteracting checks will fill us with exceeding joy. We therefore get ourselves deliberately and artificially into the hot impulsive state. It takes the presence of various instinct-arousing conditions to excite it; but little by little, once we are in the field, it reaches its paroxysm; and we reap the reward of our exertions in that pleasure of successful achievement which, far more than the dead fox or the goal-got ball, was the object we originally pursued. So it often is with duties. Lots of actions are done with heaviness all through, and not till they are completed does pleasure emerge, in the joy of being done with them. Like Hamlet we say of each such successive task,

> O cursed spite,
> That ever I was born to set it right!

and then we often add to the original impulse that set us on, this additional one, that "we shall feel so glad when well through with it," that thought also having its impulsive spur. But because a pleasure of achievement *can* thus become a pursued pleasure upon occasion, it does not follow that everywhere and always that pleasure must be what is pursued. This, however, is what the pleasure-philosophers seem to suppose. As well might they suppose, because no steamer can go to sea without incidentally consuming coal, and because some steamers may occasionally go to sea to *try* their coal, that therefore no steamer *can* go to sea for any other motive than that of coal-consumption.[18]

As we need not act for the sake of gaining the pleasure of achievement, so neither need we act for the sake of escaping the uneasiness of arrest. This uneasiness is altogether due to the fact that the act is *already tending to occur* on other grounds. And these original grounds are what impel to its continuance, even though the uneasiness of the arrest may upon occasion add to their impulsive power.

To conclude, I am far from denying the exceeding prominence and importance of the part which pleasures and pains, both felt and represented, play in the motivation of our conduct. But I must insist that it is no exclusive part, and that co-ordinately with these mental objects innumerable others have an exactly similar impulsive and inhibitive power.[19]

If one must have a single name for the condition upon which the impulsive and inhibitive quality of objects depends, one had better call it their *interest*. 'The interesting' is a title which covers not only the pleasant and the painful, but also the morbidly fascinating, the tediously haunting, and even the simply habitual, inasmuch as the attention usually travels on habitual lines, and what-we-attend-to and what-interests-us are synonymous terms. It seems as if we ought to look for the secret of an idea's impulsiveness, not in any peculiar relations which it may have with paths of motor discharge,—for *all* ideas have relations with some such paths,—but rather in a preliminary phenomenon, the *urgency, namely, with which it is able to compel attention and dominate in consciousness.* Let it once so dominate, let no other ideas succeed in displacing it, and whatever motor effects belong to it by nature will inevitably occur—its impulsion, in short, will be given to boot, and will manifest itself as a

---

[18] How much clearer Hume's head was than that of his disciples'! "It has been proved beyond all controversy that even the passions commonly esteemed selfish carry the Mind beyond self directly to the object; that though the satisfaction of these passions gives us enjoyment, yet the prospect of this enjoyment is not the cause of the passions but, on the contrary, the passion is antecedent to the enjoyment, and without the former the latter could never possibly exist," etc. (*Essay on the Different Species of Philosophy,* § 1, note near the end.)

[19] In favor of the view in the text, one may consult H. Sidgwick, *Methods of Ethics,* book I. chap. IV; T. H. Green, *Prolegomena to Ethics,* bk. III. chap. I. p. 179; Carpenter, *Mental Physiol.,* chap. VI; J. Martineau, *Types of Ethical Theory,* part II, bk. I, chap. II. i, and bk. II, branch I. chap. I. i. § 3. Against it see Leslie Stephen, *Science of Ethics,* chap. II. § II; H. Spencer, *Data of Ethics,* §§ 9–15; D. G. Thompson, *System of Psychology,* part IX, and *Mind,* VI. 62. Also Bain, *Senses and Intellect,* 338–44; *Emotions and Will,* 436.

matter of course. This is what we have seen in instinct, in emotion, in common ideo-motor action, in hypnotic suggestion, in morbid impulsion, and in *voluntas invita*,—the impelling idea is simply the one which possesses the attention. It is the same where pleasure and pain are the motor spurs—they drive other thoughts from consciousness at the same time that they instigate their own characteristic 'volitional' effects. And this is also what happens at the moment of the *fiat,* in all the five types of 'decision' which we have described. In short, one does not see any case in which the steadfast occupancy of consciousness does not appear to be the prime condition of impulsive power. It is still more obviously the prime condition of inhibitive power. What checks our impulses is the mere thinking of reasons to the contrary—it is their bare presence to the mind which gives the veto, and makes acts, otherwise seductive, impossible to perform. If we could only *forget* our scruples, our doubts, our fears, what exultant energy we should for a while display!

## WILL IS A RELATION BETWEEN THE MIND AND ITS 'IDEAS'

In closing in, therefore, after all these preliminaries, upon the more *intimate* nature of the volitional process, we find ourselves driven more and more exclusively to consider the conditions which make ideas prevail in the mind. With the prevalence, once there as a fact, of the motive idea the *psychology* of volition properly stops. The movements which ensue are exclusively physiological phenomena, following according to physiological laws upon the neural events to which the idea corresponds. The *willing* terminates with the prevalence of the idea; and whether the act then follows or not is a matter quite immaterial, so far as the willing itself goes. I will to write, and the act follows. I will to sneeze, and it does not. I will that the distant table slide over the floor towards me; it also does not. My willing representation can no more instigate my sneezing-centre than it can instigate the table to activity. But in both cases it is as true and good willing as it was when I willed to write.[20] In a word,

[20] This sentence is written from the author's own consciousness. But many persons say that where they disbelieve in the effects ensuing, as in the cas of the table, they cannot will it. They "cannot exert a volition that a table should move." This personal difference may be partly verbal. Different people may attach different connotations to the word 'will.' But I incline to think that we differ psychologically as well. When one knows that he has no power, one's desire of a thing is called a *wish* and not a will. The sense of impotence inhibits the volition. Only by abstracting from the thought of the impossibility am I able energetically to imagine strongly the table sliding over the floor, make the bodily 'effort' which I do, and to will it to come towards me. It may be that some people are unable to perform this abstraction, and that the image of the table stationary on the floor inhibits the contradictory image of its moving, which is the object to be willed.

volition is a psychic or moral fact pure and simple, and is absolutely completed when the stable state of the idea is there. The supervention of motion is a supernumerary phenomenon depending on executive ganglia whose function lies outside the mind.

In St. Vitus' dance, in locomotor ataxy, the representation of a movement and the consent to it take place normally. But the inferior executive centres are deranged, and although the ideas discharge them, they do not discharge them so as to reproduce the precise sensations anticipated. In aphasia the patient has an image of certain words which he wishes to utter, but when he opens his mouth he hears himself making quite unintended sounds. This may fill him with rage and despair—which passions only show how intact his will remains. Paralysis only goes a step farther. The associated mechanism is not only deranged but altogether broken through. The volition occurs, but the hand remains as still as the table. The paralytic is made aware of this by the absence of the expected change in his afferent sensations. He tries harder, i.e., he mentally frames the sensation of muscular 'effort,' with consent that it shall occur. It does so: he frowns, he heaves his chest, he clinches his other first, but the palsied arm lies passive as before.[21]

We thus find that *we reach the heart of our inquiry into volition when we ask by what process it is that the thought of any given object comes to prevail stably in the mind.* Where thoughts prevail without effort, we have sufficiently studied in the several chapters on sensation, association, and attention, the laws of their advent before consciousness and of their stay. We will not go over that ground again, for we know that interest and association are the words, let their worth be what it may, on which our explanations must perforce rely. Where, on the other hand, the prevalence of the thought is accompanied by the phenomenon of effort, the case is much less clear. Already in the chapter on attention we postponed the final consideration of voluntary attention with effort to a later place. We have now brought things to a point at which we see that attention with effort is all that any case of volition implies. *The essential achievement of the will, in short, when it is most 'voluntary,' is to* ATTEND *to a difficult object and hold it fast before the mind.* The so-doing *is the fiat;* and it is a mere physiological incident that when the object is thus attended to, immediate motor consequences should ensue. A *resolve,* whose contemplated motor consequences are not to ensue until some possibly far distant future condition shall have been fulfilled, involves all the psychic elements of a motor fiat except the word *'now;'* and it is the

[21] A normal palsy occurs during sleep. We will all sorts of motions in our dreams, but seldom perform any of them. In nightmare we become conscious of the non-performance, and make a muscular 'effort.' This seems then to occur in a restricted way, limiting itself to the occlusion of the glottis and producing the respiratory anxiety which wakes us up.

same with many of our purely theoretic beliefs. We saw in effect in the appropriate chapter, how in the last resort belief means only a peculiar sort of occupancy of the mind, and relation to the self felt in the thing believed; and we know in the case of many beliefs how constant an effort of the attention is required to keep them in this situation and protect them from displacement by contradictory ideas.[22]

*Effort of attention is thus the essential phenomenon of will.*[23] Every reader must know by his own experience that this is so, for every reader must have felt some fiery passion's grasp. What constitutes the difficulty for a man laboring under an unwise passion of acting as if the passion were unwise? Certainly there is no physical difficulty. It is as easy physically to avoid a fight as to begin one, to pocket one's money as to squander it on one's cupidities, to walk away from as towards a coquette's door. The difficulty is mental; it is that of getting the idea of the wise action to stay before our mind at all. When any strong emotional state whatever is upon us the tendency is for no images but such as are congruous with it to come up. If others by chance offer themselves, they are instantly smothered and crowded out. If we be joyous, we cannot keep thinking of those uncertainties and risks of failure which abound upon our path; if lugubrious, we cannot think of new triumphs, travels, loves, and joys; nor if vengeful, of our oppressor's community of nature with ourselves. The cooling advice which we get from others when the fever-fit is on us is the most jarring and exasperating thing in life. Reply we can-

---

[22] Both resolves and beliefs have of course immediate motor consequences of a quasi-emotional sort, changes of breathing, of attitude, internal speech movements, etc.; but these movements are not the *objects* resolved on or believed. The movements in common volition are the objects willed.

[23] This *volitional* effort pure and simple must be carefully distinguished from the *muscular* effort with which it is usually confounded. The latter consists of all those peripheral feelings to which a muscular 'exertion' may give rise. These feelings, whenever they are massive and the body is not 'fresh,' are rather disagreeable, especially when accompanied by stopped breath, congested head, bruised skin of fingers, toes, or shoulders, and strained joints. And it is only *as thus disagreeable* that the mind must make its *volitional* effort in stably representing their reality and consequently bringing it about. That they happen to be made real by muscular activity is a purely accidental circumstance. A soldier standing still to be fired at expects disagreeable sensations from his muscular passivity. The action of his will, in sustaining the expectation, is identical with that required for a painful musclar effort. What is hard for both is *facing an idea as real.*

Where much muscular effort is not needed or where the 'freshness' is very great, the volitional effort is not required to sustain the idea of movement, which comes then and stays in virtue of association's simpler laws. More commonly, however, muscular effort involves volitional effort as well. Exhausted with fatigue and wet and watching, the sailor on a wreck throws himself down to rest. But hardly are his limbs fairly relaxed, when the order 'To the pumps!' again sounds in his ears. Shall he, can he, obey it? Is it not better just to let his aching body lie, and let the ship go down if she will? So he lies on, till, with a desperate heave of the will, at last he staggers to his legs, and to his task again. Again, there are instances where the fiat demands great volitional effort though the muscular exertion be insignificant, e.g., the getting out of bed and bathing one's self on a cold morning.

not, so we get angry; for by a sort of self-preserving instinct which our passion has, it feels that these chill objects, if they once but gain a lodgment, will work and work until they have frozen the very vital spark from out of all our mood and brought our airy castles in ruin to the ground. Such is the inevitable effect of reasonable ideas over others—*if they can once get a quiet hearing;* and passion's cue accordingly is always and everywhere to prevent their still small voice from being heard at all. "Let me not think of that! Don't speak to me of that!" This is the sudden cry of all those who in a passion perceive some sobering considerations about to check them in mid-career. *"Hæc tibi erit janua leti,"* we feel. There is something so icy in this cold-water bath, something which seems so hostile to the movement of our life, so purely negative, in Reason, when she lays her corpse-like finger on our heart and says, "Halt! give up! leave off! go back! sit down!" that it is no wonder that to most men the steadying influence seems, for the time being, a very minister of death.

The strong-willed man, however, is the man who hears the still small voice unflinchingly, and who, when the death-bringing consideration comes, looks at its face, consents to its presence, clings to it, affirms it, and holds it fast, in spite of the host of exciting mental images which rise in revolt against it and would expel it from the mind. Sustained in this way by a resolute effort of attention, the difficult object erelong begins to call up its own congerers and associates and ends by changing the disposition of the man's consciousness altogether. And with his consciousness, his action changes, for the new object, once stably in possession of the field of his thoughts, infallibly produces its own motor effects. The difficulty lies in the gaining possession of that field. Though the spontaneous drift of thought is all the other way, the attention must be kept strained on that one subject until at last it *grows,* so as to maintain itself before the mind with ease. This strain of the attention is the fundamental act of will. And the will's work is in most cases practically ended when the bare presence to our thought of the naturally unwelcome object has been secured. For the mysterious tie between the thought and the motor centres next comes into play, and, in a way which we cannot even guess at, the obedience of the bodily organs follows as a matter of course.

In all this one sees how the immediate point of application of the volitional effort lies exclusively in the mental world. The whole drama is a mental drama. The whole difficulty is a mental difficulty, a difficulty with an object of our thought. If I may use the word *idea* without suggesting associationist or Herbartian fables, I will say that it is an idea to which our will applies itself, an idea which if we let it go would slip away, but which we will not let go. Consent to the idea's undivided presence, this is effort's sole achievement. Its only function is to get this feeling of consent into the mind. And for this there is but one way. The idea to be consented to must be kept from flickering and going out. It must be held steadily before the mind until it *fills* the mind. Such filling of the mind by an idea, with its congruous associates, *is* consent to the idea and to the fact which the idea represents. If the idea be that, or include that, of a bodily movement of our own, then we call the consent thus laboriously gained a motor volition. For Nature here 'backs' us instantaneously and follows up our inward willingness by outward changes on her own part. She does this in no other instance. Pity she should not have been more generous, nor made a world whose other parts were as immediately subject to our will!

In describing the 'reasonable type' of decision, it was said that it usually came when the right conception of the case was found. Where, however, the right conception is an anti-impulsive one, the whole intellectual ingenuity of the man usually goes to work to crowd it out of sight, and to find names for the emergency, by the help of which the dispositions of the moment may sound sanctified, and sloth or passion may reign unchecked. How many excuses does the drunkard find when each new temptation comes! It is a new brand of liquor which the interests of intellectual culture in such matters oblige him to test; moreover it is poured out and it is sin to waste it; or others are drinking and it would be churlishness to refuse; or it is but to enable him to sleep, or just to get through this job of work; or it isn't drinking, it is because he feels so cold; or it is Christmas-day; or it is a means of stimulating him to make a more powerful resolution in favor of abstinence than any he has hitherto made; or it is just this once, and once doesn't count, etc., etc., *ad libitum*— it is, in fact, anything you like except *being a drunkard. That* is the conception that will not stay before the poor soul's attention. But if he once gets able to pick out that way of conceiving, from all the other possible ways of conceiving the various opportunities which occur, if through thick and thin he holds to it that this is being a drunkard and is nothing else, he is not likely to remain one long. The effort by which he succeeds in keeping the right *name* unwaveringly present to his mind proves to be his saving moral act.[24]

Everywhere then the function of the effort is the same: to keep affirming and adopting a thought which, if left to itself, would slip away. It may be cold and flat when the spontaneous mental drift is towards excitement, or great and arduous when the spontaneous drift is towards repose. In the one case the effort has to inhibit an explosive, in the other to arouse an obstructed will. The exhausted sailor on a wreck has a will which is obstructed. One of his ideas is that of his sore hands, of the nameless exhaustion of his whole frame which the act of farther pumping

---

[24] Cf. Aristotle's *Nichomachæan Ethics*, VII. 3; also a discussion of the doctrine of 'The Practical Syllogism' in Sir A. Grant's edition of this work, 2d ed. vol. I. p. 212 ff.

involves, and of the deliciousness of sinking into sleep. The other is that of the hungry sea ingulfing him. "Rather the aching toil!" he says; and it becomes reality then, in spite of the inhibiting influence of the relatively luxurious sensations which he gets from lying still. But exactly similar in form would be his consent to lie and sleep. Often it is the thought of sleep and what leads to it which is the hard one to keep before the mind. If a patient afflicted with insomnia can only control the whirling chase of his thoughts so far as to think of *nothing at all* (which can be done), or so far as to imagine one letter after another of a verse of scripture or poetry spelt slowly and monotonously out, it is almost certain that here, too, specific bodily effects will follow, and that sleep will come. The trouble is to keep the mind upon a train of objects naturally so insipid. *To sustain a representation, to think,* is, in short the only moral act, for the impulsive and the obstructed, for sane and lunatics alike. Most maniacs know their thoughts to be crazy, but find them too pressing to be withstood. Compared with them the sane truths are so deadly sober, so cadaverous, that the lunatic cannot bear to look them in the face and say, "Let these alone be my reality!" But with sufficient effort, as Dr. Wigan says,

Such a man can for a time *wind himself up*, as it were, and determine that the notions of the disordered brain shall not be manifested. Many instances are on record similar to that told by Pinel, where an inmate of the Bicêtre, having stood a long cross-examination, and given every mark of restored reason, signed his name to the paper authorizing his discharge "Jesus Christ," and then went off into all the vagaries connected with that delusion. In the phraseology of the gentleman whose case is related in an early part of this [Wigan's] work he had "held himself tight" during the examination in order to attain his object; this once accomplished he "let himself down" again, and, if even *conscious* of his delusion, could not control it. I have observed with such persons that it requires a considerable time to wind themselves up to the pitch of complete self-control, that the effort is a painful tension of the mind. . . . When thrown off their guard by any accidental remark or worn out by the length of the examination, they *let themselves go,* and cannot gather themselves up again without preparation. Lord Erskine relates the story of a man who brought an action against Dr. Munro for confining him without cause. He underwent the most rigid examination by the counsel for the defendant without discovering any appearance of insanity, till a gentleman asked him about a princess with whom he corresponded in cherry-juice, and he became instantly insane.[25]

[25] *The Duality of the Mind,* pp. 141–2. Another case from the same book (p. 123): "A gentleman of respectable birth, excellent education, and ample fortune, engaged in one of the highest departments of trade, . . . and being induced to embark in one of the plausible speculations of the day . . . was utterly ruined. Like other men he could bear a sudden overwhelming reverse better than a long succession of petty misfortunes, and the way in which he conducted himself on the occasion met with unbounded admiration from his friends. He withdrew, however, into rigid seclusion, and being no longer able to exercise the generosity and indulge the benevolent

To sum it all up in a word, *the terminus of the psychological process in volition, the point to which the will is directly applied, is always an idea.* There are at all times *some* ideas from which we shy away like frightened horses the moment we get a glimpse of their forbidding profile upon the threshold of our thought. *The only resistance which our will can possibly experience is the resistance which such an idea offers to being attended to at all.* To attend to it is the volitional act, and the only inward volitional act which we ever perform.

I have put the thing in this ultra-simple way because I want more than anything else to emphasize the fact that volition is primarily a relation, not between our Self and extra-mental matter (as many philosophers still maintain), but between our Self and our own states of mind. But when, a short while ago, I spoke of the filling of the mind with an idea as being equivalent to consent to the idea's object, I said something which the reader doubtless questioned at the time, and which certainly now demands some qualifications ere we pass beyond.

It is unqualifiedly true that if any thought *do* fill the mind exclusively, such filling is consent. The thought, for that time at any rate, carries the man and his will with it. But it is not true that the thought *need* fill the mind exclusively for consent to be there; for we often consent to things whilst thinking of other things, even of hostile things; and we saw in fact that precisely what distinguishes our 'fifth type' of decision from the other types is just this coexistence with the triumphant thought of other thoughts which would inhibit it but for the effort which makes it prevail. The effort to *attend* is therefore only a part of what the word 'will' covers; it covers also the effort to *consent* to something to which our attention is not quite complete. Often, when an object has gained our attention exclusively, and its motor results are just on the point of setting in, it seems as if the sense of their imminent irrevocability were enough of itself to start up the inhibitory ideas and to make us pause. Then we need a new stroke of effort to break down the sudden hesitation which seizes upon us, and to persevere. So that although attention is the first

---

feelings which had formed the happiness of his life, made himself a substitute for them by daydreams, gradually fell into a state of irritable despondency, from which he only gradually recovered with the loss of reason. He now fancied himself possessed of immense wealth, and gave without stint his imaginary riches. He has ever since been under gentle restraint, and leads a life not merely of happiness, but of bliss; converses rationally, reads the newspapers, where every tale of distress attracts his notice, and being furnished with an abundant supply of blank checks, he fills up one of them with a munificent sum, sends it off to the sufferer, and sits down to his dinner with a happy conviction that he has earned the right to a little indulgence in the pleasures of the table; and yet, on a serious conversation with one of his old friends, he is quite conscious of his real position, but the conviction is so exquisitely painful that *he will not let himself believe it.*"

and fundamental thing in volition, *express consent to the reality of what is attended to* is often an additional and quite distinct phenomenon involved.

The reader's own consciousness tells him of course just what these words of mine denote. And I freely confess that I am impotent to carry the analysis of the matter any farther, or to explain in other terms of what this consent consists. It seems a subjective experience *sui generis*, which we can designate but not define. We stand here exactly where we did in the case of belief. When an idea *stings* us in a certain way, makes as it were a certain electric connection with our self, we believe that it *is* a reality. When it stings us in another way, makes another connection with our Self, we say, *let it be* a reality. To the word 'is' and to the words 'let it be' there correspond peculiar attitudes of consciousness which it is vain to seek to explain. The indicative and the imperative moods are as much ultimate categories of thinking as they are of grammar. The 'quality of reality' which these moods attach to things is not like other qualities. It is a relation to our life. It means *our* adoption of the things, *our* caring for them, *our* standing by them. This at least is what it practically means for us; what it may mean beyond that we do not know. And the transition from merely considering an object as possible, to deciding or willing it to be real; the change from the fluctuating to the stable personal attitude concerning it; from the 'don't care' state of mind to that in which 'we mean business,' is one of the most familiar things in life. We can partly enumerate its conditions; and we can partly trace its consequences, especially the momentous one that when the mental object is a movement of our own body, it realizes itself outwardly when the mental change in question has occurred. But the change itself as a subjective phenomenon is something which we can translate into no simpler terms.

.     .     .     .     .     .     .

## THE EDUCATION OF THE WILL

The education of the will may be taken in a broader or a narrower sense. In the broader sense, it means the whole of one's training to moral and prudential conduct, and of one's learning to adapt means to ends, involving the 'association of ideas,' in all its varieties and complications, together with the power of inhibiting impulses irrelevant to the ends desired, and of initiating movements contributory thereto. It is the acquisition of these latter powers which I mean by the education of the will in the narrower sense. And it is in this sense alone that it is worth while to treat the matter here.[26]

[26] On the education of the Will from a pedagogic point of view, see an article by G. Stanley Hall in the *Princeton Review* for November 1882, and some bibliographic references there contained.

Since a willed movement is a movement preceded by an idea of itself, the problem of the will's education is the problem of how the idea of a movement can arouse the movement itself. This, as we have seen, is a secondary kind of process; for framed as we are, we can have no *a priori* idea of a movement, no idea of a movement which we have not already performed. Before the idea can be generated, the movement must have occurred in a blind, unexpected way, and left its idea behind. *Reflex, instinctive,* or *random execution* of a *movement* must, in other words, precede its voluntary execution. Reflex and instinctive movements have already been considered sufficiently for the purposes of this book. 'Random' movements are mentioned so as to include *quasi*-accidental reflexes from inner causes, or movements possibly arising from such overflow of nutrition in special centres as Prof. Bain postulates in his explanation of those 'spontaneous discharges' by which he sets such great store in his derivation of the voluntary life.[27]

Now *how can the sensory process which a movement has previously produced, discharge, when excited again, into the centre for the movement itself?* On the movement's original occurrence the motor discharge came first and the sensory process second; now in the voluntary repetition the sensory process (excited in weak or 'ideational' form) comes first, and the motor discharge comes second. To tell how this comes to pass would be to answer the problem of the education of the will in physiological terms. Evidently the problem is that of the formation of *new paths;* and the only thing to do is to make hypotheses, till we find some which seem to cover all the facts.

How is a fresh path ever formed? All paths are paths of discharge, and the discharge always takes place in the direction of least resistance, whether the cell which discharges be 'motor' or 'sensory.' The *connate* paths of least resistance are the paths of instinctive reaction; and I submit as my first hypothesis that *these paths all run one way, that is from 'sensory' cells into 'motor' cells and from motor cells into muscles, without ever taking the reverse direction.* A motor cell, for example, never awakens a sensory cell directly, but only through the incoming current caused by the bodily movements to which its discharge gives rise. And a sensory cell *always* discharges or normally tends to discharge towards the motor region. Let this direction be called the 'forward' direction. I call the law an hypothesis, but really it is an indubitable truth. No impression or idea of eye, ear, or skin comes to us without occasioning a movement, even though the movement be no more than the accommodation of the sense-organ; and all our trains of sensation and sensational imagery have their terms alternated and interpenetrated with motor processes, of most of

---

[27] See his *Emotions and Will,* 'The Will,' chap. i. I take the name of random movements from Sully, *Outlines of Psychology,* p. 593.

which we practically are unconscious. Another way of stating the rule is to say that, primarily or connately, all currents through the brain run towards the Rolandic region, and that there they run out, and never return upon themselves. From this point of view the distinction of sensory and motor cells has no fundamental significance. All cells are motor; we simply call those of the Rolandic region, those nearest the mouth of the funnel, the motor cells *par excellence.*

A corollary of this law is that 'sensory' cells do not awaken each other connately; that is, that no one sensible property of things has any tendency, in advance of experience, to awaken in us the idea of any other sensible properties which in the nature of things may go with it. *There is no a priori calling up of one 'idea' by another;* the only *a priori* couplings are of ideas with movements. All suggestions of one sensible fact by another take place by secondary paths which experience has formed.

The diagram (Fig. 9.1)[28] shows what happens in a nervous system ideally reduced to the fewest possible terms. A stimulus reaching the

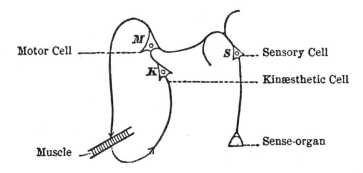

Motor Cell

Sensory Cell

Kinæsthetic Cell

Sense-organ

Muscle

Figure 9.1

sense-organ awakens the sensory cell, S; this by the connate or instinctive path discharges the motor cell, M, which makes the muscle contract; and the contraction arouses the second sensory cell, K, which may be the organ either of a 'resident' or 'kinæsthetic,' or of a 'remote,' sensation: (See above, p. 152.) This cell K again discharges into M. If this were the entire nervous mechanism, the movement, once begun, would be self-

[28] This figure and the following ones are purely schematic, and must not be supposed to involve any theory about protoplasmatic and axis-cylinder processes. The latter, according to Golgi and others, emerge from the base of the cell, and each cell has but one. They alone form a nervous network. The reader will of course also understand that none of the hypothetical constructions which I make from now to the end of the chapter are proposed as definite accounts of what happens. All I aim at is to make it clear in some more or less symbolic fashion that the formation of new paths, the learning of habits, etc., is in *some* mechanical way conceivable. Compare what was said in Vol. I. p. 81, note.

maintaining, and would stop only when the parts were exhausted. And this, according to M. Pierre Janet, is what actually happens in *catalepsy*. A cataleptic patient is anæsthetic, speechless, motionless. Consciousness, so far as we can judge, is abolished. Nevertheless the limbs will retain whatever position is impressed upon them from without, and retain it so long that if it be a strained and unnatural position, the phenomenon is regarded by Charcot as one of the few conclusive tests against hypnotic subjects shamming, since hypnotics can be made cataleptic, and then keep their limbs outstretched for a length of time quite unattainable by the waking will. M. Janet thinks that in all these cases the outlying ideational processes in the brain are temporarily thrown out of gear. The kinæsthetic sensation of the raised arm, for example, is produced in the patient when the operator raises the arm, this sensation discharges into the motor cell, which through the muscle reproduces the sensation, etc., the currents running in this closed circle until they grow so weak, by exhaustion of the parts, that the member slowly drops. We may call this circle from the muscle to K, from K to M, and from M to the muscle again, the 'motor circle.' *We should all be cataleptics and never stop a muscular contraction once begun, were it not that other processes simultaneously going on inhibit the contraction. Inhibition is therefore not an occasional accident; it is an essential and unremitting element of our cerebral life.* It is interesting to note that Dr. Mercier, by a different path of reasoning, is also led to conclude that we owe to outside inhibitions exclusively our power to arrest a movement once begun.[29]

One great inhibiter of the discharge of K into M seems to be the painful or otherwise displeasing quality of the sensation itself of K; and conversely, when this sensation is distinctly pleasant, that fact tends to further K's discharge into M, and to keep the primordial motor circle agoing. Tremendous as the part is which pleasure and pain play in our psychic life, we must confess that absolutely nothing is known of their cerebral conditions. It is hard to imagine them as having special centres; it is harder still to invent peculiar forms of process in each and every centre, to which these feelings may be due. And let one try as one will to represent the cerebral activity in exclusively mechanical terms, I, for one, find it quite impossible to enumerate what seem to be the facts and yet to make no mention of the psychic side which they possess. However it be with other drainage currents and discharges, the drainage currents and discharges of the brain are not purely physical facts. They are *psychophysical* facts, and the spiritual quality of them seems a codeterminant of their mechanical effectiveness. If the mechanical activities in a cell, as they increase, give pleasure, they seem to increase all the more rapidly for that fact; if they give displeasure, the displeasure seems to dampen the activities. The psychic side of the phenomenon thus seems, somewhat

[29] *The Nervous System and the Mind* (1888), pp. 75–6.

like the applause or hissing at a spectacle, to be an encouraging or adverse *comment* on what the machinery brings forth. The soul *presents* nothing herself; *creates* nothing; is at the mercy of the material forces for all *possibilities;* but amongst these possibilities she *selects;* and by reinforcing one and checking others, she figures not as an 'epiphenomenon,' but as something from which the play gets moral support. I shall therefore never hesitate to invoke the efficacy of the conscious comment, where no strictly mechanical reason appears why a current escaping from a cell should take one path rather than another.[30] But the *existence* of the current, and its *tendency* towards either path, I feel bound to account for by mechanical laws.

Having now considered a nervous system reduced to its lowest possible terms, in which all the paths are connate, and the possibilities of inhibition not extrinsic, but due solely to the agreeableness or disagreeableness of the feeling aroused, let us turn to the conditions under which new paths may be formed. Potentialities of new paths are furnished by the fibres which connect the sensory cells amongst themselves; but these fibres are not originally pervious, and have to be made so by a process which I proceed hypothetically to state as follows: *Each discharge from a sensory cell in the forward direction* [31] *tends to drain the cells lying behind the discharging one of whatever tension they may possess. The drainage from the rearward cells is what for the first time makes the fibres pervious. The result is a new-formed 'path,' running from the cells which were 'rearward' to the cell which was 'forward' on that occasion; which path, if on future occasions the rearward cells are independently excited, will tend to carry off their activity in the same direction so as to excite the forward cell, and will deepen itself more and more every time it is used.*

Now the 'rearward cells,' so far, stand for all the sensory cells of the brain other than the one which is discharging; but such an indefinitely broad path would practically be no better than no path, so here I make a third hypothesis, which, taken together with the others, seems to me to cover all the facts. It is that *the deepest paths are formed from the most drainable to the most draining cells;* that *the most drainable cells are those which have just been discharging;* and that *the most draining cells are those which are now discharging or in which the tension is rising towards the point of discharge.*[32] Another diagram, Fig. 9.2, will make the

[30] Compare Vol. I. pp. 137, 142.

[31] That is, the direction towards the motor cells.

[32] This brain scheme seems oddly enough to give a certain basis of reality to those hideously fabulous performances of the Herbartian *Vorstellungen.* Herbart says that when one idea is inhibited by another it fuses with that other and thereafter helps it to ascend into consciousness. Inhibition is thus the basis of association in both schemes, for the 'draining' of which the text speaks is tantamount to an inhibition of the activity of the cells which are drained, which inhibition makes the inhibited revive the inhibiter on later occasions.

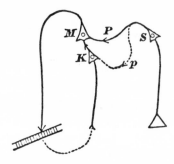

Figure 9.2

matter clear. Take the operation represented by the previous diagram at the moment when, the muscular contraction having occurred, the cell K is discharging forward into M. Through the dotted line $p$ it will, according to our third hypothesis, drain S (which, in the supposed case, has just discharged into M by the connate path P, and caused the muscular contraction), and the result is that $p$ will now remain as a new path open from S to K. When next S is excited from without it will tend not only to discharge into M, but into K as well. K thus gets excited directly by S *before* it gets excited by the incoming current from the muscle; or translated into psychic terms: *when a sensation has once produced a movement in us, the next time we have the sensation, it tends to suggest the idea of the movement, even before the movement occurs.*[33]

The same principles also apply to the relations of K and M. M, lying in the forward direction, drains K, and the path KM, even though it be no primary or a connate path, becomes a secondary or habitual one. Hereafter K may be aroused in any way whatsoever (not as before from S or from without) and still it will tend to discharge into M; or, to express it again in psychic terms, *the idea of the movement M's sensory effects will have become an immediately antecedent condition to the production of the movement itself.*

Here, then, we have the answer to our original question of how a sensory process which, the first time it occurred, was the effect of a movement, can later figure as the movement's cause.

It is obvious on this scheme that the cell which we have marked K may stand for the seat of either a resident or a remote sensation occasioned by the motor discharge. It may indifferently be a tactile, a visual, or an auditory cell. The idea of how the arm *feels* when raised may cause it to rise; but no less may the idea of some *sound* which it makes in rising, or of some *optical* impression which it produces. Thus we see that the 'mental cue' may belong to either of various senses; and that what

[33] See the luminous passage in Münsterberg: *Die Willenshandlung*, pp. 144–5.

our diagrams lead us to infer is what really happens; namely, that in our movements, such as that of speech, for example, in some of us it is the tactile, in others the acoustic, *Effectsbild,* or memory-image, which seems most concerned in starting the articulation. The *primitive* 'starters,' however, of all our movements are not *Effectsbilder* at all, but sensations and objects, and subsequently ideas derived therefrom.

Let us now turn to the more complex and serially concatenated movements which oftenest meet us in real life. The object of our will is seldom a single muscular contraction; it is almost always an orderly sequence of contractions, ending with a sensation which tells us that the goal is reached. But the several contractions of the sequence are not each distinctly willed; each earlier one seems rather, by the sensation it produces, to call its follower up, after the fashion described earlier, where we spoke of habitual concatenated movements being due to a series of secondarily organized reflex arcs. The first contraction is the one distinctly willed, and after willing it we let the rest of the chain rattle off of its own accord. How now is such an orderly concatenation of movements originally learned? or in other words, how are paths formed for the first time between one motor centre and another, so that the discharge of the first centre makes the others discharge in due order all along the line?

The phenomenon involves a rapid alternation of motor discharges and resultant afferent impressions, for as long a time as it lasts. They must be associated in one definite order; and the order must once have been *learned,* i.e., it must have been picked out and held to more and more exclusively out of the many other random orders which first presented themselves. The random afferent impressions fell out, those that felt right were selected and grew together in the chain. A chain which we actively teach ourselves by stringing a lot of right-feeling impressions together differs in no essential respect from a chain which we passively learn from someone else who gives us impressions in a certain order. So to make our ideas more precise, let us take a particular concatenated movement for an example, and let it be the recitation of the alphabet, which someone in our childhood taught us to say by heart.

What we have seen so far is how the idea of the sound or articulatory feeling of A may make us say 'A,' that of B, 'B,' and so on. But what we now want to see is *why the sensation that A is uttered should make us say 'B,' why the sensation that B is uttered should make us say 'C,' and so on.*

To understand this we must recall what happened when we first learned the letters in their order. Someone repeated A, B, C, D to us over and over again, and we imitated the sounds. Sensory cells corresponding to each letter were awakened in succession in such wise that each one of them (by virtue of our second law) must have 'drained' the cell just previously excited and left a path by which that cell tended ever afterwards to discharge into the cell that drained it. Let $S^a$, $S^b$, $S^c$ in figure 9.3 stand for three of these cells. Each later one of them, as it discharges motorwards, draws a current from the previous one, $S^b$ from $S^a$, and $S^c$ from $S^b$. Call $S^b$ having thus drained $S^a$, if $S^a$ ever gets excited again, it tends to discharge into $S^b$; whilst $S^c$ having drained $S^b$, $S^b$ later discharges into $S^c$, etc., etc.—all through the dotted lines. Let now the idea of the letter A arise in the mind, or, in other words, let $S^a$ be aroused: what happens? A current runs from $S^a$ not only into the motor cell $M^a$ for pronouncing that letter, but also into the cell $S^b$. When, a moment later, the effect of $M^a$'s discharge comes back by the afferent nerve and re-excites $S^a$, this latter cell is inhibited from discharging again into $M^a$ and reproducing the 'primordial motor circle' (which in this case would be the continued utterance of the letter A), by the fact that the process in $S^b$, already under headway and tending to discharge into its own motor associate $M^b$, is, *under the existing conditions,* the stronger drainage-channel for $S^a$'s excitement. The result is that $M^b$ discharges and the letter B is pronounced; whilst at the same time $S^c$ receives some of $S^b$'s overflow; and, a moment later when the sound of B enters the ear, discharges into the motor cell for pronouncing C, by a repetition of the same mechanism as before; and so on *ad libitum.* Figure 9.4 represents the entire set of processes involved.

The only thing that one does not immediately see is the reason why 'under the existing conditions' the path from $S^a$ to $S^b$ should be the stronger drainage-channel for $S^a$'s excitement. If the cells and fibres in the figure constituted the entire brain we might suppose either a mechanical or a psychical reason. The mechanical reason might lie in a general law that cells like $S^b$ and $M^b$, whose excitement is in a rising phase, are stronger drainers than cells like $M^a$, which have just discharged; or it might lie in the fact that an irradiation of the current beyond $S^b$ into $S^c$

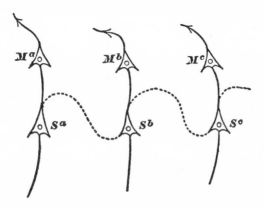

Figure 9.3

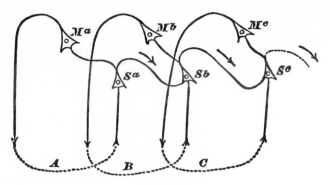

Figure 9.4

and M<sup>c</sup> has already begun also; and in a still farther law that drainage tends in the direction of the widest irradiations. Either of these suppositions would be a sufficient mechanical reason why, having once said A, we should not say it again. But we must not forget that the process has a psychical side, nor close our eyes to the possibility that the *sort of feeling* aroused by incipient currents may be the reason why certain of them are instantly inhibited and others helped to flow. There is no doubt that before we have uttered a single letter, the general intention to recite the alphabet is already there; nor is there any doubt that to that intention corresponds a widespread premonitory rising of tensions along the entire system of cells and fibres which are later to be aroused. So long as this rise of tensions *feels good*, so long every current which increases it is furthered, and every current which diminishes it is checked; and this may be the chief one of the 'existing conditions' which make the drainage-channel from $S^a$ to $S^b$ temporarily so strong.[34]

The new paths between the sensory cells of which we have studied the formation are paths of 'association,' and we now see why associations run always in the forward direction; why, for example, we cannot say the alphabet backward, and why, although $S^b$ discharges into $S^c$, there is no tendency for $S^c$ to discharge into $S^b$, or at least no more than for it to discharge into $S^a$.[35] The first-formed paths had, according to the principles which we invoked, to run from cells that had just discharged to

[34] L. Lange's and Münsterberg's experiments with 'shortened' or 'muscular' reaction-time (see Vol. I. p. 432) show how potent a fact dynamically this anticipatory preparation of a whole set of possible drainage-channels is.

[35] Even as the proofs of these pages are passing through my hands, I receive Heft 2 of the *Zeitschrift für Psychologie u. Physiologie der Sinnesorgane*, in which the irrepressible young Münsterberg publishes experiments to show that there is no association between successive ideas, apart from intervening movements. As my explanations have assumed that an earlier excited *sensory* cell drains a later one, his experiments and inferences would, if sound, upset all my hypotheses. I therefore can (as this late moment) only refer the reader to Herr M.'s article, hoping to review the subject again myself in another place.

those that were discharging; and now, to get currents to run the other way, we must go through a new learning of our letters with their order reversed. There will *then* be two sets of association-pathways, either of them possible, between the sensible cells. I represent them in Fig. 9.5,

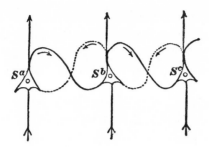

Figure 9.5

leaving out the motor features for simplicity's sake. The dotted lines are the paths in the backward direction, newly organized from the reception by the ear of the letters in the order C B A.

The same principles will explain the formation of new paths successively concatenated to no matter how great an extent, but it would obviously be folly to pretend to illustrate by more intricate examples. I will therefore only bring back the case of the child and flame, to show how easily it admits of explanation as a 'purely cortical transaction.' The sight of the flame stimulates the cortical centre $S^1$ which discharges by an instinctive reflex path into the centre $M^1$ for the grasping-movement. This movement produces the feeling of burn, as its effects come back to the centre $S^2$; and this centre by a second connate path discharges into $M^2$, the centre for withdrawing the hand. The movement of withdrawal stimulates the centre $S^3$, and this, as far as we are concerned, is the last

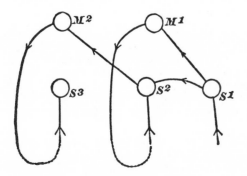

Figure 9.6

thing that happens. Now the next time the child sees the candle, the cortex is in possession of the secondary paths which the first experience left behind. $S^2$, having been stimulated immediately after $S^1$, drained the latter, and now $S^1$ discharges into $S^2$ before the discharge of $M^1$ has had time to occur; in other words the sight of the flame suggests the idea of the burn before it produces its own natural reflex effects. The result is an inhibition of $M^1$, or an overtaking of it before it is completed, by $M^2$.— The characteristic physiological feature in all these acquired systems of paths lies in the fact that the new-formed sensory irradiations keep *draining things forward,* and so breaking up the 'motor circles' which would otherwise accrue. But, even apart from catalepsy, we see the 'motor circle' every now and then come back. An infant learning to execute a simple movement at will, without regard to other movements beyond it, keeps repeating it till tired. How reiteratively they babble each new-learned word! And we adults often catch ourselves reiterating some meaningless word over and over again, if by chance we once begin to utter it 'absent-mindedly,' that is, without thinking of any ulterior train of words to which it may belong.

One more observation before closing these already too protracted physiological speculations. Already I have tried to shadow forth a reason why collateral innervation should establish itself after loss of brain-tissue, and why incoming stimuli should find their way out again, after an interval, by their former paths. I can now explain this a little better. Let $S^1$ be the dog's hearing-centre when he receives the command 'Give your paw.' This *used* to discharge into the motor centre $M^1$, of whose discharge $S^2$ represents the kinæsthetic effect; but now $M^1$ has been destroyed by an operation, so that $S^1$ discharges as it can, into other movements of the body, whimpering, raising the wrong paw, etc. The kinæsthetic centre $S^2$

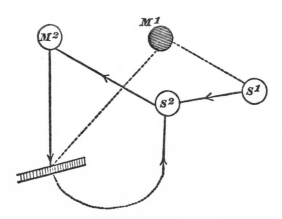

Figure 9.7

meanwhile has been awakened by the order $S^1$, and the poor animal's mind tingles with expectation and desire of certain incoming sensations which are entirely at variance with those which the really executed movements give. None of the latter sensations arouse a 'motor circle,' for they are displeasing and inhibitory. But when, by random accident, $S^1$ and $S^2$ *do* discharge into a path leading through $M^2$, by which the *paw is again given*, and $S^2$ is excited at last from without as well as from within, there are no inhibitions and the 'motor circle' is formed: $S^1$ discharges into $M^2$ over and over again, and the path from the one spot to the other is so much deepened that at last it becomes organized as the regular channel of efflux when $S^1$ is aroused. No other path has a chance of being organized in like degree.

# 10 • Edwin B. Holt

## *The Physiology of Wishes; and Their Integration*

In the work of Holt can be seen the influence of two streams of thought
which appeared after William James. Obvious in this selection is the influence
of psychoanalysis as newly formulated by Sigmund Freud. Secondly, there is
the point of view which can broadly be termed *behavioristic*. In the Freudian
concept of the "wish," Holt saw a basic unit of analysis for all psychology. In
positing an objective, behavioristic (Pavlovian), and even physiological sub-
structure for wishes, Holt carried the psychology of purpose to a new and more
sophisticated level. By looking upon the wish as a "readiness for a course of
action," Holt went far toward removing the mentalistic overtones of the word
and paved the way for experimental studies of goal-directed behavior. His
thoughts about the integration of reflexes and the recession of the stimulus
added to the reasonableness of the linkage of molecular reflex psychology to
molar, purposive psychology.

*The foregoing pages* will have sufficiently illustrated, I trust, what Freud
means by his very comprehensive term 'wish.' I have dwelt on it at great
length, because it is this 'wish' which transforms the principal doctrines
of psychology and recasts the science; much as the 'atomic theory,' and
later the 'ionic theory,' have reshaped earlier conceptions of chemistry.
This so-called 'wish' becomes the unit of psychology, replacing the older
unit commonly called 'sensation'; which latter, it is to be noted, was a
*content* of consciousness unit, whereas the 'wish' is a more dynamic affair.
In attempting to expound the change in psychology which is effected
by this concept of the 'wish,' I shall have to go somewhat beyond anything which Freud himself has said or written, for he has mainly devoted
himself to reshaping the science of psychiatry, *abnormal* psychology; and
has not discussed at anything like so great length the general field of
normal mind. But I shall try to limit myself to the *necessary implications*

of his discoveries, in the field of normal psychology. And in doing this I am quite aware that the rank and file of psychologists to-day neither understand nor accept, if indeed they have ever dreamt of, these essential and, as I think, very illuminating implications. It shall be for the reader to judge whether the picture which emerges bears the stamp of truth.

Unquestionably the mind is somehow 'embodied' in the body. But how? Well, if the unit of mind and character is a 'wish,' it is easy enough to perceive how it is incorporated. It is, this 'wish,' something which the body as a piece of mechanism can *do:* a course of action with regard to the environment which the machinery of the body is capable of carry-ing out.[1] This capacity resides, clearly, in the parts of which the body consists and in the way in which these are put together; not so much in the matter of which the body is composed, as in the forms which this matter assumes when organized. If, now, the wishes *are* the soul, then we can understand in all literalness Aristotle's dictum, that the soul "is the *form* of a natural body endowed with the capacity of life"; soul is indeed the entelechy. Just as the spirit of any piece of machinery lies in what it can do, and this specific capacity lies in its plan and structure rather than in the brute matter through which this plan is tangibly realized, so precisely it is with the human spirit and the human body. The spirit and the matter of the body are two things: and in the case of machinery and engineering enterprises we can plan, alter, revise, estimate, purchase, and patent the spirit, before this is ever materially incorporated. Yet on the other hand, the spirit needs to be realized in a tangible body before it can effectively operate. In living human beings, certainly, the spirit *is* embodied.

In order to look at this more closely we must go a bit down the evolu-tionary series to the fields of biology and physiology. Here we find much talk of nerves and muscles, sense-organs, reflex arcs, stimulation, and muscular response, and we feel that somehow these things do not reach the core of the matter, and that they never can: that spirit is not nerve or muscle, and that intelligent conduct, to say nothing of conscious thought, can never be reduced to reflex arcs and the like; just as a printing-press is not merely wheels and rollers, and still less is it chunks of iron. If, then, we insist on there being a soul which nevertheless the biologist says that he cannot discover anywhere in the living tissues of the animal he studies, we are quite right. And the biologist has only himself to thank if he has overlooked a thing which lay directly under his nose. He has overlooked the *form of organization* of these his reflex

---

[1] Here the reader may raise the query—"Carry out without the directing influ-ence of an intelligent soul?" To this I will ask the reader to accept provisionally the answer—Yes, *without.* But this merely because the question as raised, although familiar, is meaningless. We are not coming out to a psychology without a soul, unless by soul one means 'ghost-soul.' Quite on the contrary, Freud's is actually the first psychology *with* a soul.

arcs, has left out of account that step which assembles wheels and rollers into a printing-press, and that which organizes reflex arcs, as we shall presently see, into an intelligent conscious creature. Evolution took this important little step of organization ages ago, and thereby produced the rudimentary 'wish.'

It was a novelty. Yet so complete is the continuity of evolution, and when we watch it closely so little critical are the 'critical points' in any process, that we may overlook the advent of a genuine novelty howsoever important. Thus in geometry the step is infinitesimal between two parallel lines and two lines which meet in infinity,[2] yet the geometrical properties of the system are astoundingly different in the two cases. Now in the reflex arc a sense-organ is stimulated and the energy of stimulation is transformed into nervous energy, which then passes along an afferent nerve to the central nervous system, passes through this and out by an efferent or motor nerve to a muscle, where the energy is again transformed and the muscle contracts. Stimulation at one point of the animal organism produces contraction at another. The principles of irritability and of motility are involved, but all further study of *this* process will lead us only to the physics and chemistry of the energy transformations: will lead us, that is, in the direction of *analysis*. If, however, we inquire in what way such reflexes are combined or 'integrated' into more complicated processes, we shall be led in exactly the opposite direction, that of *synthesis*, and here we soon come, as is not surprising, to a synthetic novelty. This is *specific response* or *behavior*. And the advent of specific response is a sufficiently critical point to merit detailed examination, since it is the birth of *awareness* and therewith of psychology itself.

In the single reflex something is done to a sense-organ and the process within the organ is comparable to the process in any unstable substance when foreign energy strikes it; it is strictly a chemical process; and so for the conducting nerve; likewise for the contracting muscle. It happens, as a physiological fact, that in this process stored energy is released, so that a reflex contraction is literally comparable to the firing of a pistol. But the reflex arc is not 'aware' of anything, and indeed there is nothing more to say about the process unless we should begin to analyze it. But even two such processes going on together in one organism are a very different matter. Two such processes require two sense-organs, two conduction paths, and two muscles: and since we are considering the result of the two in combination, the relative anatomical location of these six members is of importance. For simplicity I will take a hypothetical, but strictly possible, case. A small water-animal has an eye-spot located on each side of its anterior end; each spot is connected by a

---

[2] It is of course not true, though often said, that "parallel lines meet in infinity"; not true, that is, if parallel lines are "lines which are everywhere equally distant from each other."

nerve with a vibratory cilium or fin on the *opposite* side of the posterior end; the thrust exerted by each fin is toward the rear. If, now, light strikes one eye, say the right, the left fin is set in motion and the animal's body is set rotating toward the right like a rowboat with one oar. This is all that one such reflex arc could do for the animal. Since, however, there are now two, when the animal comes to be turned far enough toward the right so that some of the light strikes the second eye-spot (as will happen when the animal comes around facing the light), the second fin, on the right side, is set in motion, and the two together propel the animal forward in a straight line. The direction of this line will be that in which the animal lies when its two eyes receive equal amounts of light. In other words, by the combined operation of two reflexes the animal swims *toward the light*, while either reflex alone would only have set it spinning like a top. It now responds specifically in the direction of the light, whereas before it merely spun when lashed.

As thus described, this first dawn of behavior seems to present nothing so very novel; it is not more novel than the infinitesimal touch that makes two parallel lines meet somewhere off in infinity. The animal, it is true, is still merely 'lashed' into swimming toward the light. Suppose, now, that it possesses a *third* reflex arc—a 'heat-spot' so connected with the same or other fins that when stimulated by a certain intensity of heat it initiates a nervous impulse which stops the forward propulsion. The animal is still 'lashed,' but nevertheless no light can force it to swim "blindly to its death" by scalding. It has the rudiments of 'intelligence.' But so it had before. For as soon as two reflex arcs capacitate it mechanically to swim *toward light,* it was no longer exactly like a pinwheel: it could respond specifically toward at least one thing in its environment.

It is this objective reference of a process of release that is significant. The mere reflex does not refer to anything beyond itself: if it drives an organism in a certain direction, it is only as a rocket ignited at random shoots off in some direction, depending on how it happened to lie. But specific response is not merely in some random direction, it is *toward an object,* and if this object is moved, the responding organism changes its direction and still moves after it. And the objective reference is that the organism is *moving with reference to some object or fact of the environment.* In the pistol or the skyrocket the process released depends wholly on factors internal to the mechanism released; in the behaving organism the process depends partly on factors external to the mechanism. This is a difference of prime significance, for in the first case, if you wish to understand all about what the rocket is doing, you have only to look inside the rocket, at the powder exploding there, the size and shape of the compartment in which it is exploding, etc.; whereas, in order to understand what the organism is doing, you will just *miss* the essential point if you look inside the organism. For the organism, while a very interesting mechanism in itself, is one whose movements turn on objects outside of itself, much as the orbit of the earth turns upon the sun; and these external, and sometimes very distant, objects are as much *constituents* of the behavior process as is the organism which does the turning. It is this *pivotal outer object*, the object of specific response, which seems to me to have been over-neglected.

The case cited, in which merely two reflex arcs enable an organism to respond specifically to the direction of a luminous object, is of course an extremely simple one. We have seen how much the addition of even a third reflex arc can contribute to the security of the animal as it navigates its environment, and to the apparent intelligence and 'purposiveness' of its movements. It is not surprising, then, that in animals as highly organized reflexly as are many of the invertebrates, even though they should possess no other principle of action than that of specific response, the various life-activities should present an appearance of considerable intelligence. And I believe that in fact this intelligence is solely the product of accumulated specific responses.[3] Our present point is that the specific response and the 'wish,' as Freud uses the term, are one and the same thing.

This thing, in its essential definition, is *a course of action which the living body executes or is prepared to execute with regard to some object or some fact of its environment.* From this form of statement it becomes clear, I think, that not only is this the very thing which we are generally most interested to discover about the lower animals—what they are doing or what they are going to do—but also that it is the most significant thing about human beings, ourselves not excepted. "Ye shall know them by their fruits," and not infrequently it is by one's own fruits that one comes to know oneself. It is true that the term 'wish' is rather calculated to emphasize the distinction between a course of action actually carried out and one that is only entertained 'in thought.' But this distinction is really secondary. The essential thing for both animal behavior and Freud's psychology is the *course of action,* the purpose with regard to environment, whether or not the action is overtly carried out.

In this whole matter the introspective tradition, which has led psychology into so many unfruitful by-paths, is prepared to mislead us. We must go cautiously. In the first place, let us bear quite clearly in mind that in any living organism, human or animal, we have a very complicated mechanism in which the property of irritability is so united with the power of motion that in a purely mechanical way the organism be-

---

[3] The reader who is interested in the development of specific response into intelligence will enjoy the small volume of A. Bethe ("Dürfen wir den Ameisen und Bienen psychische Qualitäten zuschreiben?" Bonn, 1898), in which the author shows how the life-activities of ants and bees can be explained in terms of reflex process.

comes, on proper stimulation, an engine that behaves in a certain way *with reference to* a specific feature of its environment.[4] This is what we can safely conclude from merely watching the doings of any living creature. And we behold invariably that every living thing is in every waking moment doing something or other to some feature or other of its environment. It is going toward or away from something, it is digging or climbing, it is hunting or eating; more developed organisms are working or playing, reading, writing, or talking, are making money or spending it, are constructing or destroying something; and at a still higher stage of development we find them curing disease, alleviating poverty, comforting the oppressed, and promoting one or another sort of orderliness. All these cases are alike in this, that the individual is doing something definite to some part or other of its environment. In exact language its activity is a "constant function" of some feature of this environment, in just the same sense (although by a different mechanism) as the orbit of our earth is a constant function of the position of the sun around which it swings. This constant function, involving always the two things—living organism and environment—is that which constitutes behavior and is also precisely that which Freud has called, with a none too happy choice of term, the 'wish': as a glance at the illustrations given in Chapter I will show. And we must not forget that 'purpose,' in any sense you may choose howsoever intellectual or indeed moral, is precisely the same thing.

Now, in an organism which is about to perform overtly a course of action with regard to its environment, the internal mechanism is more or less completely set for this performance beforehand. The purpose about to be carried out is already embodied in what we call the 'motor attitude' of the neuro-muscular apparatus; very much as a musical composition is embodied in a phonographic record. And this is why it is in some respects irrelevant whether the individual actually carries out its wish, or not. Something may intervene so that the mechanism is not finally touched off, the stimulus may not be quite strong enough on this occasion, etc.; but that the individual ever developed such a set of its mechanism is the important point. It will be touched off some day, and even if it is not, its presence cannot fail to react on other mechanisms, other motor attitudes. We blame a man who is prepared to tell a lie, nearly if not quite as much as one who actually tells one.

There is indeed excellent ground for believing that the one difference between thought and will is the difference between a motor attitude prepared and one that is touched off. In other words, the essential physiological condition for thought (whatever view one may otherwise hold as to the nature and place of consciousness) is the lambent interplay of motor attitudes, in which some *one* finally gains the ascendency, and goes

---

[4] I would not for a moment minimize the actuality of 'thought.' For the moment we are considering another aspect of the matter.

over into overt conduct. This is no new doctrine, since it is just this which Spinoza had in mind when he declared that "The will and the intellect are one and the same." [5] Herbert Spencer gives us a somewhat closer view of this fact,[6] and modern psychology as a whole has begun to recognize it, as the remarkable tendency of otherwise divergent schools toward some form of 'motor theory of consciousness' shows. Thus, too, William James writes: "Beliefs, in short, are rules for action; and the whole function of thinking is but one step in the production of active habits." [7] And all this is undoubtedly why it is true that as a man thinketh in his heart, so is he. For Freud these motor attitudes of the body, whether they emerge in overt behavior or not, are the will of the individual. And the development of character, in fact the whole drama of life, hinges on the development and reciprocal modification of motor settings, that is of purposes and wishes incorporated in the body. The manner of this interaction is our main theme, for it has a practical bearing on ethics.

Remarkably enough this reduces to an extremely simple principle which will be found to underlie anything which can be called behavior or conduct, from the silent bending of the sensitive tip of a plant's rootlet to the most subtly motivated act of man. Darwin describes, in his book on "The Power of Movement in Plants," [8] how the growing tip of a radicle is sensitive to gravity, moisture, and light, and when subject to one of these influences it transmits an impulse to an adjoining upper part of the rootlet which then bends in such a way that the tip is turned toward the center of the earth, or toward moisture or (in the third case) away from light. If all three forces are present at once, the tip is bent in that direction which provides the most moisture compatible with the greatest depth and the least light. Here we have a very simple case in which three reflexes combine to produce one movement which is a plain mechanical resultant of the movements which the three reflexes would have produced if each had acted alone. They combine because the three reflexes converge on the same motile tissue that bends the rootlet, and this contractile tissue obeys as well as it can the simultaneous commands of all three irritable centers. It is significant that Darwin concludes the volume with these words (p. 573): "It is hardly an exaggeration to say that the tip of the radicle thus endowed, and having the power of directing the movements of the adjoining parts, acts like the brain of one of the lower animals; the brain being seated within the anterior end of the body, receiving impressions from the sense-organs, and directing the several movements."

In the lower forms of animal life we find likewise that reflexes com-

---

5 "Ethics." Part II, Prop. LXIX, Corol. See also the Scholium which follows.
6 "The Principles of Psychology," 2d edition, Vol. I, Part IV, Chap. IX.
7 "The Varieties of Religious Experience." 1902, p. 444.
8 New York, 1888, Chap. XII.

bine to diminish (interference) or to augment each other in the response. H. S. Jennings writes of infusorians,[9] that "under the simultaneous action of the two stimuli the infusorian may either react to the more effective of the two, whichever it is, without regard to the other, or its behavior may be a sort of compromise between the usual results of both." Of course in the former case the less effective stimulus is not without its effect, although this effect may be largely masked by the greater strength of the other factor. "If specimens showing the contact reaction [of settling down on solid objects] are heated, it is found that they do not react to the heat until a higher temperature has been reached than that necessary to cause a definite reaction in free swimming specimens. . . . On the other hand, both heat and cold interfere with this contact reaction. . . . Specimens in contact with a solid react less readily to chemicals than do free specimens, so that a higher concentration is required to induce the avoiding reaction." In these ways the planarians are found to respond to specific temperatures, degrees of chemical concentration, and to specific *amounts of change* in the vital conditions which surround them. Always, stimuli which if given separately would produce the same response, augment each other when they are given simultaneously; while stimuli which separately would produce opposed responses, interfere with or cancel each other when given together.

In the case of such wonderful little creatures as bees we see the same principle extended. As we all know, one prominent part of the behavior of the worker bee is that it fares forth every warm morning, visits the flowers, and returns laden with honey to its hive; to its own hive and no other. It does this throughout the day. This is no simple mode of behavior, and we know that it rests on elaborate neuro-muscular mechanisms. The bee is guided by the characteristic odor of its hive, and of the flowers, by the visible appearance of its own hive and of the surroundings, and by that of the flowers which it selects to visit, by a sense of the sun's warmth, of the state of the atmosphere, of the downward pull of gravity (as it flies), perhaps by some not yet fully understood 'sense of direction,' and by many other sense-data. All these sensory impulses converging on the motor apparatus of the bee's legs, wings, and proboscis guide and impel it moment by moment through its daily rounds. There is no reason to believe, as so careful an observer as Bethe assures us, that any more mysterious (as, say, 'psychic') factors than such plain sensori-motor reflexes are at any moment of the process involved. The fact is that just as in the case of our hypothetical little creature (p. 188), which by two reflex arcs was enabled to swim toward light and by a third was made to avoid too high a temperature (a very 'purposive' response), so in the case of the bee several thousand reflex paths cooperating produce a be-

9 "Behavior of the Lower Organisms." New York, 1906, pp. 92–3.

havior which both looks and is startlingly 'purposive.' The question arises at once, Is this purposiveness really the result of a merely mechanical interplay of reflex arcs, or has an invisible little 'soul' already crept into the bee's 'pineal gland' to direct operations? This we shall have to answer in no uncertain tone: the bee is a purely reflex creature. We have seen purposiveness arise from the mere presence in one organism of three reflex arcs, which cause an organism to seek light and to avoid being scalded; these are already two purposes.[10] In fact, as C. S. Sherrington has said, "In light of the Darwinian theory every reflex *must* be purposive." [11] And a combination of reflexes is even more markedly so. We have then no reason to doubt that Bethe is correct in saying of so complicated an organism as the bee, that all its (so highly purposive) activities are the work of integrated reflexes.

I have stated that the mechanical interaction of reflexes on one another reduces to a very simple principle, and before we consider reflex integration in vertebrates, it will be well to have this principle definitely in mind. The reciprocal influence of reflexes can be exerted, of course, only where they come together, and that is where they converge on a common motor-organ, or on a common efferent nerve leading out to the motor-organ. Now, as the physiologist Sherrington says,[12] "each receptor [sense-organ] stands in connection not with one efferent only but with many—perhaps with all, though as to some of these only through synapses [nerve junctions] of high resistance." It is "approximately true" that "each final common path is in connection with practically each one of all the receptors of the body." This generalization is made of vertebrates, but it is fairly certain that a similar state of things holds throughout the animal and plant kingdoms (for plants, also, have sense-organs, nerves, and muscles). Now nature has not found it convenient to equip us with rotary means of locomotion, like the propeller of a ship; but has provided that every motion shall be made by the to-and-fro play of a member—fin, arm, or leg. Therefore the muscles exist in pairs, in each one of which one muscle moves the limb in a direction opposite to that in which the other muscle moves it; that is, the two muscles of a pair are antagonists. While the nervous impulse generated by any stimulus goes (or under certain circumstances can go) to any muscle of the body, the nervous paths are of different degrees of resistance, so that the main force of the impulse goes in certain few directions rather than in all. And one stimulus will effect somewhere a muscular contraction: some member of the body is moved. But many outer forces are simultaneously playing on the many sense-organs of the body, and they prompt the muscles to many

---

[10] "Yes, but not *conscious* purposes," I seem to hear the reader say. This is a point which I shall take up a little further on.

[11] "The Integrative Action of the Nervous System." New York, 1906, p. 235.

[12] *Op. citat.*, pp. 145–6.

different motions. Wherever these impulses converge to contract the same muscle, that muscle contracts with all the more force, and the limb moves. But when the sensory impulses run equally to the antagonistic muscles of a pair, the limb is naturally unable to move in opposite directions at the same time. If the two impulses are equal in amount the limb will not move at all. Such impulses cancel each other, and *do not contribute* to *behavior*. If we call the sum of all sense impulses at any moment the 'sensory pattern,' we shall practically always find that some portions of this pattern cancel themselves out by interference, in the way described, while the remaining portions augment one another and produce the individual's overt behavior and conduct. The impulses of the sensory pattern may be so weak as to produce no gross muscular contractions, but they will then cause varying degrees of muscular tonus; and this is that play of motor attitude which I have previously mentioned. It is thought. It differs from overt behavior only in the small degree of muscular action which it involves. The one fundamental principle is that no member can move in opposed directions at once, and impulses that impel to this efface each other. This is very simple: the complications to which it gives rise, both physiologically and behavioristically, are far from simple.

An interesting problem of a partially conflicting sensory pattern is 'the Meynert scheme' of the child and the candle-flame, which has become generally familiar owing to its having been quoted by James.[13] Meynert aims to show by a diagram how a child learns not to put his finger into a candle-flame. Two original reflexes are assumed: one in which the visual image of the candle causes the child's finger to go out to touch the flame; the other in which the painful heat on the finger causes the child's arm to be withdrawn. A fanciful series of nerve-paths, fabricated in the interests of the 'association theory,' purports to show why after once burning himself the child will in future put out his hand, on seeing a candle, but draw it back again *before* he burns himself. The explanation is beautifully accomplished by begging the whole question; that is, by resting the 'explanation' on certain time (and strength) relations between the two reflexes of extension and retraction—relations which neither diagram nor text accounts for. In fact, apart from the passage in which the whole question is begged, both diagram and text show that on every subsequent occasion the child will infallibly put out his hand, burn it, and then withdraw it, just as he had done the first time; for the reflex path for extending the hand is the shorter and the better established of the two, and it remains entirely vague as to how the impulse to withdraw shall arrive in time to save the hand.

But Meynert's explanation is not only unsuccessful, it is wrong in its

[13] The Principles of Psychology." New York, 1890, Vol. I, pp. 24–7.

intent. If achieved, it would show that a child once burned will on merely seeing a candle, and before it feels the candle's heat, draw back its hand. And this, Meynert thinks, is the process of learning. Whereas in fact a child that shrinks on merely *seeing* a candle has not *learned* anything; it has acquired a morbid fear. So far from being a step in learning, such a reaction will gravely impede the child in acquiring the use of this innocent utensil. It is true that one severe experience of being burned can establish the morbid cringing at the mere sight of fire, but every teacher knows how disastrous this is to a child's progress; and the mechanism of such a response will not be found in any such figment of the imagination as that which Meynert adduces.[14] I know of nothing in this 'Meynert scheme' that tallies with fact, and, as James well says, it is "a mere scheme" and "anything but clear in detail." Nothing but the authority of the association theory ever loaned it plausibility.

The normal process of learning to deal with a candle is the process of establishing a response to an object which is both luminous and hot, if we consider only the two properties so far brought in question. The successful response will be one which is controlled directly by the actual properties of the candle, for this alone means precision and nicety in handling it. The normal child learns the properties of objects, without acquiring a fear of these properties; for fear is *not* 'wholesome.' The case in hand is simple. The child has in fact the two original tendencies, to put out its hand to touch any pretty, bright object, and to draw back its hand when the nerves of pain are stimulated. But these are at first not coördinated; and coordination (learning) is the establishment of a just balance between the openness of the two paths; where 'just' means proportioned to the actual properties of the candle. On first seeing a candle the child puts out its hand; the second reaction (of withdrawal) is touched off by stimulation of the heat-pain nerves in the hand,[15] and the moment at which this shall happen depends on the sensitiveness of the heat-pain end-organs, and the openness of the path connecting them with the muscles that retract the arm; of which probably the openness of path is the modifiable factor. The warmth of the candle begins to stimulate this retraction reflex, and stimulates it more, and at an increasing rate of increase, as the hand approaches the candle. All that is needed to save the child from burning its hand, and this is what Meynert's scheme aims to explain, is an openness of the retraction reflex path sufficient to stop the hand before it actually reaches the flame. If the act of extension excited through the eye is not too impetuous, the retraction reflex will

[14] Theodor Meynert was an Austrian. And in both Austria and Germany, despite the efforts of Froebel, the tradition survives that fear is a normal and necessary ingredient of the learning process.

[15] Whether the organs of heat and pain are identical or distinct, the stimulation and sensation, is a single continuous series running from warmth to heat and pain.

from the outset protect the hand; but if the former is a very open path, the advancing arm may get a momentum which the retraction reflex will not be sufficiently quick and strong to counterbalance in time to save the hand from being burned. A few repetitions of the experience will give this retraction path an openness which will safeguard the hand for the future; and this process is aided by the prolonged pain yielded by a burn, which continues the retraction stimulus for a considerable period and so 'wears' down the retraction path more than a great many merely momentary stimuli could do. In this way a single experience of burning is often sufficient for all time. Thus experience establishes a balance between the two opposed reflexes, of extension and of pain avoidance, such that the organism carries on its further examination of the candle in safety. If it be thought that this balance will never come about because each repetition will 'wear' the path for extension as much as that for retraction, it must be remembered, firstly, that the prolonged pain stimulation applies only to the latter path; and, secondly, that the opening, or '*Bahnung*,' of reflex paths is, like almost all processes in nature, a process which proceeds most rapidly at first. It is 'asymptotic.' The passage of a first nervous impulse over a path of high resistance 'wears' it down more than the same impulse would wear an already opened tract: just as the first five pedestrians across a snow-covered field do more toward making a path than do the next twenty-five.

The explanation which I have given does not account for all varieties of the learning process, of course, nor for the child's 'concept' of a candle. But it explains, I believe, how in point of fact a child learns not to burn its hands, and this is all that the fantastic Meynert scheme undertakes to do. The mechanism of learning is by no means understood as yet; that is to say, that the manner in which reflex paths are integrated to produce the more complicated forms of behavior is still a matter for investigation. Yet from the observation of behavior itself certain important facts have already been made out. One of these is that the principle of the mutual interference of opposed reflexes and the mutual augmentation of synergic reflexes holds throughout. This principle, indeed, although it becomes endlessly complicated and in some cases (as in the production of reflex stepping and other alternating movements by means of 'reciprocal innervation') is even partly obscured, seems to be the one general formula for reflex integration. This can be seen in operation in all cases of behavior from the most purely reflex to the most highly 'conscious.' Thus, just as the leaves of certain plants, which are subject to the two impulses of facing the sunlight but also of avoiding desiccating heat, will spread themselves out broadly toward the sun in the morning and afternoon, but in the heat of noonday will partially fold up, so under the teacher's eye the pugnacious impulse of the small boy is subdued to the furtive expedient of the spit-ball; and so, too, the man who yearns for worldly power but yet in *personal* contact with his fellows is unconquerably timid will become a renowned inventor, or a shrewd manipulator of stock-markets, or in politics will work into some important position 'behind the throne.'

Another feature incidental to the integration of reflexes, which is seen from the observation of behavior, is what I may call the *recession of the stimulus*. This is a point not insisted on by Freud, but one which is of vast importance to a clear understanding of the dynamic psychology which Freud has so immensely furthered. The single reflex is of course always touched off by some stimulus, and if only reflex process is in question the immediate stimulus is the inciting and controlling factor. But where even two reflexes are working together to produce specific response or behavior, the case is altered: the stimulus is now merely an agent, a part of a higher process. We have already seen this in the case of our water animal which was enabled by two eye-spots and two fins to swim toward light. Now this light toward which it swims is not the *immediate* stimulus, which rather is the light quanta which at any moment have entered the cells of the eye-spot. And one could not describe what the animal *as a whole* is *doing* in terms of the immediate stimuli; but this can be described only in terms of the environing *objects* toward which the animal's response is directed. This is precisely the distinction between reflex action and specific response or behavior. As the number of component reflexes involved in response increases, the immediate stimulus itself recedes further and further from view as the significant factor.

This is very evident in the case of the bee. We may grant with Bethe that the bee is only, in the last analysis, a reflex mechanism. But it is a very complex one, and when we are studying the bee's behavior we are studying an organism which by means of integrated reflexes has become enabled to respond specifically to the objects of its environment. It may be doubted whether Bethe, or any other of the biologists, fully realizes the significance of this; fully realizes, that is, how completely in behavior the stimulus recedes from its former position of importance. To study the behavior of the bee is of course to put the question, "What is the bee doing?" This is a plain scientific question. Yet if we should put it thus to Bethe, his answer would probably be: "It is doing of course a great many things; now its visual organ is stimulated and it darts toward a flower; now its olfactory organ is stimulated and it goes for a moment to rub antennæ with another bee of its own hive; and so forth." But this is not an answer. We ask, "What is the bee doing?" And we are told, "Now its visual . . . and now its olfactory, . . ." etc., etc. With a little persistence we could probably get Bethe to say, "Why, the *bee* isn't doing anything." Whereas an unbiased observer can see plainly enough that "The *bee* is laying by honey in its home."

My point is that the often too materialistically-minded biologist is so fearful of meeting a certain bogy, the 'psychic,' that he hastens to analyze every case of behavior into its component reflexes without venturing first to observe it as a whole. In this way he fails to note the recession of the stimulus and the infallibly objective reference of behavior. He does not see that in any case of behavior no immediate sense stimulus whatsoever will figure in a straightforward and exact description of what the creature is doing: and 'What?' is the first question which science puts to any phenomenon. This was the case even in the first instance which we looked at (p. 188), where two eye-spots and two vibratory cilia enabled an animal to *swim toward a light*. It is equally true in the cases of the rootlet, and of the planarian which responds specifically to an amount of change, or even a rate of change. It is a thousand times more marked in the case of the bee, for here not only would it not be possible to describe what the bee does in terms of sensory stimuli, but also in much of the bee's conduct it would not be possible to point out any *physical* object on which the bee's activities turn or toward which they are directed. It lays up a store of honey in its home. If we suppose that here the parental hive is the physical object around which the bee's activities center, we soon find ourselves wrong, for when the swarm migrates the bee knows the old hive no more but continues its busy life of hoarding in some other locality. The fact is that the specific object on which the bee's activities are focused, and of which they are a function, its 'home,' is a very complex *situation*, neither hive, locality, coworkers, nor yet flowers and honey, but a situation of which all of these are the related components. In short we cannot do justice to the case of the bee, unless we admit that he is the citizen of a state, and that this phrase, instead of being a somewhat fanciful metaphor or analogy, is the literal description of what the bee demonstrably is and does. Many biologists shy at such a description; they believe that these considerations should be left to Vergil and to M. Maeterlinck, while they themselves deem it safer to deal with the bee's olfactory and visual organs. They will not describe the bee's behavior as a whole, will not observe what mere reflexes when coöperating integrally in one organism can accomplish, because they fear, at bottom, to encounter that bogy which philosophers have set in their way, the 'subjective' or the 'psychic.' They need not be afraid of this, for all that they have to do is to describe in the most objective manner possible what the bee is doing.

But our present point is that even two reflexes acting within one organism bring it about that the organism's behavior is no longer describable in terms of the immediate sensory stimulus, but as a function of objects and of situations in the environment, and even of such aspects of objects as positions, directions, degrees of concentration, rates of change, etc. While as the number of integrated reflexes increases, in the higher organisms, the immediate stimulus recedes further and further from view, and is utterly missing in an exact description (merely that) of what the organism does.

Thus it comes about that in the description of the behavior of creatures as complicated as human beings it has been quite forgotten that sensory stimuli and reflexes are still at the bottom of it *all*. Indeed, such a suggestion has only to be made and it will be instantly repudiated, especially by those philosophers and psychologists who deem themselves the accredited guardians of historic truth. In other words, the study of the integration of reflexes has been so neglected, and it is indeed difficult, that we have come to believe that an unfathomable gulf exists between the single reflex movement and the activities of conscious, thinking creatures. The gap in our knowledge is held to be a gap in the continuity of nature. And yet if we face the matter frankly, we see that history, biography, fiction, and the drama are all descriptions of what men do, of human behavior. We are wont to say, "Ah, yes, but the true interest of these things lies in what the men are meanwhile *thinking*." So be it. But are thought and behavior so *toto caelo* different? And what did Spinoza mean by saying that "The will and the intellect are one and the same"? And, further, have those who so confidently assert that thought is a principle distinct from integrated reflex activity ever succeeded in telling what 'thought' is? We meet here, of course, the profoundest question in psychology, and the one which for more than a hundred years has been the central problem of philosophy—What is cognition? Or, Is cognition different in principle from integrated reflex behavior?

I must state that Freud has never raised this question in so explicit a form. He has also not answered it. But by discovering for us the way in which the 'thoughts' of men react on one another, in actual concrete fact, he has given us the key that fits one of the most ancient and most baffling of locks. What I shall say in the remainder of this section is confessedly more than Freud has said; it is, however, as I believe, the inevitable and almost immediate deduction from what he has said. This view of mind as integrated reflex behavior is subversive of much that is traditional in philosophy and psychology, and particularly of the dualistic dogma which holds that the mechanical and spiritual principles, so unmistakable in our universe, are utterly alien to each other, and even largely incompatible. This newer view, however, instead of being subversive, is unexpectedly and categorically confirmatory of certain ancient doctrines of morals and of freedom:—verities which have been well-nigh forgotten in a so-called 'scientific' age. Let us consider, then, the higher forms of behavior, in human beings, and the question of consciousness and thought.[16]

---

[16] This new theory of cognition can of course be treated here only in outline. I have written further of it under the title of "Response and Cognition" in *The Journal of Philosophy, Psychology, and Scientific Methods*, 1915, Vol. XII, pp. 365–372; 393–409. The article is reprinted as a Supplement to this book.

If one sees a man enter a railway station, purchase a ticket, and then pass out and climb on to a train, one feels that it is clear enough what the man is doing, but it would be far more interesting to know what he is thinking. One sees clearly that he is taking a train, but one cannot see his thoughts or his intentions and these contain the 'secret' of his actions. And thus we come to say that the conscious or subjective is a peculiar realm, private to the individual, and open only to his *in*trospection. It is apart from the world of objective fact. Suppose, now, one were to apply the same line of reasoning to an event of inanimate nature. At dawn the sun rises above the eastern ridge of hills. This is the plain fact, and it is not of itself too interesting. But what is the 'secret' behind such an occurrence? "Why this is, as everybody knows, that the sun is the god Helios who every morning drives his chariot up out of the East, and he has some magnificent purpose in mind. We cannot tell just what it is because his thoughts and purposes are subjective and not open to our observation. We suspect, however, that he is paying court to Ceres, and so cheers on by his presence the growing crops." Or again, the same line of reasoning as used in a somewhat later age. The stream flows through the field, leaps the waterfall, and goes foaming onward down the valley. The fact is that it has always done so. And the secret? "Well, they used to say that the stream was a daughter of Neptune and that she was hurrying past to join her father. We know better than that now; we know that water always seeks its own level, and the only secret about it is that the water is urged on from behind by an impulse which some call the *vis viva*. We've never seen this *vis viva*, for it is invisible; but it is the secret of all inanimate motion; and of course it must be there, for otherwise nothing would move."

It has taken man ages to learn that the gaps in his knowledge of observed fact cannot be filled by creatures of the imagination. It is the most precious achievement of the physical sciences that the 'secrets behind' phenomena lie in the phenomena and are to be found out by *observing* the *phenomena* and in no other way. The 'mental' sciences have yet to learn this lesson. Continued observation of the rising and setting sun revealed that the secret behind was not the gallantry of Helios, but the rotation of our earth which, by simple geometry, caused the sun relatively to ourselves to rise in the East. Continued observation of water showed that neither a nature god nor yet a *vis viva* is the secret behind the flowing stream; but that the stream is flowing as directly as the surface of the earth permits, toward *the center of the earth*. And that this is merely a special instance of the fact that all masses move toward one another. There is indeed a mystery behind such motion, but science calls this mystery neither Helios, Neptune, nor *vis viva*, but simply motion; and science will penetrate this mystery by more extended observation of motion. Now the inscrutable 'thought behind' the actions of a man, which is the invisible secret of those actions, is another myth, like the myths of the nature gods and the *vis viva*. Not that there are not actual thoughts, but tradition has turned thought into a myth by utterly misconceiving it and locating in the wrong place.

On seeing the man purchase a ticket at the railway station, we felt that there was more behind this action, 'thoughts' that were the invisible secret of his movements. Suppose, instead, we inquire whether the more is not ahead. More is to come; let us watch the man further. He enters the train, which carries him to a city. There he proceeds to an office, on the door of which we read 'Real Estate.' Several other men are in this office; a document is produced; our man takes a sum of money from his pocket and gives this to one of the other men, and this man with some of the others signs the document. This they give to our man, and with it a bunch of keys. All shake hands, and the man whom we are watching departs. He goes to the railway station and takes another train, which carries him to the town where we first saw him. He walks through several streets, stops before an empty house, takes out his bunch of keys, and makes his way into the house. Not long afterwards several vans drive up in front, and the men outside proceed to take household furniture off the vans and into the house. Our man inside indicates where each piece is to be placed. He later gives the men from the vans money.

All this we get by observing what the man does, and without in any way appealing to the 'secret' thoughts of the man. If we wish to know more of what he is doing we have only to observe him more. Suppose, however, that we had appealed to his inner thoughts to discover the 'secret' of his movements, when we first saw him buying a ticket at the railway station. We approach him and say, "Sir, I am a philosopher and extremely anxious to know what you are doing, and of course I cannot learn that unless you will tell me what you are thinking." "Thinking?" he may reply, if he condones our guileless impertinence. "Why, I am thinking that it's a plaguey hot day, and I wish I had made my morning bath five degrees colder, and drunk less of that hot-wash that my wife calls instant coffee." "Was that all?" "Yes, that was all until I counted my change; and then I heard the train whistle.—Here it is. Good-by! And good luck to your philosophy!"

Thought is often a mere irrelevance, a surface embroidery on action. What is more important, the very best that the man could have told us would have been *no better* than what we have learned by watching the man. At best he could have told us, "I am intending to buy a house and to get my furniture in to-day"; exactly what we have observed. And if he told us his further intentions, these in turn could be as completely learned by watching his movements; and *more* reliably, since men do both think and speak lies.

Freud makes, however, the further point that thought, that is, conscious thought, is so little complete as to be scarcely any index to a man's character or deeds. This is Freud's doctrine of the unconscious; although Freud is by no means the first to discover or to emphasize the unconscious. A man's conscious thoughts, feelings, and desires are determined by unconscious thoughts or 'wishes' which lie far deeper down, and which the upper, conscious man knows nothing of. I have illustrated this doctrine at length in the first part of this volume. In fact, conscious thought is merely the surface foam of a sea where the real currents are well beneath the surface. It is an error, then, to suppose that the 'secret behind' a man's actions lies in those thoughts which he (and he alone) can 'introspectively survey.' We shall presently see that it is an error to contrast thought with action at all.

But what are we to do when 'thought' has receded to so impregnable a hiding-place? We are to admit, I think, that we have misunderstood the nature of thought, and predicated so much that is untrue of it, that what we have come to call 'thought' is a pure myth. We are to say with William James: [17] "I believe that 'consciousness,' when once it has evaporated to this estate of pure diaphaneity, is on the point of disappearing altogether. It is the name of a nonentity, and has no right to a place among first principles. Those who still cling to it are clinging to a mere echo, the faint rumor left behind by the disappearing 'soul' upon the air of philosophy." This is the keynote of his Radical Empiricism, the principle that of all those which he enunciated was dearest to him; and it is his final repudiation of dualism. With this we return to the facts.

It is just one error which has prevented us from seeing that the study of what men *do*, i.e., how they 'behave,' comprises the entire field of psychology. And that is the failure to distinguish essence from accident. If one holds out one's hand and lets fall a rubber ball, it moves down past the various parts of one's person and strikes the floor; now it is opposite one's breast, now at the level of the table-top, now at the level of the chair-seat, and now it rests on the floor. This, we say, is what the ball does, and all this is as true as it is irrelevant. For if the same ball had been dropped by some other means from the same point it would have fallen in just the same way if neither oneself, nor the table, nor the chair had been there. It was all accident that it fell past one's breast and past the table; accident even that it hit the floor, for had there been no floor there it would have continued to fall. What the ball is *essentially* doing, although it took science a long time to find this out, is *moving toward the center of the earth;* and in this lies significance, for if the earth's mass were displaced or abolished, the motion of the ball would indeed be concomitantly displaced or abolished. Mathematics and science conveniently designate that which is thus essential in any process as 'function.' It is accident that the ball moves parallel to the table-leg, for essentially the

[17] "Essays in Radical Empiricism." New York, 1912, p. 2.

movement of the ball is a function of the earth's center. *This* is what the ball is *really 'doing.'* We have adumbrated this same fact in connection with the bee. It is in the present respect accidental that the bee sips at this flower, or that; pluck them aside and the bee will turn as well to other flowers. What is, however, not accidental is that the bee is laying up honey in its home; for the bee's life-activities are a function of its home,—and home is a complicated but purely objective state of things. All this is but a different aspect of that which I have called the recession of the stimulus; the latter giving place, as reflexes become more and more integrated, to objects and to *relations* between objects as that of which the total body-activity is a function.

Now it is the same case with the man whom we saw buying a railway ticket. What he is thinking at the moment is likely to be a most irrelevant gloss on what he is actually doing, and will be far from being the 'secret' of his movements. At the very most favorable moment his thought can do no more than reveal to us what he is doing; for notoriously introspection gives us no clew as to *how* we achieve even the least voluntary movement. Therefore what the man is doing is the sole question to be considered. But on the other hand, while it is true that the man is buying a ticket it is only a subordinate and insignificant matter, for essentially the man is purchasing a house, and this latter statement shows us that of which the man's total behavior is a true function. The purchase of a railway ticket is as accidental to this process as a body's striking the floor is irrelevant to the law of gravitation; and if there were no railway in existence the man would purchase his house, and go to secure his deed by stage-coach, chaise, or on his legs. Just as the stimulus recedes, so the component activities recede from their primary position in the total process, as integration advances. Both stimulus and component process are there and are necessary, but they are only parts of a larger whole.

These considerations make it clear, I trust, why the dualistic philosophical view, which contrasts physical motion with a secret, inscrutable, 'psychical' process 'behind,' is mischievous.[18] It totally ignores the work of integration, and to assuage this ignorance it fabricates a myth. With that view falls also the entire subject of 'psychophysical parallelism'; which was a complete misapprehension from the outset. It is not that we have two contrasted worlds, the 'objective' and the 'subjective'; there is but one world, the objective, and that which we have hitherto not understood, have dubbed therefore the 'subjective,' are the subtler workings of integrated objective mechanisms.

The same considerations give light on another, though cognate, issue. The man who buys a ticket is said to do so in the interest of some 'end' which he has in mind. In this way action is, again, contrasted (as the

---

[18] The view which I am outlining has, per contra, nothing to do with 'materialism,' as I have shown at length in "The Concept of Consciousness."

'means') with the mental secret of action (the 'end'). This is an unfortunate way of looking at the matter, since in reality, as I have tried to show, that which is so contrasted with the subordinate action ('means'), and is said to be a mentally entertained 'end' and quite different in nature from the means, is after all precisely another action—the purchase of a home. It is not true that we do something in order to attain a dead and static 'end'; we do something as the necessary but subordinate moment in the *doing* of something more comprehensive. The true comparison then is not between deed or means and thought or end, but between part deed and whole deed. This is of importance, and we shall consider it again; but I will point out, in passing, that without this fallacy of 'ends' we should never have been afflicted with that fantastic whimsy called 'hedonistic ethics'; which, I incline to think, is responsible for much of modern deviltry.

We return now to the main line of our argument. It is clear that this *function* which behavior or conduct is of the external situation is the very same thing which Freud deals with under the name of 'wish.' It is a course of action which the body takes or is prepared (by motor set) to take with reference to objects, relations, or events in the environment. The prophetic quality of thought which makes it seem that thought is the hidden and inner secret of conduct is due to the fact that thought is the preceding labile interplay of motor settings which goes on almost constantly, and which differs from overt conduct in that the energy involved is too small to produce gross bodily movements. This is a piece of nature's economy.

Now in this wish or function we have the pure essence of human will, and of the soul itself. No distinction can be found between function, wish, and purpose; in every case we are dealing with a dynamic relation between the individual's living body, as subject of the relation (or mathematically speaking the 'dependent variable'), and some environmental fact, as object of the relation (or 'independent variable'). The mechanism of the body incorporates the wish or purpose. And this view gives a concrete meaning to Aristotle's dictum that the soul is the '*form*' or "entelechy of a natural body endowed with the capacity of life." [19] The living body through a long process of organization has come at length to 'embody' purpose. But the soul is of course always and forever the *purpose* that is embodied, and not the mere matter (Aristotle's 'potentiality') that as a mechanism embodies. The distinction is the same as that between the design which an inventor patents and the steel and brass in which the plan is tangibly realized.

Such a view of the soul departs widely from the academic dogmas of the present day and from popular psychology; and it has the apparent

[19] "De Anima," 412a.

novelty that any restatement of the views of Plato and Aristotle must
have in an age which has forgotten the classics. One or two further deviations from current psychological notions must be briefly mentioned. The
first and most important is in regard to 'consciousness.' This actually figures in all modern discussions as a substance which, constrasted with the
substance of matter, is that of which sensations, ideas, and thoughts are
composed: the ego, mind, and soul are thought to be made of it, it is the
'subjective' essence, and the question of cognition is concerned with the
relations between consciousness and matter. In the view now before us,
consciousness and 'the subjective as such' are done away with. Consciousness is not a substance but a relation—the relation between the living organism and the environment to which it specifically responds; of
which its behavior is found to be this or that constant function; or, in
other words, to which its purposes refer. This is the relation of awareness,
and the cognitive relation. There will be no consciousness except in a
situation where *both* living organism and environment are present and
where the functional relation already described exists between them.
It has always been admitted that cognition involves a knower and a
known, and if we look for these in this situation, we see at once that the
body is the knower, and the environing objects responded to are the
known. In short, those objects or aspects toward which we respond, of
which our purposes are functions—these are the 'contents of consciousness.' And these immediately, not some pale 'representations' thereof.
This is a return to the obvious fact that what a man knows are the actual
things around him, the objects and events with which he has to deal; it is
a return also to Aristotle, who said, "Actual knowledge is identical with
its object"; [20] and again, "The mind *is* the thing when actually thinking
it." [21] Here it is of secondary importance whether there is overt and
grossly visible conduct or only the less energetic play of motor setting
and attitude, for the two are equally describable only as functions of
something in the outside situation; and that about which a man thinks
is clearly, even for introspection, numerically identical with that upon
which his actions turn, and with that which, when he comes near enough,
he sees and handles.

Thought is, however, more than the object thought about: there is
active thinking about the objects. If we look once more at the least manifold in which cognition occurs—a living organism in, and responsive to,
an environment—we see that this further active element is the active
play of motor attitude, which eventually resolves itself into the less labile
but more forceful phenomenon, conduct. Thus *thought is latent course of
action with regard to environment* (i.e., is motor setting), or a procession
of such attitudes. But we have already found that will is also course of

20 "De Anima," 431a.
21 *Ibidem,* 431b.

action with regard to environment, so that the only difference between thought and volition is one of the intensity of nerve impulse that plays through the sensori-motor arcs—a difference of minimal importance for either psychology or *ethics*. From this appears the literal truth of Spinoza's dictum that "The will and the intellect are one and the same"; a saying that is verifiable on many sides, and one which early moralists recognize in such maxims as, "As a man thinketh in his heart, so is he"; but one which, on the other hand, is made unintelligible in the scheme of the mind offered by current psychology.

The scheme that I have been suggesting could be elucidated and fortified by the consideration of attention, memory, emotion, illusions, and the other phenomena studied by psychology. But I have discussed these at some length elsewhere,[22] and enough has been said, I think, to show what sort of a dynamic theory of will and cognition Freud's doctrine of the 'wish,' as I believe, implies. We have seen that the wish is purpose embodied in the mechanism of a living organism, that it is necessarily a wish about, or a purpose regarding, some feature of the environment; so that a total situation comprising *both organism and environment* is always involved. We have seen that will, thought, and the object of knowledge are all integral and inseparable parts of this total situation. Inseparable because, if organism and environment are sundered, the cognitive relation is dissolved, and merely matter remains; precisely as only water remains when a rainbow is pulled apart. Mind is a relation and not a substance.

---

[22] "Response and Cognition." *The Journal of Philosophy, Psychology, and Scientific Methods.* 1915, Vol. XII, pp. 365–372; 393–409. Cf. Supplement. "The Concept of Consciousness." George Allen and Macmillan, 1914. "The Place of Illusory Experience in a Realistic World." An essay in "The New Realism." Macmillan, 1912.

# 11 • Ralph Barton Perry

## Docility and Purposiveness

Ralph Barton Perry was known primarily as a philosopher and the biographer of William James. In this article he became enough of a psychologist to express the next step in the analysis of purpose after James and Holt. He extends the idea of the recession of the stimulus to a point where it can be seen more clearly as a "goal" and not an object, however globally defined, in the environment. His notion of the general motor set as a "higher propensity" which determines action in terms of the prospective congruence of the action with a set is of interest as a precurser to contemporary thinking which sees behavior as a resultant of some matching of input against internal standards. The T.O.T.E. units of Miller, Galanter, and Pribram, Festinger's theory of cognitive dissonance, and Hunt's postulation of incongruity as the generic motivator are cases in point. Perry's use of docility as a criterion for purpose is also of import because of its subsequent adoption by Tolman.

In two earlier papers,[1] I have discussed various conceptions which have been proposed as definitions of purpose, such as *systematic unity, tendency,* and *adaptation.* None of these appears to give any meaning to such phrases as 'in order to' or 'for the sake of,' which I have selected as the most unmistakably and unqualifiedly teleological expressions in common use. Adaptation, or complementary adjustment may, if one so desires, be regarded as purposive in a broad sense. But I have thought it important to show that such processes may be construed as complex cases of ordinary automatism or mechanism. Complementary adjustment means a give and take between environment and organism, in which the environment makes the first move, and in which the exchange of actions obeys a constant law. Given the law, and any state of the varying environment (stimulus), the response of the organism can be predicted. The law itself is like any mechanical law, and is simply obeyed by the responding

[1] Purpose as Systematic Unity, *Monist.* 1917, *27,* 352–375; and Purpose as Tendency and Adaptation, *Phil. Rev.,* 1917, *26,* 477–495.
This article is reproduced in full from the *Psychological Review,* 1918, *25,* 1–20. Reprinted by permission of the American Psychological Association.

organism. The response *is* complementary; but it means nothing to say that it occurs *in order to be* complementary, or *for the sake of* the complementary outcome.

In the case of plastic or modifiable behavior, we meet with a new and important principle. The organism *acquires* or *learns* complementary adjustments. The proverbial burnt child, for example, acquires a response that is appropriate to the stimulus of fire. It is not that the child does so respond, but that the response has been selected *owing to* its complementary character. To do full justice to the complexity of this total process it is necessary to recognize two propensities, which we may for the present call the *selective* or *higher* propensity and the *eligible,* or *lower* propensity. Let us illustrate these from a case of animal learning described by Professor Thorndike.

We take a box twenty by fifteen by twelve inches, replace its cover and front side by bars an inch apart, and make in this front side a door arranged so as to fall open when a wooden button inside is turned from a vertical to a horizontal position. . . . A kitten, three to six months old, if put in this box when hungry, a bit of fish being left outside, reacts as follows: It tries to squeeze through between the bars, claws at the bars and at loose things in and out of the box, stretches its paws out between the bars, and bites at its confining walls. Some one of all these promiscuous clawings, squeezings and bitings turns round the wooden button, and kitten gains freedom and food. By repeating the experience again and again, the animal comes gradually to omit all the useless clawing and the like, and to manifest only the particular impulse (e.g., to claw hard at the top of the button with the paw, or to push against one side of it with the nose) which has resulted successfully. It turns the button around without delay whenever put in the box.[2]

The eligible propensity in this case is the acquired propensity or habit which proves 'successful,' such as clawing hard at the top of the button with the paw. This eligible propensity is complementary to the environment in that it so combines with the environment and with reflexes such as seizing, chewing and swallowing, as to restore the vitality of the hungry organism to par. But in the course of acquiring this propensity the kitten cannot as yet be determined by it. We need therefore to recognize another or higher propensity to account for the kitten's 'trying.' This higher or selective propensity dominates the whole process. It accounts for the animal's activity, and it also accounts for that form of activity which is chosen to be the stereotyped and recurrent activity. It excites the animal to efforts that continue *until* a certain specific act occurs; and it determines what character that specific act shall possess in order to become recurrent. In the maxim 'if at first you don't succeed, try, try again,' the higher propensity both accounts for the repeated

2 E. L. Thorndike, 'Educational Psychology,' Vol. II., The Psychology of Learning, p. 9.

trials and defines what shall constitute success. Or, in the saying 'he won't be happy till he gets it,' the selective propensity accounts for the unhappiness, and for that specific thing which alone will remove it.

Although its peculiar importance has not, I think, been recognized, this governing or selective propensity is familiar enough to psychologists. Professor Thorndike calls it "the learner's *Set* or *Attitude* or *Adjustment* or *Determination*." [3] Professor Woodworth describes it as follows:

> We must assume in the animal an adjustment or determination of the psychophysical mechanism toward a certain end. . . . His behavior shows that he is, as an organism, set in that direction. This adjustment persists till the motor reaction is consummated; it is the driving force in the unremitting efforts of the animal to attain the desired end. [4]

It is manifestly the same thing which some psychologists refer to as conation. Speaking of instinctive behavior, Professor McDougall says:

> The process, unlike any merely mechanical process, is not to be arrested by any sufficient mechanical obstacle, but is rather intensified by any such obstacle and only comes to an end either when its appropriate goal is achieved, or when some stronger incompatible tendency is excited, or when the creature is exhausted by its persistent efforts. [5]

Professor Watson has recently attempted a rigorously physiological interpretation of the learning process. He is especially anxious to avoid any appeal to conscious guidance, or to conscious pleasure and displeasure, and 'to account for the elimination of useless movements upon purely objective grounds.' [6] It is not clear that he would wish to reject teleology of the sort that is here proposed. In any case, I cannot see that his account of the matter, assuming it to be correct, is in essential disagreement with the above analysis.

Professor Watson proposes to account for the formation of habit solely by the laws of *frequency* and *recency*. The so-called 'successful' movement of the animal is the movement which terminates each trial, as does movement 10 in the series, 1, 2, 3, 4, 5, 6, 7, 8, 9, *10* and 1, 3, 7, 13, 14, 8, *10*. Where there are repeated trials, *10* is then the movement which occurs in all, and hence most frequently; and it is the movement which, upon each new trial, has occurred most recently. Hence it comes to occur more promptly with each successive trial, and eventually to become a fixed habit.

[3] *Op. cit.*, p. 13.

[4] G. T. Ladd and R. S. Woodworth, 'Elements of Physiological Psychology,' p. 551.

[5] W. McDougall, 'Social Psychology,' p. 27. Professor McDougall, to be sure, reserves the term 'conation' for the consciousness or 'experience' which he believes attends behavior of this type; but in any case the process described above would represent the behaviorist aspect or criterion of conation.

[6] 'Behaviorism,' p. 251.

But the important point, as I see it, is the fact that movement 10 *does terminate* each trial, without the interference of the experimenter. A series of movements is repeatedly inaugurated, and each series continues until a certain end-state is reached. The animal then ceases to try. The important phenomenon is that of effort persisting until a situation is reached which evokes no further response; or which inaugurates a new series of trials which terminate differently, and lead to the formation of another and independent habit. The learning animal is in each case being *driven* by something (as when 'hunger is driving the animal'[7]), the peculiar reactivity of the animal being due not merely to a specific stimulus-reflex, but to a general propensity which has its own specific and determined lapse or quietus.

Professor Holt, in a recent discussion of 'The Physiology of Wishes,' has followed Sherrington and Freud in emphasizing the antagonism, reinforcement and integration of reflexes. He rightly insists that the behavior of a living organism is a *doing of something*, and is therefore describable only by reference to that environmental object toward which the act addresses itself. Even simple reflexes have this character of transcending the organism in which they occur. All responses are responses 'to' something, and that something is a part of their essential character. Where two or more responses are excited they may augment one another, inhibit one another, or give way to a resultant response in which they are both partially present. The process of integration is fairly intelligible in terms of muscular antagonism, resistance in the nerve cells or synapses, and distribution of nervous energy.

While the view which I am proposing is in fundamental agreement with that of Professor Holt, there are two important differences of emphasis. In the first place, Professor Holt uses the term 'purpose' for any organic response having specific objective reference. "This thing," he says, "in its essential definition, is *a course of action which the living body executes or is prepared to execute with regard to some object or some fact of its environment*."[8] "The purpose about to be carried out is already embodied in what we call the 'motor attitude' of the neuro-muscular apparatus."[9] The author accepts Sherrington's statement that "in the light of the Darwinian theory every reflex *must* be purposive."[10] The integrated response is more distinctively purposive only because the objective reference is more unmistakable or more necessary for the definition of the response. "As the number of component reflexes involved in response increases, the immediate stimulus itself recedes further and further from view as the significant factor."[11]

[7] According to Professor Watson himself. Cf. *ibid.*, p. 265, note.
[8] 'The Freudian Wish,' ch. 2 on The Physiology of Wishes, pp. 56–57. (This text, p. 190, ed.)
[9] *Op. cit.*, p. 59. (This text, p. 191, ed.)
[10] *Op. cit.*, p. 66. (This text, p. 194, ed.)
[11] *Op. cit.*, pp. 76–77. (This text, p. 198, ed.)

But in the view which I have proposed above the emphasis is placed on the dominance of the general motor set over the subordinate reflexes which are assimilated to it. Professor Holt illustrates his views by the case of the burnt child who learns to respond both to the body's luminousness and also to its hotness. The integrated response is a balance or resultant of the extension reflex and the retraction reflex, 'such that the organism carries on its further examination of the candle in safety.' [12] But if I were using this illustration I should call attention to the dominance of the exploration or curiosity reflex, and say that the child learns how to satisfy that impulse. To extend the hand to the vicinity of the object, to look at it more attentively, or in the case of a more advanced intelligence, to put on asbestos gloves—these are means by which the organism learns to complete or facilitate its primary response. The organism is acting under the control of one response; and this response is modified and amplified by the absorption or rejection of other responses which are incidental to the general reactivity which the primary response incites. In this way it is possible to attach some significance to the terms 'means' and 'end' which tend to drop out altogether in Professor Holt's account.[13] But the case of the burnt child would be doubtfully purposive in this sense, and I should not regard it as a peculiarly illuminating example of the principle. The type of learning process with which I propose to identify purpose, is better exemplified by cases like the one cited from Thorndike, in which there is clear evidence of a strong and persistent impulse, like hunger; which gradually articulates and completes itself, by communicating its energy to reflexes which facilitate it, and turning its energy against reflexes which retard it. In such cases an organism not only does something, but *it learns how to do something;* the 'how' being selected and consolidated under the control of the 'something-to-be-done.'

Or, still more unmistakable examples abound in the operations of more advanced intelligences. If one is hunting for a pin, the 'Aufgabe' is clearly in command of the situation from beginning to end. Sundry responses, such as walking about, probing corners, lifting objects, etc., are *sub*ordinate, and not *co*ordinate reflexes. They are due to the increased reactivity to which the problem gives rise; they acquire a liability to

---

[12] *Op. cit.*, p. 73.

[13] Cf. *op. cit.*, pp. 100–101: "The only semblance of 'end' is found where one purpose is yoked into the service of another purpose, and here the latter might roughly be called the 'end' of the former; yet only roughly and inexactly so, since the whole is process and the subordinate purposes are only its articulate phases." But there must be some difference between the superior purpose and the subordinate purposes, for two reasons: first, because the former exists before the latter, and determines their selection; second, because the subordinate purposes may afterwards be replaced, in which case the superior purpose is not changed but rather is more effectually 'realized.' I think it more in keeping with usage, and on the whole more illuminating, to reserve the term 'purpose' for the superior response, in respect of the selective and controlling function which it exercises.

recurrence according as they do or do not facilitate the finding; interruptions are repelled; and eventually there is built up the integrated response of finding a pin. There would be a specific difference between hunting a pin for the sake of exercise, and moving about for the sake of finding a pin; and this difference would depend upon the origin of the general excitation, the tendency to fixation in the minor reflexes, and the parts of the whole process which would be interchangeable.

The second respect in which I should depart from Professor Holt's statement concerns the object of response. Professor Holt speaks of the organism's responding to 'some object or fact of its environment.' That the response is often directed to a non-existent or generalized object, would not, I presume, be denied by Professor Holt. But this is a matter of great importance for the theory of value, and needs greater emphasis. In the case of hunting for a pin, the organism is not, strictly speaking, responding to an object or fact of its environment. The organism is not hunting for any particular pin; and is quite capable of carrying on the hunt, even though there be as a matter of fact no pin in its environment. The finding of any particular pin is the *hypothetical* complement to its present response. It is related to it as a hypothetical key is related to some lock which it *would* fit if it did exist. We cannot deal adequately with this matter here, but it evidently requires an epistemological construction that lies beyond the scope of a strictly physiological behaviorism. The recognition of this fact, though it does not, I think, in the least contradict the fundamental thesis of behaviorism, does forbid any hasty or contemptuous dismissal of the traditional association of purpose with non-physical or 'ideal' entities. And it suggests the danger of confining our analysis too closely to the lower forms of mind. As a matter of fact most human purposes deal with 'objects' of hope, fear, or aspiration that find no place at all in the field of nature as that is defined by the physical sciences.

Let us now consider some recent accounts of the learning process offered by a group of experimentalists in animal psychology.[14] "Apparently we have to do," says Professor S. J. Holmes, "with a selective agency which preserves or repeats certain activities and rejects others on the basis of their results."[15] All the writers of this group avoid the popular explanation in terms of the pleasurableness and painfulness of the results, and for a cumulative variety of reasons. Such an explanation imputes causal efficacy to mental states; and it introduces into the field of animal psychology a mental factor which, because it is incapable of objective description, is inconsistent with the accepted technique of the science. Furthermore, to explain behavior by pleasure and pain is to commit the fallacy of *obscurum per obscurius*. Feeling still remains the

[14] L. T. Hobhouse, S. J. Holmes, J. Peterson, and others.
[15] Pleasure, and Pain and Intelligence, *Comp. J. of Neurol.*, 1910, 20, p. 147.

*terra minime cognita* of psychology. The behaviorist hopes to be able to throw light on the physiological correlates of pleasure and pain, rather than to receive light from the very inconclusive theories on that subject which have already been proposed.[16]

Instead, however, of falling back upon the simpler mechanical explanation in terms of frequency, recency and intensity,[17] the writers of the present group emphasize the mutually reinforcing and inhibiting relations of responses. The earliest statement of this view is to be found in Hobhouse's 'Mind in Evolution.'[18] When the chick pecks at the yolk of egg or at green caterpillars, 'the "result"—the tasting or swallowing— is such as to *confirm* the original mode of reaction'; whereas when the chick pecks at orange peel or cinnabar larvæ, the effect is to *inhibit* the original reaction. For the future the chick is more likely to peck at objects of the first sort, because the excitement which they would arouse independently is now enhanced by the 'assimilation' of the excitement characteristic of the confirmatory sequel. Similarly, objects of the second sort will have lost their former power to excite, through its now being neutralized or overbalanced by the associated inhibitory excitement.[19]

But this is evidently an imperfect account of the matter. The reaction of rejection is no more inhibitory to that of pecking than is the reaction of swallowing. What the chick learns is not the simultaneous performance of two confirmatory acts, but a sequence of inhibitory acts. Why, then, should the chick not learn to pick up and reject, rather than to pick up and swallow? Or why should it acquire either of these habits to the exclusion of the other? To explain the prepotence of one of these sequences over the other, it is evident that what we need is some original connection uniting the pecking reaction with the swallowing reaction, but not with the rejecting reaction. The connection cannot be one of simultaneous compatibility or incompatibility between the reactions as such. It must be a connection between successive movements. We must conceive the pecking reaction as part of a total response of which the swallowing is the complementary *after*-part. Swallowing must be regarded as a prolongation or completion of the pecking response, in the direction of first intent, whereas rejection is an interruption or reversal of it. We must say that a pecking chick is an eating chick; and that it is

[16] Cf. J. Peterson, Completeness of Response, *Psychol. Rev.*, 1916, 23, 157–158: "The pleasurable tone which accompanies certain of our acts is of course only a subjective indication that the response is along the line of least resistance. . . . We are coming to the point now in psychology at which we cannot look upon states of feeling as *causes* of action." Cf. also S. J. Holmes, *op. cit.*, passim.

[17] I refer to the account offered by Watson, *op. cit., sup;* H. A. Carr, Principles of Selection in Animal Learning, *Psychol. Rev.*, 1914, 21; M. Meyer, 'Fundamental Laws of Human Behavior.'

[18] First published in 1901. The view as expounded here is developed more explicitly in the second edition, 1915.

[19] Hobhouse, *op. cit.*, second edition, pp. 118, 121.

this total eating response which selects the objects habitually to be pecked at. In other words, in this case *eligible* means *edible*.

It is not necessary to suppose that any mysterious psychic force is at work. If pecking is a part of eating, then it will be accompanied by the partial excitement of the swallowing reaction,—by a 'getting ready' to swallow. This anticipatory reaction will be brought to completion by certain stimuli such as the yolk of egg, inhibited by others, such as the orange peel. In the future the former will awaken these anticipatory reactions more strongly, and so reinforce the pecking reaction; whereas the latter will partially excite the rejecting reflex, which will diminish the force of the pecking reaction by inhibiting the anticipatory swallowing with which that reaction is normally correlated. This would not be the case unless swallowing were in some sense the natural sequel to pecking, unless the two were somehow already organized in the animal's nervous and muscular structure.

This view of the matter finds expression in some of Hobhouse's statements, as when he speaks of 'confirmatory movement tending to prolong the reaction, or *carry it out* strenuously *to its final development.*' Similarly, he speaks of the result of the first reaction as following 'closely enough to impinge upon and so confirm or inhibit *the conational impulse by which that reaction is initiated and sustained.*' [20]

Professor Holmes, who follows Hobhouse in the main, states the view as follows: "Pecking and swallowing form the normal elements of a chain reflex; when one part of the structure concerned is excited it tends to increase the tonus of the associated parts and thus reinforce the original response." [21] But while this statement recognizes the necessity of presupposing some original connection between the first reaction and the 'successful' reaction which is selected, that connection still remains too external. He finds it necessary to suppose that the second reaction somehow modifies the first owing merely to a 'close temporal relation'; as though, apparently, the second reacted upon the first by a sort of back set. He fails here, I think, sufficiently to recognize that the two responses are really parts of one response. This appears also in his allusions to instinct. "A response," he says, "which results in setting into action a strong instinctive proclivity is reinforced or inhibited, as the case may be, according to its congruity or incongruity with the proclivity thus aroused. . . . Ordinarily a response A that is followed closely by an instinctive reaction B involving the liberation of a considerable amount of energy, is reinforced, probably as a result of the influence of this energy on the nervous connections simultaneously excited by the response B." [22] He should, it appears to me, have included the first response within the in-

[20] *Op. cit.,* pp. 120, 123. The italics are mine.
[21] *Op. cit.,* pp. 135–136.
[22] 'Studies in Animal Behavior,' pp. 148–149.

stinct or proclivity, and regarded the first and second responses as congruent parts of it. The instinct dominates the performance throughout, initiating it, and selecting the congruent sequel, the whole instinctive performance being under way from the beginning, in its tentative, as well as in its successful and habitual stages.

The most explicit statement of the view is to be found in a recent article by J. Peterson.[23] This writer formulates what he calls 'the *principle of completeness of response.*' Learning processes 'involve more or less complex *attitudes.*' "The total reaction is in a degree incomplete, tentative. It is conditioned by various muscular 'sets,' or tensions, partial responses to immediately distracting stimuli, which cannot relax wholly until relief is obtained from confinement, or food is reached." [24] In other words, there is a 'general' or 'main' response, marked by tension and nascent activity. This tension is relieved only when 'the act as a whole is complete.' "There is . . . a continuous overlapping of responses, some of which are in opposition while others are mutually helpful and *serve to the main response as additional stimuli, the latter leading to a more easy and complete expression.*" [25]

If the above analysis is substantially correct, we find in the learning process a species of behavior that gives an empirical and objective meaning to the teleological vocabulary. A docile or corrigible organism is acting under the influence of a controlling impulsion which selects and acquires the specific instrumentalities through which it may be realized and completed. In so far as its behavior is thus determined, the organism may be said to be acting in the interested or purposive manner named for the general impulsion. In so far as the organism adopts a specific course of action because the expectation or preparatory response which it arouses coincides with that of the general controlling propensity, it may be said to act *for the sake* of the latter, or *in order to* realize it.

I have not thought it necessary for present purposes to discuss the extent to which purposive or teleological processes are hereditary. Theoretically instincts are supposed, like reflexes, to be altogether hereditary. But there are no clear cases of instinct of which this is true. Such responses as fear, pugnacity and the like are formed as they go, out of reflexes which are themselves highly modifiable. That hereditary structure defines the range of possibilities from which choice is made is doubtless

[23] Referred to above, p. 8, note. Cf. also Stevenson Smith, *Jour. Comp. Neur. and Psychol.*, 1908, 18.

[24] *Op. cit.*, p. 158.

[25] *Op. cit.*, pp. 156, 159. The writer goes on to say: "In our observation of animal behavior we have been too much interested in the principal response of the animal and have neglected to note sufficiently all the subordinate attitudes and responses." I should say rather that there had been too much neglect of the principle of subordination itself, whether through attention to the constituent reflexes or to the total performance.

true; but choice *is* made through the results of the organism's present experience. Similarly, the appetites signify certain hereditary and recurrent impulses which set the organism to acting until a specific relief is obtained; but just how any individual organism under given circumstances shall satisfy its craving for food or sexual intercourse is ordinarily determined by the results of tentative movements. It is this margin of modifiability, be it great or small, to which we must look for the factor of purpose. This interpretation will carry purposiveness far down in the phylogenetic and ontogenetic scale, but I cannot see that that argues against it.

It is essential that the action should be thus determined by its relation of prospective congruence with a controlling propensity which is both prior and more general. In other words the purposiveness is to be seen neither in the higher nor in the lower propensity regarded by itself, but in the interrelation of the two. The peculiar character of action in this case lies not in its merely having the character of complementary adjustment, but in its multiple and ulterior determination. We may now say of the 'successful' act, not merely that it is successful, in the sense, for example, of securing the food which the organism needs, but that it occurs *because it is successful*. Its being complementary to the environment, in a certain respect, accounts for its performance. It has actually been selected on this account.

Once the lesson is learned, the force of habit begins to operate; but behind the habit lies the higher propensity which has selected it, and which still exercises a certain control upon it. The lower propensity is always on trial or sufferance, so to speak; the acts which it determines occur only so long as they agree with the higher propensity. An organism in so far as acting purposively is always docile; while a purpose is always capable of inciting to new and untried efforts, and of exercising a selective function with reference to the tentative acts which it instigates. In other words, it is essential to behavior of this type that the higher propensity should be alive, or actually at work in the organism. At the moment when the habit becomes independent of this higher control, it becomes automatic. It can no longer be said to operate owing to its success. Its success accounts for its genesis; but the habit has now been weaned and is no longer answerable to the conditions with which it had to comply at birth and during its period of dependence. Herein lies the essential difference between the learning process and natural selection. According to the latter principle the character of hereditary structure is accounted for by its having been adaptive in ancestral organisms. But in so far as natural selection alone is predicated, the action of the organism cannot be said to be presently governed by this condition. In so far as its hereditary structure ceases to be adaptive through a change in the environment, the organism tends to weakness or death, and is not likely to transmit its traits; but it goes on with its maladjustment none the less. There is nothing in its constitution to forbid, or to prompt to new and more successful modes of adjustment. The organism cannot in this case be said to be *trying* to cope with its environment.

When a lesson has been learned, and a new habit established, it is quite possible that this in turn should become a higher propensity. If the kitten should be excited to effort by the the mere appearance of a button in a vertical position; if these efforts should continue until a way was hit upon to turn it horizontally; and if the random efforts should then be replaced by a stable propensity to perform the successful act, then we could say that the kitten was *trying to turn the button,* or that what it did was due to its producing the effect of a button in the horizontal position.

The variability of purposive action is not an accidental feature. What is required, as I have pointed out, is to be able to say that an act's performance is somehow conditioned by its having or promising a certain result. In order that this shall be possible, it is necessary that acts of the preferred sort should be actually selected from a larger class of acts. The rejected acts must actually occur so that the preference or selection may be manifested. An organism which reacted in one way, having a certain result, could not be said to prefer that way or to choose that result simply because other ways, having other results, were *conceivable.* It is necessary that these other ways should occur, in order to provoke the organism to the rejection of them. In order that an organism may be said to act in a certain way *because* of a certain result, it is necessary that acts, proving themselves to have a certain result, should derive a tendency to occur from this fact; and that other acts, proving not to have the result, should derive from that fact a tendency to be excluded. It is necessary that acts of the eligible type and of the ineligible type should occur *tentatively,* and then take on a stable or dispositional character according to the result. The occurrence of the experimental acts which this operation predicates is provided for only by the variability of behavior under the excitement of a deep-seated and persistent propensity.

We may consider this variability under three aspects. (1) In the first place, *the behavior is variable in respect of the response itself.* This is what Professor Thorndike terms 'the fact of multiple response to the same external situation,' and which he says pervades 'at least nine tenths of animal and human learning.' [26] In other words, it is not the constancy of the organism's behavior that is here remarkable, but its resourcefulness. Many acts are called, though few be chosen. It is a well-known fact that in the ascending scale of animal development this variability of response becomes more and more pronounced. In man, and in those men

[26] *Op. cit.,* p. 12.

whose conduct would be said to exhibit a relatively high degree of purposefulness or intelligence, this resourcefulness becomes well-nigh inexhaustible. The 'fertility' of mind which characterizes invention, is the same thing in principle, the difference lying in the fact that the lessons already learned, and the process of inference, render it unnecessary that more than a few of the responses should be carried through in order that their result should be proved.

(2) In the second place, *the behavior of learning is variable in respect of the feature of the environment to which the organism responds.* This is what Professor Thorndike calls the 'Law of Partial Activity,' according to which "a part or element or aspect of a situation may be prepotent in causing response, and may have responses bound more or less exclusively to it regardless of some or all of its accompaniments." [27] The situation in which the organism is operating is highly complex, and contains many features to which the organism's sensory apparatus qualifies it to respond. In the case of the kitten already described there are the button, the bars, the sides, the experimenter himself, etc., to one or another of which attention may be shifted. The possibilities are proportional to the mobility of attention, to the fineness of discrimination, and to the variety and delicacy of sensory capacity. Among the stimuli in the case of the kitten is the smell of the food itself. But the essential feature of the process as one of trying and learning, is that the simple reflex excited by this stimulus gives place momentarily to other reflexes excited by other stimuli. Thus though the first impulse be one of motion toward the food, this gives way presently to the impulse to push away the bars with which the animal comes into contact, and which stimulate its tactual or muscular senses.

(3) Being thus excited to various responses by the various aspects of the situation, acts occur which have different results. In other words, the *consequences of action are variable.* Some of these consequences or end-results are of the character defined by the higher or controlling propensity, some are not. Thus $e_1 + r_1 = a$, $e_1 + r_2 = b$, $e_2 + r_2 = c$, $e_3 + r_3 = m$, etc. But of these acts that which results in $m$ is unique. It terminates the process of trying, and tends to recur more promptly when that process is renewed. When $e_3 + r_3 = m$ does thus recur, bearing the peculiar relation which it does to the general set $E + R = M$, it may be said to be performed for the sake of $M$. This peculiar relation to $E + R = M$ is both a matter of past history and also of future tendency. On the one hand, $e_3 + r_3 = m$ is selected, and brings the propensity $E + R + M$ to rest, because $m$ has proved to be a case of $M$. On the other hand, $e_3 + r_3 = m$ owes its own stability as a propensity to the persistence of the propensity $E + R + M$, and to $m$'s continuing to be the result of $e_3 + r_3$.

[27] *Op. cit.*, p. 14.

Although the matter cannot be fully dealt with here, it is desirable to make at least a brief reference to what would usually be regarded as the mental aspect of this process. But believing as I do that to explain this process by a reference to what is commonly regarded as consciousness would be to commit the fallacy of *obscurum per obscurius,* I shall rather attempt to obtain light on the problem of consciousness by reference to certain aspects of this process.

Whatever excites endeavor or conation in the behavioristic sense already described, inaugurates the very state in which that endeavor is to terminate. As Professor Warren has pointed out, although "the dog certainly does not eat the rabbit before he catches it, . . . nevertheless, the act of eating is begun before the appropriate food stimulus appears." [28] As even Professor Warren appears not sufficiently to recognize, the process of eating is actually commenced in so far as the dog is trying to eat the rabbit. I refer, of course, to the secretion of gastric juices, the incipient muscular contractions required for seizing and tearing the prey, etc. In this sense what the animal is trying to do may be said to be what Thorndike calls 'Associative Shifting' it is possible to 'get *any response of which a learner is capable* associated with *any situation to which he is sensitive.*' [29] Thus the arbitrary combination of sounds which constitute the spoken word 'food' may excite the food-getting reflex, and similarly the expectation of food. It is probable, to my mind, that the primary function of a word is to excite the attentive act which is appropriate to a given stimulus. In other words, when the word 'food' is spoken, the organism is beginning to see food, and then over and above this to deal with it in the manner determined by the food-eating propensity. Certainly in the case of man, to 'understand' a word, is to be put in readiness for certain stimuli.

Or it is possible, if one prefers, to restrict the term idea to centrally stimulated signs. Such signs may consist of visual images resembling the object signified; or they may, as in the case of vocal-motor images, be quite arbitrary. The important thing is that they should excite anticipation or arouse expectation. This is sufficient to make them ideas. That they should be centraliy stimulated is practically important, in that it makes it possible for the individual to proceed to act upon any propensity, independently of present circumstances in the environment. Thus one may in this way seek food, whether or not either food or anything to suggest it happens to stimulate the organism from without.

There is one further consideration which is too important to omit even in this hasty summary. Endeavor, especially in the case of man, is often terminated, not by the end result toward which the organism is set, but by a belief which may, as it happens, be mistaken. In such cases, we

[28] H. C. Warren, A Study of Purpose, *J. of Phil., Psychol.,* etc., 1916, 23.
[29] *Op. cit.,* p. 15.

must say that the real object of endeavor is a situation which in turn creates certain new expectations. These expectations may in any given case be doomed to disappointment. Thus the animal may store away against the winter's famine what he takes to be food; whereas the objects collected may as a matter of fact not be edible, being made to deceive by their resemblance to familiar forms of food. We must then say that the endeavor of the animal was to reach a condition in which there is an anticipation of eating; the anticipation being excited, the endeavor comes to rest. The successful means employed to collect the spurious food is learned, and tends to become stable, just as if it were really edible. We must therefore predicate a set that is satisfied independently of the actual edibility of the objects in question. And this satisfaction must be held to consist in the animal's expectation. It is upon this model, I believe, that we must construct our account of the higher purposive processes of man, in which the purpose is none the less present even when misled and founded on error.

In the present paper I have put together certain notions of the learning process in the belief that they afford an account of behavior to which the term purpose is properly and significantly applicable, but without implying any factor out of keeping with the most rigorous scientific method. The important feature of docility is not adaptation to the environment, but the acquiring of specific modes of adaptation, and performance determined by the experience of adaptation. It appears to be necessary to predicate two springs of action in the docile organism: (1) the more deep-seated, sustained and general propensity, which accounts for the increased reactivity called 'trying' and which prescribes when this shall be brought to rest; (2) the more superficial, transitory, and specific propensities, which are rendered hyperexcitable by the former, but are ordinarily released by sense stimuli. The former we may call the selective, dominant or higher propensity, and the latter the tentative, subordinate or lower propensity. That one among the tentative propensities which is selected, and which we may term the eligible propensity, is one which confirms, facilitates and amplifies the selective propensity. When a tentative propensity has thus proved congruent with a selective propensity, then in future when that same selective propensity is moving the organism, or is dominant, then the tentative propensity in question has a prepotence over others, past and present, because of the greater compatibility between the expectation which it now arouses and the general direction or set of the dominant propensity. Expectation or set can, I think, be construed physiologically in terms of nascent adjustments. Action so performed can fairly be said to be performed owing to the agreement of its promise or prospective sequel with that of a more fundamental but more flexible propensity, which in this relation and function may be called a purpose. Action determined by an eligible propensity, is done 'on purpose.' Docility thus construed requires that the behavior of the organism shall be variable in all three in the aspects into which it can be analyzed; namely, feature of the environment attended and responded to, physical movement and effect. Purposiveness thus appears in life *pari passu* with variability or modifiability of behavior. Finally, the same mechanism which is implied in the learning process when so construed, will serve also as a crude account of the so-called 'higher processes' in which one solves a problem, or conceives and executes a plan.

# 12 • Edward C. Tolman

## Behavior, a Molar Phenomenon

Tolman considered purpose to be a descriptive feature of behavior. He saw it, however, as a molar phenomenon which was in correspondence with underlying molecular facts and hence nothing to be eschewed by objective psychologists. His acceptance of docility as the criterion of purpose led him quite naturally to study learning, which was the process through which behavior became "docile," or modifiable, with respect to experience. Thus Tolman's purposive behaviorism was to some extent turned from the strict analysis of purpose as such to a concern for the major issues of learning which occupied theoretical psychology to such a marked degree in the twenties and thirties. Indeed, Tolman's views provided the major counterpoint to the learning theory of Clark Hull.

### 1. MENTALISM vs. BEHAVIORISM

*The mentalist is* one who assumes that "minds" are essentially streams of "inner happenings." Human beings, he says, "look within" and observe such "inner happenings." And although sub-human organisms cannot thus "look within," or at any rate cannot report the results of any such lookings within, the mentalist supposes that they also have "inner happenings." The task of the animal psychologist is conceived by the mentalist as that of inferring such "inner happenings" from outer behavior; animal psychology is reduced by him to a series of arguments by analogy.

Contrast, now, the thesis of behaviorism. For the behaviorist, "mental processes" are to be identified and defined in terms of the behaviors to which they lead. "Mental processes" are, for the behaviorist, naught but inferred determinants of behavior, which ultimately are deducible from behavior. Behavior and these inferred determinants are both objectively defined types of entity. There is about them, the behaviorist would declare, nothing private or "inside." Organisms, human and sub-human, are biological entities immersed in environments. To these environments they must, by virtue of their physiological needs, adjust. Their "mental processes" are functionally defined aspects determining their adjustments. For the behaviorist all things are open and above-board; for him, animal psychology plays into the hands of human psychology.[1]

## 2. BEHAVIORISMS AND BEHAVIORISMS

The general position adopted in this essay will be that of behaviorism, but it will be a behaviorism of a rather special variety, for there are behaviorisms and behaviorisms. Watson, the arch-behaviorist, proposed one brand. But others, particularly Holt, Perry, Singer, de Laguna, Hunter, Weiss, Lashley, and Frost, have since all offered other rather different varieties.[2] No complete analysis and comparison of all these can be attempted. We shall here present merely certain distinctive features as a way of introducing what is to be our own variety.

## 3. WATSON: THE MOLECULAR DEFINITION

Watson, in most places, seems to describe behavior in terms of simple stimulus-response connections. And these stimuli and these responses he also seems to conceive in relatively immediate physical and physiological terms. Thus, in the first complete statement of his doctrine, he wrote:

We use the term *stimulus* in psychology as it is used in physiology. Only in psychology we have to extend somewhat the usage of the term. In the psy-

---

[1] It is obvious that we have oversimplified the views of both "mentalist" and "behaviorist." One ought no doubt to eschew any attempt to envisage progress as a too simple contest between "movements" (cf. E. G. Boring, Psychology for Eclectics, *Psychologies of 1930* [Worcester, Mass., Clark Univ. Press, 1930], pp. 115–127). But the temptation is too great.

[2] W. McDougall (Men or Robots, *Psychologies of 1925* [Worcester, Mass., Clark Univ. Press, 1926], p. 277) declares that he was the first to define psychology as the study of behavior. He says: "As long ago as 1905 I began my attempt to remedy this state of affairs [i.e., the inadequacies of an "Idea" psychology] by proposing to define psychology as the positive science of conduct, using the word 'positive' to distinguish it from ethics, the normative science of conduct." Cf. also, his *Psychology, the Study of Behavior* (New York, Henry Holt and Company, 1912), p. 19, "We may then define psychology as the positive science of the behavior of living things." But the credit or discredit for the raising of this definition of psychology to an *ism* must certainly be given to Watson (Psychology as a behaviorist views it, *Psychol. Rev.*, 1913, 20, 158–177; Image and affection in behavior, *J. Philos. Psychol. Sci. Meth.*, 1913, 10, 421–428). For the best analysis and bibliography of the different varieties of behaviorism extant to 1923, see A. A. Roback, *Behaviorism and Psychology* (Cambridge, Mass., Sci.-Art, 1923), pp. 231–242.

chological laboratory, when we are dealing with relatively simple factors, such as the effect of ether waves of different lengths, the effect of sound waves, etc., and are attempting to isolate their effects upon the adjustment of men, we speak of stimuli. On the other hand, when factors leading to reactions are more complex, as, for example, in the social world, we speak of *situations*. A situation is, of course, upon final analysis, resolvable into a complex group of stimuli. As examples of stimuli we may name such things as rays of light of different wave lengths; sound waves differing in amplitude, length, phase, and combination; gaseous particles given off in such small diameters that they affect the membrane of the nose; solutions which contain particles of matter of such size that the taste buds are thrown into action; solid objects which affect the skin and mucous membrane; radiant stimuli which call out temperature response; noxious stimuli, such as cutting, pricking, and those injuring tissue generally. Finally, movements of the muscles and activity in the glands themselves serve as stimuli by acting upon the afferent nerve endings in the moving muscles. . . .

In a similar way we employ in psychology the physiological term "response," but again we must slightly extend its use. The movements which result from a tap on the patellar tendon, or from stroking the soles of the feet are "simple" responses which are studied both in physiology and in medicine. In psychology our study, too, is sometimes concerned with simple responses of these types, but more often with several complex responses taking place simultaneously.[3]

It must be noted, however, that along with this definition of behavior in terms of the strict physical and physiological *muscle-twitches* which make it up, Watson was apt to slip in a different and somewhat conflicting notion. Thus, for example, at the end of the quotation just cited he went on to say:

In the latter case [that is, when in psychology our study is with several complex responses taking place simultaneously] we sometimes use the popular term "act" or adjustment, meaning by that that the whole group of responses is integrated in such a way (instinct or habit) that the individual does something which we have a name for, that is, "takes food," "builds a house," "swims," "writes a letter," "talks." [4]

Now these "integrated responses" have, perhaps, qualities different from those of the physiological elements which make them up. Indeed, Watson himself seems to suggest such a possibility when he remarks in a footnote to this chapter on "Emotions":

It is perfectly possible for a student of behavior entirely ignorant of the sympathetic nervous system and of the glands and smooth muscles, or even of

---

[3] J. B. Watson, *Psychology from the Standpoint of a Behaviorist* (Philadelpia, J. B. Lippincott Company, 1919), pp. 10 ff. (References same for 1929 edition.)

[4] *Op. cit.*, pp. 11 f.

the central nervous system as a whole, to write a thoroughly comprehensive and accurate study of the emotions—the types, their interrelations with habits, their rôle, etc.[5]

This last statement seems, however, rather to contradict the preceding ones. For, if, as he in those preceding citations contended, the study of behavior concerns nothing "but stimuli as the physicist defines them," and "muscle contraction and gland secretion as the physiologist describes them," it certainly would *not* be possible for a "student of behavior entirely ignorant of the sympathetic nervous system and of the glands and smooth muscles, or even of the central nervous system as a whole, to write a thoroughly comprehensive and accurate study of the emotions."

Again, in his most recent pronouncement,[6] we find Watson making statements such as the following:

Some psychologists seem to have the notion that the behaviorist is interested only in the recording of minute muscular responses. Nothing could be further from the truth. Let me emphasize again that the behaviorist is primarily interested in the behavior of the whole man. From morning to night he watches him perform his daily round of duties. If it is brick-laying, he would like to measure the number of bricks he can lay under different conditions, how long he can go without dropping from fatigue, how long it takes him to learn his trade, whether we can improve his efficiency or get him to do the same amount of work in a less period of time. In other words, the response the behaviorist is interested in is the commonsense answer to the question "what is he doing and why is he doing it?" Surely with this as a general statement, no one can distort the behaviorist's platform to such an extent that it can be claimed that the behaviorist is merely a muscle physiologist.[7]

These statements emphasize the whole response as contrasted with the physiological elements of such whole responses. In short, our conclusion must be that Watson has in reality dallied with two different notions of behavior, though he himself has not clearly seen how different they are. On the one hand, he has defined behavior in terms of its strict underlying physical and physiological details, i.e., in terms of receptor-process, conductor-process, and effector-process per se. We shall designate this as the *molecular* definition of behavior. And, on the other hand, he has come to recognize, albeit perhaps but dimly, that behavior, as such, is more than and different from the sum of its physiological parts. Behavior, as such, is an "emergent" phenomenon that has descriptive

---

[5] *Op. cit.*, p. 195. (References for 1929 ed., p. 225.)
[6] J. B. Watson, *Behaviorism* (New York, W. W. Norton and Company, rev. ed., 1930).
[7] *Op. cit.*, p. 15.

and defining properties of its own.[8] And we shall designate this latter as the *molar* definition of behavior.[9]

## 4. THE MOLAR DEFINITION

It is this second, or molar, conception of behavior that is to be defended in the present treatise. It will be contended by us (if not by Watson) that "behavior-acts," though no doubt in complete one-to-one correspondence with the underlying molecular facts of physics and physiology, have, as "molar" wholes, certain emergent properties of their own. And it is these, the molar properties of behavior-acts, which are of prime interest to us as psychologists. Further, these molar properties of behavior-acts cannot in the present state of our knowledge, i.e., prior to the working-out of many empirical correlations between behavior and its physiological correlates, be known even inferentially from a mere knowledge of the underlying, molecular, facts of physics and physiology. For, just as the properties of a beaker of water are not, prior to experience, in any way envisageable from the properties of individual water molecules, so neither are the properties of a "behavior-act" deducible directly from the properties of the underlying physical and physiological processes which make it up. Behavior as such cannot, at any rate at present, be deduced from a mere enumeration of the muscle twitches, the mere motions *qua* motions, which make it up. It must as yet be studied first hand and for its own sake.

An act *qua* "behavior" has distinctive properties all its own. These are to be identified and described irrespective of whatever muscular, glandular, or neural processes underlie them. These new properties, thus distinctive of molar behavior, are presumably strictly correlated with,

[8] For a very clear summary of the various different notions of "emergence" which are now becoming so popular among philosophers see W. McDougall, *Modern Materialism and Emergent Evolution* (New York, D. Van Nostrand Company, Inc., 1929). It should be emphasized, however, that in here designating behavior as having "emergent" properties we are using the term in a descriptive sense only. We are not here aligning ourselves with any philosophical interpretation as to the ultimate philosophical status or such emergents.

"Emergent" behavior phenomena are correlated with physiological phenomena of muscle and gland and sense organ. But descriptively they are different from the latter. Whether they are or are not ultimately in some metaphysical sense completely reducible to the latter we are not here attempting to say.

[9] The distinction of molar and molecular behaviorism originates with C. D. Broad (*The Mind and Its Place in Nature* [New York, Harcourt, Brace and Company, 2nd impression, 1929], pp. 616 f.), and was suggested to us by Dr. D. C. Williams (A metaphysical interpretation of behaviorism, Harvard Ph.D. thesis, 1928). Broad intends primarily to distinguish behaviorism which appeals only to *some* gross observable activity, from behaviorism which must appeal to hypothetical processes among the molecules of the brain and nervous system.

and, if you will, dependent upon, physiological motions. But descriptively and per se they are other than those motions.

A rat running a maze; a cat getting out of a puzzle box; a man driving home to dinner; a child hiding from a stranger; a woman doing her washing or gossiping over the telephone; a pupil marking a mental-test sheet; a psychologist reciting a list of nonsense syllables; my friend and I telling one another our thoughts and feelings—*these are behaviors* (qua *molar*). And it must be noted that in mentioning no one of them have we referred to, or, we blush to confess it, for the most part even known, what were the exact muscles and glands, sensory nerves, and motor nerves involved. For these responses somehow had other sufficiently identifying properties of their own.

## 5. OTHER PROPONENTS OF A MOLAR DEFINITION

It must be noted now further that this molar notion of behavior—this notion that behavior presents characterizable and defining properties of its own, which are other than the properties of the underlying physics and physiology—has been defended by other theorists than ourselves. In particular, acknowledgement must be made to Holt, de Laguna, Weiss, and Kantor.

*Holt.* The often too materialistically-minded biologist is so fearful of meeting a certain bogy, the "psyche," that he hastens to analyse every case of behavior into its component reflexes without venturing first to observe it as a whole.[10]

The phenomena evinced by the integrated organisms are no longer merely the excitation of nerve or the twitching of muscle, nor yet the play merely of reflexes touched off by stimuli. These are all present and essential to the phenomena in question, but they are merely components now, for they have been integrated. And this integration of reflex arcs, with all that they involve, into a state of systematic interdependence has produced something that is not merely reflex action. The biological sciences have long recognized this new and further thing, and called it "behavior." [11]

*De Laguna.* The total response initiated by the distance receptor and reinforced by the contact stimulus (e.g., reaching out toward, pecking at, and swallowing) forms a functional unit. The act is a *whole* and is stimulated or

[10] E. B. Holt, *The Freudian Wish* (New York, Henry Holt and Company, 1915), p. 78.

[11] *Op. cit.*, p. 155. The present chapter, as well as most of the subsequent ones, was written before the appearance of Holt's most recent book (*Animal Drive and the Learning Process* [New York, Henry Holt and Company, 1931]).

inhibited as a whole . . . Where behavior is more complex, we still find a similar relationship.[12]

The functioning of the group [of sensory cells] as a whole, since it is a *functioning*, and not merely a "chemical discharge" is not in any sense a resultant of the functioning of the separate cells which compose it.[13]

*Weiss.* The investigation of the internal neural conditions form part of the behaviorist's programme, of course, but the inability to trace the ramifications of any given nervous excitation through the nervous system is no more a restriction on the study of effective stimuli and reactions in the educational, industrial or social phases of life, than is the physicist's inability to determine just what is going on in the electrolyte of a battery while a current is passing, a limitation that makes research in electricity impossible.[14]

*Kantor.* Psychologists are attempting to express facts more and more in terms of the complete organism rather than in specific parts (brain, etc.) or isolated functions (neural).[15]

Briefly, psychological organisms, as differentiated from biological organisms, may be considered as a sum of reactions plus their various integrations.[16]

## 6. THE DESCRIPTIVE PROPERTIES OF BEHAVIOR AS MOLAR

Granting, then, that behavior *qua* behavior has descriptive properties of its own, we must next ask just what, in more detail, these identifying properties are.

The first item in answer to this question is to be found in the fact that behavior, which is behavior in our sense, always seems to have the character of getting-to or getting-from a specific goal-object, or goal-situation.[17] The complete identification of any single behavior-act re-

[12] Grace A. de Laguna, *Speech, Its Function and Development* (New Haven, Yale Univ. Press, 1927), pp. 169 f.

[13] Grace A. de Laguna, Sensation and perception, *J. Philos. Psychol. Sci. Meth.*, 1916, 13, 617–630, p. 630.

[14] A. P. Weiss, The relation between physiological psychology and behavior psychology, *J. Philos. Psychol. Sci. Meth.*, 1919, 16, 626–634, p. 634. Cf. also *A Theoretical Basis of Human Behavior* (Columbus, Ohio, R. G. Adams Company, 1925), esp. Chapter VI.

[15] J. R. Kantor, The evolution of psychological textbooks since 1912, *Psychol. Bull.*, 1922, 19, 429–442, p. 429.

[16] J. R. Kantor, *Principles of Psychology* (New York, Alfred A. Knopf, 1924) I, p. 3.

[17] For convenience we shall throughout use the terms *goal* and *end* to cover situations being got away from, as well as for situations being arrived at, i.e., *termini a quo* as well as for *termini ad quem*.

quires, that is, a reference first to some particular goal-object or objects which that act is getting to, or, it may be, getting from, or both. Thus, for example, the rat's behavior of "running the maze" has as its first and perhaps most important identifying feature the fact that it is a getting to food. Similarly, the behavior of Thorndike's kitten in opening the puzzle box would have as its first identifying feature the fact that it is a getting away from the confinement of the box, or, if you will, a getting to the freedom outside. Or, again, the behavior of the psychologist reciting nonsense syllables in the laboratory has as its first descriptive feature the fact that it is a getting to (shall we say) "an offer from another university." Or, finally, the gossiping remarks of my friend and myself have as their first identifying feature a set of gettings to such and such mutual readinesses for further behaviors.

As the second descriptive feature of a behavior-act we note the further fact that such a getting to or from is characterized not only by the character of the goal-object and this persistence to or from it, but also by the fact that it always involves a specific pattern of commerce-, intercourse-, engagement-, communion-with such and such intervening means-objects, as the way to get thus to or from.[18]

For example, the rat's running is a getting to food which expresses itself in terms of a specific pattern of running, and of running in some alleys rather than in others. Similarly the behavior of Thorndike's kitten is not merely a getting from the confinement of the box but it is also the exhibition of a specific pattern of biting, chewing, and clawing such and such features of the box. Or, again, the man's behavior is not merely that of getting from his office to his bewife-ed and be-pantry-ed home; it is also the doing so by means of such and such a specific pattern of commerce with the means-objects—automobile, roads, etc. Or, finally, the psychologist's behavior is not merely that of getting to an offer from another university; but also it is characterized in that it expresses itself as a specific pattern of means-activities or means-object commerces, viz., those of reading aloud and reciting nonsense syllables; of recording the results of these, and a lot of other bosh besides, in a *Protokoll,* and later in a typed manuscript, etc.

As the third descriptive feature of behavior-acts we find that, in the service of such gettings to and from specific goal-objects by means of commerces with such and such means-objects, behavior-acts are to be characterized, also, in terms of a *selectively greater readiness* for *short* (i.e., easy) means activities as against *long* ones. Thus, for example, if a rat is presented with two alternative spatial means-object routes to a

---

[18] These terms, *commerce-, intercourse-, engagement-, communion-with,* are attempts at describing a peculiar sort of mutual interchange between a behavior-act and the enivronment which we here have in mind. But for convenience we shall hereafter use for the most part the single term *commerce-with.*

given goal-object, one longer and one shorter, he will within limits select the shorter. And so in similar fashion for temporally and gravitationally shorter means-object routes. And what thus holds for rats will hold, no doubt, in similar and even more distinctive fashion for still higher animals and for man. But this is equivalent to saying that this selectiveness towards means-objects and means-routes is relative to the means-end "direction" and "distance" of the goal-object. The animal when presented with alternatives always comes sooner or later to select those only which finally get him to, or from, the given demanded, or to-be-avoided, goal-object or situation and which get him there by the shorter commerce-with routes.

To sum up, the complete descriptive identification of any behavior-act per se requires descriptive statements relative to (a) the goal-object or objects, being got to or from; (b) the specific pattern of commerces with means-objects involved in this getting to or from; and (c) the facts exhibited relative to the selective identification of routes and means-objects as involving short (easy) commerces with means-objects for thus getting to or from.

## 7. PURPOSIVE AND COGNITIVE DETERMINANTS

But surely any "tough-minded" reader will by now be up in arms. For it is clear that thus to identify behaviors in terms of goal-objects, and patterns of commerces with means-objects as selected short ways to get to or from the goal-objects, is to imply something perilously like purposes and cognitions. And this surely will be offensive to any hard-headed, well-brought-up psychologist of the present day.

And yet, there seems to be no other way out. Behavior as behavior, that is, as molar, *is* purposive and *is* cognitive. These purposes and cognitions are of its immediate descriptive warp and woof. It, no doubt, is strictly and completely dependent upon an underlying manifold of physics and chemistry, but initially and as a matter of first identification, behavior as behavior reeks of purpose and of cognition. And such purposes and such cognitions are just as evident, as we shall see later, if this behavior be that of a rat as if it be that of a human being.[19]

[19] McDougall, in his lecture entitled "Men or Robots" (*Psychologies of 1925* [Worcester, Mass., Clark Univ. Press, 1926]), divided all behaviorists into "Strict Behaviorists," "Near Behaviorists," and "Purposive Behaviorists." He classed the present writer and Professor R. B. Perry in the last group. It is then to Professor McDougall that we owe the title "Purposive Behavior," while it is primarily to Professor Perry (see below) that we are indebted for the original notions both of the immediate purposiveness and of the immediate cognitiveness of behavior.

Finally, it is to be noted that purposiveness and cognitiveness seem to go together, so that if we conceive behavior as purposive we *pari passu* conceive it also as cognitive. This complementary character of purpose and cognition has likewise been emphasized by McDougall (*Modern Materialism and Emergent Evolution* [New York,

Finally, however, it must nonetheless be emphasized that purposes and cognitions which are thus immediately, immanently,[20] in behavior are wholly objective as to definition. They are defined by characters and relationships which we observe out there in the behavior. We, the observers, watch the behavior of the rat, the cat, or the man, and note its character as a getting to such and such by means of such and such a selected pattern of commerces-with. It is we, the independent neutral observers, who note these perfectly objective characters as immanent in the behavior and have happened to choose the terms *purpose* and *cognition* as generic names for such characters.

## 8. THE OBJECTIVE DEFINITION OF BEHAVIOR PURPOSES

Let us consider these immediate dynamic characters which we call purpose and cognition in more detail; we begin with purpose. By way of illustration, take the case of Thorndike's cat. The cat's purpose of getting to the outside, by bursting through the confinement of the box, is simply our name for a quite objective character of his behavior. It is our name for a determinant of the cat's behavior which, it will now appear, is defined in the last analysis by certain facts of learning. Thorndike's description of the actual behavior reads:

> When put into the box the cat would show evident signs of discomfort and of an impulse to escape from confinement. It tries to squeeze through any opening; it claws and bites at the bars of wire; it thrusts its paws out through any opening and claws at everything it reaches; it continues its efforts when it strikes anything loose and shaky; it may claw at things within the box . . . The vigor with which it struggles is extraordinary. For eight or ten minutes it will claw and bite and squeeze incessantly. . . . And gradually all the other non-successful impulses will be stamped out and the particular impulse leading to the successful act will be stamped in by the resulting pleasure, until, after many trials, the cat will, when put in the box, immediately claw the button or loop in a definite way.[21]

We note two significant features in this description: (a) the fact of the behaving organism's readiness to persist through trial and error, and

---

D. Van Nostrand Company, Inc., 1929], Chapter III); and by Perry, who also points out in some detail that "there is no purpose without cognition" (The cognitive interest and its refinements, *J. Philos.*, 1921, 18, 365–375). And that "all forms of purposive behavior depend on beliefs for the issue" (The independent variability of purpose and belief, *J. Philos.*, 1921, 18, 169–180). See also R. B. Perry, The appeal to reason, *Philos. Rev.*, 1921, 30, 131–169.

[20] The term *immanent* is used by us in a purely colorless sense to mean merely directly in behavior.

[21] E. L. Thorndike, *Animal Intelligence* (New York, The Macmillan Company, 1911), p. 35 f.

(b) the fact of his tendency on successive occasions to select sooner and sooner the act which gets him out easily and quickly—i.e., the fact of *docility*.[22] And it is these two correlative features which, we shall now declare, define that immediate character which we call the cat's purpose to get to the freedom outside. The doctrine we here contend for is, in short, that wherever a response shows docility relative to some end—wherever a response is ready (a) to break out into trial and error and (b) to select gradually, or suddenly, the more efficient of such trials and errors with respect to getting to that end—such a response expresses and defines something which, for convenience, we name as a purpose. Wherever such a set of facts appears (and where save in the simplest and most rigid tropisms and reflexes does it not?), there we have objectively manifested and defined that which is conveniently called a purpose.

The first clear recognition and pronouncement of this fact that the docility of behavior is an objective definition of something appropriately to be called its purposiveness, we owe to Perry. In an article published in 1918 he wrote:

If the kitten should be excited to effort by the mere appearance of a button in a vertical position; if these efforts should continue until a way was hit upon to turn it horizontally; and if the random efforts should then be replaced by a stable propensity to perform the successful act, then we could say that the kitten was *trying to turn the button*. . . . [i.e., purposing the turning of the button] In order that an organism may be said to act in a certain way because of [by virtue of purposing] a certain result, it is necessary that acts, proving themselves to have a certain result, should derive a tendency to occur from this fact; and that other acts, proving not to have the result, should derive from that fact a tendency to be excluded. It is necessary that acts of the eligible type and of the ineligible type should occur *tentatively*, and then take on a stable or dispositional character according to the result.[23]

Finally, it must be noted that McDougall has also sponsored a seemingly similar doctrine. For he, like Perry (and ourselves), finds that behavior, as such, has distinctive properties of its own, and these distinctive properties he cites as six:

[22] Webster defines *docility* as (a) teachableness, docileness; (b) willingness to be taught or trained; submissiveness, tractableness. We use it throughout in the sense of "teachableness."

[23] R. B. Perry, Docility and purposiveness, *Psychol. Rev.*, 1918, 25, 1–20, p. 13 f. This emphasis upon the docility of behavior as the definition of its purposiveness (and also of its cognitiveness) has been expanded by Perry in other places, to wit: Purpose as systematic unity, *Monist*, 1917, 27, 352–375; and Purpose as tendency and adaptation, *Philos. Rev.*, 1917, 26, 477–495; A behavioristic view of purpose, *J. Philos.*, 1921, 18, 85–105; The independent variability of purpose and belief, *J. Philos.*, 1921, 18, 169–180; The cognitive interest and its refinements, *J. Philos.*, 1921, 18, 365–375; The appeal to reason, *Philos. Rev.* 1921, 30, 131–169; and *General Theory of Value* (New York, Longmans, Green & Co., 1926), pp. 288 f.

(1) "a certain spontaneity of movement"; (2) "the persistence of activity independently of the continuance of the impression which may have initiated it"; (3) "variation of direction of persistent movements"; (4) [the] "coming to an end of the animal's movements as soon as they have brought about a particular kind of change in its situation"; (5) "preparation for the new situation toward the production of which the action contributes"; (6) "some degree of improvement in the effectiveness of behavior, when it is repeated by the animal under similar circumstances." [24]

And the first five of these, he says, indicate purpose. McDougall's doctrine also seems, therefore, at least superficially, very similar to ours.

It must be noted, however, that he does not particularly emphasize the sixth character, "some degree of improvement"—i.e., the "docility" of behavior which, as we see it, following Perry, is the crown and significance of the other five.[25]

And one further difference must also be emphasized. For whereas, for Professor Perry and for us, purpose is a purely objectively defined variable, which is defined by the facts of trial and error and of resultant docility; for Professor McDougall, purpose seems to be an introspectively defined subjective 'somewhat,' which is a something other, and more than, the manner in which it appears in behavior; it is a "psychic," "mentalistic" somewhat, behind such objective appearances, and to be known in the last analysis through introspection only. This difference tween our

[24] W. McDougall, *Outline of Psychology* (New York, Charles Scribner's Sons, 1923), Chapter II, pp. 44–46; see also his Purposive or mechanical psychology, *Psychol. Rev.*, 1923, 30, 273–288.

[25] In this connection it may be remarked parenthetically that we formerly tended to side with McDougall (E. C. Tolman, Instinct and purpose, *Psychol. Rev.*, 1920, 27, 217–233; also Behaviorism and purpose, *J. Philos.*, 1925, 22, 36–41). That is, we then tended to hold that purpose might be said to inhere in mere trial and error and in mere persistence-until, irrespective of whether or not these tended to produce resultant learning. This seems to us now, however, an error. We have come to accept Professor Perry's *dictum* as to the need of *docility* for a true definition of purpose. It is only because there is implied in the category of trial and error and of persistence-until the further category of a resultant docility that trial and error and persistence-until have the meaning they do. Mere variability of response which involved no resultant selection among the "tries" would not be one's ordinary notion of "trial and error." Nor would mere keeping-on-ness seem a real "persistence-until." It is only when such variations and such persistences have implicit within them the further character of a resultant selection of the more efficient of the tries (i.e., *docility*) that they have their usual significance and are to be said to define purpose.

It should be noted that Singer also seems to hold much the same notion as that presented here of behavior as such and of purpose as one of its most fundamental characters. He says, to cite at random: "The history of my body's behavior reveals a purpose running through its various acts, a purpose quite like that which characterizes my neighbor, my dog, the moth which flutters by me." E. A. Singer, "Mind as behavior," *Studies in Empirical Idealism* (Columbus, Ohio, R. G. Adams Company, 1924), p. 59. See also E. A. Singer, On the conscious mind, *J. Philos.*, 1929, 26, 561–575..

point of view and McDougall's is fundamental and implies a *bouleverse-ment complet.*[26]


## 9. THE OBJECTIVE DEFINITION OF BEHAVIOR COGNITIONS

Consider, now, the fact of cognition. The docility feature of behavior also objectively defines, we shall declare, certain immediate, immanent characters for which the generic name *cognitions* or *cognition-processes* is appropriate. More specifically, our contention will be that the characteristic patterns of preferred routes and of commerces-with which identify any given behavior-act can be shown to be docile relative to, and may *pari passu* be said cognitively to assert: (a) the character of a goal-object, (b) this goal-object's initial "position" (i.e., direction and distance) relative to actual and possible means-objects, and (c) the characters of the specifically presented means-object as capable of supporting such and such commerces-with. For, if any one of these environmental entities does not prove to be so and so, the given behavior-act will break down and show disruption. It will be followed by subsequent alteration. It is, then, such contingencies in the continuance of any given behavior-act upon environmental characters actually proving to be so and so, which define that act's cognitive aspects.

The fact of these cognitive aspects is readily illustrated in the case of a rat's behavior in the maze. After a rat has once learned a given maze his behavior is a very specific dashing through it. But the continued release upon successive occasions of this same very specific dashing can easily be shown, experimentally, to be contingent upon the environmental facts *actually proving to be so and so.* It is contingent upon the food at the goal-box actually proving to have such and such a character. It is also contingent upon such and such alleys actually proving to be the best and shortest way to that food. And, finally, this dashing is contingent upon these alleys actually being shaped the way they are. For, if any of these environmental facts be unexpectedly changed, i.e., no longer prove to be so and so, this given behavior, this given dashing, will break down. It will exhibit disruption. Its continuing to go off as it does constitutes, then, the objective expression of a set of immediate contingencies. Its continuing to go off as it does asserts that the environmental features have those characters for which such behavior does not break down. And it is

---

[26] This was written before the appearance of McDougall's chapter entitled "The Hormic Psychology" in *Psychologies of 1930* (Worcester, Mass., Clark Univ. Press, 1930). In this latter place McDougall seems to deny any necessary connection between his doctrine of purpose and an animism.

such contingencies (assertions) for which the generic name cognitions seems appropriate.

## 10.  THE ORGANISM AS A WHOLE

The above doctrine that behavior is docile and, as thus docile, purposive and cognitive, also means, it should now be pointed out, that behavior is always an affair of the organism as a whole and not of individual sensory and motor segments going off *in situ,* exclusively and by themselves. For such docilities, as we have illustrated, mean shifts and selections and substitutions among motor responses and among sensory activities often widely distributed throughout the parts of the organism. The readiness to persist can involve wide shifts from one sensory and motor segment to another. Behavior as a type of commerce with the environment can take place only in a whole organism. It does not take place in specific sensory and motor segments, which are insulated and each by itself.

Indeed, this fact that behavior is an adjustment of the whole organism and not a response of isolated sensory and motor segments, going off, each in lonely isolation, can readily be demonstrated for organisms even lower in the scale than rats. Thus, for example, the behavior of crayfish in a simple T-maze led Gilhousen to conclude:

> No definite evidence was found to substantiate *any* doctrine of learning that would conceive it, even in the case of these relatively low animals, as primarily a reënforcement or inhibition of a particular reaction to a given stimulus. As has been illustrated . . . in the analysis of runs, the learning was characterized by continuously *differing* reactions to the maze situation. Intact crayfish which performed in a superior manner did so, *not by reacting invariably to the same specific cues with some invariable reaction,* but, as far as could be observed, by *reacting in properly modified ways to different cues on different trials.*[27]

In this connection, it must be noted that certain behaviorists have tended to take this fact that behavior is of the whole organism as *the* fundamentally distinctive feature of behavior, as molar. For example, Perry, to whom we owe the original emphasis upon the docility of behavior, often tends to emphasize as the one distinctive thing about behavior the fact that it is of the *whole* organism. He writes:

> Psychology [i.e., behaviorism] deals with the grosser facts of organic behavior, and particularly with those external and internal adjustments by which the organism acts as a unit, while physiology deals with the more elementary constituent processes, such as metabolism or the nervous impulse. But in so far

[27] H. C. Gilhousen, The use of vision and of the antennæ in the learning of crayfish, *Univ. Calif. Publ. Physiol.,* 1929, 7, 73–89. Final italics ours.

as psychology divides the organism it approaches physiology, and in so far as physiology integrates the organism it approaches psychology.[28]

He says further:

The central feature of this conception of human behavior is that general state of the organism which has been termed a determining tendency. The organism as a whole is for a time preoccupied with a certain task which absorbs its energy and appropriates its mechanisms.[29]

And again:

In proportion as the organism is unified and functions as a whole its behavior is incapable of being translated into simple reactions correlated severally with external events.[30]

Weiss and de Laguna also emphasize this same point.[31]

It may be noted finally, however, that from the point of view here presented the fact that behavior is of the whole organism seems to be derivative rather than primary. It is a mere corollary of the more fundamental fact that behavior *qua* behavior, as molar, is docile and that successful docility requires mutual interconnections between all the parts of an organism.

## 11. THE INITIATING CAUSES AND THE THREE VARIETIES OF BEHAVIOR DETERMINANT

We have sought to show that immanent in any behavior there are certain immediate "in-lying" purposes and cognitions. These are functionally defined variables which are the last step in the causal equation determining behavior. They are to be discovered and defined by appropriate experimental devices. They are objective and it is we, the outside observers, who discover—or, if you will, infer or invent—them as immanent in, and determining, behavior. They are the last and most immediate causes of behavior. We call them, therefore, the "immanent determinants."

But these immanent determinants, it must now briefly be pointed out, are, in their turn, caused by environmental stimuli and initiating physiological states. Such environmental stimuli and such organic states we designate as the ultimate or "initiating causes" of behavior. The im-

---

[28] R. B. Perry, A behavioristic view of purpose, *J. Philos.*, 1921, 18, 85–105, p. 85.

[29] R. B. Perry, A behavioristic view of purpose, *J. Philos.*, 1921, 18, 85–105, p. 97.

[30] *Op. cit.*, p. 102.

[31] A. P. Weiss, *A Theoretical Basis of Human Behavior* (Columbus, Ohio, R. G. Adams Company, 1925), p. 346. G. A. de Laguna, *Speech, Its Function and Development* (New Haven, Yale Univ. Press, 1927), esp. Chapter VI.

manent determinants intermediate in the causal equation between the initiating causes and the final resultant behavior.

Further, however, it must now also be made clear that besides the intermediating immanent determinants there are really two other classes of behavior-determinants intervening between stimuli (and the initiating physiological states) and behavior. They are to be designated as "capacities" and "behavior-adjustments." Such capacities and behavior-adjustments will be discussed at length in various later portions of the book. For the present it must suffice to draw attention to the fact of them and to suggest a few preliminary characterizations.

First, as to capacities. It is fairly evident in these days of mental tests and the insistence upon individual and genetic differences that the nature of the finally aroused immanent determinants will themselves on any given occasion be dependent not only upon the characters of the initiating causes—stimuli and physiological states—occurring on that occasion, but also upon the capacities of the individual organism or species of organism in question. Stimuli and initiating states work through capacities to produce the immanent purposive and cognitive determinants and thus the final resulting behavior.

Second, as to behavior-adjustments. It must also be noted that in certain special types of situation it will appear that the immanent purposes and cognitions eventually allowed to function may depend for their characters upon a preliminary arousal in the organism of something to be called behavior-adjustments. Behavior-adjustments constitute our be- havioristic substitute for, or definition of, what the mentalists would call conscious awareness and ideas. They are unique organic events which may on certain occasions occur in an organism as a substitute, or surrogate, for actual behavior. And they function to produce some sort of modifications or improvements in what were the organism's initially aroused immanent determinants, such that his final behavior, corresponding to these new modified immanent determinants, is different from what it otherwise would have been.

To sum up. The first initiating causes of behavior are environmental stimuli and initiating physiological states. These operate on or through the behavior-determinants. The behavior-determinants are, it appears further, subdivisible into three classes: (a) immediately "in-lying" objectively defined purposes and cognitions—i.e., the "immanent determinants"; (b) the purposive and cognitive "capacities" of the given individual or species, which mediate the specific immanent determinants as a result of the given stimuli and the given initiating states; (c) "behavior-adjustments," which, under certain special conditions, are produced by the immanent determinants in place of actual overt behavior and which serve to act back upon such immanent determinants, to remould and "correct" the latter and thus finally to produce a new and different overt behavior from that which would otherwise have occurred.

## 12. RECAPITULATION

Behavior, as such, is a molar phenomenon as contrasted with the molecular phenomena which constitute its underlying physiology. And, as a molar phenomenon, behavior's immediate descriptive properties appear to be those of: getting to or from goal-objects by selecting certain means-object-routes as against others and by exhibiting specific patterns of commerces with these selected means-objects. But these descriptions in terms of gettings to or from, selections of routes and patterns of commerces-with imply and define immediate, immanent purpose and cognition aspects in the behavior. These two aspects of behavior are, however, but objectively and functionally defined entities. They are implicit in the facts of behavior docility. They are defined neither in the last analysis, nor in the first instance, by introspection. They are envisaged as readily in the behavior-acts of the cat and of the rat as in the more refined speech reactions of man. Such purposes and cognitions, such docility, are, obviously, functions of the organism as a whole.[32] Lastly, it has also been pointed out that there are two other classes of behavior-determinants in addition to the immanent determinants, viz., capacities and behavior-adjustments. These also intervene in the equation between stimuli and initiating physiological states on the one side and behavior on the other.

## REFERENCES

Boring, E. G. Psychology for eclectics. *Psychologies of 1930*. Worcester, Mass.: Clark Univer. Press, 1930. Pp. 115–127.

Broad, C. D. *The mind and its place in nature*. New York: Harcourt, Brace, and Company, 2nd impression, 1929.

Gilhousen, H. C. The use of vision and of the antennæ in the learning of crayfish. *Univ. Calif. Publ. Physiol.*, 1929, 7, 73–89.

Holt, E. B. *The Freudian wish*. New York: Henry Holt and Company, 1915.

Holt, E. B. *Animal drive and the learning process*. New York: Henry Holt and Comanpy, 1931.

Kantor, J. R. The evolution of psychological textbooks since 1912. *Psychol. Bull.*, 1922, 19, 429–442.

Kantor, J. R. *Principles of psychology*. New York: Alfred A. Knopf, 1924. Vol I.

Koffka, K. *The growth of the mind*. (2d ed. rev.) New York: Harcourt, Brace and Company, 1928.

[32] It should be noted that both Koffka (*The Growth of the Mind*, 2d ed. rev. [New York, Harcourt, Brace and Company, 1928] and Mead (A behavioristic account of the significant symbol, *J. Philos.*, 1922, 19, 157–163) have suggested the term *conduct* for much the same thing, it would seem, that we here designate as behavior *qua* behavior, that is, behavior as a molar phenomenon.

Laguna, Grace A. de.   Sensation and perception. *J. Philos., Psychol. Sci. Meth.,* 1916, *13,* 533–547; 617–630.

Laguna, Grace A. de.   *Speech, its function and development.* New Haven: Yale Univer. Press, 1927.

McDougall, W.   *Psychology, the study of behavior.* New York: Henry Holt and Company, 1912.

McDougall, W.   *Outline of psychology.* New York: Charles Scribner's Sons, 1923.

McDougall, W.   Purposive or mechanical psychology. *Psychol. Rev.,* 1923, *30,* 273–288.

McDougall, W.   Men or robots? I and II, *Psychologies of 1925.* Worcester, Mass.: Clark Univer. Press, 1926. Pp. 273–305.

McDougall, W.   *Modern materialism and emergent evolution.* New York: D. Van Nostrand Company, Inc., 1929.

McDougall, W.   The hormic psychology. *Psychologies of 1930.* Worcester, Mass.: Clark Univer. Press, 1930. Pp. 3–36.

Mead, G. H.   A behavioristic account of the significant symbol. *J. Philos.,* 1922, *19,* 157–163.

Perry, R. B.   Purpose as systematic unity. *Monist.* 1917, *27,* 352–375.

Perry, R. B.   Purpose as tendency and adaptation. *Philos. Rev.,* 1917, *26,* 477–495.

Perry, R. B.   Docility and purposiveness. *Psychol. Rev.,* 1918, *25,* 1–21.

Perry, R. B.   A behavioristic view of purpose. *J. Philos.,* 1921, *18,* 85–105.

Perry, R. B.   The independent variability of purpose and belief. *J. Philos.,* 1921, *18,* 169–180.

Perry, R. B.   The cognitive interest and its refinements. *J. Philos.,* 1921, *18,* 365–375.

Perry, R. B.   The appeal to reason. *Philos. Rev.,* 1921, *30,* 131–169.

Perry, R. B.   *General theory of value.* New York: Longmans Green & Co., 1926.

Roback, A. A.   *Behaviorism and psychology.* Cambridge, Mass.: Sci-Art, 1923.

Singer, E. A.   *Mind as behavior and studies in empirical idealism.* Columbus, O.: R. G. Adams Company, 1924.

Singer, E. A.   On the conscious mind. *J. Philos.,* 1929, *26,* 561–575.

Thorndike, E. L.   *Animal intelligence.* New York: The Macmillan Company, 1911.

Tolman, E. C.   Instinct and purpose. *Psychol. Rev.,* 1920, *27,* 217–233.

Tolman, E. C.   A new formula for behaviorism. *Psychol. Rev.,* 1922, *29,* 44–53.

Tolman, E. C.   Behaviorism and purpose. *J. Philos.,* 1925, *22,* 35–41

Tolman, E. C.   A behavioristic theory of ideas. *Psychol. Rev.,* 1926, *33,* 352–369.

Watson, J. B.   Psychology as a behaviorist views it. *Psychol. Rev.,* 1913, *20,* 158–177.

Watson, J. B.   Image and affection in behavior. *J. Philos., Psychol. Sci. Meth.,* 1913, *10,* 421–428.

Watson, J. B.   *Psychology from the standpoint of a behaviorist.* Philadelphia: Lippincott, 1919. Rev. ed. 1929.

Watson, J. B. *Behaviorism.* (rev. ed.) New York: W. W. Norton and Company, 1930.

Weiss, A. P. The relation between physiological psychology and behavior psychology. *J. Philos., Psychol. Sci. Meth.,* 1919, *16,* 626–634.

Weiss, A. P. *A theoretical basis of human behavior.* Columbus, O.: R. G. Adams Company, 1925.

Williams, D. C. A metaphysical interpretation of behaviorism. Harvard Ph.D. Thesis, 1928.

# 13 • Clark L. Hull

## Knowledge and Purpose as Habit Mechanisms

As motivational psychology turned toward the concept of generalized drive and away from antiquated formulations of instinct, it became customary to hold that the particular behaviors manifested by an organism were a function of the habit systems it possessed. This seemed a narrow avenue of escape to those who with Tolman viewed behavior as "reeking with purpose." And, indeed it was, as long as the advocate of habit failed to specify exactly how apparent instances of purposive behavior could be explained in terms of habit factors alone.

In two brilliant articles published in 1930 and 1931, Clark L. Hull met this problem head on. He first demonstrated how the construct, habit $(H)$ could be used as a psychological basis for knowledge, foresight, and purpose. It introduced the notion of the pure stimulus act, the principle of their "short-circuiting," and a first formulation of the role of what came to be known as drive stimuli $(S_D)$. The second article dealt with the anticipatory goal response as a physical mechanism for "ideas" which guide an organism to a goal. All of these formulations have had a profound effect on subsequent thinking concerning the mechanisms of purpose.

*It is only* with the greatest difficulty that scientists are able to maintain a thorough naturalistic attitude toward the more complex forms of human behavior. Our intellectual atmosphere is still permeated in a thousand subtle ways with the belief in disembodied behavior functions or spirits. The situation is aggravated by the fact that the details of the more complex action patterns are so concealed as to be almost impossible of observation. Even so, the outlook is hopeful. The work of many ingenious investigators is bringing to light important details of the hidden processes, and enough evidence has already accumulated to enable us in a number of cases to discern with tolerable clearness the broad naturalistic outlines of their operation.

This article is reproduced in full from the *Psychological Review*, 1930, 37, 511–525. Reprinted by permission of the American Psychological Association.

I

One of the oldest problems with which thoughtful persons have occupied themselves concerns the nature and origin of knowledge. How can one physical object become acquainted with the ways of another physical object and of the world in general? In approaching this problem from the point of view of habit, it is important to recognize that knowledge is mediated by several fairly distinct habit mechanisms. In the present study but one of these will be elaborated.

Let us assume a relatively isolated inorganic world sequence taking place as shown in Fig. 13.1. Here $S_1$, $S_2$, etc., represent typical phases of

$$\text{The World:} \quad S_1 \longrightarrow S_2 \longrightarrow S_3 \longrightarrow S_4 \longrightarrow S_5 \text{ ---}$$

Figure 13.1

a sequential flux, the time intervals between successive $S$'s being uniform and no more than a few seconds each. Let us suppose, further, that in the neighborhood of this world sequence is a sensitive redintegrative organism. The latter is provided with distance receptors and is so conditioned at the outset as to respond characteristically to the several phases of the world sequence. Each $S$ accordingly becomes a stimulus complex impinging simultaneously on numerous end organs. As a result, each phase of the world sequence now becomes a cause, not only of the succeeding phase in its own proper series, but also of a functionally parallel event (reaction) within the neighboring organism. The organismic responses of the series thus formed have no direct causal relationship among themselves.[1] $R_1$ in itself has no power of causing (evoking) $R_2$. The causal relationship essential in the placing of $R_2$ after $R_1$ is that of the physical world obtaining in the $S$-sequence; $R_2$ follows $R_1$ because $S_2$ follows $S_1$. The situation is represented diagrammatically in Fig. 13.2.

Now a high-grade organism possesses internal receptors which are stimulated by its own movements. Accordingly each response $(R)$ produces at once a characteristic stimulus complex and stimuli thus originated make up to a large extent the internal component of the organism's

---

[1] This neglects the original dynamic influence of the ever-present internal component of the organismic stimulus complex into which each phase of the world sequence enters to evoke the corresponding organismic reaction. The excitatory potency of this internal component is here supposed to be minimal. Its influence is neglected in the interest of simplicity of exposition. Its undeniable presence clearly introduces an element of subjectivity into reactions which appear superficially to be evoked purely by the external world.

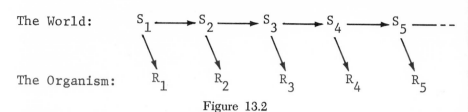

Figure 13.2

stimuli complexes. Let these internal stimulus components be represented by $s$'s. If we assume, in the interest of simplicity of exposition, that the time intervals between the phases of the world flux selected for representation are exactly equal to those consumed by the $S{\to}R{\to}s$ sequences, the situation will be as shown in Fig. 13.3, $S_2$ coinciding in time with $s_1$, $S_3$ with $s_2$ and so on.

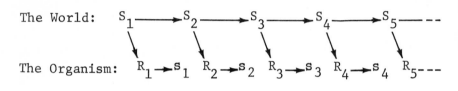

Figure 13.3

Now, by the principle of redintegration, all the components of a stimulus complex impinging upon the sensorium at or near the time that a response is evoked, tend themselves independently to acquire the capacity to evoke substantially the same response. We will let a dotted rectangle indicate that what is enclosed within it constitutes a redintegrative stimulus complex; and a dotted arrow, a newly acquired excitatory tendency. After one or more repetitions of the world sequence, the situation will be as shown in Fig. 13.4.

As a result of the joint operation of the several factors summarized in Fig. 4, the organismic reactions ($R$'s) which at the outset were joined

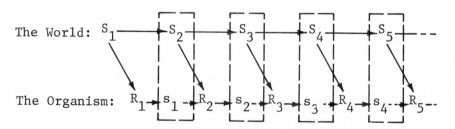

Figure 13.4

only by virtue of the energies operating in the outer world sequence of S's, are now possessed of a genuine dynamic relationship lying within the organism itself. To make this clear, let it be assumed that the world sequence begins in the presence of the organism, but is at once interrupted. The resulting situation is shown diagrammatically in Fig. 13.5.

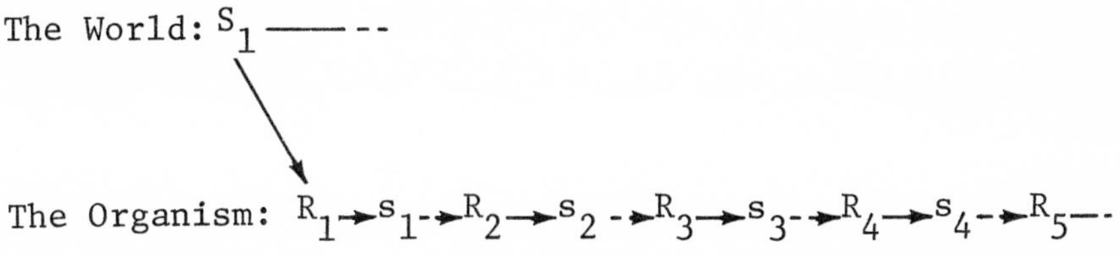

The World: $S_1$ ———

The Organism: $R_1 \rightarrow s_1 \rightarrow R_2 \rightarrow s_2 \rightarrow R_3 \rightarrow s_3 \rightarrow R_4 \rightarrow s_4 \rightarrow R_5$—-

Figure 13.5

The newly acquired excitatory tendencies, unless interrupted by some more potent influence, should continue the organismic sequence of response very much as when they were first called forth as the result of the stimulation by the world sequence.

In summary it may be said that through the operation of a variety of principles and circumstances, the world in a very important sense has stamped the pattern of its action upon a physical object. The imprint has been made in such a way that a functional parallel of this action segment of the physical world has become a part of the organism. Henceforth the organism will carry about continuously a kind of replica of this world segment. In this very intimate and biologically significant sense the organism may be said to know the world. No spiritual or supernatural forces need be assumed to understand the acquisition of this knowledge. The process is entirely a naturalistic one throughout.

## II

Once the organism has acquired within its body this subjective parallel to the ways of the physical world, certain other activity patterns or habit mechanisms at once become operative. One of the more important of these is the power of foresight or fore-knowledge. A great deal of mystery has surrounded this problem. Foresight may be defined for our present purpose as *the reaction to an event which may be impending, but which has not as yet taken place.* The difficulty seems largely to have been concerned with the problem of how an organism can react to an event not yet in existence. The reasoning runs: An event not yet in existence cannot be a stimulus; and how can an organism react to a stimulus which does not exist? In terms of our diagram, how can $R_5$, which is a reaction to the stimulating event $S_5$, take place before $S_5$ itself has occurred?

An important circumstance connected with foresight is the fact that the tempo of the acquired subjective parallel to the outer world sequence is not limited to that of the latter. Indeed, there is evidence indicating a tendency for a primary conditioned reaction to run off at a higher speed than that of the master world sequence which it parallels.[2] Thus it comes about that, even when both series begin at the same instant, the end-reaction of the subjective series may actually antedate the stimulus in the world sequence which exclusively evoked it previous to the conditioning shown in Fig. 13.4. It is evident that this possibility of the heightened tempo on the part of the organismic act sequence is intimately connected with the possession by the organism of knowledge of events before they actually take place.

The biological advantage of antecedent knowledge of impending events is great. This is particularly clear in the case of defense reactions. These latter fall into two main types—flight and attack. Let us suppose that in the example elaborated above, $S_5$ is a seriously nocuous stimulus and $R_5$ is a successful flight reaction. Foresight will result from the reeling off of the $R$-series faster than the $S$-series so that $s_4$ will evoke $R_5$ before $S_5$ has occurred. In this event, $S_5$, when it does occur, will not impinge on the organism for the reason that the latter will have withdrawn from the zone of danger as the result of the act $R_5$. In case $R_5$ is an act of attack rather than flight it must, to be successful, bring the organismic series into contact with the world sequence in such a manner as to interrupt the latter before $S_5$ is reached. In this case also, the organism clearly escapes the injury. Thus the supposed impossibility of an organismic reaction to a situation before it exists as a stimulus is accomplished quite naturally through the medium of an internal substitute stimulus.

## III

A reflective consideration of the habit mechanisms involved in anticipatory defense reactions reveals a phenomenon of the greatest significance. This is the existence of acts whose sole function is to serve as stimuli for other acts. We shall accordingly call them *pure stimulus acts*.

---

[2] C. L. Hull, A functional interpretation of the conditioned reflex. *Pyschol. Rev.*, 1929, *36*, p. 507 *ff.* A quite distinct mechanism serving much the same function as that here emphasized has its basis in the peculiar advantage afforded by distance receptors. The stimulus of a distant object through a distance receptor is often sufficiently like that when the object is near and nocuous to evoke a successful defense reaction before the source of danger can get near enough to produce injury. This has been discussed in detail by Howard C. Warren, *J. Phil., Psychol. & Scient. Meth.*, 1916, *23*, p. 35 *ff.*

Under normal conditions practically all acts become stimuli, but ordinarily the stimulus function is an incidental one. The consideration of the approach of an organism to food may clarify the concept. Each step taken in approaching the food serves in part as the stimulus for the next step, but its main function is to bring the body nearer the food. Such acts are, therefore, primarily instrumental. By way of contrast may be considered the anticipatory defense sequence presented above. $R_5$, the actual defense reaction, obviously has instrumental value in high degree. $R_4$, on the other hand, has no instrumental value. This does not mean that it has no significance. Without $R_4$ there would be no $s_4$, and without $s_4$ there would be no $R_5$ i.e. no defense. In short, $R_4$ is a pure stimulus act. In the same way $R_3$ and $R_2$ serve no instrumental function but, nevertheless, are indispensable as stimulus acts in bringing about the successful defense response.

A simple experiment which can be performed by anyone in a few moments may still further clarify the concept of the pure stimulus act. Ask almost any psychologically naïve person how he buttons his coat with one hand—which finger, if any, he puts through the buttonhole, what the last act of the sequence is—and so on. The average person can tell little about it at first. If wearing a coat, he will usually perform the act forthwith. If warned against this, the hand may quite generally be observed to steal close to the position at which the buttoning is usually performed and to go through the buttoning behavior sequence *by itself*. After this the nature of the final buttoning act may be stated with some assurance. Clearly, the earlier acts of this pseudo-buttoning sequence are pure stimulus acts since they serve no function whatever, except as stimuli to evoke succeeding movements and ultimately, the critical final movement which is sought.

It is evident upon a little reflection that the advent of the pure stimulus act into biological economy marks a great advance. It makes available at once a new and enlarged range of behavior possibilities. The organism is no longer a passive reactor to stimuli from without, but becomes relatively free and dynamic. There is a transcendence of the limitations of habit as ordinarily understood, in that the organism can react to the not-here as will as the not-now. In the terminology of the Gestalt psychologists, the appearance of the pure stimulus act among habit phenomena marks a great increase in the organism's 'degrees of freedom.' The pure stimulus act thus emerges as an organic, physiological—strictly internal and individual—symbolism.[3] Quite commonplace instrumental

[3] This peculiarly individual form of symbolism is not to be confused with the purely stimulus acts of social communication. Neither is it to be confused with what appears to be a derivative of the latter by a reduction process, the subvocal speech emphasized by Watson. The special stimulus-response mechanisms by which the evolution of these latter forms of symbolism take place, together with their peculiar potentialities for mediating biological adjustment and survival, are so complex as to preclude consideration here.

acts, by a natural reduction process, appear transformed into a kind of *thought*—rudimentary it is true, but of the most profound biological significance.

Thus the transformation of mere action into thought, which has seemed to some as conceivable only through a kind of miracle, appears to be a wholly naturalistic process and one of no great subtlety. Indeed, its obviousness is such as to challenge the attempt at synthetic verification from inorganic materials. It is altogether probable that a 'psychic' machine, with ample provision in its design for the evolution of pure stimulus acts, could attain a degree of freedom, spontaneity, and power to dominate its environment, inconceivable alike to individuals unfamiliar with the possibilities of automatic mechanisms and to the professional designers of the ordinary rigid-type machines.

## IV

Pure stimulus-act sequences present certain unique opportunities for biological economy not possessed by ordinary instrumental-act sequences. In the first place, there is the ever present need of reducing the energy expenditure to a minimum while accomplishing the ordinary biological functions in a normal manner. It is clear that pure stimulus-act sequences, since they no longer have any instrumental function, may be reduced in magnitude to almost any degree consistent with the delivery of a stimulus adequate to evoke the final instrumental or goal act.[4] Observation seems to indicate that this economy is operative on a very wide scale. It may even be observed in the buttoning experiment previously cited. The hand while going through the buttoning sequence by itself will ordinarily make movements of much smaller amplitude than when performing the instrumental act sequence with a real button.

A significant observation made by Thorndike in the early days of animal experimentation illustrates the same tendency, though in a very different setting. He placed cats in a confining box from which they sought to escape. Some he would release only when they licked themselves, others only when they scratched themselves. After an unusually long training period the cats finally learned to perform the required acts and thus to escape fairly promptly. In this connection, Thorndike remarks:

---

[4] Movements greatly reduced in magnitude tend to become vestigial. This suggests a possible explanation of the extreme subjectivity of imagery. Just how far the weakening of pure stimulus acts may go and still serve their stimulus function is a question which may yield to experimental approach. That they should diminish to an actual zero, with nothing but a neural vestige remaining to perform the stimulus function, is conceivable though hardly probable. It is believed that the present hypothesis is general enough to fit either alternative.

There is in all these cases a noticeable tendency, of the cause of which I am ignorant, to diminish the act until it becomes a mere vestige of a lick or a scratch. After the cat gets so it performs the act soon after it is put in, it begins to do it less and less vigorously. The licking degenerates into a mere quick turn of the head with one or two motions up and down with tongue extended. Instead of a hearty scratch the cat waves its paw up and down rapidly for an instant.[5]

The ordinary scratch of a cat is an instrumental act. It must have a certain duration and intensity to serve its function. In the present instance the scratch served only as a visual stimulus to Dr. Thorndike. As such, a small movement was presumably quite as effective as a large one.

In the second place there is, particularly in the case of primitive defense acts, the need to economize time so as to increase the promptness of the defense reaction. This desideratum appears to be accomplished by the same means as the first—the reduction in the magnitude of the acts. A movement of small amplitude should be more quickly performed than one of large amplitude.

But the maximum of economy, both as to energy and as to time, demands not only that the units of the stimulus-act sequence shall be small in amplitude, but that they shall also be as *few* as possible. If a single stimulus act is sufficient to furnish the necessary stimulus for the defense reaction, the existence of all the other stimulus acts in the series is a sheer waste, both of time and energy. This means that biological efficiency demand on two separate counts the dropping out of large sections of purely stimulus-act sequences.

## V

The importance of the serial-segment elimination tendency in pure stimulus-act and other complex learning sequences raises very insistently the question as to what stimulus-response mechanisms may bring it about. Observations suggests that one condition favorable for 'short circuiting' is that the process shall be strongly 'purposive.' *In the present study the purpose mechanism shall be understood as a persisting core of sameness in the stimulus complexes throughout the successive phases of the reaction sequence.* We will symbolize this persisting stimulus by $S_p$. This may be thought of concretely as a continuous strong red light, or a continuous gripping of a dynamometer, or the continuous knitting of the brows, or (more typically) the continuously recurring crampings of the digestive tract as in hunger.

When the principle of the persisting stimulus is joined to the set of principles represented as operating in Fig. 13.5, a number of novel con-

[5] E. L. Thorndike, *Animal Intelligence*, Macmillan, 1911, p. 48.

sequences at once appear. The situation is represented in Fig. 13.6. An examination of this diagram shows that $S_p$ has a unique advantage over all the other components in the several stimulus complexes. Thus, $S_1$, $S_2$, etc. and $s_1$, $s_2$, etc. can get conditioned, except for remote associative tendencies,[6] only to the response in each case which immediately follows *i.e.* to but a single response each. But $S_p$, since it is present in all the stimulus complexes of the series, *gets conditioned to all the reactions* taking place in it.

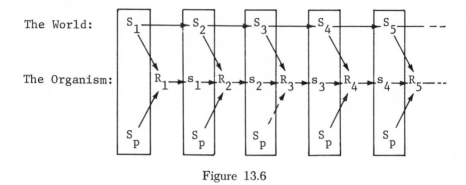

Figure 13.6

This multiplicity of excitatory tendencies resulting from the situation shown in Fig. 13.6, is represented diagrammatically in Fig. 13.7.

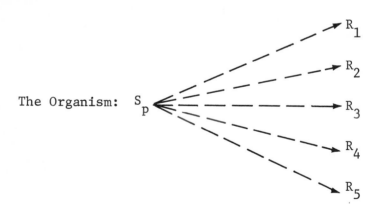

Figure 13.7

## VI

It is evident that in a situation such as is presented in Fig. 13.7, a competition of the several excitatory tendencies will follow. Since this

[6] These are here neglected in order to simplify the exposition. Ultimately they must, of course, be taken fully into account.

competition must be between the several parts of the series, it will be called *intraserial competition*. We may safely assume that the several excitatory tendencies radiating from $S_p$ will have varying strengths. There also enter into this competition, of course, the stimulus elements which may be present in the stimulus complex from other sources at any particular moment. We will simplify the stimulus situation somewhat by assuming that the world sequence is interrupted at once after its first phase, $S_1$. What, then, will be the state of this intraserial competition at the second stimulus complex of the diagram?

If we assume that $s_1$ has an excitatory tendency toward $R_2$ of 2 units, that $S_p$ also has an excitatory tendency toward $R_2$ of 2 units, towards $R_3$ of 3 units, towards $R_4$ of 4 units and towards $R_5$ of 5 units, the competition among the several segments of the series will be that shown in Fig. 13.8. From this diagram it may be seen that the immediately follow-

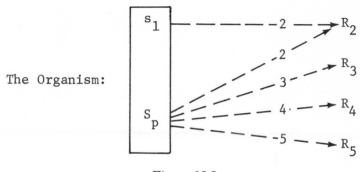

The Organism:

Figure 13.8

ing reaction ($R_2$) in the original action sequence has the advantage of a double excitatory tendency, whereas the more distant reactions such as $R_3$, $R_4$, and $R_5$, have but a single excitatory tendency each, that arising only from $S_p$. But if at any time one of the single ($S_p$) excitatory tendencies should chance to be stronger than the combination of the two tendencies leading to the immediately following act of the original sequence, the elimination of a segment of the pure stimulus-act sequence will take place.

In order to understand how the purposive mechanism, through intraserial competition, may bring about serial segment elimination, let us observe the sequel to the following hypothetical situation. It may very well prove to be the case that $S_p$ gets conditioned more strongly as the final or critical response in a behavior cycle is approached.[7] Accordingly

[7] It would not appear to be an over difficult task to test this hypothesis experimentally. If it should prove true it would have extensive theoretical implications and would clear up a number of questions in the theory of learning. However, almost any other hypothesis which provides considerable variation in the strength of the excitatory

a rough approximation to such a system of excitatory tendencies has been assigned to the bonds presented in Fig. 13.8. We may summarize the several competing excitatory tendencies radiating from the second stimulus complex as follows:

$$R_2 = 4,$$
$$R_3 = 3,$$
$$R_4 = 4,$$
$$R_5 = 5.$$

This shows that the reaction following the second stimulus complex must be, not $R_2$ as in the original act sequence, but $R_5$. But if $R_5$ follows immediately after $R_1$, the behavior segment shown in Fig. 13.9 drops completely out of the series. This is inevitable because no stimulus now remains in the series adequate to evoke it.

The Organism:    $R_2 \longrightarrow S_2 \longrightarrow R_3 \longrightarrow S_3 \longrightarrow R_4 \longrightarrow S_4$

Figure 13.9

One of the most baffling theoretical problems related to experimental psychology has been that of explaining how errors or unnecessary acts in behavior sequences get eliminated. Nevertheless, few psychological phenomena are more common. One is asked the product of 49 × 67. He writes the numbers down on paper, certain multiplication-table and addition-table habits of childhood are evoked in an orderly succession, and at length there is written down by successives stages the number, 3283. If, not too long afterwards, the individual is again asked the product of 49 × 67, he may respond by saying 3283 at once. In thus passing directly from the question to the answer, the behavior sequence of pure stimulus acts which constituted the detailed multiplication of 49 × 67 has completely dropped out of the sequence.

The difficulty of accounting for this phenomenon has been due to a considerable extent to the fact that the serial segment elimination must take place in the face of the so-called law of use or frequency. According to this principle (alone) practice or repetition might be expected blindly to fix the undesirable behavior segment in its place more firmly than ever. Perhaps such inadequacies as these have contributed much to bringing the simple chain reaction theory into its deserved ill repute as a universal

---

tendencies radiating from $S_p$ will produce substantially similar results. It may be added that an irregular distribution of intensities of excitatory tendencies from $S_p$ offers special opportunities for backward serial segment elimination as contrasted with the more usual forward variety here emphasized.

explanatory principle. As a matter of plain fact, the principle of redintegration from which may be derived the simple chaining of reactions, implies with equal cogency the evolution of a stimulus-response mechanism which appears to be capable on occasion of completely transcending the chaining tendency.[8] According to this principle any stimulus such as an organic craving which persists as a relatively constant component throughout the otherwise largely changing stimulus complexes of a behavior sequence, must become conditioned to every act of the series. The implications of this for complex adaptive behavior are far reaching. It is our present concern only to point out that the persisting stimulus, through the sheaf of excitatory tendencies emanating from it to every act of the series, provides a unique dynamic relationship between each part of the series and every other part. This, as we have seen above, gives rise to a significant competition among the several potential action tendencies within the series. While final decision must be reserved until the facts are determined by experiment, the probability seems to be that this intraserial competition may easily become sufficiently potent to over-ride the simple chain-reaction tendency and produce a leap in the behavior sequence from the beginning of a series at once to the final or goal reaction, thus eliminating the intervening unnecessary action segment.

## VII

The results of the present inquiry may be briefly summarized.

Sequences in the outer world evoke parallel reaction sequences in sensitive organisms. By the principle of redintegration the organismic sequences acquire a tendency to run off by themselves, independently of the original world sequences. The organism has thus acquired an intimate functional copy of the world sequence, which is a kind of knowledge.

In case the two sequences begin at the same time but the organismic or behavior sequence runs off at a faster rate, the knowledge becomes fore-knowledge or foresight. This has great significance in terms of biological survival.

The possibility of more or less extended functional habit sequences being executed by the organism with an instrumental act only at the end, gives rise to the concept of the pure stimulus act. Such behavior sequences have great biological survival significance because they enable the organism to react both to the not-here and not-now. Incidentally it accounts for a great deal of the spontaneity manifested by organisms.

The concept of the pure stimulus act appears to be the organic basis

[8] See E. L. Thorndike, *The Original Nature of Man,* New York, 1913, 186–187.

of symbolism but is believed to be a more fundamental one than that of symbolism as ordinarily conceived.

Pure stimulus-act sequences offer possibilities of biological economy, both of energy and of speed, through the reduction in the amplitude of the acts in the sequence. Further analysis reveals the fact that both energy and time would be economized with no incidental sacrifice if the acts between the beginning of an action cycle and its goal act should drop out of the sequence. Observation seems to show that the dropping out of such intervening pure stimulus acts occurs very extensively.

The problem arises as to how this dropping out of undesirable behavior segments may come about, since it appears to be a violation of the 'law of use.' A plausible explanation is found in the peculiar potentialities of stimuli which persist relatively unchanged throughout a behavior sequence. A persisting stimulus component is regarded as one of the characteristic mechanisms of purposive behavior. We should expect such a stimulus to get conditioned to every act of the sequence, presumably most strongly to the goal act and those acts immediately preceding the goal act. The resulting multiplicity of excitatory tendencies emanating from the persisting stimulus is found to generate an important phenomenon—the competition among the several potential segments of the behavior series. This intraserial competition, if sufficiently strong, could easily over-ride the simple chaining of contiguous acts produced by the 'law of use' and enable the final act of the original series to be evoked at once after the first act of the series, thus producing what is rather inappropriately called 'short-circuiting.' Thus may a persistent problem in the theory of mammalian adaptive behavior be on its way to solution.

The general plausibility of the foregoing theoretical deductions as well as the probable biological significance of several of the deduced mechanisms, suggests strongly the desirability of an intensive program of experimental research designed to test their actuality. In that way the true function of theoretical analysis may be realized.

# 14 • Clark L. Hull

## Goal Attraction and Directing Ideas Conceived as Habit Phenomena

In this second article by Hull, it is noteworthy that there is explicit recognition that the fractional anticipatory goal response may be the "actual basis of what has long been known as ideo-motor action." This brings this group of articles full cycle, for it was William James in the first article of this section who made systematic use of the postulate of ideo-motor action. In a sense, then, this selection may be interpreted as a fruition of a continuing line of thought which had developed over a span of more than 40 years.

I

*When an animal* long without food is first placed in a maze or other problem situation it will usually, after a momentary pause, move about vigorously but more or less at random. These seeking movements are understood without great difficulty as the result of the combination of (A) the changing sensory stimulation emanating from the environment as the animal moves from place to place; (B) the changing proprioceptive stimulation resulting from the immediately preceding movements of the animal itself; and (C) a sensibly *non*-changing dynamic internal core of stimulation emanating from the continually recurring hunger cramps of the digestive tract. The changing stimulus components account to a considerable extent for the variability characteristic of the trial-and-error seeking behavior, the particular acts taking place at each instant being determined by the nature of the habituation tendencies set up in the previous history of the organism. The unchanging stimulus component, on the other hand, gives the various action segments of the behavior flux its characteristic unity by tending largely to limit the behavior to acts which in the past have been associated with the securing of food and which are therefore more likely than pure chance to result

This article is reproduced in full from the *Psychological Review*, 1931, 38, 487–506. Reprinted by permission of the American Psychological Association.

in securing it again. And when, at length, the food is found and eaten and the digestive crampings have ceased, the food-seeking behavior naturally comes to an end because its stimulus motivation has ended. Such, in brief, is the account of trial-and-error behavior conceived as motivated primarily by physiological drive.

But this is by no means the whole story. While probably accurate enough so far as it goes, the above account presents but the first part of the learning process. Experimenters report that once the animal has found food at the end of the maze a few times, his behavior undergoes a striking qualitative change. The new behavior is often characterized as appearing to be more 'purposeful' than at the beginning; he acts, as Gengerelli remarks, as if he were 'going somewhere.' Beneath this rather vague characterization there may be discerned certain fairly concrete and definite behavior tendencies, the most notable of which involve anticipatory movements. When an animal is approaching his goal (the food box) he is apt progressively to speed up his pace. Another significant observation is that when an animal is approaching a familiar 90° turn in a maze, he quite generally begins his turning movements some time before he reaches the corner. Perhaps most significant of all is the phenomenon observed not only in all sorts of vertebrates but in young children and naive adults as well, that as a food goal is neared the organism tends to make mouth movements of a masticatory nature. It is probably not without significance that such movements are particularly prominent in cases where the sequence of acts leading to the goal is, for some reason, interrupted.

To casual observation such acts as the premature or anticipatory movements just cited are likely to appear as interesting symptoms of an obscure psychic tendency but in themselves to be of no functional value whatever to the organism. If this were the case they would, of course, be positively detrimental, since they would involve a wasteful expenditure of energy. In direct contrast to this view, it is the purpose of the present paper to elaborate the hypothesis that anticipatory goal reactions, as distinct from organic drives, play an indispensable rôle in the evolution of certain of the more complex forms of mammalian adaptive behavior and that the understanding of this rôle will render explicable on a purely naturalistic and physical basis the profoundly significant influence of rewards, goals, and guiding ideas upon behavior sequences.

## II

Let it be assumed that a relatively isolated inorganic world flux takes place in time. Characteristic phases of the world sequence, separated from each other by but a few seconds each, are represented by $S_1$, $S_2$, $S_3$, etc., as they appear in Fig. 14.1. In the neighborhood of this world sequence is a sensitive redintegrative organism provided with

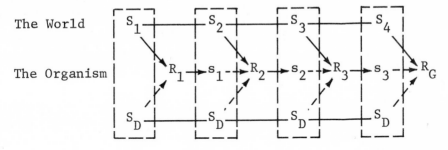

Figure 14.1

distance receptors and so constituted as to respond characteristically to the several phases of the world flux with a parallel behavior flux. Phases of the response flux corresponding to the world-stimulus flux are represented in Fig. 14.1 by $R_1$, $R_2$, etc., the final or goal reaction being indicated by $R_G$. Let it be assumed, further, that within the organism there is a source, such as hunger, which produces the continually recurring stimulation represented in Fig. 14.1 by $S_D$. Now, according to the principle of redintegration, all the components of a stimulus complex which may be impinging on the sensorium at or near the time that a response is evoked tend themselves independently to acquire the capacity to evoke substantially the same response. The stimulus complexes in Fig. 14.1 which fall under this principle are each enclosed within a dotted rectangle. It may be seen from an examination of the diagram that $S_D$, owing to the fact that it persists throughout the entire behavior sequence, will acquire a tendency to the evocation of $R_1$, $R_2$, $R_3$, and $R_G$, *i.e.*, to the evocation at any moment of every part of the reaction sequence. These newly acquired excitatory tendencies are indicated in the diagram by dotted arrows.

To amplify this part of the picture, there must be added the fact that each act, as $R_1$, gives rise to a proprioceptive stimulus, $s_1$. These proprioceptive stimuli are added to the diagram in Fig. 14.2. Through the operation of redintegration, they likewise tend to acquire the capacity to evoke the reactions immediately following them. This second group of newly acquired excitatory tendencies is also represented by dotted arrows.

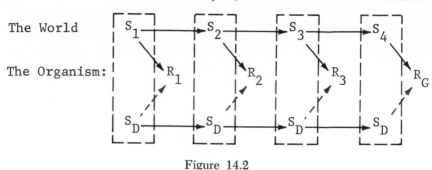

Figure 14.2

## III

It has been shown elsewhere [1] that under certain conditions, notably when the behavior sequence is made up of symbolic or pure-stimulus acts, the multiple excitatory tendency of the persisting stimulus, $S_D$, may evoke the final or goal reaction of the series almost or quite at the outset of the movement, thus dropping out the useless and actually wasteful intervening acts formerly leading to the goal. But in cases where the intervening acts are mainly instrumental in nature, as is obviously the case with the locomotor activities involved in maze running, it is physically impossible to drop out any of the acts involved in traversing the *true* pathway and at the same time reach the goal.[2] With the maze remaining constant, the space between the starting point and the goal must, somehow, be gotten over if the food is to be obtained. Consequently, if the anticipatory invasion by the goal reaction of the instrumental behavior sequence normally leading to the goal should result in the interruption of the sequence, the actual goal will never be reached and the episode will be biologically abortive. Such an interruption will

[1] C. L. Hull, Knowledge and purpose as habit mechanisms, *Psychol. Rev.*, 1930, 37, 511–525.

It should be noted that the mechanism of short circuiting behavior sequences there described is not adequate, as it stands, to explain the dropping of blind-alley entrances in maze learning. Space is here lacking for the elaboration of the particular mechanism involved in that specialized form of behavior sequence. Contrary to what seems to have been assumed by some, maze learning, instead of being a relatively simple process, is in reality one of great complexity. See C. L. Hull, The goal gradient hypothesis and maze learning, This journal (In press).

[2] Perhaps this difference in short circuiting of pure-stimulus acts as contrasted with instrumental acts is their most revealing distinction. Pure-stimulus acts are defined as acts whose sole function is to evoke other acts through the proprioceptive stimuli which they give rise to. They thus conform in a physical sense to the concept of symbolism though the entire process may be confined to a single organism in contrast to communicational symbolism which involves the acts of one organism serving as stimuli to another. The pure stimulus acts considered in the present paper are entirely of the first or individual type.

inevitably take place either when (A) the invading goal reaction is of such a nature that it cannot be performed by the organism at the same time as the antecedent instrumental acts leading up to it, or (B) when the execution of the goal reaction results in the removal of the source of the physiological drive stimulus ($S_D$).

In view of the ever-present potentiality of a strong drive stimulus for producing anticipatory invasions of behavior sequences by goal reactions, it should not occasion surprise if these invasions should occasionally take place even in genuinely instrumental sequences. Those common wish-fulfilling delusions so characteristic of certain forms of dementia precox are probably cases where the miscarriage of this mechanism has led to its natural maladaptive issue. Indeed, all wish fulfillments appear to be of this nature, which doubtless explains their bad repute among psychopathologists. The sexual orgasm which takes place during the ordinary erotic dream is evidently of the same nature. Extreme *ejaculatio precox* in anticipation of the sex relationship is a still clearer example of the abortive results of the goal reaction being displaced forward in time, producing the typical biologically disastrous result of preventing the completion of a reproductive cycle.

That this abortive anticipatory invasion of the antecedent instrumental sequence by the goal reaction does not take place with as great frequency as does the biologically valuable short-circuiting of pure-stimulus-act sequences raises an important theoretical question. A plausible explanation of this difference is found in the nature of the stimuli complexes operative in the two cases. Except for remote excitatory tendencies, which are here neglected in the interest of simplicity of exposition, the typical stimulus complex of the instrumental sequence leading to a goal is shown in Fig. 14.2. Consider, for example, the stimulus complex immediately preceding $R_2$. It consists of the external stimulus $S_2$, the proprioceptive stimulus, $s_1$, arising from the preceding activity, and the persisting or drive stimulus, $S_D$. The typical symbolic series, on the other hand, being ordinarily an internal process, characteristically lacks in its stimulus complex the external factor, $S_1$, at least as a dynamic and coercive component. The significance of this stimulus difference becomes apparent when it is observed that the $S_2$- and $s_1$-components operate in the direction of a simple and stable chain-reaction tendency whereas the $S_D$, in addition to a chaining tendency, may have at the same time a very strong tendency to evoke other reactions, and especially the goal reaction. The relative potentialities of the two stimulus systems may be seen very readily by an inspection of Fig. 14.3, where arbitrary numerical values have been assigned to the several excitatory tendencies. The simple summation of the potentialities of the several excitatory tendencies of the instrumental stimulus complex, $S_2\ s_1\ S_D$, yields the following values:

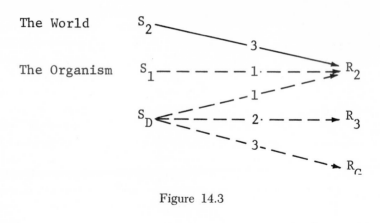

Figure 14.3

$$R_2 = 5$$
$$R_3 = 2$$
$$R_G = 3$$

Here $R_2$ is definitely prepotent and the original sequence will not be interrupted. Clearly the chaining tendency is greatly stabilized by the presence of $S_2$. A similar casting up of the action potentialities when $S_2$ is neutral or functionally absent (as in symbolic sequences) shows the following:

$$R_2 = 2$$
$$R_3 = 2$$
$$R_G = 3$$

In this case, $R_G$ becomes prepotent. Here the chaining tendency is very obviously threatened with disruption as the result of $R_G$ following immediately after $R_1$ with the consequent dropping out of $R_2$ and $R_3$.

From the foregoing it is evident that in genuinely instrumental sequences the goal reaction is not likely to be displaced backward in the behavior sequence if it is of such a nature as seriously to compete with the latter for control of the final common path. The powerful influence of the external component of the stimulus complex $(S_2)$ ought normally to prevent this. But in case the goal reaction does not, either as a whole or in part, compete with the instrumental sequence, there seems to be no reason why the former should not undergo such displacement. In that case, the anticipatory goal reaction would not disrupt the instrumental sequence, but the two would take place concurrently. Presumably, however, goal reactions spread rather widely and ordinarily involve a large part of the organism. A wide involvement of the organism in the goal act would naturally tend strongly to interfere with any other complex concurrent activities with which it might be associated. Thus the appearance of complete goal reactions simultaneously with what previously were their antecedents should be rare.

There remains the more likely alternative that a split-off portion of the goal reaction which chances not to be in conflict with the antecedent instrumental series may be so displaced. Unfortunately, little is known experimentally of the dynamics of this fascinating possibility. Observation, however, supporting theoretical expectation, seems to indicate that anticipatory goal reactions appearing in the midst of normally antecedent instrumental act sequences are generally incomplete, fractional, imperfect, and feeble. Fortunately, with pure-stimulus acts, weakness within limits is of no disadvantage.[3]

Moreover, anticipatory goal reactions appear to manifest themselves with special frequency, vigor and completeness on occasions when, for any reason, the smooth flow of the instrumental sequence has been interrupted. This, again, is in harmony with theoretical expectation, since at such times there would presumably be less competition for the final common path. As an illustration of this there may be mentioned a recent observation made in a Boston restaurant. A man and woman were leisurely eating their dinner. Sitting bolt upright at the table on a third chair was a handsome bull terrier. Throughout the meal the dog watched his master and mistress consuming the tempting morsels without himself making the slightest overt instrumental act leading to the obvious goal. Moreover, all overt anticipatory goal reactions (such as masticatory movements) appeared also to have been inhibited, quite in accordance with the best New England traditions. After a time, however, an implicit fractional component of the anticipatory goal reaction manifested itself; a long, thick thread of saliva was observed hanging from each corner of the dog's mouth. The carefully studied salivation of Pavlov's dogs evidently also represents anticipatory goal or terminal reactions. The less inhibited Russian dogs executed gross mouth movements such as vigorous licking of the lips as well.[4]

Despite the superficial appearance of a lack of physiological conflict between two such processes as locomotion and the goal activity of mastication, general observation leads rather strongly to the expectation that there would be considerable interference even in such cases. Carefully controlled experiments will probably show, for example, that salivation is more active when the normally antecedent instrumental acts are temporarily interrupted than when they are proceeding in full vigor. If this principle can be established experimentally it will have special theoretical significance.

[3] C. L. Hull, Knowledge and purpose as habit mechanisms, *Psychol. Rev.*, 1930, 37, p. 515.
[4] I. P. Pavlov, Conditioned reflexes, p. 22.

## IV

Having the phenomenon of the anticipatory goal reaction clearly before us, we may proceed to the consideration of some of its functional potentialities. Let us assume that in the dynamic situation represented in the diagram of Fig. 14.3, one portion of the goal reaction is not in conflict (competition) with its antecedent reactions, whereas the remainder is so. For convenience we may designate this non-conflicting component as $r_G$ and the conflicting component as $R'_G$. It is assumed that as learning proceeds, $S_D$ gets conditioned to the several phases of the reaction sequence and with an intensity roughly proportional to the proximity of each to the goal, the goal reaction itself possessing the most strongly conditioned excitatory tendency of all.[5] It is assumed, further, that this tendency, at least occasionally, will be sufficiently strong to evoke a weak $r_G$-reaction even at the outset of the series. This movement of the fractional goal reaction to the beginning of the behavior sequence together with its subsequent persistence throughout the cycle is indicated diagrammatically in Fig. 14.4. The persistence of $r_G$ is due to the parallel persistence of $S_D$ which continuously evokes it.

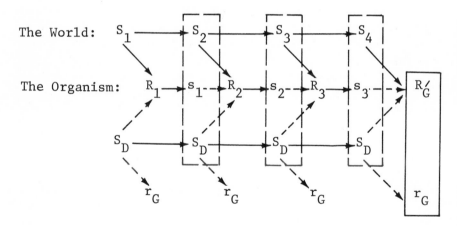

Figure 14.4

Like all other movements, $r_G$ causes characteristic proprioceptive stimulations to arise from the muscles involved. This complex of stimulation flowing from $r_G$ may be represented conveniently by $s_G$ (Fig. 14.5).

[5] C. L. Hull, Knowledge and purpose as habit mechanisms, *Psychol. Rev.*, 1930, 37, p. 521. This as yet hypothetical drive stimulus excitatory gradient will be taken up in some detail in a forthcoming paper. A rather numerous and varied assortment of experimental observations substantiates the hypothesis.

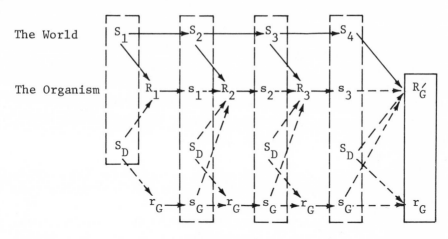

Figure 14.5

It is obvious that since $r_G$ persists throughout the behavior sequence, $s_G$ must also do so. It thus comes about that our dynamic situation is possessed of two persisting stimuli, $S_D$ and $s_G$. Some of the potentialities of the drive stimulus ($S_D$), have been elaborated elsewhere.[6] The second persisting stimulus ($s_G$), by way of contrast, will be called the *goal stimulus.*

It is at once apparent from an examination of Fig. 14.5 that, just as in the case of the drive stimulus, the principle of redintegration ought to set up excitatory tendencies from $s_G$ to every reaction of the behavior sequence including, apparently, tendencies to both components of the goal reaction, the one to $r_G$ being circular. The multiple excitatory tendencies in question are represented diagrammatically in Fig. 14.6.

Despite the very significant similarity of the goal stimulus to the drive stimulus there are equally significant differences which need carefully to be noted. In the first place, the two stimuli differ radically in their source, or origin. The drive stimulus, in the typical case of hunger already before us, evidently has its origin in the physico-chemical processes involved in nutrition. The goal stimulus, on the other hand, is dependent, in the main at least, upon the existence of the drive stimulus and the conditioning of it to the goal reaction. The drive stimulus thus has an essentially non-redintegrative origin, whereas the goal stimulus is preeminently a redintegrative phenomenon. The drive stimulus is not likely to be greatly disturbed by either the presence or absence of the

[6] C. L. Hull, Knowledge and purpose as habit mechanisms, *Psychol. Rev.*, 1930, 37, p. 519. In that article the drive stimulus, here represented by $S_D$, was represented by $S_p$. The present notation is believed to be the more appropriate.

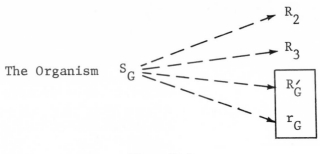

The Organism

Figure 14.6

goal stimulus, but anything which terminates the drive stimulus will automatically bring the goal stimulus to an end.[7]

A second significant difference between the drive stimulus and the goal stimulus arises from the fact that from a single drive stimulus there may evolve many tolerably distinct goals. A rat, for example, will, when hungry, eat many different kinds of food. The eating of each kind of food may become a different goal with the goal reaction in each case presumably in some sense distinct. Moreover, the same kind of food may constitute the goal in many different mazes. It is evident that this possibility of a multiplicity of goal stimuli for each drive stimulus has important dynamic potentialities, especially in view of the small number of drives as contrasted with the immense variety of mammalian goals.

V

With the contrasted concepts of the drive stimulus and the goal stimulus well before us, we may now turn to the consideration of the rôles played by them in certain typical situations which are known rather well on the basis of specific experiment. The first situation to be studied is the well known one where an animal which has learned a maze with a reward of food consistently given, for a number of trials receives no reward of any kind. Under such circumstances the maze habit progressively disintegrates. Our interest is concerned with the mode of this disintegration. There is, of course, nothing surprising in the fact that a food reaction should suffer experimental extinction upon consistent failure of reinforcement. Nothing is more common in the conditioned reflex

[7] This neglects the possibility that once $S_D$ has brought $r_G$ into the antecedent reaction sequence, stimuli there resident may acquire a tendency to evoke $r_G$ themselves and thus bring into existence $s_G$ independently of $S_D$. An example of such a possibility would be the excitatory tendency represented by $s_1 \to r_G$.

literature.[8] But this, as it stands, would seemingly account for nothing but the inhibition of the act immediately preceding the failure of the customary reward. The particular question which primarily interests us here is: Why does the habit sequence disintegrate as a whole? Why should an event (failure to receive food) taking place at the conclusion of a long series of reactions produce a disintegration of those habit segments most remote from the active origin of disintegration, quite as promptly and completely as of the segment (goal reaction) immediately adjacent? In terms of our diagrams (Figs. 14.4 and 14.5) why should an event taking place at $S_4$ produce a disintegration of habit organization at $S_1$?

The first hypothesis which appears to offer anything in the way of explaining this extensive disintegration is that the drive stimulus might acquire generalized inhibitory properties. Specifically, once the drive stimulus ($S_D$) has suffered experimental extinction as regards its goal reaction, this inhibition might conceivably spread to every other reaction into which $S_D$ enters as a stimulus. But since $S_D$ is present throughout the series the tendency to inhibition would thus spread from the termination of the sequence at once throughout its whole length and might, therefore, produce the generalized disintegration known to exist.[9]

As yet our knowledge of secondary inhibitory tendencies is too meager for us to express an opinion with any confidence as to whether a spread of inhibition would be brought about by the mechanism sketched above, and, if so, whether the tendency would be strong enough to produce the disintegration just referred to. The following consideration makes it seem doubtful: If the inhibitory tendency to reactions emanating from $S_D$ were strong enough to over-ride the chaining excitatory tendencies holding the behavior segments together in the series in which the frustration took place, it should also be strong enough to produce a similar disintegrative tendency in every other sequence which this drive ($S_D$) enters as a stimulus. This means that if the organism were consistently disappointed in finding food in one accustomed place until it would no longer seek it in that location there would also result a similar paralysis of all attempts to seek food in any place at all, at least until the inhibitory tendency should have subsided. And in that event the organism would be about as likely to seek food in the place previously proven disappointing as in some alternative place which has consistently yielded food. Since these deductions are obviously contrary to fact, at

---

[8] It is here tacitly assumed as a useful working hypothesis that principles found to be operative in conditioned reflexes are also operating in maze learning. This paper may be regarded as essentially an exploration of what might be expected in a complex learning situation in case this were true. Once the implications have been drawn, the way will be open for the setting up of critical experiments which may clarify the present unfortunate uncertainty concerning the relationship between the two phenomena.

[9] I. P. Pavlov, Conditioned reflexes, pp. 48 ff.

least in this extreme form,[10] we must seek some further or supplementary mechanism for the explanation of habit disintegration which results from withdrawal of reward.

A second mechanism which appears with somewhat greater probability as mediating the generalized disintegration of maze habit organization at the failure of the reward is the *goal stimulus*. We have already pointed out in connection with the discussion of the rôle of the drive stimulus that the goal reaction ($r_G$) would naturally be the one to be eliminated at once as the result of failure of reinforcement by food. But when $r_G$ is eliminated, there is automatically eliminated $s_G$ also, together with the influence of its multiple excitatory tendencies (Fig. 14.5). And, since $s_G$ is a stimulus component of all the reactions of the sequence, they will all be correspondingly weakened by its absence, thus accounting for the spread of the effects of the failure of reward so effectively throughout the entire series.

The extent to which this weakening takes place will depend to a considerable degree upon whether the stimuli throughout the action sequence are in the state of mere unorganized complexes or whether they are organized more or less perfectly into stimulus patterns. In the former case any stimulus component, by dropping out of the complex, will withdraw from its joint excitatory tendency no more than what it would exert if acting alone. But in case the stimuli have become organized into patterns the dropping out of any customary component may result in the profound weakening of the joint excitatory tendency and even its complete abolition.[11]

Our main objective, however, is to emphasize a radical and significant difference between the habit mechanisms of drive stimulus and goal reaction stimulus respectively. We have already seen that a strictly generalized inhibitory tendency from $S_D$ alone, if such exists, would spread alike to all reaction sequences which are mediated by this drive and would not permit of the differentiation of a successful series from an unsuccessful one. This would present an impossible biological dilemma. The goal stimulus supplies the key to the situation. Since $r_G$ is peculiar to the one sequence of which it is the terminal action, the effect

10 The *a priori* probability that the inhibition resulting from failure of reward in one situation should inhibit to a certain extent other tendencies to action from the same drive stimulus, at least for a time, is sufficient to warrant the setting up of a carefully controlled experiment to determine whether or not it exists. If, for example, a rat has learned two distinct mazes to a known and equal degree and then the habit of running maze No. 1 is disintegrated by failure of reward, the rat should show a perceptible tendency to disintegration of the second maze habit when comparison is made with a suitable control. A fundamental principle of considerable importance may thus emerge.

11 Presumably habits range everywhere between these two extremes of degree of patterning and any given stimulus may be in a constant state of flux in this respect. The experimental determination of the factors governing this fundamental tendency offers a rich field for systematic exploration.

of its inhibition will weaken its own series alone. This will leave all other series, even when motivated by the same drive, essentially intact except possibly for weak inhibitory radiation effects. Thus an animal disappointed in finding food at one place, will no longer seek it there but will, nevertheless, proceed to seek it elsewhere. The disintegration of maze habits under the influence of withdrawal of reward thus serves nicely to illustrate both the inadequacy of the drive stimulus as a sole explanatory concept and the distinct explanatory possibilities of the goal-stimulus concept.

## VI

The concept of anticipatory or premature goal reactions appearing in fragmentary form concurrently with acts originally antedating them presents a very striking similarity to what has long been known as ideo-motor action. Some concrete cases of what is meant by this latter term may assist in the grasping of this point. A familiar example of ideo-motor action is found in the pressure of the inexperienced billiard player against the edge of the table while observing the movement of a ball which he has just activated, particularly when the ball threatens not quite to reach the mark at which he has aimed. A somewhat similar example is seen in the common tendency of people when watching a football game to lean and even push in the direction that they wish the play to move.

To most psychologists in the past, ideo-motor action has been regarded as no more than an interesting curiosity—a kind of abortive activity having no functional value in itself but serving, perhaps in large part by virtue of its very maladaptive nature, to indicate strikingly the existence of a tendency which might be really adaptive under other circumstances.[12] From the point of view of instrumental behavior the maladaptive nature of most ideo-motor acts is evident. Nothing could well be conceived as more stupid and less calculated to influence the course of a billiard ball than a gentle pressure on the side of the billiard table. Few things could be imagined which would be more futile as regards the outcome of a football play than the sympathetic movements on the part of the spectators. In this, ideo-motor action presents an exact parallel to implicit anticipatory goal reactions such as the licking

---

[12] This seems to have been true even of William James, despite the fact that he regarded ideo-motor action as intimately related to will. "Wherever movement follows *unhesitatingly and immediately* the notion of it in the mind, we have ideo-motor action. . . We think the act and it is done. . . Dr. Carpenter, who first used, I believe, the name of ideo-motor action, placed it, if I mistake not, among the curiosities of our mental life. The truth is that it is no curiosity but simply a normal process stripped of disguise." (William James, *Principles of Psychology*, 1908, Vol. II, p. 522.)

of the lips and the salivation of the dogs of the conditioned reflex experiments. Indeed if we consider that the pressure delivered to the side of the billiard table really would function on the ball if the hand had traversed the distance from the edge of the table to the position of the ball, and that the movements of the spectator of a football game really would affect the outcome of the play if he had traversed the distance separating him from the players, these movements appear quite literally as anticipatory goal reactions. As instrumental acts they are, and must always be, abortive, maladaptive, wasteful and stupid.

It by no means follows from the foregoing, however, that ideo-motor action is really maladaptive. On the contrary the view is here put forward that ideo-motor reactions and anticipatory goal reactions in general are really guiding and directing pure-stimulus acts and as such perform the enormously important functions ordinarily attributed to ideas. Considered merely as acts they are negligible; as pure-stimulus acts and sources of stimuli to control other action, they at once take on the very greatest importance. While indubitably physical they occupy at the same time the very citadel of the mental. The classical view was that a non-physical idea of an act preceded the act and somehow commanded the energy to evoke it, such act in consequence being called ideo-motor. In contrast to that view, the hypothesis here put forward is (1) that ideo-motor acts are in reality anticipatory goal reactions and, as such, are called into existence by ordinary physical stimulation; and (2) that these anticipatory goal reactions are pure-stimulus acts and, as such, guide and direct the more explicit and instrumental activities of the organism. In short, ideo-motor acts, instead of being *evoked* by ideas, *are* ideas. Thus the position of the classical psychology in this field is completely inverted.

Healthy individuals, uncontaminated by psychological and metaphysical theory, generally have quite simply and naturally held that ideas were dynamic—that somehow they exert a physical control over instrumental activity. The prevailing metaphysics, with its roots far back in the unscientific past, has insisted that ideas are not physical. The combination of the two points of view produced the logical absurdity of hypothesizing a physical interaction where one of the two entities involved was non-physical. Among other difficulties, such an interaction found itself in direct conflict with the principle of the conservation of energy. The present hypothesis, according to which the idea [13] is physical

---

[13] It is not to be understood that the anticipatory goal reaction is the only physical basis for what have in the past been called ideas. There certainly are some others and probably a good many others, particularly with human subjects. What was lumped together by the classical psychologists as a single thing is turning out to include a number of fairly distinct things. Thus the old terminology becomes inadequate for modern needs.

and at the same time an action and a stimulus, completely dissolves this logical absurdity, opens the door for an objective study of ideas, and offers a legitimate and unambiguous status for them in science.

But granting, for the sake of argument, that a non-physical idea could somehow evoke physical movements, there still remains the fundamental question of how, in detail, such an idea could evoke the particular actions which would be necessary to lead to a particular goal even in the relatively simple situations considered above. Schools of psychology dominated by metaphysical idealism have been peculiarly insistent upon the obligation of physical psychological theories to explain the guidance or control of action by ideas. The fact that the mentalists themselves have not been able to do this seems hardly to have been noticed, either by themselves or anyone else. Possibly in a system already filled with the incredible an additional incredibility attracts little notice. The fact remains that there exists no magic which absolves *any* system which purports to give a thoroughgoing account of human nature from the obligation of showing how purposive ideas [14] are able automatically to guide and direct action to the realization of a goal or reward. The problem is admittedly a difficult one. However, considerations already put forward in this paper furnish some grounds for optimism concerning its final solution on a strictly physical basis. At any rate the challenge is accepted.

## VII

We may now briefly summarize the results of our discussion:

The drive stimulus accounts very well for the random seeking reactions of a hungry organism, but alone it is not sufficient to produce the integration of complex behavior sequences such as is involved in maze learning. There must always be a reward of some kind. Once the reward has been given, however, the behavior undergoes a marked change most definitely characterized by evidences of actions anticipatory of the goal, which actions tend to appear as accompaniments to the sequence ordinarily leading to the full overt goal reaction.

It is shown how these fractional anticipatory goal reactions could be drawn to the beginning of the behavior sequence and maintained throughout it by the action of the drive stimulus ($S_D$). The kinaesthetic stimulus resulting from this persistent anticipatory action should furnish

---

[14] In a previous paper purpose was tentatively identified with the drive stimulus ($S_D$). Upon more mature consideration the writer is inclined to revise this judgment in favor of the goal stimulus ($s_G$), largely on the ground that the latter stimulus both represents the goal and provides the more intimate mechanism of its attainment, even though the goal stimulus is ultimately dependent for its existence upon the drive.

a second stimulus ($s_G$) which would persist very much like $S_D$. These two persisting stimuli alike should have the capacity of forming multiple excitatory tendencies to the evocation of every reaction within the sequence. They should differ, however, in that the anticipatory goal reaction stimulus would be dependent for its existence upon the integrity of the drive stimulus. A second difference is that a single drive stimulus may generate many distinct goal stimuli.

The general *a priori* probability of the existence of the goal stimulus finds confirmation in the fact that it affords a plausible explanation of a class of experimentally observed facts hitherto inexplicable. It enables us to understand, for example, why withholding the usual reward at the end of an accustomed maze run will cause a disintegration of that particular habit sequence while leaving the organism free to pursue alternative sequences based on the same drive. It offers an explanation of why, during a maze learning process, the substitution of one reward for another presumably of about the same attractiveness should produce a transitory slump in the learning scores. It throws light on why an animal evidently motivated by the anticipation of one kind of food will leave untouched a different but otherwise acceptable type of food which has been surreptitiously substituted. There is reason to believe that as the experimental literature on the motivating influence of rewards increases the goal stimulus mechanism will find enlarged application.

Moreover, there is strong reason for believing that the fractional anticipatory goal reaction is the actual basis of what has long been known as ideo-motor action. This latter phenomenon emerges from the analysis as a dynamic mechanism, a pure-stimulus act, rather than an end product as was formerly supposed. This means that ideo-motor acts are not caused by ideas. On the contrary, they are themselves ideas. It has long been recognized that one of the prime functions of ideas is to guide and control instrumental acts in cases where the situation to which the acts really function is absent and, as a consequence, is unable to stimulate the organism directly. The capacity of anticipatory goal reactions as stimuli to control and direct other activity renders intelligible on a purely physical basis the dynamic guiding power of ideas. This, in turn, makes still more plausible the hypothesis that anticipatory goal reactions are the physical substance of purposive ideas.

For the sake of definiteness and additional clarity the hypotheses elaborated above may be assembled in brief dogmatic form: Pure-stimulus acts are the physical substance of ideas. Ideas, however, are of many varieties. Among them are goal or guiding ideas. The physical mechanism constituting these particular ideas is the anticipatory goal reaction. This appears to be substantially the same as ideo-motor action. The anticipatory goal reaction seems also to constitute the physical basis of the somewhat ill-defined but important concept of purpose, desire, or wish, rather than the drive stimulus as has sometimes been supposed, notably by Kampf. This interpretation of purpose explains its dynamic nature and at the same time removes the paradox arising under the classical psychology where the future appeared to be operating causally in a backward direction upon the present. This hypothesis also renders intelligible the 'realization of an anticipation' by an organism. It is found in situations where a fractional anticipatory goal reaction as a stimulus has motivated a behavior sequence which culminates in a full overt enactment of a goal-behavior complex of which it is a physical component.

# 15 • Edward B. Titchener

## Brentano and Wundt: Empirical and Experimental Psychology

The dynamics of purpose, as the phrase is used here, has to do with the consequences of motives once they have become operative. As has been mentioned, many psychologists have assumed that purpose and intention are so fundamental to organismic action as to provide the unit of all psychological description. The preceding selections on the analysis of purpose have examined the work of men who were concerned with how behavior may become purposeful. The following group deals with contributions which have examined the effects of purpose. These have come most consistently from psychologists like Brentano who have considered psychic phenomena to be basically *activities*—imagining, judging, wishing, and the like. Motivation has always been central to act psychology, but act psychologists have not always been well understood by American students. E. B. Titchener, the author of this selection, was not an act psychologist himself, but an advocate of the content psychology of Wundt. In this simple introduction to the psychologies of the act psychologist, Franz Brentano, and the content psychologist, Wilhelm Wundt, Titchener points up the fundamental differences between these two schools in an eminently fair-minded way.

I

*The year 1874* saw the publication of two books which, as the event has shown, were of first-rate importance for the development of modern psychology. Their authors, already in the full maturity of life, were men of settled reputation, fired as investigators with the zeal of research, endowed as teachers with a quite exceptional power to influence younger minds, ready as polemists to cross swords with a Zeller or a Helmholtz. Yet one would look in vain for any sign of closer intellectual kinship between them; hardly, indeed, could one find a greater divergence either

This article is reproduced in full from *The American Journal of Psychology*, 1921, 32, 108–120. Reprinted by permission of *The American Journal of Psychology*.

of tendency or of training. Psychology, seeing how much their work and example have done to assure her place among the sciences, may gladly confess her debt to both. The student of psychology, though his personal indebtedness be also twofold, must still make his choice for the one or the other. There is no middle way between Brentano and Wundt.[1]

Franz Brentano began his career as a catholic theologian. In 1867 he published an outline of the history of philosophy within the mediaeval church which sets forth, as clearly and sharply as the essay of thirty years later, his famous doctrine of the four phases.[2] Early and late, however, his intellectual interest has centered in the philosophy of Aristotle. He came to psychology by way of an intensive study of the *De Anima*, and he has made the Aristotelian method his pattern of scientific procedure. We possess, unfortunately, only the first volume of his *Psychologie:* Brentano seems always to have preferred the spoken to the written word: but this volume, like everything else that he has given to the press, is complete in itself, the finished expression of his mature thought.

Wilhelm Wundt started out as a physiologist, interested in the special phenomena of nerve and muscle. In 1862 he had sought to lay the foundations of an 'experimental psychology' (the phrase now appears in print for the first time)[3] in a theory of sense-perception. Here he fell into the mistake to which every student of natural science is liable who turns, without due preparation, to the things of mind: the mistake, namely, of supposing that psychology is nothing more than an applied logic; and the mistake was repeated in a popular work upon human and animal psychology which followed on the heels of the technical volume. By 1874 he had definitely discarded this earlier view for the conception of psychology as an independent science. He still maintained, however, that the path to it leads through the anatomy and physiology of the nervous system.

Such, in briefest outline, were the conditions under which the two psychologies acquired their form and substance. We see, on the one hand, a man who has devoted his 'hours of solitary reflection' to ancient and

---

[1] F. Brentano, *Psychologie vom empirischen Standpunkte* (henceforth cited as *PES*), i, 1874. Cf. the Biographical Note in F. Brentano, *The Origin of the Knowledge of Right and Wrong*, trs. C. Hague, 1902, 119 ff.; M. Heinze, F. *Ueberwegs Grundriss der Geschichte der Philosophie*, iv, 1906, 332 ff. W. Wundt, *Grundzüge der physiologischen Psychologie* (henceforth cited as *PP*), 1874. The first ten chapters of Wundt's work were issued in 1873 and are utilised by Brentano. For a bibliography of Wundt's scientific writings see *Amer. Jour. Psych.*, xix (1908) ff.; cf. Heinze, *op. cit.*, 322 ff.

[2] J. A. Möhler, *Kirchengeschichte*, ii, 1867, 539 f.; F. Brentano, *Die vier Phasen der Philosophie und ihr augenblicklicher Stand*, 1895. The four phases, repeated in the three great philosophical periods, are those of scientific construction, failure or perversion of the scientific interest, scepticism and mysticism.

[3] W. Wundt, *Beiträge zur Theorie der Sinneswahrnehmung*, 1862, vi.

mediaeval philosophy; we see, on the other hand, a man who has wrought out in the laboratory his contributions to the latest-born of the experimental sciences. They are both professors of philosophy, and they are both to range widely, in the future, over the varied fields of philosophical enquiry. Yet it would be wrong to suppose that the psychology to which they have now attained, and which, by a happy chance, they give to the world in the same year, represents merely an incident, even if it were the central incident, of their philosophical history. Psychology, on the contrary, has laid strong hands upon them, and is to dominate all their further thinking. Wundt, a generation later, will round off the manifold list of his books with the encyclopaedic folk-psychology, and Brentano never gives up the hope of a descriptive—to be followed, perhaps, at long last by a genetic—psychology as the ripe fruit of his studious old age.

## II

We shall better understand the nature of this choice which lies before us if we first note the points of resemblance between the two systems. For even in 1874 psychology was not in such bad case that Brentano and Wundt are always at variance. They agree that psychology holds a place of high importance in the fellowship of the sciences, and that it is logically prior to natural science.[4] They agree that it may dispense with the concept of substance and confine itself to an account of phenomena.[5] They reject the unconscious as a principle of psychological explanation.[6] They define the unity of consciousness in substantially the same terms.[7] So far there is agreement: and though the agreement is largely of a formal kind, and though a good deal of it has a negative ground in the reaction against Herbart, it serves nevertheless to mark out a common universe of discourse.

On the material side there is also agreement, with such difference of emphasis as the difference of authorship would lead us to expect. We find, for instance, that Brentano deals at length with the general method of psychology, and is at pains to distinguish inner perception from inner observation, while Wundt takes inner observation for granted and describes in detail only those special procedures which raise it to the rank of experiment.[8] We find that Wundt devotes much space to Fechnerian psychophysics, and interprets the psychophysical law as a general psychological law of relativity, while Brentano makes only incidental and

[4] *PES*, 24 ff., 119; *PP*, 4, 863.
[5] *PES*, 10 ff.; *PP*, 9, 12, 20.
[6] *PES*, 133 ff.; *PP*, 644 f., 664, 708 f., 712, 790 ff.
[7] *PES*, 204 ff.; *PP*, 715 ff., 860 ff.
[8] *PES*, 34 ff., 184; *PP*, 1 ff.

critical mention of Fechner's work.[9] The differences are striking enough, but behind them lies agreement regarding the subject-matter of psychology. Even in the extreme case, where the one book emphasises what the other omits, difference does not of necessity mean disagreement. We find, again, that Wundt says nothing of a question which for Brentano is the essential problem of psychology as it was the first problem of psychophysics, the question of 'immortality,' of the continuance of our mental life after death, and conversely that Brentano fails to discuss Wundt's cardinal problem of attention. Yet Wundt had touched upon the question of immortality in his earlier writing, and Brentano plainly recognises that there is a problem of attention, although (as we may suppose) he has put off its discussion to his second volume.[10]

So the student of psychology who read these two books in their year of issue might, if he had made due allowance for the training and natural tendencies of the authors, have entertained a reasonable hope for the future of his science; and we ourselves, who see their differences far more plainly than was possible for him, may still hope that the main issue can be taken on common ground and fought out at close quarters.

## III

Brentano entitles his book 'psychology from the empirical standpoint,' and Wundt writes 'physiological psychology' on his title-page and suggests 'experimental psychology' in his text.[11] The adjectives do not greatly help us. For all experimental psychology is in the broad sense empirical, and a psychology which is in the narrow sense empirical may still have recourse to experiment. To show the real difference between the books, the difference that runs through their whole texture and composition, we need at this stage terms that are both familiar and clear; the time has not yet come for technicalities and definitions. We may say, as a first approximation, that Brentano's psychology is essentially a matter of argument, and that Wundt's is essentially a matter of description.

At the end of his discussion of method Brentano refers with approval to Aristotle's use of *aporiae*, of difficulties and objections, wherein a subject is viewed from various sides, and opinion is weighed against opinion and argument against argument, until by comparison of pros and

---

[9] *PP*, 421; *PES*, 9 f., 87 ff.

[10] *PES*, 17 ff., 32 f., 95 f.; Wundt takes up the question of immortality (indirectly, it is true) in *Vorlesungen*, etc., ii, 1863, 436, 442; cf. the direct treatment in the later edition, 1892, 476 ff. Brentano recognises the problem of attention in *PES*, 91, 155; cf. 263, and C. Stumpf, *Tonpsychologie*, i, 1883, 68; ii, 1890, 279 f.

[11] *PP*, 3.

cons a reasonable conclusion is reached.[12] This is, in the large, his own
way of working. He appeals but rarely, and then only in general terms,
to facts of observation. His rule is to find out what other psychologists
have said, to submit their statements to a close logical scrutiny, and so by
a process of sifting to prepare the reader's mind for a positive determination. When the ground has thus been cleared Brentano's doctrine,
novel though it may be, has the appearance (so to say) of a necessary
truth; we feel that we have duly considered the possibilities in the case
and have come to the one rational decision; and if for conscience' sake
we go on to deduce and to verify, we still are assured beforehand that
everything will fit together within the system. Minor points may need to
be expanded; even, perhaps, in the light of further *aporiae*, to be corrected; but the whole exposition gives the impression of finality.[13] It is
no wonder, then, that many students have judged the author successful
in his aim of writing, not Brentano's psychology, nor yet a national psychology, but—psychology.[14]

Wundt's book, on the contrary, abounds in facts of observation:
anatomical facts, physiological facts, results of psychophysical and psychological experiment. Its introductory chapter is brief to the point of
perfunctoriness, and criticism of psychological theories is packed away
into fine-print paragraphs that, to all intents and purposes, are a series
of appendices. There is, to be sure, a great deal of argument. Where the
facts are scanty, they must not only be generously interpreted but must
also be eked out by hypothesis; if a leading physiologist has mistaken the
problem of sense-perception, he must be argued into a better way of

---

[12] *PES*, 96 f.; cf. J. S. Mill, Grote's Aristotle, *Fortnightly Rev.*, N. S. xiii, 1873,
48 ff. Brentano had earlier noted, with the same approval, the use of *aporiae* by
Thomas Aquinas: see J. A. Möhler, *Kirchengeschichte*, ii, 1867, 555.

[13] I know of only three corrections that Brentano has made to his psychology.
(1) In *PES* 292 degree of conviction, as intensity of judgment, is declared analogous
to degree of intensity of love and hate (cf. 203); in the notes to *The Origin of the
Knowledge of Right and Wrong* (1889), 1902, 52 f., this analogy is denied. (2) In
*PES* 202 f. feeling is said to be always present along with ideation; the belief to the
contrary is due to the mistaken preference of memory over inner perception (44); but
in *Untersuchungen zur Sinnespsychologie*, 1907, 119, 124, the acts of the two higher
senses are not intrinsically emotive. (3) In *PES* 115 the object upon which a psychical
phenomenon is directed is not to be understood as *eine Realität;* but the notes appended to the reprinted section *Von der Klassifikation der psychischen Phänomene*
(1911, 149) lay it down that "nie etwas anderes als Dinge, welche sämtlich unter
denselben Begriff des Realen fallen, für psychische Beziehungen ein Objekt abgibt."—
There would, no doubt, if the book were rewritten, be many other modifications of
detail, and yet others if the second volume were undertaken; the discussion of the
modi of ideation in the *Klassifikation* shows that Brentano had not in 1874 thought
out the doctrine of his Bk. iii. In the main, nevertheless, the doctrine of 1874 has
stood the test of Brentano's own continued reflection and of the attacks of critics.
Such an achievement is worthy of all admiration. Only we must add—those of us
who challenge Brentano's premises—that even isolated changes are disconcerting. The
first statement is so serenely confident, and the changes are again so confidently made!

[14] *PES*, vi.

thinking; in any case, the new science of experimental psychology must offer a bold front to her elder sisters.[15] The argument, none the less, is always secondary and oftentimes plainly tentative; so that the book as a whole gives the impression of incompleteness, of a first essay which can be improved when more work (and a great many suggestions of further work are thrown out [16]) has been accomplished. Hence it is no accident, but rather a direct reflex of the spirit in which the authors approached their task, that Brentano's volume still bears the date 1874 while Wundt's book, grown to nearly triple its original size, has come to a sixth edition.[17]

This thorough-going difference of argument and description means, of course, a radical difference of attitude toward psychology itself. It means that Brentano and Wundt, in spite of formal and material agreement, psychologise in different ways. Our next step, therefore, is to place ourselves inside the systems and to realise, so far as we may without too much detail, what manner of discipline they intend psychology to be. We have to choose: and the illustrations that follow will show the alternatives of choice in concrete and tangible form.

## IV

Brentano defines psychology as the science of psychical phenomena. The term may easily be misleading: for the phenomena in question are very far from being static appearances. Generally they are activities; in the individual case they are acts. Hence they can properly be named only by an active verb. They fall into three fundamental classes: those, namely, of Ideating (I see, I hear, I imagine), of Judging (I acknowledge, I reject, I perceive, I recall), and of Loving-Hating (I feel, I wish, I resolve, I intend, I desire). We may use substantives if we will, and may speak of sensation and idea, memory and imagination, opinion, doubt, judgment, joy and sorrow, desire and aversion, intention and resolution; but we must always bear in mind that the psychical phenomenon is active, is a sensing or a doubting or a recalling or a willing.

It is true that we never have act without content. When we ideate, we sense or imagine something; when we judge, we perceive something, acknowledge the truth of something, recall something; when we love or hate, we take interest in something, desire or repudiate something. This, however, is precisely the difference between psychical and physical phenomena. The latter are blank and inert: the color or figure or land-

---

[15] *PP*, Vorwort.

[16] *PP*, 284, 293, 314, 317, 373, 394, 399, etc., etc.

[17] See the prefaces to the successive editions of the *PP*. Even the sixth edition, as I have shown elsewhere (*Psych. Rev.*, xxiv, 1917, 52 f.), has not attained to systematic completion, and only in the fifth (*PP*, i, 1902, ix) did Wundt set himself definitely to the task of system-making.

scape that I see, the chord that I hear, the warmth or cold or odor that I sense, the like objects that I imagine, all these things are described when their given appearance is described; their appearance sums them up and exhausts them; they have no reference, and do not carry us beyond themselves. Psychical phenomena, on the other hand, are precisely characterised by relation to a content, by reference to an object; they contain an object intentionally within them; and this character of immanent objectivity, in virtue of which they are active, marks them off uniquely from the physical phenomena upon which they are directed or toward which they point. Even in cases where the content of a psychical phenomenon is not physical, but is another psychical phenomenon, the distinction holds good. For the act which becomes content or object of another act is not thereby deprived of its essential character; it is still active in its own right; and it is therefore by no means confusable with bare physical appearance.[18]

These are Brentano's views of the subject-matter of psychology. He begins by considering the alleged differences between physical and psychical, finds an adequate *differentia* of the psychical, and is therefore able to define psychology in terms of the matter with which it deals. He then reviews the principal classifications hitherto made of psychical phenomena, and arrives at a classification of his own, in which judgment is accorded independent rank, and feeling and will are bracketed under a single heading. Throughout the discussion his chief reliance is upon argument. To be sure, he takes the testimony of inner perception; but inner perception is not observation; it is rather a self-evident cognition or judgment; and as such it is, if we may use the phrase, of the same stuff as argument.[19] Psychological observation is possible for Brentano only when past acts are recalled in memory; then indeed, as he admits, even a sort of experimentation becomes possible. Not only, however, is memory subject to gross illusion, but the act of memory, once more, falls under the category of judgment, so that experiment itself takes place in the world of argument.[20] The empirical psychology thus employs the same psychical activities to establish the nature of its subject-matter and to discuss the variety of psychological opinion.

## V

For Wundt, psychology is a part of the science of life. Vital processes may be viewed from the outside, and then we have the subject-matter of

---

[18] *PES*, 23 f., 35, 101 ff., 161, 167, 256 ff. On the problem of natural science as an explanatory discipline, see 127 ff.

[19] *PES*, 35 ff., 181 ff. (summary 202 f.), 262. Cf. *Klassifikation*, 1911, 129.

[20] *PES*, 42 ff., 162, 169, 262; *Klassifikation*, 130.

physiology, or they may be viewed from within, and then we have the subject-matter of psychology.[21] The data, the items of this subject-matter, are always complex, and the task of experimental psychology is to analyse them into "the elementary psychical processes." If we know the elements, and can compare them with the resulting complexes, we may hope to understand the nature of integration, which according to Wundt is the distinguishing character of consciousness.[22]

Analysis of the processes of the inner life brings us, in the last resort, to pure sensations, constituted originally of intensity and quality. Sensations carry no reference; they look neither before nor after; they tell us nothing of their stimuli, whether external or organic, and nothing of their point of excitation, whether peripheral or central, nor do they forecast the ideas in which we find them synthetised. They simply run their course, qualitatively and intensively, and may be observed and described as they proceed.[23] Ideas, in their turn, are originally constituted of these sensations; there is nothing within or upon them to show whether they are ideas of imagination or perceptions.[24] Individual ideas differ psychologically from general ideas solely in the nature of their sensory constitutents: in the former the complex of sensations is constant, in the latter it is variable.[25] Concepts are not "psychical formations" at all; if we psychologise them, we discover only their substitutes in consciousness, spoken or written words, accompanied by a vague and indeterminate feeling.[26] Judgments, in the same way, belong to logic, and not primarily to psychology; logic and psychology approximate only as a result of the parallel growth, long continued, of conceptual thinking and its expression in language; our "conscious psychological processes" consist originally of nothing more than ideas and their connections.[27]

The trend of all this analysis is clear: Wundt is trying to describe mind, to show the stuff of which it is made, to reduce it to its lowest terms. When, however, he turns from analysis to synthesis, the exposition is less easy to follow. Sensations are integrated into ideas by a "psychical synthesis" which Wundt himself compares to a chemical synthesis and which critics have assimilated to Mill's "mental chemistry." [28] Ideas gain

[21] *PP*, 1 ff.

[22] *PP*, 5, 20, 717.

[23] *PP*, 273 ff., 484 f. When sensations enter into connection with one another, the third attribute of affective tone or sensory feeling is added. Intensity and quality are, however, the "more original" constituents.

[24] *PP*, 464 f.

[25] *PP*, 468.

[26] *PP*, 672.

[27] *PP*, 709 ff.

[28] *PP*, 484 f.; J. S. Mill, *A System of Logic*, 1843, bk. vi, ch. iv (ii, 1856, 429); *An Examination of Sir William Hamilton's Philosophy*, 1865, 286 f.; note in J. Mill, *Analysis of the Phenomena of the Human Mind*, i, 1869, 106 ff. The original source is D. Hartley, *Observations on Man*, 1749, pt. i, ch. i, sect. 2, prop. 12, cor. 1 (i, 1810, 77 f.).

their objective reference by a "secondary act" which seems to consist, psychologically, in the simple addition of further ideas; [29] yet the objective reference is itself put, later on, to psychological purposes. Concepts and forms of intuition are made 'postulates' of advancing thought,[30] as if the logical and practical aspects of mind were necessarily implied in its given or phenomenal aspect, and as if the psychologist might shift from one aspect to another without breach of scientific continuity. But though we may puzzle over details, there is nothing obscure in the general situation. Wundt, like many others of his generation, is dazzled by the vast promise of the evolutionary principle; [31] 'original' is for him more or less what 'nascent' is for Spencer; the later must derive from the earlier, because that is the way of things, and the later has no other basis. Let us remember, all the same, that Wundt's primary effort is to describe, and that he falls back upon 'genetic explanation' only when some phase of the traditional subject-matter of psychology proves to be indescribable.

That, then, is one of the threads of Wundt's system. Even a descriptive psychology cannot, however, be written simply in terms of sensations and their modes and levels of psychological integration. For the field of consciousness, Wundt reminds us, is not uniformly illuminated; it shows a small bright area at its centre and a darker region round about; the ideas which occupy it differ in their conscious status. So arises the problem of atention. Descriptively—Wundt takes up the task of description piecemeal, in different contexts, as if it were 'on his conscience'—attention reduces to clearness of ideas and characteristic feelings of effort or strain.[32] It has two concrete manifestations, apperception and voluntary action; we speak of apperception when we are considering the internal course of ideas, and of voluntary action when we are considering the issue of an emotion in external movement.[33] Both forms of the attentional process are subject to conditions, and both are strictly correlated with physiological processes in the cerebral cortex; they therefore fall within the limits of a scientific psychology.[34] Yet psychologists have neglected them, and have paid the penalty of this neglect in inadequate psychology and untenable philosophy.[35]

We need not here trace the doctrine of attention further; we need not either debate whether the problem of attention is included in Wundt's formal statement of the task of experimental psychology. We may, however, as an illustration of the interweaving of the two system-

---

[29] *PP*, 465.
[30] *PP*, 672, 680.
[31] *PP*, vi.
[32] *PP*, 717 ff., esp. 724.
[33] *PP*, 831, 835.
[34] *PP*, 720 f., 723 f., 834 f.
[35] *PP*, 792 f., 831 ff.

atic threads, glance at his treatment of the association of ideas. He begins, as we might expect, with mode of integration; and under this heading declares that the recognised laws, of similarity and of frequency of connection in space and time, are imperfect even as empirical generalisations. We find, it is true, two forms of association, distinguishable in the free play of fancy and in reflective thought. But the one is wider than association by similarity, in that the effective resemblance may reside in any and every sensory constituent of the ideas concerned, and especially in their affective tone, while the other reveals itself simply as an affair of habit. Wundt therefore proposes to term them, respectively, 'association by relationship' and 'association by habituation.' The new names, he maintains, are not indifferent; for they do fuller justice than the old to the facts of self-observation, and they also point us to the conditions of association in the central nervous substance.[36]

Here then is an improvement on the side of analysis and synthesis; but that is not enough. For ideas do not associate automatically, as it were of their own motion; the laws of association are, on the contrary, under the universal dominance of attention. And now there opens up, for experimental attack, a whole series of special problems which an empirical psychology, following only the single line of enquiry, must naturally miss. In their light we pass beyond associationism to a more faithful transcript of the 'course and connection of ideas'; [37] and in like manner we avoid, in our psychology of will, the philosophical *impasse* of indeterminism.[38]—

These paragraphs express, in rough summary, the teaching of the Wundt of 1874. He does not give psychology a distinct and peculiar subject-matter; the difference between physiology and psychology lies simply in our point of view. Wundt had already published a comprehensive work upon physiology, and now that he has turned to psychology he carries his knowledge and method with him; he is convinced that the processes of the inner life are best set forth in close connection with those of the outer life, and that the results of inner observation are surest when the appliances of external observation, the procedures of physiology, are pressed into psychological service. He spends little time upon preliminaries, but gets as quickly as may be to the exposition of facts. Where facts are few or lacking, he seeks to supplement or to supply them by observations of his own. His primary aim in all cases is to describe the phenomena of mind as the physiologist describes the phenomena of the living body, to write down what is there, going on observably before him: witness his treatment of idea, of concept, of attention, of association. There is still great space for argument, and the argument, we must admit,

[36] *PP*, 788 ff.
[37] *PP*, 793; cf. the earlier sections of ch. xix.
[38] *PP*, 837 f.

is often influenced by previous habits of thought, by psychological tradition, by a certain tendency to round things off to a logical completeness, by a somewhat naïve trust in the principle of evolution. The argument, however, does not impress the reader as anything but secondary: Wundt is at once too dogmatic and too ready to change his views. The recurring need of further facts and the patchwork character of the argument suggest, both alike, that psychology, under his guidance, has still a long systematic road to travel.

## VI

We have now viewed our two psychologies from within. Brentano, we have found, looks back over the past, weeds out its errors with a sympathetic hand, accepts from it whatever will stand the test of his criticism, and organises old truth and new into a system meant, in all essentials, to last as long as psychology shall be studied; Wundt, after he has acknowledged his debt to the past, turns away from it and plunges into the multifarious and detailed work of the laboratories, producing a psychology that is as much encyclopaedia as system, and that bears on its face the need for continual revision. Which of the two books holds the key to a science of psychology?

Brentano has all the advantage that comes with historical continuity. His doctrine of immanent objectivity goes back to Aristotle and the Schoolmen, and the classification of psychical acts into ideas, judgments, and phenomena of love and hate goes back to Descartes.[39] More than this: he can claim kinship with every psychologist, of whatever school, who has approached his subject from the technically 'empirical' standpoint. For the 'empirical' psychologist means to take mind as he finds it; and like the rest of the world, who are not psychologists, he finds it in use; he finds it actively at work in man's intercourse with nature and with his fellow-man, as well as in his discourse with himself. Terms may change and classifications may vary, but the items of classification are always activities, and the terms employed—faculties, capacities, powers, operations, functions, acts, states—all belong to the same logical universe. Brentano, innovator though he is, takes his place as of right in a great psychological community.[40]

---

[39] *PES*, 115 f.; *The Origin of the Knowledge of Right and Wrong*, 47.

[40] In spite of the remarks in §3 and in §6 below it may seem unjust to Brentano if, even in this preliminary sketch of the psychological issue, his interest in experiment is left without record. We note, then, that as early as 1874 he urged the establishment at Vienna of a psychological laboratory (*Ueber die Zunkunft der Philosophie*, 1893, 47 f.); that he has published *Untersuchungen zur Sinnespsychologie* (1907) and in particular that he brought the Müller-Lyer illusion to the attention of psychologists (*Zeits. f. Psych. u. Phys. d. Sinnesorgane*, iii, 1892, 349); and that Stumpf, who was

To offset this advantage, and to justify his own break with tradition, Wundt holds out the promise of an experimental method. He should have been more explicit: for technology as well as science—medicine as well as physiology, engineering as well as physics—makes use of experiment. His actual purpose, as we trace it in the chapters of his book, is to transform psychology into an experimental science of the strict type, a science that shall run parallel with experimental physiology.[41] He failed, no doubt, to see all that this purpose implied, and his earlier readers may be excused if they looked upon his work as an empirical psychology prefaced by anatomy and physiology and interspersed with psychophysical experiments. There is plenty of empirical psychology in the volume. If, however, we go behind the letter to the informing spirit; if we search out the common motive in Wundt's treatment of the familiar topics; if we carry ourselves back in thought to the scientific atmosphere of the seventies, and try in that atmosphere to formulate the purpose that stands out sharp and clear to our modern vision; then the real significance of the *Physiological Psychology* cannot be mistaken. It speaks the language of science, in the rigorous sense of the word, and it promises us in this sense a science of psychology.

But Brentano also speaks of a 'science' of psychology. Which of the two authors is in the right?

---

his pupil (Ueberweg-Heinze, iv, 1906, 334 f.), has given us the experimental *Tonpsychologie*. All this, however, does not prevent his being, in the narrow sense, an 'empirical' psychologist. Stumpf tells us that his own work is to "describe the psychical functions that are set in action by tones" (*Tonpsych.*, i, 1883, v) and declares later that "there cannot be a psychology of tones; only a psychology of tonal perceptions, tonal judgments, tonal feelings" (*Zur Einteilung der Wissenschaften*, 1907, 30). Brentano, even with a laboratory, would not have been, in Wundt's sense, an 'experimental' psychologist. We know, besides, something of Brentano's systematic programme. The empirical psychology is not to be concluded; it is to be supplemented and replaced by a 'descriptive' psychology (*The Origin*, etc., vii, 51 f.), fragments of which have appeared in *The Origin of the Knowledge of Right and Wrong* (dealing with the phenomena of love and hate and, in the Notes, with judgment) and in the *Untersuchungen* sense-perception). This in turn is to be followed by an 'explanatory' or 'genetic' psychology, a sample of which is given in *Das Genie*, 1892 (see *The Origin*, etc., 123).

[41] The substitution of folk-psychology for experiment in the study of the more complicated mental processes appears in the fourth edition (*PP*, i, 1893, 5); the reservation in regard to psychophysical parallelism in the fifth edition (*PP*, iii, 1903, 775 ff.).

# 16 • Henry J. Watt

## Experimental Contribution to a Theory of Thinking

The Wuerzburg School of psychologists began with a Wundt-like content orientation but were led by their results to an act-like position which recognized the influence of what might now be termed *motivational sets* upon the course of thinking. Henry Watt contributed the only publication of the Wuerzburg School written in the English language. It was the article reproduced here, based on his doctoral dissertation at Wuerzburg. What Watt refers to as the *task* later became Ach's *determining tendency* and this in turn was the forerunner of the later construct of set. Watt's article also stresses the insufficiency of analysis of conscious processes alone to deal with motivational effects.

*For this thesis* a long series of experiments was carried out. *Several hundred nouns* of common occurrence were printed in big type on cards and were shown to the observing subject one at a time by means of an

This paper, which is to be regarded as an abstract of a thesis entitled, "Experimentelle Beiträge zu einer Theorie des Denkens" (Doctor Dissertation, Würzburg, 1904, *Archiv für die gesamte Psychologie*, vol. iv. Leipzig: Engelmann, 1904. Pp. 154), was accompanied by a letter from the author addressed to Professor M'Kendrick, of which the following is a paragraph:—

"I have made no attempt to sketch a physiological theory which would give a basis for the psychological factors I distinguish in my thesis. It is only just to those who know the possibilities of such physiological theories better than I do, to allow a clear account of psychological analysis to tempt *them* to any such undertaking. In several points, besides, as will be evident to you, my work goes rather to strengthen the hands of those who, for the present, want to work out their physiological material directly without any conclusions from psychological theory. The most we psychologists can hope meanwhile is, that some analysis of ours may suggest a new idea to some physiologist which he might try and investigate directly on physiological material. That would be something to be proud of! It will also be good if the impression gains ground that experimental psychology is an intelligible and exact science and not a mere play with dreams."

This article is reproduced in full from the *Journal of Anatomy and Physiology*, 1906, *40*, 257–266. Reprinted by permission of the Journal of Anatomy.

automatic *card-changer* (Dr. Ach's). A metal plate, which covered the card, sprang up, when a string was pulled, and by so doing closed an electric current, which flowed through a Hipp *chronoscope* and a *speaking tube* (Cattell's). The chronoscope therefore marked the time which passed from the appearance of the printed word until the first vibrations from the subject's voice broke the current in the speaking tube. This constituted the measure of the duration of the reaction and formed, with a full account of all the reproducible experiences of the observing subject, which were at once written down in full, and any other remarks he had to make, the experimental data of the thesis.

In contrast to previous experiments, on association definite *tasks* (*Aufgaben*) were given, which the subject had to accomplish in the reaction. These referred to what the printed word on the card signified, and were as follows: to classify it, to name an example of it, to name a whole to which it belonged, to name a part, to name another of the same class or another part of the same whole. Each subject performed the experiments separately, and every care was taken, both in regard to technical details and to the way the experiments were carried out, that no disturbing factors should be present. The most of the work was done by four practised observers, and over three thousand experiments were made in all.

The following are *the results*. In almost every case the subject is able to accomplish his task correctly. His description of his experiences shows that there are in the main *three kinds of complexes of experiences*. Most frequently the subject follows one line right through the experiment, which then leads to the spoken word. In the other cases, he may seek a word which he does not find, and which he even afterwards cannot name, or he may have intended to say a certain word, but for some reason or other, wittingly or unwittingly, have said another. In general the first class, the *simple reproductions*, take place in a good deal less time than the other two classes, the *complex reproductions*, of which two the second named usually and naturally last longer.

Within each of these classes there are *three groups*. In the *first* of these the spoken word follows directly on the given optical stimulus, sometimes after a pause which can be described in no particularly definite way, sometimes with the assurance of the subject that between the stimulus and the reaction nothing whatever has been experienced. Such a reaction lasts in general a very short time, and in the second form a shorter time than any other kind of association reaction. In a *second* and very large class, a *visual representation* follows the stimulus. Directly after that, or after a short pause or a so-called search, comes the spoken word. These are a good deal longer than the first set, and sometimes longer, sometimes shorter, among themselves according to the detail and vividness of the representation and the frequency of occurrence of such reactions containing visual representations for the particular subject. *Last* of all come those reactions in which a *word-representation,* or some experience which could only be described in conceptual terms and not analytically according to its psychological content—call it a thought— appeared between the presentation of the word and the spoken reaction. These were often shorter than those containing visual representations and sometimes longer. It is not, however, contended in this classification that the reaction could take no other course. On the contrary, it is easy to see that we could have tone, smell, taste, touch and other such representations playing a part in the reaction, provided the conditions of experiment produced them. None of these were clearly present among these experiments.

But what are these *conditions of experiment?* How does any one particular reaction come about and not another? The *first influence* at work on the subject is the given *task.* This he hears spoken by the experimenter, and generally repeats to himself in words, *e.g.* "find a part!" "name an example!" or he may exemplify the experiment to himself, *e.g.* "animal—dog," and so on. The scanty description of the preparation for the experiment given in the subject's account of it does not help us to form a very clear idea of what the process itself is. It was found, however, as a series of detailed curves show, that of all the simple reproductions the percentage of occurrence of each of the three above-named classes changes regularly and similarly with each subject from one task to another. This leads to the assertion that the task has a regular influence on the *nature* of the experiences of each subject, which becomes particularly evident between the two larger groups of simple reproductions, those containing visual representations and those containing nothing at all. The change of task has a most decisive influence on the percentage of these classes, and a subject who has hardly a single visual representation when the task "classify" is given, may have them in 50 per cent of the cases when the task "find a part" is given. Alongside this, a subject with 50 per cent visual representations in the first case, may have 90–100 per cent in the second. Moreover it is found that the *duration* of the reaction in each of these classes is also on the average dependent on the nature of the task. So too is the duration of the complex reproductions, but the percentage occurrence of these, out of all experiments made, is, curiously enough, quite *independent* of the nature of the task, as curves show. The attempt is made to explain this by a fairly probable consideration. The number of tendencies to reproduction which diverge from any one stimulus, must depend on the number of ideas with which the stimulus is associated. It is impossible to conceive how the task should change these, as an association must be presupposed before the task working with the stimulus could produce any reaction. The occurrence of a complex reproduction would depend then on the nature of the stimulus-word given and not on that of the task. The influence of the *task* has therefore to be carefully differentiated from that of the *stimulus*.

An analysis of the experiments worked with the fifth and sixth tasks shows that an experience which plays an *important* part in producing or leading to a reaction makes the reaction longer than when the experience only comes along with the stimulus or the reaction-word, that is, when it is only side-play, as it were.

States of consciousness *tend to persist* and to return more easily once they have been experienced. It is found that they come *more rapidly* after the first time. It is found, besides, that the task also tends to persist, for it also often comes to consciousness, in the form of a word-presentation or the like, during the course of the experiment. In the great majority of cases this occurs only where some disturbing factor has been present, while the normal reproduction runs its course smoothly from beginning to end, as soon as the regular preparation for the experiment, *i.e.* the given task, has worked on the stimulus without any repetition during the experiment. The *repetition of the task* is therefore, we suppose, made necessary as soon as the task ceases to operate sufficiently well. This shows the exchange which goes on between representations and the task in operation. A suitable representation may introduce the task, which then, when it has ceased to operate effectually, may come to consciousness in similar representations. By means of such exchange it is possible to modify, strengthen, restrain, or check the task which is operating.

It has already been shown in experimental work on memory that the *rapidity of a reproduction* is dependent on the number of times the reproduction has occurred. In accordance with this it is found that the rapidity of such reproductions as those here described is dependent to a very large degree on the number of subjects who make any particular reproduction. The dependence is, of course, not supposed to be direct, but the co-ordination and the result presupposes that the number of subjects who make any given reproduction is a fair sign of the frequency of its repetition.

The result is very distinct and the exceptions can, as a rule, be explained by the record the subject gave of his experiences or by other experimental data. Further, if the average duration of each grade of frequency is co-ordinated with the change in the task for each subject, the *influence of the task* on the duration of the reaction *in each grade of frequency* is seen to be surprisingly similar to its influence in the previous cases. This means that the influence of the task is *independent* of the rapidity of the tendency to reproduction in itself, so that the influence of the stimulus-word is for the second time differentiated from that of the task. It is, then, probable that the rapidity of a tendency to reproduction from one point to another in the stream of succeeding ideas is something by itself, independent of the influence of the task operating at the moment. Whether the latter be to the increase of the former in every case remains to be settled.

It has often been asserted that over and above more or less mechanical reproductions, which are often to be found in our mental experience, there is a large number of cases in which the decision is not uniformly and completely determined by regular laws, but in which a greater or less amount of scope is allowed for the usually indefinite activity called choice or selection by the attention and the like. But a thorough examination of the complex reproductions, in which no particular description was given of the second tendency to reproduction, produces a large mass of evidence, partly from the record of the subject and partly from manifold combinations of the various experimental data, much too detailed to be described, in favour of the reproduction which actually took place. This shows that, if other conditions remain the same, it is the individual strength or *rapidity* of the tendency to reproduction *which determines the reproduction*, and not anything else. In other words, the influence of the task is the same for all the reproductions it makes possible. It is not meant, of course, that our everyday conception of choice has no meaning, but only that the influences which determine every event in our mental experience fall into two large groups, the operating task and the individual strength of the reproductions which come thereby in question. On the one hand, the task may find no reproductions, in which case no reaction can occur; and, on the other hand, the strength of the tendency to reproduction may be too great for the task to operate, in which case it forces its way out in spite of the task, or before any reproduction which the task favours has had time to become actual: in other words, a wrong reaction takes place. Otherwise, more or less suitable reactions occur. This is thought to be *valid for the whole of our mental experience*, because the very few cases which offered no explanation, contained no indication of any other determining factors, and are therefore to be placed alongside the others with the remark that in these cases the record of the subject or the experimental data were probably deficient, as can always occur in such experiments.

A detailed examination shows further that the general content, the vividness, and the frequency of our *visual representations* is dependent on the nature of the *task* in question. It is therefore probable that rather hasty generalisations have been made of the possible *types of mental imagery*. It could very well be, according to this result, that a subject who showed an entire absence of visual representation with the kind of task which has hitherto been given to determine the types of mental imagery, would with other tasks show quite a lively and detailed visual imagination. An example of almost such a case occurred among the subjects used for these experiments. It is probable, however, that one who has fewer and less vivid imagery than another with one task, will with another task again have less vivid and detailed imagery than the other.

The attempt to establish an *association by contrast* or by *similarity* is then discussed, on the basis of the experiments, and is rejected, because it is found to be impossible to show that similarity as such could determine an association. Apparent determinations of reproductions by similarity are found to dissolve into more detailed reproductions, which are themselves determined by the factors already discovered. There is no reason to expect that the subject in his record should be able to give the reason for any reaction, or even always the previous mental experience by which the reproduction in question under the operation of the task was determined.

A detailed examination of the experiments with each task by themselves, leads to interesting results which tend to separate the task as a psychological factor still more from the tendency to reproduction in itself and from other factors. Interesting connections are shown between the logical relations contained in the tasks given and the psychological processes found in the experiments, in which the psychological simplicity and rapidity of happening are shown to be sometimes on the side of the logical simplicity and sometimes not.

In a lengthy *summary* the results are brought together under various points of view and several *theories* formulated.

After a short summary of *individual differences, a criticism of the distinction between motor and sensory reaction* is given. First of all, the facts are brought together to show that this distinction is a fairly good description of some differences between the subjects. The first basis of the distinction was the usual arithmetical mean, but of late it has been thought that the *curve of distribution* of the reaction-times gives a better foundation. This curve is formed by making a time equal to the probable error of all time-observations of the series the unit in the horizontal, and by setting the number of cases which occur at each such unit on the perpendicular. If the number of factors involved is small and limited, then this curve ought to rise to one or more symmetrical points. This is sometimes the case, especially in the motor reaction, according to the latest researches. It is evident, according to the last two of these, that the time of even the motor reaction can be shortened a good deal with practice, and the curves seem to show points at somewhat regular periods, —these periods being, however, liable to minimal displacements when the nature or quantity of the stimulus is changed. It is also indisputably true, that the *class* to which any experiment is to be reckoned, is not determined by the nature of the experiment after it has been made, but by the nature of the given *preparation*, the direction of the attention to sensory or motor elements. Here, then, we have again differences between what we call the task and the mere tendency to reproduction or any physiological basis for the latter. A *motor reaction* is, therefore, merely the quickest and most constant reaction possible, which constancy and rapidity are achieved by simple and constant conditions of experiment and of task especially. The long-practised so-called *natural reaction,* in which the task directs the attention specially neither to the stimulus nor to the movement which is to be carried out, also shows a regular curve of distribution. It is evident that in this natural reaction, too, the factors involved are constant and regular. The *sensory reaction,* however, is not nearly so liable to be regular, and it is supposed that this lies in the *greater complexity of factors,* because the curve of distribution contains not one, but several high points. This is made probable by its being shown that, in the curves of distribution of the experiments made, the average times of most of the big classes of experiments found and distinguished on the basis of the records, lie under the larger rises, and *vice versa.* It is then likely that, if the conditions could be kept as constant as they are in the shortest possible reactions, the curves of distribution would be quite as regular for any set of conditions whatever. Peculiarities in the form of the curve of distribution would then be *symptomatic* of peculiarities in the reactions or in the factors which bring about these, and thereby an aid to discovery. The distinction between sensory and motor reactions is, therefore, *not physiological but psychological* in the prime instance, and is not an exact distinction. It has to be split up into its elements, and when this is done nothing new is found.

This result leads to a more decisive way of looking at those reactions which, through frequent repetition, are held by many to become *unconscious* or *mechanical.* It is evident that, if reflexes be excluded from this class, a task is always necessarily presupposed for the accomplishment of such a reaction. The task may not have been given before each experiment, but it must at least have become operative. The stimulus is given and the reaction follows without any conscious links intervening whatsoever. There is no need to appeal to the unconscious even when everything else falls away except the essentials, task and stimulus.

The *method of subtraction* of different sets of reactions from one another, in order to find the duration of an act of recognition, of distinction, and of association, is subjected to a criticism. In order to find the duration of elementary acts, it is no guarantee to suppose that the contents of all experiments carried out with the same task are the same. First of all, those experiments which are really similarly composed, must be collected with the help of the experimental data and the records. An ideally complete reaction, made up of bits out of many different reactions, is of no use for this purpose. The scheme which has been the basis of this method of subtraction is, besides, very mechanical, much too mechanical for any one to suppose it to be based on data which are true, or likely to be found true in physiology. But even if the number and nature of the elements in an experiment were experimentally determined, it has to be remembered that it is not yet settled how exactly the task affects each element which goes to make up the reaction. All this does not make the method impossible, but only for a long time purposeless.

If *association* be understood as the cause of the known fact and experience of reproduction, it may be *defined* as that means of which it first becomes possible for one experience to be reproduced by another. Other definitions are found to rest on logical divisions, and to give no guarantee of unity in research. There can be only one kind of association, as far as we know, and on the basis of the previous results the later experience is never reproduced by the earlier by means of the *value* of the logical relations between them but only by the factors described above. The only conceivable condition for the origin of association is, that the two experiences shall have once been together or immediately successive in consciousness.

It is evident that, to form a *judgment*, the subject must have at the moment some experience, and, besides, some experience which consists of reproductions, because an absolutely new experience and nothing else could not be held to form a judgment by itself. An absolutely fixed and rigid system of reproductions, however, gives no judgments, but merely a succession of experiences under the one principle of association. Even the subjects themselves tend to decline the responsibility for judgments in which the reaction which constituted the judgment was determined by the overwhelming strength of a tendency to reproduction. The experimental conclusion drawn by Marbe is accepted, that if one confines oneself to the experiences between the stimulus and the reaction, there is no psychological criterion of the judgment. Outside of this limit, however, stands the *task* which, even if it is not identical in the sense of being always either visual representation or word-representation or the like, is yet *functionally identical*, and is the one factor which goes beyond the rigidity which the single tie of association would give. *The operaton of a task makes the reaction* which is determined by or in spite of it, *a judgment* in reference to this task. This position must be met before the attempt can be made to set up hidden unconscious or rare experiences as the criterion of the judgment. It is also evident that the agreement of ideas with their objects, whether these be themselves ideas or not, can never be directly the aim in view. Such agreement, if it exists, can be only and merely the result of the operation of the factors enumerated, of which the one, the task, may of course include the conception agreement. For how would it be possible to proceed to obtain such agreement psychologically?

A *theory of thinking* has, then, to start from our experience as we know it. This presents to us no sharply defined states with beginning and end like printed letters, but only continued observation leads us to a more and more detailed and exact description of our experiences. By means of experimental data we can work ourselves out beyond this position and formulate our factors more precisely. We decline to accept choice and apperception or contrast and similarity as exact or useful scientific conceptions any further. The tendency to reproduction which realises itself, *ceteris paribus,* is that one which, by reason of more frequent actualisation, possesses a greater speed of reproduction. The task, which is no doubt itself a wider and stronger tendency to reproduction, has been sketched in detail as an operative force, and its sphere of operation is doubtless much larger than we have been able to determine it to be. Over against any tendency to reproduction, the task can only overpower a limited amount of force, a circumstance which makes false reactions possible. Any theory of association which operates only with associations between two experiences immediately following one another, is thus seen to be insufficient, though this much must be presupposed in any theory. Physiology can, perhaps, not offer us more than this at present, but a more exact definition of psychological factors and their sphere of operation can only be welcome to physiology, while the prospect that physiology and psychology will one day be able to give an account of their material which they will find to be much more intelligible to one another than it is now, is by no means excluded. It seems probable at present that the *variable factor* is the strength or rapidity of reproduction and *not the task,* which is supposed to favour in equal strength all tendencies to reproduction which come under its influence. The operations of these two classes of factors on one another, which seems to be confined to a small area which contains at least our fully conscious experiences, is what we know as thinking.

It must not be supposed that the picture of his mental experience given in a subject's record is by any means complete. We see from these results that besides mere suppression of parts of a record, which is not presupposed, the subject may have forgotten something, or the tendencies to reproduction and the tasks which would have enabled him to give a full and accurate record may not have been present, or, for want of practice, very poorly developed. Even if forgetfulness is put aside, we have therefore no right to suppose that what is not in the record was not experienced. But granting this, what can we say about that part of experience which does not come fully to consciousness in reproductions and judgments? A mere mechanical succession of events in consciousness seems to us obviously intelligible, as soon as it happens in fact. What we do not understand is the *meaning* contained in the reference of one experience to another, whether it reproduce or be reproduced by this other. The reaction refers to the stimulus, and, under the influence of the task, brings to fuller consciousness something which was latent in it, although, as we have seen, no other fully conscious elements need be found either in the record or by experimental investigation. There are, besides, several elementary experiences which cannot be further analysed into psychological components, but can only be rendered by one or many reproductions. Such experiences are the more indefinite conceptual states of consciousness, what is often called feeling (other than pleasure and pain). Such experiences may besides be introduced by representations, for example, word-representations, and they are then to be exemplified by conceptions and tasks. All this points to an *insufficiency of consciousness* to give a full knowledge of our subjective experience. The only means we possess for supplementing this deficiency, is to contrive that every part of our consciousness shall be operated on by tasks capable of bringing as much as possible to full consciousness in reactions or judgments. At the same time, this conception of the insufficiency of consciousness starts out from conscious experience and does not necessarily imply notions like the *unconscious,* which lie further afield and are as yet more or less indefinite and unsettled. The *great advantage of the experimental method* is, that it enables us, by grouping of data and by a more exact knowledge of the elementary factors of experience, to overcome the insufficiency of our direct introspection.

The thesis closes with a critical discussion of general representations and conceptions.

# 17 • Kurt Lewin

## *Behavior and Development as a Function of the Total Situation*

Kurt Lewin began his psychological career with an attack on the position of the Wuerzburg School. He contended that they had not gone far enough in their motivational analysis of thinking and behavior. He placed the concept of force—a directed tendency with a given strength and a point of application —at the core of his psychology, and went on to develop a dynamic system which enabled him to deal with problems, such as conflict, in a manner which has stimulated continuing research to this day. This selection was an influential presentation of his position to an American audience.

### Constructs Basic for Representing the Psychological Field

*It seems to be* possible to represent the essential properties of the life space with the help of relatively few (perhaps a dozen) related constructs. To some degree it is a matter of convenience which of a group of interrelated constructs are to be considered the basic ones (Reichenbach, 1928). For the purpose of this representation we shall use mainly the following constructs: psychological *force*, psychological *position*, and *potency* of a situation.

(1) The concept of force in psychology refers to phenomena which have been called *drive, excitatory tendency*, or by any other name expressing "tendency to act in a certain direction." The term *force* intends to express this directed element, attributing to it, in addition, a magnitude (strength of force) and a point of application, without assuming any additional implications (Lewin, 1938).

(2) The position of the person within the total psychological field and the position of the other parts of the field in relation to one another are of prime importance. This holds for the relative position of various

From *Manual of Child Psychology*, Leonard Carmichael, Ed. Copyright, 1946, by John Wiley and Sons, Inc. Reprinted by permission of John Wiley and Sons, Inc. This material represents a part of Chapter 16, pages 796–815.

areas of activities the child might enter, the relative position of social groups to which the child belongs, or would like to belong, and of areas of security and insecurity. Although it is not possible today to measure psychological distance or direction quantitatively, it is possible to treat some problems of position by means of the qualitative geometry called topology.

(3) *Potency* refers to the weight which a certain area of the life space has for a child relative to other areas. This concept is particularly valuable in case of "overlapping situtions," that is, when the belongingness to two groups or the involvement in two or more activities at the same time is pertinent.

## THE BEHAVIOR IN A GIVEN PSYCHOLOGICAL FIELD

### Cognitive Structure of the Life Space

#### THE LIFE SPACE AS A WHOLE DURING DEVELOPMENT

*Differentiation of the various dimensions of the life space.* An outstanding characteristic of the change of the life space during development is an increasing differentiation. The importance of this factor has been shown in regard to the development of language (Gesell and Thompson, 1934), knowledge (Tolman, 1932), social interrelations (Murphy, 1937), emotions (Jersild, 1936), and actions (Fajans, 1933).

The life space of the newborn child may be described as a field which has relatively few and only vaguely distinguishable areas (Koffka, 1928). The situation probably corresponds to a general state of greater or less comfort. No definite objects or persons seem to be distinguished. No area called "my own body" exists. Future events or expectations do not exist; the child is ruled by the situation immediately at hand.

Some of the first areas which get a definite character seem to be connected with food and elimination. As early as three to six days the child reacts to being prepared for nursing (Marquis, 1931). A similar increase in size and differentiation of the life space occurs in other respects. The child studies his own body (Bühler, 1939) and his immediate physical surroundings. Within the first few months, certain social relations develop.

The increase of the life space in regard to the psychological time dimension continues into adulthood. Plans extend farther into the future, and activities of increasingly longer duration are organized as one unit. For instance, between two and six years of age the duration of play units increases (Barker, Dembo, and Lewin, 1941).

The differentiation of the life space also increases in the dimension of reality-irreality. The different degrees of irreality correspond to different degrees of fantasy. They include both the positive wishes and the fears. Dynamically, the level of irreality corresponds to a more fluid medium (J. F. Brown, 1933; Erikson, 1940) and is more closely related to the central layers of the person. This fact is particularly important for the psychology of dreams (Freud, 1916; T. French, 1939). Play can be understood as an action on the level of reality closely related to the irreal level (Sliosberg, 1934). The play technique (Homburger, 1937), in the study of personality, makes use of the fact that the irreal level is closely related to the central layers of the person.

The level of irreality in the psychological future corresponds to the wishes or fears for the future; the level of reality, to what is expected. The discrepancy between the structure of the life space on the levels of irreality and of reality is important for planning and for the productivity of the child (Barker, Dembo, and Lewin, 1941). Hope corresponds to a sufficient similarity between reality and irreality somewhere in the psychological future; guilt to a certain discrepancy between reality and irreality in the psychological past. In the young child, truth and lying, perception and imagination are less clearly distinguished than in an older child (Piaget, 1932; Sliosberg, 1934; L. K. Frank, 1935). This is partly due to the fact that the younger child has not yet developed that degree of differentiation of the life space into levels of reality and irreality which is characteristic of the adult.

The speed with which the life space increases in scope and degree of differentiation during development varies greatly. A close relation seems to exist between intelligence or, more specifically, between mental age and the degree of differentiation of the person and the psychological environment (Lewin, 1935; Kounin, 1939). If this is correct, differences in IQ should be considered as different rates of increasing differentiation of the life space. Similar considerations apply to motor development (Mc-Graw, 1935) and to social development.

The growth of the life space has a different rate at different times. Such differences are particularly important for the so-called developmental crises, as in adolescence (Dimock, 1937; Lewin, 1939).

Figure 17.1a and 17.1b represents schematically the scope and degree of differentiation of the life space as a whole at two developmental stages. The differentiation concerns the psychological environment as well as the person. The increasing differentiation of needs, for instance, can be represented as an increase in the differentiation of certain intrapersonal regions. The main differences between these developmental stages are: (1) an increase in the *scope* of the life space in regard to (*a*) what is part of the psychological present; (*b*) the time perspective in the direction of the psychological past and the psychological future; (*c*) the reality-irreality dimension; (2) an increasing *differentiation* of every level of the life space into a multitude of social relations and areas of activities; (3) an increasing *organization;* (4) a change in the general *fluidity* or *rigidity* of the life space.

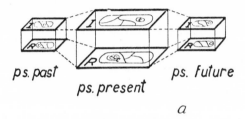

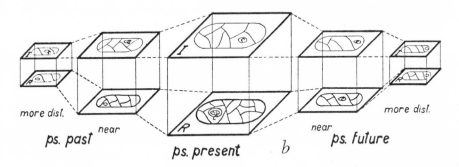

Figure 17.1. The life space at two developmental stages.

Figure 17.1*a* represents the life space of a younger child. Figure 17.1*b* represents the higher degree of differentiation of the life space of the older child in regard to the present situation, the reality-irreality dimension, and the time perspective. *C*, child; *R*, level of reality; *I*, level of irreality; *Ps Past*, psychological past; *Ps Present*, psychological present; *Ps Future*, psychological future.

Not all the areas of this life space are accessible to the child. He sees older children engaged in certain activities, which he would like to do himself, but into which he finds he cannot enter because he is not strong or clever enough. Additional limitations of his space of free movements are established by the prohibitions of the adult or by other social taboos.

The relation between accessible and inaccessible regions in the life space, the size of the space of free movement, and the precision of boundary between accessible and inaccessible areas are of great importance for behavior and development of the normal and abnormal child (Lewin, 1936*a*).

*Regression.* A change of the life space as a whole in the direction opposite to that characteristic of development may be called *regression.* Regression may include a decrease in time perspective, dedifferentiation or disorganization, leading to behavior more or less typical for children on a younger age level.

Regression may be either permanent or temporary. It is a common phenomenon and may be due, for instance, to sickness (Jersild, 1936), frustration (Barker, Dembo, and Lewin, 1941), insecurity (Murphy,

1937), or emotional tension (Dembo, 1931; Jersild, 1936). Regression, in the sense of a narrowing-down of the psychologically present area, may result from emotional tension, for instance, if the child is too eager to overcome an obstacle (Köhler, 1925).

Regression may occur not only as a result of such frustration in the immediate situation but also as the result of a background of frustration. Barker, Dembo, and Lewin (1941) have shown that the constructiveness of play of a five-and-one-half-year-old child may regress to the level of a three-and-one-half-year-old child as a result of a background of frustration. This is due to the fact that constructiveness of play is closely related to time perspective, the degree of differentiation within an organized unit of play, and the functional relation between irreality and reality. The amount of regression increases with the potency of the background of frustration (Figure 17.2).

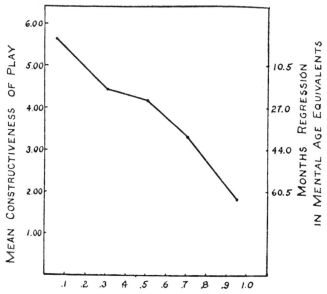

Figure 17.2.  Decrease in constructiveness with a background of various degrees of frustration. (From "Studies in Topological and Vector Psychology: II. Frustration and Regression," by R. Barker, T. Dembo, and K. Lewin. *University of Iowa Studies in Child Welfare*, 1941, 18, 166. By permission of the publisher.)

THE POSITION OF THE PERSON. BEING INSIDE AND OUTSIDE A REGION

*Position, neighboringness, and locomotion.*  The determination of the position of the person within the life space is the first prerequisite for understanding behavior. His social position within or outside of various groups should be known; his position in regard to various activities, in regard to his goal regions, and in regard to physical areas should be determined. This is fundamental because the region in which the person is located determines (1) the quality of his immediate surroundings, (2) what kinds of regions are adjacent to the present region—that is, what possibilities the individual has for his next step—and (3) what step has the meaning of an action toward his goal and what step corresponds to an action away from his goal.

Most behavior can be conceived of as a change of position—in other words, as a locomotion of the person. (The other cases of behavior are changes of structure.) In turn, every behavior changes the situation. We shall mention only a few examples of the effect of the region in which the person is located.

*"Adaptation" to a situation.* A common phenomenon is what is usually called adaptation in the sense of "getting tuned to the present atmosphere." H. Anderson (1939) found that children of preschool age reacted to an aggressive approach with aggression, to a friendly approach in a friendly manner. Ronald Lippitt's (1940) study on democratic and autocratic atmospheres found similar adaptation of the children to the cultural atmosphere produced by the leader. J. R. P. French, Jr. (1944) found adaptation to group atmospheres in experiments with college freshmen. There are many indications from case studies that the tenseness of the mother easily affects the emotional state of the young child. There are indications that this occurs even during the first few months of life. It is a common observation that children who are learning bladder control may resume bed-wetting if exposed to the sound of running water.

The adaptation to the present region is frequently employed to make a child do something "against his will." A child of a few weeks may be induced to drink at the breast when he does not like to by keeping his head pressed to the breast in the position of feeding. Waring, Dwyer, and Junkin (1939) describe how the child and the adult both commonly use this technique for their own purposes when they differ about the desirability of eating a certain food. The child tries to avoid the pressure of the adult by leaving the eating-situation (for instance, by going to the toilet) or by making the adult leave the eating-situation psychologically (for instance, by starting conversations about noneating topics). On the other hand, the adult frequently uses one of two methods of coercion. He may lower the potency of the eating-situation (see later), and thus the resistance of the child, by "distracting his attention" from the eating (that is, by making the child enter a psychologically different region) and then slip in the food. Or he may heighten the potency of the eating-situation and of his own pressure, and in this way induce the child to eat. In the latter case he frequently uses the "step-by-step method": having the child sit at the table, then putting the food on the spoon, and so on.

J. D. Frank (1944) has found, in an experiment with college students, that the step-by-step method is more efficient in coercing the person to eat than the attempt to make him go the whole way at one step. The effectiveness of the step-by-step method seems to be based on the gradual acceptance of the situation in which the person finds himself so that he resists less the making of the next step. A similar method is frequently used in domestic and international politics. People who are ready to fight against being pushed into a situation may accept the *fait accompli*.

*Group belongingness.* Most social goals can be characterized as a wish to belong or not to belong to a certain group. This group may be a group of friends, an athletic organization, or a favorite subgroup within a larger group. It may be a group of only two persons, as with the friendship between mother and child. Belonging or not belonging to the group is equivalent to having a position inside or outside this group. This position determines the rights and duties of the individual and is decisive for the ideology of the individual.

The feeling of belonging to certain groups is a crucial factor for the feeling of security in children of minorities (Dollard, 1937; Lewin, 1940b). MacDonald (1940) found that the security of the child is greatly increased by the presence of the mother. The tendency to enter a certain group and to keep certain children in and other children out of that group plays a great rôle in the behavior of the nursery school child (Murphy, 1937; Rosemary Lippitt, 1940). This tendency is important for the children's gang (Shaw, 1933). Juveniles in the reformatory who have not fully accepted their belonging to the criminals have a tendency to name as their best friends persons outside the reformatory (Kephart, 1937).

Ronald Lippitt (1940) found that the feeling of group belongingness (as expressed, for instance, by the use of the term "we" instead of "I") is stronger in democratic than in autocratic clubs. In the autocratic atmosphere the larger group is actually composed of a number of subgroups containing the leader and one child each, whereas in the democratic group the group as a whole has a greater potency (Figure 17.3a and b). This is one of the reasons why children in these autocracies are more likely to be aggressive against their fellows although submissive to the leader. M. E. Wright (1940) found that friendship between two children increases in certain situations of frustration partly because these situations favor a group structure in which the children see themselves opposed to the adult.

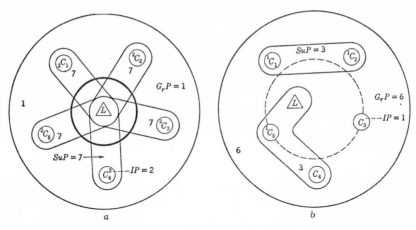

Figure 17.3. Subgrouping and potency of the group as a whole in (a) an autocratic and (b) a democratic setting. (Derived from "Studies in Topological and Vector Psychology: I. An Experimental Study of the Effect of Democratic and Authoritarian Group Atmospheres," by Ronald Lippitt. *University of Iowa Studies in Child Welfare*, 1940, 16, 133-135. By permission of the publisher.)

In the autocratic situation two distinct social strata exist, a higher one containing the leader ($L$) and a lower containing the children ($C$). (The social distance between these strata is indicated by the heavy black circle.) In democracy the status differences are less marked (dotted line). In the autocratic setting distinct subgroups of two exist containing one child and the leader. Therefore, if the leader is taken away, no strong bond between the members remains. In democracy the subgrouping is varying and less rigid. The potency of the group as a whole ($GrP$) is higher there than in the autocratic setting where the potency of the individual goal ($IP$) and of the subgroup ($SuP$) is relatively higher.

Bavelas (1942a) found that the degree of cooperation between children in a day camp increased after their adult leaders were retrained from autocratic to democratic leadership techniques.

Moreno (1934) has developed a technique which permits an easy determination of group structure and group belongingness under certain circumstances. Other techniques have been developed, for instance, by Bogardus (1933) and by Ronald Lippitt (1940).

The difference between being inside and outside a region is basic not only for social groups but for all goal-seeking activities, and for the problem of frustration. Seeking a certain goal is equivalent to a tendency to enter a region outside of which one is located. We shall take up this question when discussing psychological forces.

### CHANGE IN COGNITIVE STRUCTURE

The structure of the life space is the positional relations of its parts. Structure may be expressed by the topology of the life space. Locomotion of the person, that is, the change of his position from one region to another region, can be viewed as one type of change in structure. Other examples are those changes which occur during "insight" or learning. The infinite variety of changes in structure may be classified roughly into (1) an increase in differentiation of a region, that is, an increase in the number of subregions; (2) a combination of separated regions into one differentiated region; (3) a decrease in differentiation, that is, a decrease in the number of subregions within a region; (4) a breaking-up of a whole, that is, previously connected subparts of a region are separated into relatively independent regions; and (5) a restructuring, that is, a change in pattern without increase or decrease of differentiation.

*Detour. Insight.* Restructuring of certain areas of the life space can be readily observed in the solution of detour problems. The basic questions can be illustrated by a simple example: A goal $G$ (Figure 17.4) lies behind a U-shaped physical barrier $B$. The child $C$, of a mental age of one year (this may be a chronologically young child, or an older feeble-

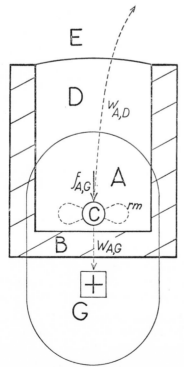

Figure 17.4. A simple detour problem as seen by the young child.

minded child) is likely to try to reach the goal by an action toward the
barrier along the path $w_{A, G}$.[1] A child of five years, under the same circumstances, will have no difficulty. It will reach the goal by way of a
roundabout route along the path $w'_{A, G}$ (Figure 17.5). What are the dif-

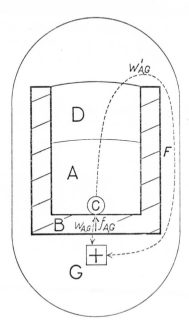

Figure 17.5. The detour problem
represented in Figure 17.4 as seen
by the older child.

ficulties of the younger child? Both children have the tendency to loco-
mote from their present situation $A$ toward the goal $G$. (As we shall see
later, we can say there exists a psychological force $f_{A, G}$ acting on the
child in the direction from $A$ toward $G$.)

We can understand the differences in difficulties if we consider what
"direction toward $G$" means for both children. For the young child the
direction from $A$ to $G$, $d_{A, G}$, is equal to the direction toward the barrier
$B$, ($d_{A, G} = d_{A, B}$). A movement from $A$ to $D$ along the path $w_{A, D}$ would
have, for this child, the meaning of going away from $G$. In other words,
the direction toward $D$, $d_{A, D}$, is opposite to the direction toward $G$, $d_{A, G}$
($d_{A, D} = d_{A, G}$). For the older child (Figure 17.5) the direction toward
$D$, $d_{A, D}$, has not the character of being opposite to the direction but of
being equal to the direction to $G$ ($d_{A, D} = d_{A, G}$), because the step from
$A$ to $D$ is seen by this child as a part of the roundabout route $w'_{A, G}$ to-

[1] A fuller discussion of the problems of direction and path in psychology may be
found in Lewin (1938).

ward G. The difference in the meaning of the direction $d_{A, G}$ toward G is due mainly to two facts:

(1) For the young child the immediate situation is less extended than for the older one (this is but one result of the fact that the life space of the younger child is smaller in many aspects than that of the older child). It includes only the regions A, B, and G (Figure 17.4). For the older child, a wider area is psychologically present, including, for instance, the areas D and F. As an effect of this difference in scope of the present situation the younger child sees the areas A and G separated by the impassable barrier B. For the older child, regions A and G are connected by way of passable regions D and F.

Directions in the psychological life space are defined by certain paths as a whole. The older child sees the step from A to D as a part of the path A, D, F, G toward G. The young child sees the step A, D as a part of the path A, E, that is, away from G. The difference in the cognitive structure of the situation for the young and older child leads, therefore, to a different meaning of the direction toward G and, accordingly, to a different locomotion resulting from the same tendencies of both children to reach G.

(2) For the young child, the path $w'_{A, G}$ simply does not exist psychologically. For the older child two paths toward G exist psychologically, namely, the roundabout route $w'_{A, G}$ and the blocked "direct" path $w_{A, G}$. The "direct" direction toward G can be interpreted, in this case, as the direction of looking toward G; the less "direct" direction as that of walking toward G. For the young child, "direction toward G" has not yet been differentiated into these two directions. (This is an example of the lesser degree of differentiation of the life space of the younger child.)

A two-year-old child placed in the same situation may at first have a cognitive structure corresponding to that of the younger child (Figure 17.4). After a few attempts the structure of the situation may change to that of the older child (Figure 17.5). These changes frequently occur as a sudden shift. They are an example of what has been called *insight* (Köhler, 1925).

Insight can always be viewed as a change in the cognitive structure of the situation. It frequently includes differentiation and restructuring in the sense of separating certain regions which have been connected and connecting regions which have been separated. For instance, to use a branch of a tree as a stick (Köhler, 1925) for reaching a goal behind a fence (Figure 17.6) it is necessary to see the branch $br$ as a relatively separate unit instead of a part within the larger unit of the tree $Tr$. In addition, it is necessary to connect this branch $br$ with the goal G behind the fence.

From the theory of insight in detour problems certain conclusions in regard to factors facilitating insight can be derived. Becoming emotional leads frequently to a narrowing-down of the psychologically existing area. A state of strong emotionality should, therefore, be detrimental

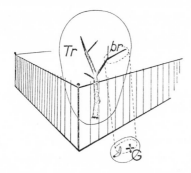

Figure 17.6. Problem solving. A case of change in cognitive structure.

to finding intellectual solutions. A distance sufficient to permit a survey of the larger situation helps in the solution of intellectual problems. Katona (1940) discusses the effect of various settings upon the change of the cognitive structure and the ability to find new solutions.

The principles of change in cognitive structure discussed here are as applicable to social and mathematical problems as to physical problems.

*Learning. Orientation.* Learning is a popular term referring to such different processes as learning to like spinach, learning to walk, and learning French vocabularies, that is, problems of changes of goals or needs, changes of posture and muscular coordination, and changes in knowledge. Therefore, no one theory of learning is possible. Problems of change in goals will be discussed later. Insight is an example of learning in the sense of change of cognitive structure. Learning, in this sense, usually involves several of those types of structural changes which we have mentioned previously, combined with a change in the degree of organization.

A change in the direction of greater differentiation takes place, for instance, when a child gets oriented in a new surrounding. Being in an unknown surrounding is equivalent to being in a region which is unstructured in the double sense that neither the quality nor the subparts of the present region, nor the immediately neighboring regions, are determined. Orientation means the structurization of the unstructured region. In this way, direction within the life space becomes determined

(Lewin, 1938). Orientation is a process which, on a smaller scale, shows significant parallels to the development of the life space of the young child.

An unstructured region usually has the same effect as an impassable obstacle. Being in unstructured surroundings leads to uncertainty of behavior because it is not clear whether a certain action will lead to or away from the goal. It is undetermined whether the neighboring regions are dangerous or friendly. Waring, Dwyer, and Junkin (1939) found that children during the meals of the first nursery school day were more ready to acquiesce to the advice of the adult than later on when they felt themselves to be on better-known ground for resisting.

The problem of learning is treated in detail in another chapter. We shall add, therefore, but one remark about the relation between repetition and learning. Repetition of a certain activity may lead to differentiation of a previously undifferentiated region of the life space, and to unification of previously separated activities. This is frequently the case in motor learning. However, if continued long enough, repetition may have the opposite effect, namely, a breaking-up of the larger units of actions, a dedifferentiation, unlearning, and disorganization similar to that of primitivation or degeneration. These processes are typical of psychological satiation and oversatiation.

## Force and Force Field

### FORCE AND VALENCE

*Resultant force, locomotion, and force field.* The structure of the life space determines what locomotions are possible at a given time. What change actually occurs depends on the constellation of psychological forces. The construct *force* characterizes, for a given point of the life space, the direction and strength of the tendency to change. This construct does not imply any additional assumptions as to the "cause" of this tendency. The combination of a number of forces acting at the same point at a given time is called the *resultant force*. The relation between force and behavior can then be summed up in the following way: Whenever a resultant force (different from zero) exists, there is either a locomotion in the direction of that force or a change in cognitive structure equivalent to this locomotion. The reverse also holds; namely, whenever a locomotion or change of structure exists, resultant forces exist in that direction.[2]

[2] We are not discussing here the complicated problems of the alien factors, that is, those physical and social factors which may be viewed as the boundary conditions of the life space (Lewin, 1936a; 1943; 1944). We keep within the realm of psychology.

Psychological forces correspond to a relation between at least two regions of the life space. A simple example is the force $f_{A,\ G}$ acting on a child $C$ in the direction toward a goal $G$ (Figure 17.7). This force de-

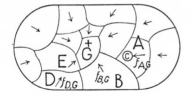

Figure 17.7. A positive central field of forces corresponding to a positive valence.

pends upon the state of the child $C$, particularly upon the state of his needs, and upon the nature of the region $G$. If the region $G$ (which may represent an activity, a social position, an object, or any other possible goal) is attractive to the person, it is said to have a positive valence $(Va(G)>0)$.

Such a valence corresponds to a field of forces which has the structure of a positive central field (Figure 17.7). If no other valences existed, the person located in any region $A, B, D, E \ldots$ would always try to move in the direction toward $G$. In other words, the valence $G$ corresponds to a force $f_{A,\ G}, f_{B,\ G}, f_{D,\ G}$, etc. The observation of behavior permits not only the determination of conscious goals but also of "unconscious goals," as Freud uses the term.

If the person is repulsed, we speak of a negative valence of $G$ $(Va(G)>0)$, corresponding to a negative central field (Figure 17.8), which is composed of forces $f_{A,\ -G}, f_{B,\ -G}, f_{D,\ -G}$, etc., away from $G$.

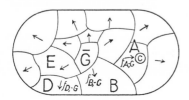

Figure 17.8. A negative central field of forces corresponding to a negative valence.

The effect of forces may be observed from earliest infancy: Movements toward or away from the breast during feeding are noted in the first weeks of life. Looking toward an object (fixation) is another example of directed action. Later on, there is grasping. More elaborate directed actions presuppose a correspondingly higher differentiation of the life space. In a young child a force is more likely to affect directly every part of the child than it is at a later age. For instance, the child of six months reaching out for a toy may move both arms and legs in this direction. He may open his mouth and bend his head toward the goal. The older, more differentiated child is likely to react in a more "controlled" way with only a part of the body.

*Strength of force and distance of valence.* We shall discuss later what factors determine a change of valence. First, let us ask what effect a given valence, or distribution of valences, has on behavior. The strength of the force toward or away from a valence depends upon the strength of that valence and the psychological distance ($e_{A, G}$) between the person and the valence [$f_{A, G} = F(Va(G), e_{A, G})$].

Fajans (1933) found that the persistence of children (ages 1 to 6 years) trying to reach a goal from various physical distances (8 to 100 cm.) increases with decreasing distance. This may mean that, with increasing distance, either the force decreases or the child sees more quickly that the barrier is insurmountable. If the first factor is dominant, emotional tension should decrease with distance. Fajans found this to be true only for the infants. For the older children, the second factor seems to be dominant, probably because these children view the obstacle as dependent upon the will of the experimenter rather than as physical distance.

In some experiments with rats, the velocity of running toward a goal was found to increase with decreasing distance (Hull, 1932). H. F. Wright (1937) found no consistent indication of such a speed gradient in experiments where nursery school children pulled the goal (a marble) toward themselves. This indicates that the relation between strength of force and bodily locomotion is rather complicated in psychology and that physical and psychological distance may be related quite differently under different circumstances.

As a particular example, the situation may be mentioned where the person "nearly" reaches a goal. In animals (Hull, 1932), as in children (H. F. Wright, 1937), a marked slowing-down has been observed at the last section before the goal is reached. If the force were related simply to the physical distance, there should be no sudden drop in velocity at this point. Obviously, after the individual is inside the goal region, the force $f_{A, G}$ can no longer have the direction "toward" the goal region but changes to a force $f_{G, G}$, which properly has to be interpreted as a tendency to resist being forced out of the goal region (for details see Lewin, 1938). Being in the goal region is frequently not equivalent to consumption of, or to bodily contact with, the goal, but it is equivalent to having the goal in one's power, to being sure of it. This is probably the reason for the slowing-down in the last section before the goal. This also explains the frequent "decrease of interest" after possession, illustrated by the following example. A nine-month-old child reaches out for two rattles lying before him. When he gets one he does not begin to play but is interested only in the rattle he does not have.

An example of a decrease of the strength of a force with the distance from the negative valence can be found in certain eating-situations

(Lewin, 1938, p. 117). For a child who dislikes his spinach, the act of eating might consist of a series of relatively separate steps, such as putting the hand on the table, taking the spoon, putting food on the spoon, etc. (Figure 17.9*a*). The strength of the force away from eating the dis-

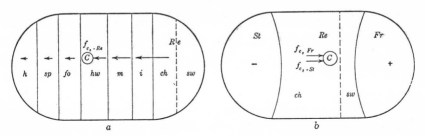

Figure 17.9. (*a*) Eating situation in case of disliked food. (*b*) Change of direction of forces after the child started real eating. (From "The Conceptual Representation and Measurement of Psychological Forces," by K. Lewin. *Contributions to Psychological Theory*, 1938, 1, 117. By permission of the Duke University Press, publisher.)

(*a*) *C*, child; *Re*, real eating; *h*, putting hand on table; *sp*, taking spoon; *fo*, putting food on spoon; *hw*, bring spoon halfway to mouth; *m*, bringing spoon to mouth; *i*, taking food into mouth; *ch*, chewing; *sw*, swallowing. Eating has a negative valence; the force away from eating $f_{C,-Re}$ increases stepwise with the decrease of distance between *C* and *Re*.

(*b*) *C*, child; *Re*, real eating; *St*, struggle with adults; *Fr*, freedom; $f_{C,Fr}$, force in the direction if freedom; $f_{C,-St}$, force away from struggle.

agreeable food and, therefore, the resistance against making the next step increases with the nearness of the step to the actual eating (*Re*). After the child starts chewing, the structure of the situation in regard to this bite usually is fundamentally changed, as shown in Figure 17.9*b*. Instead of resisting the child tries to finish the bite. This is an example of how the direction and strength of the forces acting on the person depend upon the region in which the person is located.

The change of the strength of the force with the distance to the valence is different for positive and for negative valences. The latter usually diminishes much faster (see later, Figure 17.14). The amount of decrease depends also upon the nature of the region which has a positive or negative valence. It is different, for example, in case of a dangerous animal which can move about, from the amount in case of an immovable unpleasant object.

The effect of temporal distance on the strength of the force seems to parallel that of physical distance in some respects. E. Katz (1938), in experiments with nursery school children, found that the frequency of resumption of interrupted tasks increases with the nearness of the interruption to the completion of the task, but that it drops for interruptions very close to the end. Institutionalized adolescents, like other prisoners, may attempt to escape shortly before they are eligible for release. Frequently they become rebellious (Farber, 1944). Their emotional tension is heightened by the temporal nearness of the goal.

### TYPE OF FORCES

*Driving and restraining forces.* The forces toward a positive, or away from a negative, valence can be called *driving forces.* They lead to locomotion. These locomotions might be hindered by physical or social obstacles. Such barriers correspond to *restraining forces* (Lewin, 1938). Restraining forces, as such, do not lead to locomotion, but they do influence the effect of driving forces.

The restraining forces, just as the driving forces, are due to a relation between two regions of the life space, namely, the nature of the barrier region and the "ability" of the individual. The same social or physical obstacle corresponds, therefore, to different restraining forces for different individuals.

*Induced forces, forces corresponding to own needs and impersonal forces.* Forces may correspond to a person's own needs. For instance, the child may wish to go to the movie or to eat certain food. Many psychological forces acting on a child do not, however, correspond to his own wishes but to the wish of another person, for instance, of the mother. These forces in the life space of the child can be called *induced forces,* and the corresponding positive or negative valence "induced valence." (A force acting on the child in the direction of the goal $G$ induced by the mother $M$ may be written $i^M f_{C, G}.$)

There are forces which psychologically correspond neither to the own wish of the child nor the wish of another person, but have, for the child, the character of something "impersonal," a matter-of-fact demand. We call them *impersonal forces.* It is of great importance for the reaction of the child and for the atmosphere of the situation whether an impersonal request or the personal will of another individual is dominant.

*Point of application.* Forces may act on any part of the life space. Frequently, the point of application is that region of the life space which corresponds to the own person. The child may, however, experience that the "doll wants to go to bed," or that "another child wants a certain toy." In these cases the points of application of the forces are regions in the life space of a child other than his own person. Such cases are most common and play an important part, for instance, in the problems of altruism.

### CONFLICT SITUATIONS

*Definition of conflict.* A conflict situation can be defined as a situation where forces acting on the person are opposite in direction and about equal in strength. In regard to driving forces three cases are possible: The person may be located between two positive valences, between two negative valences, or a positive and negative valence may lie in the same direction. There may be, also, conflicts between driving and restraining forces. Finally, there may be conflicts between own forces and various combinations of induced and impersonal forces. The effect and the development of conflicts vary with these different constellations, although all conflicts have certain properties in common.

*Conflicts between driving forces.* What is usually called a *choice* means that a person is located between two positive or negative valences which are mutually exclusive. The child has to choose, for example, between going on a picnic ($G^1$, Figure 17.10a) and playing ($G^2$) with his comrades. (Figure 17.10 and some of the later figures represent situations where the physical directions and distances are sufficiently important psychologically to be used as frames of reference for the life space. One can speak in these cases of quasi-physical fields.) An example of a child standing between two negative valences is a situation in which punishment ($G^1$) is threatened if he does not do a certain dis-

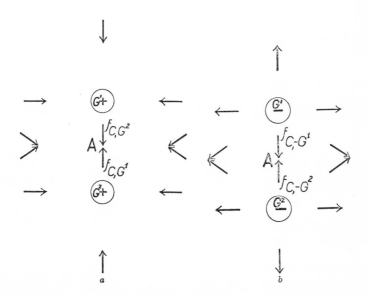

Figure 17.10.   (*a*) Force field corresponding to two positive valences. (*b*) Force field corresponding to two negative valences.

agreeable task ($G^2$, Figure 17.10$b$). Figure 17.10$a$ and $b$ represents the corresponding force fields. If the child is located at $A$ and the strength of the valences are equal, he will be exposed to forces which are equal in strength but opposite in direction. In the first example, the opposing forces $f_{A, G^1}$ and $f_{A, G^2}$ are directed toward the picnic and play. In the second example, the opposing forces $f_{A, -G^1}$ and $f_{A, -G^2}$ are directed away from the task and the punishment.

From these force fields certain differences of behavior can be derived. In the case of two negative valences, there is a resultant force in the direction of "leaving the field" altogether. If the two negative valences are very great, the child may run away from home, or try to avoid the issue. To be effective, the threat of punishment has to include the creation of a set-up which prohibits this avoidance (Lewin, 1935), that is, the creation of a prisonlike situation, where barriers $B$ prohibit leaving the situation in any other way than by facing the task $T$ or the punishment $P$ (Figure 17.11). If there is a choice between two positive

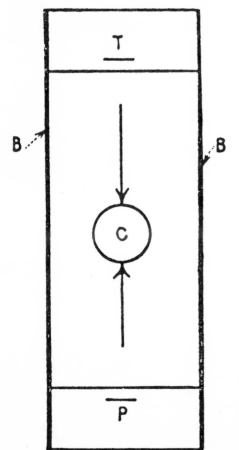

Figure 17.11. Threat of punishment. (From *Dynamic Theory of Personality*, by K. Lewin. New York: McGraw-Hill, 1935, 91. By permission of the publisher.)

$T$, disagreeable task; $P$, threat of punishment; $C$, child; $B$, barrier preventing the child from leaving the situation through other regions than $T$ or $P$.

valences, no force in the direction of leaving the field exists. Instead, the child will try to reach both goals if possible.

An example of a conflict due to the presence of a negative and a positive valence is the promise of reward for doing a disagreeable task (Figure 17.12). Here a conflict is brought about by the opposition of the force $f_{A, R}$ toward the reward $R$ and the force $f_{A, -T}$ away from the disagreeable activity $T$. The structure of the situation is similar to that characteristic of a detour problem. Indeed, the child frequently tries to reach the reward $R$ along a roundabout route $w_{A, C, R}$ without passing through the disagreeable activity. The reward will be effective only if all other paths to $R$ are blocked by an impassable barrier $B$ which permits entrance to $R$ only by way of $T$. The barriers in this case, as in the case of the threat of punishment (Figure 17.11), are usually social in nature: The child knows that the adult will prevent certain actions by social force.

The necessity for setting up a barrier around the reward indicates one of the differences between this method of making the child perform a disagreeable activity $T$ and the methods which try to change the negative valence of $T$ itself into a positive one. A "change of interest" in $T$ may be brought about by imbedding the activity $T$ (for instance, the disliked figuring) into a different setting (for instance, into playing store), so that the meaning, and consequently the valence, of $T$ is changed for the child. Such a method makes the creation of a barrier unnecessary and secures spontaneous actions of the child toward the previously disliked activity as a result of the newly created positive central field.

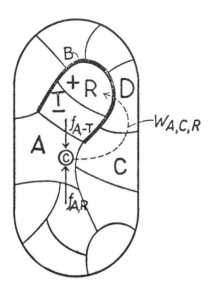

Figure 17.12. Offer of a reward.

Another example of a conflict between a positive and a negative valence can be observed in a setting where a child of three years is trying to seize a toy swan S from the waves W on the seashore (Figure 17.13). Following the forces $f_{C, \ S}$, the child will approach the swan. If, however, he comes too close to the waves W, the force away from the waves $f_{C, \ -W}$ may be greater than those toward the swan. In this case the child will retreat. The force corresponding to the negative valence of the waves decreases rather rapidly with the increasing distance because of the limited range of the effect of the waves (Figure 17.14). The forces corresponding to the positive valence of the swan diminish much more slowly with the distance. There exists, therefore, an equilibrium between the opposing forces at point E where their strengths are equal ($f_{E, \ s} = f_{E, \ -W}$). The children may be observed wavering around this point of equilibrium until one of these forces becomes dominant as a result of changes of circumstances or of a decision. In this example the force field corresponding to the swan is a positive central field; the forces corresponding to the waves have a direction perpendicular to the shore.

*Conflicts between driving and restraining forces.* A most common type of conflict arises when a child is prevented from reaching a goal G by a barrier B. Two basic cases may be distinguished: (1) the child is surrounded by a barrier with the goal outside (Figure 17.11); (2) the goal is surrounded by a barrier with the child outside (Figure 17.15). The first case is a prison-like situation which gives the child little space

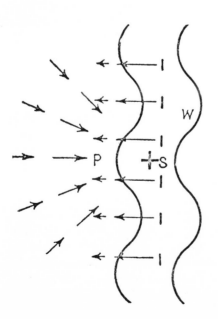

Figure 17.13. Force field in a conflict resulting from a positive and negative valence. (From *Dynamic Theory of Personality*, by K. Lewin. New York: McGraw-Hill, 1935, 92. By permission of the publisher.)

S, attractive toy; W, waves perceived as dangerous; P, point of equilibrium.

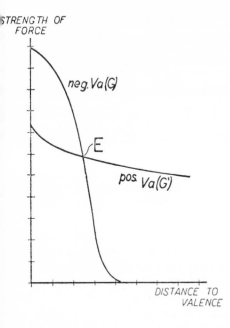

STRENGTH OF
FORCE

neg. Va(G)

E

pos. Va(G')

DISTANCE TO
VALENCE

Figure 17.14. Schematic representation of the change of the strength of a force with the distance to a positive and a negative valence.

of free movement. In the second case, the child is free except in regard to the region $G$. Each of these cases leads to specific reactions (Lewin, 1935). We shall now discuss in greater detail a sequence of behavior typical of the second case.

At first, a certain amount of change in structure usually occurs: The child tries to investigate the nature of the obstacle with the purpose of finding a sector $s$ within the barrier which will permit passage. Such a change in cognitive structure is similar to that observed in detour problems. It is very common for a child to be in situations where an obstacle could be overcome with the help of an adult. In these situations the barrier is composed of at least two sectors, one corresponding to the physical obstacle ($ph$, Figure 17.15), the other to the social obstacle ($sl$). In the experiment of Fajans, mentioned above, practically all children conceived of the barrier at first as a physical obstacle (as too great a physical distance). For the children above two years, after some time the social aspect of the situation became clear and led to social approaches toward the goal (the children asked the adult for help).

The barrier acquires a negative valence for the child after a number of unsuccessful attempts to cross it. This change is equivalent to a change in the force field from the structure represented in Figure 17.16 to that of Figure 17.17. If the barrier is an obstacle but has no negative valence, the corresponding force field does not reach much beyond the barrier (Fig. 17.16). The restraining forces $rf/\overline{c,\ B}$ merely hinder a locomotion in

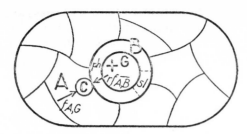

Figure 17.15. Conflict between driving and restraining forces in the case of a physical and social obstacle to a goal.

$f_{A,G}$, driving force; $rf/_{\overline{A,B}}$, restraining force; *ph*, physical sector of the barrier $(B)$; *sl*, social sector of the barrier.

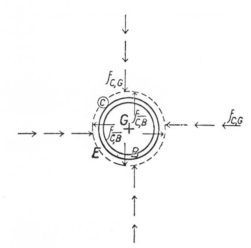

Figure 17.16. Line of equilibrium between driving and restraining forces in case of a circular barrier.

the direction of the force $f_{C, B}$ without driving the person away from $B$. The line of equilibrium $E$ between driving and restraining forces lies, therefore, close to the barrier region. If, after failure, the barrier acquires a negative valence, the corresponding negative central force field will reach out farther (Figure 17.17) so that the line of equilibrium $E$ between the force $f_{C, G}$ toward the goal and the force $f_{C -B}$ away from the barrier is located at a greater distance.

With increasing failure, the negative valence tends to increase. This enlarges the distance between the line of equilibrium and the barrier until the child leaves the field altogether.

Fajans (1933) has given a detailed report about the form and sequence of events in such a situation. Usually the child leaves the field at first only temporarily. After some time, the forces toward the goal again become greater than the forces away from the barrier, and the child returns. If the new attempts are still unsuccessful, the negative valence increases again until the child leaves. On the average, these later attempts show less duration. Finally, the child leaves the field permanently; he gives up. Barker, Dembo, and Lewin (1941) report similar

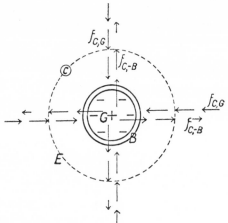

Figure 17.17.   Line of equilibrium after the barrier has acquired a negative valence.

sequences of behavior in children between two and six years in a slightly different setting of frustration.

Active children, on the average, are more persistent than passive one (Fajans, 1933). Some active children, however, are particularly quick to leave the situation, probably because they decide soon that the barrier is impassable. A state of equilibrium in such a conflict can lead to passive, gesturelike action toward the goal: The child stays below the goal with his arm erect but he makes no actual attempts to reach it. Children frequently leave the field psychologically without leaving the room bodily. They may try to enter a different activity, may daydream, or start self-manipulation with their clothes or their body (Fajáns, 1933; Sliosberg, 1934; MacDonald, 1940).

A conflict between driving and restraining forces may also occur if the child is prevented by an obstacle from leaving the field of a negative valence. Such a situation exists, for instance, if a child is oversatiated with an activity but prevented from leaving it, or in any other prisonlike situation. The sequence of behavior is, in many respects, similar to that discussed above. Attempts to leave are followed by the giving-up of such attempts as the result of the relation between the strength of the force $f_A$, $_{-A}$ away from the region $A$ and the increasing negative valence of the barrier. Frequently a state of high emotional tension results.

*Conflicts between own and induced forces.*   Every one of the conflict situation discussed above might be due to the opposition of two forces corresponding to the child's own needs, to the opposition of two induced forces, or to the opposition between an own and an induced force. Many effects of conflict situations are independent of these differences. Certain effects, however, are typical of conflicts between own and induced forces.

A force induced by a person P on a child C can be viewed as the result of the power field of that person over the child (Figure 17.18).

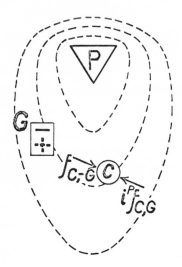

Figure 17.18.   Power field.

P, stranger; C, child; G, activity having positive valence for the child and an induced negative valence; $f_{C,G}$, own force away from G; $i^{P}f_{C,G}$, force induced by P in the direction of G. ———, lines corresponding to equal strength of power field.

The person having power over the child is able to induce positive and negative valences by giving orders. By a restraining command, he can change the character of a region which would be passable according to the child's own ability into an impassable barrier. In other words, "the power of P over C" means that P is able to create induced driving or restraining forces $i^{P}f_{C,\ G}$ which correspond to P's will.

A conflict between own and induced forces always permits at least one other solution in addition to those discussed above: The child may attempt to undermine the power of the other person, at least in the area of conflict. The tendency of a conflict between own and induced forces to lead to fights has been observed by Waring, Dwyer, and Junkin (1939) in nursery school children in an eating-situation. Dembo (1931) and J. D. Frank (1944) have observed similar tendencies in students. M. E. Wright (1940) found an increasing aggression against the experimenter in pairs of nursery school children in a setting of frustration induced by the experimenter. The children showed greater cooperation among themselves. This might be interpreted as due partly to the tendency to increase their own power relative to the power of the experimenter. Lewin, Lippitt, and White (1939) found a strong tendency toward aggression in autocratic atmospheres which are dominated much more by induced forces than by forces corresponding to the own needs of the children. This aggressiveness, however, was usually not directed against the supreme powers of the leader but diverted toward their fellows or toward material objects. If the suppressive power of the leader is too great, even this aggression ceases.

# IV
# Clinical and Descriptive Approaches to Motivation

In the culture at large, the most influential treatments of motivation have been those offered by men who have studied highly complex manifestations of human motivation at first hand. This is not surprising since such manifestations are obviously the focus of great interest and are in themselves of immediate practical significance for society. The relevance of motivation in everyday life is so great as to make the more abstract and intellectual concerns of the psychological systematists seem pale in comparison. Those clinicians and insightful observers of human activity who have sought to deal with their subject in the whole as it is found around them have frequently had to sacrifice a certain neatness and elegance in the presentation of their results, but they have nonetheless provided the challenge of a living description of what they have seen or experienced. From their material more meticulous formalizers have gauged the magnitude of their task and found leads to the necessary directions for further theoretical development. Both clinical-descriptive and systematic-experimental approaches contribute to motivation. In this section are found some of the significant statements of the clinical-descriptive approach.

First in line, of course, comes Sigmund Freud. With his vast clinical experience and profound originality, he was able to revolutionize the whole field of motivation. Here we find two examples of his work. In one, he relates his view of instincts. Freud's description of the characteristics of instincts and his recognition of the pervasiveness of sexual motives at all stages of development from infancy through adulthood stand as cornerstones in his thinking. Fully as important was Freud's emphasis on unconscious motivation, as is illustrated in his article, "The Unconscious."

In spite of the revolutionary character of Freud's contributions and the unusual observational evidence which his psychoanalytic techniques provided, there were still common elements in his positions and those taken by drive theorists and more conventional instinct theorists. There was agreement that all motivation derived from innate, primary sources and a consensus to the effect that motivation was essentially an aversive condition, a state of unrest which persisted until relief occurred. The implication was that the absence of motivation would lead to a condition of quiescence. The organism was seen as basically a stimulus-avoiding mechanism, with behavior ultimately tending toward the reduction of all motive states. Later clinical-descriptive psychologists tended to challenge this apparently pessimistic interpretation. Allport, for example, in his postulation of the functional autonomy of motives, held that the dependence of acquired social motives upon innate sources was only a developmental one and that, once formed, such motives could perpetuate themselves without further linkage to innate sources. Functionally autonomous motives carried their own continuing satisfactions and in a sense were self-rewarding. H. A. Murray stressed that an adequate taxonomy of motives would include many more than the primary, viscerogenic drives. His effort to describe the array of motives necessary for the description of personality is presented in this section. His descriptive system has provided the background for more than a generation of research on the measurement and effects of the specific motives, such as the need for achievement, which he postulated.

Out of this tradition has come the emphasis by humanistic psychologists upon the positive character of many human motives. Motivation, it has been held, is not always aversive, but includes as well propensities, such as curiosity and pleasure-seeking, which do not tend toward quiescence and stimulus reduction, but toward activity and increased stimulation. Advocates of this position have called themselves a "third force" to emphasize their differences with psychoanalysis and behavioristic drive theory. Maslow, who is not represented in this section, has proposed that motives are hierarchically ordered such that positive or growth motives can only be manifested when aversive or deficit motives have been substantially satisfied. A prominently suggested growth motive has been that of self-actualization. The article by Carl Rogers reports a point of view which is more radical than that of Maslow in that it contends self-actualization to be "the substratum of anything we might term motivation." Thus, in Rogers' formulation, positive motivation does not supplement, but replaces the classic aversive instincts and drives.

# 18 • Sigmund Freud

## Instincts and Their Vicissitudes

As an instinct theorist, Freud dwelt much more on the mental or psychic aspects of the problem than did the instinct theorists represented in the group of articles under the heading of instinct. His description of instincts in terms of their source, pressure (strength), object, and aim is well known. Less recognized, perhaps, is his profound grasp of the requirements of scientific description and conceptualization. Both are demonstrated in the following selection.

*We have often* heard it maintained that sciences should be built up on clear and sharply defined basic concepts. In actual fact no science, not even the most exact, begins with such definitions. The true beginning of scientific activity consists rather in describing phenomena and then in proceeding to group, classify and correlate them. Even at the stage of description it is not possible to avoid applying certain abstract ideas to the material in hand, ideas derived from somewhere or other but certainly not from the new observations alone. Such ideas—which will later become the basic concepts of the science—are still more indispensable as the material is further worked over. They must at first necessarily possess some degree of indefiniteness; there can be no question of any clear delimitation of their content. So long as they remain in this condition, we come to an understanding about their meaning by making repeated references to the material of observation from which they appear to have been derived, but upon which, in fact, they have been imposed. Thus, strictly speaking, they are in the nature of conventions—although everything depends on their not being arbitrarily chosen but determined by their having significant relations to the empirical material, relations

Acknowledgment is made to Sigmund Freud Copyrights Ltd., the Estate of Mr. James Strachey, and the Hogarth Press Ltd. for permission to quote from 'Instincts and Their Vicissitudes' (1915), Volume 14 of the Standard Edition of *The Complete Psychological Works of Sigmund Freud.* Reprinted for the American market by permission of Basic Books, Inc., from Chap. IV of Vol. 4 of *The Collected Papers of Sigmund Freud,* edited by Ernest Jones, M.D., Basic Books, Inc., Publishers, New York, 1959.

that we seem to sense before we can clearly recognize and demonstrate them. It is only after more thorough investigation of the field of observation that we are able to formulate its basic scientific concepts with increased precision, and progressively so to modify them that they become serviceable and consistent over a wide area. Then, indeed, the time may have come to confine them in definitions. The advance of knowledge, however, does not tolerate any rigidity even in definitions. Physics furnishes an excellent illustration of the way in which even 'basic concepts' that have been established in the form of definitions are constantly being altered in their content.[1]

A conventional basic concept of this kind, which at the moment is still somewhat obscure but which is indispensable to us in psychology, is that of an 'instinct'.[2] Let us try to give a content to it by approaching it from different angles.

First, from the angle of *physiology*. This has given us the concept of a 'stimulus' and the pattern of the reflex arc, according to which a stimulus applied to living tissue (nervous substance) *from* the outside is discharged by action *to* the outside. This action is expedient in so far as it withdraws the stimulated substance from the influence of the stimulus, removes it out of its range of operation.

What is the relation of 'instinct' to 'stimulus'? There is nothing to prevent our subsuming the concept of 'instinct' under that of 'stimulus' and saying that an instinct is a stimulus applied to the mind. But we are immediately set on our guard against *equating* instinct and mental stimulus. There are obviously other stimuli to the mind besides those of an instinctual kind, stimuli which behave far more like physiological ones. For example, when a strong light falls on the eye, it is not an instinctual stimulus; it is one, however, when a dryness of the mucous membrane of the pharynx or an irritation of the mucous membrane of the stomach makes itself felt.[3]

We have now obtained the material necessary for distinguishing between instinctual stimuli and other (physiological) stimuli that operate on the mind. In the first place, an instinctual stimulus does not arise from the external world but from within the organism itself. For this reason it operates differently upon the mind and different actions are necessary in order to remove it. Further, all that is essential in a stimulus is covered if we assume that it operates with a single impact, so that it can be disposed of by a single expedient action. A typical instance of this is motor flight from the source of stimulation. These impacts may, of course, be repeated and summated, but that makes no difference to

1 [A similar line of thought had been developed in the paper on narcissism (1914c).]

2 ['*Trieb*' in the original.]

3 Assuming, of course, that these internal processes are the organic basis of the respective needs of thirst and hunger.

our notion of the process and to the conditions for the removal of the stimulus. An instinct, on the other hand, never operates as a force giving a *momentary* impact but always as a *constant* one. Moreover, since it impinges not from without but from within the organism, no flight can avail against it. A better term for an instinctual stimulus is a 'need'. What does away with a need is 'satisfaction'. This can be attained only by an appropriate ('adequate') alteration of the internal source of stimulation.

Let us imagine ourselves in the situation of an almost entirely help-less living organism, as yet unorientated in the world, which is receiving stimuli in its nervous substance.[4] This organism will very soon be in a position to make a first distinction and a first orientation. On the one hand, it will be aware of stimuli which can be avoided by muscular action (flight); these it ascribes to an external world. On the other hand, it will also be aware of stimuli against which such action is of no avail and whose character of constant pressure persists in spite of it; these stimuli are the signs of an internal world, the evidence of instinctual needs. The perceptual substance of the living organism will thus have found in the efficacy of its muscular activity a basis for distinguishing between an 'outside' and an 'inside'.[5]

We thus arrive at the essential nature of instincts in the first place by considering their main characteristics—their origin in sources of stimulation within the organism and their appearance as a constant force—and from this we deduce one of their further features, namely, that no actions of flight avail against them. In the course of this discussion, how-ever, we cannot fail to be struck by something that obliges us to make a further admission. In order to guide us in dealing with the field of psy-chological phenomena, we do not merely apply certain conventions to our empirical material as basic *concepts;* we also make use of a number of complicated *postulates.* We have already alluded to the most important of these, and all we need now do is to state it expressly. This postulate is of a biological nature, and makes use of the concept of 'purpose' (or perhaps of expediency) and runs as follows: the nervous system is an apparatus which has the function of getting rid of the stimuli that reach

---

[4] [The hypothesis which follows concerning the behaviour of a primitive living organism, and the postulation of a fundamental 'principle of constancy', had been stated in similar terms in some of the very earliest of Freud's psychological works. See, for instance, Chapter VII, Sections C and E, of *The Interpretation of Dreams* (1900a), *Standard Ed.*, 5, 565 *ff.* and 598 *ff.* But it had been expressed still earlier in *neurological* terms in his posthumously published 'Project' of 1895 (1950a, Part 1, Section 1), as well as, more briefly, in his lecture on the Breuer and Freud 'Pre-liminary Communication' (1893h) and in the penultimate paragraph of his French paper on hysterical paralyses (1893c). Freud returned to the hypothesis once more, in Chapters I and IV of *Beyond the Pleasure Principle* (1920g), *Standard Ed.*, 18, 1 *ff.* and 26 *ff.*; and reconsidered it in 'The Economic Problem of Masochism' (1924c). Cf. footnote, p. 327 below.]

[5] [Freud dealt with the subject later in his paper on 'Negation' (1925h) and in Chapter I of *Civilization and its Discontents* (1930a).]

it, or of reducing them to the lowest possible level; or which, if it were feasible, would maintain itself in an altogether unstimulated condition.[6] Let us for the present not take exception to the indefiniteness of this idea and let us assign to the nervous system the task—speaking in general terms—of *mastering stimuli*. We then see how greatly the simple pattern of the physiological reflex is complicated by the introduction of instincts. External stimuli impose only the single task of withdrawing from them; this is accomplished by muscular movements, one of which eventually achieves that aim and thereafter, being the expedient movement, becomes a hereditary disposition. Instinctual stimuli, which originate from within the organism, cannot be dealt with by this mechanism. Thus they make far higher demands on the nervous system and cause it to undertake involved and interconnected activities by which the external world is so changed as to afford satisfaction to the internal source of stimulation. Above all, they oblige the nervous system to renounce its ideal intention of keeping off stimuli, for they maintain an incessant and unavoidable afflux of stimulation. We may therefore well conclude that instincts and not external stimuli are the true motive forces behind the advances that have led the nervous system, with its unlimited capacities, to its present high level of development. There is naturally nothing to prevent our supposing that the instincts themselves are, at least in part, precipitates of the effects of external stimulation, which in the course of phylogenesis have brought about modifications in the living substance.

When we further find that the activity of even the most highly developed mental apparatus is subject to the pleasure principle, i.e. is automatically regulated by feelings belonging to the pleasure-unpleasure series, we can hardly reject the further hypothesis that these feelings reflect the manner in which the process of mastering stimuli takes place—certainly in the sense that unpleasurable feelings are connected with an increase and pleasurable feelings with a decrease of stimulus. We will, however, carefully preserve this assumption in its present highly indefinite form, until we succeed, if that is possible, in discovering what sort of relation exists between pleasure and unpleasure, on the one hand, and fluctuations in the amounts of stimulus affecting mental life, on the other. It is certain that many very various relations of this kind, and not very simple ones, are possible.[7]

---

[6] [This is the 'principle of constancy'. See footnote 4 above, p. 326].

[7] [It will be seen that two principles are here involved. One of these is the 'principle of constancy' (see above, p. 327, and footnote 4, p. 326). It is stated again in *Beyond the Pleasure Principle*, 1920g, Chapter I (*Standard Ed.*, *18*, 9), as follows: 'The mental apparatus endeavours to keep the quantity of excitation present in it as low as possible or at least to keep it constant.' For this principle Freud, in the same work (ibid., 56), adopted the term 'Nirvana principle'. The second principle involved is the 'pleasure principle', stated at the beginning of the paragraph to which this note is appended. It, too, is restated in *Beyond the Pleasure Principle* (ibid., 7): 'The course taken by mental events is automatically regulated by the pleasure principle.

If now we apply ourselves to considering mental life from a *bio-logical* point of view, an 'instinct' appears to us as a concept on the frontier between the mental and the somatic, as the psychical representative of the stimuli originating from within the organism and reaching the mind, as a measure of the demand made upon the mind for work in consequence of its connection with the body.

We are now in a position to discuss certain terms which are used in reference to the concept of an instinct—for example, its 'pressure', its 'aim', its 'object' and its 'source'.

By the pressure [*Drang*] of an instinct we understand its motor factor, the amount of force or the measure of the demand for work which it represents. The characteristic of exercising pressure is common to all instincts; it is in fact their very essence. Every instinct is a piece of activity; if we speak loosely of passive instincts, we can only mean instincts whose *aim* is passive.[8]

The aim [*Ziel*] of an instinct is in every instance satisfaction, which can only be obtained by removing the state of stimulation at the source of the instinct. But although the ultimate aim of each instinct remains unchangeable, there may yet be different paths leading to the same ultimate aim; so that an instinct may be found to have various nearer or intermediate aims, which are combined or interchanged with one another. Experience permits us also to speak of instincts which are 'in-

---

. . . [That course] takes a direction such that its final outcome coincides with . . . an avoidance of unpleasure or a production of pleasure.' Freud seems to have assumed to begin with that these two principles were closely correlated and even identical. Thus, in his 'Project' of 1895 (Freud, 1950a, Part I, Section 8) he writes: 'Since we have certain knowledge of a trend in psychical life towards avoiding unpleasure, we are tempted to identify that trend with the primary trend towards inertia [i.e. towards avoiding excitation].' A similar view is taken in Chapter VII (E) of *The Interpretation of Dreams* (1900a), *Standard Ed.*, 5, 598. In the passage in the text above, however, a doubt appears to be expressed as to the completeness of the correlation between the two principles. This doubt is carried farther in *Beyond the Pleasure Principle* (*Standard Ed.*, 18, 8 and 63) and is discussed at some length in 'The Economic Problems of Masochism' (1924c). Freud there argues that the two principles cannot be identical, since there are unquestionably states of increasing tension which are pleasurable (e.g. sexual excitement), and he goes on to suggest (what had already been hinted at in the two passages in *Beyond the Pleasure Principle* just referred to) that the pleasurable or unpleasurable quality of a state may be related to a *temporal* characteristic (or rhythm) of the changes in the quantity of excitation present. He concludes that in any case the two principles must not be regarded as identical: the pleasure principle is a *modification* of the Nirvana principle. The Nirvana principle, he maintains, is to be attributed to the 'death instinct', and its modification into the pleasure principle is due to the influence of the 'life instinct' or libido.]

[8] [Some remarks on the active nature of instincts will be found in a footnote added in 1915 to Section 4 of the third of Freud's *Three Essays* (1905d), *Standard Ed.*, 7, 219.—A criticism of Adler for misunderstanding this 'pressing' characteristic of instincts appears at the end of the second Section of Part III of the 'Little Hans' analysis (1909b), *Standard Ed.*, 10, 140–1.]

hibited in their aim', in the case of processes which are allowed to make some advance towards instinctual satisfaction but are then inhibited or deflected. We may suppose that even processes of this kind involve a partial satisfaction.

The object [*Objekt*] of an instinct is the thing in regard to which or through which the instinct is able to achieve its aim. It is what is most variable about an instinct and is not originally connected with it, but becomes assigned to it only in consequence of being peculiarly fitted to make satisfaction possible. The object is not necessarily something extraneous: it may equally well be a part of the subject's own body. It may be changed any number of times in the course of the vicissitudes which the instinct undergoes during its existence; and highly important parts are played by this displacement of instinct. It may happen that the same object serves for the satisfaction of several instincts simultaneously, a phenomenon which Adler [1908] has called a 'confluence' of instincts [*Triebverschränkung*].[9] A particularly close attachment of the instinct to its object is distinguished by the term 'fixation'. This frequently occurs at very early periods of the development of an instinct and puts an end to its mobility through its intense opposition to detachment.

By the source [*Quelle*] of an instinct is meant the somatic process which occurs in an organ or part of the body and whose stimulus is represented in mental life by an instinct. We do not know whether this process is invariably of a chemical nature or whether it may also correspond to the release of other, e.g. mechanical, forces. The study of the sources of instincts lies outside the scope of psychology. Although instincts are wholly determined by their origin in a somatic source, in mental life we know them only by their aims. An exact knowledge of the sources of an instinct is not invariably necessary for purposes of psychological investigation; sometimes its source may be inferred from its aim.

Are we to suppose that the different instincts which originate in the body and operate on the mind are also distinguished by different *qualities,* and that that is why they behave in qualitatively different ways in mental life? This supposition does not seem to be justified; we are much more likely to find the simpler assumption sufficient—that the instincts are all qualitatively alike and owe the effect they make only to the amount of excitation they carry, or perhaps, in addition, to certain functions of that quantity. What distinguishes from one another the mental effects produced by the various instincts may be traced to the difference in their sources. In any event, it is only in a later connection that we shall be able to make plain what the problem of the quality of instincts signifies.[10]

What instincts should we suppose there are, and how many? There is

[9] [Two instances of this are given by Freud in the analysis of 'Little Hans' (1909*b*), *Standard Ed.*, *10*, 106 and 127.]

[10] [It is not clear what 'later connection' Freud had in mind.]

obviously a wide opportunity here for arbitrary choice. No objection can be made to anyone's employing the concept of an instinct of play or of destruction or of gregariousness, when the subject-matter demands it and the limitations of psychological analysis allow of it. Nevertheless, we should not neglect to ask ourselves whether instinctual motives like these, which are so highly specialized on the one hand, do not admit of further dissection in accordance with the *sources* of the instinct, so that only primal instincts—those which cannot be further dissected—can lay claim to importance.

I have proposed that two groups of such primal instincts should be distinguished: the *ego,* or *self-preservative,* instincts and the sexual instincts. But this supposition has not the status of a necessary postulate, as has, for instance, our assumption about the biological purpose of the mental apparatus (p. 327); it is merely a working hypothesis, to be retained only so long as it proves useful, and it will make little difference to the results of our work of description and classification if it is replaced by another. The occasion for this hypothesis arose in the course of the evolution of psycho-analysis, which was first employed upon the psychoneuroses, or, more precisely, upon the group described as 'transference neuroses' (hysteria and obsessional neurosis); these showed that at the root of all such affections there is to be found a conflict between the claims of sexuality and those of the ego. It is always possible that an exhaustive study of the other neurotic affections (especially of the narcissistic psychoneuroses, the schizophrenias) may oblige us to alter this formula and to make a different classification of the primal instincts. But for the present we do not know of any such formula, nor have we met with any argument unfavourable to drawing this contrast between sexual and ego-instincts.

I am altogether doubtful whether any decisive pointers for the differentiation and classification of the instincts can be arrived at on the basis of working over the psychological material. This working-over seems rather itself to call for the application to the material of definite assumptions concerning instinctual life, and it would be a desirable thing if those assumptions could be taken from some other branch of knowledge and carried over to psychology. The contribution which biology has to make here certainly does not run counter to the distinction between sexual and ego-instincts. Biology teaches that sexuality is not to be put on a par with other functions of the individual; for its purposes go beyond the individual and have as their content the production of new individuals—that is, the preservation of the species. It shows, further, that two views, seemingly equally well-founded, may be taken of the relation between the ego and sexuality. On the one view, the individual is the principal thing, sexuality is one of its activities and sexual satisfaction one of its needs; while on the other view the individual is a temporary and transient appendage to the quasi-immortal germ-plasm, which is entrusted to him by the process of generation.[11] The hypothesis that the sexual function differs from other bodily processes in virtue of a special chemistry is, I understand, also a postulate of the Ehrlich school of biological research.[12]

Since a study of instinctual life from the direction of consciousness presents almost insuperable difficulties, the principal source of our knowledge remains the psycho-analytic investigation of mental disturbances. Psycho-analysis, however, in consequence of the course taken by its development, has hitherto been able to give us information of a fairly satisfactory nature only about the *sexual* instincts; for it is precisely that group which alone can be observed in isolation, as it were, in the psychoneuroses. With the extension of psycho-analysis to the other neurotic affections, we shall no doubt find a basis for our knowledge of the ego-instincts as well, though it would be rash to expect equally favourable conditions for observation in this further field of research.

This much can be said by way of a general characterization of the sexual instincts. They are numerous, emanate from a great variety of organic sources, act in the first instance independently of one another and only achieve a more or less complete synthesis at a late stage. The aim which each of them strive for is the attainment of 'organ-pleasure'; only when synthesis is achieved do they enter the service of the reproductive function and thereupon become generally recognizable as sexual instincts. At their first appearance they are attached to the instincts of self-preservation, from which they only gradually become separated; in their choice of object, too, they follow the paths that are indicated to them by the ego-instincts. A portion of them remains associated with the ego-instincts throughout life and furnishes them with libidinal components, which in normal functioning easily escape notice and are revealed clearly only by the onset of illness. They are distinguished by possessing the capacity to act vicariously for one another to a wide extent and by being able to change their objects readily. In consequence of the latter properties they are capable of functions which are far removed from their original purposive actions—capable, that is, of 'sublimation'.

11 [The same point is made near the beginning of Lecture XXVI of the *Introductory Lectures* (1916–17.)]

12 [This hypothesis had already been announced by Freud in the first edition of his *Three Essays* (1905d), *Standard Ed.*, 7, 216 n. But he had held it for at least ten years previously. See, for instance, Draft I in the Fliess correspondence (1950a), probably written in 1895.]

# 19 · Sigmund Freud

## *The Unconscious*

To the layman, Freud's contention that significant purposive motives may be unconscious has been difficult to accept, as have his related hypotheses concerning the relevance of dreams, slips of the tongue, accidents, and free association for the uncovering of psychological "complexes." Where his stress on sexuality was scandalous in his time, his challenge to the supremacy of conscious experience may seem even more demeaning to latter-day students. The fact of unconscious motivation has become so well established among psychologists, however, that it is no longer a subject of debate.

*We have learnt* from psycho-analysis that the essence of the process of repression lies, not in putting an end to, in annihilating, the idea which represents an instinct, but in preventing it from becoming conscious. When this happens we say of the idea that it is in a state of being 'unconscious', and we can produce good evidence to show that even when it is unconscious it can produce effects, even including some which finally reach consciousness. Everything that is repressed must remain unconscious; but let us state at the very outset that the repressed does not cover everything that is unconscious. The unconscious has the wider compass: the repressed is a part of the unconscious.

How are we to arrive at a knowledge of the unconscious? It is of course only as something conscious that we know it, after it has undergone transformation or translation into something conscious. Psychoanalytic work shows us every day that translation of this kind is possible. In order that this should come about, the person under analysis must overcome certain resistances—the same resistances as those which, earlier,

Acknowledgment is made to Sigmund Freud Copyrights Ltd., the Estate of Mr. James Strachey, and the Hogarth Press Ltd. for permission to quote from 'The Unconscious' (1915), Volume 14 of the Standard Edition of *The Complete Psychological Works of Sigmund Freud*. Reprinted for the American market by permission of Basic Books, Inc., from Chap. VI of Vol. 4 of *The Collected Papers of Sigmund Freud*, edited by Ernest Jones, M.D., Basic Books, Inc., Publishers, New York, 1959.

made the material concerned into something repressed by rejecting it from the conscious.

## I. JUSTIFICATION FOR THE CONCEPT OF THE UNCONSCIOUS

Our right to assume the existence of something mental that is unconscious and to employ that assumption for the purposes of scientific work is disputed in many quarters. To this we can reply that our assumption of the unconscious is *necessary* and *legitimate,* and that we possess numerous proofs of its existence.

It is *necessary* because the data of consciousness have a very large number of gaps in them; both in healthy and in sick people psychical acts often occur which can be explained only by presupposing other acts, of which, nevertheless, consciousness affords no evidence. These not only include parapraxes and dreams in healthy people, and everything described as a psychical symptom or an obsession in the sick; our most personal daily experience acquaints us with ideas that come into our head we do not know from where, and with intellectual conclusions arrived at we do not know how. All these conscious acts remain disconnected and unintelligible if we insist upon claiming that every mental act that occurs in us must also necessarily be experienced by us through consciousness; on the other hand, they fall into a demonstrable connection if we interpolate between them the unconscious acts which we have inferred. A gain in meaning is a perfectly justifiable ground for going beyond the limits of direct experience. When, in addition, it turns out that the assumption of there being an unconscious enables us to construct a successful procedure by which we can exert an effective influence upon the course of conscious processes, this success will have given us an incontrovertible proof of the existence of what we have assumed. This being so, we must adopt the position that to require that whatever goes on in the mind must also be known to consciousness is to make an untenable claim.

We can go further and argue, in support of there being an unconscious psychical state, that at any given moment consciousness includes only a small content, so that the greater part of what we call conscious knowledge must in any case be for very considerable periods of time in a state of latency, that is to say, of being psychically unconscious. When all our latent memories are taken into consideration it becomes totally incomprehensible how the existence of the unconscious can be denied. But here we encounter the objection that these latent recollections can no longer be described as psychical, but that they correspond to residues of somatic processes from which what is psychical can once more arise. The obvious answer to this is that a latent memory is, on the contrary, an unquestionable residuum of a *psychical* process. But it is more important to realize clearly that this objection is based on the equation—not, it is true, explicitly stated but taken as axiomatic—of what is conscious with what is mental. This equation is either a *petitio principii* which begs the question whether everything that is psychical is also necessarily conscious; or else it is a matter of convention, of nomenclature. In this latter case it is, of course, like any other convention, not open to refutation. The question remains, however, whether the convention is so expedient that we are bound to adopt it. To this we may reply that the conventional equation of the psychical with the conscious is totally inexpedient. It disrupts psychical continuities, plunges us into the insoluble difficulties of psycho-physical parallelism,[1] is open to the reproach that for no obvious reason it over-estimates the part played by consciousness, and that it forces us prematurely to abandon the field of psychological research without being able to offer us any compensation from other fields.

It is clear in any case that this question—whether the latent states of mental life, whose existence is undeniable, are to be conceived of as conscious mental states or as physical ones—threatens to resolve itself into a verbal dispute. We shall therefore be better advised to focus our attention on what we know with certainty of the nature of these debatable states. As far as their physical characteristics are concerned, they are totally inaccessible to us: no physiological concept or chemical process can give us any notion of their nature. On the other hand, we know for certain that they have abundant points of contact with conscious mental processes; with the help of a certain amount of work they can be transformed into, or replaced by, conscious mental processes, and all the categories which we employ to describe conscious mental acts, such as ideas, purposes, resolutions and so on, can be applied to them. Indeed, we are obliged to say of some of these latent states that the only respect in which they differ from conscious ones is precisely in the absence of consciousness. Thus we shall not hesitate to treat them as objects of psychological research, and to deal with them in the most intimate connection with conscious mental acts.

The stubborn denial of a psychical character to latent mental acts is accounted for by the circumstance that most of the phenomena concerned have not been the subject of study outside psycho-analysis. Anyone who is ignorant of pathological facts, who regards the parapraxes of normal people as accidental, and who is content with the old saw that dreams are froth [*'Träume sind Schäume'*][2] has only to ignore a few more problems of the psychology of consciousness in order to spare him-

---

[1] [Freud seems himself at one time to have been inclined to accept this theory, as is suggested by a passage in his book on aphasia (1891*b*, 56 *ff*.). This will be found translated below in Appendix B (p. 206).]

[2] [Cf. *The Interpretation of Dreams* (1900*a*), *Standard Ed.*, 4, 133.]

self any need to assume an unconscious mental activity. Incidentally, even before the time of psycho-analysis, hypnotic experiments, and especially post-hypnotic suggestion, had tangibly demonstrated the existence and mode of operation of the mental unconscious.[3]

The assumption of an unconscious is, moreover, a perfectly *legitimate* one, inasmuch as in postulating it we are not departing a single step from our customary and generally accepted mode of thinking. Consciousness makes each of us aware only of his own states of mind; that other people, too, possess a consciousness is an inference which we draw by analogy from their observable utterances and actions, in order to make this behaviour of theirs intelligible to us. (It would no doubt be psychologically more correct to put it in this way: that without any special reflection we attribute to everyone else our own constitution and therefore our consciousness as well, and that this identification is a *sine qua non* of our understanding.) This inference (or this identification) was formerly extended by the ego to other human beings, to animals, plants, inanimate objects and to the world at large, and proved serviceable so long as their similarity to the individual ego was overwhelmingly great; but it became more untrustworthy in proportion as the difference between the ego and these 'others' widened. To-day, our critical judgment is already in doubt on the question of consciousness in animals; we refuse to admit it in plants and we regard the assumption of its existence in inanimate matter as mysticism. But even where the original inclination to identification has withstood criticism—that is, when the 'others' are our fellow-men—the assumption of a consciousness in them rests upon an inference and cannot share the immediate certainty which we have of our own consciousness.

Psycho-analysis demands nothing more than that we should apply this process of inference to ourselves also—a proceeding to which, it is true, we are not constitutionally inclined. If we do this, we must say: all the acts and manifestations which I notice in myself and do not know how to link up with the rest of my mental life must be judged as if they belonged to someone else: they are to be explained by a mental life ascribed to this other person. Furthermore, experience shows that we understand very well how to interpret in other people (that is, how to fit into their chain of mental events) the same acts which we refuse to acknowledge as being mental in ourselves. Here some special hindrance evidently deflects our investigations from our own self and prevents our obtaining a true knowledge of it.

This process of inference, when applied to oneself in spite of internal opposition, does not, however, lead to the disclosure of an unconscious;

---

[3] [In his very last discussion of the subject, in the unfinished fragment 'Some Elementary Lessons in Psycho-Analysis' (1940*b*), Freud entered at some length into the evidence afforded by post-hypnotic suggestion.]

it leads logically to the assumption of another, second consciousness which is united in one's self with the consciousness one knows. But at this point, certain criticisms may fairly be made. In the first place, a consciousness of which its own possessor knows nothing is something very different from a consciousness belonging to another person, and it is questionable whether such a consciousness, lacking, as it does, its most important characteristic, deserves any discussion at all. Those who have resisted the assumption of an unconscious *psychical* are not likely to be ready to exchange it for an unconscious *consciousness*. In the second place, analysis shows that the different latent mental processes inferred by us enjoy a high degree of mutual independence, as though they had no connection with one another, and knew nothing of one another. We must be prepared, if so, to assume the existence in us not only of a second consciousness, but of a third, fourth, perhaps of an unlimited number of states of consciousness, all unknown to us and to one another. In the third place—and this is the most weighty argument of all—we have to take into account the fact that analytic investigation reveals some of these latent processes as having characteristics and peculiarities which seem alien to us, or even incredible, and which run directly counter to the attributes of consciousness with which we are familiar. Thus we have grounds for modifying our inference about ourselves and saying that what is proved is not the existence of a second consciousness in us, but the existence of psychical acts which lack consciousness. We shall also be right in rejecting the term 'subconsciousness' as incorrect and mis-leading.[4] The well-known cases of *'double conscience'* [5] (splitting of consciousness) prove nothing against our view. We may most aptly de-scribe them as cases of a splitting of the mental activities into two groups, and say that the same consciousness turns to one or the other of these groups alternately.

In psycho-analysis there is no choice for us but to assert that mental processes are in themselves unconscious, and to liken the perception of them by means of consciousness to the perception of the external world by means of the sense-organs.[6] We can even hope to gain fresh knowledge from the comparison. The psycho-analytic assumption of unconscious mental activity appears to us, on the one hand, as a further expansion of the primitive animism which caused us to see copies of our own con-

---

[4] [In some of his very early writings, Freud himself used the term 'subconscious', e.g. in his French paper on hysterical paralyses (1893c) and in *Studies on Hysteria* (1895), *Standard Ed.*, 2, 69 n. But he disrecommends the term as early as in *The Interpretation of Dreams* (1900a), *Standard Ed.*, 5, 615. He alludes to the point again in Lecture XIX of the *Introductory Lectures* (1916–17), and argues it a little more fully near the end of Chapter II of *The Question of Lay Analysis* (1926e).]

[5] [The French term for 'dual consciousness'.]

[6] [This idea had already been dealt with at some length in Chapter VII (F) of *The Interpretation of Dreams* (1900a), *Standard Ed.*, 5, 615–17.]

sciousness all around us, and, on the other hand, as an extension of the corrections undertaken by Kant of our views on external perception. Just as Kant warned us not to overlook the fact that our perceptions are subjectively conditioned and must not be regarded as identical with what is perceived though unknowable, so psycho-analysis warns us not to equate perceptions by means of consciousness with the unconscious mental processes which are their object. Like the physical, the psychical is not necessarily in reality what it appears to us to be. We shall be glad to learn, however, that the correction of internal perception will turn out not to offer such great difficulties as the correction of external perception—that internal objects are less unknowable than the external world.

## II. VARIOUS MEANINGS OF 'THE UNCONSCIOUS'— THE TOPOGRAPHICAL POINT OF VIEW

Before going any further, let us state the important, though inconvenient, fact that the attribute of being unconscious is only one feature that is found in the psychical and is by no means sufficient fully to characterize it. There are psychical acts of very varying value which yet agree in possessing the characteristic of being unconscious. The unconscious comprises, on the one hand, acts which are merely latent, temporarily unconscious, but which differ in no other respect from conscious ones and, on the other hand, processes such as repressed ones, which if they were to become conscious would be bound to stand out in the crudest contrast to the rest of the conscious processes. It would put an end to all misunderstandings if, from now on, in describing the various kinds of psychical acts we were to disregard the question of whether they were conscious or unconscious, and were to classify and correlate them only according to their relation to instincts and aims, according to their composition and according to which of the hierarchy of psychical systems they belong to. This, however, is for various reasons impracticable, so that we cannot escape the ambiguity of using the words 'conscious' and 'unconscious' sometimes in descriptive and sometimes in a systematic sense, in which latter they signify inclusion in particular systems and possession of certain characteristics. We might attempt to avoid confusion by giving the psychical systems which we have distinguished certain arbitrarily chosen names which have no reference to the attribute of being conscious. Only we should first have to specify what the grounds are on which we distinguish the systems, and in doing this we should not be able to evade the attribute of being conscious, seeing that it forms the point of departure for all our investigations. Perhaps we may look for some assistance from the proposal to employ, at any rate in writing, the abbreviation *Cs.* for consciousness and *Ucs.*

for what is unconscious, when we are using the two words in the systematic sense.[7]

Proceeding now to an account of the positive findings of psycho-analysis, we may say that in general a psychical act goes through two phases as regards its state, between which is interposed a kind of testing (censorship). In the first phase the psychical act is unconscious and belongs to the system *Ucs.*; if, on testing, it is rejected by the censorship, it is not allowed to pass into the second phase; it is then said to be 'repressed' and must remain unconscious. If, however, it passes this testing, it enters the second phase and thenceforth belongs to the second system, which we will call the system *Cs.* But the fact that it belongs to that system does not yet unequivocally determine its relation to consciousness. It is not yet conscious, but it is certainly *capable of becoming conscious* (to use Breuer's expression)[8]—that is, it can now, given certain conditions, become an object of consciousness without any special resistance. In consideration of this capacity for becoming conscious we also call the system *Cs.* the 'preconscious'. If it should turn out that a certain censorship also plays a part in determining whether the preconscious becomes conscious, we shall discriminate more sharply between the systems *Pcs.* and *Cs.* For the present let it suffice us to bear in mind that the system *Pcs.* shares the characteristics of the system *Cs.* and that the rigorous censorship exercises its office at the point of transition from the *Ucs.* to the *Pcs.* (or *Cs.*).

By accepting the existence of these two (or three) psychical systems, psycho-analysis has departed a step further from the descriptive 'psychology of consciousness' and has raised new problems and acquired a new content. Up till now, it has differed from that psychology mainly by reason of its *dynamic* view of mental processes; now in addition it seems to take account of psychical *topography* as well, and to indicate in respect of any given mental act within what system or between what systems it takes place. On account of this attempt, too, it has been given the name of 'depth-psychology'.[9] We shall hear that it can be further enriched by taking yet another point of view into account.

If we are to take the topography of mental acts seriously we must direct our interest to a doubt which arises at this point. When a psychical act (let us confine ourselves here to one which is in the nature of an idea [10]) is transposed from the system *Ucs.* into the system *Cs.* (or *Pcs.*),

---

[7] [Freud had already introduced these abbreviations in *The Interpretation of Dreams* (1900a), *Standard Ed.*, 5, 540 ff.]

[8] [See *Studies on Hysteria*, Breuer and Freud (1895), *Standard Ed.*, 2, 225.]

[9] [By Bleuler (1914). See the 'History of the Psycho-Analytic Movement' (1914d).]

[10] [The German word here is 'Vorstellung', which covers the English terms 'idea', 'image' and 'presentation'.]

are we to suppose that this transposition involves a fresh record—as it were, a second registration—of the idea in question, which may thus be situated as well in a fresh psychical locality, and alongside of which the original unconscious registration continues to exist? [11] Or are we rather to believe that the transposition consists in a change in the state of the idea, a change involving the same material and occurring in the same locality? This question may appear abstruse, but it must be raised if we wish to form a more definite conception of psychical topography, of the dimension of depth in the mind. It is a difficult one because it goes beyond pure psychology and touches on the relations of the mental apparatus to anatomy. We know that in the very roughest sense such relations exist. Research has given irrefutable proof that mental activity is bound up with the function of the brain as it is with no other organ. We are taken a step further—we do not know how much—by the discovery of the unequal importance of the different parts of the brain and their special relations to particular parts of the body and to particular mental activities. But every attempt to go on from there to discover a localization of mental processes, every endeavour to think of ideas as stored up in nerve-cells and of excitations as travelling along nerve-fibres, has miscarried completely.[12] The same fate would await any theory which attempted to recognize, let us say, the anatomical position of the system *Cs.*—conscious mental activity—as being in the cortex, and to localize the unconscious processes in the subcortical parts of the brain.[13] There is a hiatus here which at present cannot be filled, nor is it one of the tasks of psychology to fill it. Our psychical topography has *for the present* nothing to do with anatomy; it has reference not to anatomical localities, but to regions in the mental apparatus, wherever they may be situated in the body.

In this respect, then, our work is untrammelled and may proceed according to its own requirements. It will, however, be useful to remind ourselves that as things stand our hypotheses set out to be no more than graphic illustrations. The first of the two possibilities which we considered—namely, that the *Cs.* phase of an idea implies a fresh registration of it, which is situated in another place—is doubtless the cruder but also the more convenient. The second hypothesis—that of a merely *functional* change of state—is *a priori* more probable, but it is less plastic, less easy to manipulate. With the first, or topographical, hypothesis is bound up

[11] [The conception of an idea being present in the mind in more than one 'registration' was first put forward by Freud in a letter to Fliess of December 6, 1896 (Freud, 1950a, Letter 52). It is used in connection with the theory of memory in Chapter VII (Section B) of *The Interpretation of Dreams* (1900a), *Standard Ed.*, 5, 539; and it is alluded to again in Section F of the same chapter (ibid., 610) in an argument which foreshadows the present one.]

[12] [Freud had himself been much concerned with the question of the localization of cerebral functions in his work on aphasia (1891b).]

[13] [Freud had insisted on this as early as in his preface to his translation of Bernheim's *De la suggestion* (Freud, 1888-9).]

that of a topographical separation of the systems *Ucs.* and *Cs.* and also the possibility that an idea may exist simultaneously in two places in the mental apparatus—indeed, that if it is not inhibited by the censorship, it regularly advances from the one position to the other, possibly without losing its first location or registration.

This view may seem odd, but it can be supported by observations from psycho-analytic practice. If we communicate to a patient some idea which he has at one time repressed but which we have discovered in him, our telling him makes at first no change in his mental condition. Above all, it does not remove the repression nor undo its effects, as might perhaps be expected from the fact that the previously unconscious idea has now become conscious. On the contrary, all that we shall achieve at first will be a fresh rejection of the repressed idea. But now the patient has in actual fact the same idea in two forms in different places in his mental apparatus: first, he has the conscious memory of the auditory trace of the idea, conveyed in what we told him; and secondly, he also has—as we know for certain—the unconscious memory of his experience as it was in its earlier form.[14] Actually there is no lifting of the repression until the conscious idea, after the resistances have been overcome, has entered into connection with the unconscious memory-trace. It is only through the making conscious of the latter itself that success is achieved. On superficial consideration this would seem to show that conscious and unconscious ideas are distinct registrations, topographically separated, of the same content. But a moment's reflection shows that the identity of the information given to the patient with his repressed memory is only apparent. To have heard something and to have experienced something are in their psychological nature two quite different things, even though the content of both is the same.

So for the moment we are not in a position to decide between the two possibilities that we have discussed. Perhaps later on we shall come upon factors which may turn the balance in favour of one or the other. Perhaps we shall make the discovery that our question was inadequately framed and that the difference between an unconscious and a conscious idea has to be defined in quite another way.

## III.  UNCONSCIOUS EMOTIONS

We have limited the foregoing discussion to ideas; we may now raise a new question, the answer to which is bound to contribute to the elucidation of our theoretical views. We have said that there are con-

[14] [The topographical picture of the distinction between conscious and unconscious ideas is presented in Freud's discussion of the case of 'Little Hans' (1909*b*), *Standard Ed.*, 10, 120 *f.*, and at great length in the closing paragraphs of his technical paper 'On Beginning the Treatment' (1913*c*).]

scious and unconscious ideas; but are there also unconscious instinctual impulses, emotions and feelings, or is it in this instance meaningless to form combinations of the kind?

I am in fact of the opinion that the antithesis of conscious and unconscious is not applicable to instincts. An instinct can never become an object of consciousness—only the idea that represents the instinct can. Even in the unconscious, moreover, an instinct cannot be represented otherwise than by an idea. If the instinct did not attach itself to an idea or manifest itself as an effective state, we could know nothing about it. When we nevertheless speak of an unconscious instinctual impulse or of a repressed instinctual impulse, the looseness of phraseology is a harmless one. We can only mean an instinctual impulse the ideational representative of which is unconscious, for nothing else comes into consideration.

We should expect the answer to the question about unconscious feelings, emotions, and affects to be just as easily given. It is surely of the essence of an emotion that we should be aware of it, i.e. that it should become known to consciousness. Thus the possibility of the attribute of unconsciousness would be completely excluded as far as emotions, feelings and affects are concerned. But in psycho-analytic practice we are accustomed to speak of unconscious love, hate, anger, etc., and find it impossible to avoid even the strange conjunction, 'unconscious consciousness of guilt',[15] or a paradoxical 'unconscious anxiety'. Is there more meaning in the use of these terms than there is in speaking of 'unconscious instincts'?

The two cases are in fact not on all fours. In the first place, it may happen that an affective or emotional impulse is perceived, but misconstrued. Owing to the repression of its proper representative it has been forced to become connected with another idea, and is now regarded by consciousness as the manifestation of that idea. If we restore the true connection, we call the original affective impulse an 'unconscious' one. Yet its affect was never unconscious; all that had happened was that its *idea* had undergone repression. In general, the use of the terms 'unconscious affect' and 'unconscious emotion' has reference to the vicissitudes undergone, in consequence of repression, by the quantitative factor in the instinctual impulse. We know that three such vicissitudes are possible: either the affect remains, wholly or in part, as it is; or it is transformed into a qualitatively different quota of affect, above all into anxiety; or it is suppressed, i.e. it is prevented from developing at all. (These possibilities may perhaps be studied even more easily in the dream-work than in neuroses.[16]) We know, too, that to suppress the development of

---

[15] [German '*Schuldbewusstsein*', a common equivalent for '*Schuldgefühl*', 'sense of guilt'.]

[16] [The main discussion of affects in *The Interpretation of Dreams* (1900a) will be found in Section H of Chapter VI, *Standard Ed.*, 5, 460–87.]

affect is the true aim of repression and that its work is incomplete if this aim is not achieved. In every instance where repression has succeeded in inhibiting the development of affects, we term those affects (which we restore when we undo the work of repression) 'unconscious'. Thus it cannot be denied that the use of the terms in question is consistent; but in comparison with unconscious ideas there is the important difference that unconscious ideas continue to exist after repression as actual structures in the system *Ucs.*, whereas all that corresponds in that system to unconscious affects is a potential beginning which is prevented from developing. Strictly speaking, then, and although no fault can be found with the linguistic usage, there are no unconscious affects as there are unconscious ideas. But there may very well be in the system *Ucs.* affective structures which, like others, become conscious. The whole difference arises from the fact that ideas are cathexes—basically of memory-traces— whilst affects and emotions correspond to processes of discharge, the final manifestations of which are perceived as feelings. In the present state of our knowledge of affects and emotions we cannot express this difference more clearly.[17]

It is of especial interest to us to have established the fact that repression can succeed in inhibiting an instinctual impulse from being turned into a manifestation of affect. This shows us that the system *Cs.* normally controls affectivity as well as access to motility; and it enhances the importance of repression, since it shows that repression results not only in withholding things from consciousness, but also in preventing the development of affect and the setting-off of muscular activity. Conversely, too, we may say that as long as the system *Cs.* controls affectivity and motility, the mental condition of the person in question is spoken of as normal. Nevertheless, there is an unmistakable difference in the relation of the controlling system to the two contiguous processes of discharge.[18] Whereas the control by the *Cs.* over voluntary motility is firmly rooted, regularly withstands the onslaught of neurosis and only breaks down in psychosis, control by the *Cs.* over the development of affects is less secure. Even within the limits of normal life we can recognize that a constant struggle for primacy over affectivity goes on between the two systems *Cs.* and *Ucs.*, that certain spheres of influence are marked off from one another and that intermixtures between the operative forces occur.

The importance of the system *Cs.* (*Pcs.*) [19] as regards access to the release of affect and to action enables us also to understand the part

[17] [This question is discussed again in Chapter II of *The Ego and the Id* (1923*b*).]

[18] Affectivity manifests itself essentially in motor (secretory and vasomotor) discharge resulting in an (internal) alteration of the subject's own body without reference to the external world; motility, in actions designed to effect changes in the external world.

[19] [In the 1915 edition only, '(*Pcs.*)' does not occur.]

played by substitutive ideas in determining the form taken by illness. It is possible for the development of affect to proceed directly from the system *Ucs.*; in that case the affect always has the character of anxiety, for which all 'repressed' affects are exchanged. Often, however, the instinctual impulse has to wait until it has found a substitutive idea in the system *Cs.* The development of affect can then proceed from this conscious substitute, and the nature of that substitute determines the qualitative character of the affect. We have asserted that in repression a severance takes place between the affect and the idea to which it belongs, and that each then undergoes its separate vicissitudes. Descriptively, this is incontrovertible; in actuality, however, the affect does not as a rule arise till the break-through to a new representation in the system *Cs.* has been successfully achieved.

# 20 · Gordon W. Allport

## *The Transformation of Motives*

Gordon Allport, who for many years seemed to be more renowned among European psychologists than among his American colleagues, was nevertheless always and universally recognized as the originator of the doctrine of the functional autonomy of motives. This principle for many years seemed isolated from and incompatible with most major theories of motivation. This chapter was written in 1937. The subsequent merging of phenomenological psychology with American objective psychology, together with the rise in emphasis upon positive motivation, makes it seem perhaps more cogent today than when it first appeared.

*Somehow in the* process of maturing the manifold potentialities and dispositions of childhood coalesce into sharper, more distinctive motivational systems. *Pari passu* with their emergence these systems take upon themselves effective driving power, operating as mature, autonomous motives quite different in aim and in character from the motivational systems of juvenile years, and very different indeed from the crude organic tensions of infancy.

One of the chief characteristics of the mature personality is its possession of sophisticated and stable interests and of a characteristic and predictable style of conduct. Convictions and habits of expression are definitely centered. Evaluations are sure, actions are precise, and the goals of the individual life are well defined.

G. K. Chesterton gives a brief but psychologically significant portrait of a thoroughly mature personality, Leo Tolstoy, in whom all motivation seems to be centered in one master-sentiment.

Tolstoy, besides being a magnificent novelist, is one of the very few men alive who have a real, solid, and serious view of life. . . . He is one of the two or three men in Europe, who have an attitude toward things so entirely their own, that we could supply their inevitable view in anything—a silk hat, a Home Rule Bill, an Indian poem, or a pound of tobacco. There are three men in existence who have such an attitude: Tolstoy, Mr. Bernard Shaw, and my friend Mr. Hillaire Belloc. They are all diametrically opposed to each other, but they all have this essential resemblance, that given their basis of thought, their soil of conviction, their opinions on every earthly subject grow there naturally, like flowers in a field. There are certain views of certain things that they must take; they do not form opinions, the opinions form themselves. Take, for instance, in the case of Tolstoy, the mere list of miscellaneous objects which I wrote down at random above, a silk hat, a Home Rule Bill, an Indian poem, and a pound of tobacco. Tolstoy would say: "I believe in the utmost possible simplification of life; therefore, this silk hat is a black abortion." He would say: "I believe in the utmost possible simplification of life; therefore this Home Rule Bill is a mere peddling compromise; it is no good to break up a centralised empire into nations, you must break the nation up into individuals." He would say: "I believe in the utmost possible simplification of life; therefore, I am interested in this Indian poem, for Eastern ethics, under all their apparent gorgeousness, are far simpler and more Tolstoyan than Western." He would say: "I believe in the utmost possible simplification of life; therefore, this pound of tobacco is a thing of evil; take it away." Everything in the world, from the Bible to a bootjack, can be, and is, reduced by Tolstoy to this great fundamental Tolstoyan principle, the simplification of life.[1]

One must, of course, dismiss as literary exaggeration Chesterton's claim that there are only "two or three men in Europe" so well integrated that one could supply their inevitable view in anything. Among our own acquaintances we can name several more. In principle, however, if not in statistics, Chesterton is right, for the *majority* of personal lives are not nearly so unified as Toltoy's; in few cases is the *Leitmotif* so entirely consistent. The difference is one of degree. For in nearly all mature personalities master-sentiments exist, and, however difficult the task may be, psychologists are bound to try to account for them.

## FUNCTIONAL AUTONOMY

To understand the dynamics of the normal mature personality a new and somewhat radical principle of growth must be introduced to supplement the more traditional genetic concepts thus far considered. For convenience of discussion this new principle may be christened the *functional autonomy of motives*.[2]

[1] From G. K. Chesterton and others, *Leo Tolstoy*, 1903, pp. 3 *f.*

[2] The authenticity of this principle has been admitted by many psychological writers, but they have neglected thus far to give it a name. Its most familiar statement to date is the oft-quoted phrase of R. S. Woodworth, "mechanisms may become drives." Another clear recognition lies in the following quotation from E. C. Tolman.

Now, any type of psychology that treats *motives*, thereby endeavoring to answer the question as to *why* men behave as they do, is called a *dynamic psychology*. By its very nature it cannot be merely a descriptive psychology, content to depict the *what* and the *how* of human behavior. The boldness of dynamic psychology in striking for causes stands in marked contrast to the timid, "more scientific" view that seeks nothing else than the establishment of a mathematical function for the relation between some artificially simple stimulus and some equally artificial and simple response. If the psychology of personality is to be more than a matter of coefficients of correlation it *must* be a dynamic psychology, and seek first and foremost a sound and adequate theory of the nature of human dispositions.

Unfortunately the type of dynamic psychology almost universally held, however sufficient it may seem from the point of view of the *abstract* motives of *abstract* personalities, fails to provide a foundation sound enough or flexible enough to bear the weight of any *single* full-bodied personality. The reason is that all prevailing dynamic doctrines refer every mature motive of personality to underlying original instincts, wishes, or needs, shared *by all men.* Thus, the concert artist's devotion to his music might be "explained" as an extension of his "self-assertive instinct," of the "need for sentience," or as a symptom of some repressed striving of "the libido." In McDougall's hormic psychology, for example, it is explicitly stated that only the instincts or propensities can be prime movers. Though capable of extension (on both the receptive and executive sides), they are always few in number, common in all men, and established at birth. The enthusiastic collector of bric-a-brac derives his enthusiasm from the parental instinct; so too does the kindly old philanthropist, as well as the mother of a brood. It does not matter how different these three interests may seem to be, they derive their energy from the same source. The principle is that a very few basic motives suffice for explaining the endless varieties of human interests. And the psychoanalyst holds the same over-simplified theory. The number of human interests that he regards as so many canalizations of the one basic sexual instinct is past computation.

Taking the case of Tolstoy, Adler would find the style of life adopted by Tolstoy to be a consequence of his compensatory striving for power, for health, or for personal integrity in the face of an unfavorable envi-

---

But neither Woodworth nor Tolman has adopted a substantive designation for the psychological process in question.

"The whole body of both what the anthropologists find in the way of specific culture-patterns and what psychologists find in the way of individual idiosyncrasies sems to consist for the most part, psychologically speaking, in acquired specifications of ultimate goals or in acquired adherences to specific types of means-objects, which latter then often set up in their own right. And such specifications and settings-up, once established, acquire a strangle hold." *Phil. Science*, 1935, *2*, p. 370.

ronment. Freud might decide that the "simplification of life" was a mere ritual evolved to escape feelings of guilt derived from an unhallowed infantile love; or perhaps he would attribute it to a Death Wish. Rank would see it as a desire to return to the peaceful pre-natal life. Kempf might say that it represented a sublimational craving, sustained by a tension produced by unfulfilled love or by some danger not successfully averted. McDougall might attribute it to the combined effects of the propensities for submission and comfort. H. A. Murray might say that there was a need for submission and inviolacy. And in the language of W. I. Thomas, the wish for security or recognition, perhaps both, would be made responsible. Any of these writers, to be sure, would admit that the original motive had become greatly extended both in the range of stimuli which provoke it and in its varieties of expression. But *the common factor in all these explanations is the reduction of every motive, however elaborate and individual, to a limited number of basic interests, shared by all men, and presumably innate.*

The authors of this type of dynamic psychology are concerning themselves only with mind-in-general. They seek a classification of the common and basic motives of men by which to explain the normal or neurotic behavior of any individual case. (This is true even though they may regard their own list as heuristic or even as fictional.) The plan really doesn't work. The very fact that the lists are so different in their composition suggests—what to a naive observer is plain enough—that motives are almost infinitely varied among men, not only in form but in substance. Not four wishes, nor eighteen propensities, nor any and all combinations of these, even with their extensions and variations, seem adequate to account for the endless variety of goals sought by an endless variety of mortals. And paradoxically enough, in certain cases the few simplified needs or instincts alleged to be the common ground for all motivation, turn out to be completely lacking.

Before describing the principle of functional autonomy, its theoretical significance should stand out clearly. The stress in this volume is constantly on the ultimate and irreducible uniqueness of personality. "But how," cry all the traditional scientists, including the older dynamic psychologists, "how are we ever to have a *science* of unique events? Science must generalize." Perhaps it must, but what the objectors forget is that *a general law may be a law that tells how uniqueness comes about.* It is manifest error to assume that a general principle of motivation must involve the postulation of abstract or general motives. The principle of functional autonomy, here described, is general enough to meet the needs of science, but particularized enough in its operation to account for the uniqueness of personal conduct.

The dynamic psychology proposed here regards adult motives as infinitely varied, and as self-sustaining, *contemporary* systems, growing out of antecedent systems, but functionally independent of them. Just as a child gradually repudiates his dependence on his parents, develops a will of his own, becomes self-active and self-determining, and out-lives his parents, so it is with motives. Each motive has a definite point of origin which may lie in the hypothetical instincts, or, more likely, in the organic tensions and diffuse irritability described earlier. Theoretically all adult purposes can be traced back to these seed-forms in infancy. But as the individual matures the bond is broken. The tie is historical, not functional.

Such a theory is obviously opposed to psychoanalysis and to all other genetic accounts that assume inflexibility in the root purposes and drives of life. (Freud says that the structure of the Id *never* changes.) The theory declines to believe that the energies of adult personality are in-fantile or archaic in nature. Motivation is *always* contemporary. The life of modern Athens is *continuous* with the life of the ancient city, but it in no sense *depends* upon it for its present "go." The life of a tree is continuous with that of its seed, but the seed no longer sustains and nourishes the full grown tree. Earlier purposes lead into later purposes, but are abandoned in their favor.

William James taught a curious doctrine that has been a matter for incredulous amusement ever since, the doctrine of the *transitoriness of instincts*. According to this theory—not so quaint as sometimes thought—an instinct appears but once in a lifetime, whereupon it promptly dis-appears through its transformation into habits. If there *are* instincts this is no doubt their fate, for no instinct can retain its motivational force unimpaired after it has been absorbed and recast under the transforming influence of learning. Such is the reasoning of James, and such is the logic of functional autonomy. The psychology of personality must be a psychology of post-instinctive behavior. If, as in this volume, instincts are dispensed with from the beginning, the effect is much the same, for whatever the original drives or "irritabilities" of the infant are, they be-come completely transformed in the course of growth into contempo-raneous systems of motives.

Woodworth has spoken of the transformation of "mechanisms" into "drives." [3] A *mechanism* Woodworth defines as any course of behavior that brings about an adjustment. A *drive* is any neural process that re-leases mechanisms especially concerned with consummatory reactions. In the course of learning, many preparatory mechanisms must be de-veloped in order to lead to the consummation of an original purpose. These mechanisms are the effective cause of activity in each succeeding

---

[3] R. S. Woodworth, *Dynamic Psychology*, 1918. Equivalent assertions are those of W. Stern concerning the transformation of "phenomotives" into "genomotives" (*Allgemeine Psychologie*, 1935, p. 569); and of E. C. Tolman regarding the "strangle hold" that "means-objects" acquire by "setting up in their own right" (ftn. p. 345).

mechanism, furnishing the drive for each stage following in the series. Originally all these mechanisms were merely instrumental, only links in the long chain of processes involved in the achievement of an *instinctive* purpose; with time and development, with integration and elaboration, many of these mechanisms become activated directly, setting up a state of desire and tension for activities and objects no longer connected with the original impulse. Activities and objects that earlier in the game were *means* to an end, now become *ends* in themselves.[4]

Although Woodworth's choice of quasi-neurological terminology is not the best, his doctrine, or one like it, is indispensable in accounting for the infinite number of effective motives possible in human life, and for their severance from the rudimentary desires of infancy. Further discussion of the operation of the principle and a critique of Woodworth's position will be more to the point after a review of the evidence in favor of the principle.

## EVIDENCE FOR FUNCTIONAL AUTONOMY

Let us begin in a common sense way. An ex-sailor has a craving for the sea, a musician longs to return to his instrument after an enforced absence, a city-dweller yearns for his native hills, and a miser continues to amass his useless horde. Now, the sailor may have first acquired his love for the sea as an incident in his struggle to earn a living. The sea was merely a conditioned stimulus associated with satisfaction of his "nutritional craving." But now the ex-sailor is perhaps a wealthy banker; the original motive is destroyed; and yet the hunger for the sea persists unabated, even increases in intensity as it becomes more remote from the "nutritional segment." The musician may first have been stung by a rebuke or by a slur on his inferior performances into mastering his instrument, but now he is safely beyond power of these taunts; there is no need to continue, yet he loves his instrument more than anything else in the world. Once indeed the city dweller may have associated the hills around his mountain home with nutritional and erotogenic satisfactions, but these satisfactions he finds in his city home, *not* in the mountains; whence then comes all his hill-hunger? The miser perhaps learned his habits of thrift in dire necessity, or perhaps his thrift was a symptom of sexual perversion (as Freud would claim), and yet the

---

[4] "The fundamental drive towards a certain end may be hunger, sex, pugnacity or what not, but once the activity is started, the means to the end becomes an object of interest on its own account" (Woodworth, *op. cit.*, p. 201). "The primal forces of hunger, fear, sex, and the rest, continue in force, but do not by any means, even with their combinations, account for the sum total of drives activating the experienced individual" (*Ibid.*, p. 104).

miserliness persists, and even becomes stronger with the years, even after the necessity or the roots of the neurosis have been relieved.

Workmanship is a good example of functional autonomy. A good workman feels compelled to do clean-cut jobs even though his security, or the praise of others, no longer depend upon high standards. In fact, in a day of jerry-building his workman-like standards may be to his economic disadvantage. Even so he cannot do a slipshod job. Workmanship is not an instinct, but so firm is the hold it may acquire on a man that it is little wonder Veblen mistook it for one. A businessman, long since secure economically, works himself into ill-health, and sometimes even back into poverty, for the sake of carrying on his plans. What was once an instrumental technique becomes a master-motive.

Neither necessity nor reason can make one contented permanently on a lonely island or on an isolated country farm after one is adapted to active, energetic city life. The acquired habits seem sufficient to urge one to a frenzied existence, even though reason and health demand the simpler life.

The pursuit of literature, the development of good taste in clothes, the use of cosmetics, the acquiring of an automobile, strolls in the public park, or a winter in Miami, may first serve, let us say, the interests of sex. But every one of these instrumental activities may become an interest in itself, held for a lifetime, long after the erotic motive has been laid away in lavender. People often find that they have lost allegiance to their original aims because of their deliberate preference for the many ways of achieving them.

The maternal sentiment offers an excellent final illustration. Many young mothers bear their children unwillingly, dismayed at the thought of the drudgery of the future. At first they may be indifferent to, or even hate, their offspring; the "parental instinct" seems wholly lacking. The only motives that hold such a mother to child-tending may be fear of what her critical neighbors will say, fear of the law, a habit of doing any job well, or perhaps a dim hope that the child will provide security for her in her old age. However gross these motives, they are sufficient to hold her to her work, until through the practice of devotion her burden becomes a joy. As her love for the child develops, her earlier practical motives are forgotten. In later years not one of these original motives may operate. The child may be incompetent, criminal, a disgrace to her, and far from serving as a staff for her declining years, he may continue to drain her resources and vitality. The neighbors may criticize her for indulging the child, the law may exonerate her from allegiance; she certainly feels no pride in such a child; yet she sticks to him. The tenacity of the maternal sentiment under such adversity is proverbial.[5]

---

[5] Most mothers, to be sure, give their babies a somewhat warmer welcome from the start, but even so, there is little evidence that the maternal instinct is a ready-

Such examples from everyday experience could be multiplied *ad infinitum*. The evidence, however, appears in sharper outline when it is taken from experimental and clinical studies. In each of the following instances some new function emerges as an independently structured unit from preceding functions. The activity of these new units does not depend upon the continued activity of the units from which they developed.

1. *The Circular Reflex.* Everyone has observed the almost endless repetition of acts by a child. The good-natured parent who picks up a spoon repeatedly thrown down by a baby wearies of this occupation long before the infant does. Such repetitive behavior, found likewise in early vocalization (babbling), and in other early forms of play, is commonly ascribed to the mechanism of the circular reflex.[6] It is an elementary instance of functional autonomy; for any situation where the consummation of an act provides adequate stimulation for the repetition of the *same* act does not require any backward tracing of motives. The act is self-perpetuating until it is inhibited by new activities or fatigue.

2. *Conative Perseveration.* Many experiments show that incomplete tasks set up tensions that tend to keep the individual at work until they are resolved. No hypothesis of self-assertion, rivalry, or any other basic need, is required. The completion of the task itself has become a quasi-need with dynamic force of its own. It has been shown, for example, that interrupted tasks are better remembered than completed tasks;[7] that an individual interrupted in a task will, even in the face of considerable opposition, return to that task;[8] that even trivial tasks undertaken in a casual way become almost haunting in character until they are completed.[9]

Conative perseveration of this order is stronger if an empty interval of time follows the period of work, showing that *left to itself*, without the inhibiting effect of other duties or activities, the motive grows stronger and stronger. The experiment of Kendig proves this point, as well as that of C. E. Smith.[10] The latter investigator demonstrated that there is more success in removing a conditioned fear if the deconditioning process is commenced immediately. After a twenty-four hour delay the fear has become set, and is more difficult to eradicate. We are reminded here of the sound advice to drivers of auto-

---

made, full-fledged and invariable possession of all women. Even those who have early learned to be fond of babies find that with practice and experience the interest becomes constantly stronger, demanding no other satisfaction for itself than its own autonomous functioning. Some women become *so* absorbed in being good mothers that they neglect being the good wives they were earlier.

6 As a means of fixating early habits of providing a foundation for future learning, this mechanism has received detailed attention by E. B. Holt, *Animal Drive and the Learning Process*, 1931, esp. chaps. vii and viii.

7 B. Zeigarnik, *Psychol. Forsch.*, 1927, 9, 1–85.

8 M. Ovsiankina, *Psychol. Forsch.*, 1928, 6, 302–379.

9 I. Kendig, "Studies in Perseveration" (in five parts), *J. Psychol.*, 1936, 3, 223–264.

10 C. E. Smith, *Change in the Apparent Resistance of the Skin as a Function of Certain Physiological and Psychological Factors* (Harvard College Library), 1934.

mobiles or airplanes who have been involved in an accident, that they drive again immediately to conquer the shock of the accident, lest the fear become set into a permanent phobia. The rule seems to be that unless specifically inhibited all emotional shocks, given time to set, tend to take on a compulsive autonomous character.

3. *"Conditioned Reflexes" Not Requiring Reinforcement.* The pure conditioned reflex readily dies out unless the secondary stimulus is occasionally reinforced by the primary stimulus. The dog does not continue to salivate whenever it hears a bell unless sometimes at least an edible offering accompanies the bell. But there are innumerable instances in human life where a single association, *never* reinforced, results in the establishment of a life-long dynamic system. An experience associated only once with a bereavement, an accident, or a battle, may become the center of a permanent phobia or complex, not in the least dependent on a recurrence of the original shock.

4. *Counterparts in Animal Behavior.* Though the validity of a principle in human psychology never depends upon its having a counterpart in animal psychology, still it is of interest to find functional autonomy in the lower organisms. For example, rats, who will first learn a certain habit only under the incentive of some specific tension, as hunger, will, after learning, often perform the habit even when fed to repletion.[11]

Another experiment shows that rats trained to follow a long and difficult path, will for a time persist in using this path, even though a short easy path to the goal is offered and even after the easier path has been learned.[12] Among rats as among human beings, old and useless habits have considerable power in their own right.

Olson studied the persistence of artificially induced scratching habits in rats. Collodion applied to the ears of the animal set up removing and cleaning movements. Four days later the application was repeated. From that time on the animals showed significantly greater number of cleaning movements than control animals. A month after the beginning of the experiment when the ears of the rats as studied by the microscope showed no further trace of irritation, the number of movements was still very great. Whether the induced habit spasm was permanently retained the experimenter does not say.[13]

5. *Rhythm.* A rat whose activity bears a definite relation to his habits of feeding (being greatest just preceding a period of feeding and midway between two such periods) will, even when starved, display the same periodicity and activity. The acquired rhythm persists without dependence on the original periodic stimulation of feeding.[14]

Even a mollusc whose habits of burrowing in the sand and reappearing depend upon the movements of the tide, will, when removed from the beach to the laboratory, continue for several days in the same rhythm without the

---

[11] J. D. Dodgson, *Psychobiology*, 1917, 1, 231–276. This work has already been interpreted by K. S. Lashley as favoring Woodworth's dynamic theory as opposed to Freud's (*Psychol. Rev.*, 1924, 31, 192–202).

[12] H. C. Gilhousen, *J. Comp. Psychol.*, 1933, 16, 1–23.

[13] W. C. Olson, *The Measurement of Nervous Habits in Normal Children*, 1929, pp. 62–65.

[14] C. P. Richter, *Comp. Psychol. Monog.*, 1922, 1, No. 2.

tide. Likewise certain animals, with nocturnal rhythms advantageous in avoiding enemies, obtaining food, or preventing excessive evaporation from the body, may exhibit such rhythms even when kept in a laboratory with constant conditions of illumination, humidity, and temperature.[15]

There are likewise instances where acquired rhythms in human life have taken on a dynamic character. Compulsive neurotics enter upon fugues or debauches, apparently not because of specific stimulation, but because "the time has come." A dipsomaniac in confinement and deprived for months of his alcohol describes the fierceness of the recurrent appetite (obviously acquired).

> Those craving paroxysms occur at regular intervals, three weeks apart, lasting for several days. They are not weak, namby-pamby things for scoffers to laugh at. If not assuaged with liquor they become spells of physical and mental illness. My mouth drools saliva, my stomach and intestines seem cramped, and I become bilious, nauseated, and in a shaky nervous funk.[16]

In such states of drug addiction, as likewise in states of hunger, lust, fatigue, there is to be sure a physical craving, but the rhythms of the craving are partially acquired, and are always accentuated by the mental habits associated with it. For instance, eating in our civilized way of life takes place not because physical hunger naturally occurs three times a day, but because of habitual rhythms of expectancy. The habit of smoking is much more than a matter of craving for the specific narcotic effects of tobacco; it is a craving for the motor ritual and periodic distraction as well.

6. *Neuroses.* Why are acquired tics, stammering, sexual perversions, phobias, and anxiety so stubborn and so often incurable? Even psychoanalysis, with its deepest of depth-probing seldom succeeds in effecting *complete* cures in such cases, even though the patient may feel relieved or at least reconciled to his difficulties after treatment. The reason seems to be that what are usually called "symptoms" are in reality something more. They have set themselves up in their own right as independent systems of motivation. Merely disclosing their roots does not change their independent activity.[17]

7. *The Relation Between Ability and Interest.* Psychometric studies have shown that the relation between ability and interest is always positive, often markedly so. A person likes to do what he can do well. Over and over again it has been demonstrated that the skill learned for some external reason, turns into an interest, and is self-propelling, even though the original reason for pursuing it has been lost. A student who at first undertakes a field of study in college because it is prescribed, because it pleases his parents, or because it comes at a convenient hour, often ends by finding himself absorbed, per-

---

[15] S. C. Crawford, *Quar. Rev. Biol.*, 1934, 9, 201–214.

[16] Inmate Ward Eight, *Beyond the Door of Delusion*, Macmillan, 1932, p. 281.

[17] The case of W. E. Leonard, *The Locomotive God*, 1927, is instructive in this regard. An intense phobia was not relieved by tracing its history backward to the start of life. Even though he could explain why he was once frightened for a very good reason (by a locomotive), the author is quite unable to explain why now he is frightened *for no particular reason*. Such neuroses, and psychotic delusional systems as well, often acquire a "strangle hold," and the task of dislodging them is usually more than therapeutic skill is equal to.

haps for life, in the subject itself. He is not happy without it. The original motives are entirely lost. What was a means to an end has become an end in itself.

And there is the case of genius. A skill takes possession of the man. No primitive motivation is needed to account for his persistent, absorbed activity. It just *is* the alpha and omega of life to him. It is impossible to think of Pasteur's concern for health, food, sleep or family, as the root of his devotion to his work. For long periods of time he was oblivious of them all, losing himself in the white heat of research for which he had been trained and in which he had *acquired* a compelling and absorbing interest.

A much more modest instance is the finding of industrial research that when special incentives are offered and work speeded up as a consequence, and then these special incentives removed, *the work continues at the speeded rate*. The habit of working at a faster tempo persists without external support.

8. *Sentiments vs. Instincts.* Every time an alleged instinct can by rigid analysis be demonstrated not to be innate but acquired, there is in this demonstration evidence for functional autonomy. It is true enough that maternal conduct, gregariousness, curiosity, workmanship, and the like, have the tenacity and compelling power that instincts are supposed to have. If they are not instincts, then they must be autonomous sentiments with as much dynamic character as has been attributed to instincts. It is not necessary here to review all the arguments in favor of regarding such alleged instincts as acquired sentiments; the problem was discussed earlier.

9. *The Dynamic Character of Personal Values.* When an interest-system has once been formed it not only creates a tensional condition that may be readily aroused, leading to overt conduct in some way satisfying to the interest, but it also acts as a silent agent for selecting and directing any behavior related to it. Take the case of people with strongly marked esthetic interests. Experiments with the word-association test have shown that such people respond more quickly to stimulus words connected with this interest than to words relating to interests they lack.[18] Likewise, in scanning a newspaper they will observe and remember more items pertaining to art; they also take a greater interest in clothes than do non-esthetic people; and when they are asked to rate the virtues of others, they place esthetic qualities high. In short the existence of a well-established acquired interest exerts a directive and determining effect on conduct just as is to be expected of any dynamic system. The evidence can be duplicated for many interests other than the esthetic.[19]

## CRITIQUE OF FUNCTIONAL AUTONOMY

Objections to the principle of autonomy may be expected from two sides. Behavioristically inclined psychologists will continue to prefer their conception of organic drive with its capacity for manifold condi-

[18] H. Cantril, "General and Specific Attitudes," *Psychol. Monog.*, 1922, No. 192.
[19] H. Cantril and G. W. Allport, *J. Abnorm. & Soc. Psychol.*, 1933, 28, 259–273.

tioning by ever receding stimuli. Whereas instinct psychology of the traditional order will be unable to accept a pluralistic principle that seems to leave purpose so largely at the mercy of learning.

The behaviorist is well satisfied with motivation in terms of organic drive and conditioning because he feels that he somehow has secure anchorage in the neural structure. (For some strange reason, the closer he approaches nervous tissue the happier the behaviorist is.) But the truth of the matter is that the neural physiology of organic drive and conditioning is no better established, and no easier to imagine, than is the neural physiology of the type of complex autonomous units of motivation we have described.

Two behavioristic principles will be said to account adequately for the instances of functional autonomy previously cited, *viz.*, the circular reflex and cross-conditioning. The former concept, acceptable enough when applied to infant behavior, merely says that the more activity a muscle engages in, the more activity of the same sort does it engender through a self-sustaining circuit.[20] This is, to be sure, a clear instance of autonomy, albeit on a primitive level, over-simplified so far as adult conduct is concerned. The doctrine of cross-conditioning refers to subtle recession of stimuli in the process of conditioning, and to the intricate possibility of cross-connections in conditioning. For instance, such ubiquitous external stimuli as humidity, daylight, gravitation, may feed collaterally into open channels of activity, arousing mysteriously and unexpectedly a form of conduct to which they have unconsciously been conditioned. For example, the angler whose fishing expeditions have been accompanied by sun, wind, or a balmy June day, may feel a desire to go fishing whenever the barometer, the thermometer, or the calandar in his city home tells him that these conditions prevail.[21] Innumerable such crossed stimuli are said to account for the arousal of earlier patterns of activity.

Such a theory is highly mechanistic. It inherits, first of all, the difficulties resident in the principle of conditioning whenever it is applied to human behavior in general. Further, though the reflex circle and cross-conditioning may in fact exist, they are really rather trivial principles. They leave the formation of interest and its occasional arousal almost entirely to chance factors of stimulation. They give no picture at all of the spontaneous and variable aspects of traits, interests, or sentiments. These dispositions are regarded as purely *reactive* in nature; the stimulus is all-important. The truth is that dispositions *sort out* stimuli congenial to them, and this activity does not in the least resemble the rigidity of reflex response.[22]

---

[20] E. B. Holt, *op. cit.*, p. 38.

[21] *Ibid.*, p. 224.

[22] The basic fact that complex "higher" centers have the power of inhibiting, selecting, and initiating the activity of simpler segmental responses is a fact too well

A variant on the doctrine of cross-conditioning is the principle of *redintegration.*[23] This concept admits the existence of highly integrated dispositions of a neuropsychic order. These dispositions can be aroused *as a whole* by any stimulus previously associated with their functioning. In this theory likewise the disposition is regarded as a rather passive affair, waiting for reactivation by some portion of the original stimulus. Here again the variability of the disposition and its urge-like quality are not accounted for. The stimulus is thought merely to reinstate a complex determining tendency. Nothing is said about how the stimuli themselves are *selected,* why a motive once aroused becomes insistent, surmounting obstacles, skillfully subordinating conflicting impulses, and inhibiting irrelevant trains of thought.

In certain respects the principle of autonomy stands midway between the behavioristic view and the thoroughgoing purposive psychology of the hormic order. It agrees with the former in emphasizing the *acquisition* of motives, in avoiding an a priori and unchanging set of original urges, and in recognizing (as limited principles) the operation of the circular response and cross-conditioning. It agrees with the hormic psychologist, however, in finding that striving-from-within is a far more essential characteristic of motive than stimulation-from-without. It agrees likewise in distrusting the emphasis upon stomach contractions and other "excess and deficit stimuli" as "causes" of mature behavior. Such segmental sources of energy even though conditioned cannot possibly account for the "go" of conduct. But functional autonomy does not rely as does hormic theory upon modified instinct, which after all is as archaic a principle as the conditioning of autonomic segmental tensions, but upon the capacity of human beings to replenish their energy through a plurality of constantly changing systems of dynamic dispositions.

The hormic psychologist, however, will not accept the autonomy of new motivational systems. If mechanisms can turn into drives, he asks, why is it that habits and skills as they become exercised to the point of perfection do not acquire an ever increasing driving force? [24] The mechanisms of walking, speaking, or dressing, cannot be said to furnish their own motive-power. One walks, speaks, or dresses in order to satisfy a motive entirely external to these learned skills.[25] The criticism is sufficiently cogent to call into question Woodworth's form of stating the principle, *viz.,* "Mechanisms may become drives." It is not an adequate statement of the case.

---

established to need elaboration here. It constitutes the very foundation of the psychophysiological theories advanced by Sherrington, Herrick, Dodge, Köhler, Troland, and many others.

[23] Cf. H. L. Hollingworth, *Psychology of the Functional Neuroses,* 1920.

[24] W. McDougall, *Mind,* 1920, N. S., 29, 277–293.

[25] Though this objection is usually valid, it is not always so, for there are cases where the liking for walks, for talking for the sake of talking, or for dressing, playing games, etc., seem to be self-sustaining motivational systems.

Looking at the issue more closely it seems to be neither the perfected talent nor the automatic habit that has driving power, but the imperfect talent and the habit-in-the-making. The child who is *just learning* to speak, to walk, or to dress, is, in fact, likely to engage in these activities for their own sake, precisely as does the adult who has an *unfinished* task in hand. He remembers it, returns to it, and suffers a feeling of frustration if he is prevented from engaging in it. Motives are always a kind of striving for some form of completion; they are unresolved tension, and demand a "closure" to activity under way. (Latent motives are dispositions that are easily thrown by a stimulus or by a train of associations into this state of active tension.) The active motive subsides when its goal is reached, or in the case of a motor skill, when it has become at last automatic. The novice in automobile driving has an unquestionable impulse to master the skill. Once acquired the ability sinks to the level of an *instrumental* disposition and is aroused only in the service of some other *driving* (unfulfilled) motive.

Now, in the case of the permanent interests of personality, the situation is the same. A man whose motive is to acquire learning, or to perfect his craft, can never be satisfied that he has reached the end of his quest, for his problems are never completely solved, his skill is never perfect. Lasting interests are recurrent sources of discontent, and from their incompleteness they derive their forward impetus. Art, science, religion, love, are never perfected. But motor skills are often perfected, and beyond that stage they seldom provide their own motive power. Only skills in the process of perfecting (mechanisms-on-the-make) serve as drives. With this emendation, Woodworth's view is corrected, and Mc-Dougall's objection is met.[26]

If the dynamic psychologist finds in such a pluralistic system a displeasing lack of unity, he may, without damage to the principle of autonomy, fall back upon the elemental horme. All motives—diverse as they are—*may* be regarded as so many channels of the original Will-to-Live. (Such a monistic under-pinning to a theory of motivation is preferable to a list of arbitrarily distinguished propensities or instincts.) But, as was previously pointed out, the Will-to-Live, however acceptable it may be in the underlying metaphysics of personality, does not itself aid in the task of psychological analysis.

Only such a principle as that under discussion can provide a flexible enough account of the plurality of motives and their countless expressions in human life. Its specific advantages stand out in the following summary:

1. It clears the way for a completely dynamic psychology of *traits,*

[26] This theory embraces very easily the work of K. Lewin and his associates upon the nature of "quasi-needs." The urgency of these needs is greatest just before a goal is reached, after which time the motive subsides completely.

*attitudes, interests,* and *sentiments,* which can now be regarded as the ultimate and true dispositions of the mature personality.

2. It avoids the absurdity of regarding the energy of life now, in the *present,* as somehow consisting of early archaic forms (instincts, prepotent reflexes, or the never-changing Id). Learning brings new systems of interests into existence just as it does new abilities and skills. At each stage of development these interests are always contemporary; whatever drives, drives *now.*

3. It dethrones the stimulus. A motive is no longer regarded as a mechanical reflex or as a matter of redintegration, depending entirely upon the capricious operation of a conditioned stimulus. In a very real sense dispositions select the stimuli to which they respond, even though *some* stimulus is required for their arousal.

4. It readily admits the validity of all other established principles of growth. Functional autonomy *utilizes* the products of differentiation, integration, maturation, exercise, imitation, suggestion, conditioning, trauma, and all other processes of development; and allows, as they do not, considered by themselves, for their *structuration* into significant motivational patterns.

5. It places in proper perspective the problems of the origin of conduct by removing the fetish of the genetic method. Not that the historical view of behavior is unimportant for a complete understanding of personality, but so far as *motives* are concerned the cross-sectional dynamic analysis is more significant. Motives being always contemporary should be studied in their present structure. Failure to do so is probably the chief reason why psychoanalysis meets so many defeats, as do all other therapeutic schemes relying too exclusively upon uncovering the motives of early childhood.

6. It accounts for the force of delusions, shell shock, phobias, and all manner of compulsive and maladaptive behavior. One would expect such unrealistic modes of adjustment to be given up as soon as they are shown to be poor ways of confronting the environment. Insight and the law of effect should both remove them. But too often they have acquired a strangle hold in their own right.

7. At last we can account adequately for socialized and civilized behavior. The principle supplies the correction necessary to the faulty logic of *bellum omnium contra omnes.* Starting life as a completely selfish being, the child would indeed remain entirely wolfish and piggish throughout his days unless genuine transformations of motives took place. Motives being completely alterable, the dogma of Egoism turns out to be a callow and superficial philosophy of behavior, or else a useless redundancy.

8. It explains likewise why a person often *becomes* what at first he merely *pretends* to be—the smiling professional hostess who grows fond

of her once irksome role and is unhappy when deprived of it; the man who for so long has counterfeited the appearance of self-confidence and optimism that he is always driven to assume it; the prisoner who comes to love his shackles. Such *personae*, as Jung observes, are often transformed into the real self. The mask becomes the *anima*.[27]

9. The drive behind genius is explained. Gifted people demand the exercise of their talents, even when no other reward lies ahead. In lesser degree the various hobbies, the artistic, or the intellectual interests of any person show the same significant autonomy.

10. In brief, the principle of functional autonomy is a declaration of independence for the psychology of personality. Though in itself a general law, at the same time it helps to account, not for the abstract motivation of an impersonal and purely hypothetical mind-in-general as do other dynamic principles, but for the concrete, viable motives of any one mind-in-particular.

## SUDDEN REORIENTATION: TRAUMA

A special instance of functional autonomy is the effect of abrupt shocks on the developing personality. Ordinarily the process of growth is gradual; it is like the slow reaching of tentacles in many directions, some of the movements being halted when they are found maladaptive, and others continued in directions found to make for successful survival. All of the processes of growth thus far described—with the possible exception of maturation—manifest themselves *as a rule* by this gradual operation. Yet, sometimes, this operation is abruptly altered. An entirely new direction is given to the person's aims, outlooks, and style of life. Growth at this moment ceases to be gradual and becomes, for the time being, saltatory.[28]

No one can tell what catastrophic events an individual will encoun-

---

[27] C. J. Jung, *Psychological Types*, 1924, p. 593.

[28] One hundred years ago Charles Fourier, the self-styled "super-omnigyne" whose novel theories of personality were described in Chapter III, offered the following rhythmic scheme for representing the alternating phases of gradual and saltatory development. Over-simplified though it is, the list has some suggestive value.

*Ascending*
- initial crisis—birth
- 1st phase of growth—childhood
- ascending crisis—puberty
- 2nd phase of growth—adolescence

*Descending*
- climax of life—virility
- 3rd phase of movement—maturity
- descending crisis—sterility
- 4th phase of movement—decline
- final crisis—death

ter in the course of his life, or what their impression will be upon him. Some life-histories seem pivoted upon one decisive event, the vision of St. Paul, for example, the illness of St. Francis, the Italian Journey of Goethe, or Nietzsche's infection by a prostitute. Yet similar experiences in the lives of others have no such radical effects. It is small wonder that William James wrote: "However closely psychical changes may conform to law, it is safe to say that individual histories and biographies will never be written in advance no matter how 'evolved' psychology may become." [29]

In each of the periods of life there fall certain characteristic emergencies that the individual must meet in his struggles for adjustment. Though these emergencies do not always result in psychic traumas, they do sometimes serve to halt abruptly one course of development and to start a distinctly new pattern of habits and traits.

In infancy, there is first of all the possibility of a birth-trauma, though in view of the immature condition of the nervous system at the commencement of life it is difficult to see how one can attach as much weight to this possibility as certain psychoanalysts do.[30] Be that as it may, there are undeniably other traumas in infancy that may leave permanent effects on personality—accidents, for example, or illnesses (*e.g.,* Jacksonian epilepsy or encephalitis). At any time in life, for that matter, the traumatic effects of accident and illness may alter the preceding direction of development and substitute an altogether different one to accord with the changed physical condition.

The pre-school child does not as a rule encounter crises outside the home-circle, but within the home many critical experiences may occur to redirect the whole course of development: the arrival of a new baby with the consequent feelings of jealousy, early experiences of shame, of bereavement, or perhaps adoption into a foster-family.

When at about the age of six the child leaves the shelter of his home for the harder environment of the school and playground, experiences of failure, ostracism, and ridicule await him, and these may provoke quite suddenly new forms of adjustment or else accentuate previously insignificant traits. The sensitive child may grow definitely morbid. Inferiority complexes may be created over night, affecting profoundly the subsequent course of life. In the development of most boys there is a critical "sissy hurdle" that must be met. Perhaps a fist-fight, a foot race, a "grown-up" haircut, or some act of daring does the trick. If so a "normal boy's" life lies ahead for him. But perhaps the hurdle is not successfully passed, and as a result the plan of life is radically altered; new compensations and new ideals develop.

Soon come the demands of the gang, relations to the opposite sex, religious interests. Experiences of success and failure, of remorse and

[29] *Principles of Psychology,* 1890, II, 576 ftn.
[30] Cf. O. Rank, *The Trauma of Birth,* trans. 1929.

guilt, of conversion, or puppy love, may be of supreme importance. Also in adolescence comes the frequently traumatic experience of leaving home, of being "psychologically weaned" from the parents. There are also new worlds to conquer, college examinations to be met, a living to be earned, where traumatic experiences of success or failure can occur.[31]

In adult years shocks due to business failure, to illness, to religious conversion,[32] to the death of loved persons, to the "descending crisis," all may make swift and profound alterations. Yet, as a rule, personality after the age of thirty is much less subject to sudden upheavals than prior to that age. Critical and abrupt changes are never so numerous as in adolescence.

Biography is full of illustrations, some of the most interesting of which concern the sudden intrusion of an *idea* into a preceding stagnant condition of thought. Gibbon dates the first occurrence of his ambition to write of the decline and fall of the Roman Empire as the evening of the 15th of October, 1764, as he sat musing among the ruins of the Capitol.[33] Alice James describes the lasting importance of an idea, conveyed to her by her literary brother when she was only eight.

I remember so distinctly the first time I was conscious of a purely intellectual process. . . . We were turned into the garden to play. . . . Harry suddenly exclaimed: "This might certainly be called pleasure under difficulties!" The stir of my whole being in response to the exquisite, original form of his remark almost makes my heart beat now with the sisterly pride which was then awakened, and it came to be in a flash—the higher nature of this appeal to the mind, as compared to the rudimentary solicitations which usually produced my childish explosions of laughter, and I can also feel distinctly the sense of self-satisfaction in that I could not only perceive but appreciate this subtlety, as if I had acquired a new sense, a sense whereby to measure intellectual things, wit as distinguished from giggling, for example.[34]

Sometimes casual remarks made by other people, especially people toward whom because of prestige one is suggestible, have lasting influence. A certain freshman in college, coming from an uncultured home with exclusively economic aspirations, had a marked supercilious atti-

---

[31] The crises of adolescence are interestingly dealt with by L. S. Hollingworth, *The Psychology of the Adolescent*, 1928. But in combating the "widespread myth that every child is a changeling, who at puberty comes forth as a different personality," the author sems to risk the opposite error of underestimating the frequency with which radical alterations of personality do occur in the period of *Sturm und Drang*.

[32] Conversions, though much more numerous in adolescence, as a rule leave a more marked impress upon personality if they come later in life. A well known example is the case of Count Tolstoy. A profound religious experience at the age of fifty resulted in a radical shift of his whole plan of life and was responsible for the development of the new and firmly knit master-motive described by Chesterton (pp. 190 *f*).

[33] G. B. Hill (editor), *The Memoirs of the Life of Edward Gibbon*, 1900, p. 167.

[34] *Alice James, Her Brothers—Her Journal*, Dodd, Mead, 1934, p. 166.

tude toward all intellectual activities. Badly adjusted to college, with poor habits of study, and as nearly illiterate as a college youth can be, he had special difficulties with his course in English composition. One day when his weary instructor was giving him a periodic berating, the boy countered with one of his customary defenses, "I don't like English, and I never did like it, and never shall." The instructor, bored but still didactic, remarked, "It isn't English I'm talking about at the moment, it's your life." The effect was wholly unpredictable. The thrust struck home. The lad not only reformed his precarious ways, but became devoted to the subject, obtained a high grade, made Phi Beta Kappa, and eventually became a teacher of English!

An older woman traces her life-long devotion to poetry largely to an episode in her Virgil class in high school. She was performing a routine translation, difficult and dreary. The teacher trying for the thousandth time to give significance to the monotonous task, asked how the passage would be expressed in the Bible. Happily the girl caught the allusion, and spontaneously revised her translation, "Incline thine ear unto my supplication." Her artistic success on this occasion was a traumatic experience, a dawn of poetic beauty, to which she was ever after devoted.

These "chambers of maiden thought," as Keats has called them, are usually entered—if they are entered at all—as the personality approaches maturity. The experience may be due to books read, or to sermons and lectures heard, to the influence of friends, parents, or teachers; it may lead further into the chambers of abstract thought and scientific research. It is, of course, not always traumatic in nature, but may be a gradual growth, or turn out to be merely abortive. However entered, if it is entered at all, the world of ideas is a factor that shapes the more complex reaches of personality, and not infrequently it is the most important factor of all.

Quick turns do then occur in personality and permanently hold the stage; the next step is to explain them. Probably the answer must be given in terms of the adaptive process.[35] A crisis is brought about by an

---

[35] One type of psychological writing, the *dialectical,* finds no difficulty whatever in accounting for the phenomenon of sudden reorientation. It holds that the entire course of life is a matter of conflict, personality being constantly assailed by tendencies to act and by negations of these tendencies, with its goal always the synthesis of these conflicting impulses if possible. Sometimes the synthesis is gradual, but it often comes as a sudden change. Especially when one of the conflicting factors is *suddenly* introduced it is normal to expect a *Katastrophenreaktion* (Künkel), whereby a novel convergence of the old and the new takes place. Good examples of the dialectical method applied to personality are found in F. Künkel, *Vitale Dialektik,* 1929, K. N. Kornilov, "Psychology in the Light of Dialectical Materialism," in *Psychologies of 1930,* chap. xiii, W. Stern, *Allgemeine Psychologie auf personalistischer Grundlage,* 1935. Dialectic runs the danger of overestimating the prevalence of sudden, and underestimating the occurrence of gradual, change.

exceedingly intense emotional stimulus. Why it is intense for the particular individual depends almost wholly upon the present condition of susceptibility of that individual (a confluence of his own temperament and previous relevant experiences). The crisis throws into new relief the factors in a situation that was already, perhaps unconsciously, of some importance to him. But though the shift occurs upon some pre-existent familiar ground the old familiar preformed habits and traits no longer meet the need. The crisis imperiously demands new and more concordant systems. It is so urgent that it cannot be set aside, and since it cannot be admitted into the older setting, a new setting must be swiftly prepared. Sometimes as in the case of a religious or moral conversion, the majority of the previous habits and attitudes may have to be radically altered. As a result the "new" personality seems utterly different from the old.

It is the nature of traumatic experiences that they are always specific, that is to say, they can be dated and defined, but their effects are always generalized, spreading into many, or sometimes all, of the recesses of personality. The newly created interests are promptly charged with dynamic power, displacing older formations, and henceforth serving as functionally autonomous systems, guiding the further development of the personality until they in turn are gradually or suddenly transformed.

# 21 • Henry A. Murray

## Needs, Viscerogenic and Psychogenic

The project of the workers at the Harvard Psychological Clinic, of which *Explorations in Personality* is the published record, was a unique effort to advance the descriptive psychology of personality. The investigation involved the combined efforts of a team of specialists who devoted themselves to the intensive long-term study of a group of college-age men. The objective was to devise a framework which would be adequate to the task of yielding a psychological characterization of each subject. A particular emphasis was placed on the taxonomy of motives. This included a more or less conventional listing of physiological, or viscerogenic, drives. More influential, from the standpoint of motivational psychology, was the classification, description, and the beginnings of assessment techniques for a set of so-called psychogenic needs, or motives. The suggested scheme, together with its set of symbols, has not only survived, but has proved to have continued heuristic value for both researchers and clinicians.

*Up to this point* only two criteria for distinguishing needs have been stressed: the kind of trend (effect) observed objectively and the kind of effect which the subject says that he intends or desires. Though these provide an insufficient basis for a satisfactory classification, we shall, nevertheless, now offer a list of the needs that we have found it profitable to distinguish, in order to assist the reader in following the further elaboration of the theory.

Needs may be conveniently divided into: 1, primary (viscerogenic) needs, and 2, secondary (psychogenic) needs. The former are engendered and stilled by characteristic periodic bodily events, whereas the latter have no subjectively localizable bodily origins; hence the term 'psychogenic.' They are occasioned by regnant tensions, with or without emotion, that are closely dependent upon certain external conditions or upon images depicting these conditions. Thus, speaking loosely, we may

From *Explorations in Personality: A Clinical and Experimental Study of Fifty Men of College Age*, edited by Henry A. Murray. Copyright 1938 by Oxford University Press, Inc. Renewed 1966 by the author. Reprinted by permission of Oxford University Press. This excerpt is from Chapter 2, pages 76–85, Part C, The Concept of Need or Drive, and is a subsection with the title given above.

say that from a subjective standpoint the viscerogenic needs have to do with physical satisfactions and the psychogenic needs with mental or emotional satisfactions.

The viscerogenic needs are: 1, n Air, 2, n Water, 3, n Food, 4, n Sex, 5, n Lactation, 6, n Urination, 7, n Defecation, 8, n Harmavoidance, 9, n Noxavoidance, 10, n Heatavoidance, 11, n Coldavoidance, and 12, n Sentience. We also recognize a need for Passivity, which includes relaxation, rest and sleep, but this may be neglected for the present.[1]

It is hard to decide whether one should concoct new words as names for the needs or attempt to get along with old and ill-used terms. In the present endeavour sometimes one and sometimes the other of these two possibilities was adopted but without conviction. It was found that no system of nomenclature could be consistently maintained: appropriate words were not forthcoming.

The words used for most of the viscerogenic needs indicate in each case what effect is brought about by the need action. The n Noxavoidance refers to the tendency to avoid or rid oneself of noxious stimuli: to look or draw away from repulsive objects, to cough, spit or vomit up irritating or nauseating substances. The needs for Heatavoidance and Coldavoidance together refer to the tendency to maintain an equable temperature: to avoid extremes of heat and cold, to clothe the body or seek shelter when necessary. The n Harmavoidance refers to the tendency to avoid physical pain: to withdraw, flee or conceal oneself from injuring agents. It includes 'startle' and 'fear' reactions generally, to loud noises, loss of support, strangers. The n Sentience refers to the inclination for sensuous gratification, particularly from objects in contact with the body: taste sensations and tactile sensations (ex: thumb-sucking). The need moves in a direction opposite to that of the n Noxavoidance and the n Harmavoidance. But it may be associated with any one of the other needs: local sensations are an important part of sexual activity and they may accompany urination and defecation; moderate changes in temperature are sensuously agreeable and food may give rise to delicious olfactory and gustatory impressions.

The effect of the need action in each case can be represented by the B–E form.

| B.S. | E.S. |
|---|---|
| Lack of food | Repletion |
| Genital tumescence | Detumescence |
| Fluid in the bladder | Evacuation |
| Pain | Absence of pain |

[1] It is heartening to discover, as P. T. Young's recent book (*Motivation of Behavior*, New York, 1936) makes evident, that psychologists are reaching agreement in regard to the most convenient classification of viscerogenic drives.

A few remarks at this point may not be amiss:

1. Some of the needs here distinguished represent gross groupings of a number of more specific needs. The n Food, for instance, could be divided into separate needs for different kinds of food. Here they are combined for convenience because they all involve 'feeding behaviour' and the objects are all nourishing.

> i. Certain animals go to salt licks—as certain tribes used to travel to salt mines—for the sole purpose of adding this necessary ingredient to their diet. ii. Diabetics have an appetite for sugar; sufferers from deficiency diseases 'need' this or that vitamin, and so forth.

2. It will be noticed that the B.S. for most of the viscerogenic needs are afferent impulses from some region of the body.

3. The viscerogenic needs are of unequal importance as variables of personality. The personological significance of a need seems to depend upon whether there are marked differences between individuals in the frequency, intensity and duration of its activity, and upon whether the strength of any psychogenic needs are functions of such differences. A need, furthermore, does not usually become a dominant element of personality if there is no obstruction to its satisfaction. If its activity and gratification can be 'taken for granted,' it may be neglected. The n Air, for example, is perhaps the most essential of all the needs from a biological standpoint, since if the organism does not attain this need's E.S. in three or four minutes, it dies. And yet the n Air is rarely of any personological importance. Air is free and most human beings get enough of it. There is little competition for air. The n Sex, on the other hand, ordinarily depends upon the co-operation of another person, is commonly interfered with by rivals, is highly unstable, and is hemmed in by all kinds of social restrictions. This is enough to account for its importance.

The viscerogenic needs enumerated above may be grouped in a number of ways. One convenient grouping (which calls for the division of the n Air into inspiration and expiration) is the following.

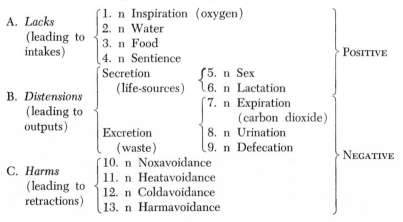

The first six needs may be called 'positive' or 'adient' needs because they force the organism in a positive way towards other objects: air, water, food, sensuous patterns, a sex object, a suckling. The last seven needs, on the other hand, may be called 'negative' or 'abient' needs because they force the organism to separate itself from objects: to eliminate waste matter or to avoid unpleasant or injuring agents. The positive needs are chiefly characterized subjectively by a desire to reach the E.S., whereas the negative needs are chiefly characterized by a desire to get away from the B.S. The division of needs into lack with intakes, distensions with outputs, and harms with retractions may also be found useful.

The secondary or psychogenic needs, which are presumably dependent upon and derived from the primary needs, may be briefly listed. They stand for common reaction systems and wishes. It is not supposed that they are fundamental, biological drives, though some may be innate. The first five pertain chiefly to actions associated with inanimate objects.[2]

n *Acquisition* (Acquisitive attitude). To gain possessions and property. To grasp, snatch or steal things. To bargain or gamble. To work for money or goods.

n *Conservance* (Conserving attitude). To collect, repair, clean, and preserve things. To protect against damage.

n *Order* (Orderly attitude). To arrange, organize, put away objects. To be tidy and clean. To be scrupulously precise.

n *Retention* (Retentive attitude). To retain possession of things. To refuse to give or lend. To hoard. To be frugal, economical and miserly.

n *Construction* (Constructive attitude). To organize and build.

Actions which express what is commonly called ambition, will-to-power, desire for accomplishment and prestige have been classified as follows:

n *Superiority* (Ambitious attitude). This has been broken up into two needs: the n Achievement (will to power over things, people and ideas) and the n Recognition (efforts to gain approval and high social status).

n *Achievement* (Achievant attitude). To overcome obstacles, to exercise power, to strive to do something difficult as well and as quickly as possible. (This is an elementary Ego need which alone may prompt any action or be fused with any other need.)

n *Recognition* (Self-forwarding attitude). To excite praise and commendation. To demand respect. To boast and exhibit one's accomplishments. To seek distinction, social prestige, honours or high office.

We have questioned whether the next need should be distinguished from the Recognition drive. In the present study the two have been combined.

---

[2] To some extent the same tendencies are exhibited towards people (acquiring friends, maintaining loyalties, possessiveness, organizing groups).

*n Exhibition* (Exhibitionistic attitude). To attract attention to one's person. To excite, amuse, stir, shock, thrill others. Self-dramatization.

Complementary to Achievement and Recognition are the desires and actions which involve the defence of status or the avoidance of humiliation:

*n Inviolacy* (Inviolate attitude). This includes desires and attempts to prevent a depreciation of self-respect, to preserve one's 'good name,' to be immune from criticism, to maintain psychological 'distance.' It is based on pride and personal sensitiveness. It takes in the n Seclusion (isolation, reticence, self-concealment) which in our study was considered to be the opposite of n Exhibition and, for this reason, was not separately considered. The n Inviolacy has been broken up into three needs: n Infavoidance (the fear of and retraction from possible sources of humiliation), n Defendance (the verbal defence of errors and misdemeanours), and n Counteraction (the attempt to redeem failures, to prove one's worth after frustration, to revenge an insult). Counteraction is not truly a separate need. It is n Achievement or n Aggression acting in the service of n Inviolacy.

*n Infavoidance* (Infavoidant attitude). To avoid failure, shame, humiliation, ridicule. To refrain from attempting to do something that is beyond one's powers. To conceal a disfigurement.

*n Defendance* (Defensive attitude). To defend oneself against blame or belittlement. To justify one's actions. To offer extenuations, explanations and excuses. To resist 'probing.'

*n Counteraction* (Counteractive attitude). Proudly to overcome defeat by restriving and retaliating. To select the hardest tasks. To defend one's honour in action.

The next five needs have to do with human power exerted, resisted or yielded to. It is a question of whether an individual, to a relatively large extent, initiates independently his own behaviour and avoids influence, whether he copies and obeys, or whether the commands, leads and acts as an exemplar for others.

*n Dominance* (Dominative attitude). To influence or control others. To persuade, prohibit, dictate. To lead and direct. To restrain. To organize the behaviour of a group.

*n Deference* (Deferent attitude). To admire and willingly follow a superior allied O. To co-operate with a leader. To serve gladly.

*n Similance* (Suggestible attitude). To empathize. To imitate or emulate. To identify oneself with others. To agree and believe.

*n Autonomy* (Autonomous attitude). To resist influence or coercion. To defy an authority or seek freedom in a new place. To strive for independence.

*n Contrarience* (Contrarient attitude). To act differently from others. To be unique. To take the opposite side. To hold unconventional views.

The next two needs constitute the familiar sado-masochistic dichotomy. Aggression seems to be either 1, the heightening of the will-to-power (Achievement, Dominance) when faced by stubborn opposition, 2, a common reaction (fused with n Autonomy) towards an O that opposes any need, or 3, the customary response to an assault or insult. In the latter case (revenge) it is Counteraction acting in the service of n Inviolacy. One questions whether n Abasement should be considered a drive in its own right. Except for the phenomenon of masochism, Abasement seems always to be an attitude serving some other end: the avoidance of further pain or anticipated punishment, or the desire for passivity, or the desire to show extreme deference.

*n Aggression* (Aggressive attitude). To assault or injure an O. To murder. To belittle, harm, blame, accuse or maliciously ridicule a person. To punish severely. Sadism.

*n Abasement* (Abasive attitude). To surrender. To comply and accept punishment. To apologize, confess, atone. Self-depreciation. Masochism.

The next need has been given a separate status because it involves a subjectively distinguishable form of behavior, namely *inhibition*. Objectively, it is characterized by the absence of socially unacceptable conduct. The effect desired by the subject is the avoidance of parental or public disapprobation or punishment. The need rests on the supposition that there are in everybody primitive, asocial impulses, which must be restrained if the individual is to remain an accepted member of his culture.

*n Blamavoidance* (Blamavoidance attitude). To avoid blame, ostracism or punishment by inhibiting asocial or unconventional impulses. To be well-behaved and obey the law.

The next four needs have to do with affection between people; seeking it, exchanging it, giving it, or withholding it.

*n Affiliation* (Affiliative attitude). To form friendships and associations. To greet, join, and live with others. To co-operate and converse sociably with others. To love. To join groups.

*n Rejection* (Rejective attitude). To snub, ignore or exclude an O. To remain aloof and indifferent. To be discriminating.

*n Nurturance* (Nurturant attitude). To nourish, aid or protect a helpless O. To express sympathy. To 'mother' a child.

*n Succorance* (Succorant attitude). To seek aid, protection or sympathy. To cry for help. To plead for mercy. To adhere to an affectionate, nurturant parent. To be dependent.

To these may be added with some hesitation:

*n Play* (Playful attitude). To relax, amuse oneself, seek diversion and entertainment. To 'have fun,' to play games. To laugh, joke and be merry. To avoid serious tension.

Finally, there are two complementary needs which occur with great frequency in social life, the need to ask and the need to tell.

n *Cognizance* (Inquiring attitude). To explore (moving and touching). To ask questions. To satisfy curiosity. To look, listen, inspect. To read and seek knowledge.

n *Exposition* (Expositive attitude). To point and demonstrate. To relate facts. To give information, explain, interpret, lecture.

On the basis of whether they lead a subject to *approach* or *separate* himself from an object, these derived needs may be divided into those which are *positive* and those which are *negative*, respectively. Positive needs may again be divided into *adient* needs: those which cause a subject to approach a *liked* object, in order to join, amuse, assist, heal, follow or co-operate with it; and *contrient* needs: those which cause a subject to approach a *disliked* object in order to dominate aggressively, abuse, injure, or destroy it. Negative needs, following Holt,[3] are *abient* needs.

This classification of needs is not very different from lists constructed by McDougall, Garnett, and a number of other writers. At first glance it is quite different from the scheme most commonly used in psychoanalysis. According to the latter there are two fundamental urges, or two classes of drives: ego instincts and sex instincts. Among the ego instincts is the hunger drive and the need for aggression. Hunger is rarely mentioned, but within recent years aggression has become one of the chief variables in the analyst's conceptual scheme. Aggression, the concomitant of hate, is considered to be the force which is operating when an individual attacks, injures and murders others. It may also be turned inward, in which case the subject may abuse, mutilate or even kill himself. Contrasting with aggression and other unnamed ego instincts are the sex instincts—the force underlying them all being termed 'libido.' Under sex has been subsumed:

1. The sex instinct proper, as biologists have described it, that is, the force which leads to the development of sexual characteristics and to intercourse between the sexes (n Sex).

2. All tendencies which seek and promote sensuous gratification (n Sentience), particularly the enjoyment of tactile sensations originating in certain sensitive regions of the body (the erogenous zones). Thus, analysts speak of oral, anal, urethral and genital erotism.

3. All desires and actions which are attended by genital excitement or by that characteristic emotional state—the palpitating, ecstatic-like feeling—which is the usual accompaniment of sexual activity. Here one speaks of the erotization of a need (fusions with n Sex).

4. All manifestations of love and humane feeling: the emotions of

---

[3] Holt, E. B. *Animal Drive and the Learning Process*, New York, 1931.

a lover, feelings of friendship, social inclinations (n Affiliation) and maternal tenderness (n Nurturance). Here the sex instinct takes the place of the biologist's herd instinct. It binds people together and leads to peace and concord.

5. Self-love, or Narcism, is also considered to be a manifestation of the sex instinct, but here it is the sex instinct turned inward upon the subject (Narcism, or Egophilia).

# 22 • Carl R. Rogers

## The Actualizing Tendency in Relation to "Motives" and to Consciousness

The positive motive of self-actualization has a history of its own which antedates by far this selection by Carl Rogers. Rogers, however, has been one of the major proponents of such a "growth" motive as opposed to the more usual "deficit" conceptions. This relatively recent article is included here to illustrate the extent to which the "third force" psychologists represent a position which is in sharp contrast to psychoanalytic or behavioristic orientations in motivation.

## THE ACTUALIZING TENDENCY

*This paper,* in its later sections, contains many ideas and beliefs which are at this point tentative and uncertain in me. They may therefore be the most profitable for discussion and clarification. This first section, however, presents a conviction which has grown stronger in me over the years. I should like to introduce it by telling of an experience, very remote from psychology, which made a strong impression on me.

During a vacation weekend some months ago I was standing on a headland overlooking one of the rugged coves which dot the coastline of northern California. Several large rock outcroppings were at the mouth of the cove, and these received the full force of the great Pacific combers which, beating upon them, broke into mountains of spray before surging into the cliff-lined shore. As I watched the waves breaking over these large rocks in the distance, I noticed with surprise what appeared to be tiny palm trees on the rocks, no more than two or three feet high, taking the pounding of the breakers. Through my binoculars I saw that these were some type of seaweed, with a slender "trunk" topped off with a head of leaves. As one examined a specimen in the intervals between the waves it seemed clear that this fragile, erect, top-

Reprinted from the *Nebraska Symposium on Motivation 1963*, Marshall R. Jones, Ed., by permission of the University of Nebraska Press and author. Copyright, 1963, University of Nebraska Press.

heavy plant would be utterly crushed and broken by the next breaker. When the wave crunched down upon it, the trunk bent almost flat, the leaves were whipped into a straight line by the torrent of the water, yet the moment the wave had passed, here was the plant again, erect, tough, resilient. It seemed incredible that it was able to take this incessant pounding hour after hour, day and night, week after week, perhaps, for all I know, year after year, and all the time nourishing itself, extending its domain, reproducing itself; in short, maintaining and enhancing itself in this process which, in our shorthand, we call growth. Here in this palmlike seaweed was the tenacity of life, the forward thrust of life, the ability to push into an incredibly hostile environment and not only to hold its own, but to adapt, develop, become itself.

Now I am very well aware that we can, as we say, "explain" many aspects of this phenomenon. Thus we can explain that the weed grows on top of the rock rather than on the protected side, because it is phototropic. We can even attempt some biochemical explanations of phototropic. We can say that the plant grows where it does because there is an ecological niche which it fills, and that if *this* plant had not developed to fill this niche, the process of evolution would have favored some other organism which would gradually have developed much these same characteristics. I am aware that we can now begin to explain why this plant assumes the form it does, and why if it is damaged in some storm, it will repair itself in a way consistent with its own basic species-form. This will all come about because the DNA molecule, as long as it is a part of, and is interacting with, a living cell, carries within it, like a program for guiding a computer, instructions to each emergent cell as to the form and function it will assume in order to make the whole a functioning organism.

Such knowledge *explains* nothing, in any fundamental sense. Yet it is very valuable as a part of the continuing differentiation, the finer description, the more accurate picture of functional relationships, which our curiosity demands, and which gives us at least a deeper respect for and understanding of the complexities of life.

But my reason for telling this story is to call attention to a more general characteristic. Whether we are speaking of this sea plant or an oak tree, of an earthworm or a great night-flying moth, or an ape or a man, we will do well, I believe, to recognize that life is an active process, not a passive one. Whether the stimulus arises from within or without, whether the environment is favorable or unfavorable, the behaviors of an organism can be counted on to be in the direction of maintaining, enhancing, and reproducing itself. This is the very nature of the process we call life. Speaking of the totality of these reactions within an organism Bertalanffy says: "We find that all parts and processes are so ordered that they guarantee the maintenance, construction, restitution, and reproduction of organic systems" (Bertalanffy, 1960, p. 13). When we speak in any basic way of what "motivates" the behavior of organisms, it is this directional tendency, it seems to me, which is fundamental. This tendency is operative at all times, in all organisms. Indeed, it is only the presence or absence of this total directional process which enables us to tell whether a given organism is alive or dead.

It was considerations of this kind which led me to formulate the actualizing tendency as the motivational construct in my own theory of personality and therapy (Rogers, 1959). I was influenced in my thinking by the work of Goldstein, Maslow, Angyal, and others. I wrote of the actualizing tendency as involving "development toward the differentiation of organs and functions, expansion and enhancement through reproduction. It is development toward autonomy and away from heteronomy, or control by external forces" (Rogers, 1959, p. 196).

Although it was ten years ago that I worked out this formulation (there was a long lag before publication), I have found no reason to change this basic notion of the process underlying all behaviors. Indeed, there seems to have been an increasing degree of support for a conception of the organism as an active directional initiator. The "empty organism" school of thought, with nothing intervening between stimulus and response, is on the decline.

Only after attempting to formulate my own theory did I become aware of some of the work in biology which supported the concept of the actualizing tendency. One example, replicated with different species, is the work of Driesch with sea urchins many years ago, quoted by Bertalanffy (Bertalanffy, 1960, p. 5). He learned how to tease apart the two cells which are formed after the first division of the fertilized egg. Had they been left to develop normally it is clear that each of these two cells would have grown into a portion of a sea urchin larva, the contributions of both being needed to form a whole creature. So it seems equally obvious that when the two cells are skillfully separated, each, if it grows, will simply develop into some portion of a sea urchin. But this is overlooking the directional and actualizing tendency characteristic of all organic growth. It is found that each cell, if it can be kept alive, now develops into a whole sea urchin larva—a bit smaller than usual, but normal and complete.

I am sure that I choose this example because it seems so closely analogous to my experience of dealing with individuals in psychotherapy. Here, too, the most impressive fact about the individual human being seems to be his directional tendency toward wholeness, toward actualization of his potentialities. I have not found psychotherapy effective when I have tried to create in another individual something which is not there, but I have found that if I can provide the conditions which make for growth, then this positive directional tendency brings about constructive results. The scientist with the divided sea urchin egg is in the same situation. He cannot cause the cell to develop in one way or another, he cannot (at least as yet) shape or control the DNA molecule, but if he focuses his skill on providing the conditions which permit the cell to survive and grow, then the tendency for growth and the direction of growth will be evident, and will come from within the organism. I cannot think of a better analogy for psychotherapy where, if I can supply a psychological amniotic fluid, forward movement of a constructive sort will occur.

Support for the concept of an actualizing tendency comes at times from surprising quarters, as in the simple but unusual experiments of Dember, Earl, and Paradise, which show that rats prefer an environment involving more complex stimuli over an environment involving less complex stimuli. It seems striking that even the lowly laboratory rat, within the range of complexity that he can appreciate, prefers a more richly stimulating setting to a more impoverished one. The authors' theory states, and is thus far confirmed, that "a shift in preference, if it occurs, will be unidirectional, toward stimuli of greater complexity" (Dember, Earl, and Paradise, 1957, p. 517).

Better known are the increasing number of studies having to do with exploratory behavior, curiosity, play—the spontaneous tendency of the organism to seek stimulation, to produce a difference in the stimulus field (Berlyne, 1960; Harlow, 1953, are examples). This concept has become well accepted during the past decade.

The work in the field of sensory deprivation underscores even more strongly the fact that tension reduction or the absence of stimulation is a far cry from being the desired state of the organism. Freud (1953, p. 63) could not have been more wrong in his postulate that "the nervous system is . . . an apparatus which would even, if this were feasible, maintain itself in an altogether unstimulated condition." On the contrary, when deprived of external stimuli, the human organism produces a flood of internal stimuli sometimes of the most bizarre sort. As Goldstein (1947, p. 141) points out, "The tendency to discharge any tension whatsoever is a characteristic expression of a defective organism, of disease."

Much of the material summarized by White (1959) in his excellent article on motivation adds up to the point I too have been making, namely, that the organism is an active initiator and exhibits a directional tendency. He puts this in very appealing terms when he says, "Even when its primary needs are satisfied and its homeostatic chores are done, an organism is alive, active, and up to something." (White, 1959, p. 315)

As a consequence of these and other developments in psychological and biological research, I feel considerably more secure than I did a decade ago in calling attention to the significance of those directions in the human organism which account for its maintenance and enhancement.

I would like to add one comment which may be clarifying. Sometimes this tendency is spoken of as if it involved the development of all of the potentialities of the organism. This is clearly not true. The organism does not, as Leeper has pointed out, tend toward developing its capacity for nausea, nor does it actualize its potentiality for self-destruction, nor its ability to bear pain. Only under unusual or perverse circumstances do these potentialities become actualized. It is clear that the actualizing tendency is selective and directional, a constructive tendency if you will.

Thus, to me it is meaningful to say that the substratum of all motivation is the organismic tendency toward fulfillment. This tendency may express itself in the widest range of behaviors, and in response to a very wide variety of needs. Maslow's hierarchy of needs manages to catch something of the fact that certain wants of a basic sort must be at least partially met before other needs become urgent. Consequently, the tendency of the organism to actualize itself may at one moment lead to the seeking of food or sexual satisfaction, and yet unless these needs are overpoweringly great, even these satisfactions will be sought in ways which enhance rather than diminish self-esteem. And other fulfillments will also be sought in the transactions with the environment—the need for exploration, for producing change in the environment, for play, for self-exploration when that is perceived as an avenue to actualization— all of these and many other behaviors are basically "motivated" by the actualizing tendency.

We are, in short, dealing with an organism which is always motivated, is always "up to something," always seeking. So I would reaffirm, perhaps even more strongly after the passage of a decade, my belief that there is one central source of energy in the human organism; that it is a function of the whole organism rather than of some portion of it; and that it is perhaps best conceptualized as a tendency toward fulfillment, toward actualization, toward the maintenance and enhancement of the organism.

## WHO NEEDS "MOTIVES"?

At this point, however, I should like to introduce an idea which, if it has gained some limited acceptance during recent years, is still far from being acceptable to most psychologists. I can introduce it by posing this question. Given the motivational substratum of the actualizing tendency, is anything added to our theories by postulating more specific motivational constructs? How helpful has it been in the past and how helpful is it likely to be in the future to specify and try to give meaning to a variety of special motives? I am not arguing that these differing types of seeking do not take place. Men do seek food, and they do tend toward increasing their competence in dealing with the environment, and most people wish to increase their self-esteem, but I am not at all sure that there is any profit to thinking of a hunger motive, a competence motive, or a self-esteem motive. Are these heuristic concepts? Do they lead to significant discovery? Are they provocative of effective research? Obviously I am dubious.

As I endeavor to discover what constitutes science in its truest sense, it seems to me clear that science has not made progress by positing forces, attractions, repulsions, causes, and the like, to explain *why* things happen. As we all know, there are very few answers to the question "why." But science has progressed and found itself on more fruitful paths when it restricts itself to the question of "how" things happen. When the theory was offered that nature abhors a vacuum, and that this explained *why* air rushes in to fill any vacuum or partial vacuum, this led to little effective research. But when science began to describe, in empirical terms, the functional relationships which hold between a partial vacuum and the atmospheric pressure outside the container, significant results accrued, and the question as to whether nature feels this particular abhorrence was forgotten. Or, as Galileo so forcefully demonstrated, when we cease trying to formulate the reasons as to *why* a stone falls, and concentrate on the exact description of its rate of fall per second, and the degree of its acceleration, then these exact descriptions of functional relationships open up whole new fields of investigation and are incredibly fruitful of further knowledge. One of the by-products is a loss of interest in *why* the stone falls.

In the same vein, I doubt if psychologists make progress in their science so long as their basic theory focuses on the formulation that man seeks food *because* he has a hunger motive or drive; that he interacts in an exploratory and manipulative manner with his environment *because* he has a competence motive; that he seeks achievement *because* he has a mastery drive or a need for achievement. Even in the area that has seemed so clear to so many, the concept of a sexual motive has not been too helpful in unraveling the vastly complex variables which determine sexual behavior even in animals—the genetic, physiological, environmental, maturational, social, perceptual, and other elements which enter in. As Beach (1955, p. 409) has pointed out in regard to instincts, such concepts of specific energy sources lead to oversimplified theories and even to an insistence upon theories rather than upon observation. His proposal regarding the improvement of the situation regarding instincts bears consideration in regard to motives:

The analysis that is needed involves two types of approach. One rests upon determination of the relationships existing between genes and behavior. The other consists of studying the development of various behavior patterns in the individual, and determining the number and kinds of factors that normally control the final form of the response.

When these methods have been applied to the various types of behavior which today are called "instinctive," the concept of instinct will disappear, to be replaced by scientifically valid and useful explanations.

In much the same fashion I believe that when we have developed and tested hypotheses as to the conditions which are necessary and sufficient antecedents to certain behaviors, when we understand the complex variables which underlie various expressions of the actualizing tendency of the organism, then the concept of specific motives will disappear.

## AN ILLUSTRATION

The point I am making could be illustrated from many areas of psychology but you will not be surprised if I speak of it from the area of my own work. I would like to sketch briefly a chain of experiences in theory and research regarding the therapeutic relationship, and endeavor to relate these experiences to what I have been saying about motivational constructs.

In a lifetime of professional effort I have been fascinated by the process of change which sometimes occurs in human beings in the therapeutic relationship when it is, as we say, "successful." Individual clients in such a relationship could be described in very general and theoretical terms as moving in the direction of actualization of their potentialities, moving away from rigidity and toward flexibility, moving toward more process living, moving toward autonomy, and the like. In more specific and empirical terms we know that they change in their observed behaviors, exhibiting more socially mature behavior, that they change in the way in which they perceive themselves, that they place a more positive value upon self, that they give more healthy responses to projective tests. Perhaps it should be stressed that these generalizations regarding the direction of the process in which they are engaged exist in a context of enormously diverse specific behaviors, with different meanings for different individuals. Thus, progress toward maturity for one means developing sufficient autonomy to divorce himself from an unsuitable marriage partner; in another it means living more constructively with the partner he has. For one student it means working hard to obtain better grades; for another it means a lessened compulsiveness and a willingness to accept poorer grades. So we must recognize that the generalizations about this process of change are abstractions drawn from a very complex diversified picture.

But the nagging question over the years has been What is it that initiates this process? Every therapist knows that it does not occur in each of his clients. What are the conditions, in the client, in the therapist, in the interaction, which are antecedent to this process of change? In trying to formulate hypotheses in regard to this, I believe that there is no substitute for close observation—with as much openness to unexpected facts and possibilities as the observer can bring to bear, with as much laying aside of defensiveness and rigidity as he can achieve. As I continued to observe therapy, the formulation at which I gradually arrived was very different from the views with which I started, though how much defensive inability to see the facts is still involved no man can say of himself. At any rate, the theoretical position to which I came hypothesized that the process of change was initiated primarily by the psychological climate created by the therapist, and not by his techniques, his therapeutic orientation, or his scholarly knowledge of personality dynamics. I have spelled out these hypotheses in different publications (Rogers, 1962a, 1959, 1957).

The point to which I would call attention is that when you become interested in the conditions which are antecedent to a given complex of behaviors, it becomes quite clear that questions regarding specific motives seem futile as leads for further work. Are differing therapist behaviors due to varying degrees of altruistic motive? or to differing amounts of the need for affiliation? or to the need for dominance? Are the client's behaviors due to his competence motive? or his need for dependence? or is there a self-exploration motive which is tapped? To me these do not seem to be heuristic questions.

On the other hand, when I begin, on the basis of observation, to hypothesize specific conditions or determinants of change, then, it seems to me, research progress is stimulated in two ways. In the first place, one attempts to describe the specific conditions which appear to operate, not to consult a list of motives. The specific conditions may conceivably be genetic or physiological or environmental. They may be strictly observable behaviors, or may be phenomenological states inferred from the behaviors. They may be interactional, although in my experience interactional variables are difficult to make operational. In the second place, it is, I believe, considerably easier to give operational definitions of observed conditions than to measure a general motivational state such as need for affiliation.

In any event, to continue with my account, the conditions which appeared on the basis of observation to be antecedent to and relevant to the process of developmental change in the client, were of quite different sorts. There were essentially five—four of them attitudinal sets in the therapist, one an element in the client.

An accurate and sensitive empathy communicated by the therapist appeared crucial. This is a variable which falls in the class of directly observable behaviors. It has been possible to assess it from the verbal behavior of the therapist and from his vocal inflections.

The warmth of positive regard for the client experienced by the therapist was postulated as a second variable of significance. This is a complex factor existing in the phenomenal field of the therapist, which may be inferred from the quality and tone of his voice. It can also be inferred from his posture and gestures, if moving pictures or direct observation can be employed.

Third, the unconditionality of the therapist's regard is a related factor deemed to be important. Is the therapist's regard relatively conditional, that is, valuing certain aspects of the client and his behavior, and devaluing other aspects, or is it unconditional? Assessment of such a variable must to some degree be an inference regarding the phenomenal field of the therapist, but to the extent that the regard is conditional, it constitutes observable behavior, evident in verbalizations, inflections, gestures.

A fourth element hypothesized to be important was the congruence of the therapist—the extent to which, in the relationship, he is integrated, whole, real, his conscious attitudes and behavior congruent with the experiencing going on in him. Assessment must be based entirely on behavioral observation—the voice qualities particularly—since a lack of congruence is usually unknown to the therapist himself at the time, being essentially a defense against feelings in himself which he senses as threatening. Thus, this seems like an extremely subtle assessment to make. We are assisted in this, however, by the fact that this type of assessment is made by every one from childhood up, as he evaluates each relationship as to whether the person is being real, or is acting a role, putting up a façade, or being a "phony."

The fifth and final condition is purely phenomenological—the client's perception of at least a minimal degree of these qualities in the therapist. We have used a paper-and-pencil inventory to get at this client perception.

Now it should be clear that these are very crude formulations of variables hypothesized to be significant. In this respect they are, I believe, representative of the primitive state of psychological science as it relates to human beings. It is a tragedy that we have not achieved any rational scientific methodology which is adequate for the study of organisms with their wholistic nature and their basic process characteristics. So these formulations I have given represent only a first awkward attempt to define the elements which nourish and facilitate psychological change, growth, development toward maturity, in the human person. I see them as roughly analogous to the early attempts to isolate the nutritional elements which promote physical growth. Just as a maturing science can now define with very considerable precision the elements necessary for physical growth, so I believe a maturing psychological science will eventually define the psychological nutriments which promote personal growth.

When I ask myself if this attempt would have proceeded more rapidly or more accurately if we had hypotheses based upon some theory of specific motives, rather than upon naturalistic observation, my answer is strongly negative. In my judgment, assessment of therapist motives, such as need for affiliation, for altruism, for dominance or mastery or competence, would have approached only very indirectly, if at all, the problem of the conditions which facilitate change. And if I turn the question around and ask myself what motive lies behind the therapist's genuineness or his sensitive empathy in the relationship, I must answer that I do not know. Nor does the question have any real importance for me. So I reiterate the idea voiced previously, that a theory involving specific motivations, no matter how they are categorized or sliced, does not seem to me to be helpful in the empirical investigations which alone can determine the patterning which exists in human behavior.

Yet when the variables are selected through subjective observation, when the scientist is willing to use his own disciplined sensitivity to his experience in the selection of variables, when he is willing to trust his experience as a tentative and perhaps intuitive guide in the formulation of hypotheses, positive results can emerge. I think we often fail to recognize the truth of Polanyi's (1958) thesis that if it were not for the pattern which the disciplined scientist senses long before he can confirm or disconfirm it, there would be no such thing as an advancing science.

So to complete very briefly the story of these particular formulations about the conditions necessary for the therapeutic process, I will attempt to summarize the results of a number of completed studies in this field, several of which are moving toward publication (Barrett-Lennard, in press; Halkides, 1958; Spotts, 1962; Truax, 1962; Truax, Liccione and Rosenberg, 1962). The studies deal with two rather different groups of clients: on the one hand, students and other adults who come voluntarily for help; and on the other hand, schizophrenic individuals who have been in a state hospital for periods ranging from a few months to many years. The first group is above the socio-educational average, well motivated, and ranging from mildly to seriously disturbed in their functioning. The second group is below the socio-educational average, not only unmotivated but resistant, unable to cope with life in the community, and often out of contact with reality.

In the different studies there have been three ways of measuring the relationship elements I have described. The first method is through the rating of brief segments of the recorded interviews, usually four minutes in length, taken in a randomized fashion from the interview. Raters, listening to these segments, judge the degree to which the therapist is, for example, being accurately empathic, and make a rating on a carefully defined scale. The raters have no knowledge as to whether the segment is from an early or late interview, or a more or less successful case. In the most recent of the studies a different group of raters has made the ratings for each of the qualities.

A second method of measurement has been through the use of the Relationship Inventory, an instrument designed to capture the client's perception of the qualities of the relationship. The third method is also based on this Inventory, filled out by the therapist to obtain *his* perception of the relationship qualities.

Various criteria of change have been used in these studies, to assess the degree of positive or negative change in personality. In all cases the criteria of change have been independent of the measures of the attitudinal elements. Some of the measures have been: assessment by clinicians, working "blind," of the changes between pre- and post-projective and other tests; changes in various MMPI scales; changes in Q-sort adjustment score and in a measure of anxiety. There have also been measures of process movement in some of the studies, based upon a process analysis of the interview segments made entirely independently of the attitudinal assessment.

The major finding from all of the studies is that clients in relationships marked by a high level of therapist congruence, empathy, and positive regard of an unconditional sort, tend to show a significant degree of constructive personality change and development. Clients in relationships characterized by a low level of these attitudinal conditions show significantly less positive change on the indices described above. In the schizophrenic group, the individuals in relationships low in these qualities show *negative* personality change. They are, at the end, worse off than their matched nontherapy controls. Clinically, this is a very sobering finding; scientifically, it is of great importance. There are various other findings which are of interest, but not relevant to our present topic.

I have given this much of the findings simply to indicate that variables abstracted from observation, quite without regard to motivational constructs, have proven to be significantly related to personality change. They are of the order which I believe has usually been of the most importance in science, namely "x is a function of y." In this case, personality change is a function of certain measured relationship qualities.

But this is not all. One of our staff has also abstracted out the construct of client likability, and has shown that the likability of the client is also associated with the degree of change (Stoler, in press). Again, motivational constructs have, I am sure, played no part in this research. In some further work we seem to be teasing out a factor which perhaps we could call client readiness, as still another predictor of change. What I am saying is that in our efforts to understand objectively a complex process of change in the personality and behavior of the individual we are making progress, but that progress has in no way come from theories of specific motivations. In fact, to have operated from a base of such theories would, I believe, only have clouded the difficult task of discovering the elements which, empirically, are associated with change.

## A Restatement

Let me summarize very briefly what I have been saying up to this point. The human organism is active, actualizing, and directional. This is the basis for all of my thinking. Once this fact is accepted, I see no virtue in imposing abstractions regarding specific motives upon man's complex and multiform behavior. It is certainly possible to categorize the behavioral phenomena into many different motives and, in fact, these phenomena may be sliced in a variety of ways, but that this is desirable or heuristic seems dubious to me. I have tried to indicate by illustration that in any actual attempt to understand the conditions antecedent to behavior it may be preferable to formulate our hypotheses on the basis of close observation of the phenomena, rather than upon a previously constructed series of motives.

## THE PROBLEM OF INCONGRUENCE OR DISSOCIATION

I should like now to turn to a very different and very puzzling cluster of questions. These questions are certainly related to the issue of motivation, but to many other aspects of personality theory as well. Anyone who delves at all into the dynamics of human behavior must deal with them in some way. I have myself found them very perplexing, and have felt quite dissatisfied with the all too easy "explanations" which have been given. They have to do with what I think of as incongruence or dissociation. In general, the questions are of this sort. How is it that man is so frequently at war within himself? How do we account for the all too common rift which we observe between the conscious aspects of man and his organismic aspects? How do we account for what appears to be two conflicting motivational systems in man?

To take a very simple example, how is it that a woman can consciously be a very submissive and compliant person, very sure that this is her goal, that such behavior represents her true values, and then at times blow up in abnormally hostile and resentful behavior which greatly surprises her, and which she does not own as a part of herself? Clearly her organism has been experiencing both submission and aggression, and moving toward the expression of both. Yet at the conscious level she has no awareness and no acceptance of one aspect of this process going on within her. This is a simple example of the rift with which every psychologist interested in human behavior must come to terms.

In the theory I advanced a decade ago I saw the rift as an incongruence between the self-perceptions held by the individual and his organismic experiencing. I said that this was brought about by distorted perceptions of self and experience, which in turn grew out of conditions of worth introjected from significant others. I expressed the view that the actualizing tendency promoted the fulfillment of the organism on the one hand, but that as the self developed it also tended to actualize the self, and that frequently the self and the experience of the organism were decidedly incongruent. Thus, we have the actualizing tendency splitting into two systems at least partially antagonistic in their directions (Rogers, 1959, pp. 196–97). I am not at all sure that this captures the facts in the way most effective for promoting investigation. I do not see any clear solution to the problem, but I think perhaps I see the issues in a larger context. So I should like to share my puzzlement with you. To do so, I would like to back away and look at the broad picture.

In nature, the working out of the actualizing tendency shows a surprising efficiency. The organism makes errors, to be sure, but these are corrected on the basis of feedback. Even the human infant, faced with natural, unflavored foods, does a quite satisfactory job of balancing his diet over time, and thus both maintains and enhances his development. This type of relatively integrated, self-regulating behavior, directed toward maintenance and fulfillment, seems to be the rule in nature rather than the exception. One can, of course, point to serious mistakes over evolutionary time. Evidently the dinosaurs, by becoming very efficiently and rigidly actualized in terms of a given environment, could not adapt, and thus effectively destroyed themselves through the perfection with which they had fulfilled themselves in a given environment. But this is the exception. On the whole, organisms behave in ways which make an awesome degree of directional sense.

In man, however—perhaps particularly in our culture—the potentiality for awareness of his functioning can go so persistently awry as to make him truly estranged from his organismic experiencing. He can become self-defeating as in neurosis, incapable of coping with life as in psychosis, unhappy and divided as in the maladjustments which occur in all of us. Why this division? How is it that a man can be consciously struggling toward one goal, while his whole organic direction is at cross purposes with this?

In puzzling over this issue, I find myself trying to take a fresh look at the place and function of awareness in the life of man. The ability to focus conscious attention seems to be one of the latest evolutionary developments in our species. It is, we might say, a tiny peak of awareness, of symbolizing capacity, based on a vast pyramid of nonconscious organismic functioning. Perhaps a better analogy more indicative of the continual change going on, is to think of man's functioning as a large, pyramidal fountain in which the very tip of the fountain is intermittently illuminated with the flickering light of consciousness, but the constant flow goes on in darkness or in the light.

In the person who is functioning well, awareness tends to be reflexive, rather than the sharp spotlight of focused attention. Perhaps it is more accurate to say that in such a person awareness is simply a reflection of something of the flow of the organism at that moment. It is only when the functioning is disrupted that a sharply self-conscious awareness arises. Speaking of the different aspects of awareness in this well-functioning person, I have said, "I do not mean that this individual would be self-consciously aware of all that was going on within himself, like the centipede who became aware of all his legs. On the contrary, he would be free to live a feeling subjectively, as well as be aware of it. He might experience love or pain or fear, living in this attitude subjectively. Or he might abstract himself from this subjectivity and realize in awareness, 'I am in pain'; 'I am afraid'; 'I do love.' The crucial point is that there would be no barriers, no inhibitions, which would prevent the full experiencing of whatever was organismically present" (Rogers, 1962b, p. 25).

In this way, as in various other ways, my thinking is similar to that of Lancelot Whyte, who comes at the same problem from a very different perspective, that of the philosopher of science and historian of ideas. He too feels that in the person who is functioning well "the free play of spontaneous vitality—as in the transitory rhythms of eating, drinking, walking, loving, making things, working well, thinking, and dreaming—evokes no persistent differentiated awareness. We feel right while it is going on, and then forget it, as a rule" (Whyte, 1960, p. 35).

When functioning in this manner the person is whole, integrated, unitary. This appears to be the desirable and efficient human way. Sharpened self-consciousness in such functioning arises, according to Whyte, only as a result of contrast or clash between the organism and its environment, and the function of such self-awareness is to eliminate the clash by modifying the environment or altering the behavior of the individual. His viewpoint is startling but challenging when he says, "The main purpose of conscious thought, its neobiological function, may be first to identify, and then to eliminate, the factors which evoke it" (Whyte, 1960, p. 37).

It will probably be evident that such views as the foregoing could be held only by individuals who see the nonconscious aspect of man's living in a positive light. I have myself stressed the idea that man is wiser than his intellect, and that well-functioning persons "accept the realization that the meanings implicit in their experiencing of a situation constitute the wisest and most satisfying indication of appropriate behavior." They have come to "trust their experiencing" (Rogers, 1962b, p. 28). Whyte places this same idea in a larger context when he says, "Crystals, plants, and animals grow without any conscious fuss, and the strangeness of our own history disappears once we assume that the same kind of natural ordering process that guides their growth also guided the development of man and of his mind, and does so still" (1960, p. 5). It is clear that these views are very remote from Freud's distrust of the unconscious, and his general view that it was antisocial in its direction. Instead, as developed in these paragraphs, when man is functioning in an integrated, unified, effective manner, he has confidence in the directions which he unconsciously chooses, and trusts his experiencing, of which, even if he is fortunate, he has only partial glimpses in his awareness.

If this is a reasonable description of the functioning of consciousness when all is going well, why does the rift develop in so many of us, to the point that organismically we are moving in one direction, and in our conscious life are struggling in another?

I am interested that Whyte and I give sharply different explanations of the way in which this dissociation comes about, but very similar descriptions of the condition itself. A brief summary can scarcely do justice to his thought, but he believes that the tendency of European or Western man to lose his proper organic integration has come about through the peculiarly Western development of static concepts—in the formation of our language, in our thought, in our philosophy. Though nature is clearly process, man has been caught in his own fixed forms of thought: "Deliberate behavior was organized by the use of static concepts, while spontaneous behavior continued to express a formative process; that special part of nature which we call thought thus became alien in form to the rest of nature . . ." (Whyte, 1949, p. 39). It is in this fashion, he believes, that a dissociation develops in which "mutually incompatible systems of behavior compete for control" (Whyte, 1949, p. 44). It is his judgment that this rift is more profound in men than in women because for various reasons, woman's special functions "link her thought more closely to those organic processes which maintain the animal harmony" (Whyte, 1949, p. 40).

My own explanation has more to do with the personal dynamics of the individual. Love by the parent or significant other is made conditional. It is given only on the condition that the child introject certain constructs and values as his own, otherwise he will not be perceived as worthwhile, as worthy of love. These constructs are rigid and static since they are not a part of the child's normal process of evaluating his experience. He tends to disregard his own experiencing process wherever it conflicts with these constructs, and thus to this degree cuts himself off from his organic functioning, becoming to this degree dissociated. If the conditions of worth imposed on him are numerous and significant, then the dissociation can become very great, and the psychological consequences serious indeed (Rogers, 1959, pp. 221–33).

I have gradually come to see this dissociation, rift, estrangement, as something learned, a perverse channeling of some of the actualizing tendency into behaviors which do not actualize. In this respect it would be similar to the situation in which sexual urges can, through learning, be channeled perversely into behaviors far removed from the physiological and evolutionary ends of these impulses. In this respect my thinking has changed during the past decade. Ten years ago I was endeavoring to explain the rift between self and experience, between conscious goals and organismic directions, as something natural and necessary, albeit unfortunate. Now I believe that individuals are culturally conditioned, rewarded, reinforced, for behaviors which are in fact perversions of the natural directions of the unitary actualizing tendency. As Whyte says, "The conflict between spontaneous and deliberate behavior would never have represented more than a normal difficulty of choice had the influence of the social tradition been favorable to the maintenance of the overriding coordination" (1949, p. 44).

Both Whyte and I see the end result as similar, in that dissociated man is best described as man consciously behaving in terms of static constructs and abstractions and unconsciously behaving in terms of the actualizing tendency. This is in sharp contrast to the healthy, well-functioning person who lives in close and confident relationship to his own ongoing organismic process, nonconscious as well as conscious. I see constructive outcomes in therapy and Whyte sees constructive developments in society as possible only in terms of the human individual who trusts his own inner directions and whose awareness is a part of and integrated with the process nature of his organic functioning. Whyte states the goal as being "the recovery of animal harmony in the differentiated form appropriate to man at this stage of history" (1949, p. 199). I have described the functioning of the psychologically mature individual as being similar in many ways to that of the infant, except that the fluid process of experiencing has more scope and sweep, and that the mature individual, like the child, "trusts and uses the wisdom of his organism, with the difference that he is able to do so knowingly" (Rogers, 1962c, p. 14).

Let me endeavor to summarize my thoughts on this matter. I have said that the extremely common estrangement of conscious man from his directional organismic processes is not a necessary part of man's nature. It is instead something learned, and to an especially high degree in our Western culture. It is characterized by behaviors which are guided by rigid concepts and constructs, interrupted at times by behaviors guided by the organismic processes. The satisfaction of fulfillment of the actualizing tendency has become bifurcated into incompatible behavioral systems, of which one may be dominant at one moment, and the other dominant at another moment, but at a continual cost of strain and inefficiency. This dissociation which exists in most of us is the pattern and the basis of all psychological pathology in man, and the basis of all his social pathology as well. This, at least, is my view.

The natural and efficient mode of living as a human being, however, a mode partially achieved by individuals whom we term psychologically mature, does not involve this dissociation, this bifurcation. Instead, such a person exhibits a trust in the directions of his inner organismic processes which, with consciousness participating in a coordinated rather than a competitive fashion, carry him forward in a total, unified, integrated, adaptive, and changing encounter with life and its challenges.

I trust that the significance which I attach to the function of the actualizing tendency is indicated by the preceding paragraph. The tragic condition of man is that he has lost confidence in his own nonconscious inner directions. Again, I cannot refrain from quoting Whyte's words which express my own view: "Western man stands out as a highly developed but bizarre distortion of the human animal" (1949, p. 46). To me the remedy for this situation is the incredibly difficult but not impossible task of permitting the human individual to grow and develop in a continuing confident relationship to the formative actualizing tendency and process in himself. If awareness and conscious thought are seen as a part of life—not its master nor its opponent, but an illumination of the developing processes within the individual—then man's total life can be the unified and unifying experience which seems characteristic in nature. If man's magnificent symbolizing capacity can develop as a part of and guided by the tendency toward fulfillment which exists in him as in every creature, then the "animal harmony" is never lost, and becomes a human harmony and human wholeness simply because our species is capable of greater richness of experience than any other.

And if the skeptical and natural question is raised, "Yes, but how? How could this possibly come about?" then it seems to me that the illustration I gave of research regarding the therapeutic relationship is a very small but hopefully a significant signpost in this respect. Our capacity for scientific investigation can help us. It seems very probable that the conditions which promote dissociation, which bifurcate the actualizing tendency, can be empirically identified. I have pointed out two types of hypotheses already formulated by Whyte and myself, which lie at hand for testing. The conditions which are associated with the restoration of unity and integration in the individual are, as I have indicated, already in process of being identified. The conditions which would promote a continuing internal harmony in children, without the all too common learning of dissociation, can also be identified and put to preventive use. We can, if we will, I believe, use our scientific skills to help us keep man whole and unified, a creature whose actualizing tendency will be continually forming him in the direction of a richer and more fulfilling relationship to life.

## SUMMARY

I have endeavored to say three things. First, there is a tendency toward fulfillment which is the most basic aspect of the life of any organism. It is the substratum of anything we might term motivation.

Second, I have questioned whether the formulation of theories of specific motives moves us forward in research. Since the major usefulness of theories is to stimulate research, I question the value of specific motivational constructs. Through an illustration, I have endeavored to indicate that the determinants of any given set of complex behaviors may perhaps be more accurately hypothesized from careful naturalistic observation than from thinking in terms of "motives."

Third, and finally, I have pointed out that in nature the actualizing tendency usually brings about a unified and integrated behavioral process, often highly complex in character. Why in man does it so often produce bifurcated systems—conscious versus unconscious, self versus the experiencing process, conceived values versus experienced values? I have hypothesized that this is due to specific types of social learning, especially predominant in Western culture, and not a *necessary* part of human living. If this type of learning is not a necessary element of human life, there would seem to be some possibility that it might be changed.

## REFERENCES

Barrett-Lennard, G. T.   Dimensions of therapist response as causal factors in therapeutic change. *Psychol. Monogr.*, in press.

Beach, F. A.   The descent of instinct. *Psychol. Rev.*, 1955, 62, 401–410.

Berlyne, D. E.   *Conflict, arousal, and curiosity*. New York: McGraw-Hill, 1960.

Bertalanffy, L.   *Problems of Life*. New York: Harper Torchbooks, 1960 (first published 1952).

Dember, W. N., Earl, R. W., & Paradise, N.   Response by rats to differential stimulus complexity. *J. comp. physiol. Psychol.*, 1957, 50, 514–518.

Freud, S.   Instincts and their vicissitudes. *Collected Papers*. London: Hogarth Press and Inst. of Psychoanalysis, 1953. Vol. IV, pp. 60–83.

Goldstein, K. *Human nature in the light of psychopathology.* Cambridge: Harvard Univer. Press, 1947.

Halkides, G. An experimental study of four conditions necessary for therapeutic change. Unpublished doctoral dissertation, Univer. of Chicago, 1958.

Harlow, H. F. Motivation as a factor in the acquisition of new responses. *Current theory and research in motivation: a symposium.* Lincoln, Neb.: Univer. of Nebraska Press, 1953. Pp. 24–49.

Polanyi, M. *Personal knowledge.* Chicago: Univer. of Chicago Press, 1958.

Rogers, C. R. The necessary and sufficient conditions of therapeutic personality change. *J. consult. Psychol.,* 1957, *21,* 95–103.

Rogers, C. R. A theory of therapy, personality, and interpersonal relationships. In S. Koch (Ed.), *Psychology: a study of a science.* New York: McGraw-Hill. Vol. III, 1959. Pp. 184–256.

Rogers, C. R. The interpersonal relationship: the core of guidance. *Harv. Educ. Rev.,* 1962, *32,* 416–429. (a)

Rogers, C. R. Toward becoming a fully functioning person. In *Perceiving, behaving, becoming.* 1962 Yearbook, Assoc. for Supervision and Curriculum Dev., Washington, D. C.: Nat. Educ. Assn., 1962, 21–33. (b)

Rogers, C. R. Toward a modern approach to values. Unpublished manuscript, 1962. (c)

Spotts, J. E. The perception of positive regard by relatively successful and relatively unsuccessful clients. Unpublished manuscript. Wisconsin Psychiatric Institute: Research Reports, 1962.

Stoler, N. Client likability: a variable in the study of psychotherapy. *J. consult. Psychol.,* in press.

Truax, C. B. The relationship between the level of accurate empathy offered in psychotherapy and case outcome. Unpublished manuscript. Wisconsin Psychiatric Institute: Research Reports, 1962.

Truax, C. B., Liccione, J., & Rosenberg, M. Psychological test evaluations of personality change in high conditions therapy, low conditions therapy, and control patients. Unpublished manuscript. Wisconsin Psychiatric Institute: Research Reports, 1962.

White, R. W. Motivation reconsidered: the concept of competence. *Psychol. Rev.,* 1959, *66,* 297–333.

Whyte, L. L. *The next development in man.* New York: Mentor Books, 1949.

Whyte, L. L. *The unconscious before Freud.* London: Tavistock Publications, 1960.

# V
## Functional Problems and the Measurement of Motivation

The gathering of systematic, experimental data relevant to the problems of the activation and direction of behavior has been a vital theme in the evolution of the many-faceted area of motivation. The plethora of theoretical contentions, the multiple levels of discourse, the range of phenomena discussed, and the proliferation of overlapping terminology have not prevented and, indeed, may have fostered the accumulation of a vast body of empirical data, particularly in recent years. In this section will be found a selection of statements of empirical issues and research results. Each article has been a milestone from which new directions in theory and research have developed. Koch's 1951 discussion of the status of motivational psychology contains a succinct statement of the imbalance which existed between motivational theory and the amount of centrally relevant supporting data, as well as an elegant delineation of the specific problem clusters which at that time comprised the major focus of empirical studies. Koch later concluded that his "theoretically neutral" map of the field was inaccurate in that it omitted reference to positive, or intrinsic, motivation. Nevertheless, he skillfully outlined the empirical domains as they then appeared and in so doing stimulated further studies on those topics.

Even before Koch had included the measurement of needs as a problem area, that issue had been recognized and a classic experimental effort to gauge the relative strength of normal drives in the white rat had been carried out by C. J. Warden. He used an obstruction box and counted the number of crossings of an electrified grill which would be made in a given period of time by motivated animals who could reach an appropriate goal object only in this way. Warden's results are still cited as part of the lore of motivational psychology, although few would regard them as successful with respect to their original aim. The ability to measure needs was not to come that easily to motivation. A more sophisticated attempt to relate strength of behavior to intensity of a particular drive, hunger, is represented in Kimble's article. His findings may represent the closest approach to a precisely specified functional relationship of this type, but it is now known to be highly restricted to the conditions of his study rather than to represent a general law.

Motivation may, as we have seen, be treated in a variety of contexts and some of the most fruitful developments have come from the interplay of different approaches. A particularly good example was the interaction between the Freudian concept of fear, or anxiety, and the learning principles of the drive theorists. It led, for one thing, to the reformulation of fear into learning theory terminology and to the treatment of fear as a learnable drive. Neal Miller's research on fear as an acquirable drive was the cornerstone of a hardy edifice of empirical studies which established the properties of fear as a behavior determinant. It led to the further elaboration of drive and learning theory and proved useful in the systematic examination of human anxiety in the laboratory as well as the clinic. Janet Taylor also conceived of anxiety as a drive and tested her conception in an eyelid conditioning situation. For this, she developed a paper and pencil test to assess anxiety, or emotionally based drive, and thereby launched a vigorous new movement in research, a movement which brought the study of individual differences as measured by standardized tests into contact with traditional experimental methodology and theory. The body of literature dealing with test-defined anxiety represents one of the two most influential areas of systematic research in human motivation over the last 20 years.

The other major area of systematic research in human motivation to have arisen following the development of a method for assessing a relevant human motive is that pertaining to achievement motivation. David C. McClelland and his collaborators set out to measure motives as revealed in fantasy. After having established the feasibility of their method by showing changes in fantasy behavior with different intensities of hunger, they determined the effects of experimentally aroused achievement motivation upon fantasy as shown in thematic apperception. These effects, which are reported in the article reproduced here, were then applied to the creation of a projective test for achievement motivation. The test has been widely used to study the origin and consequences of achievement motivation in individuals and in cultures as a whole. Moreover, work in this area has provided the starting point for laboratory studies of the dynamics of task choice and perseverance, particularly in the work of men like John Atkinson.

While students of motivation must naturally keep informed of the results of current research, it is from a knowledge of germinal investigations such as those included here that the relevance of the many derivative studies which have since appeared may be evaluated.

# 23 • Sigmund Koch

## *The Current Status of Motivational Psychology*

The criticisms by Sigmund Koch of the adequacy of the methodological and theoretical orthodoxies of the Hullian era were among the first of a long line and heralded the end of what he called the "Golden Age" of learning theory. The style of his general attack upon the hypothetico-deductive method of the time is anticipated in this selection as he deplores the state of motivation theories in particular. In 1951, however, Koch was still thinking within the frame of problems set by the orientation he was to criticize more extensively at a later date. In this article, then, can be seen the shadow of new developments as well as a statement of what many psychologists have considered to be the major functional problems of motivational psychology.

*Disorientation is* the natural condition of psychology, but the quality and amount of this commodity change at different periods. During the two decades or so before the war, when the tidy trinity of S–R, Gestalt and Psychoanalytic types of theory dominated the scene, disorientation was a property of the whole body psychological, rather than its component parts. Members of each theoretical school had a clear, if over-optimistic, sense of direction; disorientation was a molar product of the "cross-purposeful" relations of each theoretical camp to the others.

With the conclusion of total war, psychology seems now to have entered an era of total disorientation. Pressures deriving from the needs of a sick society, and, more directly, the unavailability, to a greatly expanded corps of psychological and social technologists, of adequate scientific tools for meeting these needs, have led to a widespread re-

The substance of this paper was presented as part of a Symposium on Motivation, held April 6, 1950, at the meeting of the Southern Society for Philosophy and Psychology in Nashville, Tenn. The paper is published exactly as given, except for an altered final paragraph and the inclusion of references. The references are included for illustrative and explicative purposes. They are not intended to provide a comprehensive, or even a representative, bibliography of the literature on motivation.

This article is reproduced in full from the *Psychological Review*, 1951, 58, 147–154. Reprinted by permission of the American Psychological Association and the author.

evaluation of theoretical and fundamental psychology. A sense that the chief pre-war theoretical programs were over-ambitious in scope, prematurely timed in relation to extant empirical knowledge, is beginning to emerge.

I feel that nothing could be, *in principle*, more salutary than this recognition of inadequacy, but the shock of recognition has been a difficult trauma to contain. The messianic impulse rules the day—psychology is to be saved, and the H bomb foiled by group dynamics, cybernetics, transactional observation, projective measurement, unified social science theory, the new look in perception; by demolition of the barricades separating learning, perception and motivation; by the exhaustive analysis of bar-pressing behavior, etc. Even the pre-war messiahs (who shall remain nameless) have lost their old buoyancy. One of them is calling ruefully for "neurological models" despite a long and checkered history of *amours* with "schematic sow bugs" and the like, and others appear to be feeling only half safe, after many years of militant confidence.

One cannot avoid strong concern over the current messianic wave. Most of the very real deficiencies of the synoptic pre-war theories seem generously compounded, not reduced, in the new messages. Apparently the important lesson has not been learned. The lesson is very simple and very painful. It reads: Psychology is not ready for high-order theory of any great range or predictive power. We lack basic areas of empirical knowledge of the sort necessary for adequate theory. We are even a long way from the resolution of many methodological problems, answers to which are crucial to adequate construction of theory. Contrary to certain of the stereotypes of the thirties and forties, we are *not* in a "Galilean era" of theoretical construction; we are closer to Thales than we are to Galileo. We are a science still groping for the identification of our basic variables.

Only *after* learning this lesson of humility will it become possible to make efficient progress towards the objectives of sound theory, and powerful technology. I believe that a sober, rational program for the rôle of theoretical psychology in working towards these objectives can already be blocked out, but this report is not the place for the discussion of such a program.[1] I shall try instead to derive a few of the implications of our "lesson of humility" for the current status of "motivational psychology."

Nowhere is disorientation—old style or new—more evident than in

---

[1] I believe that progress towards adequate theory can only be achieved by substituting for the continued, undisciplined spinning of *comprehensive psychological "theories,"* the pursuit of theoretical psychology, as defined in terms of a set of modest objectives geared to a realistic estimate of the status of our knowledge. I have attempted to outline such a set of *feasible* objectives for theoretical psychology in an article (*18*) which will appear in this JOURNAL.

the field of motivation. Every major theory of behavior of the modern period makes some provision for the incorporation of variables which represent motivational processes. Concepts of the most diverse sorts carry this systematic burden in the different theories. They vary in every possible dimension. They vary in level of analysis, from assorted degrees of the molar in behavioral theories, to assorted degrees of the molecular in physiological theories. They vary in *generality* from Freud's *libido* and McDougall's *horme*, to the tension systems which Lewin correlates with his quasi-needs and intentions. To these concepts may be imputed the most widely divergent properties: In some theories they may represent a class of persisting stimuli (*e.g.*, Guthrie, earlier Hull); in others an energy source (Freud, McDougall, instinct theory); in still others a class of regulating and directing mechanisms (Morgan's C.M.S., Köhler's brain-field vectors, Hull's $r_G$, etc.). Again, there is wide variation in the way in which motivational variables are interrelated with other classes of variables (learning, perceptual, etc.) in the different theories.

To this cacophony of theoretical "be-bop," the "new disorientation" has added some new dissonances. Krech, for instance, would save the day by proposing, as the central construct of psychology, a notion of "dynamic systems" which "vary along the dimensions of Isolation, Differentiation and Tension" (*19*, p. 78). The arbitrarily discriminated fields of motivation, learning and perception immediately wither away, everything now becoming a global matter of dynamic systems. Of course, "variations of . . . Tension will contribute to the conscious correlate of . . . desire, need, demand," and "these particular conscious correlates are the aspects of experience to which most of us refer when we speak about 'motivation'" (*19*, pp. 78–79). Hochberg and Gleitman, too, have a way out. They "would subsume motivational phenomena under perceptual laws" (*12*, p. 183).

Confronted with this over-profusion of conflicting "theory," the hygienic thing to do is to turn towards the facts. What we find is a ridiculously meager set of scattered experimental findings and empirical observations. Moreover much of this material proves, on close analysis, to be ambiguous, unreliable, of indeterminate generality, or downright trivial.

The rate of progress in the accumulation of basic empirical relationships has been fantastically slow. Take as a single example of his creeping development the history of the research on the rôle of differential intensities of primary needs or drives in what was called "learning." This, after all, is not an unimportant problem; every theory of behavior must make some commitment with regard to learning-motivation interrelations. In 1918 Szymansky (*43*) reported that mice learn a simple maze with increasing rapidity as hunger is increased from ½ to 21–24 hours. Learning rate is therefore a positive function of strength of motivation. During the next 15 years or so, a few more experiments of similar design were made, with similar conclusions, despite the fact that Ligon's (*24*) 6- and 12-hour groups showed an inversion. By the mid-thirties, psychology had finally, via the latent learning experiments, won its way to the distinction between learning and performance. With this distinction nothing was done for another dozen years or thereabouts, except for the prosecution of a violent quarrel over whether latent learning demonstrates the latent death of reinforcement theory. It was, in any case, a well-known reinforcement theorist (*14*), who, by the early forties, helped psychologists see that the initial question must be broken down into two major problem clusters—one concerning the rôle of drive strength in the *acquisition* of habit structures, and the other having to do with the rôle of drive strength in the utilization (performance) of habit structures already learned. By 1950 we have accumulated some slight evidence, far from quantitatively exact, about the form of the relationship between drive intensity and *vigor* of performance, at least in the case of a single drive (hunger), a single organism (the rat), and a single response (bar pressing) (*37, 40*). With regard to the effect of variations in drive strength on the rate of trace or habit acquisition, we have not been quite so fortunate. The past decade has yielded some half dozen rat experiments in two standard situations (*e.g., 9, 17, 26, 41*). Most of these studies show *no effect* of varied food-deprivation periods on the indirect measure of acquisition rate; some, however, *do*.

Now, I submit that it is absurd to proceed with the construction of theories, resembling in any degree the ambitiousness of extant formulations, on the basis of experimental material of this order. The alternative is the drab one of working modestly *towards* theory, and this must be done on a number of fronts. In the area of motivation perhaps the most important need is for a sharp acceleration of progress in the accumulation of "theoretically neutral" empirical knowledge.[2]

Thus I cannot discharge the obligation imposed on me by this symposium in any direct way. The systematic status of "motivation" cannot be defined by anyone; it can only emerge, along with some future emergence of systematic psychology. What I can do is to examine, briefly, the status of the empirical facts in the field, because the status of motivation is defined by these facts, and not by the empty super-struc-

---

[2] The expression "theoretically neutral" may require explanation. Without getting twisted in the epistemology of bias, reference frames, etc., I may say this: There is good evidence to suggest that, at those points where the major theoretical programs have been in contact with empirical materials, there has been a growing convergence towards the identification, manipulation and recording of *common experimental variables*, both independent and dependent. Such commonly acknowledged experimental variables may be regarded as "theoretically neutral," and experiments designed to explore relations among such variables may be said to give "theoretically neutral" knowledge.

tures of current theory. Since this empirical material, however limited, must provide the starting point for the accelerated development we are calling for, it will be well to present an outline of the way in which the major problem clusters have planlessly evolved.

Any "theoretically neutral" map of the field of motivation must cope with an amorphous and gappy terrain. Any such map must be selective, but my map will try to avoid the kind of selectivity that springs from a desire to chart the field as it should be, rather than as it is. There is no implication that all areas listed are important or indispensable; I imply only that they exist. All that I can squeeze into this report is a map of my map.

As I see it, there are five major problem clusters in the current psychology of motivation. Summarily, these are: I *Functional Problems* (concerning the rôles of needs in behavior), II *Genetic Problems,* III *Problems Concerning Need Interaction and Conflict,* IV *"Mensurational" Problems,* and V *Problems Relating to the Organization of Needs in Personality.*

These areas have emerged independently of coöperative research planning or coördination. They are complexly interrelated, but we do not know how. Advance in any one of these areas often presupposes the application of knowledge that we do not have in some one or more of the others. But this is what we have, and we might as well admit it.

Let us briefly identify these areas.


# I.  FUNCTIONAL PROBLEMS

The problems here are central to the development of behavior theory. The concern is with the general relations between needs and: (a) other behavior determinants (relating to learning, perception, etc.), and (b) final behavior or performance. Functional research has been concentrated in four main sub-areas:

(1) *The Relations between Needs and Activity* (both general and specific) (32, pp. 368–381, 39). This has long existed as a semi-independent field. In the present state of motivation research, logic would seem to demand the subsumption of this field under the relations between needs and performance.

(2) *The Relations between Needs and Perception* (and allied processes). Here, until recently, we have had only a series of demonstration experiments (2, 4). Currently the sultry glare of the "new look" is producing a flare-up of *conditional* research interest (3, 38, 44) even to the point of a search for "intervening mechanisms." Worthy as such a search may be, my guess is that success in this quest for mediating mechanisms must await *general* advance in psychological theory.

(3) *Relations between Needs and Learning.* Progress in this intricate field has been mainly a matter of achieving the ability to ask *some* of the meaningful questions. We have practically none of the answers. Two principal classes of questions have arisen: The first concerns the rôle of needs in the selective determination of the content of learning (*e.g.*, the extensive literature of "latent learning"). This set of questions is qualitative. The second concerns the rôle of needs in determining the rate of acquisition of learning structures (habits, traces) (*9, 17, 26, 41*). These questions are, of course, quantitative.

(4) *Relations between Needs and Performance.* This area has also bifurcated into two as yet almost entirely unexplored sets of questions. One of them has to do with the rôle of needs in determining which learning structures are activated under given conditions of stimulation (*e.g.*, *13, 20*, and certain of the "latent learning" experiments). The other looks into the effects of differential need intensity on the vigor with which preëxistent learning structures are activated (*e.g.*, *37, 40*).

## II. GENETIC PROBLEMS

The genetic research cluster deals with the analysis of: (1) primary need systems, (2) acquired need systems, and (3) the learning mechanisms responsible for the modification of primary and the development of acquired needs.

*(1) Primary needs.* A mass of research, most of it at the physiological level, and a little at the psychological level, has been accumulated. At the physiological level some progress has been made in the analysis of biological and neural mechanisms associated with primary need states, most conspicuously in the cases of hunger and sex (*32*, pp. 390–401, 418–438). But what we know about even these needs is microscopic in comparison to what we still have to learn. At the psychological level we have some descriptive material on the behavior tendencies connected with primary needs and their learned patterning. The need for increasing this pathetically limited knowledge has been sharply undervalued.

*(2) Acquired needs.* Social psychologists, sociologists and cultural anthropologists have provided us with descriptive identifications of major acquired need systems as the latter operate in the statistically defined "individuals" of various cultures and sub-cultures (*15, 28*). Clinical psychologists and psychiatrists have contributed cross-sectional and longitudinal descriptions of acquired need systems as the latter operate uniquely in individuals (*34, 36, 42*). I doubt that the specific findings here are of significance to fundamental psychology, although certain of the descriptive and "mensurational" techniques used in these studies *may be.*

*(3) Learning mechanisms responsible for need development.* The problems in this group are crucial to adequate motivational theory. They are perhaps the most knotty problems that behavior theory must confront. But what do we have? A handful of studies built around a series of vague speculations on (a) "functional autonomy" (*1*), (b) "response produced stimulation" (*6, 30, 31, 33*) and (c) "secondary reinforcement" (*7, 8, 11, 14*).

## III.  NEED INTERACTION AND CONFLICT

Behavior is never motivated by a single need; it is always a complex function of a plurality of co-acting needs. In this immensely complex area we have virtually no soundly established knowledge. Psychoanalysts and clinicians have given us a few orienting insights and some scattered clinical data. But from experiments we have nothing more than a few surface-scratching studies of irrelevant drive (*45*), drive combination (*16, 17*) and conflict (*6, 29*). Some of these studies come from fundamental psychologists, who, as a group, have shown insufficient interest in these problems; others come from the psychopathologists (*25, 27*).

## IV.  NEED MEASUREMENT

"Measurement" is a metaphor in this connection, as it usually is in psychology. Of course, we have our well-known 86 techniques for estimating the strength and qualitative character of needs in humans and other animals (*5, 14, 23, 35*), but we have not even begun to tackle those scaling problems, solutions to which are most vital to *fundamental* advance. For instance, we still have not explored the possibility of expressing strength of primary motivation in units which permit translation from one drive to others.

## V.  ORGANIZATION OF NEEDS IN PERSONALITY

This area can only arbitrarily be separated from the general problems of need measurement. Ability to measure or estimate isolated need systems is only a part of what we require, if psychology is to be able to represent its "initial conditions" in a way necessary for prediction. We need also descriptive tools for representing the *interrelations* of needs within the individual. Freud (*10*) and Lewin (*21, 22, 23*) (and certain of the personality theorists) have given us some crude, if illuminating, leads in this direction. But they are crude, and they are only leads. The problems of this and the preceding cluster are partly methodological in nature, but concrete solutions will involve much experimentation.

It should be clear by now that what we are mapping can hardly be called "terrain." The subject-matter of our map is still in the gaseous stage, to borrow a geophysical metaphor, and will require much cooling before it assumes determinate form. That cooling can only be precipitated by tough-minded research, and it is redundant to add that the rate of cooling will depend on the rate of research.

There may be a danger in concentrating, as I necessarily have, on only one of the preconditions to sound progress in a field like motivation— the need for an accelerated rate of fundamental research. I hope that my position will not be interpreted as merely another of the indiscriminate invitations to research of the sort connected with the usual laments about the backward condition of the social sciences. If I have asked for research, it is research of a special kind. It is research designed to provide the inductive materials for theory in some non-illusory sense of the word. Thus, it is research guided by a strategy based on an analysis of the prerequisites of adequate theory. The programming of such research must start from an assessment of what is useful and what expendable, what is common and what specific in extant theoretical sallies. It must presuppose a search for those "theoretically neutral" empirical variables which have emerged as common components of the concrete research inspired by our pre-theoretical and quasi-theoretical thinking; it must also presuppose an effort to chart the contours of existing knowledge in terms of the interrelations among such variables. The research I have in mind would be calculated to increase the accuracy, fill in the finer details, and enlarge the boundaries of such "theoretically neutral" knowledge. Yet it would not preclude *conceptual* experimentation with independent theoretical hypotheses or limited-scope postulate sets which have a domain corresponding to some part of this knowledge. Indeed, our fund of theoretically neutral knowledge could not grow without the continuous and intensive prosecution of such theoretical endeavors. One of the main functions of our inventory of theoretically neutral knowledge would be to make attempts at concrete theory-construction feasible, and one of the main results of these concrete, if limited, theoretical attempts would be the enrichment of such knowledge. Only in this way, by continual interplay between restricted, even fragmentary, theoretical attempts, and our inventory of theoretically neutral knowledge, can we purchase our slow way towards theory of a scope and predictive fertility sufficient to justify the business of psychology.

## REFERENCES

1. Allport, G. *Personality*. New York: Henry Holt and Co., 1937.
2. Ansbacher, H. Perception of number as affected by the monetary value of the objects. *Arch. Psychol.*, 1937, No. 215.
3. Bruner, J. S., & Postman, L. Perception, cognition, and behavior. *J. Personality*, 1949, *18*, 14–31.
4. Carmichael, L., Hogan, H. P., & Walter, A. A. An experimental study of the effect of language on the reproduction of visually perceived form. *J. exp. Psychol.*, 1932, *15*, 73–86.
5. Cattell, R. B. *Description and measurement of personality*. Yonkers: World Book Co., 1946.
6. Dollard, J., & Miller, N. E. *Personality and psychotherapy: an analysis in terms of learning, thinking and culture*. New York: McGraw-Hill, 1950.
7. Estes, W. K. Generalization of secondary reinforcement from the primary drive. *J. comp. physiol. Psychol.*, 1949, *42*, 286–295.
8. Estes, W. K. A study of motivating conditions necesary for secondary reinforcement. *J. exp. Psychol.*, 1949, *39*, 306–310.
9. Finan, J. L. Quantitative studies in motivation. I. Strength of conditioning in rats under varying degrees of hunger. *J. comp. Psychol.*, 1940, *29*, 119–134.
10. Freud, S. *The ego and the id*. London: Hogarth, 1927.
11. Grice, G. R. The relation of secondary reinforcement to delayed reward in visual discrimination learning. *J. exp. Psychol.*, 1948, *38*, 1–16.
12. Hochberg, J. E., & Gleitman, H. Towards a reformulation of the perception-motivation dichotomy. *J. Personality*, 1949, *18*, 180–191.
13. Hull, C. L. Differential habituation to internal stimuli in the albino rat. *J. comp. Psychol.*, 1933, *16*, 255–273.
14. Hull, C. L. *Principles of behavior*. New York: Appleton-Century, 1943.
15. Kardiner, A. *The psychological frontiers of society*. New York: Columbia Univer. Press, 1945.
16. Kendler, H. H. Drive interaction. I. Learning as a function of the simultaneous presence of the hunger and thirst drive. *J. exp. Psychol.*, 1945, *35*, 96–109.
17. Kendler, H. H. Drive interaction. II. Experimental analysis of the role of drive in learning theory. *J. exp. Psychol.*, 1945, *35*, 188–198.
18. Koch, S. Theoretical psychology, 1950: an overview. *Psychol. Rev.*, 1951, *58*, in press.
19. Krech, D. Notes toward a psychological theory. *J. Personality*, 1949, *18*, 66–87.
20. Leeper, R. The role of motivation in learning: a study of the phenomenon of differential motivational control of the utilization of habits. *J. genet. Psychol.*, 1935, *46*, 3–40.
21. Lewin, K. *Dynamic theory of personality*. New York: McGraw-Hill, 1935.

22. Lewin, K. *Principles of topological psychology.* New York: McGraw-Hill, 1936.

23. Lewin, K. The conceptual representation and the measurement of psychological forces. *Contr. Psychol. Theory,* Vol. 1, No. 4. Durham, N. C.: Duke Univer. Press, 1938.

24. Ligon, E. M. A comparative study of certain incentives in the learning of the white rat. *Comp. Psychol. Monogr.,* 1929, 6(2), 1–95.

25. Luria, A. R. *The nature of human conflicts.* New York: Liveright, 1932.

26. MacDuff, M. N. The effect on retention of varying degrees of motivation during learning in rats. *J. comp. Psychol.,* 1946, 39, 207–240.

27. Masserman, J. H. *Behavior and neurosis.* Chicago: Chicago Univer. Press, 1943.

28. Mead, M. *Cooperation and competition among primitive people.* New York: McGraw-Hill, 1937.

29. Miller, N. E. Experimental studies of conflict. In J. McV. Hunt (Ed.), *Personality and the behavior disorders.* New York: Ronald Press, 1944. Vol. 1.

30. Miller, N. E. Studies of fear as an acquirable drive. I. Fear as motivation and fear-reduction as reinforcement in the learning of new responses. *J. exp. Psychol.,* 1948, 38, 89–101.

31. Miller, N. E., & Dollard, J. *Social learning and imitation.* New Haven: Yale Univer. Press, 1941.

32. Morgan, C. T. *Physiological psychology.* (2nd ed.) New York: McGraw-Hill, 1950, Chap. 17.

33. Mowrer, O. H. A stimulus-response analysis of anxiety and its role as a reinforcing agent. *Psychol. Rev.,* 1939, 46, 553–565.

34. Mullahy, P. (Ed.) *A study of interpersonal relations.* New York: Hermitage Press, 1949.

35. Murphy, G. *Personality.* New York: Harper & Bros., 1947.

36. Murray, H. A. *Explorations in personality.* New York: Oxford Univer. Press, 1938.

37. Perin, C. T. Behavior potentiality as a joint function of the amount of training and the degree of hunger at the time of extinction. *J. exp. Psychol.,* 1942, 30, 93–113.

38. Proshansky, H., & Murphy, G. The effects of reward and punishment on perception. *J. Psychol.,* 1942, 13, 295–305.

39. Reed, J. D. Spontaneous activity of animals: a review of the literature since 1929. *Psychol. Bull.,* 1947, 44, 393–412.

40. Saltzman, I., & Koch, S. The effect of low intensities of hunger on the behavior mediated by a habit of maximum strength. *J. exp. Psychol.,* 1948, 38, 347–370.

41. Strassburger, R. C. Resistance to extinction of a conditioned operant as related to drive level at reinforcement. *J. exp. Psychol.,* 1950, 40, 473–487.

42. Sullivan, H. S. *Conceptions of modern psychiatry.* Washington, D. C.: The William Alanson White Psychiatric Foundation, 1947.

43. Szymanski, J. S. Ein experimenteller Beitrag zur Analyse der bei Entste-

hung neuer Gewohnheiten mitwirkenden Faktoren. *Pflüg. arch. ges. Physiol.*, 1918, *170*, 197–220.

44. Wallach, H.   Some considerations concerning the relation between perception and cognition. *J. Personality*, 1949, *18*, 6–13.

45. Webb, W.   The motivational aspect of an irrelevant drive in the behavior of the white rat. *J. exp. Psychol.*, 1949, *39*, 1–14.

# 24 • Carl J. Warden

## The Relative Strength and Persistence
## of the Normal Drives
## in the White Rat

The effort to assess the strength of a drive by pitting it against a standard obstacle is not patently unreasonable, and it offers the intriguing possibility of comparing the strengths of various drive states in terms of their results against the same obstacle. The Columbia Obstruction Method was devised with this strategy in mind. It failed for a number of reasons. There was the issue of how to determine when drive strength in any modality was at a maximum. There was the problem of drive interaction, that is, the likelihood that the pain of the electric shock was a drive which differentially affected the intensities of other drives which were to be gauged against it. There was the difficulty that learned fear became an additional motivational factor in the situation after the initial crossings had been made. Other factors, too, led to the abandonment of the obstruction method as a means of measuring drive. The empirical information gained from the Columbia technique has retained interest, however, and the project represented a courageous effort from which much was learned.

*The central purpose* of the project, as stated in the preceding section, was to determine the relative strength and persistence of the more important drives in the white rat when tested under the most natural conditions, e.g., with all conditions normal except for some definite and measurable deprivation of the incentive. We shall speak of the drives as tested under these conditions as "normal" drives. The value of the present study over previous studies of dynamic behavior lies not merely in the fact that a more direct and controlled method (The Columbia Obstruction Method) was used in the measurement of the several drives, but even more in the fact that the project was so standardized throughout that the scores of the various drives may be directly compared with one another. This standardization makes possible a fairly definite ranking of the drives and thus gives us a picture of the natural dynamic behavior patterns of the white rat, within the limitations of a single test method.

Before entering upon an analysis and comparison of the actual scores, it will be necessary to direct attention to the extent to which standardization was carried in method and procedure—since the validity of comparing the scores directly from drive to drive must depend, in the last analysis, upon the thoroughness of such standardization. This aspect of the problem will be covered in the first sub-section, and this will be followed by a second sub-section dealing with the comparison of the scores indicating the ranking of the different drives.

## STANDARDIZATION OF EXPERIMENTAL CONDITIONS

Our interest here is not to establish the validity of the Columbia Obstruction Method as an instrument for the measurement of animal drives. Our present concern is merely to show that the method was adapted to the measurement of the various drives under such uniform conditions that the scores from drive to drive may be directly compared. For the sake of clearness the conditions of uniformity adopted will be presented, in so far as possible, in tabular form. The conditions enumerated below were uniform for all the drives except for certain necessary variations as indicated.

### A. Apparatus Conditions

(See Fig. 24.1, for general diagram of apparatus)

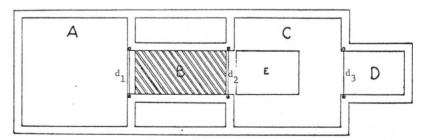

Figure 24.1.   Diagram of floor plan of the obstruction box.

A, entrance compartment; B, obstruction compartment; C, D, divided incentive compartment; E, release plate; $d_1$, manually operated door of entrance compartment; $d_2$, automatic door (operated by release plate) between two divisions of incentive compartment.

1. Compartment A (Entrance) empty except for test animal.

2. Compartment B (Obstruction) grid giving standard shock; alternating current of 60 cycles, with terminal pressure of 475 volts, external resistance of 10,100,000 ohms, and current of 0.047 milliamperes.

3. Compartment C (Incentive response-chamber) empty except for test animal.

4. Compartment D (Incentive container). Identical box used in tests on hunger, thirst, and sex.

5. Doors separating the different compartments, including the automatic release door between compartments C and D, were operated in the same manner in testing all drives, regardless of whether the incentive required the use of a given door or not.

## B. Animals Employed

1. Wistar Institute experimental colony strain throughout.

2. Animals reared at Wistar Institute until approximately 150 days of age, or first and second generation of this strain reared in our own laboratory.

3. Animals weaned at approximately 30 days; males and females reared together until 150 days of age, at which time they were segregated as to sex for 35 days (range, 33–39 days) to eliminate pregnancies. Exception: groups used in study of the maternal drive were not segregated until near term, normally the fact of pregnancy being sufficient to prevent copulation during this period; this exception was necessary in order to make the primiparous and multiparous groups strictly comparable.

4. Standard age for testing was 185 days (range, 175–196 days) or the age reached at the end of the 35-day segregation period. Exceptions: (a) Male sex drive, 28-day group were of standard age but for the longer period of sex deprivation (28 days) involved; this group can be eliminated without affecting the comparisons to be made in this section. (b) First litter, maternal drive group in which age of testing was necessarily determined by the factor of primiparity (range, 79–150 days).

5. Animals shipped to us from the Wistar Institute at approximately 150 days were thus allowed about 5 weeks to become accustomed to living conditions in our laboratory before reaching the standard test age.

## C. Incentive Conditions

1. The general plan was to deprive the animal of some one of the factors (food, water, sex, litter, etc.) of the standardized set of living conditions, keeping all other factors of the normal living conditions constant and uniform from drive to drive.

2. A summary of incentive conditions is presented in Table 24.1 of

TABLE 24.1. Summary of experimental and test conditions for normal drives.

| Drive Condition Tested | Size of Group | | | Incentive (Compartment D) | Incentive Response | Method of Keeping Other Drives Quiescent | | | | |
| | M. | F. | Comb. | | | Hunger | Thirst | Sex | Maternal | Exploratory |
|---|---|---|---|---|---|---|---|---|---|---|
| (Hunger) | | | | Sample of regular diet (McCollum's mixture) in compart. | Nibble of powdered food; 30 sec. limit | Drive being tested | Regular water supply to hour of test | Males seg. 35 days; Females in dioestrum | Only non-pregnant females without litters | Specific incentive objects present; no place to explore |
| 0 days | 10 | 10 | 20 | | | | | | | |
| 2 days | 10 | 10 | 20 | | | | | | | |
| 3 days | 10 | 10 | 20 | | | | | | | |
| 4 days | 10 | 10 | 20 | | | | | | | |
| 6 days | 10 | 10 | 20 | | | | | | | |
| 8 days | 10 | 10 | 20 | | | | | | | |
| (Thirst) | | | | Regular water bottle in compart. | Moistening tongue on damp nipple; 30 sec. limit | Regular diet, except greens omitted | Drive being tested | Same as above | Same as above | Same as above |
| 0 days | 10 | 10 | 20 | | | | | | | |
| 1 day | 10 | 10 | 20 | | | | | | | |
| 2 days | 10 | 10 | 20 | | | | | | | |
| 4 days | 10 | 10 | 20 | | | | | | | |
| 6 days | 10 | 10 | 20 | | | | | | | |
| (Sex—male) | | | | Female in cornified stage, except compart. empty for control group | Nipping, biting, nosing genitalia, mounting, etc.; 30 sec. limit | Regular diet to hour of test | Same as thirst above | Drive being tested | Same as above | Same as above |
| 0 hours | 20 | | | | | | | | | |
| 6 hours | 20 | | | | | | | | | |
| 12 hours | 20 | | | | | | | | | |
| 1 day | 20 | | | | | | | | | |
| 1 day (control) | 20 | | | | | | | | | |
| 4 days | 20 | | | | | | | | | |
| 7 days | 20 | | | | | | | | | |
| 28 days | 20 | | | | | | | | | |

| | | | | | | | | |
|---|---|---|---|---|---|---|---|---|
| (Sex—female) | | | | | | | | |
| Early congestive | 7 | Normal male, except compart. empty for control group | Nipping, biting, nosing genitalia, exposing vulva; 30 sec. limit | Same as above | Same as above | Drive being tested | Same as above | Same as above |
| Oestrum (cornified) | 21 | | | | | | | |
| Same (control) | 22 | | | | | | | |
| Late cornified | 3 | | | | | | | |
| Post-ovulative | 6 | | | | | | | |
| Dioestrum (4 stages) | 32 | | | | | | | |
| (Maternal) | | | | | | | | |
| First litter | 9 | Litter in maternity cage | Attending to litter; 30 sec. limit | Same as above | Same as above | Females with litter | Drive being tested | Same as above |
| Multiparous (stand. age) | 10 | | | | | | | |
| (Exploratory) | | | | | | | | |
| Males (stand. age) | 20 | Exploration box | Random activity; 30 sec. limit | Same as above | Same as above | Males seg. 35 days | Males only | Drive being tested |

this study. The incentives used in the apparatus were samples of usual food (McCollum's diet), water supply (metal nipple bottle system), sex object, etc., so that the incentive response was always to the sort of stimulus to which the animals had been accustomed in cage life.

3. Isolation of a given drive for testing was accomplished, in so far as isolation could be secured, by keeping drives, other than the one being tested quiescent, or at a physiological minimum during the test period. A summary of the controls utilized are shown in the last five columns of Table 24.1 of this study. The conditions for keeping any one of the given drives at a minimum while testing some other drive was constant and uniform throughout. In the testing of any drive, four of these controls were operative, so that, even if the controls should be considered inadequate, they were uniform for all normal drive conditions investigated. The adequacy of the various controls will be discussed at some length later.

## D. Procedure

1. The experimenter was eliminated by making the tests in a dark room with observation made possible by means of a specially constructed illumination hood which operated to place the experimenter outside the visual field of the test animal.

2. All tests were made between the hours of 9 P.M. and 4 A.M., or during the period when the white rat is normally most active; it was felt that maximum drive scores were most likely to be secured at this time when diurnal activity is also at a maximum. This time of day also favored better general laboratory conditions for testing.

3. The test period proper was standardized at 20 minutes immediately following the preliminary period to be next described. The advantages of a temporal over other forms of limiting the testing will be shown in the later discussion.

4. During the preliminary period, the incentive was indicated to the animal by allowing four crossings from compartment A into compartment C, with access to the incentive object in compartment D, with no shock present in compartment B. This tended to make the specific incentive dominant in the stimulation conditions afforded by the apparatus. The presence and nature of the shock was indicated to the animal by a fifth crossing, with the standard current turned on in compartment B. The testing proper followed immediately.

Exception: In testing the exploratory drive, the animal was not allowed to proceed into compartment *D*, except on the fourth and fifth crossings of the preliminary period, in order not to lower the value of the exploration box as an incentive and to allow compartment C to be thoroughly explored in the preliminary period and thus enhance the incentive value of the exploration box in the test proper. This change in procedure favored the exploratory drive somewhat, perhaps, but the scores for this drive were extremely low anyway, so that the ranking of drives is not disturbed thereby.

5. The general method of handling the animals was kept uniform; the mode of lifting the animal from incentive compartment and the rate of movement in transferring it back into the entrance compartment was developed into an automatic habit by the experimenter before being allowed to take data in connection with the project.

6. Scores were taken during the test period, covering the following types of response to the obstruction-incentive situation:

(a) Approaches—Tip of nose across threshold of door between compartments A and B, but without touching the grid, facing incentive.

(b) Contacts—Touching grid with nose or stepping upon it; partial crossings involving shock.

(c) Crossings—Complete passage over grid into incentive compartment.

7. Only one sex was tested on a given day and the apparatus washed out thoroughly at the close of each test period.

It will be noted, in checking over the above summary of conditions, that strict uniformity was had from drive to drive, with the following exceptions: (1) The maternal groups were not segregated as to sex 35 days previous to testing. This variation in conditions may well be ignored in view of the fact that they were pregnant for a period of 22 days of the 35-day period, on the average, during which time copulation would naturally be avoided. Furthermore, as Jenkins has shown, a segregation period of 35 days is of slight consequence in the case of the adult white rat. (2) One group of males (28-day sex deprived) were, on account of the long period of sex deprivation beyond the standard age at the time of testing. We have eliminated this group from the comparisons of this section, so that this variation in conditions can be entirely ignored. (3) The first litter, maternal group was younger than the standard age at time of testing, since age was necessarily determined by the factor of primiparity. In ranking the drives, this group may also be eliminated, and the standard age, maternal group score be taken as the maximum score for the maternal drive, under our standard conditions. (4) passing the threshold into compartment D was allowed only on the fourth and fifth crossings, in testing the exploratory drive. As we have elsewhere stated, this variation in conditions favored the exploratory drive, and since the score for this drive is extremely low even with this advantage, this variation does not influence the rank order of the drives at all, and so may be disregarded.

Much more important than the above mentioned slight variations in procedure certain problems raised by the methods of control utilized to keep other drives at a minimum while a given drive was being tested, the comparability of the incentive-response (Table 24.1) from drive to drive, and the validity of a test period of set length. The questions raised here do not arise in so far as the method is utilized in the measurement of a single drive, but are of major consequence in any attempt to compare the scores and rank the different drives. These points will now be discussed in order.

It is manifestly impossible to isolate, in any absolute sense, a single drive in a complex organism like the white rat. Obviously, the different physiological systems upon which drives are based are more or less interdependent and operate simultaneously when the organism is maintained in a normal or natural state. The best that can be done is to keep drives, other than the one being tested in a minimum status of quiesence, and such a status must be empirically determined for each drive and with reference to the general living conditions which prevail during the investigation. Standardization of method covering the manner of securing the quiescence of a given drive is of as much importance as standardization of test procedure. Furthermore, in a project such as the present one in which the central aim is the ranking of drives, it is necessary to make use of the same method of allaying a given drive throughout the entire investigation.

Such standardization was accomplished in the present case in the following manner: (1) Except when the hunger drive was itself being tested, the animal was taken from a cage which had been continuously supplied with the usual diet of the laboratory. (2) Except when the thirst drive was itself being tested, the animal was taken from a cage which had been continuously supplied with water. (3) Except when the male sex drive was itself being tested, the male had been segregated from females for 35 days, and at approximately this time the male sex drive is at a minimum within the limits of our tests on male sex deprivation. (4) Except when the female sex drive was itself being tested, only females in dioestrum, at which stage the female sex drive is at a minimum, were used. This does not apply, obviously, to the maternal groups, but the same principle holds here, since females are sexually inactive while carrying the young. (5) Except when the exploratory drive was itself being tested, the animals were prevented from exploratory excitation by the small size of compartment D, by the preliminary crossings into compartments C and D, and by the dominance of appropriate incentive objects in compartment D, whenever they entered these compartments. The chief value of the Columbia Obstruction Method as a means of measuring definite incentive-drive conditions lies in the directness and dominance of the incentive-object stimulation. (See Warden, The Columbia Obstruction Method.) Even if these controls were inadequate in maintaining at an absolute minimum all drives, other than the one being tested, whatever lack of control there may have been operated uniformly throughout and hence does not argue against the comparability of the scores from drive to drive.

Some question may arise as to the comparability of the incentive-response from drive to drive. The response of an organism to food, water, sex object, etc., naturally differs considerably not only qualitatively, but also as to the directness with which it is called out when brought in contact with the incentive object, as in compartments C and D. The hungry or thirsty animal reacts promptly enough to food or water, and likewise the maternal and exploratory response is usually prompt; at least this was true under our conditions in which the animals had gotten over the normal tendency to investigate a novel place during the five preliminary crossings into these compartments. But the completed sex act is not prompt in either male or female and we found it necessary to use some latitude in deciding when the animal had made an appropriate sex response so that it might be returned to the entrance compartment again. Such preliminary sex activities as biting the sex object or nosing the external genitalia rather than the act of copulation were the criteria adopted. In the case of the female, the familiar response of elevating the vulva under the nose of the male was considered sufficient. Mounting, or attempted mounting, in the male, if it occurred before the usual nosing or biting was also checked as a response to the sex object. The white rat exhibits no small degree of individual difference in the matter of preliminary sex activities, and it was necessary to use common sense in the matter of a criterion in the case of both male and female sex drive. It might be argued that, since the complete sex act was not permitted, the test conditions for the sex drive differed in an important manner from that for the other drives. But, as a matter of fact, deprivation during the test is necessary was the rule for all the drives; the incentive object was utilized as a stimulus to excite the drives rather than as a means of satiation. In the case of hunger, only the merest nibble of powdered food was permitted upon entering the incentive compartment; only the damp nipple of the water bottle could be licked in testing the thirst drive; only the merest attention to the young was allowed in the maternal group, and only the slightest running about was permitted in the exploration box in testing the exploratory drive. We cannot, of course, contend that the stimulation conditions from drive to drive were of the same degree, in so far as the incentive-response in compartments C and D are concerned, but we made use of the best criteria of response to the different types of incentive that we could devise after a large amount of preliminary observation of the animals in the apparatus. Further observation during the progress of the testing confirms us in our opinion that, when taken in connection with our method of scoring, to be next discussed, the criteria were sufficiently comparable as not to involve any question regarding the validity of ranking the different drives. This view of the matter is further strengthened by the fact that the ranking of the drives, in the last analysis, will be based upon the maximum scores for each drive; but, when a given drive is strongly aroused, the response to the incentive tends to be definitely and prompt as might be expected.

The advantages of a test period of definite length has many obvious advantages, and among these, the matter of ease in scoring is of considerable importance. The amount of work done in a given time, or the number of repetitions accomplished within a definite practice period are well established methods of scoring human performance. The only questions that might arise regarding the validity of such a set test period as we used in this project (20 min.) would be: (1) Was the test period long enough to include a sufficient amount of behavior characteristic of a given drive to yield an adequate index of the strength of the drive; (2) since the incentive responses varied in promptness from drive to drive, was a test period of the same length equally fair to the various drives investigated?

The first question can be answered clearly in the positive. Preliminary work indicated that a test period of only 10 minutes by this method would give valid indices of drive conditions, the curves following the same general lines as those obtained by our standard 20-minute test period. We have checked through the results of several drives and have found that the ranking of drive conditions would not be disturbed at all by discarding the results obtained during the last half (10 min.) of the standard test period. In the case of each drive, approaches, contacts, and crossings were checked on the record card for each minute of the 20-minute test period so that this matter is open to the most complete analysis. The test period was set at 20 minutes so as to insure the inclusion of any drive behavior of significance in the score.

The second point cannot be so clearly disposed of. For, as we have said, the incentive response varied not only as to general type from drive to drive, but also as to promptness, and this latter factor would be expected to influence the score since the test period was limited. In order to equalize the value of a crossing to the incentive from drive to drive, the animal was allowed to remain in the incentive compartment, after crossing over the grid, for not longer than 30 seconds, regardless of whether he had met the criterion of an appropriate incentive response for the given drive or not. That is to say, the time allowed for an incentive response was limited just as was the total period of the test. This was done with a view to standardizing the method so as to take account of differences in promptness in responding to the incentive from drive to drive. Again we must suggest that, in ranking the drives, we are directly comparing the maximum scores only, and that when strongly aroused the response to the incentive tended to be prompt and uniform in the case of each of the drives. As a matter of fact, the act of crossing and making an appropriate response to the incentive did not seem to vary any more from drive to drive than from one condition to another within the same drive. In any case, the incentive response could not last longer than 30 seconds, and in most cases actually occurred much sooner than that in each of the drives, and especially so when these were at a maximum.

From the above discussion it will appear that our apparatus and mehod was sufficiently well standardized to warrant the use of the scores in ranking the normal drives as proposed.

## ANALYSIS OF RESULTS

Our main interest, in the present section, will be in a comparison of the maximum scores of the different drives with a view to ranking them in a definite order on the basis of strength and persistence. Nevertheless, it seems best as a matter of convenience to the reader to bring togther in tabular form the results of each normal drive condition investigated, and so to present the maximum scores in their appropriate setting.

The averages for each of the normal groups, covering approaches, contacts, and crossings, are given in Table 24.2, together with the usual statistical values for the several averages. These scores represent the full 20-minute test period. Separate indices have been entered for the two sexes in the case of hunger and thirst, in addition to the combined scores for these two drives.

In Table 24.3 will be found a set of values representing a grouping of the scores on the basis of successive five-minute parts of the 20-minute test period, and percentage scores, following the same grouping comprise Table 24.4. A finer temporal distribution of the scores (minute by minute) is available in the original reports, but no summary of this analysis has been included at this point, since even the five-minute grouping seems to be of little significance. The data were taken and reported in these temporal groupings in the hope that such temporal distribution would throw some light upon the persistence of the drive during the test period. It was thought possible that some useful measure of the *persistence* of a given drive might be thus secured, corresponding to the *strength* score based upon the total score. However, it appears to be very doubtful whether the distinction between strength and persistence of drive is defensible—at least in so far as these may be indicated by total score and temporal distribution respectively. It is true, as an examination of Tables 24.3 and 24.4 will show, that when a drive is at its maximum as indicated by the maximum score in crossings, the score tends to be uniformly maintained throughout the test period; the one exception to be noted is the maximum score for the thirst drive. Scores representing other than

TABLE 24.2. Showing results for the various drive conditions.

| Drive Condition Tested | Size of Group | Approaches | | | Contacts | | | Crossings | | |
|---|---|---|---|---|---|---|---|---|---|---|
| | | Average | Standard Deviation | Coefficient of Variation | Average | Standard Deviation | Coefficient of Variation | Average | Standard Deviation | Coefficient of Variation |
| (Hunger–male) | | | | | | | | | | |
| 0 period | 10 | 1.5 | 1.34 | 89 | 2.2 | 1.20 | 55 | 2.7 | 3.37 | 125 |
| 2 days | 10 | 3.3 | 1.47 | 44 | 4.9 | 1.59 | 32 | 16.1 | 6.56 | 41 |
| 3 days | 10 | 5.0 | 1.41 | 28 | 5.7 | 1.58 | 28 | 18.0 | 7.52 | 42 |
| 4 days | 10 | 3.6 | 2.20 | 61 | 2.8 | 1.17 | 42 | 19.1 | 5.87 | 31 |
| 6 days | 10 | 3.6 | 1.59 | 44 | 3.0 | 1.55 | 52 | 14.2 | 5.98 | 42 |
| 8 days | 10 | 4.6 | 1.79 | 39 | 5.5 | 2.18 | 40 | 9.8 | 5.33 | 54 |
| (Hunger–female) | | | | | | | | | | |
| 0 period | 10 | 2.0 | 1.34 | 67 | 3.5 | 1.55 | 44 | 2.1 | 2.07 | 98 |
| 2 days | 10 | 3.4 | 1.56 | 46 | 6.9 | 1.87 | 27 | 19.0 | 8.91 | 47 |
| 3 days | 10 | 5.2 | 1.25 | 24 | 8.0 | 1.41 | 76 | 18.4 | 7.63 | 41 |
| 4 days | 10 | 5.2 | 2.04 | 39 | 5.7 | 1.10 | 19 | 17.0 | 5.92 | 35 |
| 6 days | 10 | 6.1 | 1.77 | 29 | 5.3 | 1.80 | 34 | 14.0 | 7.18 | 51 |
| 8 days | 10 | 6.8 | 1.69 | 25 | 7.3 | 2.29 | 31 | 6.0 | 4.69 | 78 |
| (Hunger–combined) | | | | | | | | | | |
| 0 period | 20 | 1.75 | 1.36 | 79 | 2.85 | 1.42 | 50 | 2.40 | 2.78 | 116 |
| 2 days | 20 | 3.35 | 2.81 | 84 | 5.90 | 3.92 | 66 | 17.60 | 7.78 | 44 |
| 3 days | 20 | 5.10 | 2.46 | 48 | 6.85 | 2.93 | 43 | 18.20 | 7.58 | 42 |
| 4 days | 20 | 4.40 | 2.37 | 54 | 4.75 | 1.91 | 40 | 18.10 | 5.98 | 33 |
| 6 days | 20 | 4.85 | 3.58 | 74 | 4.15 | 3.61 | 87 | 14.10 | 6.61 | 47 |
| 8 days | 20 | 5.70 | 3.77 | 66 | 6.40 | 5.71 | 89 | 7.90 | 5.07 | 64 |
| (Thirst–male) | | | | | | | | | | |
| 0 period | 10 | 3.0 | 1.6 | 53 | 1.7 | 2.1 | 123 | 3.7 | 4.0 | 108 |
| 1 day | 10 | 7.3 | 3.3 | 45 | 5.6 | 5.4 | 96 | 21.1 | 11.6 | 54 |
| 2 days | 10 | 5.0 | 3.7 | 74 | 4.5 | 4.3 | 95 | 16.7 | 12.3 | 74 |
| 4 days | 10 | 3.0 | 1.8 | 60 | 1.8 | 2.0 | 111 | 12.7 | 9.0 | 71 |
| 6 days | 10 | 0.8 | 0.7 | 87 | 0.9 | 1.2 | 133 | 7.5 | 5.5 | 73 |
| (Thirst–female) | | | | | | | | | | |
| 0 period | 10 | 3.1 | 2.9 | 94 | 0.8 | 0.9 | 112 | 4.6 | 3.8 | 83 |
| 1 day | 10 | 7.3 | 4.7 | 64 | 4.7 | 3.9 | 83 | 19.7 | 11.1 | 56 |
| 2 days | 10 | 4.0 | 3.5 | 87 | 3.8 | 3.4 | 89 | 15.3 | 11.7 | 76 |
| 4 days | 10 | 3.2 | 3.3 | 103 | 1.1 | 1.4 | 127 | 14.5 | 8.3 | 57 |
| 6 days | 10 | 1.7 | 1.9 | 111 | 1.8 | 1.9 | 105 | 6.9 | 6.9 | 100 |
| (Thirst–combined) | | | | | | | | | | |
| 0 period | 20 | 3.05 | 2.3 | 75 | 1.25 | 1.3 | 104 | 4.15 | 3.9 | 94 |
| 1 day | 20 | 7.30 | 4.1 | 56 | 5.15 | 4.7 | 91 | 20.40 | 11.4 | 56 |
| 2 days | 20 | 4.50 | 3.6 | 80 | 4.15 | 3.9 | 94 | 16.0 | 12.0 | 75 |
| 4 days | 20 | 3.10 | 2.7 | 87 | 1.45 | 1.7 | 117 | 13.6 | 8.7 | 64 |
| 6 days | 20 | 1.25 | 1.5 | 120 | 1.35 | 1.6 | 119 | 7.2 | 6.0 | 83 |

TABLE 24.2 (*Continued*)

| (Sex—male) | | | | | | | | | | |
|---|---|---|---|---|---|---|---|---|---|---|
| 0 period | 20 | 1.2 | 1.36 | 113 | 0.35 | 0.7 | 200 | 3.6 | 4.08 | 114 |
| 6 hours | 20 | 4.15 | 3.26 | 79 | 4.50 | 2.77 | 62 | 8.1 | 5.20 | 64 |
| 12 hours | 20 | 2.70 | 2.03 | 75 | 2.65 | 1.98 | 75 | 12.2 | 4.80 | 39 |
| 1 day | 20 | 2.30 | 2.35 | 102 | 1.5 | 1.5 | 100 | 13.45 | 4.03 | 30 |
| 1 day (control) | 20 | 1.20 | 1.03 | 86 | 1.05 | 1.18 | 112 | 2.95 | 1.80 | 61 |
| 4 days | 20 | 1.80 | 1.90 | 106 | 1.85 | 1.56 | 84 | 12.60 | 6.24 | 50 |
| 7 days | 20 | 2.25 | 1.50 | 67 | 3.10 | 2.50 | 81 | 12.25 | 7.07 | 58 |
| 28 days | 20 | 2.50 | 2.90 | 116 | 2.00 | 1.97 | 99 | 10.55 | 7.10 | 66 |
| (Sex—female) | | | | | | | | | | |
| Early congestive Oestrum | 7 | 6.71 | 5.39 | 80 | 4.86 | 2.31 | 48 | 11.14 | 6.08 | 55 |
| (cornified) | 21 | 5.43 | 3.63 | 67 | 3.14 | 2.73 | 87 | 14.14 | 5.14 | 36 |
| Same (control) | 22 | 3.23 | 2.70 | 84 | 2.27 | 1.91 | 84 | 5.05 | 2.55 | 51 |
| Late cornified | 3 | 2.33 | 1.39 | 60 | 3.66 | 1.39 | 38 | 8.66 | 5.55 | 64 |
| Post-ovulative | 6 | 1.17 | 1.04 | 89 | 4.00 | 2.92 | 73 | 4.66 | 5.28 | 113 |
| Dioestrum (4 stages) | 32 | 1.16 | 1.42 | 117 | 1.47 | 1.27 | 86 | 1.34 | 1.57 | 117 |
| (Maternal) | | | | | | | | | | |
| First litter | 9 | 3.89 | 2.68 | 69 | 0.78 | 0.63 | 81 | 28.33 | 7.73 | 27 |
| Multiparous (stand. age) | 10 | 4.10 | 3.67 | 89 | 1.30 | 1.90 | 146 | 22.40 | 9.14 | 41 |
| (Exploratory) | | | | | | | | | | |
| Males (stand. age) | 20 | 5.20 | 3.85 | 74 | 1.8 | 1.66 | 92 | 6.00 | 4.89 | 81 |

maximum conditions of the drives usually show either an increase or a decrease through successive five-minute parts of the test period. But what this may mean in terms of the loose concept of *persistence of drive* is not at all clear, and we shall omit further discussion of these data from this section.

In comparing the various normal drives we shall limit ourselves to the scores for crossings, in which a complete response to the obstruction-incentive situation occurred. As a matter of fact, this plan was followed in the original reports on the several drives, since the other two types of response (approaches, contacts) appeared to be of little or no significance as between different drive conditions. From the first, approaches and contacts were checked in the hope that these partial crossings would reveal something of importance regarding strength of drive, and the practice was continued in the interests of uniformity in all later studies. However, we can find no indication of any significance in these two types of partial crossing to the incentive. From an inspection of the values for approaches and contacts in Table 24.2, it appears that they exhibit relatively slight variations from one condition to another within the same drive, and from one drive to another, sharply contrasting with markedly variable crossing scores. There seems to be no legitimate method by which the three types of reaction to the obstruction-incentive situation

TABLE 24.3. Showing temporal distribution in five-minute intervals of approaches, contacts, and crossings during the twenty-minute test period.

| Drive Condition Tested | Approaches Minutes of test period | | | | Contacts Minutes of test period | | | | Crossings Minutes of test period | | | |
|---|---|---|---|---|---|---|---|---|---|---|---|---|
| | 0–5 | 6–10 | 11–15 | 16–20 | 0–5 | 6–10 | 11–15 | 16–20 | 0–5 | 6–10 | 11–15 | 16–20 |
| (Hunger—combined) | | | | | | | | | | | | |
| 0 days | 15 | 10 | 7 | 3 | 28 | 18 | 4 | 7 | 31 | 9 | 5 | 3 |
| 2 days | 17 | 8 | 18 | 22 | 16 | 23 | 42 | 37 | 130 | 109 | 86 | 33 |
| 3 days | 42 | 25 | 17 | 18 | 54 | 37 | 28 | 18 | 75 | 91 | 100 | 98 |
| 4 days | 23 | 34 | 10 | 21 | 41 | 22 | 8 | 14 | 94 | 89 | 87 | 91 |
| 6 days | 28 | 20 | 18 | 31 | 18 | 14 | 13 | 33 | 64 | 65 | 77 | 76 |
| 8 days | 30 | 28 | 16 | 40 | 27 | 29 | 29 | 46 | 31 | 40 | 42 | 45 |
| (Thirst—combined) | | | | | | | | | | | | |
| 0 days | 20 | 18 | 13 | 10 | 8 | 6 | 4 | 7 | 42 | 21 | 7 | 13 |
| 1 day | 74 | 31 | 22 | 19 | 38 | 24 | 20 | 10 | 153 | 106 | 84 | 65 |
| 2 days | 24 | 31 | 16 | 20 | 28 | 22 | 14 | 19 | 153 | 81 | 60 | 26 |
| 4 days | 18 | 17 | 20 | 7 | 14 | 3 | 6 | 6 | 115 | 70 | 48 | 39 |
| 6 days | 8 | 8 | 4 | 5 | 10 | 6 | 4 | 7 | 39 | 31 | 42 | 32 |
| (Sex—male) | | | | | | | | | | | | |
| 0 hours | 4 | 3 | 12 | 5 | 2 | 2 | 2 | 1 | 10 | 19 | 18 | 25 |
| 6 hours | 26 | 17 | 24 | 16 | 31 | 22 | 19 | 18 | 52 | 61 | 28 | 21 |
| 12 hours | 6 | 22 | 15 | 7 | 13 | 13 | 8 | 19 | 74 | 76 | 44 | 50 |
| 1 day | 19 | 16 | 6 | 5 | 9 | 9 | 8 | 4 | 76 | 63 | 60 | 70 |
| 1 day (control) | 3 | 4 | 9 | 9 | 8 | 7 | 3 | 3 | 28 | 17 | 9 | 5 |
| 4 days | 15 | 8 | 9 | 4 | 12 | 5 | 8 | 3 | 62 | 55 | 65 | 70 |
| 7 days | 12 | 11 | 11 | 9 | 17 | 9 | 24 | 12 | 47 | 33 | 58 | 107 |
| 28 days | 9 | 8 | 15 | 18 | 4 | 9 | 22 | 5 | 16 | 40 | 54 | 101 |
| (Sex—female) | | | | | | | | | | | | |
| Early congestive | 11 | 17 | 13 | 6 | 6 | 3 | 8 | 17 | 11 | 18 | 21 | 28 |
| Oestrum (cornified) | 49 | 29 | 23 | 13 | 8 | 16 | 16 | 26 | 59 | 45 | 81 | 22 |
| Same (control) | 19 | 32 | 14 | 6 | 17 | 13 | 15 | 5 | 48 | 36 | 17 | 10 |
| Late cornified | 3 | 1 | 1 | 2 | 4 | 1 | 3 | 3 | 5 | 3 | 7 | 11 |
| Post-ovulative | 3 | 2 | 1 | 1 | 5 | 9 | 9 | 1 | 9 | 10 | 3 | 5 |
| Dioestrum | 12 | 17 | 5 | 3 | 15 | 18 | 9 | 5 | 18 | 13 | 9 | 3 |
| (Maternal) | | | | | | | | | | | | |
| First litter | 11 | 16 | 5 | 3 | 4 | 1 | 1 | 1 | 64 | 59 | 65 | 67 |
| Multiparous (Standard age) | 12 | 14 | 8 | 7 | 1 | 5 | 5 | 2 | 63 | 50 | 53 | 58 |
| (Exploratory) | | | | | | | | | | | | |
| Males (Standard age) | 38 | 29 | 19 | 18 | 12 | 12 | 4 | 8 | 48 | 29 | 23 | 20 |

TABLE 24.4. Showing temporal distribution in five-minute intervals of approaches, contacts, and crossings, (percentages) during the twenty-minute test period.

| Drive Condition Tested | Approaches Minutes of test period | | | | Contacts Minutes of test period | | | | Crossings Minutes of test period | | | |
|---|---|---|---|---|---|---|---|---|---|---|---|---|
| | 0–5 | 6–10 | 11–15 | 16–20 | 0–5 | 6–10 | 11–15 | 16–20 | 0–5 | 6–10 | 11–15 | 16–20 |
| (Hunger–combined) | | | | | | | | | | | | |
| 0 days | 43 | 28 | 20 | 9 | 49 | 32 | 7 | 12 | 65 | 19 | 10 | 6 |
| 2 days | 26 | 12 | 28 | 34 | 14 | 19 | 36 | 31 | 37 | 29 | 25 | 9 |
| 3 days | 41 | 24 | 17 | 18 | 39 | 27 | 21 | 13 | 21 | 25 | 27 | 27 |
| 4 days | 26 | 38 | 12 | 24 | 48 | 26 | 9 | 17 | 26 | 25 | 24 | 25 |
| 6 days | 29 | 21 | 18 | 32 | 23 | 18 | 17 | 42 | 23 | 23 | 27 | 27 |
| 8 days | 26 | 25 | 14 | 35 | 21 | 22 | 22 | 35 | 20 | 25 | 27 | 28 |
| (Thirst–combined) | | | | | | | | | | | | |
| 0 days | 33 | 30 | 21 | 16 | 32 | 24 | 16 | 28 | 51 | 25 | 8 | 16 |
| 1 day | 51 | 21 | 15 | 13 | 41 | 26 | 22 | 11 | 37 | 26 | 21 | 16 |
| 2 days | 26 | 34 | 18 | 22 | 34 | 26 | 17 | 23 | 48 | 25 | 19 | 8 |
| 4 days | 29 | 28 | 32 | 11 | 48 | 10 | 21 | 21 | 42 | 26 | 18 | 14 |
| 6 days | 32 | 32 | 16 | 20 | 37 | 22 | 15 | 26 | 28 | 22 | 28 | 22 |
| (Sex–male) | | | | | | | | | | | | |
| 0 hours | 17 | 12 | 50 | 21 | 29 | 29 | 28 | 14 | 14 | 26 | 25 | 35 |
| 6 hours | 31 | 21 | 29 | 19 | 35 | 24 | 21 | 20 | 32 | 38 | 17 | 13 |
| 12 hours | 12 | 44 | 30 | 14 | 24 | 25 | 15 | 36 | 30 | 31 | 18 | 21 |
| 1 day | 41 | 35 | 13 | 11 | 30 | 30 | 27 | 13 | 28 | 24 | 22 | 26 |
| 1 day (control) | 12 | 16 | 36 | 36 | 38 | 34 | 14 | 14 | 48 | 29 | 15 | 8 |
| 4 days | 42 | 22 | 25 | 11 | 43 | 18 | 28 | 11 | 24 | 22 | 26 | 28 |
| 7 days | 28 | 26 | 25 | 21 | 27 | 15 | 39 | 19 | 19 | 13 | 24 | 44 |
| 28 days | 18 | 16 | 30 | 36 | 10 | 22 | 55 | 13 | 8 | 19 | 25 | 48 |
| (Sex–female) | | | | | | | | | | | | |
| Early congestive Oestrum | 23 | 36 | 28 | 13 | 18 | 9 | 23 | 50 | 14 | 23 | 27 | 36 |
| (cornified) | 43 | 26 | 20 | 11 | 12 | 24 | 24 | 40 | 19 | 15 | 26 | 40 |
| Same (control) | 27 | 45 | 20 | 8 | 34 | 26 | 30 | 10 | 43 | 32 | 15 | 10 |
| Late cornified | 43 | 14 | 14 | 29 | 36 | 10 | 27 | 27 | 19 | 12 | 27 | 42 |
| Post-ovulative Dioestrum | 43 | 29 | 14 | 14 | 21 | 38 | 37 | 4 | 32 | 36 | 11 | 21 |
| (4 stages) | 32 | 46 | 14 | 8 | 32 | 38 | 19 | 11 | 42 | 30 | 21 | 7 |
| (Maternal) | | | | | | | | | | | | |
| First litter Multiparous | 29 | 34 | 20 | 17 | 8 | 38 | 38 | 16 | 28 | 22 | 24 | 26 |
| (Standard age) | 31 | 46 | 14 | 9 | 58 | 14 | 14 | 14 | 25 | 23 | 26 | 26 |
| (Exploratory) Males (Standard age) | 37 | 28 | 18 | 17 | 34 | 33 | 11 | 22 | 40 | 24 | 19 | 17 |

might be combined into a single index of strength of drive. A crossing always includes, of course, both an approach to, and a contact with the obstruction (grid). It is logical to suppose that any type of score for partial crossings would be reduced by actual crossings, as when the drive is strong. There is some evidence for an inverse relationship between scores for partial crossings, particularly approaches, and actual crossings, although this relationship is not very consistent. This argues against any method of weighting the three types of incentive response and resorting to pooling in order to reduce all to a common index of strength of drive, aside from the element of arbitrariness that would enter into any such weighting of scores that are so disparate in significance. We did pool the averages for approaches, contacts, and crossings, without weighting, as a matter of information to ourselves, comparing these pooled scores with the scores for crossings, and while such a pooling is certainly not legitimate, we may as well report the result. There was no displacement of rank among the group averages of a given drive, except in the case of the male and female sex drive, where the grouping represents finer divisions in experimental analysis, and even here the displacements were based upon slight differences. This comparison serves at least to show the neutral character of partial crossing scores and their consequent insignificance in any index of drive. We feel justified in suggesting that, in later studies of drive in the white rat by means of the Columbia Obstruction Method, scoring be limited to crossings only, since it seems a mere waste of time to take account of partial crossings of any sort.

Since we are interested at this point primarily in the maximum scores as these may be useful in ranking the normal drives, further discussion of Tables 24.2, .3 and .4 will be unnecessary. In so far as the values there summarized relate to a particular drive, detailed analyses and comparisons will be found in the full reports under the appropriate sections. We may turn at once to an examination of the maximum scores covering the number of crossings to the incentive, considering the same a common index for the ranking of the various drives. It will be convenient to deal separately with the group of male and of female drives, as well as with the group of drives in which the sexes are combined.

The rank order of the several drives, according to these groupings will be found in Table 24.5, together with the maximum score in crossings upon which the ranking was based. Since, as we shall see, the sex differences for the hunger, thirst, and sex drives are too small to be of much significance, the ranking of the drives in the last grouping of the table (male and female combined) are of most interest to us.

Before dealing with the reliability of the maximum scores in comparisons from drive to drive, it may be well to discuss briefly the significance of the maximum scores for a given drive. In each case these indicate the number of crossings to the incentive when the drive was most strongly

TABLE 24.5. Showing maximum scores (crossings) for the various drives, arranged in rank order.

| Drives Tested | Condition of Maximum Drive | M. | F. | Comb. | Average | Standard Deviation | Coefficient of Variation |
|---|---|---|---|---|---|---|---|
| (Male) | | | | | | | |
| Thirst | 2nd day | 10 | | | 21.10 | 11.60 | 54 |
| Hunger | 4th day | 10 | | | 19.10 | 5.87 | 31 |
| Sex | 1st day | 20 | | | 13.45 | 4.03 | 30 |
| Exploratory | Only 1 tested | 20 | | | 6.00 | 4.89 | 81 |
| (Female) | | | | | | | |
| Maternal | Standard age | | 10 | | 22.40 | 9.14 | 41 |
| Thirst | 1st day | | 10 | | 19.70 | 11.10 | 56 |
| Hunger | 3rd day | | 10 | | 19.00 | 8.91 | 47 |
| Sex | Oestrum | | 21 | | 14.14 | 5.14 | 36 |
| (Combined) | | | | | | | |
| Maternal | Standard age | | 10 | | 22.40 | 9.14 | 41 |
| Thirst | 1st day | 10 | 10 | 20 | 20.40 | 11.40 | 56 |
| Hunger | 3rd day | 10 | 10 | 20 | 18.20 | 7.58 | 42 |
| Sex | 1st day & Oestrum | 20 | 21 | 41 | 13.80 | 4.64 | 34 |
| Exploratory | Only 1 tested | 20 | | | 6.00 | 4.89 | 81 |

aroused. Except for the maternal and the exploratory drives, no less than five conditions, representing systematic changes in the variable, were tested in the case of each drive. The curves covering the successive changes in the variable (water, food, sex deprivation, etc.) comprise Figures 24.2, .3, and .4, of this study. The first value on each curve represents an approximate physiological zero for the given drive. Thus hunger and thirst begin with zero deprivation; male sex with a zero established by copulating with a female in heat until completely satiated, while dioestrum constituted a zero point for the female sex drive. In thirst, hunger, and male sex, deprivation was carried far beyond the point of the maximum drive condition as the curves clearly indicate; each of the eight recognized stages of the oestrus cycle were tested in the female. We are able to say, then, that for each of these four drives, we secured the true maximum score under our conditions, within the limits of the unit of change adopted for the several variables. A finer unit of change might show the true maximum point to lie somewhere near rather than precisely at the points we indicate in each instance. For example, it is possible that a finer working of the field might result in showing that the maximum point for thirst is somewhat less or somewhat more than the one-day point where our maximum score was found; and so with the other drives. But, in any case, it must be admitted that our maximum points are approximately true, and are clearly established as true by the general trend

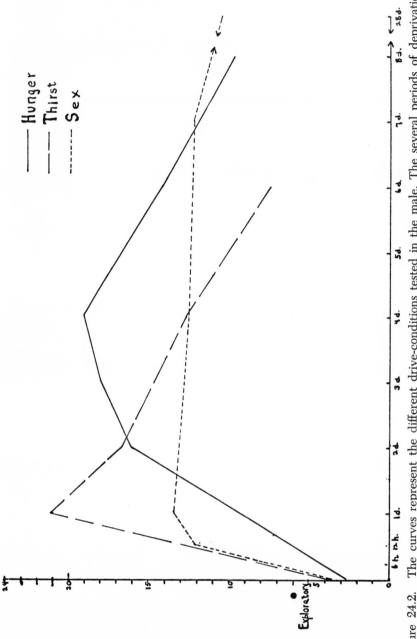

Figure 24.2. The curves represent the different drive-conditions tested in the male. The several periods of deprivation are indicated on the abscissa and the average number of crossings on the ordinate.

of the scores downward in either direction from these maximum points, as may be observed in Figures 24.2, 3, and 4.

Only a single condition was tested in the case of the maternal drive, and the exploratory drive, under our normal standardization, and therefore, we cannot insist that the scores included for these two drives are true maxima. So far as the maternal drive is concerned, it is quite doubtful

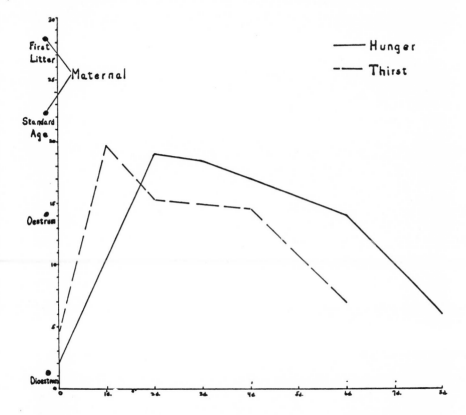

Figure 24.3. The curves represent the different drive-conditions tested in the female. The several periods of deprivation (thirst, hunger) are indicated on the abscissa and the average number of crossings on the ordinate.

whether the score in Table 24.5 is the highest possible maternal score, even under our standard conditions. The score for first litter is considerably higher (28.33) but this score could not be used here because the animals tested were naturally younger than our standard age. However, there is one important factor that might be varied in animals of standard age which might give a higher score than we secured, e.g., length of time between parturition and testing. Our standard age, maternal group were tested on the average 15 hours (range 12–20 hours) after casting the

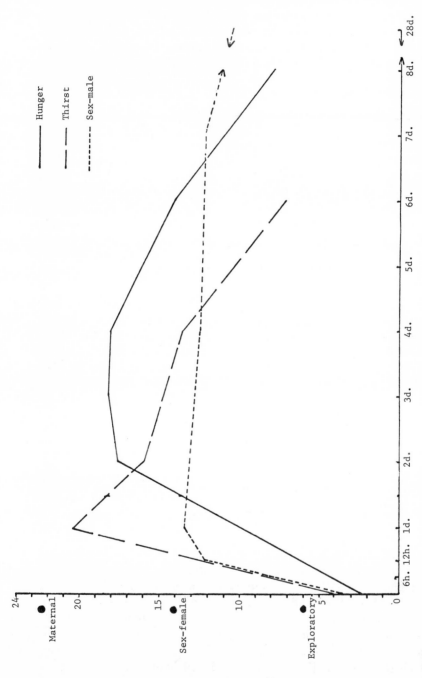

Figure 24.4. The curves represent the different drive-conditions tested, with thirst and hunger scores for male and female combined. The several periods of deprivation are indicated on the abscissa and the average number of crossings on the ordinate.

litter, and this may not have been the best time to have tested them so far as strength of maternal drive is concerned. But, the admission of the possibility of an even higher score than we secured for the maternal drive does not disturb our table of ranking, since the maximum score we show is high enough to place the maternal drive at the top of the list any way. On the other hand, the score for the exploratory drive is so low that further tests are not likely to shift it from the position of the lowest in our table of ranks. So far, then, as general considerations are involved, the ranking of the drives as shown in Table 24.5, and as indicated by the graphs of Figures 24.2, .3, and .4, must be regarded as based upon sound principles. This is of importance as establishing the basic method of comparing drives in terms of a common type of response to a well standardized obstruction-incentive situation.

The relation of the maximum scores for each drive to the scores obtained when the drive was tested at other than maximum strength is shown in Table 24.6. In every instance, the difference between the maximum score and some one or more scores on a given drive curve at points on either side of the maximum point are large enough to pass the most rigorous test of statistical validity. It is true that the differences between the maximum point and points near the maximum are, in many cases, too small to be statistically valid, but such small differences must be interpreted not independently but in the light of the general trend of the scores on either side of the maximum. The clear cut trends in every instance establish the validity of the maximum score within the limitation of the unit of change in the variable, or the fineness of the experimental analysis, for a given drive.

Accepting the maximum scores as valid indices of the strength of the several drives, we must now inquire as to the significance of the differences between these scores from drive to drive. As previously mentioned, the ranking of the drives upon the basis of the maximum score is indicated in Table 24.5, and can also be seen by an inspection of the graphs of Figures 24.2, .3, and .4. The reliability of the differences between the maximum scores for the several male drives will be found in Table 24.7; similar values for the several female drives comprise Table 24.8, while Table 24.10 covers the same point with the drives grouped together without regard to sex. The relations of these reliabilities to rank order are summarized in Table 24.11.

Before discussing these data we shall examine Table 24.9 and dispose of the matter of sex differences in strength of drive. Separate scores for the sexes are available in the thirst, hunger, and sex drives only. The difference in both hunger and thirst favors the male, but is too small to be considered significant, while the sex drive is higher in the female by only a small margin of questionable validity. These findings refer only to the height of the curve for the drives and do not imply that the maxi-

TABLE 24.6.  Showing the reliability of the difference between the maximum score (crossings) for each drive and all the other scores for the given drives.

| Drive Conditions Tested | S. D. of Difference | Difference Between Averages | Difference / S. D. of Difference | Chances in 100 of a True Difference |
|---|---|---|---|---|
| (Hunger—male) | | | | |
| 4 days and 0 days | 2.14 | 16.4 | 7.66 | 100 |
| 4 days and 2 days | 2.78 | 3.0 | 1.08 | 86 |
| 4 days and 3 days | 3.02 | 1.1 | 0.36 | 64 |
| 4 days and 6 days | 2.65 | 4.9 | 1.85 | 97 |
| 4 days and 8 days | 2.51 | 9.3 | 3.71 | 100 |
| (Hunger—female) | | | | |
| 2 days and 0 days | 2.89 | 16.9 | 5.84 | 100 |
| 2 days and 3 days | 3.71 | 0.6 | 0.16 | 56 |
| 2 days and 4 days | 3.38 | 2.0 | 0.59 | 72 |
| 2 days and 6 days | 3.62 | 5.0 | 1.38 | 92 |
| 2 days and 8 days | 3.18 | 13.0 | 4.08 | 100 |
| (Hunger—combined) | | | | |
| 3 days and 0 days | 1.81 | 15.8 | 8.73 | 100 |
| 3 days and 2 days | 2.43 | 0.6 | 0.25 | 60 |
| 3 days and 4 days | 2.16 | 0.1 | 0.05 | 52 |
| 3 days and 6 days | 2.25 | 4.1 | 1.82 | 97 |
| 3 days and 8 days | 2.04 | 10.3 | 5.05 | 100 |
| (Thirst—male) | | | | |
| 1 day and 0 days | 3.88 | 17.4 | 4.48 | 100 |
| 1 day and 2 days | 5.35 | 4.4 | 0.82 | 80 |
| 1 day and 4 days | 4.64 | 8.4 | 1.81 | 96 |
| 1 day and 6 days | 4.06 | 13.6 | 3.35 | 100 |
| (Thirst—female) | | | | |
| 1 day and 0 days | 3.71 | 15.1 | 4.07 | 100 |
| 1 day and 2 days | 5.10 | 4.4 | 0.86 | 81 |
| 1 day and 4 days | 4.38 | 5.2 | 1.19 | 88 |
| 1 day and 6 days | 4.13 | 12.8 | 3.10 | 100 |
| (Thirst—combined) | | | | |
| 1 day and 0 days | 2.69 | 16.3 | 6.06 | 100 |
| 1 day and 2 days | 3.70 | 4.4 | 1.19 | 88 |
| 1 day and 4 days | 3.21 | 6.8 | 2.12 | 98 |
| 1 day and 6 days | 2.88 | 13.2 | 4.58 | 100 |
| (Sex—male) | | | | |
| 1 day and 0 hours | 1.28 | 9.9 | 7.68 | 100 |
| 1 day and 6 hours | 1.47 | 5.4 | 3.64 | 100 |
| 1 day and 12 hours | 1.40 | 1.3 | 0.89 | 81 |
| 1 day and 4 days | 1.65 | 0.9 | 0.51 | 69 |
| 1 day and 7 days | 1.82 | 1.2 | 0.66 | 75 |
| 1 day and 28 days | 1.83 | 2.9 | 1.60 | 95 |
| 1 day and control | 0.99 | 10.5 | 10.61 | 100 |
| (Sex—female) | | | | |
| Cornified and control | 1.25 | 9.1 | 7.28 | 100 |
| Cornified and dioestrum | 1.16 | 12.8 | 11.00 | 100 |
| Control and dioestrum | 0.61 | 3.7 | 6.08 | 100 |
| (Maternal) | | | | |
| First litter and standard age | 3.87 | 5.9 | 1.53 | 94 |

TABLE 24.7. Showing the reliability of the difference between maximum scores (crossings) of the different drives in males.

| Drive Conditions Tested | S. D. of Difference | Difference Between Averages | Difference / S. D. of Difference | Chances in 100 of a True Difference |
|---|---|---|---|---|
| Hunger and thirst | 4.11 | 2.00 | 0.49 | 69 |
| Hunger and sex | 2.06 | 5.65+ | 2.74 | 99.7 |
| Hunger and exploration | 2.15 | 13.10+ | 6.08 | 100 |
| Thirst and sex | 3.78 | 7.65+ | 2.03 | 98 |
| Thirst and exploration | 3.83 | 15.10+ | 3.95 | 100 |
| Sex and exploration | 1.42 | 7.45+ | 5.26 | 100 |

LEGEND: The plus sign indicates that the first drive of the pair has the higher score.

TABLE 24.8. Showing the reliability of the difference between the maximum scores (crossings) of the different drives in females.

| Drive Conditions Tested | S. D. of Difference | Difference Between Averages | Difference / S. D. of Difference | Chances in 100 of a True Difference |
|---|---|---|---|---|
| Hunger and thirst | 4.50 | 0.70 | 0.16 | 56 |
| Hunger and sex | 3.03 | 4.86+ | 1.60 | 95 |
| Hunger and maternal | 4.04 | 3.40 | 0.84 | 80 |
| Thirst and sex | 3.69 | 5.56+ | 1.51 | 93 |
| Thirst and maternal | 4.55 | 2.70 | 0.59 | 72 |
| Sex and maternal | 3.10 | 8.26 | 2.66 | 99.6 |

LEGEND: The plus sign indicates that the score is higher than the female score.

TABLE 24.9. Showing the reliability of the difference between the maximum scores (crossings) of the male and female groups.

| Drive Conditions Tested | S. D. of Difference | Difference Between Averages | Difference / S. D. of Difference | Chances in 100 of a True Difference |
|---|---|---|---|---|
| Hunger | 3.37 | 0.10+ | 0.03 | 51 |
| Thirst | 5.08 | 1.40+ | 0.28 | 61 |
| Sex | 1.44 | 0.69 | 0.48 | 68 |

LEGEND: The plus sign indicates that the male score is higher than the female score.

mum point was identical for the two sexes. As will be seen by comparing the graphs of Figures 24.2 and 24.3, the peak of the thirst drive came at the same point (1 day) for both sexes, but this was not true in the case of the hunger drive. The peak for the females, in the latter drive, came after 2 days of starvation, while that for males came after 4 days of starvation. From the showing in Table 24.9, we may conclude that the hunger, thirst, and sex drives are about equally strong in the two sexes when at their maximum.

A detailed examination of Tables 24.7, 24.8, and 24.10 does not seem

TABLE 24.10.   Showing the reliability of the difference between the maximum scores (crossings) of the different drives with sexes combined.

| Drive Conditions Tested | S. D. of Difference | Difference Between Averages | Difference / S. D. of Difference | Chances in 100 of a True Difference |
|---|---|---|---|---|
| Hunger and thirst | 3.06 | 2.20 | 0.72 | 76 |
| Hunger and sex | 1.84 | 4.40+ | 2.39 | 99 |
| Hunger and maternal | 3.35 | 4.20 | 1.25 | 89 |
| Hunger and exploration | 2.02 | 12.20+ | 6.03 | 100 |
| Thirst and sex | 2.65 | 6.60+ | 2.49 | 99.4 |
| Thirst and maternal | 3.85 | 2.00 | 0.52 | 70 |
| Thirst and exploration | 2.77 | 14.40+ | 5.19 | 100 |
| Sex and maternal | 2.98 | 8.60 | 2.89 | 99.8 |
| Sex and exploration | 1.31 | 7.80+ | 5.95 | 100 |
| Maternal and exploration | 3.09 | 16.40+ | 5.31 | 100 |

LEGEND: The plus sign indicates that the first drive of the pair has the higher score.

to be especially called for, since the main results in so far as the matter of the validity of the rank order of the various groupings of drives have been summarized in Table 24.11. In column 1, of this table, the rank order for the several male drives tested, based upon the maximum scores is given; following this the rank order of the female drives, and finally the rank order for the drives as such without regard to sex. That is, the maximum scores for the two sexes covering the hunger, thirst, and sex drives are here combined; we have already found, in connection with the discussion of Table 24.9, that there is apparently no significant sex difference in maximum score, so that such combination seems thoroughly justifiable. The reliability of the difference between a given drive score (maximum) and that for each drive of lower rank, taken singly, in terms of probability is shown for each drive in the next four columns of the table. The position of the sex drive, both male and female, as lower than either hunger or thirst, appears to be practically certain by this method of comparison. The exploratory drive is shown to be certainly lower than any of the other drives. The probability that thirst is higher than hunger is the least satisfactory, while the chances that maternal is higher than hunger and thirst, taken singly, are not any too good.

The problem of the validity of the rank order may be dealt with

TABLE 24.11.   Showing the reliability of the differences between maximum scores, as related to rank order. The difference between a given score and that for each drive of lower rank, taken singly, is treated in columns 2, 3, 4, and 5; in the last column the scores for all the drives of lower rank have been combined.

| Drive Tested | Rank Order | Chances in 100 of a True Difference Greater Than 0 | | | | |
| | | Thirst | Hunger | Sex | Exploratory | Combination |
|---|---|---|---|---|---|---|
| (Male) | | | | | | |
| Thirst | 1. | | 69 | 98 | 100 | 99.4 |
| Hunger | 2. | | | 99.7 | 100 | 100 |
| Sex | 3. | | | | 100 | 100 |
| Exploratory | 4. | | | | | |
| (Female) | | | | | | |
| Maternal | 1. | 72 | 80 | 99.6 | | 96 |
| Thirst | 2. | | 56 | 89 | | 86 |
| Hunger | 3. | | | 95 | | 95 |
| Sex | 4. | | | | | |
| (Combined) | | | | | | |
| Maternal | 1. | 70 | 89 | 99.8 | 100 | 99.6 |
| Thirst | 2. | | 76 | 99.4 | 100 | 99.7 |
| Hunger | 3. | | | 99 | 100 | 100 |
| Sex | 4. | | | | 100 | 100 |
| Exploratory | 5. | | | | | |

by the method of combining averages rather than by the method of single comparisons. By this method the score of a given drive is compared, not with the score of the next lowest drive, but with the average score of all the drives of lower rank. This method is more pertinent to the present discussion because it deals simply with the factor of rank position within a group of values, such as we have here. The probability of the ordinal positions worked out by this method is much higher than that obtained by comparing the obtained differences singly, as will appear from an inspection of the last column of Table 24.11. The rank order as listed in this table amounts to practical certainty for the group of male drives, and for the group of drives in combination, while the chances that the listed rank order for the female drives is a true ranking is very high. The most general statement that can be made, then, is that for the white rat, tested under our conditions, and within the limitations of the scope of our investigation, the normal drives rank as follows in strength: Maternal, thirst, hunger, sex, exploratory.

The fact that the maternal drive ranks highest comes as something of a surprise, since several investigators using other methods have rated the maternal tendency rather low. In some cases, at least, the normal maternal drive has been more or less disturbed by the method employed. A common error in technique is to have the litter born in the living cage, and then transfer it for test to the apparatus used. We tested a group, following this procedure, and obtained a score only about half as high as in our regular group in which the small maternity cage in which the litter had been born was attached directly to the apparatus, as compartment D. It may be argued that, in such a case, we are testing the maternal drive plus the tendency to return to the home nest. But the truth seems to be that when the normal conditions of maternity are disturbed by transferring the litter to an unfamiliar apparatus, the tendency to explore the novel surroundings of the litter interferes with the maternal drive. Then, too, many animals ignore young that have been moved about—this is true of many species of birds such as the quail. Our purpose was to test the maternal drive, along with the other drives discussed in this section, under normal conditions, in order to secure maximum indices, and we feel that our ranking of the maternal drive is the only defensible one from this point of view. The fact that the score for first litter, maternal drive, was higher than the score for standard age, maternal is a further argument for the placing of the maternal drive at the top of the list. We have not used the score for first litter in the comparisons of this section relative to ranking the several drives, since the animals were younger than standard age.

The conclusions drawn above regarding the relative rank of the several normal drives in the white rat, must be, of course, qualified by the general and specific conditions representing the standardization of the project as a whole. In the strict sense, these conclusions apply only to the adult white rat, of the strain and age employed, and reared unsegregated as to sex until approximately the standard test age. The fact should be recognized that relative strength of drive is very likely a function of the age of the animal within wide limits, and there may be other factors also that enter here, such as strain, the precise incentive object used, and specific aspects of our method of testing and scoring. Our results, at any rate, justify the extension of the Columbia Obstruction Method, as a means of analyzing the dynamics of behavior, to other species, and further work in this direction has been planned by this laboratory for the immediate future. The importance of indices of motivation for typical animal forms, and secured by the same method of testing, can scarcely be overestimated for systematic comparative psychology.

# 25 • Gregory A. Kimble

## Behavior Strength as a Function of the Intensity of the Hunger Drive

Researchers often distinguish between exploratory investigations and functional studies. In the former an experiment may be carried out to determine whether or not a given variable has any effect at all upon some dependent variable. Granted that a drive such as hunger may influence the strength of a learned response tendency, there still remains the functional question of how variation in the strength of hunger may differentially affect a given measure of response. Some theories have specified what the shape of the curve relating magnitudes of two such variables should be. The Kimble study reported below represented an effort to determine empirically, under well-specified conditions, the functional relationship between time of food deprivation and the latency of a conditioned operant response.

*The strength of* the tendency to perform a learned reaction, according to current learning theory, depends upon the strength of motivation. The present study was designed to investigate the nature of the function which relates the latency of a conditioned operant response to the strength of the hunger drive. In the terminology of Hull (2) the problem is that of determining the relationship between response latency ($_st_R$) and drive strength ($D$) when hours of food deprivation ($h$) and amount of food last eaten ($A$) are the determiners of drive. In the case of the hunger drive ($D_H$) it is often said that the intensity of this motive increases with the number of hours that the animal has been deprived of food ($D_H = f[h]$). But it is also possible to control hunger by varying the amount of food ingested, a technique employed by Skinner (8) and Reynolds (6). The latter investigator, for example, produced a low and a high drive state in two groups of animals by feeding the low-drive group 12 gm. of food 24 hr. prior to a learning experiment, and the high-

This article is reproduced in full from the *Journal of Experimental Psychology*, 1951, *41*, 341–348. Reprinted by permission of the American Psychological Association and the author.

drive group 3 gm. of food 24 hr. before the same experiment. The proper formula for the strength of the hunger drive, thus, may be $D_H = f(A,h)$.

Response latency should vary as a function of time since eating (amount last eaten constant) or as a function of amount eaten (time since eating constant) since either of these influences the intensity of hunger. Hunger in turn is a drive and determines, with habit strength ($_sH_R$), the value of an intervening variable, $_sE_R$, upon which response latency depends directly. Thus, even if the strength of habit is constant, latency should vary with drive, which partially determines the magnitude of $_sE_R$.

The relationship between response latency and hunger has not been traced adequately experimentally. Investigations of the relationship between behavior potentiality and the strength of hunger have presented results mainly in terms of numbers of trials to extinction and have reported latencies only incidentally. Such studies include those of Perin (5), Koch and Daniel (4), and Saltzman and Koch (7). The results of these investigations, as summarized by Saltzman and Koch, suggest that the curve relating trials to extinction to hours of food deprivation is one which rises rapidly during the first 2 hr., and then continues to rise at a much slower rate, at least up to 24 hr. If response latency reflects the same thing as number of trials to extinction, it is to be predicted that the *reciprocal* of reaction latency and number of trials to extinction will be related to drive strength in similar ways.

A special problem arising in connection with the functional relationship between hunger and its determining conditions, as pointed out by Zeaman and House (11), involves the concept of satiation. Hull's (2) earlier statement about behavior under satiation was based upon an extrapolation of the function obtained by Perin (5) to zero hours, of food deprivation. His conclusion was that, at this point, resistance to extinction is about 28 per cent of its value at 24 hr. of deprivation. More recently Koch and Daniel (4) and Saltzman and Koch (7) have taken experimental issue with this conclusion. In an experiment similar to the Perin experiment they found that resistance to extinction was very low at low drive intensities. At zero hours of deprivation, the median number of trials of extinction was 1.0. Hull's (1) more recent account of the function which relates hunger to number of hours of food deprivation has been presented only in a very brief form. But apparently it is in line with the findings of Koch and his co-workers. Hull writes that "The functional relationship of drive ($D$) to one drive condition (food privation) is: from $h = 0$ to about 3 hours drive rises in an approximately linear manner until the function abruptly shifts to a near horizontal, then to a concave-upward course, gradually changing to a convex-upward curve reaching a maximum of $12.36\sigma$ at about $h = 59, \ldots$" (1, p. 176). This statement is not, however, specific with respect to the characteristics of behavior under food satiation.

## PURPOSE OF THE EXPERIMENT

The foregoing introduction poses three questions which identify the threefold purpose of this experiment: (1) What is the nature of the function relating behavior potentiality (reflected in reciprocal latency) to number of hours of food deprivation? (2) Are there changes in the strength of the tendency to perform a learned response correlated with the ingestion of food? (3) What are the characteristics of behavior acquired on the basis of the hunger drive when this drive is reduced to zero?

## EXPERIMENTAL PROCEDURE

*Apparatus.*—The response required of the Ss in this experiment was a panel-pushing reaction similar to that previously employed by Webb (*10*). The apparatus was designed to measure the latency of this reaction as accurately as possible. This apparatus consisted of a box 11 in. long by 6¼ in. high by 5¼ in. wide with a masonite guillotine door in one end. When this door was raised, a black panel was presented. This panel, which was 4¾ in. high by 2⅛ in. wide, was pivoted so that a very light pressure against it exposed a food cup and the food reward. A counterbalance kept the panel open after the response was made.

Raising the guillotine door 1 in. depressed a microswitch and started a Springfield timer. Opening the panel closed another switch improvised from a telegraph key, activated a holding relay which stopped the timer, and thus recorded the latency of the response to the nearest .01 sec. Except for the counterbalancing arrangement, the important details of the apparatus are shown in Fig. 25.1.

*Subjects.*—Twelve female rats from the inbred strain of Wistar stock maintained by the Department of Psychology at Brown University were the Ss in the experiment. They were 73 to 75 days old at the beginning of training. One additional animal was discarded for failure to learn the panel-pushing reaction.

*Scheduling.*—The relationship between behavior potentiality and hunger is probably partly (and perhaps importantly) a function of the maintenance schedule of the animal. For this reason, it appeared to be important to establish a constant motivational state under 24 hr. of deprivation before beginning the experiment. To this end, the animals were put on a feeding schedule for 11 days prior to the experiment. During this period, a record of the amount of food eaten in a 20-min. feeding period was taken on days 1, 3, 5, 7, 9, 10, and 11. The assumption was that a constant motivational state had been reached when the food intake became essentially constant from day to day. Eleven days on the 24-hr. deprivation schedule seemed to have accomplished this. On the ninth day, the animals ate slightly less than they had on the sev-

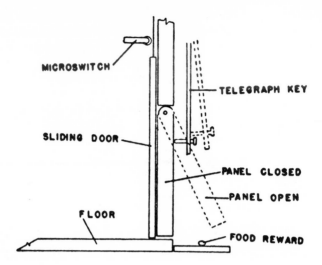

Figure 25.1. Apparatus. This figure shows only the portion of the apparatus involved in the recording of the rat's response latency. When the sliding door is raised, the microswitch is depressed and a .01 sec. clock started. When the panel is pushed open, the telegraph key switch breaks the clock circuit by activating a holding relay.

enth day; and on the eleventh day, they ate an average of .2 gm. more than they had on the tenth day and 2.2 gm. more than on day 7. Food intake seemed to have stabilized at about 21 gm. of mash per day.

The Ss were allowed to eat 20 min. per day on a mash composed by weight of 40 per cent ground Purina dog checkers and 60 per cent water. To this mixture a small amount of cod-liver oil had been added. The Ss were fed on platforms near the experimental apparatus. On days when weight measures were taken, the feeding period was divided into four sessions. At the end of each 5 min., the food was removed and Ss were weighed to determine their intake. This periodic interruption of eating is believed to be particularly effective as a preliminary to the use of a satiation technique, in that Ss learn to eat rapidly. During the fourth 5-min. eating period they ate almost nothing.

*Training.*—After this scheduling procedure, Ss were taught the panel-pushing habit in a single session involving 3 pretraining trials and 15 learning trials. On the pretraining trials, the panel was held open, and S was allowed to discover and to eat a small pellet of mash thus presented. On each of the 15 training trials, E waited until S was facing and had its forepaws in the half of the box containing the guillotine door. When this criterion position was assumed, the door was raised and the trial begun. Under this training procedure, learning is very rapid; response latency reached an asymptote on trial 11 at a median value of .4 sec.

*Tests under varying numbers of hours of deprivation.*—After preliminary training, the experiment proper was begun. In a random order on different days, Ss were tested after 0, 2, 8, 15, and 24 hr. of food deprivation. Under each condition, Ss were given five trials under the same conditions as training. Food was present in the food cup, and the same criterion based upon the animals' position in the box was used to determine when to raise the guillotine door and start a trial.

In all these conditions, except for the satiation condition, the reported number of hours of food deprivation is the length of time since the end of the last regularly scheduled 20-min. eating period. Because of certain precautions taken with the zero-hour condition, it requires additional comment. It seemed desirable to make every effort to produce complete satiation (if this is possible) and to obtain enough data upon each S's behavior to form the basis for dependable statements. Three different procedures were employed for these two purposes. The first involved the treatment of the animals during the eating period. As already mentioned, most of the animals finished eating in 15 min. of their allotted 20 min. In an effort to encourage further eating, the food was removed from the feeding platforms after 20 min., stirred, and returned after 1 min. This occasionally produced more eating for a few seconds. When the animals had again ceased to eat, they were lifted and placed before the food cups. This never produced any additional eating, nor did attempts to feed them by spoon.

The second special procedure was designed to obtain more data under satiation than under the other motivational levels. For this purpose, the satiated animals were given four blocks (instead of the usual *one*) of five trials each on successive days. On these trials, an animal which did not respond to the panel within 5 min. of its exposure on any trial was removed from the apparatus and assigned an arbitrary latency of 5 min. for that trial and for the remaining trials in that five-trial series. Fortunately, this procedure was never necessary for as many as half the animals. Median latencies are, therefore, obtainable for this condition as well as for each of the others.

For the tests under satiation, all Ss were fed at the same time. This meant that some Ss were run under satiation later than others. This procedure, which looks more hazardous from the point of view of experimental design than it actually is, was employed for three reasons: (1) to aid in the mechanical details of running the experiment and keeping the Ss on feeding schedule; (2) because previous observations upon the eating behavior of the Ss had indicated that they would not eat for an hour or more after the satiation procedure used in this experiment; and (3) because this procedure provided latency measures at several points during the period immediately after eating. Of these three considerations, the last was the most important.

Specifically, Ss tested under satiation could be regarded as being run under different (short) periods of deprivation ranging from 10 min. to 60 min. These values were arrived at by dividing the 12 Ss into four groups of three Ss determined by the order in which they were run. Since the order of testing under satiation was randomly determined from day to day, it seemed proper to combine data for these days, thus providing 60 latencies

(3 animals × 5 trials × 4 days) upon which to compute a median latency. By averaging the times after satiation at which each of these subgroups was run, and by rounding to the nearest multiple of 5, we thus obtain latency measures corresponding roughly to 10 min., 30 min., 50 min., and 60 min. deprivation.

As a third special procedure employed in the tests under satiation, a check on the possibility that the animals might not have been completely satiated in spite of our precautions was attempted on a fifth day. They were fed according to the usual satiation procedure. When S was satiated, it was given a single trial in the panel-pushing apparatus. But in this case, one of the food cups was placed in the apparatus to provide an easily accessible supply of food. If S ate this food (3 Ss), it was removed from the apparatus to the feeding platform, allowed to eat, and run again later. If it did not eat (9 Ss), the single test-trial was administered immediately.

*Tests after various amounts eaten.*—Two further sets of measurements were made on the same Ss. In this phase of the experiment, the Ss were interrupted in their eating and run within 1 min. after this interruption. The conditions used were one in which the Ss had been allowed to eat for 10 min., and another in which they had been allowed to eat for 15 min. These two conditions, together with the 24-hr. deprivation condition and the satiation condition, provide a sample of behavior after various amounts of prefeeding.

*Summary of experimental conditions.*—The experiment provides data on the behavior of the Ss under 11 different motivational conditions. There are three conditions in which the drive-controlling variable is the amount of time allowed for eating after 24 hr. of deprivation. These times are 0 min., 10 min., and 15 min. In the other eight conditions drive strength is determined by the time since last eating to satiation. These times are 10 min., 30 min., 50 min., 60 min., 2 hr., 8 hr., 15 hr., and 24 hr. For each condition, the dependent variable is the latency of the conditioned reaction.

## RESULTS

The major findings of the experiment are presented in Fig. 25.2, where the reciprocal of the median latency is plotted as a function of time either since the beginning of eating or since the termination of eating, depending upon the section of the graph. Median latencies are used because of the occasional indeterminate latencies under the low-drive conditions which make the use of other averages inappropriate. The reciprocal of the median latency is used for purely aesthetic reasons. This measure increases where we would want to consider drive as increasing and decreases where we would want to consider drive as decreasing.

Figure 25.2 is divided into three sections. The portion of the figure at the left shows latency changes which accompany the ingestion of food. In terms of time allowed for eating prior to their determination, the three points represent 0 min., 10 min., and 15 min. The first of these

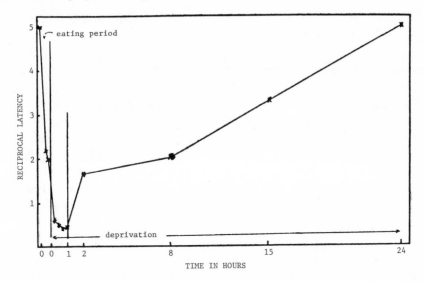

Figure 25.2. Median reciprocal response latency as a function of time allowed for eating and time of deprivation. The left-hand portion of the graph represents changes in behavior strength associated with ingestion of food. The second and third sections present reciprocal latency as a function of number of hours of food deprivation.

points (0 min.) is, of course, the same value as that plotted for 24-hr. deprivation. The expected rapid decrease in reciprocal latency as a function of time allowed for eating is readily seen.

Orthodox statistical tests are not applicable to the data of this experiment for three reasons: (1) Variability under low drive is many times as great as under high drive; (2) latency distributions under low drive are very badly skewed; and (3) when a criterion of no response is used, indeterminate latencies are sometimes obtained. For these reasons, the results of the experiment have been evaluated statistically by means of the non-parametric sign test described by Dixon and Mood (3). The sign test is a special application of the binomial theorem in which one merely counts the number of positive and negative differences obtained when one subtracts measures under one condition from those under another and determines the significance of the departure from a 50-50 distribution. For example, in this experiment, when one subtracts the median latency produced in the 10-min. prefeeding condition from the same value for the 15-min. prefeeding condition for each animal, eight positive differences are obtained. Using a single-tailed test (since we have made predictions of direction) this result is significant at only the .20 level of confidence. By the same test the difference between the median latencies obtained under the 24-hr. deprivation condition and either of the above prefeeding conditions is significant beyond the .01 level of confidence. Similarly, the difference between median latencies for either prefeeding condition and the satiation condition is significant beyond the .01 level.

The second, intermediate, portion of the graph shows the changes in reciprocal latency which occur in the first hour after satiation. These points are considered separately because the values they represent were determined in a manner somewhat different from that used in the determination of the points plotted in the other portions of the graph. The most striking thing suggested by the trend apparent in these points is that response strength may continue to decrease for the first hour following satiation. This finding is not unique. Saltzman and Koch (7) showed a similar effect for the first 30 min. after satiation. Thus, this finding confirms their result and suggests that it persists for 1 hr. or longer.

The reliability of this trend was also evaluated by the sign test. The method was to compare the median response latency of each S when it was run in the first block of Ss with the same measure obtained on another day when the S was run in the last squad of three animals. As a result of the random assignment of order, it happened that only nine of the Ss supplied data in both conditions. Of these, seven produced longer latencies in the second condition. The probability of such an outcome on the basis of chance is 46 in 512, a result significant at the .10 level of confidence.

Thus we have obtained no evidence for an increase in behavior strength during the first hour of deprivation. And, while the evidence for a decrease is not impressive, it does permit us to suggest this as a possibility. Between 1 and 2 hr. of deprivation, a sharp increase in behavior strength occurs. Beyond 2 hr., the function is one which increases more slowly up to the next regularly scheduled feeding period. The initial increase in behavior strength occurred in all Ss, making a statement of statistical dependability superfluous. The difference between the 2- and 8-hr. performance is not statistically reliable. By the sign test the difference between the 8- and 15-hr. results is significant at the .01 level; that between the 15- and 24-hr. conditions is significant at about the .10 level. An examination of the individual latency distributions indicates a possible explanation for this latter result, in that some Ss were apparently responding with maximal speed under the drive produced by 15-hr. food deprivation.

A final set of observations obtained in this investigation was that during the five-trial tests under satiation, the response latency becomes progressively longer. Median latencies for the five trials are .9, 12.0, 37.3, 123.5, and 145.9 sec. That this trend is reliable is indicated by the fact that when median latencies, based on all trials under satiation, are examined S by S, there is a consistent tendency for this measure to be larger on the last two than on the first two trials. To make this comparison, two Ss were disregarded for producing so many indeterminate latencies as to make it impossible to determine the trend. Of the ten remaining Ss, nine show the effect, a finding significant at about the .01 level of confidence. The elimination of the two Ss for whom median latencies could not be determined also has the effect of demonstrating that this increase in latency is not merely an artifact of the procedure of assigning latency values of 5 min. for all trials beyond the one on which the first such latency appears. For the ten Ss remaining, the trend being evaluated was not affected by the presence or absence of such indeterminate latencies.

## DISCUSSION

The experiment just reported was designed to provide information on behavior strength as a function of drive intensity when the drive-controlling operation is either prefeeding or deprivation.

Associated with prefeeding, it was found that there occurs a rapid drop in the reciprocal latency of a conditioned response based upon food reward. This finding is easily predicted upon the basis of any of the current learning theories. Hull's (2) theory, which makes the matter most specific, would hold that hunger ($D$) decreases with the ingestion of food, thus decreasing the magnitude of an intervening variable, $_sE_R$. This latter decrease is reflected directly in an increased latency or a decreased reciprocal latency. The only importance which attaches to our findings is that the predicted has been demonstrated in a new experimental situation.

Somewhat more surprising is the finding that there is no increase (perhaps some decrease) in behavior strength for about 1 hr. after eating to satiation, when satiation is defined as refusal to eat. This finding confirms that of Saltzman and Koch (7). To the physiologically minded psychologist it should certainly suggest that satiation depends in part upon bodily absorption of food products.

For the period from 1 hr. to 24 hr. after satiation, the curve relating reciprocal latency to the number of hours of food deprivation is one which rises rapidly to 2 hr., and then more slowly to 24 hr. of deprivation. In its gross aspect, this curve is much like that presented by Saltzman and Koch (7) and also resembles that described by Hull (1). It, therefore, appears that the function relating the strength of the hunger drive to food deprivation is not restricted to a single apparatus, or a single response measure, or a single strain of rats. The most important question raised by such functions concerns the sudden shift in acceleration which appears at 2 or 3 hr. of deprivation. One possibility is that this represents a residual effect of the rat's 2-4 hr. ad lib. feeding schedule.

Of special interest is the behavior observed under satiation. In addition to the expected protracted latencies, it was noted that these latencies increased regularly through a five-trial test series run under satiation. This finding appears to be more difficult to explain than any of our other results. The very long latencies on trials 4 and 5 present no difficulty. They may be interpreted as simply reflecting the reduction of drive and, therefore, of $sE_R$, to nearly zero. It is the short latencies on the early trials which present a problem. One first suspects incomplete satiation. This explanation, however, cannot account for the behavior observed on the fifth day of testing under satiation, when food was available in the apparatus. Under this condition, the available food was never eaten; but all Ss responded to the panel. The median latency of these responses was .2 sec. Thus, when there is an additional criterion in terms of which to justify the statement that the Ss were satiated, it is found that they make at least one short-latency response. In the light of this evidence, one is forced to accept the view that some motive other than hunger in the usual sense was energizing this behavior, and (more important) that this motive functions in the absence of the original motive under which the habit was learned. One possibility is the operation of an acquired drive of the sort postulated by Tolman (9), whose general position is that techniques or responses which have, in the past, led to primary reinforcement somehow become ends in themselves. However, the acceptance of this position raises at least two questions: (1) Why should this acquired drive "extinguish" as rapidly as the latency changes observed in the trials under satiation lead one to suppose it does? (2) In about 50 per cent of the responses obtained under satiation, the Ss ate the available food, even though they just refused the same kind of food in a familiar container in the apparatus. How shall this be explained? One suggestion is that behavior which has previously terminated in eating tends to complete itself; i.e., to continue to terminate in eating, even when the animal is satiated. But this is no explanation—rather, it is a restatement of an observation.

Fortunately, these questions are amenable to experimentation. If the behavior observed under satiation is mediated by a secondary drive, it should be possible to increase the strength of a response tendency tested under satiation by increasing the number of trials for the acquisition of this drive. And, if behavior which has, in the past, terminated in eating tends to complete itself under satiation, then the presence or absence of food should influence performance even under satiation when the food presumably has no drive-reduction value. One would predict a greater persistence of the response tendency under satiation for conditions where the food is present than for conditions where the food is absent.

## SUMMARY

Twelve female albino rats were taught a panel-pushing response to obtain food after 24 hr. of food deprivation. Then they were tested under different amounts of drive when the drive-controlling operations were prefeeding or deprivation. Measurements of behavior strength in terms of median reciprocal latency of the response were obtained after 0, 10, and 15 min. of prefeeding, and after deprivations of 10 min., 30 min., 50 min., 60 min., 2 hr., 8 hr., 15 hr., and 24 hr. Associated with prefeeding there occurred a rapid decrease in reciprocal latency which persisted for the first hour after eating to satiation. Between 1 hr. and 2 hr. of deprivation a rapid increase in reciprocal latency occurred. Beyond 2 hr. this measure increased more slowly up to 24 hr. The shape of the function resembles that presented by Saltzman and Koch (7) for resistance to extinction. It also is like a curve described by Hull (1). The characteristics of the behavior observed under satiation suggest the operation of a motive other than hunger, perhaps an acquired drive of the sort postulated by Tolman (9).

## REFERENCES

1. Hull, C. L. Behavior postulates and corollaries—1949. *Psychol. Rev.* 1950, *57*, 173–180.
2. Hull, C. L. *Principles of behavior.* New York: D. Appleton Century, 1943.
3. Dixon, W. J., & Mood, A. M. The statistical sign test. *J. Amer. statist. Ass.,* 1946, *41*, 557–566.
4. Koch, S., & Daniel, W. J. The effect of satiation on the behavior mediated by a habit of maximum strength. *J. exp. Psychol.,* 1945, *35*, 167–185.
5. Perin, C. T. Behavior potentiality as a joint function of the amount of training and the degree of hunger at the time of extinction. *J. exp. Psychol.,* 1942, *30*, 95–109.
6. Reynolds, B. The relationship between the strength of a habit and the degree of drive present during acquisition. *J. exp. Psychol.,* 1949, *39*, 296–305.
7. Saltzman, I., & Koch, S. The effect of low intensities of hunger on the behavior mediated by a habit of maximum strength. *J. exp. Psychol.,* 1948, *38*, 347–370.
8. Skinner, B. F. *The behavior of organisms.* New York: D. Appleton Century, 1938.
9. Tolman, E. C. *Drives toward war.* New York: D. Appleton Century, 1942.
10. Webb, W. B. The motivational aspect of an irrelevant drive in the behavior of the white rat. *J. exp. Psychol.,* 1949, *39*, 1–14.
11. Zeaman, D., & House, B. J. Response latency at zero drive after varying numbers of reinforcements. *J. exp. Psychol.,* 1950, *40*, 570–583.

# 26 • Neal E. Miller

## Studies of Fear as an Acquirable Drive

How motives are learned has always been a central motivational issue, and fear, in particular, has long been regarded as a highly significant (and by some, the only) learnable drive. This study by Miller has had its impact, not because it demonstrates how fear is learned, for this is open to alternative explanations. Rather it stands as a prototype of a methodology which has produced a total literature concerning fear and avoidance learning that is one of the most impressive accomplishments in psychology. It has produced a subject matter which has had major influence on clinical therapeutic practice as well as animal studies of elementary learning processes.

*An important role* in human behavior is played by drives, such as fears, or desires for money, approval, or status, which appear to be learned during the socialization of the individual (*1, 12, 16, 17, 18,*). While some studies have indicated that drives can be learned (*2, 8, 15*), the systematic experimental investigation of acquired drives has been scarcely begun. A great deal more work has been done on the innate, or primary drives such as hunger, thirst, and sex.

Fear is one of the most important of the acquirable drives because it can be acquired so readily and can become so strong. The great strength which fear can possess has been experimentally demonstrated in studies of conflict behavior. In one of these studies (*3*) it was found that albino rats, trained to run down an alley to secure food at a distinctive place and motivated by 46-hour hunger, would pull with a force of 50 gm. if they were restrained near the food. Other animals, that had learned to run away from the end of the same alley to escape electric shock, pulled with a force of 200 gm. when they were restrained near that place on trials during which they were not shocked and presumably were motivated only by fear. Furthermore, animals, that were first trained to run to the end of the alley to secure food and

This article is reproduced in full from the *Journal of Experimental Psychology,* 1948, *38,* 89–101. Reprinted by permission of the American Psychological Association and the author. The original title was *Studies of Fear as an Acquirable Drive: I. Fear as Motivation and Fear-reduction as Reinforcement in the Learning of New Responses.*

then given a moderately strong electric shock there, remained well away from the end of the alley, demonstrating that the habits motivated by fear were prepotent over those motivated by 46-hour hunger (9)[1]. This experimental evidence is paralleled by many clinical observations which indicate that fear (or anxiety as it is called when its source is vague or obscured by repression) plays a leading role in the production of neurotic behavior (5, 6).

The purpose of the present experiment was to determine whether or not once fear is established as a new response to a given situation, it will exhibit the following functional properties characteristic of primary drives, such as hunger: (a) when present motivate so-called random behavior and (b) when suddenly reduced serve as a reinforcement to produce learning of the immediately preceding response.

## APPARATUS AND PROCEDURE

The apparatus used in this experiment is illustrated in Fig. 26.1. It consisted of two compartments: one white with a grid as a floor and the other black with a smooth solid floor. Both of these had a glass front to enable the experimenter to observe the animal's behavior. The two compartments were separated by a door which was painted with horizontal black and white stripes. This door was held up by a catch operated by a solenoid and could be caused to drop in any one of three different ways: (a) by the E pushing a button, (b) by the rat moving a little cylindrical wheel made of horizontal rods stretched between bakelite disks and exposed above the right hand half of the door, (c) by a bar projecting 1¼ in. from the side of the apparatus in front of the upper left hand corner of the door.

The support of the grid was pivoted at the end near the door and held slightly above a contact by a little spring at the far end. Placing the rat into the apparatus caused the grid to move down a fraction of an inch and close the contact. This started an electric clock. When the animal caused the door to drop by rotating the wheel a fraction of a turn or pressing the bar (depending upon the way the apparatus was set), he stopped the clock which timed his response. The wheel was attached to a ratchet in such a way that the part of it facing the rat could only be moved downward. A brush riding on a segment of the wheel which projected through the back of the apparatus was arranged in such a way that each quarter of a revolution was recorded on an electric counter.

The animals used in this experiment were male albino rats approximately six months old. They had been tamed by handling but had not been used in any other experiment. They were allowed plenty of food and water in their home cages at all times.

[1] In both of these experiments the 46-hour food deprivation was made more effective by the fact that the animals had been habituated to a regular feeding schedule and maintained on a diet that was quantitatively restricted enough to keep them very thin but qualitatively enriched with brewer's yeast, cod liver oil, and greens to keep them healthy.

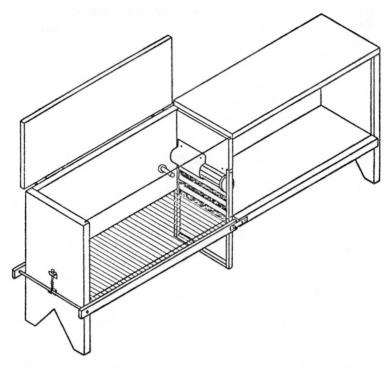

Figure 26.1.  Acquired drive apparatus. The left compartment is painted white, the right one black. A shock may be administered through the grid which is the floor of the white compartment. When the animal is placed on the grid which is pivoted at the inside end, it moves down slightly making a contact that starts an electric timer. When the animal performs the correct response, turning the wheel or pressing the bar as the case may be, he stops the clock and actuates a solenoid which allows the door, painted with horizontal black and white stripes, to drop. The *E* can also cause the door to drop by pressing a button. The dimensions of each compartment are $18 \times 6 \times 8\frac{1}{2}$ in.

The procedure involved the following five steps:

1. *Test for initial response to apparatus.*—The animals were placed in the apparatus for approximately one min. with the door between the two compartments open and their behavior was observed.

2. *Trials with primary drive of pain produced by electric shock.*—The procedure for administering shock was designed to attach the response of fear to as many as possible of the cues in the white compartment instead of merely to the relatively transient stimulus trace of just having been dropped in. This was done so that the animal would remain frightened when he was restrained in the compartment on subsequent non-shock trials. The strength of shock used was 500 volts of 60 cycle AC through a series resistance of 250,000 ohms. The animals were given 10 trials with shock. On the first trial they

were allowed to remain in the white compartment for 60 sec. without shock and then given a momentary shock every five sec. for 60 sec. At the end of this period of time the E dropped the door and put a continuous shock on the grid.

As soon as the animal had run into the black compartment, the door was closed behind him and he was allowed to remain there for 30 sec. Then he was taken out and placed in a cage of wire mesh approximately nine in. in diameter and seven in. high for the time between trials. Since the animals were run in rotation in groups of three, the time between trials was that required to run the other two animals, but was never allowed to fall below 60 sec. This procedure was followed on all subsequent trials.

On the second trial the animal was placed into the center of the white compartment facing away from the door, was kept there for 30 sec. without shock, at the end of which time the shock was turned on and the door opened. On trials 3 through 10 the grid was electrified before the animal was dropped on it and the door was opened before he reached it. On odd numbered trials the animal was dropped at the end of the compartment away from the door and facing it; on even numbered trials he was dropped in the center of the compartment facing away from the door.

3. *Non-shock trials with experimenter dropping door.*—The purpose of these trials was to determine whether or not the animals would continue to perform the original habit in the absence of the primary drive of pain from electric shock, and to reduce their tendency to crouch in the white compartments and to draw back in response to the sound and movement of the door dropping in front of them.[2] Each animal was given five of these non-shock trials during which the E dropped the door before the animal reached it. As with the preceding trials the animals were dropped in facing the door on odd numbered trials and facing away from it on even numbered ones; they were allowed to remain in the black compartment for 30 sec. and were kept in the wire mesh cage for at least 60 sec. between trials.

4. *Non-shock trials with door opened by turning the wheel.*—The pur-

---

[2] During the training in the next step (learning to rotate the wheel), crouching would interfere with the type of responses necessary in order to hit the wheel and withdrawing would prevent the animals from going into the black compartment and having their fear reduced immediately after hitting the wheel. Apparently crouching occupies a dominant position in the innate hierarchy of responses to fear. Similarly withdrawing seems to be either an innate or a previously learned response to the pattern of fear plus a sudden stimulus in front of the animal. During the shock trials the response of fear is learned to the pattern of shock plus white compartment and the responses of running are learned to the pattern of shock plus stimuli produced by the fear response plus the cues in the white compartment. When the shock stimulus drops out of the pattern, the generalized fear and running responses elicited by the remainder of the pattern are weaker. The innate crouching response to fear is then in conflict with the generalized running responses to the pattern of fear plus cues in the alley. If the door is closed, the extinction of running and other related responses may reduce their strength to the point where crouching becomes dominant. If the door is dropped in front of the animal so that he can immediately run out of the white compartment, the reduction in the strength of fear will be expected to strengthen the relative dominance of running and related responses to the stimulus of fear plus the cues in the white compartment and the sight and sound of the door dropping.

pose of these trials was to determine whether the continued running without shock was the mere automatic persistence of a simple habit, or whether an acquired drive was involved which could be used to motivate the learning of a new habit. During these trials the E no longer dropped the door. The apparatus was set so that the only way the door could be dropped was by moving the wheel a small fraction of a turn. The bar was present but pressing it would not cause the door to drop. The animals that moved the wheel and caused the door to drop were allowed to remain 30 sec. in the black compartment. Those that did not move the wheel within 100 sec. were picked out of the white compartment at the end of that time. All animals remained at least 60 sec. between trials in the wire mesh cage. All animals were given 16 trials under these conditions. On each trial the time to move the wheel enough to drop the door was recorded on an electric clock and read to the nearest 10th of a sec.

5. *Non-shock trials with door opened by pressing the bar.*—The purpose of these trials was to determine whether or not animals (a) would unlearn the first new habit of turning the wheel if this habit was no longer effective in dropping the door, and (b) would learn a second new habit, pressing the bar, if this would cause the door to drop and allow them to remove themselves from the cues arousing the fear. Animals that had adopted the habit of crouching in the white compartment till the end of the 100 sec. limit and so had not learned to rotate the wheel were excluded from this part of the experiment. These trials were given in exactly the same way as the preceding ones except that the apparatus was set so that turning the wheel would not cause the door to drop but pressing the bar would. During these trials there was no time limit; the animals were allowed to remain in the white compartment until they finally pressed the bar.[3] The time to press the bar was recorded on an electric clock to the nearest 10th of a sec. and the number of revolutions of the wheel was recorded on an electric counter in quarter revolutions.

## SUGGESTED IMPROVEMENTS IN PROCEDURE

In the light of further theoretical analysis and experimental results it is believed that the above procedure could be improved by the following changes: (a) Have the door drop down only part of the way so that it remains as a hurdle approximately two in. high over which the animals have to climb, thus introducing components of standing up and reaching into the initial response. This should favor the subsequent occurrence of wheel turning or bar pressing. (b) Connect the door to an electronic relay so that it will fall when touched and require the animals to touch it in order to make it fall during steps 2 and 3 of the experiment. This should tend to accomplish the same purpose as the preceding change and also insure that the animals have the response of running through the

[3] One animal which did not hit the bar within 30 min. was finally discarded.

door attached to the stimulus produced by its dropping when they are very close to it. (c) Increase the number of non-shock trials in step 3 to approximately 12 in order to further counteract crouching. (d) At the end of the time limit in step 4, drop the door in front of the animal instead of lifting him out of the white compartment. This should tend to maintain the strength of the habit of going through the door and make it less likely that crouching or sitting will be learned.

## RESULTS

In the test before the training with electric shock, the animals showed no readily discernible avoidance or preference for either of the two chambers of the apparatus. They explored freely through both of them.

During the trials with primary drive of pain produced by electric shock, all of the animals learned to run rapidly from the white compartment through the door, which was dropped in front of them by the *E*, and into the black compartment. On the five trials without shock, and with the *E* still dropping the door, the animals continued to run. The behavior of the animals was markedly different from what it had been before the training with the primary drive of pain from electric shock.

When the procedure of the non-shock trials was changed so that the *E* no longer dropped the door and it could only be opened by moving the wheel, the animals displayed variable behavior which tended to be concentrated in the region of the door. They would stand up in front of it, place their paws upon it, sniff around the edges, bite the bars of the grid they were standing on, run back and forth, etc. They also tended to crouch, urinate, and defecate. In the course of this behavior some of the animals performed responses, such as poking their noses between the bars of the wheel or placing their paws upon it, which caused it to move a fraction of a turn and actuate a contact that caused the door to open. Most of them then ran through into the black compartment almost immediately. A few of them drew back with an exaggerated startle response and crouched. Some of these eventually learned to go through the door; a few seemed to learn to avoid it. Other animals abandoned their trial-and-error behavior before they happened to strike the wheel and persisted in crouching so that they had to be lifted out of the white compartment at the end of the 100 sec. period. In general, the animals that had to be lifted out seemed to crouch sooner and sooner on successive trials.

Thirteen of the 25 animals moved the wheel enough to drop the door on four or more out of their first eight trials. Since, according to theory, a response has to occur before it can be reinforced and learned, the results of these animals were analyzed separately and they were the only ones which were subsequently used in the bar-pressing phase of the experiment.[4] The average speed (reciprocal of time in seconds) with which these animals opened the door by moving the wheel on the 16 successive trials is presented in Fig. 26.2. It can be seen that there is a

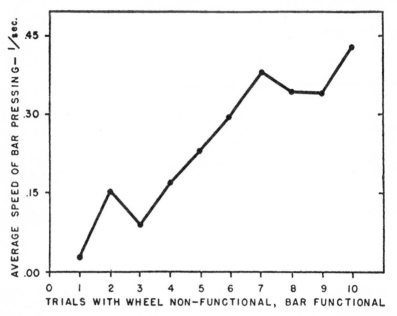

Figure 26.2.   Learning the first new habit, turning the wheel, during trials without primary drive. With mild pain produced by an electric shock as a primary drive, the animals have learned to run from the white compartment, through the open door, into the black compartment. Then they were given trials without any electric shock during which the door was closed but could be opened by turning a little wheel. Under these conditions the 13 out of the 25 animals which turned the wheel enough to drop the door on four or more of the first eight trials learned to turn it. This figure shows the progressive increase in the average speed with which these 13 animals ran up to the wheel and turned it enough to drop the door during the 16 non-shock trials.

definite tendency for the animals to learn to turn the wheel more rapidly on successive trials. Eleven out of the 13 individual animals turned the wheel sooner on the 16th than on the first trial, and the two animals which did not show improvement were ones which happened to turn the wheel fairly soon on the first trial and continued this performance

[4] In a subsequent experiment (*13*) in which further steps suggested by the theoretical analysis (see footnote 2 and Suggested Improvements in Procedure) were taken to get rid of the crouching, none of the 24 animals in the group which had received the strong shock had to be eliminated for crouching; all of them learned to perform the new response during the non-shock trials.

throughout. The difference between the average speed on the first and 16th trials is of a magnitude ($t = 3.5$) which would be expected to occur in the direction predicted by theory, less than two times in 1000 by chance. Therefore, it must be concluded that those animals that did turn the wheel and run out of the white compartment into the black one definitely learned to perform this new response more rapidly during the 16 trials *without* the primary drive of pain produced by electric shock.

When the setting on the apparatus was changed so that the wheel would not open the door but the bar would, the animals continued to respond to the wheel vigorously for some time. It was obvious that they had learned a strong habit of responding to it. Eventually, however, they stopped reacting to the wheel and began to perform other responses. After longer or shorter periods of variable behavior they finally hit the bar, caused the door to drop, and ran through rapidly into the black compartment. On the first trial the number of complete rotations of the wheel ranged from zero to 530 with a median of 4.75. On successive trials during which turning the wheel did not cause the door to drop, the amount of activity on it progressively dropped till by the tenth trial the

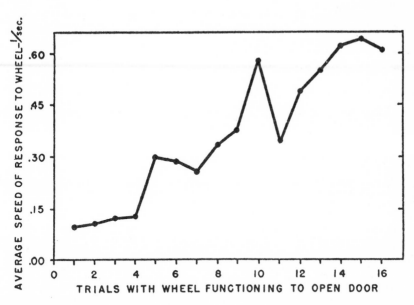

Figure 26.3. Unlearning of the habit of turning the wheel during trials on which it no longer serves to reduce the acquired drive. When conditions were changed so that turning the wheel was ineffective (and pressing the bar was effective) in causing the door to drop and allowing the animal to run from the white into the black compartment, the animals showed a progressive decrement in the response of rotating the wheel. Each point is based on the median scores of 13 animals.

range was from 0 to 0.25 rotations with a median of zero. The progressive decrease in the amount of activity on the wheel is shown in Fig. 26.3. It is plotted in medians because of the skewed nature of the distribution. Twelve out of the 13 rats which were used in this part of the experiment gave fewer rotations of the wheel on the tenth than on the first trial. From the binomial expansion it may be calculated that for 12 out of 13 cases to come out in the direction predicted by the theory is an event which would be expected to occur by chance less than one time in 1000. Thus, it may be concluded that the dropping of the door, which is presumed to have produced a reduction in the strength of fear by allowing the animals to escape from the cues in the white compartment which elicited the fear, was essential to the maintenance of the habit of rotating the wheel.

The results on bar pressing are presented in Fig. 26.4. It can be seen that the speed of bar pressing increased throughout the 10 non-shock

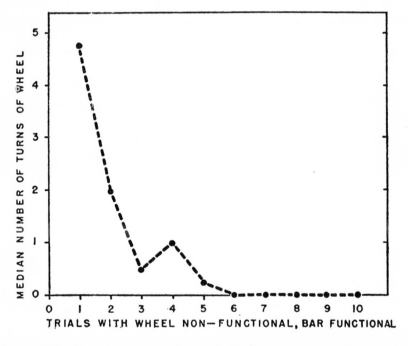

Figure 26.4. Learning a second new habit, bar pressing, under acquired drive. Conditions were changed so that only pressing the bar would cause the door to drop and allow the animals to run from the white compartment where they had been previously shocked, into the black one where they had escaped shock. During non-shock trials under these conditions, the animals learned a second new habit, pressing the bar. Each point is based on the average speed of 13 animals.

trials during which that response caused the door to drop. Since the last trial was faster than the first for 12 out of the 13 animals, the difference was again one which would be expected by chance less than one time in 1000.

## DISCUSSION

On preliminary tests conducted before the training with electric shock was begun, the animals showed no noticeable tendency to avoid the white compartment. During training with the primary drive of pain produced by electric shock in the white compartment, the animals learned a strong habit of quickly running out of it, through the open door, and into the black compartment.

On non-shock trials the animals persisted in running from the white compartment through the open door into the black one. On additional non-shock trials during which the door was not automatically dropped in front of the animals, they exhibited so-called random behavior and learned a new response, turning the wheel, which caused the door to drop and allowed them to escape into the black compartment. This trial-and-error learning of a new response demonstrated that the cues in the white compartment had acquired the functional properties of a drive and that escape from the white into the black compartment had acquired the functional properties of a reward.

At this point the results of two later experiments which serve as controls should be briefly mentioned. One of these (13) demonstrated that the capacity of the cues in the two compartments to motivate and reinforce new learning was a function of the strength of the primary drive involved in the previous stage of the training. Animals put through the same procedure in every respect except that the primary drive was a weak one produced by a 90 volt electric shock showed no tendency to learn a new habit (which in this case was bar pressing) on subsequent non-shock trials. Animals, given their initial training with a stronger primary drive produced by a 540 volt shock, showed rapid learning of the new response on subsequent non-shock trials. For these two groups all other features of the experiment were exactly the same including possible initial preferences for the different features of the two compartments and trials of running in the apparatus with the last response to the cues in the white compartment being going through the door into the black one, etc. Therefore, the difference in learning during the non-shock trials must have been a function of the previous training, and more specifically a function of the strength of the primary drive involved in that training.

The second experiment which serves as a control demonstrated that if the non-shock trials were continued long enough, the new habit of pressing the bar and the older response of running through the door would both eventually extinguish (*11*). Thus, in this situation the primary drive of pain is essential not only to the establishment of the acquired drive, but also to its maintenance.

In the present experiment, when the animals were dropped into the white compartment on the non-shock trials following their training with shock, they exhibited urination, defecation, tenseness, and other forms of behavior which are ordinarily considered to be symptoms of fear. Furthermore, the procedure of having been given a number of moderately painful shocks in this compartment would be expected to produce fear. Therefore, it seems reasonable to conclude that the acquirable drive motivating the learning of the new response of turning the wheel was fear and that a reduction in the strength of this fear was the reinforcing agent. Thus, this experiment confirms Mowrer's (*14*) hypothesis that fear (or anxiety) can play a role in learning similar to that of a primary drive such as hunger.

In terms of the hypothesis put forward in Miller and Dollard (*12*) the cues in the white compartment acquire their drive value by acquiring the capacity to elicit an internal response which produces a strong stimulus. Whether this strong stimulus is produced by peripheral responses, such as those involved in the blanching of the stomach and the tendency for hair to stand on end, or by central impulses which travel from the thalamus to sensory areas of the cortex is a matter of anatomical rather than functional significance. Fear may be called a stimulus-producing response if it shows the functional characteristics of such responses, in brief, obeys the laws of learning and serves as a cue to elicit learned responses such as the verbal report of fear.

The general pattern of the fear response and its capacity to produce a strong stimulus is determined by the innate structure of the animal. The connection between the pain and the fear is also presumably innate. But the connection between the cues in the white compartment and the fear was learned. Therefore the fear of the white compartment may be called an acquired drive. Because fear can be learned, it may be called acquirable; because it can motivate new learning, it may be called a drive.

Running through the door and into the black compartment removed the animal from the cues in the white compartment which were eliciting the fear and thus produced a reduction in the strength of the fear response and the stimuli which it produced. This reduction in the strength of the intense fear stimuli is presumably what gave the black compartment its acquired reinforcing value.

If the reduction in fear produced by running from the white into the black was the reinforcement for learning the new habit of wheel turning, we would expect this habit to show experimental extinction when that reinforcement was removed. This is exactly what happened. During the first trial on which turning the wheel no longer dropped the door, the animals gradually stopped performing this response and began to exhibit other responses. As would be expected, the one of these responses, pressing the bar, which caused the door to drop and allowed the animal to remove himself from the fear-producing cues in the white compartment, was gradually learned in a series of trials during which the wheel turning was progressively crowded out. Thus, it can be seen that the escape from the white compartment, which presumably produced a reduction in the strength of the fear, played a crucial role, similar to that of a primary reward, in the learning and maintenance of the new habits.

Some of the implications of the principles which this experiment has demonstrated should be mentioned briefly. It can be seen that being able to learn a response (fear of the white compartment) which in turn is able to motivate the learning and performance of a whole category of new responses (turning the wheel, pressing the bar, and any other means of escape from the white compartment) greatly increases the flexibility of learned behavior as a means of adapting to a changing environment.

The present experiment has demonstrated the drive function of fear as a response which presumably produces a strong stimulus. But if fear is a strong response-produced stimulus, it will be expected to function, not only as a drive, but also as a cue mediating secondary generalization. Thus, when fear is learned as a new response to a given situation, all of the habits which have been learned elsewhere in response to fear, as well as the innate responses to fear, should tend to be transferred to that new situation. Evidence supporting this deduction has been secured in a recent experiment by May (7).

It seems possible that the potentialities of response-produced stimuli as mediators of secondary generalization and sources of acquirable drive may account in stimulus-response, law-of-effect terms for the type of behavior which has been described as 'expectancy' and considered to be an exception to this type of explanation. If it should turn out that all of the phenomena of expectancy can be explained on the basis of the drive and cue functions of response-produced stimuli, expectancy will of course not vanish; it will be established as a secondary principle derivable from more primary ones.

The mechanism of acquired drives allows behavior to be more adaptive in complex variable situations. It also allows behavior to appear more baffling and apparently lawless to any investigator who has not had the opportunity to observe the conditions under which the acquired drive was established. In the present experiment the learning and performance of the responses of turning the wheel and pressing the bar are readily understandable. An *E* dealing with many rats, a few of which without his knowledge had been shocked in the white compartment, might be puzzled by the fact that these few rats became so preoccupied with turning the wheel or pressing the bar. In the present experiment, the white and black compartments are very obvious features of the animal's environment. If more obscure external cues or internal ones had been involved, the habits of turning the wheel and pressing the bar might seem to be completely bizarre and maladaptive. One hypothesis is that neurotic symptoms, such as compulsions, are habits which are motivated by fear (or anxiety as it is called when its source is vague or obscured by repression) and reinforced by a reduction in fear.[5]

## SUMMARY

Albino rats were placed in a simple apparatus consisting of two compartments separated by a door. One was white with a grid as a floor; the other was black without a grid. Before training, the animals showed no marked preference for either compartment. Then they were placed in the white compartment, received an electric shock from the grid, and escaped into the black compartment through the open door. After a number of such trials, the animals would run out of the white compartment even if no shock was on the grid.

To demonstrate that an acquired drive (fear or anxiety) had been established, the animals were taught a *new* habit *without further shocks*. The door (previously always open) was closed. The only way that the door could be opened was by rotating a little wheel, which was above the door, a fraction of a turn. Under these conditions, the animals exhibited trial-and-error behavior and gradually learned to escape from the white compartment by rotating the wheel.

If conditions were changed so that only pressing a bar would open the door, wheel turning extinguished, and a second new habit (bar pressing) was learned.

Control experiments demonstrated that the learning of the new habits was dependent upon having received moderately strong electric shocks during the first stages of training.

The following hypotheses were discussed: that responses which produce strong stimuli are the basis for acquired drives; that such responses

---

[5] The author's views on this matter have been materially strengthened and sharpened by seeing the way in which Dollard (*4*), working with symptoms of war neuroses, has independently come to a similar hypothesis and been able to apply it convincingly to the concrete details of the case material.

may be the basis for certain of the phenomena of learning which have been labeled 'expectancy,' thus reducing this from the status of a primary to a secondary principle and that neurotic symptoms, such as compulsions, may be motivated by anxiety and reinforced by anxiety-reduction like the two new responses learned in this experiment.

## REFERENCES

1. Allport, G. W. *Personality*. New York: Henry Holt, 1937.
2. Anderson, E. E. The externalization of drive. III. Maze learning by nonrewarded and by satiated rats. *J. genet. Psychol.*, 1941, 59, 397–426.
3. Brown, J. S. Generalized approach and avoidance responses in relation to conflict behavior. Dissertation, Yale Univer., 1940.
4. Dollard, J. Exploration of morale factors among combat air crewmen. *Memorandum to Experimental Section, Research Branch, Information and Education Division, War Department*, 9 March 1945.
5. Freud, S. *New introductory lectures on psychoanalysis*. New York: Norton, 1933.
6. Freud, S. *The problem of anxiety*. New York: Norton, 1936.
7. May, M. A. Experimentally acquired drives. *J. exp. Psychol.*, 1948, 38, 66–77.
8. Miller, N. E. An experimental investigation of acquired drives. *Psychol. Bull.*, 1941, 38, 534–535.
9. Miller, N. E. Experimental studies of conflict behavior. In J. McV. Hunt (Ed.), *Personality and the behavior aisorders*. New York: Ronald Press, 1944. Pp. 431–465.
10. Miller, N. E. Theory and experiment relating psychoanalytic displacement to stimulus-response generalization. *J. abnorm. soc. Psychol.*, in press.
11. Miller, N. E. Studies of fear as an acquirable drive. II. Resistance to extinction. (In preparation.)
12. Miller, N. E., & Dollard, J. *Social learning and imitation*. New Haven: Yale Univer. Press, 1941.
13. Miller, N. E., & Lawrence, D. H. Studies of fear as an acquirable drive. III. Effect of strength of electric shock as a primary drive and of number of trials with the primary drive on the strength of fear. (In preparation.)
14. Mowrer, O. H. A stimulus-response analysis of anxiety and its role as a reinforcing agent. *Psychol. Rev.*, 1939, 46, 553–565.
15. Mowrer, O. H., & Lamoreaux, R. R. Fear as an intervening variable in avoidance conditioning. *J. comp. Psychol.*, 1946, 39, 29–50.
16. Shaffer, L. F. *The psychology of adjustment*. Boston: Houghton Mifflin, 1936.
17. Watson, J. B. *Psychology from the standpoint of a behaviorist*. Philadelphia: Lippincott, 1924.
18. Woodworth, R. S. *Dynamic psychology*. New York: Columbia Univer. Press, 1918.

# 27 • Janet A. Taylor

## The Relationship of Anxiety to the Conditioned Eyelid Response

Experimental studies of human motivation have often proved difficult to perform and to replicate because of the lack of techniques for assessing human motives or standard methods of manipulating motive strength in the laboratory. This study by Taylor brought a new impetus to laboratory studies by introducing an easily administered test based on items related to manifest anxiety and showing how such a test could be reliably used in standard experimental situations. Her approach had the added advantage of suggesting ways in which drive theory formulated largely from studies of lower organisms could be applied to situations employing human subjects. The effect has been to spawn another body of literature which has added materially to the intricacy of psychological treatments of emotionally based drive.

A *number of* contemporary psychological theorists, such as Hull (2), Tolman (9), and Lewin (5), are in agreement that behavior is a function of two principal classes of variables: learning or cognitive on the one hand, and motivation on the other. These classes of variables are further conceived by Hull (2) as combining according to some multiplicative function, implying that a zero value of either will lead to failure of response occurrence. Hull has specifically proposed the following:

$$R = f(_sE_R) = f\frac{(_sH_R \times D)}{100}$$

where $R$ = response measure (e.g., latency, frequency of response)

$_sE_R$ = excitatory potential, a theoretical construct

$_sH_R$ = habit strength, a theoretical construct

$D$ = drive strength, a theoretical construct.

This article is reproduced in full from the *Journal of Experimental Psychology*, 1951, *41*, 81–92. Reprinted by permission of the American Psychological Association and the author.

In Hull's formulations, $_sH_R$ represents the hypothetical learning factor resulting from the operation of such experimental variables as the number and amount of reinforcements, etc. The hypothetical construct $D$ represents the total effective drive strength operating in the organism at a given moment. Thus, in a particular experimental situation, the value of $D$ is assumed to be determined not only by the relevant need (i.e., the one which is reduced by the response under consideration) but also by the aggregate strength of all other primary and secondary needs operative at the moment. These latter are referred to as irrelevant needs. Needs, in turn, are a function of certain antecedent conditions (e.g., environmental deficiencies, noxious stimulation).

There is now available concrete evidence supporting the chief implications of Hull's assumption that needs combine to produce drive strength, although there is still considerable doubt concerning the precise form of the summation equation. Kendler (4), Webb (10), and Amsel (1) have all found that two needs will summate to produce a greater drive strength than will either one alone. In the Kendler and Webb studies, two appetitional needs, hunger and thirst, were involved, while in the Amsel study a hunger need was combined, in one instance, with a primary need to escape pain, and in the second instance, with a secondary need to escape anxiety.[1]

In many experimental learning situations, e.g., salivary conditioning, instrumental reward and escape learning, problem solving, etc., the drive strength is primarily a function of a relevant need, one produced by the $E$'s manipulation of a maintenance schedule or by administration of a noxious stimulus. The response to be learned leads either to the needed goal object or to escape from the noxious stimulus. A quite different situation exists, however, in the case of classical defense conditioning in which a noxious stimulus of very brief duration is administered. The identification of the drive operative at the time of the conditioned response is much more difficult in this situation. As the conditioned response anticipates the occurrence of the noxious stimulus, one cannot appeal to the latter as the direct basis of the drive.

One suggested answer to this problem is that offered by Mowrer (7). He has assumed that the drive is a secondary one, anxiety. According to his analysis, stimuli which are consistently present when a noxious stimulus occurs come to evoke an emotional response of fear in anticipation of the noxious stimulus. This anticipatory fear reaction, termed anxiety, is assumed to provide the motivational state, or drive ($D$).

Further analysis, however, suggests difficulties in this explanation which Mowrer (8) himself later considered. The fear response is mediated by the autonomic nervous system which has a longer latency and a

---

[1] Amsel (1), following Mowrer (7) defined anxiety as the conditioned form of the pain reaction.

slower rate of responding than the skeletal reactions mediated by the central nervous system. In those defense conditioning situations in which the temporal interval between onset of the conditioned and unconditioned stimulus is small, shorter than the latency of the fear response, and the unconditioned response is a skeletal reaction of short duration, the CS, UCS, and CR have all taken place *before* the fear response has occurred. Appeal to such an anxiety reaction as the motivational factor operating at the time the conditioned response occurs therefore cannot be made.

Several other possibilities can be suggested in solution of this problem. It is an oversimplification to consider that only the conditioned stimulus has become associated with the unconditioned response: the total experimental situation also becomes associated with the fear or anxiety reaction. While differentiation between total situation and total situation-plus-CS (which is followed by the noxious stimulus) may be expected to take place in the course of time, initially, at least, the anxiety level of the S is heightened and is therefore available as a motivator at the time of the onset of the CS. In human Ss, a further source of anxiety would be that elicited by verbal reactions. Depending on the extent to which the emotional responses have been conditioned to verbal cues, Ss will exhibit different amounts of anxiety.

A further possible source of drive for the conditioned response may be the residual effects of the internal emotional response to the noxious stimulus of the preceding trial. The duration of such an emotional response is relatively long and extends beyond the range of temporal intervals usually employed in conditioning experiments. Since the effects have not worn off completely between trials, these residual effects may be cumulative and possibly serve to raise the total drive level of the S during the course of the experimental session.

A third suggested source of the motivation comes from the aggregate of primary and secondary needs that are, in a sense, brought to, but not specifically induced by, the experimental situation, i.e., what was referred to above as irrelevant needs. These needs are also regarded as contributing to the total drive strength ($D$) operative at the moment of the conditioned response. An investigation by Welch and Kubis (11) gives some support to these suggestions. These experimenters studied the rate of conditioning of the PGR in normal Ss, and in Ss from a hospital population diagnosed psychiatrically as exhibiting pathological anxiety. The criteria used in the selection of the anxious Ss, in agreement with general psychiatric thought, were behavioral symptoms which we could describe as overt manifestations of a persistently heightened emotional level. Their results indicated that there was almost no overlap between groups, the anxiety Ss being far superior to the normal group in reaching the conditioning criterion. The difference in mean scores of the groups was significant at a high level of confidence.

The hypothesis suggested in the present investigation is that such sources of drive as those hitherto discussed combine in some such manner as assumed by Hull to produce a total effective drive state ($D$), and that it is this drive value that determines the strength of the conditioned response in the classical defense conditioning situation.[2] In testing this hypothesis it is, of course, impossible to arrange a situation in which no drive is present at the time of occurrence of the conditioned response. If, however, differences in drive level among groups of Ss can be produced either experimentally or by some selection procedure, a comparison of the rate and level of development of the CR in these groups should provide data bearing on the hypothesis proposed.

## PLAN OF EXPERIMENT

The present experiment was designed to provide data on the effect that differing levels of total effective drive would have on the development of a conditioned defense response. The rate of the development of the conditioned eyelid response was measured as a function of (1) the general anxiety (drive) level of the S, defined independently of the experimental situation, and (2) differential instructions, aimed at raising or lowering anxiety level, given to the S during the course of the conditioning trials.

An attempt was made to secure different levels of drive by two means: (1) selection of two groups of Ss, hereafter designated as anxious and non-anxious, on the basis of extreme scores made on a test to be described below, and (2) administration of differential instructions, designated as anxiety-producing or anxiety-relieving, introduced during the course of the conditioning trials. The effect of these two sets of variables on the development of the conditioned eyelid response was then studied.

*Selection of anxious and non-anxious subjects.*—On the assumption that variations in what is described psychiatrically as "manifest anxiety" reflect variations in generalized levels of drive, a test of manifest anxiety was constructed for the purpose of selecting Ss for the experimental groups.

Approximately two hundred items from the Minnesota Multiphasic Personality Inventory were submitted to clinical staff members with instructions to designate those items that they judged to be indicative of manifest anxiety according to a definition furnished them. The 65 items on which there was 80 per cent agreement or better were selected for the final anxiety scale.

These 65 items, supplemented by 135 additional items from the MMPI tapping some dimension other than anxiety, were administered in group form to 352 students in a course in Introductory Psychology. The

---

[2] In terms of Hull's theory, this drive value ($D$) multiplies the learning *factor* ($H$) to determine the excitatory potential ($E$). Different response measures are then assumed to be a direct function of the excitatory potential value.

measures, based only on the 65 anxiety items, ranged from a low anxiety score of 1 to a high anxiety score of 36, with a median score of 14. The form of the distribution was slightly skewed in the direction of high anxiety.

The selection of subjects for the anxious and non-anxious groups was made by taking the individuals who scored in the upper 12 and lower 9 percentiles of the distribution.[3] The raw test scores for the non-anxious group ranged from 1 to 7, and for the anxious group from 24 to 36.

It was presumed that Ss from the anxious end of the scale would be at a relatively higher drive level ($D$) than the Ss from the low end of the scale. In terms of Hull's assumptions as to the role of drive strength in determining response strength, this would imply that the anxious subjects would exhibit a relatively higher level of conditioning.

*Experimental manipulation of anxiety level of subjects.*—During the course of the conditioning trials, half of the Ss in each group was told that the intensity of the UCS would be increased on subsequent trials, although the actual intensity remained the same. The other half of each group was told that the intensity would be decreased, but again the actual intensity was kept constant. Those receiving instructions designed to heighten anxiety were designated as a plus group, while those receiving instructions aimed at lowering anxiety were designated as a minus group.

## EXPERIMENTAL METHOD

*Subjects.*—Sixty-seven Ss were run in the experiment, but 7, 3 from the anxious group and 4 from the non-anxious group, did not meet certain criteria established for their performance, and for this reason, their records were excluded from the experimental results. Three of the anxious Ss and 1 of the non-anxious Ss thus eliminated exceeded the criterion determined for spontaneous blinking rate. This criterion will be discussed in a later section. Of the 3 remaining Ss, all in the non-anxious group, 1 was eliminated because of equipment failure, 1 because of misunderstanding of instructions, and 1 because he gave initial CR's to the CS alone, prior to paired presentation of the CS and UCS.

Of the remaining Ss, 30 were from the high (anxious) end of the distribution and 30 from the low (non-anxious) end.

*Apparatus and method of recording.*—The S was seated in a dental chair in a semi-darkened room adjoining that in which the recording apparatus and stimulus controls were located. Fixed in a reclining position in the chair with his head braced against a headrest, the S was instructed, on receiving a ready signal, to fixate a 6-cm. circular milk glass window, or disc, placed at a

---

[3] All students in the introductory course are required to serve a certain number of hours as experimental Ss, so that no connection was made by the students between the test and their selection as Ss. Furthermore, each S was told that his name had been selected at random in order to secure a representative sample of the class.

distance of 132 cm. in front of him. The brightness of the glass window between trials was .05 apparent foot-candles.

The conditioned stimulus consisted in an increase in brightness of the disc to 1.51 apparent foot-candles. The duration of the conditioned stimulus on each trial was 550 msec. Five hundred msec. following the onset of the CS, the unconditioned stimulus, a puff of air, was administered in the region of the external canthus of the right eye. The air puff was produced by the fall of an 80-mm. column of mercury, magnetically released, in a manometer. Intertrial intervals of 15, 20, and 25 sec., averaging 20 sec. and fixed according to a pre-arranged schedule, were employed.

The onset of the CS was controlled by the closing of a switch on an electronic timer (3). The latter, in turn, controlled the onset of the US at the appropriate time interval and the duration of the conditioned stimulus. An electromagnetic marker recorded the onset of the two stimuli on a Grass polygraph.

The closing of the eyelid was recorded by a combination of mechanical and electrical means. A modified Burlington Model 435 Power Level Meter was used in conjunction with a Thordarson type T 30W55 amplifier. The meter was mounted on an adjustable headband in such a position that the thread attached to the point of the meter could be fastened directly to a formed plastic extension fastened on the upper eyelid of the S. Thus any motion of the eyelid caused a voltage to be generated in the armature of the meter, which was amplified by the amplifier and ink-recorded on the polygraph paper as a deviation from a straight line by means of a Brush BL 902 Pen Motor. The latter was operated directly from the 500-ohm output tap of the amplifier output transformer.

Closure of the eyelid was recorded on the moving paper as a deviation from a horizontal line, the extent of this deviation being a function of both the amplitude and speed of the eyelid movement. A CR was recorded whenever the record showed a deflection of 1 mm. or more in the interval 200 to 500 msec. following the onset of the CS. Responses occurring less than 200 msec. after the onset of the CS were classified as original responses (alpha or beta) and were not included in the data.

*Conditioning procedure.*—Conditioning was carried out in two sessions, approximately 24 hr. apart. On day 1, each S first received three presentations of light alone. Subjects exhibiting more than one CR to the light were automatically excluded from the experimental groups. A single puff of air, unaccompanied by the light, was then administered and spontaneous blinking recorded for 40 sec. following onset of the puff. Any S who blinked (i.e., whose record showed deviation from a straight line) more than 20 per cent of the final 30 sec. of this period was also excluded from the experimental groups, although complete conditioning records were obtained for each of these Ss.[4]

[4] Since it is impossible to distinguish between conditioned responses and spontaneous blinks occurring in the same time range of the CR, Ss who show high blinking rates spuriously inflate conditioning data, especially in the earlier blocks of trials. For this reason, Ss with a high blinking rate were eliminated from the experimental groups. Of the 4 Ss exceeding the criterion, 3 were from the anxious group, so that this criterion did not favor the group for which the prediction of superior conditioning had been made.

Immediately following the preliminary trials, all Ss were given 20 paired presentations of the light and air puff. At the conclusion of trial 20, differential instructions were introduced as described above, half of each group receiving anxiety-producing instructions, half anxiety-relieving. Following administration of the instructions, conditioning trials 21–70 were given in the same fashion as trials 1–20.

In a second experimental session on the following day, 10 additional conditioning trials were given. After the final conditioning trial, half of each group was given extinction trials to a criterion of 10 successive response failures. The remaining half of each group was subjected to a special set of conditions that will not be discussed here as they are concerned with a problem outside the scope of the present experiment.

The same initial instructions prior to the conditioning trials were given to all Ss. These were originally designed to acquaint the S with the general experimental situation and to produce a more or less neutral set so that responses would be neither inhibited nor facilitated. No additional instructions were given at the beginning of the second session. At the end of the first experimental session all Ss were given a questionnaire in which their understanding of instructions and reactions to the experimental situation were ascertained.

## RESULTS

### Effects of Differential Instructions on Development of the CR

Curves of acquisition of the CR based on the percentage of anticipatory responses occurring in successive blocks of 10 trials for the four subgroups are presented in Fig. 27.1. The two upper curves show the course of conditioning for the anxious subgroups (anxious plus and anxious minus). It will be noted that the two curves overlap, neither showing any consistent superiority. The same overlapping and lack of difference is also apparent in the lower pair of curves which represent the learning of the two non-anxious subgroups.

That the total amount of conditioning, the per cent of CR's in all 80 trials, did not differ for the plus and minus groups is apparent from Table 27.1. The differences, it will be noted, are very small and without significance.

TABLE 27.1. Mean percentage of CR's exhibited on 80 conditioning trials.

| Group | Mean Percentage of Total CR's | $\sigma_M$ |
|---|---|---|
| Anxious plus | 59.75 | 4.767 |
| Anxious minus | 59.45 | 6.261 |
| Non-anxious plus | 29.14 | 4.968 |
| Non-anxious minus | 26.63 | 6.749 |

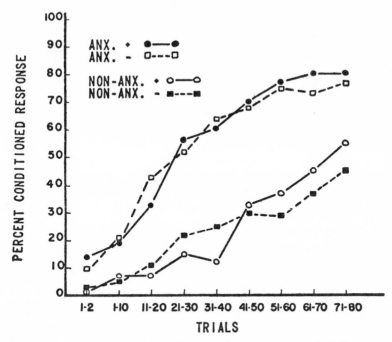

Figure 27.1. Acquisition curves showing the percentage of CR's in successive blocks of 10 trials for the four experimental groups.

On the possibility that the effect of the instructions may have been only temporary, a further analysis was made of the magnitude of the increase in percentage of CR's made from the block of trials (11–20) preceding the instructions to the blocks (21–26 and 21–30) immediately following. Table 27.2 presents the means of increases. It will be seen that in every instance but one, the plus groups made a greater increase than the corresponding minus group. Furthermore, the differences were greater

TABLE 27.2. Mean increase in percentage of CR's made from blocks of trials preceding the instructions, to the blocks immediately following.

| | Increase of CR's | | | |
| | Trials 11–20 vs. 21–26 | | Trials 11–20 vs. 21–30 | |
| Group | Mean Percent | $\sigma_M$ | Mean Percent | $\sigma_M$ |
|---|---|---|---|---|
| Anxious plus | 20.3 | 7.2 | 17.7 | 5.2 |
| Anxious minus | 4.7 | 7.5 | 12.7 | 6.4 |
| Non-anxious plus | 13.7 | 4.3 | 10.7 | 5.8 |
| Non-anxious minus | 5.7 | 5.4 | 12.0 | 6.0 |

for the shorter 5-trial period than for the longer 10-trial period. These results suggest that the instructions may have had a very brief differential effect. However, none of the differences was statistically significant, the largest $t$, that obtained for the difference between the anxious plus and anxious minus groups for trials 11–20 versus 21–25, was 1.61, significant at only the 20 percent level of confidence.

While the instructions may have had a slight and very temporary effect on the conditioning, the data indicate that the hypothesis that there is no difference between subgroups cannot reasonably be rejected. Accordingly, the data of the two anxious and the two non-anxious subgroups have been combined so that only two groups of 30 subjects, an anxiety and a non-anxiety group, will be treated in further discussion of the results.

### Effect of Anxiety and Non-anxiety on the Strength of the CR

The distributions of percentages of CR's for the anxious and non-anxious Ss occurring in trials 21–50, 51–80, and 1–80 are presented in Fig. 27.2, and the corresponding medians of the percentages in Table 27.3.

TABLE 27.3. Median percentage of CR's given for the specified trial blocks by the anxious and non-anxious groups.

|  | Anxious | Non-anxious |
| --- | --- | --- |
| Trials 21–50 | 69.0 | 13.3 |
| Trials 51–80 | 81.7 | 41.7 |
| Trials 1–80 | 64.7 | 22.6 |

Although there is overlapping between the two groups in each of the three sets of conditioning scores, the anxious group is clearly superior in amount of conditioning. A non-parametric test, described by Mann and Whitney (6), was employed to test the hypothesis that there was no difference with respect to the distribution of scores for each of the three sets of CR measures. On the basis of this hypothesis the probability that the obtained differences between the anxious and non-anxious groups would occur is, in each case, less than .0001.

Inspection of the curves in Fig. 27.3, representing the development of the CR's throughout the course of conditioning in terms of median number of CR's in successive 10-trial blocks, reveals that the anxious group was above the non-anxious in the number of CR's for every block.[5]

---

[5] The median number of CR's was used because it does not distort the conditioning scores as does the mean percentage of CR's. In the early blocks of trials, the latter measure tends to be high, while on the last blocks, the mean per cent score tends to be distorted downward.

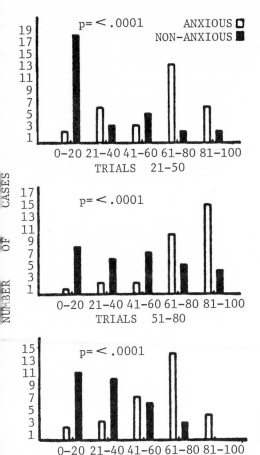

Figure 27.2. Distributions showing the percentage of CR's given by the anxious and non-anxious groups in different trial blocks.

Furthermore, it will be seen that the 50 per cent level of conditioning (median of 5 CR's) barely attained by the non-anxious groups in the final block of 10 trials was reached in the anxious Ss as early as trials 21–30. The shape of the conditioning curves suggests that the anxious Ss had reached an asymptote or limit of conditioning by the end of the training trials, whereas the curve for the non-anxious group was still showing an increase.[6]

[6] In a subquent experiment by the writer and K. W. Spence in which 100 conditioning trials were given, it was found that the asymptote of the non-anxious group was reached by 80 trials.

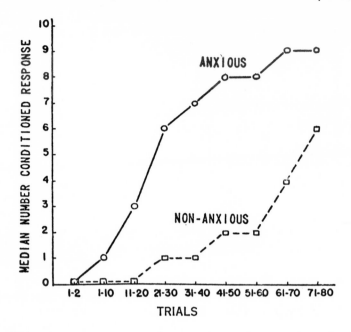

Figure 27.3. Acquisition curves showing the median number of CR's for the anxious and non-anxious groups in successive blocks of 10 trials.

The data on resistance to extinction, obtained from 14 anxious and 14 non-anxious Ss, are presented in Table 27.4.[7] Although the anxious

TABLE 27.4. Mean number of CR's and mean number of trials to the extinction criterion of ten response failures.

| Group | No. of CR's to Extinction Criterion | | No. of Trials to Extinction Criterion | |
|---|---|---|---|---|
| | Mean | $\sigma_M$ | Mean | $\sigma_M$ |
| Anxious | 2.35 | .49 | 15.43 | 1.45 |
| Non-anxious | 1.50 | .41 | 12.35 | .20 |

group is higher in both the mean number of responses and mean number of trials to the extinction criterion of 10 response failures, the difference between the means in neither case is significant. However, the *t* computed for the trial measure is between the 5 and 10 per cent level of confidence, while the *t* for the number of CR's is at the 20 per cent level. It is possible

[7] As was stated previously, approximately half of the Ss in each group was given extinction trials, the remaining Ss being subjected to experimental conditions in connection with a problem outside the scope of the present experiment.

that the differences would be more significant with a greater number of Ss.

## DISCUSSION

### Anxiety Level in Relation to the Development of the Conditioned Response

The consistent superiority of the anxious group in all measures of conditioning and extinction strongly indicates that there is a marked difference in the rate with which the strength of the CR is developed under the two conditions of drive (anxiety) level. This might be interpreted to mean that anxious Ss have a more rapid conditioning rate, or, in Hull's terms, develop habit strength ($_sH_R$) at a faster rate. While this is a possibility, it should be noted that in Hull's theoretical formulation of the assumed relations between response strength, excitatory potential ($_sE_R$), habit and drive strength, $R = f(_sE_R) = f(H \times D)$, the slope of the rise of the $_sE_R$ value, and hence the response measure, is a direct function of *both* H and D values. Thus, it is theoretically possible for the habit growth curves for two groups of Ss to be identical and yet have both the $_sE_R$ and response curves increase at two quite different rates in the two groups because of different D values.

In the present experiment an attempt was made to manipulate the variable D by obtaining varying strengths of an independent response measure (anxiety) in two groups of Ss. That is, it was assumed that drive level (D) varies directly with differing degrees of anxiety, the latter being defined in terms of the number of positive verbal responses made to test items judged to be indicative of anxiety.

In terms of Hull's formulations, higher levels of D should lead to a more rapid growth of the $_sE_R$ curve and hence to a more rapid rise in the frequency curve of CR's. The results of the experiment are in agreement with these assumptions in that the frequency of response curve for the high drive (anxious) group was considerably higher than that for the low drive group.

It is also theoretically possible, however, to interpret the experimental results in terms of the second variable, $_sH_R$, i.e., the different performance curves for the two groups could be the result of more rapid learning (increase in H) in the anxious group, as well as higher drive level. It might be argued that the anxious group reacts more strongly to the UCS so that while the UCS is physically equal for the two groups, it is a more intense stimulus psychologically for the anxious Ss. If this were the case, then the cessation of the UCS would result in a greater reduction in D in the anxious group, and hence in greater increments of $_sH_R$ ($\Delta H$), as the magnitude of the reward is postulated by Hull to be one of the variables determining the increment of $_sH_R$. The present experiment offers no conclusive evidence favoring one or the other of these alternative interpretations.

## Clinical Concepts of Anxiety and Their Relation to Amount of Conditioning

In clinical usage, the concept of anxiety is employed in at least two very different ways: (1) as the term applied to a particular behavior syndrome, and (2) as a hypothetical construct that is assumed to determine certain types of overt behavioral adjustments.

In the first sense, the definition of anxiety seems to be fairly unambiguous: a group of widespread, directly observable overt reactions (e.g., restlessness, tenseness, excessive perspiration, etc.) are identified as "manifest anxiety" and considered as the definition of anxiety neurosis. Further, these symptoms are assumed to be accompanied or paralleled by internal emotional responses (primarily controlled by the autonomic nervous system). It is this definition of anxiety which was adopted in the present experiment, the test items being descriptions of the response syndrome clinically termed "anxiety." Thus, different numbers of positive responses to the test items were assumed to reflect different degrees of manifest anxiety and of the parallel internal responses as well. It will be recalled that the assumption made earlier was that Hull's intervening variable, drive ($D$) is some positive function of the intensity of this internal emotional response.

The theoretical construct of anxiety has reference to a hypothetical state or event occurring under the skin of the organism. The construct is introduced in connection with behavior disorders (e.g., hysteria, paranoia, compulsions) in which the overt symptoms are considered to be a defense against the hypothetical internal anxiety state. The occurrence of these response symptoms is assumed to reduce the anxiety at least partially and temporarily.

Thus, in the case of manifest anxiety, as the result of past experiences, the internal response and the overt anxiety behavior occur, the former presumably determining the drive level. In the second instance, as a result of previous experience, the hypothetical anxiety state is aroused and followed by the occurrence of defense reactions reducing the anxiety.

What relationship this second hypothetical anxiety construct has to Hull's drive is a question. It might be postulated that the functional properties of the internal anxiety state are similar to those of the internal responses occurring in manifest anxiety so that different degrees of the hypothetical anxiety will be accompanied by different levels of drive. If this is the case, then the defense reactions can be considered to be a function of a high drive level. However, to the extent that the defense responses are effective in reducing drive, drive level will be low.

If these assumptions are correct, then the conditioning procedure provides a valuable technique for the investigation of this hypothetical anxiety state in the various behavior disorders. That is, the effectiveness of a particular defense syndrome in reducing the internal anxiety should be reflected in the strength of the conditioned responses exhibited by individuals with these symptoms, as compared with a group of normals. For example, the classic hysteric should show an equal or lesser amount of conditioning than the normal, since the hysterical symptoms are postulated to be more or less completely and continuously effective in reducing anxiety. On the other hand, if the repetitive act can be prevented from occurring, individuals exhibiting a repetitive compulsion should be superior conditioners, since these responses are believed to be preceded by an increasingly higher amount of anxiety. Thus, by the conditioning technique, an indirect measure is provided so that speculations concerning the role of the hypothetical anxiety in the behavior disorders can be subjected to experimental test.[8]

## SUMMARY

The present experiment attempted to evaluate the hypothesis that the amount of conditioning exhibited in a defense conditioning situation is a direct function of the level of total effective drive.

Two groups of 30 Ss each were chosen on the basis of extreme scores made on a test of manifest anxiety, those with high scores being the anxious (high drive) group, and those with low scores being the non-anxious (low drive) group. Both groups were run in a conditioned eyelid situation. During the course of the conditioning trials, differential instructions, designed to raise or to lower anxiety level, were administered, half of each group receiving anxiety-producing, and half anxiety-relieving instructions.

The results indicate that the subgroups receiving differential instructions did not differ in the amount of conditioning in the subsequent course of the training trials, showing that the instructions had little or no effect. The data from the anxious and non-anxious groups show that the anxious group was consistently superior in amount of conditioning throughout the course of the conditioning trials, the difference between the two groups being highly significant statistically.

The data on resistance to extinction, obtained from 14 of the anxious and 14 of the non-anxious Ss, indicate that although the anxious group was

---

[8] A study utilizing this technique is currently being carried out by the writer and K. W. Spence to test these hypotheses with several diagnostic groups.

higher in both measures of extinction, the difference between the two groups was in neither case significant.

The results are interpreted to mean that such sources of drive as those employed in the present experiment combine in some manner to produce a total effective drive state, and that this value is a determiner of the strength of the conditioned response.

## REFERENCES

1. Amsel, A.   The combination of a primary appetitional need with primary and secondary emotionally derived needs. *J. exp. Psychol.*, 1950, *40*, 1–14.
2. Hull, C. L.   *Principles of behavior.* New York: D. Appleton-Century, 1943.
3. Hunter, T. A., & Brown, J. S.   A decade-type electronic interval-timer. *Amer. J. Psychol.*, 1949, *62*, 570–575.
4. Kendler, H. H.   Drive interaction. I. Learning as a function of the simultaneous presence of hunger and thirst drives. *J. exp. Psychol.*, 1945, *35*, 96–109.
5. Lewin, K.   The conceptual representation and the measurement of psychological forces. *Contrib. psychol. Theor.*, 1938, *1* (4).
6. Mann, H. B., & Whitney, D. R.   On a test of whether one of two random variables is stochastically larger than the other. *Ann. math. Statist.*, 1947, *18*, 50–60.
7. Mowrer, O. H.   A stimulus-response analysis of anxiety and its role as a reinforcing agent. *Psychol. Rev.*, 1939, *46*, 553–565.
8. Mowrer, O. H.   On the dual nature of learning—a reinterpretation of "conditioning" and "problem-solving." *Harv. educ. Rev.*, Spring, 1947, 102–148.
9. Tolman, E. C.   The determiners of behavior at a choice point. *Psychol. Rev.*, 1938, *45*, 1–41.
10. Webb, W. B.   An experimental study of the role of an irrevelant drive in the behavior of the white rat. Unpublished doctoral dissertation, State Univer. Iowa, 1948.
11. Welch, L., & Kubis, J.   The effect of anxiety on the conditioning rate and stability of the PGR. *J. Psychol.*, 1947, *23*, 83–91.

# 28 • David C. McClelland, Russell A. Clark, Thornton B. Roby, and John W. Atkinson

## *The Projective Expression of Needs*

Where Taylor recognized a debt to Hullian drive theory in developing her techniques for studying human motivation, McClelland and his colleagues built on the earlier work of motivational psychologists such as Freud, Lewin, and Murray. Followers of both Taylor and McClelland, in spite of their use of different testing strategies and different working hypotheses, nevertheless showed similarities in their mutual concern for combining experimental and psychological testing techniques in programs having fundamentally theoretical aims. This early study by the McClelland group has been, like Taylor's, among the first in an accelerating series of related studies having far-reaching implications for the growth of understanding in human motivation.

*Previous experiments* in this series have been concerned with establishing principles for the interpretation of projective behavior. The method has been to note changes in perception (*13*) and apperception (*2*) resulting from different intensities of the hunger drive. A number of shifts in perception and in the thematic content of stories have been established which provide important clues for the detection of the strength of the hunger drive from projective records.

But the crucial experiment in the series remains to be performed. No one is particularly interested in diagnosing hunger from projective responses. The point is, do the same kinds of shifts occur for an experimentally controlled psychogenic need, or are the clues which have been discovered applicable only to some simple physiological tension like hunger?

The present experiment was designed to answer this crucial question. It was decided to choose a psychogenic need which could be aroused experimentally and to see whether it produced perceptive and

This article is reproduced in full from the *Journal of Experimental Psychology*, 1949, 39, 242–255. Reprinted by permission of the American Psychological Association. The original title was *The Projective Expression of Needs: IV. The Effect of the Need for Achievement on Thematic Apperception.*

apperceptive changes similar to those already noted for hunger. The need chosen was 'need achievement' or 'need mastery,' the need which *presumably* is aroused by experimentally inducing ego-involvement, according to a technique which by now is fairly well standardized among psychologists experimenting in the field of personality (*1, 16, 17*). The word 'presumably' is used advisedly. No one knows for certain that there is a unitary n Achievement [1] which can be satisfied by success and aroused by failure in the same way that hunger is satisfied by food and aroused by deprivation of food. However, if manipulation of the conditions of ego-involvement produces the same kinds of effects on projection as manipulation of hours of food deprivation, there will be some basis for considering the psychogenic state aroused as a need, at least to the extent that it functions like a physiological one. It was to establish this kind of parallelism of function that work began in this series with a simple physiological tension which nearly everyone would accept as a need or drive. Consequently, if the results in this experiment are in substantial agreement with those obtained in earlier ones in the series, it will provide evidence for the existence of higher order psychogenic needs which at least function like those at a simpler physiological level.

One of the crucial problems in this type of experiment is to find a scoring system for thematic stories which is objective enough to provide high observer agreement and sensitive enough to reflect changes in motivational states. So a further purpose of this experiment is to develop the scoring system further which was found useful for hunger (*2*) and to test its applicability to a more complex psychogenic need. The standardization of an objective scoring system for projective records should ultimately make possible some general principles for interpreting them. What is even more important, it should open up for experimentation the whole field of imagination which has been more or less neglected, except by the clinicians, since introspection was discredited as a fruitful approach to arriving at psychological principles.

## PROCEDURE

The materials used in the experiment consisted of some simple paper and pencil tests and some slides for thematic apperception. There were seven short tests: anagrams (4 min.), scrambled words I (3 min.), scrambled words II (4 min.), and four motor perseveration tests (*4*) in each of which the subject performed a writing task as often as possible in the normal manner for one min. and then backwards or in some unusual manner for one min. The total time taken including pauses between tests for instructions was about

---

[1] The convention adopted by Murray (*15*) of shortening need to n will be followed throughout this paper.

25 min. The tests were chosen on the basis of past experience (4, 5) for a factor analysis, in connection with which they will be described in detail (6). Their chief function here was to provide the basis for inducing ego-involvement. That is, there were two main fundamentally different conditions under which the tests were administered. In one (hereafter referred to as *relaxed*), the test administrators were introduced by the instructor at a regular class session as some graduate students who were trying out some tests. This orientation was reinforced by further remarks by the 'graduate student' to the effect that these tests had been recently devised, were still in the developmental stage, and that data were being collected in order to perfect them. Throughout, the emphasis was clearly on the fact that the experimenters were interested in testing the tests and not the students. These instructions were designed to create an easy relaxed atmosphere in which the need for achievement was at a minimum.

In the other main condition (hereafter referred to as *failure*), the administration of the preliminary tests was quite different. After the experimenters had been introduced to the class by the instructors they began passing out the text booklets with no explanation as to the purpose of the experiment. The only remarks made dealt with the first test—anagrams—and the necessity of paying close attention to directions as the tests were timed. After completing the first test, the subjects calculated and recorded their scores on it. Then they filled out a short questionnaire which asked for: name, high school and college attended with estimated class standing in each, IQ (if known), and an estimate of their general intelligence (above average, average or below average). The purpose of the questionnaire was only incidentally to obtain information. It was primarily to get a subject ego-involved in the situation by making his test score known to himself and outsiders in relation to a lot of other achievement-related facts about him.

This aim was further supported by the following remarks then made by one of the experimenters (RAC) given from memory so as to give the impression of spontaneity:

> The tests which you are taking directly indicate a person's general level of intelligence. These tests have been taken from a group of tests which were used to select people of high administrative capacity for positions in Washington during the past war. Thus in addition to general intelligence, they bring out an individual's capacity to organize material, his ability to evaluate crucial situations quickly and accurately; in short, these tests demonstrate whether or not a person is suited to be a leader.
>
> The present research is being conducted for the Navy to determine which educational institutions turn out the highest percentage of students with the administrative qualifications shown by superior scores on these tests. For example, it has been found that Wesleyan University excels in this respect. You are being allowed to calculate your own scores, so that you may determine how well you do in comparison with Wesleyan students.

At this point the experimenter quoted norms for Test I that were so high that practically everyone in the class failed and placed in the lowest quarter of the Wesleyan group. It was then explained that Test I was the single most diagnostic test in the battery and thus an individual's standing on this first test would be a good indication of how well he might expect to do on the test as a whole. The rationale of giving these instructions after the first test rather than before was partly to place their first scores near the actual comparison with the norms and partly to provide a basis for testing the initial comparability of the groups in another part of the experiment (6).[2]

After this the subjects went on and completed all the paper and pencil tests. At the end they added up individual test scores to obtain a total score and again were given falsely high norms "so that they could see how well they had done as a whole in comparison with Wesleyan students."

That these instructions succeeded in producing very different effects on the students was obvious to even the most casual observer. Under the ego-involving instructions, they worked hard and quietly, and there were various obvious expressions of dismay when the norms were announced. There was no indication that the instructions were disbelieved. Under relaxed conditions the subjects were as a whole more relaxed and gave the impression of enjoying the tasks as they would a series of parlor games.

At the conclusion of the paper and pencil tests used to arouse different need states the other experimenter (JWA) read the following instructions:

This next test is a test of your creative imagination. A number of pictures will be projected on the screen before you. You will have 20 seconds to look at the picture and then five minutes to make up a story about it. Notice that there is one page for each picture. The same four questions are asked. They will guide your thinking and enable you to cover all the elements of a plot in the time allotted. Plan to spend about a minute on each question. I will keep time and tell you when it is about time to go on to the next question for each story. You will have a little time to finish your story before the next picture is shown.

Obviously there are no right or wrong answers, so you may feel free to make up any kind of a story about the pictures that you choose. Try to make them vivid and dramatic, for this is a test of creative imagination. Do not merely describe the picture you see. Tell a story about it. Work as fast as you can in order to finish in time. Make them interesting. Are there any questions? If you need more space for any question use the reverse side.

In addition to the two major conditions of administration so far described, four other attempts were made to arouse a third intensity of n Achieve-

---

[2] It goes without saying that the instructions contained nothing that was true, or for that matter nothing that was completely false. The references to the Navy and to the Washington administrators (cf. *18*) were all partly true and could be checked by over-curious psychology students. Every other precaution was taken to prevent leaks about these instructions since they were crucial to the whole experiment. Different classes at the same institution were run on the same day and the procedure was not 'exposed' to the students at the end or even to the instructors (whose kindness in cooperating under the circumstances is greatly appreciated).

ment which would provide the three points desirable for establishing trends and for making the data comparable with the hunger experiment (2). In the first place a *success* group was created by announcing norms after the first test and at the end which were so low that all or nearly all the students succeeded as compared with Wesleyan students. This was supposed to satiate n Achievement; but a preliminary analysis of the results indicated that while this seemed to be partly true, the need aroused by the ego-involving instructions persisted into the subsequent thematic apperception test which was interpreted as a further test of ability. Consequently, the position of this group on the need continuum was not clear and the results from it did not seem worth reporting here. Secondly, there was a simple *ego-involved* group in which no norms were announced. It was expected that these Ss would reflect an aroused n Achievement which would be purer and not contaminated by recent experiences of failure or success. However, the stories written under this condition were so tense, inhibited, and cautious (cf. *14*) that it proved difficult to analyze them, and the results from this group will also not be reported here.

The results from the final two variants on the major conditions proved meaningful and will be reported. In the first of these a group of Wesleyan students was run in a *neutral* but not 'relaxed' atmosphere. That is, they were task-oriented rather than ego-oriented (cf. *1*), but they were asked to cooperate seriously and to work hard on the tasks so that adequate norms for them could be established. The reason for these instructions was to get a somewhat higher n Achievement tension than under the relaxed condition in order to maximize individual differences as part of another experiment (6). In the final group an attempt was made to get an intenser n Achievement aroused, by giving the Ss a taste of success by quoting low norms after the first test followed by an even greater failure at the end induced by quoting high norms. This will be referred to as the *success-failure* group.

There was no indication in the ego-involved groups that the projective tests were not still part of the program of testing for administrative ability. The slides used for eliciting the written stories consisted of two especially chosen for this experiment (two men in overalls looking or working at a machine; a young man looking into space seated before an open book), followed by two taken from the Murray Thematic Apperception Test ('father' talking to 'son'—TAT 7 BM; boy and surgical operation—TAT 8 BM). The pictures were chosen to suggest achievement—either at a specific task or general level and in school-related and unrelated situations.

The Ss were all male, a majority veterans, and all college students taking various psychology courses at the University of Connecticut (at Storrs and the Ft. Trumbull extension); New Britain State Teachers College, Trinity College, and Wesleyan University. They were run in regular class room periods either in the summer of 1947 or the Spring of 1948. The entire testing time which included some tests of perceptual inference reported elsewhere (*14*) took from 70–80 min., except for the *success-failure* condition in which it was necessary to cut out the last three of the motor perseveration tests to finish within a normal 50-min. class period.

*Scoring.*—The stories were scored according to the same general system used in the hunger experiment (2) with additions and modifications necessitated by the more complex nature of the need involved. Detailed scoring criteria cannot be given here for lack of space, but they have been reported in full elsewhere (12). The following brief descriptions will serve at least to identify the major categories used.

*g, t, or u I:* Achievement imagery is scored either general (g I) or task (t I); stories with no achievement imagery are scored as unrelated (u I). To be general, achievement imagery must deal with some long term problem of getting ahead at the ego ideal level (career, schooling, inventing something, etc.). Everything else, particularly the specific task situation, was classified as t I.

*Ach or D th:* Themas or plots are scored if the achievement imagery is central to the story. If the plot is concerned with someone who is in an achievement difficulty which has or is anticipated as having serious long term effects, it is scored as deprivation thema (D th); otherwise it is an achievement thema (Ach th), though there may be many difficulties in the way of the goal.

*d p or w:* Deprivations or blocks in the path of progress or indications of past failures, i.e., things not running smoothly. If the trouble is with the person himself it is scored d p; if it is with the world it is scored d w. D th was not scored for d also unless there was some secondary and separate source of hindrance.

*N p or g:* Need for achievement is stated in the story either at the personal level ("He wants to be a doctor") or at the general level ("He wants to serve humanity").

*I +, −, or o:* Instrumental activity which is either successful (I +) unsuccessful (I −) or of doubtful outcome (I o). The person in the story must do something (even if only think or decide) about achieving his goal which is separate from the statement of the situation and the statement of outcome: e.g., "the boy graduates from school" is scored for outcome but considered too passive to represent instrumental activity.

*Ga +, −, or o:* Anticipations of outcomes (goal responses) which may be either of success (Ga +, "He is thinking of the day when he'll be famous") or failure (Ga −, "He is worried about what will happen") or neither (Ga o, "He is wondering what will happen").

*nu or ho P:* Nurturant or hostile press. Some person in the story is either actively helping or hindering the person working for achievement. The hindrance must be more hostile than a static block (see d w above).

*S:* Substitution. A person who meets with an obstacle in his achievement instigation-action sequence adopts a substitute instrumental act or substitute goal response ("He drowns his sorrows in a tavern").

*G or G′ + or −:* Goal responses which occur either within the story (G) or at the end (G′) and which may be either positive affect ("He was happy in his new job") or negative affect ("The boy is worried over having flunked his exam").

*O +, −, or o:* Outcomes of the whole story are judged according to whether they are happy (O +), unhappy (O −), or doubtful (O o). Finer breakdowns were made but did not prove useful. The total outcome was not necessarily the same as that for the instrumental activity and was also separate from the final affect (G'). For example, "They fixed the machine" is scored O + but not G' +, because it doesn't say they were pleased about it.

The following story illustrates how the scoring was used. After each word or phrase scored is written in parenthesis the scoring symbol applicable:

1. What is happening? Who are the persons?—"The boy is being talked to by his father, maybe something about what has happened in school, or he may be planning to get married."

2. What has led up to the situation—that is, what has happened in the past?—"He may have flunked out of school (D th) and is being lectured on what is expected of him (nu P)."

3. What is being thought—what is wanted? By whom?—"The father wants the boy to make good (N p), he is thinking that he wants his son to follow in his footsteps and make good in life (Ga +, g I)."

4. What will happen? What will be done?—"The boy will do his best, will go back to school because he has learned a lesson he will never forget (I +). He will make good this time and be a success (O +)."

As this example shows, the scoring was not done from the viewpoint of a single character with whom the writer supposedly identified, although this is the usual method of procedure. Thus the father's wish for the son's success is scored N p (father's viewpoint) and the father's help is scored nu P (son's viewpoint). The rationale for this was the conviction that determination of the person with whom the writer identified was often difficult and that it was not necessary—e.g., in this instance it is just as possible to suppose that the writer is projecting his wish to do well into the father figure as into the son. Note also that the second statement of the father's wish is not scored again. A given category is scored only once per story no matter how many times it appears.

This example shows how decisions on the scoring of a specific item were affected by the total context and by the scoring of other items. Thus, it is not until the whole story is read that the thema is clearly one of achievement and not marriage, and it is not until the third paragraph that the decision can be made that the imagery is general and the thema one of deprivation. The factors which lead to this decision are the presence of Ga + and N p (see above definitions). It was recognized that the interdependence of scoring categories was not wholly desirable from the statistical viewpoint, but it soon became obvious that the interdependence existed at the intuitive level for categories like g I and D th, no matter how discretely the definitions might be drawn. Hence, it seemed best to state as explicitly as possible any other categories that were usually taken into account in the normal process of arriving at a judgment on a given category.

The way in which all the stories were scored will be described in full under results in the section on reliability of the scoring. It involved two judges working together without knowledge of which of three groups (neutral, failure, and success-failure) the stories belonged to.

## RESULTS

The main results of the experiment are shown in Tables 28.1, 28.2, 28.3, and 28.4, which summarize the frequency of appearance of various scoring categories for the relaxed, failure, and success-failure conditions. The results from the neutral condition, which generally fell between the relaxed and failure conditions, will be reported only in summary form. In all the tables increases or decreases from the relaxed to the failure condition are tested for significance by means of chi-square.[3]

TABLE 28.1. The number and percentage of achievement-related stories written under relaxed, failure, and success-failure conditions. The number of stories in each condition is 156 (39 Ss × 4 stories).

|                |      | Relaxed |      | Failure |      | Chi-square | Success-Failure |      |
|----------------|------|---------|------|---------|------|------------|---------|------|
|                |      | N       | %    | N       | %    |            | N       | %    |
| Imagery        |      |         |      |         |      |            |         |      |
| task           | t I  | 73      | 46.8 | 56      | 35.9 | 3.82       | 47      | 30.1 |
| general        | g I  | 26      | 16.7 | 75      | 48.1 | 35.16      | 85      | 54.5 |
| unrelated      | u I  | 57      | 36.5 | 25      | 16.0 | 16.94      | 24      | 15.4 |

NOTE: Chi-square is 3.84 and 6.64 at the .05 and .01 levels of significance, respectively.

Table 28.1 shows that there is a large and very significant increase in the number of stories dealing with general or long term achievement while there is a decrease in the number of stories with no achievement imagery and of those with task achievement imagery.

Because of this shift the method of computing percentages in Tables 28.2, 28.3, and 28.4 has been changed. Since there were significantly more stories with achievement imagery in the two failure conditions, there is a correspondingly greater opportunity for other achievement-related characteristics to appear in these conditions. But the important question is: given an achievement story, are there significant differences

[3] It should be noted that the population considered here is number of stories, rather than, as in the hunger experiment, the number of Ss showing a characteristic at least once. The latter measure, while easier to interpret statistically, is not as applicable to the data of this experiment because of the much greater frequencies obtained for many of the need-related categories. The authors realize that a chi-square test of significance applied to repeated measures from the same Ss is hard to interpret because of the peculiar nature of the universe to which the inference is made, but have decided to use it for two reasons: (1) other statistics appear to have even more serious objections, and (2) the differences found to be significant for all four pictures and used in calculating the final n Achievement score were also significant when only the results from the single most diagnostic picture (TAT 7 BM) were used.

in its internal characteristics when written under different conditions? Hence, the results for further characteristics are presented as percentages not of all stories but only of the achievement stories in each condition.

Table 28.2 shows only a significant increase in the number of deprivation themas. A comparison of the failure with the success-failure

TABLE 28.2.   The number and percentage of the achievement-related stories written under different conditions showing various story characteristics related to the description of the situation.

| Number of Stories: | Relaxed 99 | | Failure 131 | | Chi-square | Success-Failure 132 | |
|---|---|---|---|---|---|---|---|
| | N | % | N | % | | N | % |
| Plot     Ach th | 59 | 59.6 | 83 | 63.4 | | 98 | 74.2 |
| D th | 6 | 6.1 | 25 | 19.1 | 8.11 | 14 | 10.6 |
| Obstacles   d p | 12 | 12.1 | 23 | 17.6 | | 24 | 18.2 |
| d w | 22 | 22.2 | 17 | 13.0 | 3.41 | 21 | 15.9 |

NOTE: Chi-square is 3.84 and 6.64 at the .05 and .01 levels of significance, respectively.

results suggests that the former reflect sensitively the Ss' greater failure experience since the combined thema totals are nearly identical for the two conditions (82.5 and 84.8 percent respectively), both being considerably larger than the same figure for the relaxed condition (65.7 percent).

Table 28.3 shows a larger number of significant shifts in the forward-

TABLE 28.3.   The number and percentage of the achievement-related stories written under different conditions showing various story characteristics related to the characters' reaction to the situation.

| Number of Stories: | Relaxed 99 | | Failure 131 | | Chi-square | Success-Failure 132 | |
|---|---|---|---|---|---|---|---|
| | N | % | N | % | | N | % |
| Need stated: | | | | | | | |
| N p&/or g | 21 | 21.2 | 58 | 44.3 | 13.30 | 64 | 48.5 |
| Instrumental acts I + | 9 | 9.1 | 41 | 31.3 | 16.29 | 31 | 23.5 |
| I − | 7 | 7.1 | 3 | 2.3 | | 6 | 4.5 |
| I o | 6 | 6.1 | 10 | 7.6 | | 7 | 5.3 |
| Anticipatory goal response | | | | | | | |
| Ga + &/or Ga − | 15 | 15.2 | 47 | 35.9 | 12.33 | 60 | 45.5 |
| Ga o | 6 | 6.1 | 11 | 8.4 | | 15 | 11.4 |

NOTE: Chi-square is 3.84 and 6.64 at the .05 and .01 levels of significance, respectively.

looking, striving aspects of the stories. This table indicates that an aroused n Achievement increases the likelihood that characters in the story will be described as wanting to get ahead (N p), as doing something successful about getting ahead (I +), and as thinking in advance about success or failure (Ga + or Ga −). In Table 28.4 the shifts appear

TABLE 28.4.   The number and percentage of the achievement-related stories written under different conditions showing various story characteristics related to the outcome of the situation.

| Number of Stories: | Relaxed 99 | | Failure 131 | | Chi-square | Success-Failure 132 | |
|---|---|---|---|---|---|---|---|
| | N | % | N | % | | N | % |
| Press: ho P &/or nu P | 10 | 10.1 | 29 | 22.1 | 5.82 | 20 | 15.2 |
| Substitution: S | 2 | 2.0 | 11 | 8.4 | 3.20* | 7 | 5.3 |
| Goal response: | | | | | | | |
|   G &/or G' + | 4 | 4.0 | 33 | 25.2 | 18.61 | 31 | 23.5 |
|   G &/or G' − | 18 | 18.2 | 34 | 26.0 | | 32 | 24.2 |
| Outcomes:  o + | 47 | 47.5 | 63 | 48.1 | | 69 | 52.3 |
|       o − | 16 | 16.2 | 12 | 9.2 | | 24 | 18.2 |
|       o  o | 36 | 36.2 | 56 | 42.8 | | 39 | 29.5 |

NOTE: Chi-square is 3.84 and 6.64 at the .05 and .01 levels of significance, respectively.
   * Corrected for continuity.

in the number of people seen as aiding or hindering achievement (nu or ho P) and in the frequency with which positive affect is specifically mentioned, either in the course of the story or at the end (G or G' +). It is interesting to note that there are no significant changes in the outcome category, despite the fact that most of the present *a priori* systems for scoring the TAT (*3, 15, 20*) lay emphasis on this characteristic, and despite the fact that a far more elaborate breakdown of different types of endings was actually made than is reported here. There is one shift in outcomes, however, for the success-failure group, which gives significantly fewer doubtful outcomes to its stories than does the failure group. This suggests that repeated failure may cause an unwillingness to state the outcome of an achievement sequence, especially an unfavorable (0 −) outcome, since this is the category which is reduced in the failure group.

A tabulation of the frequency of appearance of each story characteristic for each S was made as a basis for obtaining a single summary n Achievement score. The characteristics which showed a significant increase in Tables 28.1–4 from the relaxed to the failure condition were scored $+ 1$ and those which decreased were scored $- 1$.[4] Thus, there were seven positive characteristics (g I, D th, N, I $+$, Ga $+$ or $-$, nu or ho P, and G or G' $+$) and two negative characteristics (t I and u I). The results from the success-failure group were not taken into account in developing the scoring system because it was felt that the need state aroused might be more complex than in the straight failure group.

Table 28.5 presents the mean n Achievement scores for each con-

TABLE 28.5. Mean n Achievement scores for the relaxed, neutral, failure, and success-failure conditions.

| N | Relaxed 39 | | Neutral 39 | | Failure 39 | | Success-Failure 39 |
|---|---|---|---|---|---|---|---|
| Mean | $-1.00$ | | 3.13 | | 5.82 | | 6.00 |
| $\sigma_m$ | .46 | | .69 | | .82 | | .73 |
| Diff. | | 4.13 | | 2.69 | | .18 | |
| $\sigma_{diff.}$ | | .83 | | 1.07 | | 1.14 | |
| Critical ratio | | 4.98 | | 2.51 | | .16 | |
| P | | $<.01$ | | $<.02$ | | $>.50$ | |

dition. The means for the relaxed and failure conditions differ very significantly as they should from the way the scoring system was devised. The success-failure condition was almost exactly equal to the failure condition as had been indicated by the comparisons in Tables 28.1–4. The neutral condition showed a moderate need strength, by this scoring system, which was significantly greater than the relaxed condition and significantly less than the two failure conditions. This last comparison is particularly important methodologically, because the papers from these three groups had been mixed together and were all scored together without the judges' knowing to which group any paper belonged. Thus, with all possibility of bias removed, there is still a significant mean difference in n Achievement score between a presumed low and high intensity of induced n Achievement.

### Reliability of the Scoring

A matter of considerable methodological importance, in view of the present tendency of experimentalists to eschew free verbal reports, is

[4] A scoring system was also tried which weighted the changes in accordance with the improbability of their having occurred by chance. However, the correlation between weighted and unweighted scores for the 39 Ss in the neutral condition was .956, confirming the high relationship found in other studies and leading to the adoption of the simpler unweighted or unit scoring.

the reliability of the scoring system used here. Consequently, reliability was studied intensively from three different angles. First, an attempt was made to determine the extent to which the judges agreed on a given category for a particular story. Since agreement is almost certainly a function of amount of the judges' experience with the scoring system, a measure of it was taken at the end of the scoring, after one of the judges had had a year's previous experience with the system amounting to the scoring of at least 3000 stories and the other had scored at least 1000 stories. The two judges always worked together, one reading the story aloud so that both could form tentative judgments independently, which were discussed, if they differed, in making the final decision. At the time the test was made they were spending on the average of two to three min. per story, or at the most from five to ten min. per S. The test consisted of drawing 10 records at random from the neutral, failure, and success-failure groups and rescoring them. The index of agreement was computed by dividing twice the agreements by the sum of the items scored on each of the two occasions. It turned out to be 291/321, or 91 percent.

Secondly, reliability was approached from a less conservative viewpoint by attempting to measure the extent to which the totals are stable for a given category on two judgments of the same records. This is more to the point in estimating the dependability of group shifts, since judges may quite possibly miss a category in one story and pick it up somewhere else leaving the total the same though not the percentage agreement. To check this, the stories written by the 39 relaxed Ss were completely rescored after all the other stories had been finished.[5] There was a nearly significant increase in the proportion of stories scored as containing achievement imagery, due to a conscious liberalization in the judges' set, but this increase did not change the ratio of general to task imagery or any of the other categories scored. Seventeen out of 22 of the category totals were within three points of each other.

Also relevant to this point is the comparability of the totals for various categories for the failure and success-failure groups. They are very close in nearly every case in Tables 28.1–4, and the mean overall n Achievement scores are practically identical. This shows that category totals are apt to be quite stable even when obtained on two different groups of Ss, and even when there are minor differences in the method of arousing n Achievement.

In the third place, the reliability of an individual's overall n Achieve-

---

[5] An attempt was made to mix the relaxed stories with others in the rescoring but it was not continued beyond the first 10, since the judges who had scored these same stories several times before easily recognized them as being very different from the others with which they were mixed. Any further attempt to conceal their identity seemed a waste of time.

ment score was tested by correlating the scores obtained for 30 individuals on two different scoring occasions. The product moment correlation was .946, indicating fairly high stability of an individual's score for his whole record. Furthermore, this correlation is probably conservative, since 20 of the 30 Ss came from the relaxed group, which reduced the range of scores, and since the scoring was done much more hastily on both occasions than it normally would be in a clinical situation.

## DISCUSSION

### Validity of n Achievement Score

No one can deny that there are differences in the story characteristics which appear in the relaxed as compared with the failure condition, but is it proper to assume that these differences represent a difference in the need for achievement in the two groups? This is the central problem of validity, of whether the score derived from these differences measures anything of importance, or more particularly of whether it measures the n Achievement which it is supposed to measure. There are two kinds of evidence which argue that it is a valid measure of n Achievement.

*The nature of the procedure* used to arouse the need provides the first basis for assuming that n Achievement was more intense in the two failure conditions. In discussing what we have labelled n Achievement, after Murray (15, p. 164), Sears states: "There are many names for this learned drive: pride, craving for superiority, ego-impulse, self-esteem, self-approval, self-assertion, but these terms represent different emphases or different terminological systems, not fundamentally different concepts. Common to all is the notion that the feeling of success depends on the gratification of this drive, and failure results from its frustration" (17, p. 236). This suggests that the experimental operations which will satiate and arouse the drive are success and failure. However, the success and failure must be in relation to some achievement goal which the Ss have set for themselves. That is, in the case of a physiological need like hunger, it is only necessary to deprive the Ss of food to arouse the drive, since the organism automatically by the consumption of energy produces in time a need for food. But in the case of a psychogenic need it is necessary first to induce Ss to want some goal like achievement. In the present experiment that was supposedly done by giving the Ss an opportunity to perform on some tests which were described to them in such a way that doing well should lead them to feel increased pride, self-esteem, self-approval, feelings of success, etc. Since these terms define what is commonly meant by the striving for success or n Achievement, if the instructions and the tests were such as to arouse these feelings, then by definition n Achievement was aroused in the failure and success-failure groups.[6] And it does seem reasonable to assume that the attainment of high intelligence and leadership as suggested in the instructions are two goals which in our society would lead to the feelings mentioned.

Granted that n Achievement was aroused by the instructions, it further seems reasonable to suppose that failure-frustration would lead to a heightened need. Although this assumption is supported by experimental evidence (8) and by the deprivation method of arousing physiological drives, we recognize that it may complicate the resulting picture here. That is, granted that failure does heighten n Achievement, it may also lead to the projection of material which is specific to the experience of failure rather than characteristic of a 'pure' heightened need.[7] It was this conviction that led to the collection of stories from an ego-involved group which had had neither success nor failure. Unfortunately, as has been reported under procedure, for reasons given fully elsewhere (cf. 14) the Ss in this group were too inhibited to write stories which could be readily analyzed. So the main comparisons had to be made between a relaxed condition and a condition in which n Achievement was augmented by failure.

*The comparison with the effect of hunger* on similar stories (2) provides the second basis for arguing that a need has been aroused by the experimental conditions. However unwise it may prove to be to have used failure to heighten the need intensity, it serves to make the need-arousal method more nearly comparable to the deprivation used to increase hunger (2). Consequently, it becomes more legitimate to ask, what is the evidence that food-deprivation and achievement-deprivation affect imagination in the same way?

Table 28.6 provides the positive evidence that the two needs have the same general effect. The case rests largely on the first three items (D th, N and I +), since failure of categories to shift may mean failure of the scoring system at some point. Even so the evidence is impressive, considering the fact that a complex psychogenic need like that for achievement might be supposed on *a priori* grounds to differ extensively from a simple primary need like hunger.

---

[6] Since these instructions are also the ones commonly called 'ego-involving' by other workers in the field (cf. *1*), it is apparent the authors believe that ego-involvement and n Achievement arousal are the same thing under certain conditions.

[7] The fact that the failure group showed more deprivation themas than the success-failure group, while both showed about the same high number of themas as compared with the relaxed group, would support this proposition. That is, one could argue that heightened need tension results in more achievement imagery central to the plot, but that failure as a method of increasing this tension shifts some of this plot or thema imagery to the deprivation category.

TABLE 28.6. A comparison of the story characteristics showing significant changes for both increased n Food and increased n Achievement.

1. An increase in the number of plots dealing primarily with deprivation of the goal in question (D th)
2. An increase in the number of times that characters in the stories were said to want or wish for the goal in question (N)
3. An increase in the mention of instrumental activities which are successful in dealing with the need-related problem (I +)
4. No change in the number of plots dealing with direct attainment of the goal (F th or Ach th)
5. No change in the amount of substitute activity, in instrumental activity of unsuccessful or doubtful outcome, or in negative affect (represented by subjective hostility in the food experiment)

There is also some negative evidence, i.e., instances of categories which shift in one experiment but not in the other. But these can rather easily be explained in terms of differences in procedure in the two experiments. For example, the biggest lack of correspondence in the two experiments was in the way a higher need decreased the favorable aspects in the food stories and increased them in the achievement stories. A case in point is the decrease in friendly press for hunger and the increase in nurturant press for n Achievement. This can be explained by the fact that the two control groups were not equivalent. The one-hour hunger group was *satiated* with respect to hunger, whereas the relaxed group in the present experiment could best be described as *unmotivated* with respect to n Achievement. Satiation undoubtedly carries over to increase the frequency of appearance of favorable story aspects, as has been shown for the n Achievement situation when success is given the Ss (12, 14). Since the low need groups therefore doubtless differed initially in the amount of favorable material projected, it is not surprising that high need groups in the two experiments produced different or even opposite effects. Other incongruencies between the two experiments are largely due to changes in the scoring system necessitated by the greater complexity of n Achievement (e.g., the general imagery category).

If one notes the major agreements and explains away in this manner the disagreements, Table 28.6 can be said to supply considerable support for the argument that the conditions of this experiment induced a state in the Ss which affected their imagination in the same general way as an increase in hunger. To the extent that one accepts hunger as a need, it would therefore seem valid to refer to the state induced by ego-involvement and failure as a need. Even if one grants this, however, it must of course still be shown that the situationally induced need affects apperception in the same way as a strong character need would, as clinically or otherwise defined. This ultimate problem of validity must await further study.

*Clinical applications.*—In the meantime, the data are sufficiently clearcut to provide some guidance for the person working with the TAT clinically. They suggest in the first place what story characteristics are apt to be important as indicators of need strength. Although the validity of these indicators is by no means finally established, they do represent an advance over the logical or *a priori* validity earlier workers in the field have been forced to assume for their scoring systems. In the second place, the data suggest to the clinician that the conditions of administration of the TAT are of considerable importance in determining the dynamic content of the stories. Stories written under relaxed, neutral, and failure conditions differed so much in the present experiment as to suggest more caution than has heretofore been indicated in assuming that the basic personality picture given by the TAT is not influenced by recent experiences (3, 7). Our results suggest strongly that the clinician should be careful to investigate such matters as how the subject conceives of the test, his reason for taking it, his relation to the testor who may or may not have given him other tests that have involved success or failure, etc.

*Nature of motivation.*—One of the most important implications of this experiment is suggested by a consideration of the categories which shifted in frequency when the need was presumably aroused. Most, if not all of them, appear to have a future reference—for instance, the stated wish for achievement, successful instrumental striving, anticipatory goal responses, and positive affect at the end of the story. Two other important characteristics—the increase in general imagery and the increase in deprivation themas—also appear to refer to the future on further scrutiny, the former because it is defined as involving a person's career or life work, and the latter because it is defined as a situation in which forces are at work against a person which would make him worse off in the future. In both instances the presence of stated need or anticipatory goal response was often useful in defining the category. On the other hand categories did not change which seemed to involve more of an objective description of the situation (plots, obstacles and outcomes) without the striving or anticipatory dimension. This, taken with similar earlier evidence (14), suggests that it is one of the major characteristics of motivation—at least achievement motivation—to be anticipatory or forward looking. This might seem to be a somewhat radical departure from the usual conception of a motive as a persisting deficit stimulus, but oddly enough Hull (9), working from entirely different data, has come to much the same conclusion—namely, that fractional anticipatory goal responses are the key to understanding purposeful and motivational phenomena. In fact, one can argue that the anticipatory goal responses observed in this experiment supply a kind of direct confirmation of Hull's view which has been very difficult to obtain with animals.

*Methodological considerations.*—Last but not least these results have an important bearing on the experimental methodology of handling verbal material. They report a method for scoring written thematic apperception stories which is sensitive enough to distinguish between the conditions under which the stories are written, which is objective enough to yield high agreement on a repeat scoring by two trained judges working together, and which is easy enough to apply quickly to an individual record. This in itself is of considerable importance in a field in which prior scoring systems have either been so complex or so dependent on clinical insight (3, 15, 20) that they are of little use to the experimental psychologist interested in studying imaginative processes.

The potential value to psychological theory of an objective scoring method for free verbal behavior is illustrated by the fact that its application in this experiment clearly indicates that phantasy does not always serve the purpose of wish-fulfillment or substitute gratification for pleasures denied in reality, an assumption which has been rather frequently made (cf. *10*, p. 93). Instead, a study of the variety of story characteristics which shifted in this experiment with an increase in need supports the parsimonious assumption that imaginative behavior is governed by the same general principles as govern any behavior. For example, a variety of experiments show the same increase in instrumental activity with increased drive at the gross motor level; others, as in the standard Pavlovian conditioning, show the same increase in anticipatory goal responses (salivation). If one grants that the principles governing imaginative behavior are no different from those governing performance when both are analyzed according to the same categories of response, then the method used here becomes a more subtle and flexible approach to the establishment and extension of those principles than the ordinary method of studying performance. Thus, for example, it would be difficult to get a performance response which would correspond to the anticipation of deprivation which follows drive arousal at the imaginative level. One might even go so far as to suggest that by the use of this method Tolman could study much more directly the 'cognitive maps' which the behavior of his rats has led him to infer are the important intervening variables in determining behavior (*19*).

## SUMMARY

Over 200 male college students wrote five-min. stories in response to four slides depicting achievement-related situations under the influence of various interpretations of the meaning of the story writing and several short pencil and paper tests taken just previously. The stories were analyzed completely for 39 Ss from each of four conditions: (1) a *relaxed* condition, in which all the tests were interpreted as being in an experimental stage, (2) a *neutral* condition, in which the tests were described as experimental but in which the Ss were urged to do their best to establish some norms, (3) a *failure* condition, in which the tests were interpreted as standardized measures of intelligence and leadership and in which the Ss wrote their stories after failing on the paper and pencil tests, and (4) a *success-failure* condition, which was the same as the failure condition except that the Ss succeeded on the first part of the paper and pencil tests and then failed on the whole test. The stories from a group who wrote under ego-involving instructions but without success and failure proved too inhibited to analyze, and those from a group who succeeded throughout are not reported because the meaning of the situation to the Ss did not seem clear. The scoring followed in general the usual analysis of an overt behavioral sequence with adaptations from Murray. The following results were obtained:

1. The scoring method, when used by two experienced judges working together, could be quickly applied (two to four min. per story), was sensitive enough to discriminate among the stories written under different conditions even when mixed together before judging, and was objective enough to yield on rescoring a 91 percent agreement for individual categories and a rescoring reliability coefficient for the n Achievement score developed of .948.

2. On the assumption that the relaxed and failure conditions represented a low and high degree of induced need for achievement, a comparison was made of the category shifts between these two groups. The following changes occurred at least at the .05 level of significance: a *decrease* in unrelated and task achievement imagery, an *increase* in general achievement imagery, achievement-related deprivation themas, stated needs, successful instrumental acts, anticipatory goal responses, nurturant or hostile press, and positive affective states. In nearly every case the success-failure condition showed the same percentages as the failure condition providing a category total stability check.

3. A single n Achievement score was computed for each individual by summing the characteristics he showed which increased reliably for the group and subtracting those which decreased reliably. The mean n Achievement scores computed in this way increased significantly in accordance with the presumed increase in induced need from relaxed, to neutral, to the failure conditions.

The validity of these results as true measures of n Achievement is discussed particularly as it derives from a comparison with similar trends obtained with hunger and from a consideration of the experimental operations performed on the Ss. The data are further interpreted as pointing to the dynamics of the test situation as an important determiner of TAT content, as supporting a theory of motivation based on anticipatory goal responses, and as providing a method for investigating such important theoretical constructs as 'cognitive maps' and 'anticipatory goal responses' which is more sensitive than that based on the usual inferences from performance responses.

## REFERENCES

1. Alper, T. G.   Task-orientation vs. ego-orientation in learning and retention. *Amer. J. Psychol.*, 1946, *59*, 236–248.
2. Atkinson, J. W., & McClelland, D. C.   The projective expression of needs. II. The effect of different intensities of the hunger drive on thematic apperception. *J. exp. Psychol.*, 1948, *38*, 643–658.
3. Bellak, L.   The concept of projection. *Psychiatry*, 1944, *7*, 353–370.
4. Cattell, R. B.   The riddle of perseveration. I. "Creative effort" and disposition rigidity. *J. Person.*, 1946, 229–238.
5. Clark, R. A.   The problem of closure in mental organization. Unpublished Honor's thesis, Wesleyan Univer., 1947.
6. Clark, R. A., & McClelland, D. C.   A factor analytic integration of apperceptive and clinical measures of n Achievement. Unpublished ONR report.
7. Coleman, W.   The Thematic Apperception Test. I. Effect of recent experience. II. Some quantitative observations. *J. clin. Psychol.*, 1947, *3*, 257–264.
8. Festinger, L.   Development of differential appetite in the rat. *J. exp. Psychol.*, 1943, *32*, 226–234.
9. Hull, C. L.   Goal attraction and directing ideas conceived as habit phenomena. *Psychol. Rev.*, 1931, *38*, 487–506.
10. Langer, W.   *Psychology and human living.* New York: Appleton-Century, 1941.
11. McClelland, D. C., & Apicella, F. S.   Reminiscence following experimentally induced failure. *J. exp. Psychol.*, 1947, *37*, 159–169.
12. McClelland, D. C., Atkinson, J. W., & Clark, R. A.   The effect of different intensities of need mastery on thematic apperception. Mimeographed ONR report, 1947.
13. McClelland, D. C., & Atkinson, J. W.   The projective expression of needs. I. The effect of different intensities of the hunger drive on perception. *J. Psychol.*, 1948, *25*, 205–232.
14. McClelland, D. C., Atkinson, J. W., & Clark, R. A.   The projective expression of needs. III. The effect of ego-involvement, success and failure on perception. *J. Psychol.*, 1949, *27*, 311–330.
15. Murray, H. A., et al.   *Explorations in personality.* New York: Oxford Univer. Press, 1938.
16. Nowlis, H. H.   The influence of success and failure on the resumption of an interrupted task. *J. exp. Psychol.*, 1941, *23*, 204–325.
17. Sears, R. R.   Success and failure: a study of motility. In *Studies in personality.* New York: McGraw-Hill, 1942. Chap. 13.
18. Thurstone, L. L.   *A factorial analysis of perception.* Chicago: Univer. Chicago Press, 1944.
19. Tolman, R. C.   Cognitive maps in rats and men. *Psychol. Rev.*, 1948, *55*, 189–208.
20. Tomkins, S. S.   *The thematic apperception test.* New York: Grune and Strutton, 1947.

# VI

# Possibilities of a Common
# General Basis for Motivation

As a final example of a continuing theme in the history of motivational psychology, a number of contributions concerning the possibility of a common general basis for motivation have been brought together. It has been usual, though not universal, to assume that the sources of motivation are multiple, that individuals may be motivated by hunger *or* thirst *or* pain or some complex of such sources. Many thinkers, however, have sought to isolate some common feature or some general characteristic which uniquely applies to the various motivational sources. Some generalization which extends across all motivators and which differentiates motivating from nonmotivating conditions has often been considered essential to a unified theory of motivation. Since it is an empirical question as to whether the determinants of activation and direction in behavior possess such a common property, it would seem unwise to cling to such a requirement as a theoretical necessity. The possibility is nevertheless an interesting one to consider and a number of stimulating hypotheses have been advanced.

Walter B. Cannon coined the term *homeostasis* to refer to a relatively stable state of equilibrium. Building on the work of Claude Bernard, who had described the tendency of organisms to maintain constancy conditions within the internal environment, Cannon showed how a number of mechanisms operated to produce homeostasis in certain bodily states such as temperature and blood pressure. It was a simple extension to apply the same line of reasoning to motivational states, particularly those with known physiological bases, and to postulate homeostatic tendencies with respect to them. Cannon, in his book, *The Wisdom of the Body*, makes a convincing case for the homeostatic character of several viscerogenic drives and suggests that all motivation may be considered to have the general feature of restoring homeostasis and to be based upon the notion of disequilibrium as a generic motivator.

Promising as it was, the homeostatic hypothesis was not the most influential conception of a common basis for motivation during the thirties and forties. This distinction went to the hypothesis that the basis of motivation lay in tissue needs. Sometimes known as the *survival-need theory*, it held that motivation was increased whenever a condition of the body existed which was related to the survival of the individual, or, in the case of sex, the survival of the species. The articles by Dashiell and Hull promote this biological conception of the origin of motivation.

The acceptance of the tissue-need basis of motivation was so great that for some years it went virtually unquestioned. When the reaction occurred, however, it was a strong one. Harry Harlow's vociferous attack was a key example. He belittled the role of viscerogenic drives and emphasized the motivational role of external stimuli. His recognition of curiosity as a primary drive violated the principles of the prevailing tissue-need theory and opened the door for the reconsideration of positive motives. We have seen how Rogers came to see self-actualization as the basis of all motivation. Less radically, J. McV. Hunt, for example, has suggested that there is motivation inherent in information-processing and Harlow himself proposes that a return to hedonism as a common basis for motivation may be in order.

D. C. McClelland and his collaborators have proposed a view which involves both the equilibratory assumptions of homeostasis and a hedonistic hypothesis which sees positive and negative affect as a common feature in motivation. They suggest that Helson's concept of variable adaptation levels may provide a more plausible center for equilibratory processes than the physiological constants of homeostasis, that deviations from adaptation levels may produce positive affect when they are minimal and negative affect when they are large. Certainly McClelland's position is a more complicated one than the others, but it may be that if any adequate common general basis for motivation is to be found, it will have to possess at least that level of complexity.

# 29 • Walter B. Cannon

## *The General Features of Bodily Stabilization*

The material below was the summary chapter of Cannon's influential book on homeostasis. Readers of the earlier sections pertaining to the analysis of purpose will understand how Cannon could meaningfully dedicate his book to Ralph Barton Perry. Perry's "higher propensities" were not far removed from the homeostatic idea of equilibration. Cannon's book contained an epilogue on "social homeostasis," but his most convincing arguments were made in connection with physiological instances.

### I

*In the previous* chapters we have witnessed an inductive unfolding of the methods employed in preserving homeostatic conditions and we have examined the evidence that these conditions are under the government of the interofective, autonomic nervous system. A review of the facts, with the purpose of drawing from them the general principles which they illustrate, will be useful in giving us an opportunity to look at them from a new point of view and also in preparing us for an inquiry into the possibly necessary prerequisites for stability in other types of organization.

One of the most striking features of our bodily structure and chemical composition that may reasonably be emphasized, it will be recalled, is extreme natural instability. Only a brief lapse in the coordinating functions of the circulatory apparatus, and a part of the organic fabric may break down so completely as to endanger the existence of the entire bodily edifice. In many illustrations we have noted the frequency of such contingencies, and we have noted also how infrequently they bring on the possible dire results. As a rule, whenever conditions are such as to affect the organism harmfully, factors appear within the organism itself that protect it or restore its disturbed balance. The *types* of arrangement by which this stabilization is accomplished is our present interest.

Although some organs are under a sort of control that keeps them from going too fast or too slowly—the heart with its inhibitor and accelerator nerves is an example—these instances may be regarded as secondary and contributory forms of self-regulation. In the main, stable states for all parts of the organism are achieved by keeping uniform the natural surroundings of these parts, their internal environment or fluid matrix. That is the common *intermedium* which, as a means of exchange of materials, as a ready carrier of supplies and waste, and as an equalizer of temperature, provides the fundamental conditions which facilitate stabilization in the several parts. This "milieu interne," as Claude Bernard pointed out, is the product of the organism itself. So long as it is kept uniform, a large number of special devices for maintaining constancy in the workings of the various organs of the body are unnecessary. The steadiness of the "milieu interne," therefore, may be regarded as an arrangement of economy. And the course of evolution of higher organisms has been characterized by a gradually increasing control of the functions of that *milieu* as an environmental and conditioning agency. Just insofar as this control has been perfected, both internal and external limitations on freedom of action have been removed and risks of serious damage or death have been minimized. The central problem in understanding the nature of the remarkable stability of our bodies, therefore, is that of knowing how the uniformity of the fluid matrix is preserved.

## II

A noteworthy prime assurance against extensive shifts in the status of the fluid matrix is the provision of sensitive automatic indicators or sentinels, the function of which is to set corrective processes in motion at the very beginning of a disturbance. If water is needed, the mechanism of thirst warns us before any change in the blood has occurred, and we respond by drinking. If the blood pressure falls and the necessary oxygen supply is jeopardized, delicate nerve endings in the carotid sinus send messages to the vasomotor center and the pressure is raised. If by vigorous muscular movements blood is returned to the heart in great volume, so that cardiac action might be embarrassed and the circulation checked, again delicate nerve endings are affected and a call goes from the right auricle, that results in speeding up the heart rate and thereby hastening the blood flow. If the hydrogen-ion concentration in the blood is altered ever so slightly towards the acid direction, the especially sensitized part of the nervous system which controls breathing is at once made active and by increased ventilation of the lungs carbonic acid is pumped out until the normal state is restored.

In previous pages we have learned of other instances in which quick and efficient corrective measures are instituted when the first intimations of disturbance appear, without our having, however, clear knowledge of what the indicator is or how it works. The operation of the sympathico-adrenal apparatus to increase blood sugar when the glycemic percentage begins to fall below the critical level is a case in point. What sets it going we do not know. And the regulation of body temperature probably belongs in this class. Although the diencephalon seems to contain the thermostat, it may be that the controlling center is there and that it is managed by an agent outside—a number of recent discoveries in physiology have deprived the brain of credit for direct action and have proved that the true *modus operandi* is a reflex. Here more information is required before we can be sure of the location of the agency which is on guard.

Indicators of variation in still other states in the fluid matrix, which are regularly held in remarkable steadiness and which, if altered, are soon restored, are unfortunately unknown. The blood proteins (on which the very existence of the normal blood volume depends), the blood calcium (of primary importance for the proper functioning of the neuromuscular system) and the red corpuscles of the blood (essential for the oxygen supply to the tissues) are examples of factors in the fluid matrix, all of which exhibit homeostasis to a surprising degree. Marked change in their concentration brings about alarming disturbances in the organism. In all probability a slight movement in the direction of change is signalled, just as in other instances which we have considered above, and then the tendency is corrected. But what sends in the signal and how the signal sends orders to the organs which make the correction, must remain a mystery until further physiological research has disclosed the facts.


III


Two general types of homeostatic regulation can be distinguished, dependent on whether the steady state involves *materials* or *processes*. We shall consider first the regulation of materials.

The homeostasis of materials, as numerous instances have shown us, is accomplished by *storage* as an adjustment between occasional or precarious supply and constant, and at times augmented, need. Storage, we we have seen, is of two kinds—*temporary*, for immediate accommodation and use, and *reserved*, for later and lasting service.

The temporary storage is apparently a consequence of simple flooding of tissue spaces. When an abundance is provided it spreads into the fine meshwork, the "spongy cobweb of delicate filaments," of which the connective tissue under the skin and around and between the muscle bundles is largely composed. In this region water is stored and all constituents of the blood which are dissolved in water—salts especially, and sugar. As the high levels which produced the flooding subside, the substances seep back into the running stream (the blood), by which they are distributed to other parts where need may exist. Or, in the case of glucose, the temporary storage may changed to the permanent form, without immediate use. This simple mode of setting aside materials we have called *storage by inundation*. It appears to have no specially developed control other than the relative concentration of the substances concerned, either in the blood or in the fluids of the alveolar connective tissue.

In the more or less permanent or reserved storage the materials are set apart inside of cells or in special places. It may be called *storage by segregation*. From what we know regarding the management of this mode of storage in certain cases, we may infer that it differs from storage by inundation in being subject to a nervous or neuro-humoral government. The best understood instance of such government is that of glucose regulation in the blood. We have seen evidence that when the blood sugar rises much above the usual level of 100 milligrams per cent, the vago-insular mechanism is stimulated, and the insulin discharged into the blood stream from the island cells of the pancreas limits the rise by favoring the use of the sugar and its storage in the cells of the liver and of muscles. On the other hand, if the glycemic percentage falls much below the usual level, a critical point is reached at which the sympathico-adrenal mechanism is brought into action. The glycogen stored in the liver cells is thereby transformed into glucose. This escapes through the cell walls into the circulating blood, and thus the tendency towards a low blood sugar and its harmful consequences is averted.

It must be admitted that, in relation to the homeostasis of other materials, our acquaintance with its regulation is largely restricted to suggestive indications. We have learned that calcium is set aside as a reserve in the spicules and trabeculae inside the long bones. Its abundance in those forms when the calcium of the food is plentiful, and its disappearance when the intake is meager, clearly prove the fact of storage. Furthermore, some evidence at hand, which points to the functioning of the parathyroid glands as influential in promoting storage and to the thyroid as a releasing agent, might offer a fairly close analogy to the regulation of blood sugar. But the relations between the glands and the hoarding or liberating of calcium are at present too loosely defined to permit any reliable conclusion to be drawn. And we are still in the dark as to factors which excite or check the activity of the glands!

The same sort of suggestive evidence can be cited with regard to the regulation of other materials. Fat and protein, like calcium, are stored by segregation; the fat inside the cells of adipose tissue, the protein, according to present testimony, inside of liver cells. We have noted that one observer has reported that the protein masses in the liver cells disappear if adrenin is injected into the circulation. If that observation is confirmed, it may lead to further insight into a sympathico-adrenal influence on the protein content of the blood. Further, we know that when the thyroid gland is deficient and also when the part of the base of the brain near the pituitary gland has been injured, a heavy layer of fat is developed under the skin and elsewhere in the body. Also we know that the fat which is stored because of thyroid deficiency is readily removed by feeding thyroid gland or an extract of it. All this information hints at interesting possibilities of regulation of the supplies of both protein and fat. The importance of securing further knowledge of the ways in which these primary substances are laid by and later mobilized for use is unquestioned. But for such knowledge we must await the progress of patient research.

Back of storage, and, indeed, as occasion for storage, are the motivators for the taking of food and water. Fundamentally these are the disagreeable experiences of hunger and thirst: the unpleasant pangs, which disappear when food is eaten; and the unpleasant dryness of the mouth, that disappears when water or watery fluid is drunk. But these automatic "drives" lead at times to delectable sensations of taste and smell. Such sensations become associated with the taking of the special foods and drinks which have occasioned them. Thus appetites are established which, by inviting to eat and to drink, may replace in part the need for the goads of hunger and thirst. But if appetites fail to keep up the supplies, the more imperious and more insistent agencies come into action and demand that the reserves be replenished.

IV

Another means of assuring constancy of the fluid matrix is by *over-flow*. This arrangement sets a limit on the upward variation of substances in the fluid matrix. Already, in relation to the homeostasis of glucose, we have noted the use of overflow as a means of checking too great a rise of that constituent of the blood. Not only excess of sugar, however, but also excess of water and of certain substances dissolved in it—sodium and chloride ions, for example—is discharged by way of the kidneys. In accordance with the modern theory of urine formation these are all "threshold substances"; they are reabsorbed by the kidney tubules only in such quantitative relations to one another as to preserve the normal status of the blood. All above these amounts is allowed to escape from the body as overflow.

It is interesting to note that the threshold substances are primarily stored by flooding or inundation. When a sufficient reserve of these supplies has been established, however, the ability of the overflow mechanism to maintain homeostasis is marvelous. I have previously called attention to the experiments of Haldane and Priestley on themselves in which during six hours an amount of water exceeding by one-third the estimated volume of the blood was allowed to overflow through the kidneys with such nicety that at no time was the blood diluted to a degree which notably reduced the percentage of hemoglobin. These experiments demonstrate vividly not only the efficacy of the kidney as a spillway but also the use of the principle of the spillway as a means of manitaining a uniform state in the fluid matrix.

In their functions as overflow organs the kidneys act to preserve the normal balance between acid and base in the blood. If non-volatile acid is produced in excess, it passes the barrier; and if there is too much alkali in the blood, it also overflows and escapes.

Not only the kidneys but also the lungs serve for overflow. As we have seen, a very slight excess of carbonic acid in the arterial blood instantly induces deeper breathing. The increased pulmonary ventilation, occasioned thereby, promptly and effectively reduces the carbon dioxide in the alveoli, so that, in spite of large production of carbonic acid, the percentage of the gas in the alveolar air is kept nearly constant. By this means provision is made for the extra carbon dioxide to stream out from the blood over a dam set at a fixed level. In consequence, under usual circumstances, the hydrogen-ion concentration of the blood is evenly maintained, and the harmful effects of an excessive shift in the acid direction is avoided.

It is noteworthy that overflow is used as a regulatory process not only for keeping down the concentration of waste material (carbon dioxide), but also for keeping down the concentration of useful material (glucose). Here again we see indicated the importance of constancy of the fluid matrix as a primary condition of the organism.

## V

The second general type of homeostatic regulation is that in which *processes*, rather than materials, are involved. The most significant instance is presented in the mechanism of heat regulation. The processes of heat production and heat loss, as we know, are going on continuously. When the body temperature starts to fall the process of heat production is accelerated and that of heat loss is diminished. And when the opposite tendency of the body temperature appears, the effects on the processes are reversed. Thus by altering the rate of continuous processes, in a manner nicely adapted to the needs of the organism, the temperature is held in a remarkably uniform balance.

Similar phenomena are found in the supply of oxygen to the tissues, and in the preservation of the normal acid-base equilibrium of the blood. Continuously oxygen is being supplied by moderate activity of the respiratory and circulatory systems, but in special circumstances the demand is greatly augmented. Thereupon, the respiration rate and the circulation rate are correspondingly accelerated, the red blood corpuscles are loaded and unloaded much faster, and the oxygen tension in the fluid matrix near the needy organs, inspite of their larger requirement, is to a high degree sustained. As the special circumstances which have roused the systems to extra action fade away, the systems, after paying any "oxygen debt" that may be left, subside into their former moderate functional speed. The same principles and many of the same phenomena are illustrated when conditions cause an increase of acid concentration in the blood. And when the reaction of the blood is moved towards the alkaline side, again a continuous process, that of respiration, is retarded or wholly stopped until enough of the continuously produced acid has accumulated to restore the normal acid-base relation.

A combination of the use of reserves and the use of the altered rate of processes is found in the complex of mechanisms which operate to assure uniformity of the oxygen tension. It will be recalled that besides the faster return of blood to the heart, the faster heart beat, and the high head of arterial pressure which results in a faster blood flow—all accelerations of continuous performances—there is a setting free of the concentrated red corpuscles from the store in the spleen. These corpuscles now join those already in the hurried current and help them to meet the exigency which confronts the laboring cells.

VI

The modes of storage and release, and the speeding up and slowing down of continuous processes, which keep steady the conditions of the internal environment, are not, as a rule, under control from the cortex. We can, to be sure, voluntarily breathe faster or slower, but ordinarily the rate of respiration is managed automatically. And in a like manner all the other homeostatic adjustments are managed. Automatically materials are set aside in the reserves by the natural functioning of the cranial division of the interofective nervous system. Automatically the reserves are called forth and the processes are accelerated when the blood sugar runs low, when extra oxygen is needed, when acid tends to accumulate or when the temperature begins to fall. It is a special part of the autonomic nervous system—the sympathico-adrenal division—which is charged with the performance of these services, quite outside of conscious direction; indeed, in ways which only elaborate physiological research has revealed.

Whether the sympathico-adrenal division is aroused by pain or excitement, by muscular effort, asphyxia or low blood pressure, by cold or hypoglycemia, the presenting situation is one in which the constancy of the fluid matrix is endangered or is likely to be endangered. In each one of these contingencies the operation of the system is such as to favor the welfare of the organism by preserving homeostasis of the internal environment. The blood flow is shifted and hastened so as to maintain uniformity of the oxygen tension and to keep level the acid-base balance during muscular exertion; the metabolic rate is raised so as to produce more heat if the heat loss is excessive; glucose is liberated from hepatic stores when the amount in the blood is dropping to a low percentage or when there may be special need for it; the capacity of the vascular system is adapted to a reduced blood volume when, after hemorrhage, the circulating blood as a common carrier is likely to become inefficient—in short, as these illustrations indicate, the sympathico-adrenal apparatus promptly and automatically makes the adjustments which are required to preserve the normal internal condition for the living parts when that is disturbed or likely to be disturbed.

The amazing feature of the rôle played by the sympathico-adrenal system is its applicability to the wide range of possible disturbances that we have just noted. As stated earlier, the system commonly works as a unit. It is very remarkable indeed that such unified action can be useful in circumstances so diverse as low blood sugar, low blood pressure, and low temperature. It would seem, however, that the utility is not always complete in details, for at times effects are produced which apparently have little or no value for the organism. Examples of these meaningless responses are seen in the sweating in hypoglycemia and in the rise of blood sugar in asphyxia. Under other circumstances, as we know, these are serviceable responses; e.g., sweating when vigorous muscular exercise produces extra heat, and liberation of sugar from the liver when the glycemic percentage falls too low. The appearance of inappropriate features in the total complex of sympathico-adrenal function is made reasonable, as I pointed out in 1928, if we consider, first, that it is, on the whole, a unitary system; second, that it is capable of producing effects in many different organs; and third, that among these effects are different combinations which are of the utmost utility in correspondingly different conditions of need. Vasoconstriction, increased heart rate, and a larger output of adrenin are a useful group of sympathico-adrenal reactions when the blood pressure is low or when the temperature must be sustained; and that group is not any less effective in the two situations because there is an attendant, perhaps useless, increase of blood sugar. The effects which, in any particular case of need, are not useful may reasonably be regarded as incidental, as lying outside the group of sympathicoadrenal agencies which, for the moment, are working for homeostasis.

## VII

In 1926 I advanced a number of tentative propositions concerned with steady states in the body, and with the maintenance of these states, that are pertinent in the present consideration of the general features of homeostasis. We shall now regard only four of them.

"In an open system, such as our bodies represent, compounded of unstable material and subjected continually to disturbing conditions, constancy is in itself evidence that agencies are acting, or ready to act, to maintain this constancy." This is an inference based on insight into the ways by which some steady states are regulated (e.g., glycemia, body temperature, and the acid-base balance), and it was expressed with confidence that other steady states, not yet fully understood, are similarly regulated. When we have learned more concerning the factors which govern the constancy of proteins, fat and calcium in the blood plasma, we shall probably see that it results from as nice devices as those operating in the better known cases of homeostasis.

"If a state remains steady it does so because any tendency towards change is automatically met by increased effectiveness of the factor or factors which resist the change." Thirst, the reaction to low blood sugar, the respiratory and circulatory responses to a blood shift towards acidity, the augmented processes of heat conservation and production, all become more intense as the disturbance of homeostasis is more pronounced, and they all subside quickly when the disturbance is relieved. Similar conditions probably prevail in other steady states.

"The regulating system which determines a homeostatic state may comprise a number of coöperating factors brought into action at the same time or successively." This statement is well illustrated by the elaborate and complex reactions in the blood itself, and simultaneously in the circulatory and respiratory system, that preserve the relative constancy of the acid-base relation in the plasma; and also by the arrangements for protection against a fall of temperature in which the defensive processes are awakened in series, one after another.

"When a factor is known which can shift a homeostatic state in one direction it is reasonable to look for automatic control of that factor, or for a factor or factors having an opposing effect." This postulate is really implied in the previous postulates and may be regarded as emphasizing the confident opinion that homeostasis is not accidental, but is a result of organized self-government, and that search for the governing agencies will be rewarded by their discovery.

# VIII

It is not supposed that the full display of homeostatic adjustments will be found in all forms of animals. The illustrations which I have given in earlier chapters have been taken from experiments and observations on mammals. Birds alone can share with mammalian forms the possession of complicated mechanisms for keeping constant the fluid matrix of the body and birds have been very little studied with reference to these mechanisms. Reptiles and amphibia are much less highly organized, in the sense of having a controlled internal environment which liberates them from the vicissitudes of the external environment. As pointed out in an earlier chapter, the amphibian is unable to preserve his water content and cannot hold steady his own temperature, independent of that of his outer world. The reptile, a higher type, does not lose water quickly to the air about him as the amphibian does, but, like the amphibian, the reptile is "cold-blooded" and therefore is limited in his activities by cold surroundings.

The evidence that homeostasis as seen in mammals is the product of an evolutionary process—that only gradually in the evolution of vertebrates has stability of the fluid matrix of the body been acquired—is interestingly paralleled in the development of the individual. Indeed, a suggestive addition to the group of facts which support the idea that the history of the individual summarizes the history of the race, or that ontogeny recapitulates phylogeny, is found in the absence or deficiency of homeostatic regulation in babies during a considerable period after birth, and the later rather slow acquirement of control. Before birth, of course, the baby has the benefit of the uniformity of the mother's "milieu interne." At birth he is suddenly exposed to very different and quite variable surroundings, when his own "milieu interne," though formed, has not been subjected to any stress which might alter it. Now it has long been known that the new born, when they are exposed to cold, have little ability to maintain a constant temperature. Instead of reacting swiftly in such ways as would keep the temperature from falling, the organism permits the fall to occur, much as it occurs in cold-blooded forms, without a quiver of resistance. The elaborate complex of adjustments for the homeostasis of temperature, that is characteristic of adults, is only gradually developed, perhaps as the consequence of exercise and training. The control of blood sugar is similarly the result of a developmental process. Recent observations by Schretter and Nevinny have shown that in the early days of babyhood the percentage of glucose in the blood varies much more, and in larger oscillations, than it does during the later periods of life. It seems not improbable that study of other homeostatic regulations would prove that they too are unstable at the start and only by experience acquire the efficiency seen in adults.

## IX

Repeatedly in foregoing chapters I have called attention to the fact that insofar as our internal environment is kept constant we are freed from the limitations imposed by both internal and external agencies or conditions that could be disturbing. The pertinent question has been asked by Barcroft, freedom for what? It is chiefly freedom for the activity of the higher levels of the nervous system and the muscles which they govern. By means of the cerebral cortex we have all our intelligent relations to the world about us. By means of it we analyze experience, we move from place to place, we build airplanes and temples, we paint pictures and write poetry, or we carry on scientific researches and make inventions, we recognize and converse with friends, educate the young, express our sympathy, tell our love—indeed, by means of it we conduct ourselves as human beings. The alternative to this freedom would be either submission to the checks and hindrances which external cold or internal heat or disturbance of any other constants of the fluid matrix would impose upon us; or, on the other hand, such conscious attention to storage of materials and to altering the rate of bodily processes, in order to preserve constancy, that time for other affairs would be lacking. It would be like limiting social activities because of domestic duties, or excluding foreign relations because of troubles in the interior. The full development and ample expression of the living organism are impossible in those circumstances. They are made possible by such automatic regulation of the routine necessities that the functions of the brain which subserve intelligence and imagination, insight and manual skill, are set free for the use of these higher services.

In summary, then, we find the organism liberated for its more complicated and socially important tasks because it lives in a fluid matrix, which is automatically kept in a constant condition. If changes threaten, indicators at once signal the danger, and corrective agencies promptly prevent the disturbance or restore the normal when it has been disturbed. The corrective agencies act, in the main, through a special portion of the nervous system which functions as a regulatory mechanism. For this regulation it employs, first, storage of materials as a means of adjustment between supply and demand, and, second, altered rates of continuous processes in the body. These devices for maintaining constancy in the organism are the result of myriads of generations of experience, and they succeed for long periods in preserving a remarkable degree of stability in the highly unstable substance of which we are composed.

## REFERENCES

Cannon. *Ergebn. d. Physiol.*, 1928, xxvii, 380.
Cannon. *Amer. J. med. Sci.*, 1926, clxxi, 1.
Barcroft. *J. exp. Biol.*, 1932, ix, 24.
Schretter and Nevinny. *Zeitschr. f. Geburtsh. u. Gynäkol.*, 1931, xcviii, 258.

# 30 • John F. Dashiell

## Tissue Needs as Sources of Drives

It can be made plausible that species in which tissue needs served as the source of adaptive activation might well have a greater probability of survival. This line of thought led, although not coercively, to the generalization that all activating drives had their original source in some survival need. The converse, that all survival needs gave rise to drive, was also sometimes implied. Of course, there was no necessity on logical grounds for either position. While evolutionary thinking might make a positive relationship between needs and drives likely, it would not demand anything close to a perfect correlation. Evolution could well permit the continuation of drives which were unrelated to survival needs, as long as they were not detrimental to them, and there could easily arise tissue needs for which sheer evolution had not prepared a species motivationally. It seems, for example, that radiation effects may be fatal without being a source of drive in humans. Such considerations, however, were not impressive enough to prevent many psychologists from concluding that the survival-need hypothesis was sufficient as a common general basis for all motivation.

*To the study* of human motives by scientific methods psychologists have addressed themselves only at intervals or only in certain schools. The structural psychology that was devoted to the analyzing of what it "feels like" or what one is aware of, when he is in the presence of certain things or when he thinks about other things, practically ignored the question of motives behind the scenes. The instinct psychologists met the question and settled it altogether too neatly with their springs of action, their jacks-in-the-box, hidden away inside the human being waiting only to be released. The behaviorists have frequently seemed too preoccupied with their mechanisms of activity to have regard to the drives energizing those mechanisms. The psychoanalysts, on the contrary, have boldly stepped out with the motivation of human conduct as their principal objective of investigation. Whatever be the final appraisal of the psychoanalysts' doctrines, certain it is that they, more than any others, have driven home the realization of the importance of untangling and identifying motives. And they have carried this type of inquiry to great lengths. Nothing in human behavior, they remind us, is uncaused, nothing is really a matter of pure chance; and if everything has its adequate causes it remains for the scientist only to find out those particular motives responsible for it. If a person dislikes shad roe or has great fondness for speckled trout, there are, of course, conditions or factors that are responsible for this. One dreams a dream: the general trend and, still more, each of the specific objects and incidents of the nocturnal drama must have its cause. One constantly mislays certain objects; he is always forgetting certain names; he makes a slip of speech or of spelling now and then: each and all of these errors have their own explanations. A psychasthenic cannot control the compulsion to count his steps as he walks, or he is kept perpetually unnerved by the doubts of a Hamlet—these are but symptoms of underlying psychological causes, the outcroppings of personal desires or aversions. We may be unwilling to go the whole length of the fantastic elaborations of theory supported by some of the followers of Freud and of Jung; but we must acknowledge the service of psychoanalysts to psychology in reminding us that a scientific knowledge of man is not complete as a description of mechanisms without recognition and measurement of the drives that propel them.

Let the reader not be misled. To place in contrast "mechanisms" and "drives" is not to imply that the latter are to be sought somehow outside the elaborate mechanistic scheme of nature. Perhaps the contrast might be more happily stated as that between "machines" and "energies": on the one hand, you have your wheels, levers, pulleys, and pistons; on the other, the coal, the live steam, the dammed-up water, the ignited gas.

External Stimuli Function Principally as Releases. One source of energy for organic activity is, of course, external stimulation. The ether or air vibrations producing sight and hearing, the chemical agencies affecting smell and taste receptors, the changes of temperature and the impact of physical masses at the skin surface are all readily recognized as moving forces in human behavior. If you would see a man get into action touch him with a needle point or sound an auto horn behind him, call him by name, slap him on the back, announce a circus parade or a fashion parade, call out the word "fire." Among the conditions that activate human nature are to be listed, then, all those classes of stimuli that we have canvassed already.

But even in the crude illustrations just offered it does not need much discernment to note that the extra-organic stimulations tell by no means the whole story. Human nature is not a football. It is not immediately and solely subject to the actions of external forces alone.[1] Rather, these *exteroceptive stimuli serve mainly to release, to touch off, the energies stored and systematized within* that *extremely complex balanced mass* we call a living organism.

To be sure, there are numerous types of reaction that are dependent only in a minor degree upon intra-organic conditions and to a major degree upon the direct, unequivocal result of exteroceptive stimulation. The knee jerk, the pupillary reflex, the flexion reflex, are examples of this order. They are to be described and explained more in terms of their immediate stimuli than in terms of the chemical disequilibrium of the whole organism or of the inadequacy of a specific organ or tissue. Such unmotivated responses, however, play only the rôle of supernumeraries on life's stage. Eyelid twitchings and finger jerks, necessary as they are to the behavior of man, have no central part in determining in what line or direction a person will act or with what energy he will act.

Let us make sure of our orientation again. In an earlier chapter of this book we saw from concrete examples that it is of the essence of animal and human behavior to seek or to maintain optimal conditions for one's self—these conditions to be determined by whether one's intra-organic processes are adequately furthered. The key to man and to subhuman forms is to be sought more in the enormously complex energy exchanges going on within him than in the fortuitous play of outside energies working upon him. You can lead a horse to water, but the sight of water will not be an effective stimulus unless he be thirsty—and in that case an untethered horse will lead himself to the trough. A mate does not excite the pigeon or the frog to sexual advances except when the latter is in a certain physiological state. It is even said that a lion must be hungry to attack a peaceful and unaggressive man. Is the child hungry? Then and only then will he approach the food. Is he tired? The bed now invites him as it did not while he was in the flush of play. It is when he is cold that the warm radiator can attract him, when he is in pain that he runs to his nurse. *The primary drives to persistent forms of animal and human conduct are tissue-conditions within the organism giving rise to stimulations exciting the organism to overt activity.* A man's interests and desires may become ever so elaborate, refined, socialized, sublimated, idealistic; but the raw basis from which they are developed is found in the phenomena of living matter. In the next few pages let us canvass the better-known tissues in the body of man or some lesser

[1] This is one reason for a common misunderstanding of a scientific psychology that seeks to know man in terms of cause and effect relationships. It is a very superficial view of the science that characterizes it as making man into a robot, a puppet, a marionette, acting out his whole drama of life merely in response to external promptings. But it is equally as impossible and absurd to suppose that the only alternative is to assume mysterious agencies, entities, dæmons implanted in man's nature and operating him.

animal, together with the more obvious conditions that furnish stimulation through the nervous system to activity—conditions that (*a*) "get a man into motion" and (*b*) determine the direction of his motions.

## TISSUE NEEDS AS SOURCES OF DRIVES

### Hunger [2]

The values of eating have always been to a degree a measure of other values in the life of man. "I would rather do that than eat" is a colloquial expression of this fact. A formal meeting of people who are called together for even a serious purpose is generally incomplete without a dinner or banquet to celebrate the occasion. Love feasts and communions solidify religious association. A recent motion picture of epic dimensions has vividly presented the true story of a whole tribe of fifty thousand people who were forced annually to migrate over glaciers and precipices and across angry rivers, with staggering losses of live stock and human life and incredible personal sufferings—all for the sake of having grass. With another Asiatic tribe, dependent solely upon their milk supply for food, the buffalo is a sacred animal, the dairy building their nearest approach to a temple, and the dairyman practically a priest. It would be an instructive exercise to try to estimate what proportion of farming and milling, of transportation, of office work and wholesale and retail counter service in America has grown out of the biological need of something to eat.

The fact that hunger operates as a drive to increase overt activity has been assumed and used experimentally in nearly all research into animal learning. A genuinely hungry rat or monkey will get into activity and keep in activity until its hunger is satisfied, and if obstacles to hunger are interposed it will show exploratory activity until it chances to surmount them.

A direct study of the connection between hunger drive and general bodily activity was made by Wada. From the work of Carlson, and of Cannon and Washburn, it was known that hunger, as distinguished from appetite, is traceable to contractions of the smooth musculature of the stomach walls, the contractions appearing and disappearing in rhythmic alternations for periods varying between a half-hour and an hour and a half. Under the bed of a subject Wada arranged a receiving tambour with the rubber diaphragm connected to the under surface of the bed by a spi-

---

[2] "Hunger" for the general reader frequently connotes an experience. From the objective point of view maintained in this book only the use of the term developed in Chapter V is permissible: vigorous rhythmic contractions of the walls of the empty stomach.

ral spring and made so sensitive that every overt bodily movement of the subject, even the moving of a finger, affected the tambour. By way of a rubber tubing the movements were communicated to a recording tambour and pointer placed in another room, and were traced on a long paper kymograph. A simultaneous record of stomach contractions (hunger) was made with an inflated balloon communicating with a recording manometer. By comparing the two lines traced upon the kymograph record, Wada was able to show that both during sleep and during a quiet waking state (that of reading a book) there was a very close correlation between the rhythmic occurrences of hunger and the rhythmic occurrences of gross striped muscular activity. (Cf. Figure 30.1.) Further, by

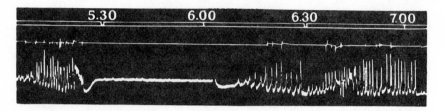

Figure 30.1. Correspondence between the periods of hunger contractions and the periods of overt bodily movements.

A sample kymograph record. Upper line: time indicated by half-hour breaks. Middle line: bodily movements indicated by vertical departures from the horizontal level. Lower line: stomach contractions shown as tonus in the long level tracing, as hunger contractions in the pronounced vertical records. (Wada, *Archives of Psychol.*, no. 57.)

awakening sleeping subjects at different times he obtained some evidence of a greater tendency to dreaming during the hunger contraction periods, and by testing waking subjects at various intervals, with a hand dynamometer and with intelligence tests, he found that hunger apparently facilitated both gross reactions and the finer thinking reactions.[3]

How does hunger (stomach contractions) and how does general bodily need of nourishment operate to produce excess activity of the striped muscles? It has been suggested [4] that when the chemical equilib-

---

[3] The writer has devised a simple method of demonstrating hunger as a drive to excess exploratory activity in the white rat. A maze was laid out on a plan allowing the animal to run about through many criss-crossing alleys. The floor was marked off lightly into squares; and the animal's total activity in a given time was counted in terms of the number of squares entered. Hungry rats were found to average a distinctly greater number of squares entered than rats that had been recently fed.

[4] By Ritcher. He also calls attention to Carlson and Luckhardt's demonstration that in spinal preparations of frogs and turtles mechanical or electrical stimulation of visceral organs such as heart, alimentary tract, and lungs induces skeletal muscle reflexes of the defensive type.

rium of the body is disturbed by the nutritive deficiency, chemical products of the deficiency may directly affect the stomach (which is known to be sensitive to chemical stimulation), setting up in the empty stomach the hunger contractions which in turn, via afferent impulses to the central nervous system, excite greater tonus and activity in the striped muscle.

## Sex Urge

Food and sex are the great interests of the individual and of society. These may work out in various secondary forms, but the ground patterns of man's life are determined by these two elemental forces. This is, of course, an over-simplification of the story of the motivating of man's behavior; but it may be said that whereas the need of food, when extreme, may become most imperious, the urge to mating has played the most dramatic part in human history and is notorious for its power often to drive men through all barriers of individual inhibitions and of social taboos. On account of the formidable, impelling character of this bodily urge on the one hand, and of the complicated restrictions that have become established by society concerning the means of its satisfaction on the other, this is nowadays recognized as the greatest of all sources of maladjustment of human beings to their social environments. Freud, indeed, once held it to be the one and only drive of importance in the genesis of mental disorders.

This organic urge arises from a condition in the sex apparatus. Wang used a revolving cage and cyclometer to confirm earlier observations that the adult female albino rat—but not the male nor the immature female—showed rhythmic changes in the amount of general bodily activity in cycles of about four days' length. What drives a female rat, he asked, to show such regular cyclic changes of overt behavior? By microscopic examination of the epithelium of the reproductive tract he then confirmed earlier findings that the periods of œstrus (heat) occurred in cycles of the same duration (cf. Figure 30.2); and, moreover, he was able to show not only that these two kinds of cycles were coincident, but that any interruption of the œstrous rhythm by pregnancy and lactation or by removal of the ovaries resulted in an interruption of the cycles of gross activity.

On an earlier page it has been stated that the findings from many physiological laboratories prove that the secondary sexual characteristics are dependent in both male and female upon internal secretions from certain cells which form parts of the sex apparatus. Let us add here that the same line of work (including removals, transplantations, and injections) has shown also that in the male not only general bodily activity but also the specific pattern of behavior in copulation depends for

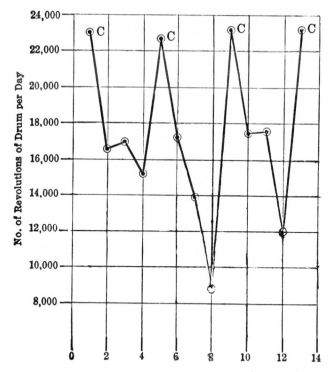

Figure 30.2. Correspondence between Oestrous rhythm and cycles of general bodily activity in a female rat.

Encircled dots indicate examinations made of reproductive tract, those marked *C* being those at which were found cornified epithelial cells, indicative of "heat." The vertical distance of each dot represents the total amount of general bodily activity of the animal on the day on which the examination was made. (Wang, *Compar. Psychol. Mono.*, no. 6.)

activation upon the internal secretions of the testes. So far as the necessary external stimulus to this behavior pattern is concerned, Stone found it to reside in the type of bodily movements exhibited by the female.

The hypertonicity excited reflexly by intra-organic stimulation from the sex apparatus, when in certain physiological conditions, is by no means limited to the striped musculature but is evident also in effectors distributed through the viscera. The tension, in other words, is not merely in overt posturings and restlessness; it is also strongly emotional. Marston offers evidence that in such a condition the organism shows a drop in blood pressure. It is common physiological knowledge that the sacral subdivision of the autonomic is in control, in part directing excess blood supply into pelvic channels. All in all, the craving called sex emotion is recognized to be a profound visceral disturbance with a wide field of irradiation.

The part played by external stimuli in sex behavior is originally very minor and secondary to the intra-organic, although early in the biography of an organism the whole pattern of emotion becomes conditioned to the sight, smell, touch or other form of stimulation from mates, so that this avenue of excitation later comes to have an increasingly important share in the generation of the sex drive.

### Unfavorable Temperature Liberation through the Skin

It has been universally recognized that the food and the sex motives have had dominating influences in setting up and establishing lines of human activity, leading to the most elaborate of customs and ceremonials. Another tissue condition that has in only slightly less degree motivated humankind is that of an inadequate exchange of energies through the integument.

One of the most delicate operations in the human organism is the maintenance of a constant body *temperature.* Summer and winter this is so effectively operated that a variation of only two or three degrees from the normal 98.6° F. is considered a symptom of illness. In part, this great mechanism is a function of the *skin.* The processes of combustion in the body liberate an enormous amount of heat, only a fraction of which is necessary to keep up the level required for the organism's metabolic functions, the remainder being released mainly through the skin surface to the outside. Sometimes the rate of release becomes excessive, owing to the chill of a disease within or to a frigid air temperature without; sometimes it becomes insufficient, owing to a raging fever within or to a torrid temperature without. In either case the condition at the skin operates as a stimulus that sets up afferent neural impulses passing into and through the connecting system and out to striped muscles and other effectors, occasioning excess activity that will be continued until either the organism's production of heat has been readjusted or the environment has been changed to a more equable one.

The amount of general initiative shown in man's behavior varies with this relation of his internal heat production to his external conditions. The torrid heat belt about the earth, extending from about 30° north latitude to about 30° south, is notorious for not producing important advances in the arts of living or in the sciences, literatures, or fine arts, while at the same time the frigidity of Arctic and Antarctic zones is directly responsible for a poverty of cultural development in those regions. The particular directions assumed by activity that is prompted by unfavorable skin conditions are in the first place the seeking and fashioning of clothing and shelter. When the primitive cave man chanced to bear upon his back the body of his prey and found that it protected him a little from a wintry blast, the stage was set for acquiring habits of covering the body, and for the gradual elaborating of clothing from skins and barks to the finely woven fabrics in linen or silk worn by civilized man. When the roving savages of the Andaman Islands retreat before severe weather to the seashore and there each hollows out a hole in the sand under some overhanging cliff, a beginning has been made in the direction of shelter construction, which we see elaborated by other men into lines of action and occupation centering about the production and transportation of fuel and of building materials, and the applied art of architecture. It is interesting to note that the gregarious form of life among some animals at least is undoubtedly an outgrowth of reactions motivated by unfavorable skin conditions: their original "sociability" is a huddling together of individuals who have been restlessly moving about until the warmth of each other's bodies furnished enough heat to allow the organisms to come to rest—as is easily observed in the nestling together of very young animals.

For experimental measurement of the driving function of skin temperature conditions we may turn to a study of an invertebrate form, the water-mite. Agar placed specimens of these Hydrachnids (spider-like forms living in water) in tubes of water kept at different constant temperatures. Each tube was marked off into five sections, named, A, B, C, D, E; and the locomotor activity of each animal was recorded in terms of the sections entered. The optimal temperature for this organism lies between 12.5° and 22.5°C. Figure 30.3 presents partial records of the same organism when placed in tubes kept at four different temperatures. It will be observed that in the tube maintained at 12.5°C. the animal after its admission near section A typically followed the tube through its full length until forced to turn, whereupon it followed it again through its length, and so on continuously. In a tube of the lower temperature, 6.5°, the animal moved through the length of the tube fewer times, such excursions being frequently interrupted by unforced reversals. In a tube at 32°, the animal again frequently turned about face; and in one 37°, its reversals were so frequent that it did not once traverse the whole tube. At optimal temperatures, then, this organism is active but in a routine straightaway manner; whereas at abnormally low and abnormally high temperatures its behavior shows *variability* in high degree. The variability in the behavior increases in direct proportion to the degree of lack of balance between internal and external temperature conditions. (Let the reader be clear on one point: action of the animal is not determined by external heat as such or by cold as such in a tropic or simple reflex fashion, but by the conditions of energy exchange in the skin tissues.)

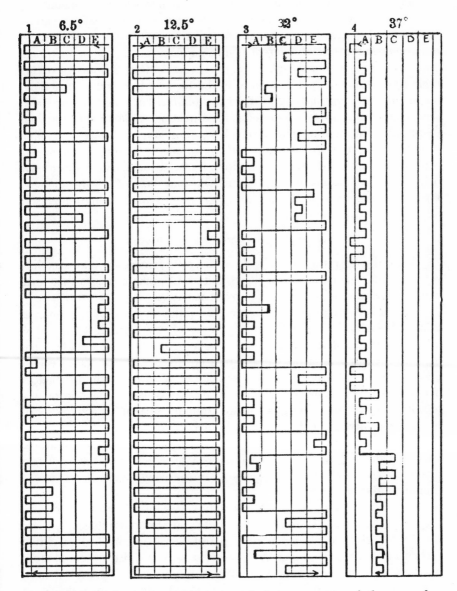

Figure 30.3.   Schematic representation of the movements of the same hydrachnid in tubes kept at different constant temperatures.

Arrowheads indicate places of introduction of the animal into the tubes, at top of figure, and the continuous lines show directions of locomotion thereafter from section to section (*A*, *B*, etc.) of the tube. The graphic records include most of the total runs at the two lower temperatures, less of the run at 32 and only the first small part of that at 37. (Agar, *J. Compar. Psychol.*, vol. 7.)

In the operation of each of these three motivations (hunger, sex urge, and unfavorable skin conditions) we can now see that *the fundamental part of the drive is to be traced to certain tissue conditions of the organism that set up afferent neural impulses passing to and through nerve centers and out to effectors,* the visceral often included, *exciting them to excess activity* (frequently in the form of preparatory reactions, *q.v.*); and that *the adequate external stimulus,* such as food or mate, *serves here as a trigger or release* for directing some of the reactions (especially the consummatory ones) *by providing the necessary environmental opportunity for their full appearance* (leading perchance to the elimination of the exciting condition in the tissue and to a subsidence of the drive). "Excess activity," moreover, may be in the form of *more vigorous* movements or in the form of *greater variation* in movements.

### Other Organic Sources of Drives

With the operation of these three drives before us we may sketchily refer to other inadequacies in the condition of organic tissues that form or may form the basis of drives to overt behavior.

Associated frequently with hunger is the dryness in the mucous lining of the back of the *throat* which impels man or beast to restless activity until the discovery of water awakens the drinking response that leads to the removal of the cause. (It is possible to remove such dryness and terminate the drive by merely swabbing the throat with citric acid.) The importunate character of *thirst* in human behavior and the degree to which it has taken the lead in determining certain aspects of social life is sufficiently evident to require no elaboration.

Distended conditions of the *bladder* and of the *colon* operate to stimulate the individual and if unrelieved may generate emotional excitement. This is shown clearly enough in the young child in whom the proper inhibitions have not been well developed.

The *striped musculature* in a condition of fatigue provides proprioceptive stimulations taking the form of the inhibitory tendency to cease activity, to rest, to sleep. In the opposite physico-chemical condition (when one is rested) the striped musculature gives rise to stimulations of excitatory nature, and the individual is urged into some kind of muscular exercise. Unquestionably, the developed interests in athletics, in hunting or in tramping, in the use of certain stimulant drugs, in "physical culture," as well as the interests in a restful bed or chair, in an "easy living," in the use of sedatives, are a few of the many lines of human behavior motivated fundamentally by opposite conditions of these muscle tissues.

Another characteristic of striped muscle that leads to the development of a drive is the rhythmic character of its contractions. When an external source of stimulation is acting rhythmically the efforts of the auditor, spectator, or hand worker to adjust himself to that stimulation are modified and influenced by the subject's own rhythms, and a tendency to follow an easily reproduced rhythm becomes strong. It is easy to see the importance of this as a component of the human interest in dancing, music, poetry, and so forth. Incidentally it is to be noted that rhythmic activity appears to have emotion-arousing value—at least if it is intense and long maintained—as is shown in the arts just mentioned, and is so dramatically exhibited in war dances, in whirling dervishes, and in camp-meeting oratory, when excitement mounts to a veritable frenzy.

Then there are the *respiratory* and *circulatory* systems. Smothering or suffocating promptly excites most vigorous skeletal movements, especially extensor thrusts, and the subject frequently develops emotional excitement of the rage type—as was shown so clearly in babies. Accelerated or retarded blood circulation, whether directly affecting receptors or not, plays a central part in the activity of other processes that furnish drives—digestion, overt muscular exertion, heat elimination, and so on.

It needs no demonstration here to show that the *skin* is so loaded with receptors that, when it is subjected to injury, violent defensive reactions are at once set up. Avoidance of *noxious* (pain) stimulation has motivated not a little of the social submissiveness of the slave, of the prisoner of war, of the convict in the turpentine camp, of the suspect in a back room at the police station, of the school child, and of the younger brother. On account of its convenience as well as its energy-releasing potency this incentive has been much used in experimental work on animal species along with that of hunger. In case the pain condition is persistent or intense, the motor effects include extensive visceral disturbances. The display of overt muscular efforts is accompanied and is in fact supported and reënforced by pronounced changes in the operations of the great organ systems of the body, a partial description of which has been offered in the preceding chapter. Of these the surgeon and the dentist are quite well aware, and for them they make provisions in the handling and nursing of a patient. These visceral tensions may lead to powerful emotional outbursts, as in the pet dog that, when his foot is caught in a trap, snaps at his own master, or the child with a cut finger who alternately cries in terror and berates his nurse. Both the rage and the fear types of excitement are to be observed in man or beast under such circumstances.

Very different conditions at the skin may arouse quite an opposite form of behavior. Skin that is *mildly stroked* and *patted,* and thus probably facilitated in its blood circulation and in other normal metabolic processes, gives rise to energy changes which as afferent impulses reflexly excite inhibitory motor innervations, leading to muscular relaxation. The effect of this on young and old is marked, and such manipulation has been used to quiet the restless baby, to bring sleep to an uneasy adult, and as a form of therapy for a definitely "nervous" patient. At particular points of the skin are to be noted special *sensitive zones* (a term suggested by Allport to replace the misleading "erotic zones" of the psychoanalysts), where gentle stimulations have special reflex effects that are more excitatory but still of a general, positive, seeking type. For a good example the well known tickling response will serve us. A light scratching on the soles of the feet or a firm rubbing of the skin over the ribs awakens quick and even vigorous laughter and wriggling movements of body and limbs. A variety of responses clearly belonging to the same category may be elicited at lips, armpits, axillæ, and other sensitive zones, in the form of smiling, gurgling, arching of back, and squirming. All such behavior involves emotional components, but at present we know little about them in detail.

Probably the reactions of *sensory apparatus* should be included here. Nearly all the receptors have associated motor tissues. Consider the eye and its six pairs of muscles to rotate the eyeball, its sphincter muscle to regulate the size of the pupil, and its ciliary muscle to adjust the lens for distances. Consider also the receptors of the skin: they may not have muscular tissues so completely identifiable as integral parts of the sense organ, but for them much the same part is played by the skeletal muscles that move exploring fingers over and around objects. The tendency of the eyes to be turned to a light, of the ears to be cocked in the direction of a sound, of the fingers to move about a mildly stimulating object, of the tongue to expose itself to a sapid substance—all such simple receptor-adjusting tendencies are strikingly evident in infancy. Such reflex adjustments seem to be set up partly as an expression of the metabolism of the receptors, for they give place to stimulus-avoiding reflexes whenever the light or noise or other external agency becomes excessively intense. It is possible that in these phenomena we have the core of the very attention-giving that, apart from any other drive to exploratory movement, is at the basis of the type of behavior denominated "curiosity."

## Concluding Note

The preceding survey has been brief and sketchy. It has probably omitted reference to many other conditions of organs and tissues which in time may be discovered to be important contributaries to the internal excitation of an organism. Two things, however, should be clear. First, the sources of the energy by which a man is set in motion are to be sought primarily in his physical bodily tissues and their physical conditions. And second, we need not depart from our $S \rightarrow R$ formula for the description of motivation, for the very operation of a drive is over sensori-motor pathways. Accordingly we need not posit any inscrutable and unanalyzable "instincts"—"reproductive" or "acquisitive" or "esthetic" or "rhythmic" or "feeling" or "curiosity"—to be accepted as ultimates behind which we cannot go. Such terms may be descriptive of general types of human behavior, but they are valueless as explanations. The sources of human motivation given in the foregoing account have been referred to as "primary" sources; but they are primary only for the psychologist, and they remain legitimate objects of further analysis by any physiologist or physiological chemist. No mystery enshrouds them.

As the term "drive" is commonly used in contemporary psychological literature it is applied in two ways: as referring (A) to a source or spring of human or animal activity, and (B) to a determinant of the direction of this activity. The various bodily demands we have described above are readily seen (A) to furnish energy and excitation for activity in general. The behavior they originally set up, however, is in greater or lesser degree random and general. Although in certain cases (as in fatigued *versus* rested musculature, or as in sensitive zones of the skin when mildly stimulated) the resulting activity is somewhat definite and recognizable as arising from the tissue-demand that is at work, we must say (B) that the activity and excitement set up by most of these drives is not very specific and peculiar to it, and that the appearance of highly definite trends of motivation and interest toward highly definite objectives must await the processes of individual learning.

# 31 · Clark L. Hull

## Characteristics of Innate Behavior
## Under Conditions of Need

Hull's formalization of need theory is nicely demonstrated in this selection. He saw animals as "aggregations of needs" and the function of drive receptors as that of transmitting impulses "corresponding to the nature and intensity of the need as it arises." He also handled the issue of activation and direction in behavior as it relates to needs and unlearned responses.

We saw in an earlier chapter that when a condition arises for which action on the part of the organism is a prerequisite to optimum probability of survival of either the individual or the species, a state of need is said to exist. Since a need, either actual or potential, usually precedes and accompanies the action of an organism, the need is often said to motivate or drive the associated activity. Because of this motivational characteristic of needs they are regarded as producing primary animal *drives*.

### DRIVES ARE TYPICAL INTERVENING VARIABLES

It is important to note in this connection that the general concept of drive $(D)$ tends strongly to have the systematic status of an intervening variable or X, never directly observable. The need of food, ordinarily called hunger, produces a typical primary drive. Like all satisfactory intervening variables, the presence and the amount of the hunger drive are susceptible of a double determination on the basis of correlated events which are themselves directly observable. Specifically, the amount of the food need clearly increases with the number of hours elapsed since the last intake of food; here the amount of hunger drive $(D)$ is a function of observable *antecedent* conditions, i.e., of the need which is measured by the number of hours of food privation. On the other hand, the amount of energy which will be expended by the organism in the securing of food varies largely with the intensity of the hunger drive existent at the time; here the amount of "hunger" is a function of observable events which are its *consequence*. As usual with unobservables, the determination of the exact quantitative functional relationship of the intervening variable to both the antecedent and the consequent conditions presents serious practical difficulties. This probably explains the paradox that despite the almost universal use of the concepts of need and drive, this characteristic functional relationship is not yet determined for any need, though some preliminary work has been done in an attempt to determine it for hunger (1).

## INNATE BEHAVIOR TENDENCIES VARY ABOUT A CENTRAL RANGE

With our background of organic evolution we must believe that the behavior of newborn organisms is the result of unlearned, i.e., inherited, neural connections between receptors and effectors ($_sU_R$) which have been selected from fortuitous variations or mutations throughout the long history of the species. Since selection in this process has been on the intensely pragmatic basis of survival in a life-and-death struggle with multitudes of factors in a considerable variety of environments, it is to be expected that the innate or reflex behavior of young organisms will, upon the whole, be reasonably well adapted to the modal stimulating situations in which it occurs.

It may once have been supposed by some students of animal behavior, e.g., by Pavlov and other Russian reflexologists, that innate or reflex behavior is a rigid and unvarying neural connection between a single receptor discharge and the contraction of a particular muscle or muscle group. Whatever may have been the views held in the past, the facts of molar behavior, as well as the general dynamics of behavioral adaptation, now make it very clear not only that inherited behavior tendencies ($_sU_R$) are not strictly uniform and invariable, but that rigidly uniform reflex behavior would not be nearly so effective in terms of survival in a highly variable and unpredictable environment as would a *behavior tendency*. By this expression is meant behavior which will vary over a certain range, the frequency of occurrence at that segment of the range most likely to be adaptive being greatest, and the frequency at those segments of the range least likely to be adaptive being, upon the whole, correspondingly rare. Thus in the expression $_sU_R$, $R$ represents not a single act but a considerable range of more or less alternative reaction potentialities.

The neurophysiological mechanism whereby the type of flexible receptor-effector dynamic relationships could operate is by no means wholly clear, but a number of factors predisposing to variability of reaction are evident. First must be mentioned the spontaneous impulse discharge of individual nerve cells, discussed above. This, in conjunction with the principle of neural interaction operating on efferent neural impulses (*efferent neural interaction*), would produce a certain amount of variability in any reaction. Secondly, the variable proprioceptive stimulation arising from the already varying reaction would, by afferent neural interaction, clearly increase the range of variability in the reaction. Finally, as the primary exciting (drive) stimulus increases in intensity, it is to be expected that the effector impulses will rise above the thresholds of wider and wider ranges of effectors until practically the entire effector system may be activated.

Consider the situation resulting from a foreign object entering the eye. If the object is *very* small the stimulation of its presence may result in little more than a slightly increased frequency of lid closure and a small increase in lachrymal secretion, two effector processes presenting no very conspicuous range of variability except quantitatively. But if the object be relatively large and rough, and if the stimulation continues after the first vigorous blinks and tear secretions have occurred, the muscles of the arm will move the hand to the point of stimulation and a considerable variety of manipulative movements will follow, all more or less likely to contribute to the removal of the acutely stimulating object but none of them *precisely* adapted to that end.

In the case of a healthy human infant, which is hungry or is being pricked by a pin, we have the same general picture, though the details naturally will differ to a certain extent. If the need be acute, the child will scream loudly, opening its mouth very wide and closing its eyes; both legs will kick vigorously in rhythmic alternation, and the arms will flail about in a variety of motions which have, however, a general focus at the mouth and eyes. In cases of severe and somewhat protracted injurious stimulation the back may be arched and practically the entire musculature of the organism may be thrown into more or less violent activity.

## SOME PRIMARY NEEDS AND THE MODAL REACTIONS TO THEM

The major primary needs or drives are so ubiquitous that they require little more than to be mentioned. They include the need for foods of various sorts (*hunger*), the need for water (*thirst*), the need for *air*, the need to avoid tissue injury (*pain*), the need to maintain an optimal temperature, the need to defecate, the need to micturate, the need for rest (after protracted exertion), the need for sleep (after protracted wakefulness), and the need for activity (after protracted inaction). The drives concerned with the maintenance of the species are those which lead to sexual intercourse and the need represented by nest building and care of the young.

The primary core or mode of the range of innate or reflex tendencies to action must naturally vary from one need to another if the behavior is to be adaptive. In cases where the rôle of chance as to what movements will be adaptive is relatively small, the behavior tendency may be relatively simple and constant. For example, the acute need for oxygen may normally be satisfied (terminated) by inspiration; the need represented by pressure in the urinary bladder is normally terminated by micturition. It is not accidental that these relatively stereotyped and invariable reactions are apt to concern mainly those portions of the external environment which are highly constant and, especially, the internal environment which is characteristically constant and predictable.

In the case of mechanical tissue injury, withdrawal of the injured part from the point where the injury began is the characteristic reflex form of behavior, and the probability of the effectiveness of such action is obvious. Environmental temperatures considerably below the optimum for the organism tend to evoke shivering and a posture presenting a minimum of surface exposed to heat loss. Temperatures above the optimum tend to produce a general inactivity, a posture yielding a maximum surface for heat radiation, and rapid panting. In certain relatively complex situations such as those associated with the need for food, water, or reproduction, the factor of search is apt to be included as a preliminary. Since extensive search involves locomotion, the preliminary activities arising from these three needs will naturally be much alike.

## ORGANIC CONDITIONS WHICH INITIATE THREE TYPICAL PRIMARY DRIVE BEHAVIORS

During recent years physiologists and students of behavior have made important advances in unraveling the more immediate conditions which are associated with the onset of the activities characteristic of the three most complex primary drives—thirst, hunger, and sex. Thirst activities appear from these studies to be initiated by a dryness in the mouth and throat caused by the lack of saliva, which in its turn is caused by the lack of available water in the blood. The hunger drive seems to be precipitated, at least in part, by a rhythmic and, in extreme cases, more or less protracted contraction of the stomach and adjacent portions of the digestive tract presumably caused by the lack of certain nutritional elements in the blood. Copulatory and maternal drives appear to be most complex of all and are not too well understood as yet. It is known that female copulatory receptivity (oestrum) is precipitated by the presence in the blood of a specific hormone secreted periodically, and that male copulatory activity is dependent upon the presence in the blood of a male hormone. Just how these hormones bring about the actual motivation is not yet entirely clear.

Because of the inherent interest of some of these studies and of their presumptive aid in enabling the reader to orient himself in this important phase of behavior, three or four typical investigations will be described.

## TYPICAL STUDIES OF HUNGER-MOTIVATED ACTIVITY

The first study to be considered concerns hunger; it was performed by Wada (3). This investigator trained human subjects to swallow a tube with a small balloon at its end, the latter entering the stomach and the other end of the tube projecting from the subject's mouth. Then the balloon was inflated and the free end of the tube was attached to a delicate pneumatic recording mechanism. The subjects slept through the night upon an experimental bed which permitted the automatic recording of any restless movements of the sleeper. A presumably typical record so obtained is reproduced as Figure 31.1. The lower tracing of this record

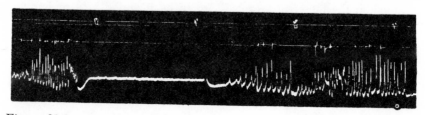

Figure 31.1. A record of the restless movements of a sleeping student (middle line) and the parallel (hunger) contractions of the student's stomach. Note that the sleeper's restless movements coincide, in general, with the periods of maximal stomach contraction. (After Wada, 3, p. 29.)

shows at the extreme left the rise of a series of rhythmic contractions of the stomach, terminating in a kind of cramp followed by a period of cessation. Presently the stomach contractions begin again, and are more or less continuous throughout the remainder of the record. But the main point of this is that the restless movements of the sleeping student (recorded as short vertical oscillations of the middle line in Figure 31.1) *occurred as a rule only when the stomach contractions were occurring, especially when they were at a maximum.*

Richter (2) attempted to secure parallel records of the stomach contractions and the restless locomotor activity of rats and other organisms to complete the proof of the presumtive relationship afforded by Wada's findings, but was unsuccessful, apparently because of technical difficulties encountered. However, he was able to show that rats are periodically rather restless in the living cage for a short time before going into a food chamber to eat, after which general activity quickly subsides. The periodicity of these restless movements is about the same as that known to occur with the stomach contractions. Richter accordingly concludes from a convincing array of such indirect evidence that the relationship between random, restless activity and the gastric hunger contractions is substantially that shown in Figure 31.2. It is to be observed that this figure is

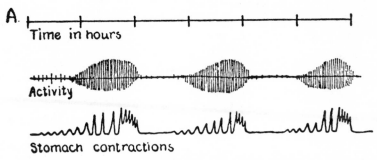

Figure 31.2.   Diagrammatic representations of the inferred relationship between the periodic stomach contractions of rats and their restless locomotor activity in the living cage. (After Richter, 2, p. 312.)

not a record but, rather, a diagrammatic representation of an inferential relationship. Nevertheless, Richter's reasoning is fairly convincing and Figure 31.2 quite probably represents the true situation.

The functional interpretation of this restless behavior is that an organism which moves about more or less continuously will in general traverse a wide area and consequently will be more likely to encounter food than if it remains quietly in one place.

## TYPICAL STUDIES OF SEXUALLY MOTIVATED ACTIVITY

Richter has also shown that the male rat displays much more restless locomotor activity when the sex drive is operating than when it is not. He placed male rats in drum-like cages pivoted on a central axis in such a way that if the animal attempted to climb the circular side of the cage its weight would turn the drum. Automatic counting devices aggregated the amount of this kind of locomotor activity by days. A graphic representation of the numerical values so obtained is shown at the left of Figure 31.3. At about the 195th day the rat was castrated. Note the abrupt

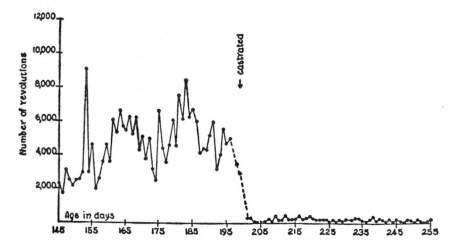

Figure 31.3. Graphic representation of restless locomotor activity of a male albino rat in a revolving cage before and after castration. (After Richter, *2*, 329.)

drop in the restless locomotor activity. Even if one makes a certain allowance for the shock produced by the operation as such, the inference is that when the hormone secreted by the testes is in the blood, the animal is generally active, but when this hormone is withdrawn through castration, generalized locomotor activity falls to a relatively low level and remains there.

Wang (*4*) has shown by analogous means that the female rat is maximally active in this same restless fashion about every fourth day, the two or three days between showing a relatively small amount of activity. A considerable number of cycles from a single female rat are represented graphically in Figure 31.4 (*2*). That these maxima of locomotor activity are coincident with periodically recurring sex drive is shown by the fact that on the occasion of the maxima such animals are receptive to the sexual advances of the male.

The functional interpretation of these studies is similar to that of the investigations involving hunger; an organism which moves about continuously will traverse a wide area and consequently will be more likely to encounter a mate than will an organism which remains in a single place.

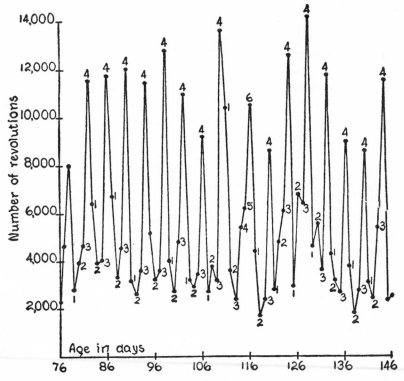

Figure 31.4. Graphic representation of the locomotor activity of a female albino rat over a series of days. Note the prevalence of a four-day cycle of activity. On the days of maximum activity these animals are sexually receptive. (After Richter, 2, 321.)

## SUMMARY

Animals may almost be regarded as aggregations of needs. The function of the effector apparatus is to mediate the satiation of these needs. They arise through progressive changes within the organism or through the injurious impact of the external environment. The function of one group of receptors (the drive receptors) is to transmit to the motor apparatus, via the brain, activating impulses corresponding to the nature and intensity of the need as it arises. Probably through the action of these drive receptors and receptor-effector connections preëstablished by the processes of organic evolution, the various needs evoke actions which increase in intensity and variety as the need becomes more acute.

Because of the inherently fortuitous nature of the environmental circumstances surrounding an organism when a state of need arises, the kind of behavior which will be required to alleviate the need is apt to be highly varied. For this reason rigid receptor-effector connections could not be very effective in terms of organismic survival. Accordingly we find, as a matter of fact, that innate molar response to a given state of need presents a considerable range of activity, the activity often consisting of a sequence of short cycles of somewhat similar yet more or less varied movements. Such behavior cycles are believed normally to show a frequency distribution in which those acts most likely to relieve the need occur most often, and those acts less likely to terminate it occur correspondingly less often. Thus reflex organization $(_sU_R)$ has more than one string to its bow; if one reaction cycle does not terminate the need, another may. The modal form of reaction will also be strongest, so that it will usually occur not only most frequently but earliest and probably will remedy the situation; but if the environment chances to be such that some other simple action sequence is required, in due course this action sequence will probably occur and the organism will survive. Finally, in still more complicated situations a particular combination of these acts may terminate the need. In this way innate behavior tendencies are organized on a genuine but primitive trial-and-error basis.

Lastly, it is to be noted that just as food-seeking activity begins long before the organism is in acute need of food, so other drives become active long before heat or cold or pain becomes seriously injurious or even in the least harmful. In short, it may be said that drives become active in situations which, if more intense or if prolonged, *would* become injurious. Once more, then, the probability aspect of primitive behavior tendencies becomes manifest.

In the light of the preceding considerations we formulate the following primary molar behavior principle:

*Postulate 3.* Organisms at birth possess receptor effector connections $(_sU_R)$ which, under combined stimulation $(S)$ and drive $(D)$, have the potentiality of evoking a hierarchy of responses that either individually or in combination are more likely to terminate the need than would be a random selection from the reaction potentials resulting from other stimulus and drive combinations.

## NOTES

### The Rôle of Adaptation in Systematic Behavior Theory

The emphasis in this and preceding chapters on the general significance of organic evolution in adapting organisms to meet critical biological emergencies calls for a word of comment, lest the reader be misled in regard to the rôle that adaptation, as such, plays in the present system. It is the view of the author that adaptive considerations are useful in making a preliminary survey in the search for postulates, but that once the postulates have been selected they must stand on their own feet. This means that once chosen, postulates or principles of behavior must be able to yield deductions in agreement with observed detailed phenomena of behavior; and, failing this, that no amount of *a priori* general adaptive plausibility will save such a postulate from being abandoned.

## Problems Associated with the Use of Drive ($D$) as an Intervening Variable

Most writers on behavior theory utilize the concept of need or some equivalent such as drive, though hardly one of them has faced squarely the associated problem of finding the two equations necessarily involved if the concept of drive is to take its place in a strict mathematical theory of behavior (5). In the case of hunger, for example, there must be an equation expressing the degree of drive or motivation as a function of the number of hours' food privation, say, and there must be a second equation expressing the vigor of organismic action as a function of the degree of drive ($D$) or motivation, combined in some manner with habit strength. A correlated task of some magnitude is that of objectively defining a unit in which to express the degree of such a motivational intervening variable.

Now it is a relatively easy matter to find a single empirical equation expressing vigor of reaction as a function of the number of hours' food privation or the strength of an electric shock, but it is an exceedingly difficult task to break such an equation up into the two really meaningful component equations involving hunger drive ($D$) or motivation as an intervening variable. It may confidently be predicted that many writers with a positivistic or anti-theoretical inclination will reject such a procedure as both futile and unsound. From the point of view of systematic theory such a procedure, if successful, would present an immense economy. This statement is made on the assumption that motivation ($D$) as such, whether its origin be food privation, electric shock, or whatever, bears a certain constant relationship to action intensity in combination with other factors, such as habit strength. If this fundamental relationship could be determined once and for all, the necessity for its determination for each special drive could not then exist, and so much useless labor would be avoided. Unfortunately it may turn out that what we now call drive and motivation will prove to be so heterogeneous that no single equation can represent the motivational potentiality of any two needs. Whether or not this is the case can be determined only by trial.

## REFERENCES

1. Perin, C. T.   Behavior potentiality as a joint function of the amount of training and the degree of hunger at the time of extinction. *J. exp. Psychol.,* 1942, *30,* 93–113.
2. Richter, C. P.   Animal behavior and internal drives. *Quar. Rev. Biol.,* 1927, *2,* 307–343.

3. Wada, T. An experimental study of hunger in its relation to activity. *Arch. Psychol.*, 1922, No. 57.

4. Wang, G. H. The relation between "spontaneous" activity and oestrous cycle in the white rat. *Comp. Psychol. Monogr.*, 1923, No. 6.

5. Young, P. T. *Motivation of behavior*. New York: John Wiley and Sons, 1936.

# 32 • Harry F. Harlow

## Mice, Monkeys, Men, and Motives

Survival-need theory led to a stress on internally aroused drives. Harlow's recognition that the distal receptors might also innately possess the potential for motivating the organism brought a new look to motivational psychology, one which initiated a lively search for primary, nonvisceral sources of drive in exploration, curiosity, information-seeking, competence, novelty, play, contact comfort, and the like. As a group, these sources seemed to hold no close relationship to survival needs. With the adequacy of the need theory shattered, the quest for some other common factor among drives began. Harlow himself advocated a return to hedonism.

*Many of psychology's* theoretical growing pains—or, in modern terminology, conditioned anxieties—stem from the behavioral revolution of Watson. The new psychology intuitively disposed of instincts and painlessly disposed of hedonism. But having completed this St. Bartholomew–type massacre, behavioristic motivation theory was left with an aching void, a nonhedonistic aching void, needless to say.

Before the advent of the Watsonian scourge the importance of external stimuli as motivating forces was well recognized. Psychologists will always remain indebted to Loeb's (21) brilliant formulation of tropistic theory, which emphasized, and probably overemphasized, the powerful role of external stimulation as the primary motivating agency in animal behavior. Unfortunately, Loeb's premature efforts to reduce all behavior to overly simple mathematical formulation, his continuous acceptance of new tropistic constructs in an effort to account for any aberrant behavior not easily integrated into his original system, and his abortive attempt to encompass all behavior into a miniature theoretical system doubtless led many investigators to underestimate the value of his experimental contributions.

Thorndike (30) was simultaneously giving proper emphasis to the

This article is reproduced in full from the *Psychological Review*, 1953, *60*, 23–32. Reprinted by permission of the American Psychological Association and the author.

role of external stimulation as a motivating force in learning and learned performances. Regrettably, these motivating processes were defined in terms of pain and pleasure, and it is probably best for us to dispense with such lax, ill-defined, subjective terms as pain, pleasure, anxiety, frustration, and hypotheses—particularly in descriptive and theoretical rodentology.

Instinct theory, for all its terminological limitations, put proper emphasis on the motivating power of external stimuli; for, as so brilliantly described by Watson (31) in 1941, the instinctive response was elicited by "serial stimulation," much of which was serial external stimulation.

The almost countless researches on tropisms and instincts might well have been expanded to form a solid and adequate motivational theory for psychology—a theory with a proper emphasis on the role of the external stimulus and an emphasis on the importance of incentives as opposed to internal drives per se.

It is somewhat difficult to understand how this vast and valuable literature was to become so completely obscured and how the importance of the external stimulus as a motivating agent was to become lost. Pain-pleasure theory was discarded because the terminology had subjective, philosophical implications. Instinct theory fell into disfavor because psychologists rejected the dichotomized heredity-environment controversy and, also, because the term "instinct" had more than one meaning. Why tropistic theory disappeared remains a mystery, particularly inasmuch as most of the researches were carried out on subprimate animal forms.

Modern motivation theory apparently evolved from an overpopularization of certain experimental and theoretical materials. Jennings' (14) demonstration that "physiological state" played a role in determining the behavior of the lower animal was given exaggerated importance and emphasis, thereby relegating the role of external stimulation to a secondary position as a force in motivation. The outstanding work in the area of motivation between 1920 and 1930 related to visceral drives and drive cycles and was popularized by Richter's idealized theoretical paper on "Animal Behavior and Internal Drives" (26) and Cannon's *The Wisdom of the Body* (3).

When the self-conscious behavior theorists of the early thirties looked for a motivation theory to integrate with their developing learning constructs, it was only natural that they should choose the available tissue-tension hypotheses. Enthusiastically and uncritically the S–R theorists swallowed these theses whole. For fifteen years they have tried to digest them, and it is now time that these theses be subjected to critical examination, analysis, and evaluation. We do not question that these theses have fertilized the field of learning, but we do question that the plants that have developed are those that will survive the test of time.

It is my belief that the theory which describes learning as dependent upon drive reduction is false, that internal drive as such is a variable of little importance to learning, and that this small importance steadily decreases as we ascend the phyletic scale and as we investigate learning problems of progressive complexity. Finally, it is my position that drive-reduction theory orients learning psychologists to attack problems of limited importance and to ignore the fields of research that might lead us in some foreseeable future time to evolve a theoretical psychology of learning that transcends any single species or order.

There can be no doubt that the single-celled organisms such as the amoeba and the paramecium are motivated to action both by external and internal stimuli. The motivation by external stimulation gives rise to heliotropisms, chemotropisms, and rheotropisms. The motivation by internal stimulation produces characteristic physiological states which have, in turn, been described as chemotropisms. From a phylogenetic point of view, moreover, neither type of motive appears to be more basic or more fundamental than the other. Both types are found in the simplest known animals and function in interactive, rather than in dominant-subordinate, roles.

Studies of fetal responses in animals from opossum to man give no evidence suggesting that the motivation of physiological states precedes that of external incentives. Tactual, thermal, and even auditory and visual stimuli elicit complex patterns of behavior in the fetal guinea pig, although this animal has a placental circulation which should guarantee against thirst or hunger (4). The newborn opossum climbs up the belly of the female and into the pouch, apparently in response to external cues; if visceral motives play any essential role, it is yet to be described (20). The human fetus responds to external tactual and nociceptive stimuli at a developmental period preceding demonstrated hunger or thirst motivation. Certainly, there is no experimental literature to indicate that internal drives are ontogenetically more basic than exteroceptive motivating agencies.

Tactual stimulation, particularly of the cheeks and lips, elicits mouth, head, and neck responses in the human neonate, and there are no data demonstrating that these responses are conditioned, or even dependent, upon physiological drive states. Hunger appears to lower the threshold for these responses to tactual stimuli. Indeed, the main role of the primary drive seems to be one of altering the threshold for precurrent responses. Differentiated sucking response patterns have been demonstrated to quantitatively varied thermal and chemical stimuli in the infant only hours of age (15), and there is, again, no reason to believe that the differentiation could have resulted from antecedent tissue-tension reduction states. Taste and temperature sensations induced by the temperature and chemical composition of the liquids seem adequate to account for the responses.

There is neither phylogenetic nor ontogenetic evidence that drive states elicit more fundamental and basic response patterns than do external stimuli; nor is there basis for the belief that precurrent responses are more dependent upon consummatory responses than are consummatory responses dependent upon precurrent responses. There is no evidence that the differentiation of the innate precurrent responses is more greatly influenced by tissue-tension reduction than are the temporal ordering and intensity of consummatory responses influenced by conditions of external stimulation.

There are logical reasons why a drive-reduction theory of learning, a theory which emphasizes the role of internal, physiological-state motivation, is entirely untenable as a motivational theory of learning. The internal drives are cyclical and operate, certainly at any effective level of intensity, for only a brief fraction of any organism's waking life. The classical hunger drive physiologically defined ceases almost as soon as food—or nonfood— is ingested. This, as far as we know, is the only case in which a single swallow portends anything of importance. The temporal brevity of operation of the internal drive states obviously offers a minimal opportunity for conditioning and a maximal opportunity for extinction. The human being, at least in the continental United States, may go for days or even years without ever experiencing true hunger or thirst. If his complex conditioned responses were dependent upon primary drive reduction, one would expect him to regress rapidly to a state of tuitional oblivion. There are, of course, certain recurrent physiological drive states that are maintained in the adult. But the studies of Kinsey (17) indicate that in the case of one of these there is an inverse correlation between presumed drive strength and scope and breadth of learning, and in spite of the alleged reading habits of the American public, it is hard to believe that the other is our major source of intellectual support. Any assumption that derived drives or motives can account for learning in the absence of primary drive reduction puts an undue emphasis on the strength and permanence of derived drives, at least in subhuman animals. Experimental studies to date indicate that most derived drives (24) and second-order conditioned responses (25) rapidly extinguish when the rewards which theoretically reduce the primary drives are withheld. The additional hypothesis of functional autonomy of motives, which could bridge the gap, is yet to be demonstrated experimentally.

The condition of strong drive is inimical to all but very limited aspects of learning—the learning of ways to reduce the internal tension. The hungry child screams, closes his eyes, and is apparently oblivious to most of his environment. During this state he eliminates response to those aspects of his environment around which all his important learned behaviors will be based. The hungry child is a most incurious child, but after he has eaten and become thoroughly sated, his curiosity and all the learned responses associated with his curiosity take place. If this learning is conditioned to an internal drive state, we must assume it is the resultant of backward conditioning. If we wish to hypothesize that backward conditioning is dominant over forward conditioning in the infant, it might be possible to reconcile fact with S–R theory. It would appear, however, that alternate theoretical possibilities should be explored before the infantile backward conditioning hypothesis is accepted.

Observations and experiments on monkeys convinced us that there was as much evidence to indicate that a strong drive state inhibits learning as to indicate that it facilitates learning. It was the speaker's feeling that monkeys learned most efficiently if they were given food before testing, and as a result, the speaker routinely fed his subjects before every training session. The rhesus monkey is equipped with enormous cheek pouches, and consequently many subjects would begin the educational process with a rich store of incentives crammed into the buccal cavity. When the monkey made a correct response, it would add a raisin to the buccal storehouse and swallow a little previously munched food. Following an incorrect response, the monkey would also swallow a little stored food. Thus, both correct and incorrect responses invariably resulted in S–R theory drive reduction. It is obvious that under these conditions the monkey cannot learn, but the present speaker developed an understandable skepticism of this hypothesis when the monkeys stubbornly persisted in learning, learning rapidly, and learning problems of great complexity. Because food was continuously available in the monkey's mouth, an explanation in terms of differential fractional anticipatory goal responses did not appear attractive. It would seem that the Lord was simply unaware of drive-reduction learning theory when he created, or permitted the gradual evolution of, the rhesus monkey.

The langurs are monkeys that belong to the only family of primates with sacculated stomachs. There would appear to be no mechanism better designed than the sacculated stomach to induce automatically prolonged delay of reinforcement defined in terms of homeostatic drive reduction. Langurs should, therefore, learn with great difficulty. But a team of Wisconsin students has discovered that the langurs in the San Diego Zoo learn at a high level of monkey efficiency. There is, of course, the alternative explanation that the inhibition of hunger contractions in multiple stomachs is more reinforcing than the inhibition of hunger contractions in one. Perhaps the quantification of the gastric variable will open up great new vistas of research.

Actually, the anatomical variable of diversity of alimentary mechanisms is essentially uncorrelated with learning to food incentives by monkeys and suggests that learning efficiency is far better related to tensions in the brain than in the belly.

Experimental test bears out the fact that learning performance by the monkey is unrelated to the theoretical intensity of the hunger drive. Meyer (23) tested rhesus monkeys on discrimination-learning problems under conditions of maintenance-food deprivation of 1.5, 18.5, and 22.5 hours and found no significant differences in learning or performance. Subsequently, he tested the same monkeys on discrimination-reversal learning following 1, 23, and 47 hours of maintenance-food deprivation and, again, found no significant differences in learning or in performance as measured by activity, direction of activity, or rate of responding. There was some evidence, not statistically significant, that the most famished subjects were a bit overeager and that intense drive exerted a mildly inhibitory effect on learning efficiency.

Meyer's data are in complete accord with those presented by Birch (1), who tested six young chimpanzees after 2, 6, 12, 24, and 48 hr. of food deprivation and found no significant differences in proficiency of performance on six patterned string problems. Observational evidence led Birch to conclude that intense food deprivation adversely affected problem solution because it led the chimpanzee to concentrate on the goal to the relative exclusion of the other factors.

It may be stated unequivocally that, regardless of any relationship that may be found for other animals, there are no data indicating that intensity of drive state and the presumably correlated amount of drive reduction are positively related to learning efficiency in primates.

In point of fact there is no reason to believe that the rodentological data will prove to differ significantly from those of monkey, chimpanzee, and man. Strassburger (29) has recently demonstrated that differences in food deprivation from 5 hours to 47 hours do not differentially affect the habit strength of the bar-pressing response as measured by subsequent resistance to extinction. Recently, Sheffield and Roby (28) have demonstrated learning in rats in the absence of primary drive reduction. Hungry rats learned to choose a maze path leading to a saccharin solution, a nonnutritive substance, in preference to a path leading to water. No study could better illustrate the predominant role of the external incentive–type stimulus on the learning function. These data suggest that, following the example of the monkey, even the rats are abandoning the sinking ship of reinforcement theory.

The effect of intensity of drive state on learning doubtless varies as we ascend the phyletic scale and certainly varies, probably to the point of almost complete reversal, as we pass from simple to complex problems, a point emphasized some years ago in a theoretical article by Maslow (22). Intensity of nociceptive stimulation may be positively related to speed of formation of conditioned avoidance responses in the monkey, but the use of intense nociceptive stimulation prevents the monkey from solving any problem of moderate complexity. This fact is consistent with a principle that was formulated and demonstrated experimentally many years ago as the Yerkes-Dodson law (32). There is, of course, no reference to the Yerkes-Dodson law by any drive-reduction theorist.

We do not mean to imply that drive state and drive-state reduction are unrelated to learning; we wish merely to emphasize that they are relatively unimportant variables. Our primary quarrel with drive-reduction theory is that it tends to focus more and more attention on problems of less and less importance. A strong case can be made for the proposition that the importance of the psychological problems studied during the last fifteen years has decreased as a negatively accelerated function approaching an asymptote of complete indifference. Nothing better illustrates this point than the kinds of apparatus currently used in "learning" research. We have the single-unit T-maze, the straight runway, the double-compartment grill box, and the Skinner box. The single-unit T-maze is an ideal apparatus for studying the visual capacities of a nocturnal animal; the straight runway enables one to measure quantitatively the speed and rate of running from one dead end to another; the double-compartment grill box is without doubt the most efficient torture chamber which is still legal; and the Skinner box enables one to demonstrate discrimination learning in a greater number of trials than is required by any other method. But the apparatus, though inefficient, give rise to data which can be splendidly quantified. The kinds of learning problems which can be efficiently measured in these apparatus represent a challenge only to the decorticate animal. It is a constant source of bewilderment to me that the neobehaviorists who so frequently belittle physiological psychology should chooose apparatus which, in effect, experimentally decorticate their subjects.

The Skinner box is a splendid apparatus for demonstrating that the rate of performance of a learned response is positively related to the period of food deprivation. We have confirmed this for the monkey by studying rate of response on a modified Skinner box following 1, 23, and 47 hr. of food deprivation. Increasing length of food deprivation is clearly and positively related to increased rate of response. This functional relationship between drive states and responses does not hold, as we have already seen, for the monkey's behavior in discrimination learning or in acquisition of any more complex problem. The data, however, like rat data, are in complete accord with Crozier's (6) finding that the acuteness of the radial angle of tropistic movements in the slug Limax is positively related to intensity of the photic stimulation. We believe there is generalization in this finding, and we believe the generalization to be that the results from the investigation of simple behavior may be very informative about even simpler behavior but very seldom are they informative about behavior of greater complexity. I do not want to discourage anyone from the pursuit of the psychological Holy Grail by the use of the Skinner box, but as far as I am concerned, there will be no moaning of farewell when we have passed the pressing of the bar.

In the course of human events many psychologists have children, and these children always behave in accord with the theoretical position of their parents. For purposes of scientific objectivity the boys are always referred to as "Johnny" and the girls as "Mary." For some eleven months I have been observing the behavior of Mary X. Perhaps the most striking characteristic of this particular primate has been the power and persistence of her curiosity-investigatory motives. At an early age Mary X demonstrated a positive valence to parental thygmotatic stimulation. My original interpretation of these tactual-thermal erotic responses as indicating parental affection was dissolved by the discovery that when Mary X was held in any position depriving her of visual exploration of the environment, she screamed; when held in a position favorable to visual exploration of the important environment, which did not include the parent, she responded positively. With the parent and position held constant and visual exploration denied by snapping off the electric light, the positive responses changed to negative, and they returned to positive when the light was again restored. This behavior was observed in Mary X, who, like any good Watson child, showed no "innate fear of the dark."

The frustrations of Mary X appeared to be in large part the results of physical inability to achieve curiosity-investigatory goals. In her second month, frustrations resulted from inability to hold up her head indefinitely while lying prone in her crib or on a mat and the consequent loss of visual curiosity goals. Each time she had to lower her head to rest, she cried lustily. At nine weeks attempts to explore (and destroy) objects anterior resulted in wriggling backward away from the lure and elicited violent negative responses. Once she negotiated forward locomotion, exploration set in, in earnest, and, much to her parents' frustration, shows no sign of diminishing.

Can anyone seriously believe that the insatiable curiosity-investigatory motivation of the child is a second-order or derived drive conditioned upon hunger or sex or any other internal drive? The S–R theorist and the Freudian psychoanalyst imply that such behaviors are based on primary drives. An informal survey of neobehaviorists who are also fathers (or mothers) reveals that all have observed the intensity and omnipresence of the curiosity-investigatory motive in their own children. None of them seriously believes that the behavior derives from a second-order drive. After describing their children's behavior, often with a surprising enthusiasm and frequently with the support of photographic records, they trudge off to their laboratories to study, under conditions of solitary confinement, the intellectual processes of rodents. Such attitudes, perfectly in keeping with drive-reduction theory, no doubt account for the fact that there are no experimental or even systematic observational studies of curiosity-investigatory-type external-incentive motives in children.

A key to the real learning theory of any animal species is knowledge of the nature and organization of the unlearned patterns of response. The differences in the intellectual capabilities of cockroach, rat, monkey, chimpanzee, and man are as much a function of the differences in the inherent patterns of response and the differences in the inherent motivational forces as they are a function of sheer learning power. The differences in these inherent patterns of response and in the motivational forces will, I am certain, prove to be differential responsiveness to external stimulus patterns. Furthermore, I am certain that the variables which are of true, as opposed to psychophilosophical, importance are not constant from learning problem to learning problem even for the same animal order, and they are vastly diverse as we pass from one animal order to another.

Convinced that the key to human learning is not the conditioned response but, rather, motivation aroused by external stimuli, the speaker has initiated researches on curiosity-manipulation behavior as related to learning in monkeys (7, 10, 12). The justification for the use of monkeys is that we have more monkeys than children. Furthermore, the field is so unexplored that a systematic investigation anywhere in the phyletic scale should prove of methodological value. The rhesus monkey is actually a very incurious and nonmanipulative animal compared with the anthropoid apes, which are, in turn, very incurious nonmanipulative animals compared with man. It is certainly more than coincidence that the strength and range of curiosity-manipulative motivation and position within the primate order are closely related.

We have presented three studies which demonstrate that monkeys can and do learn to solve mechanical puzzles when no motivation is provided other than presence of the puzzle. Furthermore, we have presented data to show that once mastered, the sequence of manipulations involved in solving these puzzles is carried out relatively flawlessly and extremely persistently. We have presented what we believe is incontrovertible evidence against a second-order drive interpretation of this learning.

A fourth study was carried out recently by Gately at the Wisconsin laboratories. Gately directly compared the behavior of two groups of four monkeys presented with banks of four identical mechanical puzzles, each utilizing three restraining devices. All four food- plus puzzle-rewarded monkeys solved the four identical puzzles, and only one of the four monkeys motivated by curiosity alone solved all the puzzles. This one monkey, however, learned as rapidly and as efficiently as any of the food-rewarded monkeys. But I wish to stress an extremely important observation made by Gately and supported by quantitative records. When the food-rewarded monkeys had solved a puzzle, they abandoned it. When the nonfood-rewarded animals had solved the puzzle, they frequently continued their explorations and manipulations. Indeed, one reason for the nonfood-rewarded monkeys' failure to achieve the experimenter's concept of solution lay in the fact that the monkey became fixated in exploration and manipulation of limited puzzle or puzzle-device components. From this point of view, hunger-reduction incentives may be regarded as motivation-destroying, not motivation-supporting, agents.

Twenty years ago at the Vilas Park Zoo, in Madison, we observed an adult orangutan given two blocks of wood, one with a round hole, one with a square hole, and two plungers, one round and one square. Intellectual curiosity alone led it to work on these tasks, often for many minutes at a time, and to solve the problem of inserting the round plunger in both holes. The orangutan never solved the problem of inserting the square peg into the round hole, but inasmuch as it passed away with perforated ulcers a month after the problem was presented, we can honestly say that it died trying. And in defense of this orangutan, let it be stated that it died working on more complex problems than are investigated by most present-day learning theorists.

Schiller [1] has reported that chimpanzees solve multiple-box-stacking problems without benefit of food rewards, and he has presented observational evidence that the joining of sticks resulted from manipulative play responses.

The Cebus monkey has only one claim to intellectual fame—an ability to solve instrumental problems that rivals the much publicized ability of the anthropoid apes (*11, 18*). It can be no accident that the Cebus monkey, inferior to the rhesus on conventional learning tasks, demonstrates far more spontaneous instrumental-manipulative responses than any old-world form. The complex, innate external-stimulus motives are variables doubtlessly as important as, or more important than, tissue tensions, stimulus generalization, excitatory potential, or secondary reinforcement. It is the oscillation of sticks, not cortical neurons, that enables the Cebus monkey to solve instrumental problems.

No matter how important may be the analysis of the curiosity-manipulative drives and the learning which is associated with them, we recognize the vast and infinite technical difficulties that are inherent in the attack on the solution of these problems—indeed, it may be many years before we can routinely order such experiments in terms of latin squares and factorial designs, the apparent *sine qua non* for publication in the *Journal of Experimental Psychology* and the *Journal of Comparative and Physiological Psychology*.

There is, however, another vast and important area of external-stimulus incentives important to learning which has been explored only

---

[1] Personal communication.

superficially and which can, and should, be immediately and systematically attacked by rodentologists and primatologists alike. This is the area of food incentives—or, more broadly, visuo-chemo variables—approached from the point of view of their function as motivating agents per se. This function, as the speaker sees it, is primarily an affective one and only secondarily one of tissue-tension reduction. To dispel any fear of subjectivity, let us state that the affective tone of food incentives can probably be scaled by preference tests with an accuracy far exceeding any scaling of tissue tensions. Our illusion of the equal-step intervals of tissue tensions is the myth that length of the period of deprivation is precisely related to tissue-tension intensity, but the recent experiments by Koch and Danil (19) and Horenstein (13) indicate that this is not true, thus beautifully confirming the physiological findings of thirty years ago.

Paired-comparison techniques with monkeys show beyond question that the primary incentive variables of both differential quantity and differential quality can be arranged on equal-step scales, and there is certainly no reason to believe that variation dependent upon subjects, time, or experience is greater than that dependent upon physiological hunger.

In defense of the rat and its protagonists, let it be stated that there are already many experiments on this lowly mammal which indicate that its curiosity-investigatory motives and responsiveness to incentive variables can be quantitatively measured and their significant relationship to learning demonstrated. The latent learning experiments of Buxton (2), Haney (9), Seward, Levy, and Handlon (27), and others have successfully utilized the exploratory drive of the rat. Keller (16) and Zeaman and House (35) have utilized the rat's inherent aversion to light, or negative heliotropistic tendencies, to induce learning. Flynn and Jerome (8) have shown that the rat's avoidance of light is an external-incentive motivation that may be utilized to obtain the solution of complex learned performances. For many rats it is a strong and very persistent form of motivation. The importance of incentive variables in rats has been emphasized and re-emphasized by Young (33), and the influence of incentive variables on rat learning has been demonstrated by Young (33), Zeaman (34), Crespi (5), and others. I am not for one moment disparaging the value of the rat as a subject for psychological investigation; there is very little wrong with the rat that cannot be overcome by the education of the experimenters.

It may be argued that if we accept the theses of this paper, we shall be returning to an outmoded psychology of tropisms, instincts, and hedonism. There is a great deal of truth to this charge. Such an approach might be a regression were it not for the fact that psychology now has adequate techniques of methodology and analysis to attack quantifiably these important and neglected areas. If we are ever to have a comprehensive theoretical psychology, we must attack the problems whose solution offers hope of insight into human behavior, and it is my belief that if we face our problems honestly and without regard to, or fear of, difficulty, the theoretical psychology of the future will catch up with, and eventually even surpass, common sense.

## REFERENCES

1. Birch, H. C.   The relation of previous experience to insightful problem solving. *J. comp. Psychol.*, 1945, *39*, 15–22.
2. Buxton, C. E.   Latent learning and the goal gradient hypothesis. *Contr. psychol. Theor.*, 1940, *2* (2).
3. Cannon, W. B.   *The wisdom of the body.* New York: Norton, 1932.
4. Carmichael, L.   An experimental study in the prenatal guinea-pig of the origin and development of reflexes and patterns of behavior in relation to the stimulation of specific receptor areas during the period of active fetal life. *Genet. Psychol. Monogr.*, 1934, *16*, 337–491.
5. Crespi, L. P.   Quantitative variation of incentive and performance in the white rat. *Amer. J. Psychol.*, 1942, *55*, 467–517.
6. Crozier, W. J.   The study of living organisms. In C. Murchison (Ed.), *The foundations of experimental psychology.* Worcester, Mass.: Clark Univer. Press, 1929.
7. Davis, R. T., Settlage, P. H., & Harlow, H. F.   Performance of normal and brain-operated monkeys on mechanical puzzles with and without food incentive. *J. genet. Psychol.*, 1950, *77*, 305–311.
8. Flynn, J. P., & Jerome, E. A.   Learning in an automatic multiple-choice box with light as incentive. *J. comp. physiol. Psychol.*, 1952, *45*, 336–340.
9. Haney, G. W.   The effect of familiarity on maze performance of albino rats. *Univer. Calif. Publ. Psychol.*, 1931, *4*, 319–333.
10. Harlow, H. F.   Learning and satiation of response in intrinsically motivated complex puzzle performance by monkeys. *J. comp. physiol. Psychol.*, 1950, *43*, 289–294.
11. Harlow, H. F.   Primate learning. In C. P. Stone (Ed.), *Comparative psychology.* (3rd ed.) New York: Prentice-Hall, 1951.
12. Harlow, H. F., Harlow, Margaret K., & Meyer, D. R.   Learning motivated by a manipulation drive. *J. exp. Psychol.*, 1950, *40*, 228–234.
13. Horenstein, Betty.   Performance of conditioned responses as a function of strength of hunger drive. *J. comp. physiol. Psychol.*, 1951, *44*, 210–224.
14. Jennings, H. S.   *Behavior of the lower organisms.* New York: Columbia Univer. Press, 1906.
15. Jensen, K.   Differential reactions to taste and temperature stimuli in newborn infants. *Genet. Psychol. Monogr.*, 1932, *12*, 361–476.
16. Keller, F. S.   Light-aversion in the white rat. *Psychol. Rec.*, 1941, *4*, 235–250.
17. Kinsey, A. C., Pomeroy, W. B., & Martin, C. E.   *Sexual behavior in the human male.* Philadelphia: W. B. Saunders, 1948.

18. Klüver, H. *Behavior mechanisms in monkeys.* Chicago: Univer. Chicago Press, 1933.
19. Koch, S., & Daniel, W. J. The effect of satiation on the behavior mediated by a habit of maximum strength. *J. exp. Psychol.*, 1945, *35*, 162–185.
20. Langworthy, O. R. The behavior of pouch-young opossums correlated with the myelinization of tracts in the nervous system. *J. comp. Neurol.*, 1928, *46*, 201–248.
21. Loeb, J. *Forced movements, tropisms and animal conduct.* Philadelphia: Lippincott, 1918.
22. Maslow, A. H. A theory of human motivation. *Psychol. Rev.*, 1943, *50*, 370–396.
23. Meyer, D. R. Food deprivation and discrimination reversal learning by monkeys. *J. exp. Psychol.*, 1951, *41*, 10–16.
24. Miller, N. E. Learnable drives and rewards. In S. S. Stevens (Ed.), *Handbook of experimental psychology.* New York: Wiley, 1951.
25. Pavlov, I. P. *Conditioned reflexes* (translated by G. V. Anrep). London: Oxford Univer. Press, 1927.
26. Richter, C. P. Animal behavior and internal drives. *Quart. Rev. Biol.*, 1927, *2*, 307–343.
27. Seward, J. P., Levy, N., & Handlon, J. H., Jr. Incidental learning in the rat. *J. comp. physiol. Psychol.*, 1950, *43*, 240–251.
28. Sheffield, F. D., & Roby, T. B. Reward value of a non-nutrient sweet taste. *J. comp. physiol. Psychol.*, 1950, *43*, 471–481.
29. Strassburger, R. C Resistance to extinction of a conditioned operant as related to drive level at reinforcement. *J. exp. Psychol.*, 1950, *40*, 473–487.
30. Thorndike, E. L. *Animal intelligence.* New York: Macmillan, 1911.
31. Watson, J. B. *Behavior: an introduction to comparative psychology.* New York: Holt, 1914.
32. Yerkes, R. M., & Dodson, J. D. The relation of strength of stimulus to rapidity of habit formation. *J. comp. Neurol. Psychol.*, 1908, *18*, 459–482.
33. Young, P. T. Food-seeking drive, affective process, and learning. *Psychol. Rev.*, 1949, *56*, 98–121.
34. Zeaman, D. Response latency as a function of amount of reinforcement. *J. exp. Psychol.*, 1949, *39*, 466–483.
35. Zeaman, D., & House, Betty J. Response latency at zero drive after varying numbers of reinforcements. *J. exp. Psychol.*, 1950, *40*, 570–583.

# 33 • David C. McClelland, John W. Atkinson, Russell A. Clark, and Edgar L. Lowell

## Toward a Theory of Motivation

While McClelland's orientation was in many ways representative of several alternatives to survival-need theory, it was unique in its claim that all motives are learned. Affect was primary. "A motive is the redintegration by a cue of a change in an affective situation." Once a motive was learned, however, it was seen as functioning in ways that could be termed both homeostatic and hedonistic. Since the demise of need theory, however, no one claim concerning a common general basis for motivation has gained wide acceptance. Indeed, only the future can tell if complex generalizations of this sort are possible.

### 2.7 THE AFFECTIVE AROUSAL MODEL

*Our reservations* with respect to contemporary motivation theory have led us to attempt to rough out proposals for an alternative theory which may now or ulimately meet some of these objections and handle the data at least as well as the other models discussed. We are well aware of the incompleteness, as of this writing, of our theoretical thinking, but we will attempt to state our views as precisely and forcefully as we can in the hope that we can stimulate more serious discussion and experimental testing of motivational theory. At several points we will be obliged to present alternative hypotheses, since we do not as yet have the data to decide between them. But we agree with Hull and others that the only way to make progress in a field is "to stick one's neck out" and to state implicit theoretical assumptions as explicitly as possible.

Our definition of a motive is this: *A motive is the redintegration by a cue of a change in an affective situation.* The word *redintegration* in this definition is meant to imply previous learning. In our system, all motives are learned. The basic idea is simply this: Certain stimuli or situations involving discrepancies between expectation (adaptation level) and perception are sources of primary, unlearned affect, either positive or negative in nature. Cues which are paired with these affective states, changes in these affective states, and the conditions producing them become capable of redintegrating a state ($A'$) derived from the original affective situation ($A$), but not identical with it. To give a simple example, this means that if a buzzer is associated with eating saccharine the buzzer will in time attain the power to evoke a motive or redintegrate a state involving positive affective change. Likewise, the buzzer if associated with shock will achieve the power to redintegrate a negative affective state. These redintegrated states, which might be called respectively *appetite* and *anxiety*, are based on the primary affective situation but are not identical with it.

The term *change in affect* is used in two separate senses. It refers on the one hand to the fact that *at the time of arousal* of a motive, the affective state which is redintegrated must be different from the one already experienced by the organism, and on the other hand to the *possibility* that *at the time of acquisition* of a motive, the affective state with which the cue gets associated must be undergoing a change. We are agreed that a "change in affect" at the time of arousal in the first sense must occur, but we see two possibilities on the acquisition side of the picture—one, that the association is with a *static* affective state; the other, that it is with a *changing* affective state. To elaborate this point further, the first alternative states simply that any cue associated with a situation producing affect will acquire the power to evoke a "model" of that situation ($A'$) which will serve as a motive. The second alternative requires that the cue be associated with a *changing* state—of going from "shock" to "no shock" or from neutrality to pleasure, and so forth. The difference between the two possibilities is illustrated in the following diagram:

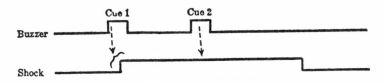

Figure 33.1

According to the first hypothesis, both cue 1 and cue 2 should be capable of evoking an avoidance motive, since they have both been paired with the affective state arising from shock. According to the second, alternative hypothesis, cue 2 should have weak or nonexistent motivating power since it has not been associated with a *change* in affect. It should be possible to determine which of these alternatives is correct by experimentation along these lines. Finally, it should be repeated that both hypotheses assume that the redintegrated affect *at the time of arousal* must represent a change over the present affective state of the organism.

In the discussion so far there has been some ambiguity as to just what is redintegrated—the affective state or change, the conditions which produced it, or both. Actually, the ambiguity reflects some uncertainty as to which alternative is correct and also some difficulty in expressing simply exactly what happens. By far the most likely possibility is that both the situation *and* the affect it produces are redintegrated. Thus the redintegrated "situation" defines the goal in the usual sense (e.g., sugar in the mouth), and the redintegrated "affect" (e.g., reaction to the sugar in the mouth) determines whether the goal is motivating or not. For the sake of simplicity, phrases like redintegrated "affective state" or "affective change" are used throughout this chapter to refer both to the affective reaction itself and the situation which produced it.

Two main questions connected with the concept of redintegrated affective state still remain to be answered. Why, first of all, should we have decided to base motives on affect? Secondly, how are we to determine the existence of affective arousal? It will be difficult to do complete justice to these questions, but a word on each may help indicate the progress of our thinking.

## 2.8 WHY AFFECT AS A BASIS FOR MOTIVES?

We have decided to base motives on affective arousal, following Young's lead (1949) for several reasons. In the first place, it seems apparent that the motive concept will be useful only if it has some kind of a limited base. That is, if all associations are motivating, then there seems no particular reason to introduce the concept of motivation to apply to a particular subclass of association. Thus the associations involved in forming motives must be in some way different from other types of associations. And we have chosen affective states as the basis for motives rather than biological needs or strong stimuli because of the limitations of those concepts already discussed. A more positive reason for choosing affective states as primary is that they are "obviously" important in controlling behavior, at least at the common-sense level. The hedonic or pleasure-pain view of motivation is certainly one of the oldest in psychological thinking and can be traced at least to Plato's *Protagoras*. Furthermore, in order to get motives in the laboratory we commonly pair cues with affective states resulting from shock, saccharine in the mouth, food deprivation, and the like. Operationally we manipulate states which we know subjectively will produce pleasure and pain when we work with motives.

Another reason for choosing affect as the basis for motives rather than tissue needs, etc., is the overwhelming evidence for the importance of selective sensitivity in guiding and directing behavior in lower animals. Tinbergen (1951) has collected dozens of cases which illustrate how special stimuli are required to release a particular "consummatory" response particularly in submammalian species. Young (1949) has repeatedly called attention to the different palatability of various foods for the white rat. Weiner and Stellar (1951) have demonstrated unlearned salt preferences in the rat. And so forth. The list could easily be extended. The usual reaction by theorists to these facts is to assume that they are not characteristic of the human animal, which is obviously much more dependent on learning than on innate reactions to particular "releasing" stimuli. The difference is nicely highlighted by Ford and Beach (1951), who show how human sexual behavior is much less dependent than the behavior of lower animals on particular external signs and internal hormonal conditions.

But all of this seems no reason to assume a sharp discontinuity between man and other animals with respect to the factors controlling behavior. Rather we have been struck by the possibility that man's behavior may also be guided by selective sensitivity to particular kinds of situations. The difference may be one of degree rather than kind. With man the "releasing" situations may be much less specific than the dot on a gull's beak which releases pecking behavior of a gull chick, but they may exist just the same (Section 2.10). And the consummatory reactions elicited by such situations may also be much less specific and rigid than the pecking, fighting, courting responses shown in lower animals; in fact, the interesting possibility pursued here is that in man these specific overt reactions to "releasing" stimuli are attenuated and occur instead as diffuse reactions of the autonomic nervous system signifying what we usually call "affect." Thus our motivational system for man has been constructed to parallel the analysis of instinctive behavior in lower animals made by Tinbergen (1951) and others. Certain types of situations (Section 2.10) innately release reactions which are diffuse and covert in man rather than specific and overt, but which are consummatory in the same sense in that they ultimately exhaust themselves. These diffuse reactions are what we mean by affect, and they can be observed either through verbal reports and autonomic reactions, or inferred from approach and avoidance behavior, as we shall see in the next section. Man's advantage over lower animals lies precisely in the wider range of situations which will produce affect and in the lack of overt specificity of the affective reaction. Thus he can build a wide variety of motives on a much broader base, but to our mind it is essentially the same base as that which is responsible for guiding and directing the behavior of lower animals.

## 2.9 BEHAVIORAL EFFECTS OF AFFECTIVE AROUSAL

But how do we propose to define pleasure and pain or affective arousal? We certainly do not intend to fall into the trap of arguing that pleasurable sensations are those that lead to survival, and painful ones those that ultimately lead to maladaptation and death. This answer lands us back in the same difficulties that face the biological need theory of motivation. Let us first attempt to define affect by anchoring it on the behavioral side. It might seem more logical to consider first the antecedent conditions of affect (see Section 2.10) rather than its behavioral consequences, but the behavioral approach is more familiar because it is the one that has been customarily employed in attempts to measure affect or pleasure and pain (cf. Lindsley in Stevens, 1951). Thus, at a certain gross level, one can distinguish affective states from other states by the effects of autonomic activity—changes in respiration rate, in electrical skin resistance, in blood pressure, and the like. Thus one might initially state as a generalization that an affective state is present whenever the *PGR* shows a significant deflection, and that anyone who wants to establish a motive can simply pair cues with such deflections or the conditions which produced them. Autonomic accompaniments of emotions may not be perfect indexes of their presence, but they are sufficiently good to provide a very practical basis for deciding in a large number of cases that affective arousal has occurred.

Since autonomic measures apparently cannot be used at the present time to distinguish sensitively between positive and negative affective states, we will need to attack this problem in some other way. There are several possibilities. Among humans, expressive movements can readily be interpreted as indicating pleasant or unpleasant feeling states, particularly facial expressions (Schlosberg, 1952). Impromptu vocalizing seems also to be a good indicator of mood. Probably the most sensitive and frequently used index to hedonic tone is verbal behavior. If the person says "I dislike it," "I'm unhappy," or "it hurts," we take it as a sign of negative affect. If he says "I feel good," or "I like it," we take it as a sign of positive affect. One difficulty with these expressive signs is that they are not infallible. They can all be "faked," or changed by learning.

And what about animals? They can't talk, it would be difficult to try to interpret the facial expression of a rat or an elephant, and no one has made a careful study of animal vocalization patterns in response to pleasure and pain. In the case of some animals, certain innate response patterns are readily interpreted as signifying positive or negative affect —e.g., purring or spitting in the cat; licking, tail-wagging, or growling in the dog, and so on. More attention should be given to the study of the expressive signs of affect, but until it is, we must be satisfied with stopgap measures. Probably the most useful of these with adult animals is simple preference or approach behavior in contrast to avoidance behavior.

Sometimes there are reflex responses that are clearly approach or avoidance in nature—e.g., sucking, grasping, swallowing, spitting, vomiting, blinking—and in some instances they may provide direct evidence of positive or negative affective arousal. That is, eye-blinking in response to a puff of air, if accompanied by an autonomic response, would give evidence that affect was present and that this affect was negative in nature. Cues paired with the air puff would in time come to elicit an avoidance motive (as indicated by the presence of an avoidance *response*—the conditional or anticipatory eye-blink). But since reflexes are few in number and sometimes hard to classify as approach or avoidance (e.g., the knee jerk), better evidence for the existence of affective arousal is to be found in *learned* approach and avoidance behavior (locomotor, manual, verbal). There is an apparent circularity here, because what we are saying is that we can tell whether affective arousal occurred only after the organism has learned an approach or avoidance response in the service of a motive. Are we not first making a motive dependent on affective arousal and then saying we can find out whether affective arousal occurred if a motive has been formed which leads to approach or avoidance behavior? The answer is "Yes, we are," but the argument is not completely circular (cf. Meehl, 1950). Thus in one experiment we can determine that salty water leads to learned approach or preference behavior in the rat and we can then *infer* from this that it produces positive affective arousal. This inference (that salty water "tastes good" to the rat) can then be used as the basis for new learning experiments, theorizing, and so on. In this way we can gradually build up classes of objects, situations, response categories, or sensations which must produce affective arousal and then try to generalize as to what they have in common, as we have later on in this chapter (Section 2.10). In brief, the notion here is to use autonomic responses to indicate the presence of affect and approach and avoidance (either learned or reflex) to distinguish positive from negative affect.

There is one misconception which may arise in connection with this definition that it is well to anticipate, however. The terms *approach* and *avoidance* must not be understood simply as "going towards" or "away from" a stimulus in a spatial sense. Thus "rage," when it goes over into attack, is an "avoidance" response, even though it involves "going towards" something. *Avoidance* must be defined in terms of its objective—

to discontinue, remove, or escape from a certain type of stimulation and not in terms of its overt characteristics. Attack has, as its objective, removal of the source of stimulation in the same sense that withdrawal does. *Approach* must also be defined functionally—i.e., it is any activity, the objective of which is to continue, maintain, or pursue a certain kind of stimulation. Because of the ambiguity involved in using these terms, it might be better to substitute others like *stimulus enhancement* or *stimulus reduction,* but approach and avoidance have the advantage of common usage and if it is understood that they are used in a functional sense, difficulties should not arise in using them as the primary means of defining positive and negative affect on the response side. It is perhaps worth noting that Dearborn (1899) and Corwin (1921) came to the same decision long ago after recording involuntary "pursuit" (extension) and "withdrawal" (flexion) movements to pleasant and unpleasant stimuli, respectively.

2.9.1 *Distinguishing the effects of affect and motive.* Analytically speaking, there are three events involved in the development of a motive, any of which may have observable and distinguishable behavioral effects. In order of occurrence, they are:

A. The situation producing affect
B. Redintegration of (A)
C. Response learned to (B)

We have discussed the problem of measuring the behavioral effects of A in the previous section. How can the effects of A and B be distinguished, if at all? The simplest assumption would seem to be the one that Hull made years ago (1931), to the effect that a cue paired with a goal response will evoke a fractional anticipatory portion of it. The notion behind this is that the redintegrated response is like the original but fractional in nature, that is, consisting of a portion of the total goal response which is perhaps less in intensity or duration. The difficulty with this idea has been discussed at some length by Mowrer (1950). In general, the objection is similar to the one made against the substitution hypothesis in conditioning experiments. That is, formerly it was commonly assumed that in conditioning the conditioned stimulus simply substituted for the unconditioned stimulus in evoking the unconditioned response. But, as Hilgard and Marquis (1940) point out, the conditioned response is in fact often quite different from the unconditioned response. It is not necessarily a miniature replica or fractional portion of the original unconditioned response. For example, there is evidence that the normal response in rats to the primary affective state produced by shock is squealing, defecating, and intense variable behavior, whereas the normal response to anticipation of shock (e.g., to fear) is different, probably crouching (Arnold, 1945). The evidence that crouching is the normal response to fear is not conclusive, as Brown and Jacobs (1949) point out, because it can be eliminated by certain experimental procedures; but the probability is still fairly great that the response to fear differs in important ways from the response to shock. Therefore it would seem unwise at this state of our knowledge to assume that the fear response is just a partial copy of the shock response. At the phenomenological level, it seems that shock produces two distinguishable response elements—pain, which is the immediate reaction to shock, and fear, which is the anticipatory redintegration of the pain response. These two responses are clearly different. That is, if one's teeth are hurt by drilling in the dentist's chair, the sight of the chair may evoke a subjective feeling we label fear, but it does not evoke a "fractional" pain in the teeth.

When we consider the third event in the sequence of motive formation—namely, the responses learned to the redintegrated affect—the picture becomes even more complex. Our position is that the genotypic responses to redintegrated positive or negative affect are "functional" approach or avoidance. Thus from avoidance we can infer that negative affect has occurred if we lack a direct independent response definition of negative affect. But at the phenotypical level, the responses learned to redintegrated negative or positive affect may be very varied. A rat can be trained to run at as well as away from a shock (Gwinn, 1949). Rage and fear are genotypically avoidance responses, but phenotypically the former involves approach and the latter withdrawal. Similarly, love and contempt or scorn are genotypically similar in that they both involve attempts to maintain a source of stimulation, but phenotypically love involves "going towards" an object and scorn involves "keeping your distance" from the scorned object. A classification of emotions on a pleasant-unpleasant dimension and on an attentive-rejective one succeeds in ordering satisfactorily nearly all the facial expressions of emotion, according to Schlosberg (1952), a fact which tends to confirm our position that one must distinguish basically between positive and negative affect on the one hand and learned reactions to it, however classified, on the other. If the learned reactions are classified as to whether they phenotypically involve "going towards" or "away from" something, as they were approximately on Schlosberg's attentive-rejective dimension, then one gets a fourfold table in which Love, Contempt, Rage, and Fear represent the four major types of emotional reactions.

But obviously such classifications of phenotypic reactions can vary tremendously. The important points to keep in mind theoretically are (1) that they are surface modes of reaction with two basic objectives— to approach or maintain pleasure and to avoid or reduce pain, and (2) that they are acquired and hence take time to develop and show characteristic individual differences.

2.9.2 *Measuring motives through their effects.* The fact that the learned reactions to motives may vary so much suggests that it may be difficult to identify motives through their effects. The first problem is to decide at what point the stream of behavior indicates the presence of a motive. It may be helpful to begin the analysis with a simple case in which the behavior produced by affect can be distinguished from that which reflects the subsequent redintegration of affect. Consider the startle reaction (Landis and Hunt, 1939). A pistol shot produces varied autonomic and reflex effects which are signs of affective arousal. The fact that this arousal is negative can be inferred after the longer latency "voluntary" avoidance responses appear which are signs of an avoidance motive cued off by the shot or its "startle" effects because of the former association of such cues with negative affect. A necessary inference from this is that the first time startle is elicited (as perhaps in the Moro reflex in infants), it should not produce the longer latency co-ordinated avoidance behavior which Landis and Hunt observed in adults.

This suggests that one of the important ways in which motivated behavior may be identified is in terms of the *co-ordination* of responses or in terms of some kind of a response *sequence,* which terminates when the organism arrives somewhere with respect to a source of affect. The terms *approach* and *avoidance* imply a sequence of responses which has a *goal*—e.g., arriving at or away from a situation producing affect. Perhaps the point can be clarified by referring to our response definitions of a motive. The general definition is "goal-oriented free choice with habit and situational factors controlled." Under this we have placed approach and avoidance behavior, the only criterion one can use with animals, and the choice of certain "classes of goal-oriented thoughts" for inclusion in fantasy, the criterion we have used in measuring achievement motivation. These criteria are similar in implying choice responses with respect to a goal. We mean by the term *goal* here the same thing we meant earlier when we were distinguishing between genotypic and phenotypic approach and avoidance, between the functional significance of an act (e.g., avoiding a stimulus) and the modality of the act itself (which may involve attacking the stimulus). The goal is the functional significance of the act. Let us be more specific. Any response an animal makes involves choice in a sense. Any succession of responses also involves co-ordination in the sense of alternation of effector pathways, and so on. But only when the succession becomes a sequence which results in approach to or avoidance of a situation can we argue that there is evidence for the existence of a motive.

In dealing with verbal responses in a story the problem is simpler. Many thoughts (e.g., "the boy is happy") indicate the presence of affect, but only those thoughts chosen for inclusion which imply affect in connection with a particular situation are evidence for the existence of a motive (e.g., "the boy wants to do a good job"). In this example, "wanting to do a good job" defines an end situation which would produce positive affect, and the fact that the subject chooses to include such a statement is taken as evidence that he is motivated for achievement. That is, he has made a "goal-oriented" choice by making a statement about an achievement situation ("good job") which would inferentially produce positive affect (the boy "wants" it). Thus with such a measure of motivation we do not need the evidence of a co-ordinated though perhaps variable sequence of responses with a certain end, since the end ("good job") is directly stated, and it is this end state, with its accompanying affect rather than mere co-ordination, which seems to be the necessary criterion for deciding that behavior is showing evidence of the existence of motivation.

In short, in verbal behavior the "redintegrated affective situation" may be reflected directly and need not be inferred from a sequence of responses signifying approach and avoidance.

But why in the definition do we insist on "free" choice with certain factors controlled? The argument runs like this. Since general locomotor approach and avoidance are learned so early and so well in the life history of the organism, they can be utilized in normal animals to test the strength of a motivational association, provided the testing situation is a "free" one—provided the rats' "habits" are normal and provided the situation is a normal one for the rat. That is, it would be fair to test for the existence and strength of a rat's hunger motive by measuring the number of times he runs toward food as compared with other objects when placed on an open table top, provided his past experience has been "normal." But obviously if his past experience has not been normal—if he has lived in a vertical cage with no chance to walk in a horizontal dimension, if he has never had the opportunity to connect the sight of food with certain affective states (taste, reduction in hunger pangs), if he has been taught to run only when mildly hungry and to sit when very hungry—then the situation will not give a "fair" measure of his hunger motive. The number of times he ends up in the vicinity of the food could still be recorded in such cases, but it might be a measure of things other than hunger. It would measure hunger according to our argument if, and only if, it made use of a highly overlearned response (i.e., a "normal" habit) in a situation which did not clearly evoke incompatible responses (i.e., a "normal" situation).

In a sense, this is fairly similar to the state of affairs when a human being is telling a story in response to a picture. That is, for most subjects putting thoughts into words or verbalizing is a highly overlearned response. Furthermore, in the fantasy situation no particular set of responses is supposed to be perceived as especially appropriate. Fantasy is a "free" response situation, provided the picture is not too structured. It might not be for a certain class of persons, for professional writers, for example, because they may have learned a particular set of responses to use in such a situation, just as the rats who have been trained to sit still when hungry have learned a particular set of responses which prevent us from measuring their motivation in the usual way. But except for professional authors, individuals should have no particular set of verbal response tendencies which seem appropriate because of past experience with such situations. In contrast, if we ask a subject if he would like to get a good grade in a course, the fact that he answers "yes" is of no particular significance for diagnosing his achievement motivation, because we can assume that he will have learned that this is an appropriate response to such a question. Here the social reality or the modal cultural pattern determines his response. It is just for this reason that we prefer pictures which are not so structured as to elicit one particular response by common social agreement. We want the restraints on the free choice of responses by the subject reduced to a certain necessary minimum.

Furthermore, the fantasy situation is "free" because the testing conditions do not place any external constraints on the responses which are possible. Thus the subject can write about anything—about killing someone, committing suicide, touring the South Seas on a pogo stick, having an illegitimate child, and so forth. Anything is symbolically possible. Thus the choice of response patterns is not limited by what can be done under the conditions in which the motive strength is to be tested. Here our measure of human motivation has a great advantage over measures of animal motivation, but in both cases the problem is the same: to minimize or know the situational and habit determinants of behavior. This position fits into the general theoretical framework described elsewhere by McClelland (1951) in which he argues that behavior is determined by situational (perceptual) factors, by habit (memory) factors, and by motivational factors. It follows that if one wants a particular response to reflect motivation primarily, the strength of the other two determinants must either be known, minimized, or randomized. In the elementary state of our present knowledge, the best procedure would appear to be to use highly overlearned responses in "free" situations. There is, therefore, some theoretical justification for our empirical finding that motives can be measured effectively in imagination.

## 2.10 ANTECEDENT CONDITIONS FOR AFFECTIVE AROUSAL

Let us now focus our attention on the all-important problem of identifying the antecedent conditions which produce affective arousal. For if we know them, we are in a position, according to the theory, of knowing how to create a motive by pairing cues with those conditions, according to the principles discussed in the next main section on *the acquisition of motives.* Considering the antecedent conditions for affective arousal inevitably gets us into some ancient controversies over what causes pleasure and pain (McDougall, 1927; Beebe-Center, 1932; Dallenbach, 1939; Hebb, 1949). There is not the space here to review these controversies or to attempt to resolve them. Instead, we can only indicate what appears to us to be a promising approach to a general theory. This approach can only be outlined roughly here in the form of a series of propositions which seem promising to us but which will require experimentation and more detailed exposition in further publications.[1]

*2.10.1 Affective arousal is the innate consequence of certain sensory or perceptual events.* It is probable (though not necessary) that the basic mechanism (see proposition 2) which gives rise to *sensory* pleasantness (e.g., sweetness) and unpleasantness (e.g., bitterness) is similar to that which gives rise to pleasantness-unpleasantness at a more complex perceptual level (pleasant music vs. dissonant music). In this connection we use the term *sensory* to refer roughly to simple variations in stimulus dimensions (e.g., stimulus intensity), whereas *perceptual* refers primarily to more complex variations in stimulus events.

*2.10.2 Positive affect is the result of smaller discrepancies of a sensory or perceptual event from the adaptation level of the organism; negative affect is the result of larger discrepancies.* The salt curve in Figure 33.2 illustrates this postulated relationship from the hedonic reactions to increasing salt concentrations in the mouth. Fifty years ago it was a commonplace assumption that increasing sensory intensity in *any* modality produced a pleasantness-unpleasantness curve like this (Beebe-Center, 1932, p. 166). The new feature of such a curve for us is that, like Hebb, we would plot it not against increasing intensity as such but against size of discrepancy between the stimulus (perception) and the adaptation level of the organism (expectation). Such a modification has several advantages which we will enumerate, but among them is the fact that it brings the "discrepancy hypothesis" as to the source of affect within the realm of quantitative testing according to Helson's formulae (1948) for determining adaptation level and discrepancies from it. In the discussion which follows we have obviously leaned heavily on Helson's formulation of the concept of adaptation level.

*2.10.3 Natural adaptation levels for various sensory receptors differ.* Such a hypothesis is apparently essential to a discrepancy hypothesis because of the known fact that some receptors give rise most readily or "naturally" to pleasantness and others to unpleasantness. In Figure 33.2

[1] D.C.McC. and R.A.C. are largely responsible for Section 2.10, which was written after the main body of the text had been completed.

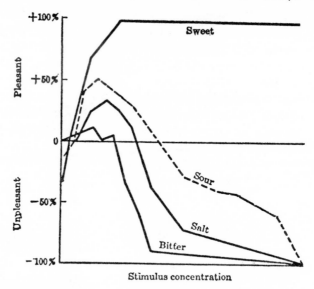

Figure 33.2. Preponderance of "pleasant" or "unpleasant" judgments in relation to the concentration of a sapid solution. The ordinate gives per cent "pleasant" minus per cent "unpleasant." The abscissa is proportional to the concentration, the full length of the baseline standing for 40 per cent cane sugar, for 10 per cent salt, and for .004 per cent quinine sulphate (all by weight). (Data of R. Engel, after Woodworth, 1938.)

the two curves for sweet and bitter sensations illustrate this point. Thus sugar appears to give rise to pleasurable sensations across the entire range of stimulus intensity. In terms of the discrepancy hypothesis, this suggests that a discrepancy from the natural adaptation level (*AL*) large enough to produce unpleasantness is not possible. The bitter curve, on the other hand, is quite different: here nearly all intensities of stimulus concentration tested give rise to negative affect. The fact that the absolute threshold for sugar is considerably above what it is for bitter (Pfaffman in Stevens, 1951) suggests the following interpretation. The threshold for sweet is relatively high and the range of stimulation to which it is sensitive sufficiently narrow so that large discrepancies from *AL* which probably lies near the threshold are impossible. With bitter the threshold is so low that small fractions of the maximum concentration used in Figure 33.2 still represent fairly large discrepancies from an *AL* near the threshold. At this stage of our knowledge easy generalizations must be avoided, but it seems obvious even now that ultimately the natural *AL* for a receptor will turn out to be somewhere near its threshold (modified perhaps by the normal stimulation impinging on it) and that the size of the discrepancies which will yield positive and negative affect will be a joint rational function of the three constants in receptor functioning—the lower threshold, the upper threshold, and the Weber fraction.

What is clearly needed is a survey of all sensory qualities in terms of the discrepancy hypothesis as to what produces positive and negative affect. Such a survey cannot be attempted here both because of space limitations and because of the obvious complexity of some of the problems to be solved. Take pitch, for example. At first glance, it would look as if a few moments at the piano would easily disprove the discrepancy hypothesis. If two notes of small discrepancy in pitch, such as C and C-sharp, are played together in the middle pitch range, the effect is normally unpleasant; whereas if two notes farther apart in pitch, such as C and E, are played together, the effect is pleasant. Isn't this just the reverse of what our hypothesis would predict? It is, unless one considers the fact that two notes fairly close together produce a larger number of audible beats per second than two notes farther apart. It has long been recognized (Woodworth, 1938, p. 515) that unpleasantness is a function of these beats which represent discrepancies from an evenly pitched sound. Thus if size of discrepancy is measured in terms of "frequency of beats," it appears that the two tones close together are *more discrepant* than those farther apart and should therefore be more unpleasant. But this is only the beginning of what could be a thorough exploration of the esthetics of music according to this principle. Variables which appear to influence the pleasantness of combinations of tones, for example, include the absolute pitch of the two tones, the pattern of overtones, simultaneity vs. succession in sounding the two tones, and the like.

Or to take one more example—that of color. If our *AL* theory is correct, one would have to predict that dark-skinned peoples of the world would have different color *AL*'s from looking at each other than would light-skinned people. Consequently, the discrepancy in wavelength terms from the *AL*'s which should yield maximum pleasure in countries like India and the United States ought to be different. In these terms one might explain the fact that in India red is the most preferred color and white is the color of mourning, whereas in the United States blue-green is most preferred and black is the color of mourning (Garth, *et al.*, 1938). It is at least suggestive that nearly complementary skin color bases should produce complementary pleasant and unpleasant colors, but the most important point to note here is that our theory would argue for a *natural* basis for color preferences based on dominant or recurrent experiences rather than for a purely accidental basis subsequently reinforced by culture, as current thinking would appear to emphasize. Obviously such natural preferences can be changed by the culture or by the individual through particular experiences (e.g., there are plenty of American children who prefer red), but the point is that U.S. and Indian populations as groups should show different color preferences according to the principle that moderate discrepancy from different skin color *AL* bases will yield pleasure in colors of different wavelength composition.

These two examples should be sufficient to illustrate the deductive fertility of the discrepancy hypothesis and also the need for the kind of careful analysis of different sensory qualities which is beyond the scope of this introductory treatment.

*2.10.4 A discrepancy between adaptation level and a sensation or event must persist for a finite length of time before it gives rise to an hedonic response.* There are several reasons for making this assumption. In the first place, Beebe-Center and others have noted that certain types of sensations—e.g., taste, smell, pain—give rise to affective responses more readily than others—e.g., sight, hearing. A possible explanation for this fact would be "receptor lag" or "*AL* lag." That is, for the first group of sensations *AL* may change rather slowly, so that the discrepancy caused by a new stimulus will last long enough to give an hedonic report. In taste and smell, for instance, there appear to be purely "mechanical" reasons for the relative slowness with which previous concentrations of stimulator substances are changed by new substances. Thus a change might occur at one point in the receptor surface while the rest of the surface was still responding to earlier chemicals. In vision and hearing, on the other hand, the *AL* appears to respond rapidly to new sensations so that only major shifts in intensity will cause a discrepancy from *AL* to persist long enough to give rise to an hedonic response.

A second reason for the discrepancy-persistence hypothesis is that the hedonic j.n.d. seems to be larger than the sensory j.n.d. That is, in all modalities the discrepancies required to produce a just noticeable difference in hedonic tone seem to be larger than those required to produce a report of a difference in sensation. Unfortunately, adequate data on this point are apparently not available at present, although the problem is one that may be attacked easily experimentally. What is needed is a repetition of some of the standard psychophysics experiments in which hedonic judgments are called for under exactly the same conditions as judgments of *heavier, brighter, longer,* and so on. Usually these two types of judgments have been made separately. It would not be surprising if the hedonic j.n.d. turned out to be some function of the Weber faction for each modality. The meaning of all this in terms of the present hypothesis is simply that a larger than just noticeable sensory difference is required to maintain a discrepancy over *AL* long enough to give rise to a just noticeable hedonic effect.

A third reason for the discrepancy-persistence hypothesis is simply to avoid making the whole of behavior affectively toned. After all, every sensory event might be considered, at least in some marginal sense, a discrepancy from some "expectation" and should therefore lead to some kind of affective arousal, were it not for some principle requiring a minimum degree of stability in the expectation or *AL* so that a discrepancy from it *could* persist. In short, the simple occurrence of an event is not sufficient to set up an *AL* such that any further modified occurrence of that same event will produce a discrepancy sufficient to cause affect. Rather the *AL* must be built up to a certain minimum level of stability through successive experiences, as in memory or psychophysical experiments, before discrepancies from it will produce affect. A case in point is provided by Hebb's young chimpanzee which did not fear a detached chimpanzee head until it had formed through experience a stable expectation of what a chimpanzee should look like ( Hebb, 1949).

2.10.5 *Discrepancies from adaptation level will give rise to a positive-negative affect function in either direction along a continuum.* In many instances, events can differ from expectation only uni-directionally. Thus after the shape of the human figure has been learned, discrepancies can occur only in the direction of being less like the expected shape. But with many dimensions, particularly intensity, discrepancies are bi-directional and may have somewhat different affective consequences depending on their direction. For example, does a decrease of so many j.n.d.'s from an *AL* have the same hedonic tone as an increase of the same number of j.n.d.'s?

The simplest assumption is that the hedonic effect is the same regardless of the direction of the discrepancy. But the evidence for the assumption is not very convincing. It consists for the most part of some early experiments in esthetics such as the one summarized in Figure 33.3. Angier (1903) simply asked his subjects to divide a 160 mm line unequally at the most pleasing place on either side of the midpoint. The results in Figure 33.3 were obtained by averaging the frequencies of choices per 5 mm unit between 5–25 mm, 25–45 mm, 45–65 mm, 65–75 mm discrepancies, and plotting them with the actual frequencies from the 5 mm discrepancies on each side of the midpoint. Since Angier did not permit his subjects to choose the midpoint and since he forced them to make half of their judgments on either side of the midpoint, the data do not really test our hypothesis crucially. He should rather have let a large number of subjects choose any division points at all along the line. Still, Angier's introspective data from his subjects led him to conclude that "most of the subjects, however, found a *slight* remove from the center disagreeable" (1903, p. 550). Furthermore it is clear that his subjects did not like to divide the line near its extremities on either side. In short, there is evidence for the typical hedonic curve for discrepancies *in both directions* from the center which must be assumed to represent some kind of an *AL* based on symmetry, balance, and so forth. A similar

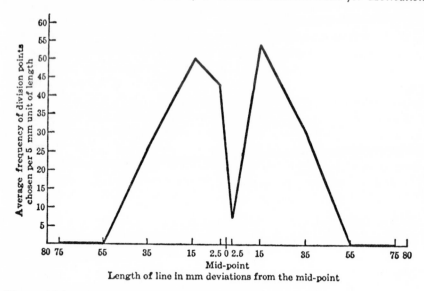

Figure 33.3.  Unequal division points of a straight line chosen as most pleasing. (From Angier, 1903.)

bimodal preference curve for rectangles of different width-length ratios is reported by Thorndike (see Woodworth, 1938, p. 386), if the exactly balanced ratio of .50 is taken as the *AL*.

When an attempt is made to discover the same principle in the operation of sensory modalities, however, the situation becomes complex. Consider Alpert's data in Figure 33.4 as an example. The lower curve, which again is the typical hedonic function for discrepancies from *AL*, was obtained in the following way. Subjects inserted one eye in a translucent "Ganzfeld" about the size of an egg cup. Around the outside of the cup, red lights were placed so as to produce inside it a diffuse red light covering the entire visual field and presumably stimulating largely only one set of receptors—the cones. In the center of the cup a small spot subtending about 18 degrees of visual arc was distinguishable from the rest of the field by a hazy dark line, produced by the fact that the spot was separately illuminated from behind. First the subject adjusted the illumination of the reddish spot until it matched the reddish "Ganzfeld" in all respects as closely as possible. Then the experimenter set a Variac which also controlled lamp voltage for the spot in such a way that if he switched off the "constant" lamp just adjusted by the subject and switched on the "variable" lamp for about two seconds, the subject got a glimpse of the spot as more or less intense than the surrounding "Ganzfeld." The subject made a judgment of pleasantness-unpleasantness on a scale of +3 to −3 *after* the "variable" lamp had been switched off and the

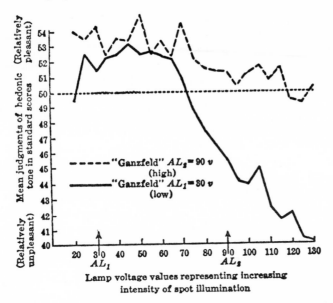

Figure 33.4. Hedonic tone judgments for discrepancies in spot illumination above and below low ($AL_1$) and high ($AL_2$) "Ganzfeld" illuminations. Red light, 10 subjects making 4 judgments at each lamp voltage value. (Data from Alpert, 1953.)

"constant" lamp back on. Each subject made four judgments at each of the lamp voltage settings shown on the abscissa of Figure 33.4. The "spots" of different intensity were presented in random order four separate times. The procedure was duplicated for different illuminations of the "Ganzfeld" (i.e., for different adaptation levels). There were 10 subjects and the two curves in Figure 33.4 represent the average judgments of all of them under two adaptation level settings—one in which the "Ganzfeld" illumination was low (< .5 foot candles) and the other in which it was high (about 3 foot candles according to G.E. photometer). Each subject's judgments under all conditions were converted to a common scale of standard scores with a mean of 50 and an *SD* of 10. Thus the fact that the dotted line in Figure 33.4 is above 50 throughout most of its course means that most of the subjects' judgments in this condition were above their individual hedonic means *for the whole series of judgments* (including a series with a moderate *AL* not reproduced here).

Three conclusions can be drawn from Figure 33.4: (1) When the *AL* is low, and the receptors are close to the "resting" state, increases in stimulation produce first positive affect and then negative affect as postulated in Section 2.10.2. See solid line in Figure 33.4. (2) When the *AL* is high, well above the resting state, all increases in stimulation tend to produce negative affect and all decreases tend to produce positive affect. See dotted line in Figure 33.4. (3) There is no marked evidence in these curves either (*a*) for large decreases in stimulation leading to negative affect or (*b*) for stimulation around the AL producing a neutral hedonic response. Neither (*a*) nor (*b*) should be considered as conclusive negative evidence, however. With respect to (*a*), common experience suggests that eating ice cream after drinking coffee is more painful than under normal conditions. On the surface, it would appear that this is because the low temperature of the ice cream represents a much larger discrepancy downwards from the heightened AL of the mouth or teeth produced by drinking coffee. But the problem is complicated by the fact that the heat and cold receptors may be different and related in an unknown way. That is, ice cream may not be a decrease in stimulation for warm receptors but an *increase* in stimulation for cold receptors. The virtue of using red illumination in the present experiment is that it presumably limits the effects of stimulation largely to one set of receptors—the cones. In short, the question of whether decreases in stimulation ever produce negative affect and of whether the hedonic curve is therefore alike on both sides of AL must be left open at the present time.

With respect to (*b*) there is a slight (though probably insignificant) dip in the lower hedonic curve for values of the spot which are close to those of the "Ganzfeld" AL. It can be argued that the reason the dip is not more striking is that at least two other AL's are operating in this situation. The first is the natural or physiological AL of the receptor which here and in other similar figures seems to lie somewhere around the threshold of the receptor. The illumination of the "Ganzfeld" was apparently close enough to this value for the lower curve in Figure 33.4 not to produce a major modification in its shape. The second AL is that produced by the *series* of spot stimuli of varying intensity. This can be calculated by Helson's formula (1947) to be equivalent to a lamp voltage value of around 63 volts, which is considerably *above* the "Ganzfeld" AL value and which may interact with it in some way to obscure further the dip in hedonic tone for values approximating AL. Generally speaking, the principle appears to hold for the lower curve if the AL is taken to be the physiological AL, and for the upper curve if the AL is taken to be the "Ganzfeld" value. Although both of these assumptions seem reasonable, once again the question must be considered open as to whether values approximating the AL always tend to take on a neutral hedonic tone, at least until we have more accurate ways of figuring out how AL's are shifted by exposure to various experiences.

*2.10.6 Increases and decreases in stimulus intensity can be related to motivation only if adaptation level and learning are taken into account.* Our view of motivation differs from Miller and Dollard's (1941) in two important ways. First, the effect of changes in stimulus intensity must always be referred to *AL*, and second, such changes produce affect immediately and motives only through learning. More specifically, an increase in stimulus intensity (a "drive" for Miller and Dollard) provides the basis for a motive only if it represents a large enough discrepancy from *AL* to produce positive or negative affect. It elicits a motive only if it or the situation producing it has been associated with such affect in the past. A decrease in stimulus intensity (a "reward" for Miller and Dollard) either provides the basis for an approach motive if it produces positive affect or removes the cues which have been redintegrating negative affect and thus eliminates an avoidance motive. Thus "drive" and "reward" in Miller and Dollard's sense are seen to be special cases of a more general theory.

Let us leave aside for the moment the question of whether motives or drives are always learned and look more closely at the question of the relation of stimulus intensity to *AL*. For us, it is not intensity per se which is important but discrepancy from *AL*. It follows that many strong stimuli will be unpleasant, but not all. It depends on over-all *AL*. Thus if a person is in dim illumination (bottom curve in Figure 33.4), a light with a lamp voltage value of 90 will produce marked negative affect; but if the illumination is already that bright, the same light will produce a rather indifferent response (upper curve in Figure 33.4). It is for this reason apparently that biting one's lips or otherwise hurting one's self helps relieve pain.

*2.10.7 Changes in adaptation level, with attendant hedonic changes, may be produced by somatic conditions.* This is an obvious point and a few illustrations will serve to demonstrate its importance. The somatic conditions may be either chemical (hormonal) or neurological in nature. Pfaffman and Bare (1950) have demonstrated that the preferences for lower salt concentrations shown by adrenalectomized rats cannot be explained by a lowering of the *sensory* threshold of the nerves responding to salt. An explanation in our terms would simply be that the central *AL* has been lowered by chemical changes in the bloodstream so that lower salt concentrations on the tongue will produce a pleasurable discrepancy from it. That is, Pfaffman and Bare found that the lower concentrations had always produced action potentials in the gustatory nerve, although they did not produce preference behavior in the normal rat. The reason for this in our terms is that they were sufficiently near the normal *AL* not to evoke preference behavior. Figure 33.5, which is plotted from Harriman's data (1952), shows in detail what happens to salt preferences in adrenalectomized rats when salt has been removed from their diet. The solid curve shows the amount of salty water of different concentrations consumed by normal rats on a normal diet (including about 1 per cent salt) when they could choose between it and distilled water. The dotted

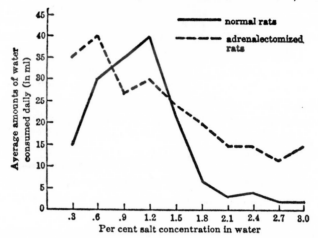

Figure 33.5. Data plotted from Harriman (1952) showing average amounts of salty water of different concentrations consumed by normal (solid line) and adrenalectomized rats (dotted line) on a salt-free diet.

curve shows the same results for the adrenalectomized animals on a salt-free diet.

The solid curve shows substantially the same relationship obtained for humans as presented in Figure 33.2 and it can be explained by the same assumptions—namely, that the *AL* for salt is somewhat below .3 per cent salt but above the absolute threshold for discrimination of salty from non-salty water which is at least as low as .01 per cent concentration of salt (Pfaffman and Bare, 1950). The *AL* empirically is that concentration which a rat will not consistently approach or avoid as compared with distilled water. The dotted curve suggests that for the operated animals the *AL* has now moved to lower concentrations, so that a .3 per cent solution represents a "pleasurable" discrepancy whereas before it was relatively "neutral." The fact that formerly preferred concentrations (.9 per cent and 1.2 per cent) are now *less* preferred also supports the idea that the *AL* has been lowered, since these now represent larger (and therefore less pleasant) discrepancies from it. But how about the tail end of the dotted curve? Should not the adrenalectomized animals find the high salt concentrations even less pleasant than the normals, if their *AL* has been lowered? According to the discrepancy hypothesis they should, but these data are not conclusive evidence that they do not. That is, the operated animals may find the strong concentrations even more unpleasant than the normals do, but drink more of them in short "swallows" because the "after-taste" remains pleasant longer. In other words, if the salt solutions dissipate according to a negative decay function, there may be an appreciable time period after exposure to a strong concentration when the stimulus is pleasant, if the $AL$ is low as in operated animals. Thus the operated animals may drink for the pleasant after-taste of strong concentrations; the normal animals may not because the dissipating solution reaches the higher $AL$ sooner. At least the possibility is worth exploring.

In this fashion, changes in positive and negative affect resulting from the same stimulation on different occasions can be accounted for by chemical effects on $AL$. Such a hypothesis should be especially valuable in accounting for changes in the pleasurableness of sexual sensations accompanying certain hormonal cycles in lower animals (cf. Ford and Beach, 1951). Similarly Head's observations on the effects of thalamic lesions show that neurological damage can affect $AL$. Take this case, for example: "In one case a tube containing water at $38°$ C applied to the normal palm was said to be warm, but the patient cried out with pleasure when it was placed on the affected hand. His face broke into smiles and he said, 'Oh! that's exquisite,' or 'That's real pleasant'" (quoted in Beebe-Center, 1932, p. 391). Or another: "When a pin was lightly dragged from right to left across the face or trunk of one of the patients suffering from a lesion affecting the left side, she exhibited intense discomfort as soon as it had passed the middle line. Not only did she call out that it hurt more, but her face became contorted with pain. Yet careful examination with algesimeters showed that on the affected side her sensitivity to such stimulation was, if anything, slightly lowered" (Beebe-Center, 1932, p. 390). It is difficult to think about such findings in any other terms but some neurological effects on a central $AL$ such that identical stimulations would produce different effects.

An interesting consequence of this proposition is that it suggests a reason why the sources of positive and negative affect may be different for different physiques. Thus if the $AL$ for kinaesthetic sensations from large well-developed muscles is higher, it would be easy to understand why more activity would be required to get pleasurable discrepancies from the $AL$ than for a weaker physique with lower kinaesthetic $AL$. In fact, one should argue that the amount of activity which produces pleasure for the mesomorphic physique (and consequently approach motives) might well produce too large a discrepancy, negative affect, and avoidance motives for the ectomorph. It might not be too far-fetched to attempt to account for the dominant sources of pleasure in each of Sheldon's somatotypes (1940) in terms of different $AL$'s set up in different sensory modalities by different types of physiques. The argument would run something like this: The endomorph appears to get most of his pleasure from his gut because the $AL$ for gut sensations is relatively high for such physiques and it takes gut sensations of greater intensity (or variety) to produce the discrepancies necessary for pleasure; the mesomorph appears to get most of his pleasure from his muscles because the $AL$ for

kinaesthetic sensations is relatively high and more variations in kinaesthetic sensations are required to give pleasure; the ectomorph appears to
get more of his pleasure from minimal sensory stimulation because the
AL for skin sensations is so low that moderate deviations from it give
pleasure, and so forth. Such hypotheses are obviously incomplete and
highly tentative, but they can certainly be tested experimentally and made
more precise by isolating such physique types and determining their
hedonic thresholds for various sensory qualities.

Finally, this proposition provides a basis for explaining Freud's libidinal development hypothesis, which has proven so fruitful clinically
but so difficult to understand in terms of traditional "objective" theories
of motivation. The explanation runs briefly as follows: "Erogenous zones"
are skin areas where AL's are so low that relatively light tactual stimulation gives rise to sufficient discrepancies from AL to yield pleasure.
If Freud is correct, it should be possible to demonstrate objectively that
a constant tactual stimulus will give rise to pleasure responses in infants
more readily in certain areas than in others. For the mouth, this seems
well established, if the sucking response is taken as indicative of pleasure
(i.e., because it is an approach response). For the anal and genital regions
the facts are less well established. Freud's second hypothesis is that the
erogenous sensitivity of these regions shifts as the child matures. In our
terms, this simply means that changes in somatic conditions, produced
here by maturation, modify AL's so that, as in the case of Head's patient,
the same stimulus has a different hedonic effect. For example, the innate
AL to mouth stimulation may increase with age so that touching the lips
in the same way no longer yields pleasure and, at the same time, the anal
region may become especially sensitive to tactual stimulation, and so on.
The rise and fall in sensitivity of these various skin areas can certainly
be measured behaviorally and understood in terms of physiologically produced changes in AL.

2.10.8 *Changes in adaptation level, with attendant hedonic changes,
may be produced by experience.* This proposition opens up a whole new
area that needs careful experimental exploration. We know some things
but not nearly enough about how this happens. Thus Helson (1948) has
demonstrated how an anchor or a series of stimuli can modify an AL in
various modalities. His formulae even make assumptions as to the relative
weights of background and figural stimulations in determining an AL
produced by a series of stimuli. Furthermore, we know that hedonic
judgments show the same type of central tendency, contrast, and assimilation effects that led Helson to formulate his notion of AL (Beebe-
Center, 1932). This is as it should be, because as AL's shift in the "physical
dimensions of consciousness" there should be corresponding shifts in
hedonic reactions if they are a function of the size of discrepancies be-

tween new stimuli and the sensory *AL*. But the most clear-cut evidence we know of which demonstrates that the hedonic curve is shifted as a function of shifts in sensory *AL* is that which has already been presented in Figure 33.4 and discussed in Section 2.10.5. (See also Beebe-Center, 1932, p. 238.)

In the absence of more such data at a more complex level, we must work with qualitative observations to some extent. Take Hebb's treatment of the "fear of the strange" as a point of departure. "About the age of four months the chimpanzee reared in the nursery, with daily care from three or four persons only and seeing few others, begins to show an emotional disturbance at the approach of a stranger (Hebb and Riesen, 1943). The disturbance increases in degree in the following months. . . . Chimpanzees reared in darkness, and brought into the light at an age when the response (to a strange face) would be at its strongest, show not the slightest disturbance at the sight of either friend or stranger. *But* some time later, after a certain amount of visual learning has gone on, the disturbance begins to appear exactly as in other animals" (Hebb, 1949, pp. 244–45). He also reports that "a model of a human or chimpanzee head detached from the body" produces marked affective arousal in half-grown or adult chimpanzees but not in younger chimpanzees. From all this he concludes that "the emotional disturbance is neither learned nor innate: a certain learning must have preceded, but given that learning the disturbance is complete on the first appearance of certain stimulus combinations" (Hebb, 1949, p. 245). This is the crux of the matter as far as our theory of the conditions necessary for affective arousal (either positive or negative) is concerned. An *AL* must be built up in certain areas of experience (though it appears to be innately given for sense modalities) and then increasing discrepancies from that *AL* give rise first to positive and then to negative affect, as in Figure 33.2. *The AL may be acquired, the affective reactions to discrepancies from it are not;* they appear maximally the first time the discrepancy occurs and with less intensity thereafter because the new experience automatically interacts with the *AL*, changes it, and thereby reduces the discrepancy. Hence there is ultimate boredom or adaptation to pain or pleasure (satiation) as we shall see in a moment.

*2.10.9 Events can differ from expectations on a variety of dimensions.* The example we have chosen from Hebb to illustrate the preceding point is important because, unlike the sensory *AL*'s which we have been discussing, it deals with changes in *patterns* of stimulation rather than with changes in *intensity* levels. Thus we have to expand the *AL* concept to include expectations about shapes (e.g., faces) or any other events that the organism has had occasion through past experience to build up expectations about. This expansion, while absolutely necessary for a complete theory, raises certain practical problems in defining the size of a discrepancy between expectation and perception—a variable which we must be able to determine quite precisely if we are going to be able to predict whether a given discrepancy will give rise to positive or negative affect.

Basically, the problem is one of isolating dimensions along which two events can differ and then attempting to define degrees of difference objectively. Thus the events can differ in intensity, extensity, clarity, quality, certainty, and so on, and traditional psychophysics gives us plenty of cues as to how degrees of difference along these dimensions can be determined. So far we have talked largely about intensity differences, but differences in quality (or similarity) can be treated the same way. Thus one would predict on the basis of the discrepancy hypothesis that an artificial language consisting of highly probable syllabic combinations would be more amusing than one consisting of highly improbable syllabic combinations, or that nonsense syllables that sounded like English (*NOQ*) would be more amusing than ones that didn't (*VOQ*). And so forth. The research along these lines that needs to be done appears almost limitless.

Most events, of course, can differ from expectation in a variety of ways. Suppose a rat runs down an alley, turns left, proceeds three or four steps further, finds and eats a food pellet of a certain size and consistency. If this series of events occurs with sufficient frequency, we argue that the rat has built up a chain of associations of high probability or certain "expectations" as to what will happen. But these expectations, redintegrated partially when the rat is placed in the maze, may fail to be exactly confirmed in a variety of ways. An obstacle may delay him so that it takes him longer to get to the food. We may substitute mash for a food pellet, or a large pellet for a small one. He may eat the food where it is or pick it up and carry it somewhere else to eat it. And so forth. According to the discrepancy hypothesis, certain predictions about this process can be made. So long as the animal is uncertain in his expectations (i.e., is still learning the habit), there will be a tendency to limit the variability of responses so as to increase the probability of expectations until events represent only moderate and hence pleasurable deviations from them. But once the habit is overlearned the animal will tend to introduce variations once more—now to *increase* uncertainty to a "pleasurable" level. In short, exactly confirming certain expectations produces boredom and a tendency to discontinue the act unless enough minor variations are permitted to produce positive affect. The evidence for this hypothesis from animal learning is considerable. Thus the tendency toward variability in routine behavior has been found by many learning psychologists and is perhaps best illustrated by Heathers' (1940) report that rats alternate the paths they choose to get food when either is equally good. They are apparently operating according to the same general principle when they prefer a path to food with a barrier in it to an unobstructed path to food (Festinger, 1943), or prefer seeds which are difficult to crack open to seeds which are not so difficult (Yoshioka, 1930). Other similar examples of "inefficient" preferences have been collected by Maltzman (1952). In these and other such cases, the rat may prefer what looks like an inefficient response because it involves minor variations from expectation along such dimensions as time delay, spatial location, size of expected object, nature of expected object, and so forth—variations which according to the discrepancy hypothesis should yield pleasure. Research on this problem has to be done with care because as soon as the modification is major (for example, when the time delay becomes too long), then, of course, negative affect results and the preference of the animal is reversed. To complicate the matter even more, one should know how certain, or overlearned, the expectations are before predicting the effects of variations from them. If the expectations are of low probability, then confirmation should produce negative affect as in "fear of the strange." If they are of moderate probability, precise confirmation should produce pleasure (as in reading a detective story or playing solitaire). If the expectations are of high probability, then precise confirmation produces boredom or indifference (as in reading over again the detective story one has just finished, to use Hebb's example). The hedonic effects of the interaction of degrees of certainty of an expectation on the one hand, and degrees of deviation of an event from that expectation on the other, have yet to be worked out experimentally, but there is no reason why they could not be, using either animal or human subjects.

*2.10.10 Frustration is a source of negative affect.* A special note is in order as to where the notion of frustration or conflict as a drive (Whiting, 1950; Brown and Farber, 1951) fits into this scheme. Frustration in their terms results essentially from competition of response tendencies in such a way that $F$ (frustration) is increased by reducing the difference in strength between the two opposed tendencies and also by increasing the absolute strength of both of them. Such statements are completely in line with our assumptions, with some exceptions to be noted in a minute. That is, we too would argue that the more nearly equal in strength two response tendencies are, the more they would give rise to negative affect $(F)$; because such competition means that if either response is made, the expectation based on the other is not confirmed; or that if neither is made, both are unconfirmed. Similarly, the effects of nonconfirmation should be greater, the greater the strength of the response tendency. There are two differences between our scheme and theirs, however: (1) We would argue that when the size of the discrepancy between the stronger and weaker response tendencies is large, there should be a stage when the competition of the weaker response tendency should give rise not to frustration but to pleasure, if the stronger tendency is confirmed. This would require a modification in their formula for computing $F$ such that for a certain range of discrepancies between the two tendencies it would yield negative $F$ values (signifying pleasure). (2) They treat $F$ as if it were a drive, whereas in our terms $F$ in itself is simply negative affect and does not become a motive until anticipations of it or by it are elicited.

2.10.11 *The achievement motive develops out of growing expectations.* So far our scheme has been stated in fairly abstract form. A concrete example involving the development of the achievement motive may help explain its application in practice. Suppose a child is given a new toy car for Christmas to play with. Initially, unless he has had other toy cars, his expectations (or $AL$'s) as to what it will do are nonexistent, and he can derive little or no positive or negative affect from manipulating it until such expectations are developed. Gradually, if he plays with it (as he will be encouraged to do by his parents in our culture), he will develop certain expectations of varying probabilities which will be confirmed or not confirmed. Unless the nonconfirmations are too many (which may happen if the toy is too complex), he should be able to build up reasonably certain expectations as to what it will do *and confirm them*. In short, he gets pleasure from playing with the car. But what happens then? Why doesn't he continue playing with it the rest of his life? The fact is, of course, that his expectations become certainties, confirmation becomes 100 per cent, and we say that he loses interest or gets bored with the car; he should get bored or satiated, according to the theory, since the discrepancies from certainty are no longer sufficient to yield pleasure. However, pleasure can be reintroduced into the situation, as any parent knows, by buying a somewhat more complex car, by making the old car do somewhat different things, or perhaps by letting the old car alone for six months until the expectations about it have changed (e.g., decreased in probability). So, if a child is to continue to get pleasure from achievement situations like manipulating toy cars, he must continually work with more and more complex objects or situations permitting mastery, since, if he works long enough at any particular level of mastery, his expectations and their confirmation will become certain and he will get bored. The situation is analogous to the experiments by Washburn, Child, and Abel (cf. Beebe-Center, 1932, p. 238) which show that pleasure decreases on successive repetitions of simple popular music, whereas it increases on successive repetitions of severely classical music. In the first instance, expectations or $AL$'s are readily formed and confirmed to the point of boredom, whereas they take much longer to form with classical music—so long in fact that some people never expose themselves to such music often enough to get pleasure from having them confirmed. Thus pleasure from anything—be it mastery, music, or modern art—depends on a moderate degree of novelty, which has to become ever greater as expectations catch up with it. But note that there are limits on this developmental process: not every child will develop a very high level achievement motive or esthetic appreciation motive. In the first place, there are limits placed by native intelligence: the possibilities of a toy car or a comic book may never be exhausted as far as a moron is concerned because they never become certain enough for him to be bored over trying them out. Thus one would expect some kind of a correlation between the mastery level involved in *n* Achievement for a given person and his intelligence.

In the second place, there are limits placed on the development of *n* Achievement by the negative affect which results from too large discrepancies between expectations and events. Thus Johnny may develop expectations as to what a model airplane or a solved arithmetic problem looks like, but he may be unable to confirm these expectations at all, or only very partially. The result is negative affect, and cues associated with these activities may be expected to evoke avoidance motives. To develop an achievement approach motive, parents or circumstances must contrive to provide opportunities for mastery which, because they are just beyond the child's present knowledge, will provide continuing pleasure. If the opportunities are too limited, boredom should result and the child should develop no interest in achievement (and have a low *n* Achievement score when he grows up). If the opportunities are well beyond his capacities, negative affect should result, and he may develop an avoidance motive as far as achievement is concerned. Since a fairly narrow range of circumstances will conspire to yield a high achievement approach motive, it would not be surprising to discover that individuals or groups of individuals in different cultures differ widely in the amount of achievement motivation they develop.

*2.10.12 In human adults adaptation levels are numerous and complex so that a single event may have several hedonic consequences.* Take flunking out of school, for example. One might argue that if the student half expected it, he should feel pleasure since his expectation is confirmed. Although it is true that he may get some fleeting satisfaction from having predicted correctly, this is more than outweighed by the nonconfirmation of other expectations built up over his whole life history such as doing a good job, being a professional man, etc. So far we have been dealing largely with low level expectations and *AL*'s taken one at a time for the sake of simplicity, but obviously in real life situations, after the person has matured, the calculus of pleasure and pain becomes exceedingly complex. Consider, for example, the traditional argument used against hedonic theories of motivation to the effect that adults at any rate frequently do things, out of a sense of duty or what not, which are distinctly unpleasant. What about the martyr, for example? Can he be seeking pleasure or avoiding pain? The answer is "yes," in the larger sense in which positive and negative affect are defined here. If a man builds up a conception of the Universe—an expectation of the way in which moral or spiritual laws govern it and his place in it—which is sufficiently firm and well defined, it may well be that the anticipated nonconfirmation of such an expectation through transgression of those laws would produce sufficient negative affect so that a man would choose the lesser negative affect of burning at the stake. One of the virtues of our view of motivation is precisely that it permits the development of new, high level motives as experience changes the person's expectations or adaptation levels. Whereas the rat or the child may be primarily governed by variations from sensory or simple perceptual expectations, the adult will be ruled by discrepancies in higher level cognitive structures (beliefs) which may lead to action in direct opposition to simple sensory pleasures and pains.

## Date Due